The Pivotal Years

Israel and the Arab World
1966 - 1977

Book One
(November 12, 1966 to October 6, 1973)

The Pivotal Years

Israel and the Arab World
1966 – 1977

Book One
(November 12, 1966 to October 6, 1973)

By Clifford B. Sobin

Text Copyright © 2017 Clifford B. Sobin

All Rights Reserved, including the right to reproduce this book or portions thereof in any form whatsoever, except for brief excerpts as part of critical reviews or other written materials without the express written permission of the author.

You may visit the website of the author at www.**CliffordSobin**.com

Print ISBN: 978-0-9986374-0-2

Dedication

Several years ago, while walking the streets of Jerusalem with my wife and two close friends, I found myself responding to their questions about the present that could not adequately be answered without them having knowledge of the past. The same has been true when talking to my children (now adults in their own right), and others close to me. It has also been the case in conversations with acquaintances and strangers alike. But, because of attention spans and the intrusions of life, the difficulty of conveying within the limited time usually available "what was then" in order to provide needed context for "what is now" has weighed on me.

Israel is so often wrongly vilified for making choices necessary for her survival because it is natural to respond to images of suffering and squalor with empathy for victims and disdain for those perceived to have caused it. And even worse, once those impressions are imprinted, they then create a false prism through which the next controversy is viewed. That is what Israel's enemies count on and foster. The best defense to such cynical manipulation is knowledge—but it is a difficult defense to wield when the knowledge required cannot be imparted in a brief conversation.

In order to remedy that problem for those closest to me, I went to libraries and bookstores searching for a book to recommend that adequately covered the pivotal years that I believed had shaped Israel's struggle to survive since. To my surprise, none satisfied me. Sure, there were plenty of books covering specific battles, policies, personalities, or ideologies—but none that wove the pivotal period between 1966 and 1977 together in a fair manner from which lessons for today can be discerned.

So, I dedicate this work to those I love, those who are my friends, and to all those who care to understand Israel's past so that they can help secure her future.

Map — Israel and Her Neighbors

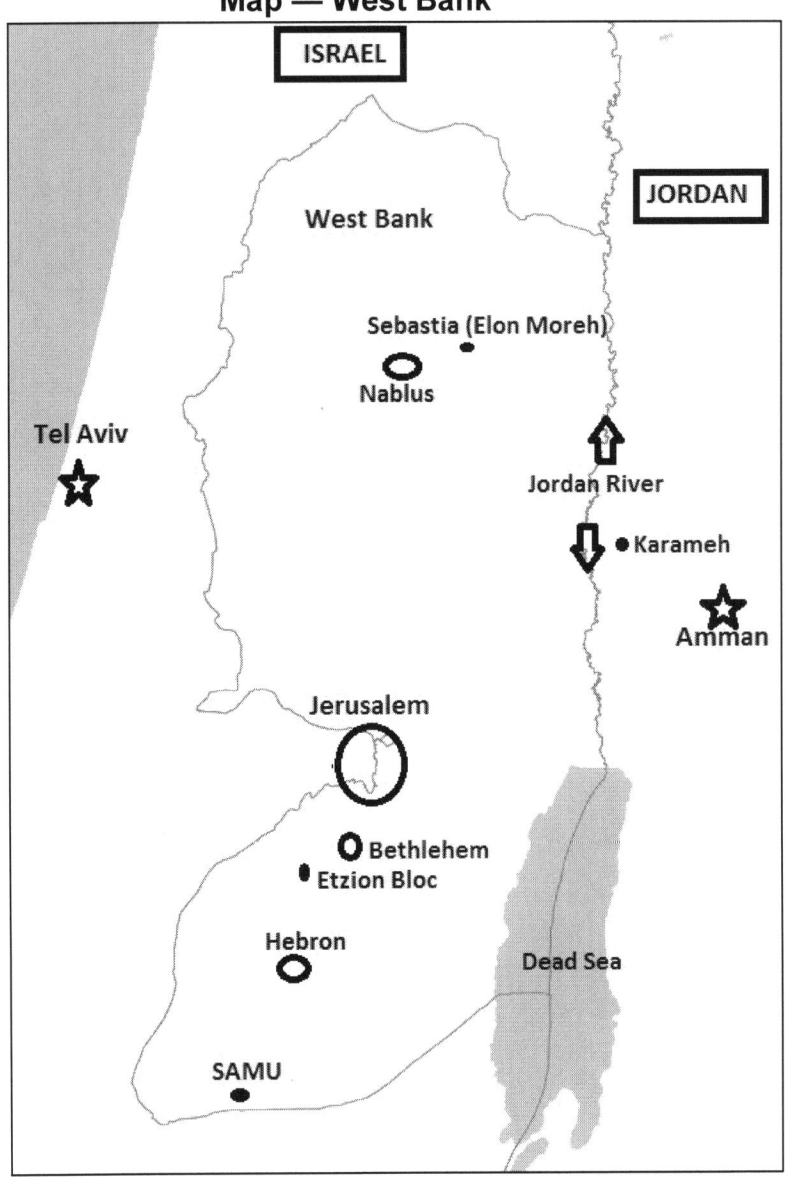
Map — West Bank

TABLE OF CONTENTS
Volume One

Introduction 1
1. Samu — November, 1966 4
2. April 7, 1967 — "Today they discovered they had made ..." 27
3. Russia Stirs and Nasser Cooks 34
4. The Independence Day Party Ends on a Bad Note 42
5. Israel Will Not Be Alone Unless She Decides To Go Alone 55
6. The Speech 67
7. Hussein and Nasser 79
8. Israel Decides 89
9. The War Plans 97
10. JUNE 5 108
11. JUNE 6 121
12. JUNE 7 134
13. JUNE 8 146
14. JUNE 9 156
15. JUNE 10 162
16. June 11 — The Day After 168
17. The West Bank — June 12 to June 19 188
18. Politics, June 12 — June 19 195
19. And so it Began 203
20. Two Months on the West Bank 215
21. Khartoum 231

22. October 21 to Early November 245
23. Resolution 242 252
24. Phantoms 268
25. Karameh 276
26. Dawn of the Settler Movement and the Rise of Fatah 284
27. The Canal Zone Heats Up in the Absence of Peace 295
28. Phantoms and the Bomb 310
29. Nixon, Kissinger, and Rogers 318
30. Eshkol Dies — Meir Emerges 328
31. The Two-Power Talks Die 333
32. The War of Attrition 342
33. The West Bank, Jordan, and Settlements 347
34. The War of Attrition Heats Up 357
35. Rogers's New Peace Plan 375
36. Hussein Takes Matters into His Own Hands 387
37. The New Arab Leaders 402
38. 1971 — Trying for Peace 410
39. Another Failed Try for Peace 425
40. Hussein and the PLO 433
41. The US and USSR Dance 438
42. Stalemate — 1972 445
43. Egypt Takes a Bold Step 461
44. Munich 470
45. Egypt Prepares for War 485

46. Preliminaries — 1973 494
47. Two Israeli Successes and One Large Failure 504
48. Hafez Ismail Comes to Washington 507
49. Meetings with Hussein and Meir 518
50. Most Favored Nation 532
51. War Approaches 535
52. Final Negotiations Before the Deluge 550
53. Final Preparations 572
54. War Approaches 585
55. The Austrian Divergence 592
56. Last Days 602
57. The Day Before 610
58. The Wrong Countdown Begins 627

Final Thoughts 642

Glossary of People, Places, Things and Entities 645

Bibliography Most Relied On 663

A Final Word 668

A Final Request 669

Introduction

On November 20, 1977, a plane touched down in Israel at Ben Gurion airport. Soon after its cabin door opened, Egyptian President Anwar Sadat appeared. Waiting below was an assemblage of Israeli political and military elite whose experiences and memories spanned the twenty-nine violent and uncertain years since Israel's independence. For them that moment was filled with promise and wonder. The unprecedented arrival of an Egyptian President on Israeli soil declared to his own people that forever more he would recognize the existence of the Jewish State. And to Israelis and Egyptians alike, Sadat's speech scheduled for the next day at the Knesset, Israel's legislative body, indicated his resolve to settle their differences, from then on, by force of argument rather than bloodshed.

It was a message of peace that depended on the courage of one man willing to face the wrath of his people by signaling a new direction. But for Syria's President, Hafez Assad, it was a nightmare that undermined his determination to recover the Golan by any means short of recognition and reconciliation with Israel. And for Yasser Arafat, it would force him to recalibrate his plans for creating a Palestinian State on Israel's ashes.

Sadat's visit changed the region and the world forever by raising hope that the enmity between the Jewish State and her Arab neighbors would be resolved by negotiation. The principle in play seemed simple—land for peace. But which land, what type of peace, and how to navigate the dangerous shoals that lay between waging war and pursuing peace? Knowing the answers to those questions is a pre-requisite for understanding what has since ensued.

This two-volume work contains the story of the pivotal years between 1966 and 1977, during which Israel and parts of the Arab World journeyed from confrontation and violence to a fragile, imperfect peace accompanied by new challenges and conflicts. It is a story told mostly through the eyes and words of the leaders and those they led. The pace of the story is driven by events: sometimes days, weeks, or months apart—and sometimes only separated by moments. It is a story of courage and fear, of struggle, of suspicion, and of self-interest. It is Israel's story of endurance. It is Egypt's story of redemption. It is Syria's story of rejection, and Jordan's story of survival. It is the story of a virulent Palestinian leadership growing in stature that used terror and cruelty for political purpose. And it is the story of the emergence of a settler movement with dreams of building new homes on ancient lands also claimed by others.

In 1966, it was almost impossible to envision a peaceful Middle East. In 1977, it was possible to hope. But until Anwar Sadat was willing, and able, to speak directly and publicly to Israel's leaders, that hope came at the cost of countless lives and immense human tragedy. However, once Sadat did, the prospect of peaceful co-existence and mutual benefit between Egypt and Israel overcame the practices of the past. His visit started a process that culminated in three crucial agreements: the peace treaty signed by Israel and Egypt in 1979, the Oslo I accords signed by Israel and the PLO in 1993, and the peace treaty concluded in 1994 between King Hussein and Israel. Sadly, however, as of 2016, hope is fading, again overcome by hatred and intolerance. In 1977, the answer to violence was leadership. The same is true today if hope is to be restored.

Therefore, since leadership is the key to change, this book focuses on many powerful, influential people and how they impacted the Israeli-Arab relationship during the climactic eleven-year period that began in 1966. They include four Israeli Prime Ministers, two Egyptian Presidents, one Syrian dictator, and a courageous but too hesitant Jordanian king. They also include a crafty Palestinian leader, two impassioned Israeli settlers, an astute American Secretary of State, and four American Presidents. Within these pages are stories of courage, cowardice, nobility and evil; all wrapped within the context of Israel's struggle to survive.

This volume begins with the saga of Samu, an almost forgotten moment that set the stage for much that bedevils the conflict between Palestinians and Israelis today. Then, in fifty-eight chapters written in a linked story format, what happened during those crucial years unfolds. **Volume Two** picks up the story with the onset of the Yom Kippur War and finishes forty-two chapters later with Sadat's arrival at Ben Gurion airport.

The period between 1966 and 1977 formed the foundation for Israel and her neighbors for all that has come since. Only by studying that time period—the many failures, constant frustrations, and few successes—is there any hope of understanding the present and divining a way forward. Shakespeare's phrase "the past is prologue" is often quoted by students of history. Perhaps in terms of the conflict between Arab and Jew, it is better to say, "The prologue is always derived from the past."

What follows is the story of that past.

CHAPTER ONE
Samu — November, 1966

In 1966, more than 2.3 million Jews were living in Israel. For the hundreds of thousands of Israelis who had managed to survive the Holocaust little more than twenty years before, the barbarism of that time remained fresh in their memories. Several hundred thousand others had a different past, but one that also left traumatic scars. Faced with hardship and intolerant Arab majority populations, they fled their ancestral homes, abandoning what they knew and loved. In addition, many middle aged and older Israelis were living with emotional scars from yet another frightening set of experiences. Since 1948, they had fought in one or more wars to protect Israel from Palestinian irregulars and the armies of surrounding Arab states. Plus, weighing heavily on all, was knowledge that for two thousand years wherever Jews lived their persecution seemed inevitable. Only by living in their own land would they be safe. Collectively, Israelis agreed they would never again passively endure the ghettos, the pogroms, or the concentration camps. Never again.

The Israeli combative mindset did not emerge without provocation. In a decades-long onslaught, Palestinian terrorists had committed atrocity after atrocity, all with the support of neighboring Arab nations. Since most Israeli population centers were within a short drive, or even walking distance, from an Arab country dedicated to Israel's destruction, almost all Israelis felt they lived on the front lines. Everyone felt the danger. And, because of their common concerns and shared terrors that intermingled with everyday life, when catastrophe struck a few, it was a catastrophe felt by all.

What was hardly bearable became intolerable in 1966. Terrorists struck targets within Israel an average of more than three times per month in a country the approximate size of New Jersey—America's fifth smallest state. The threat of random violence occupied the minds of the Israeli people, impacting their daily lives. The pace of the onslaught increased in October. Half of the attacks emanated from Jordan.

On October 7, 1966, only good fortune averted disaster. Fedayeen (a word commonly used to identify Palestinians that participated in violent operations—generally against Israeli military and civilian targets) placed explosive devices against the weight-bearing foundations of an apartment building in Jewish Jerusalem. They hoped that the collapsing structure would kill many of the residents. Three packets exploded—the fourth failed. The explosions injured several occupants, but the building did not collapse. When Israel's Prime Minister, Levi Eshkol, viewed the rubble he warned, "The ledger is open and the hand is recording."

Eighteen days later, the ledger received a new entry. Palestinian saboteurs placed a mine that exploded on a busy rail line running from Jerusalem to Tel Aviv. The detonation caused a cargo train to derail resulting in extensive damage. Just two hours earlier a train filled with passengers used the same tracks. Good fortune had again averted catastrophe.

The Catalyst and the Response

King Hussein should have been happy on November 12, 1966. His thirty-first birthday was the next day. But within minutes of awakening he received reports that Palestinian guerillas had killed three Israeli soldiers during the night.

Hussein did not consider it noteworthy for Palestinian Fedayeen to have Israeli blood on their hands. But he instantly recognized the problem this attack posed. The frequency and ferocity of Palestinian raids into Israel had been increasing. This time, Fedayeen entered Israel from a spot in the Jordanian-controlled West Bank south of Hebron. Hussein sensed Israel's tolerance had reached its limit even though the Israelis knew he did not support terrorism. He feared that their instinctive urge to retaliate against a target located in Jordan might overwhelm any thoughts of forbearance.

In hopes of slaking Israel's thirst for revenge, Hussein sent a letter of condolence to Prime Minister Eshkol, reaffirming his commitment to maintain a secure border with Israel. Government personnel delivered the letter to the American Embassy in Amman, Jordan's capital, and American embassy employees cabled it to the U.S. Ambassador to Israel. There it sat for an entire day. Eshkol did not receive the note until near 9:00 a.m. on Sunday, November 13.

The letter arrived too late.

The bomb that killed three soldiers during the night had also injured six others. The soldiers had hidden most of the night in the foothills that extended from Mount Hebron into Israel, hoping to ambush Arab infiltrators sneaking into the country from Jordan. They headed back to their base after midnight. The dark night, barely illuminated by a sliver of moon, made it impossible for them to detect the buried mine. It detonated when their vehicle passed over the explosive. A rescue team found the tracks of the perpetrators shortly after the blast. They led a few short miles to the Jordanian-controlled West Bank.

News that three more soldiers had died at the hands of Fedayeen struck deep into the emotional core of Israel's close-knit society already alarmed by the increasing frequency and audacity of Palestinian terrorist activity. During the early hours of November 12, the highest ranking officer in Israel's army, Chief of Staff Yitzhak Rabin, met with his General Staff to agree on a response to the attack. Rabin knew that Prime Minister Eshkol and his cabinet would expect him to recommend a course of action at their meeting scheduled for later that morning.

Israel had learned the hard way that complaining to the United Nations (UN) rarely advanced her cause. A month before, four Israeli border policemen died when their vehicle ran over a mine placed by Fedayeen close to the Syrian border. Israel complained to the UN that terrorists supported by Syria were responsible; ten of the eleven members of the Security Council voted in favor of censuring Syria, but the Soviet Union vetoed the resolution. Israel's leadership knew the outcome would be the same if they again relied on the UN.

Rabin and his generals agreed that the situation demanded more than a pinprick response. They also knew Syria was indirectly responsible for the recent attack. Syria provided significant financial and material support to the terrorists based in Jordan. But without convincing proof they understood world opinion would not tolerate a punitive military action against the Syrians. And an attack on Syria would mean that infantry and armor moving up and into the Golan Heights would face significant enemy fire; heavy casualties were inevitable. In addition, the mutual-defense pact concluded by Syria and Egypt a week earlier presented a problem. The General Staff did not want to risk war with Egypt by attacking Syria. Therefore, the generals advised Rabin against striking the Syrians even though they were complicit.

Jordan was another matter. The generals trusted King Hussein's desire to control their mutual border but not his ability to do so. Terrorists moved freely with little restriction within the country; they had already taken many Israeli lives, and there was little likelihood Hussein would successfully hold the Fedayeen in check in the future. Therefore, since Hussein could not seal the border, the generals decided their best option was to obstruct the terrorists' ability to initiate attacks. If the terrorists were no longer able to base themselves close to Israel and lost their ability to move about as freely, their efforts to penetrate Israel's defenses would grow complicated. That would reduce the number of terrorist missions they could launch. It was a matter of numbers; the fewer alternatives they had and the fewer missions they could mount, the safer Israelis would be.

To achieve their goal, the generals hoped to dissuade Palestinians living in Jordan from helping the terrorist organizations. Previously, in keeping with his desire to avoid confronting Hussein, Eshkol had only approved limited stealthy night attacks against specific targets in Jordan to interdict the terrorists. But those strikes failed to stem the tide of Fedayeen; terrorist incursions into Israel were increasing. A new strategy was required. No country willingly endures repeated attacks launched from its neighbor's territory without responding in kind. Nor would Israel.

Several months earlier, the Israeli Defense Forces (IDF) had requested Eshkol's permission to strike a hard, retaliatory blow against a Jordanian village that was helping the Fedayeen. The IDF argued that villagers in Jordan would not stop helping the terrorists until a cost was imposed for doing so. The IDF planned a daylight strike that would destroy the homes of known Fedayeen supporters. Those planning the attack hoped to avoid confronting the Jordanian military by moving quickly before the Jordanians could confront the IDF; they also wanted to avoid inflicting Arab civilian casualties. The planners knew it was a risky business but believed the threat of more terrorist attacks on Israel justified taking both of those risks. They knew that if nothing were done, terrorists would kill more Israelis.

Rabin went to Eshkol's home on November 12 to brief the Prime Minister before the cabinet meeting. He requested permission to launch an attack on Samu, a village in the West Bank less than five miles from Israel's border and almost fifteen miles south of Hebron. Samu had a population of 4,000, and Israeli intelligence believed that its inhabitants harbored terrorists who used the town as a base for operations against Israel. Rabin told Eshkol of his plan to use overwhelming force in broad daylight but to avoid any confrontation with the Jordanian military. He predicted it would take little more than three hours to blow up dozens of Arab residents' homes and to destroy a police station. Rabin explained further that the goal was not to kill civilians but to destroy property, and that the operation would teach Arab villagers the price of supporting terrorists.

Seventy-one-year-old Eshkol left for the cabinet meeting after seeing Rabin. The increasing ferocity and effectiveness of Arab infiltrators weighed heavily on the Prime Minister. Many constituents doubted that Eshkol's government could protect them; they needed assurance. Pressure to find a solution was widespread. Previously, debate centered on the merits of retaliatory raids into Syria or Jordan. Some proposed building a robust fence along the border, an idea that would take fruit in the 1990's. Others counseled patience and perseverance. Until November of 1966, Eshkol's policy had been to avoid major escalations that might lead to war and international sanctions. The army had had to content itself, for the most part, with establishing a porous defense. That ran contrary to the IDF's creed: Always take the fight to the enemy.

Israel's Foreign Minister, Abba Eban, perhaps best described the prevailing mood of Israelis when he later wrote, "There [was] an increasing impression in the country of 'open season' for murders and attacks, as our neighbors sit by securely." Thirty-six years afterwards, people living in the Washington, D.C. area faced the threat of random death when a sniper killed ten people over three weeks. The pervasive apprehension and fear throughout the nation's capital triggered a massive police and government response. Israeli citizens not only lived with similar threats of violence at the hand of Palestinian terrorists but did so for years rather than weeks. It could not be tolerated any longer. The public demanded a strong response.

Some of Eshkol's cabinet ministers were much older than the highest-ranking generals in the IDF. Compared to the younger, aggressive IDF officers, they were cautious and politically moderate.

Another cabinet grouping, largely composed of Eshkol's political opponents, had a different perspective. Eager to return to power, they aimed to take advantage of any opportunity to do so. If the government was too cautious, they would pounce. If the government was overzealous, and failed, they would take political advantage of that; too.

Eshkol felt pressure to respond to the soldiers deaths forcefully. His "ledger" had filled. The Prime Minister told the cabinet, "Israel's patience is not unlimited." He argued persuasively that the government must do everything possible to ensure that Israelis could live normal lives, free of fear. Forbearance had given rise to more terror, not less. Eshkol said the IDF's plan offered a solution through deterrence rather than perseverance. His argument resonated with the ministers. Although they knew Syria's long arm wielded the terrorists, Eshkol's cabinet agreed to target the West Bank villagers providing direct support to the Fedayeen. Some more moderate ministers were concerned by the scale of destruction called for, but none could propose a viable alternative. The IDF scheduled the attack, code named Operation Shredder, for the next day.

King Hussein

A king's rule is almost always endangered when there are many hostile and aggressive nations on his borders. The threat is even more if those countries possess armies more powerful than his own. That is especially so if those external threats are coupled with a domestic majority that would rejoice at the king's demise and that includes individuals, supported by foreign powers both materially and with venomous propaganda, that mount assassination attempts and incite riots. In circumstances such as these, the chances of a monarch surviving his full natural reign are slim. These were the challenges Jordan's King Hussein Ibn Talal had faced for the thirteen years since he ascended the throne at the age of seventeen in 1953. But even though he lacked the caution and wisdom drawn from experience and age, Hussein clung tenuously to power despite persistent efforts to overthrow him by Syria, Egypt, Iraq, and many of his Palestinian subjects.

Hussein had many admirable qualities. Crucial was his sixth sense that served well to balance the powerful forces arrayed against him. Perhaps, almost equally important, his charismatic deep voice resonated and commanded respect that his youthful appearance and slight five feet four inch stature did not. And Hussein was courageous. Whether engaging in his passion for driving fast cars and piloting airplanes, or facing an assassin's gun, he consistently faced death with the determination to prevail. Even so, it was far from certain in 1966 that he would survive the trials of strength and leadership that loomed before him.

Jordan's geography provided no favors for the embattled king; his country's long borders were difficult to defend. Syria, much stronger and ever opportunistic, lay to the north. To the east, Jordan shared a long border with the growing economic powerhouse of Saudi Arabia and a short border with the much more powerful Iraq. Israel stood astride Jordan's long western boundary, lengthened considerably by an area called the West Bank, which bulged deeply into the center of the Jewish State. And a short distance across the Red Sea lurked Egypt led by the strident, confrontational, leader of the Arab world, President Gamal Abdel Nasser. In many ways Hussein's map looked similar to Israel's—enemies at every turn.

Hussein's greatest threat, however, came from within. His country was poor, its small population divided. Although he could count on loyalty and respect from the Bedouin tribes that lived within Jordan, his rule also extended over more than a million disgruntled Palestinians who lived both east and west of the Jordan River.

Several hundred thousand of those Palestinians lived on the western side of the river, closer to Israel. They resided in several cities, including the Arab-populated portion of Jerusalem and in many villages that dotted the arid hills of the West Bank. They had become Jordanian subjects in 1950 after Hussein's grandfather annexed the region. Many of those Palestinians yearned for their former homes located in what had become Israel. They had fled for a variety of reasons during the 1948 War initiated by the Arabs: misplaced fears, exhortations to temporarily leave for their own safety by Arab leaders confident they would win, and, at times, intimidation by victorious Jewish soldiers. They wanted to return to their homes and did not want to be Jordanians. Some despised Hussein, others tolerated him, but few loved him.

Hussein knew he needed to address his Palestinian problem with care. On January 13, 1964, at an Arab League Summit in Cairo, delegates made a decision that would have long-term repercussions. They announced that they favored creating a Palestinian entity devoted to liberating Palestinian land and determining its own future. The declaration prepared the ground for an organization with two major policy objectives—the destruction of Israel and, from its ashes, the rise of a Palestinian State. But that placed Hussein's future control of Jordan at risk as well. Hussein knew that Palestinians would one day covet dominion over the West Bank and perhaps the rest of Jordan, too, in addition to Israel. Nevertheless, in May of 1964, due to political pressure more than conviction, Hussein permitted a founding Congress to meet in Jerusalem for the express purpose of creating a new entity, the Palestinian Liberation Organization (PLO), despite the clear threat it presented to him.

The Congress chose Ahmad Shuqayri for its leader. He was a buffoon who excelled at making bombastic statements predicting the demise of Israel and the death of Jews living there, but he proved incapable of harnessing Palestinians into a force capable of accomplishing that. He also was a puppet who followed the dictates of his main benefactor,

Egyptian President Nasser, who was not yet willing to wield PLO terrorists as a weapon because he feared Israel's response.

Nasser convened a second Arab Summit on the shores of the Mediterranean in Alexandria, Egypt in September of 1964. This time, the Arab nations in attendance committed to assist the PLO and endorsed creation of a Palestinian Liberation Army (PLA) to be the vanguard of the Arab struggle to liberate Israel from the Jews. The decision disturbed Hussein because he foresaw that the PLA would evolve into an army composed mainly of Jordanian Palestinian subjects operating on Jordanian soil but independent of his control.

After the Summit, Shuqayri tried to alleviate Hussein's concern. He renewed his promise made several months before that the PLO would only look west towards Israel, not east towards Jordan or the West Bank. Shuqayri sought to further mollify Hussein by telling him that Jordan and the PLO were "two wings of the same bird." He hoped to convince Hussein of their mutual dependence. But Shuqayri overplayed his hand when he proposed establishment of PLA regiments on the West Bank housed at military training camps in fortified villages. Then he made matters worse by advocating for a five percent tax to be levied on Palestinian employees of Hussein's government to pay for PLO activities and personnel he called "soldiers in the army of return." Those requests exposed Shuqayri's plans to create a nation within a nation. Not only did he want his own army, he also wanted the power that would stem from a taxing authority independent of Jordanian control. Not surprisingly, Hussein rejected both ideas, and, in 1965, Hussein took another step to maintain his control. He disbanded the Jordanian National Guard, composed mainly of Palestinians that provided security for villages, because he viewed it as a potential vehicle for establishing the PLA on the West Bank. Hussein's actions thwarted the first Palestinian attempt to establish an autonomous self-governing entity within a host nation that would provide them shelter and sustenance. Unfortunately, for both Jordan and Lebanon, it would not be the last.

At the same time that Hussein was fighting to prevent a Palestinian cancer from growing within, he resisted an infectious process from outside Jordan's borders. When Nasser pushed him to permit Saudi and Iraqi troops to station themselves on Jordanian soil, Hussein deflected the request. Hussein knew that his defiance of the Palestinians and the wishes of the Arab World entailed risks for him. However, he also understood the dynamics of his rule. His support came from the Bedouin tribes, but they did not constitute the vast majority of his subjects. Therefore, he had to pay lip service to Palestinian aspirations while preventing them from becoming too strong to control. He also could not afford to antagonize Israel. Jordan lay astride the political fault line of the conflict between Arabs and Israel. He would fall victim if he made one false move.

Complicating matters even further, the PLO was not the only Palestinian organization; and Shuqayri was not the only Palestinian leader Hussein needed to placate. Yasser Arafat was a leading member of Fatah, one of several Palestinian groups that refused to follow the dictates of the PLO. Arafat viewed the PLO with disdain. He believed it to be an artificial creation of Arab states, especially Egypt, designed to control Palestinians' aspirations to establish their own nation on the ruins of Israel. Arafat thought that Arab nations would wield the PLO in a manner that suited them, not in a manner that would put the needs of his people first. He regarded Shuqayri as Nasser's stooge. Arafat thought only Fatah took the well-being of Palestinians to heart. Since Fatah believed in action rather in than the reticence and subservience the group observed in the PLO, the organization decided to use terrorism to goad Israel into retaliating against neighboring Arab nations. Fatah hoped Israel's response would spark a war with those nations, a war that would end with Israel's destruction. Any collateral damage suffered by Syria, Jordan, or Egypt was of little consequence.

In 1965 and 1966, Hussein also faced increasing domestic Palestinian pressure to actively confront Israel. In addition, Syrian supported Palestinian guerillas stepped up the frequency of their raids into Israel from Jordanian territory. Then, as time passed, Palestinians grew increasingly frustrated with Hussein because of his refusal to help the terrorists. But Hussein knew that terrorist attacks emanating from Jordan into Israel would inevitably cause an armed confrontation between the two nations. Exasperated, the king declared on June 14, 1966, "All hopes have vanished for the possibility of cooperation with [the PLO] in its recent form."

By the morning of November 12, 1966, Hussein had been married to his second wife for five years. He also had been engaged in a secret relationship far more dangerous than a liaison with a mistress for more than three years. The Arab world refused to recognize Israel's existence and thirsted for her destruction. But Hussein knew his tiny army could not match Israel's in a war; therefore, he pursued a dual policy. Publicly, he fully conformed to the Arab party line vilifying his Jewish neighbor. Privately, he acted quite differently. At Hussein's request in 1963, Dr. Emmanuel Herbert, a Jewish physician in London whom the king relied upon for medical advice, arranged for him to meet secretly in the British capital with Israel's Deputy Director of the Foreign Ministry, Yaacov Herzog. Hussein knew his life would be at risk if any Arab nations or his own subjects learned of the meetings. But to survive, he needed to avoid a confrontation with Israel he would lose while simultaneously balancing the demands of Arab extremism against the limits of Israeli tolerance.

Hussein's perspective, more moderate than that of other Arab leaders, coupled with his personal courage, fortified his determination to find an accommodation with the Jewish State that would keep his enemies at bay. His grandfather traveled the same path between 1948 and

1952, and lost his life at the hands of an Arab assassin because of it. Therefore, it was not surprising that Hussein appeared nervous during his first meeting with Herzog. However, after their first secret discussion remained secret, Hussein was more relaxed during two subsequent meetings with Herzog in 1964 and a third with Israeli Foreign Minister Golda Meir in 1965.

Herzog and Meir assured Hussein that Israel had no designs on the West Bank. However, they insisted that Hussein must stop terrorists from using Jordanian soil to attack Israel. They also were clear; Israel would not tolerate other Arab nations placing their military forces within Jordan. Hussein responded that he would prevent the PLO from training and basing soldiers within his country, that he would not permit foreign troops to enter Jordan, and that he would not permit his army to base its tanks on the West Bank. In return, Hussein pleaded, Israel must patiently absorb any Palestinian terrorist attacks. Otherwise, he warned, Israeli military retaliation into Jordanian territory might destabilize his throne. After refusing permission for the PLA to operate in the West Bank, Hussein knew he would be blamed for leaving Palestinians helpless if Israel attacked them. While Herzog and Meir appeared to understand, the king remained uneasy.

His anxiety was justified. To the north, the Syrians were planning for a future—a future without Israel. And a future with little regard for how their plans would impact the king's chances of surviving.

Syria plotted to inflict pain on her Jewish neighbor, but sought to avoid a direct confrontation until the Arab nations possessed the collective strength to win an all-out war. The Syrians coveted the territories of both Israel and Lebanon. Syria's leaders hoped to join those lands with their own to create a "greater Syria." Their scheme first required emergence of a Palestinian State, on top of Israel's ruins, indebted to Syria. Achieving that interim goal required arming, training, and financing Palestinians willing to attack the Jewish State. The Syrians saw the Palestinians as surrogates, useful for furthering Syrian ambitions. The surrogates were happy to oblige because doing so fit their objectives. After Israel fell, the Syrians believed their prestige would increase, affording them the opportunity to wrest leadership of the Arab world from Nasser. The Palestinians thought differently. They believed they would have an independent country. Few had any interest in being part of Syria.

The Syrians decided to base most Palestinian terrorists in Jordan and to require them to launch their attacks into Israel from there because other alternatives were less promising. Lebanon had a short, more easily controlled border with Israel. The long border between Israel and Egypt offered a better opportunity, but, with the exception of Gaza, it ran on both sides through a remote, sparsely populated desert that lacked easy access to Israeli population centers. And even more problematic for the Syrians, Egypt kept her Palestinian refugees secure under its autocratic thumb. Nasser's inflammatory speeches were for public consumption; they did not reflect any imminent plans. The Syrians knew Nasser had no interest in provoking Israel to start a war Egypt was not yet able to win.

Nor did Syria relish supporting extensive terrorist activities emanating from Syrian soil. The high hills of the Golan Heights overlooking Jewish farming communities were far better for shooting at Israeli farmers below than for Fedayeen bases because the short border between Syria and Israel contained natural barriers, including Lake Kinneret (also known as the Sea of Galilee), that made stealthy entry difficult. Nor did the Syrians want to tempt the powerful Israelis to respond militarily. Syria's army was not up to the challenge.

The West Bank, however, was a tremendous location to establish bases for a sustained terrorist campaign. It jutted deep into Israel's midsection. In places it came within ten miles of cutting the Jewish nation in two between its rocky ridges and the Mediterranean Sea. The West Bank's 191 mile perimeter facing Israel twisted through mostly rugged terrain with no significant natural obstacles such as rivers or tall mountain ranges. Equally important, terrorists could operate from Arab villages and towns only a few miles from the border which could provide them cover and support. The Syrians knew it would be impossible for Israel to block all terrorist infiltration attempts from the West Bank into Israel. Nor could Jordan's weak army. And from those bases the Fedayeen would have easy access to soft, Jewish civilian targets. Also, Israel's capital, Jerusalem, sat at the apex of a finger of land squeezed by West Bank territory; and many other Jewish towns and settlements lay within an easy day's walk from the border. Access to Israel's soft underbelly was there for the taking.

In addition, Syria hoped that basing terrorists in Jordan would give rise to one more benefit—gun-wielding Fedayeen would destabilize Hussein's authority. If terrorist successes caused Israel to retaliate, the king would face even more pressure to permit the Palestinians to arm themselves for defensive purposes. But those same arms could also be used to overthrow him. Syria's leaders had little love for the Hashemite King. His demise would not have bothered them.

Meanwhile, the Syrians planned to deny any involvement with terrorist operations. They had no desire to give Israel an excuse to attack them, and they wanted to avoid any international opprobrium. Thus, the Syrians saw Jordan as the perfect cauldron within which Syria's rhetoric and material support could bring terror to a boil—with impunity for themselves.

The Attack

On November 13, 1966, an IDF battalion, composed of 400 soldiers—supported by tanks, planes and artillery—started towards Jordan about 5:30 a.m. The soldiers wore coats to ward off the frigid air. Vapor marked each exhalation of breath. When the sun began its inevitable rise, the first rays of light revealed ridges, gullies, and mountains at odd angles to each other. The IDF column turned onto a dirt track within Israel and, then, crossed the border. The path became increasingly rocky and rutted. Forty-five minutes later red streaks of dawn in the sky mingled with brilliant bursts of light from shells fired from the turrets of Israeli tanks which demolished a Jordanian police station. Within an hour Israeli troops arrived at the village center of Samu. Other soldiers peeled off to man defensive positions pre-selected to prevent Jordanian soldiers from reaching the area.

More than 2,000 years old, Samu was a village at the intersection of two deserts, the Israeli Negev to the south and the parched lands of Judea to the east. Its peasant farmers grazed sheep and goats on the rocky ground near their homes. The residents habitually awakened early to fetch water and to bake bread. On November 13, after hearing tank fire in the distance, most hurriedly abandoned the village in favor of the open fields and limestone caves that dotted the area. When Israeli soldiers arrived, they saw smoke streaming from some chimneys and the adobe walls of village homes painted in a variety of colors; but they encountered few people. In the town center they came across residential structures built of white stone. Frayed ropes attached to buckets hung over scattered wells throughout the town. Donkeys strolled unconcerned on the streets, and roosters called out the new day.

The Israelis gathered the remaining villagers in the city center and checked to make sure that stragglers did not linger in the buildings. Sappers then placed and set off explosives destroying residences, a school, and a medical clinic. The sturdy houses built of stone blew apart, but some rocky sections blasted into the air stubbornly stuck together until they inevitably crashed to the ground.

Outside of the village, however, the plan to avoid a clash with the Jordanian army went awry. Twenty truckloads of Jordanian troops rushed south on winding roads to aid the beleaguered town. Israeli troops lay in wait to stop them. At 7:00 a.m. the quiet morning on the road burst into the melee of blood and fire that Rabin had hoped to avoid. Four Jordanian warplanes also appeared over the battlefield to support the Jordanian ground forces, but Israeli interceptors thwarted them and shot down a Jordanian plane in the process. Its pilot, a friend of King Hussein, died. Even so, some Jordanian soldiers successfully reached the southern outskirts of Samu before Israeli tanks drove them back. By 8:00 a.m. the fighting ceased. Forty-five minutes later the Israeli soldiers withdrew. The last Israeli troops exited Jordan by 9:45 a.m.

Left behind, at least fourteen Jordanian soldiers lay dead; many more were wounded. The ruins of more than 120 buildings marred the landscape, and a furious and politically weakened King Hussein contemplated what he perceived as Israel's treachery.

The IDF did not suffer many casualties. Many of the victorious troops passed through Beersheba, an Israeli town, in a victory parade of sorts on their way back to base. The IDF had fulfilled the mission's tactical goals but inadvertently caused a geopolitical disaster. The repercussions would not be evident for several months but would last for decades.

The Aftermath

News of the raid ruined Hussein's birthday. That morning, shortly after the battle ended, Hussein received an unsolicited communication from Israel's government meant to reassure the Jordanian monarch that Israel had no intention of attacking Jordan. It probably was written before the death of the three soldiers that sparked the attack on Samu but like the letter Hussein had sent the day before, it did not arrive in time.

Hussein felt humiliated and betrayed.

His humiliation welled from his country's failure to defend herself. His sense of betrayal stemmed from the assurances he had received from Israel over the years. Hussein concluded that Israel, if given the opportunity or excuse, planned to conquer the West Bank. Although he was wrong, what Hussein believed mattered far more than the truth. Hussein refrained from retaliating because he thought it would give Israel an excuse to respond by taking the West Bank from him. Instead he restrained his fury and just referred the matter to the UN.

Eshkol was not happy either. Even though three out of four Israeli citizens supported his decision to retaliate, the raid's results angered him. The attack was supposed to convince West Bank residents to withhold support from the guerillas. However, instead of an object lesson to civilians, the planned surgical strike resulted in a pitched battle between armies. The death of so many Jordanian soldiers and the degree of destruction undercut Eshkol's tacit policy of supporting Hussein. Rather than fortifying Hussein's struggle against the Palestinian terrorists, the attack emasculated the king. Six of Eshkol's cabinet ministers expressed anger over the operation. Rabin admitted he was wrong to believe that the Jordanian army would not react.

During the acrimonious aftermath, despite his private misgivings, Eshkol supported the army. He also realized, upon reflection, he should have retaliated against Syria, not Jordan. Later, he expressed his feelings in his unique, cryptic style, commenting that you don't beat up the bride when you mean to punch your mother-in-law in the face. Meanwhile, Foreign Minister Eban attempted damage control. He admitted privately to other countries that the scope of the mission had unexpectedly expanded. Nobody questioned Israel's objective, but everyone regretted the result.

The American government was disconcerted by the attack on Samu. The United States considered Hussein a friend. President Johnson, furious by some accounts and extremely unhappy according to others, found Israel's excuses unacceptable. American diplomats pointed to Hussein's promise to keep Jordanian tanks out of the West Bank as evidence Israel had violated a tacit agreement with the king to refrain from aggressive actions. They threatened that if the Israelis attacked

Jordan again the United States would re-examine whether America would continue supplying military supplies to Israel.

America's response alarmed Eshkol. He sent a written message to Johnson in which he admitted Israel had made a mistake. Johnson did not reply. Eshkol also wrote a condolence letter to Hussein. He sent it to the U.S. State Department for forwarding. The State Department refused to deliver it to the king.

The UN Security Council unanimously condemned Israel for the attack. The condemnation included a warning that the UN would consider adopting other steps to prevent any future retaliatory attacks. And, in accordance with other UN condemnations of Israeli actions, the resolution failed to address the impetus for the armed incursion: Palestinian terrorists preying on Israeli soldiers and civilians. That was routine. What changed was that the United States did not veto the lopsided resolution.

As Hussein had predicted during his secret meetings with the Israelis, Jordan's Palestinian "guests" and Arab brethren in other countries challenged him after Samu. Domestic protests coupled with bitter denunciations from without threatened his continued rule. Angry Palestinians felt they could have protected Samu had their National Guard not been dismantled in 1965 and their weapons confiscated. Many thought Hussein cowardly to rely on UN resolutions rather than retaliating. Some accused the king of working in concert with the Israelis in order to destroy Palestinian opposition to him. It was the same accusation his assassinated grandfather had endured. As Palestinians leaned towards open revolt rather than towards demands for increased protection, Hussein's monarchy teetered due to their discontent.

Because of the unrest the PLO saw opportunity. On November 24, Shuqayri called for the Jordanian army to join the people in open rebellion. Mass Palestinian demonstrations began in Ramallah and spread to other large cities on the West Bank. Protestors carried Palestinian nationalist placards and shouted pro-Nasser slogans. Their leaders called for the establishment of a Palestinian State on the West Bank.

To mollify the protesters, Hussein issued small arms to villagers living along the border with Israel. When that failed to calm the masses, Hussein called on the Jordanian army to forcefully stop the disturbances. Two weeks of shooting live ammunition and tear gas canisters into restive crowds restored a sullen calm.

Syria and Egypt took full advantage of Jordan's humiliation to push their own agendas. Syria, looking to promote herself over her larger ally, denounced Egypt for not helping Jordan when Israel struck Samu. Both countries slandered Hussein after the attack, much of it of a personally insulting nature. They riled the "Arab street" by accusing Hussein of working with Israel and the American CIA to create an incident that would justify a crackdown on the Palestinians, and they called the king a coward for his failure to retaliate against Israel. Of course, pointing out cowardice is easier than displaying courage, and national leaders are no exception. The Syrians made no effort to practice what they preached. They, like the Egyptians, did not make any threatening moves towards Israel.

On December 15, the Arab League Defense Council met in Cairo to discuss the Samu incident. The delegates declared that Jordan had failed to fulfill her obligation to protect Palestinians living in her territory when Hussein denied Iraq and Saudi Arabia permission to establish bases within the country. The Jordanian representative responded that since Israel would consider the entry of outside forces into Jordan a reason to attack, foreign Arab armies could only enter the country to respond to imminent threats. Shuqayri then inflamed the atmosphere, already incendiary from hurled invective, by charging Jordan with obstructing the PLO, and demanding unfettered freedom for the PLO to launch terrorist operations against Israel from bases on the West Bank.

The Jordanian representative responded with verbal attacks of his own. He derided Egypt for failing to come to Jordan's aid as the Egyptians had committed to do years before when Nasser had joined with many Arab nations, including Jordan, to create the ineffectual United Arab Command. He mockingly questioned why Egypt would not let Palestinians attack Israel from Egyptian territory. He then accused the Egyptians of hiding behind the UN peacekeeping force strung out along the Egyptian-Israeli border. The peacekeepers had been installed there following the ceasefire between Israel and Egypt after their war in 1956. This was an accusation Nasser remembered six months later, a broadly held belief that contributed to the calamity that eventually befell Egypt. The Jordanian delegate also challenged Egypt to concentrate her strength against Israel rather than continuing to fight a war in Yemen. The Jordanian delegate's accusations exposed the hypocrisy of charging his country with abdicating her responsibility to confront Israel when more powerful Arab nations critical of the king fecklessly refrained from doing so. Not surprisingly, when the meeting was over, the relationship between Hussein and Nasser had deteriorated to a new low.

The Impact

Although Israel's attack on Samu was a tactical military victory, it was a strategic political disaster for Israel. It aggravated relations with the United States and left the UN fuming. It also alienated Hussein and constrained Israel's future options for deterring terror. Israel had struck the wrong country for the wrong reason. Meanwhile, the animosity between Israel and Syria, Israel's most hated and implacable enemy, festered.

Unfortunately, King Hussein drew two lessons from the attack, but both of them were catastrophically wrong. **First** and foremost, he decided Jordan must be part of a regional Arab defense pact to deter Israel. He would seek that relationship in the future if the level of animosity between Jordan and the other Arab countries ever diminished. Until then, Hussein resolved to continue castigating his Arab brethren in the ongoing war of words for as long as they did the same to him. **Second**, Hussein concluded that he could not trust Israel. He thought Israel yearned to conquer the West Bank and had schemed to manufacture a rift between Jordan and her neighboring countries to accomplish it. Nevertheless, Hussein recognized that Palestinian terrorism produced dangerous flashpoints. To avoid giving Israel a pretext to invade, he redoubled his efforts to stop guerillas crossing from Jordan into Israel.

Thus, thanks to Hussein's anxiety, Israel's short-term goal to enlist Jordan's active cooperation in the fight against the terrorists was achieved, but her success came at the cost of losing a potential secret partner in the Arab world. And, most unfortunately, Hussein misinterpreted Israel's intent. Israel did not have any plans to take the West Bank from Jordan. Ironically, it was Hussein's mistaken analysis, not Israel's machinations that ultimately led to what the king most feared.

The Samu attack did, however, increase Egypt's and Syria's confidence. A week before the battle they had signed a defense pact. When Israel attacked Samu rather than retaliating against Syria after the death of the three soldiers, both countries concluded that their mutual defense pact had deterred Israel. They saw Israel's strike on Samu as evidence of Israeli weakness rather than steely determination. They also reasoned that Syria's friendship with the Soviet Union helped shield Syria from an Israeli attack. They were not entirely wrong. Israel took the easy way out by attacking Jordan. Syria was a client state of the Soviet Union, and Israel remembered the lesson of the 1956 Suez Crises. She did not want to risk confronting a superpower without unwavering international, and most especially, American support. As a result, Russia's influence in the region grew.

The war of words and blood escalated at the start of 1967. Syria continued to support Palestinian terrorism, and the Syrian army intermittently fired artillery shells into Israel targeting civilians. And even when shooting in the north paused, Syria emphasized she would not restrain the Palestinians. On January 16, 1967, Syrian state-controlled radio announced, "Syria has changed its strategy, moving from defense to attack ... we will carry out operations until Israel is eliminated." Then, on February 13, Syrian Defense Minister Assad said, "The mere existence of Zionism in Palestine constitutes aggression and aggression and peace cannot coexist in the same territory." The Syrian Information Ministry also told a Lebanese newspaper that there is "no alternative for Arabs but to liquidate Israel or be liquidated by her."

In response to Syrian provocations, the Israeli government issued a statement that Syria's hope to "hit us without being hit" would fail. Eshkol also added that Israel would respond "with arms and methods of our choosing." The UN was of no help. It tried and failed to broker a ceasefire that would end the numerous border clashes between the IDF and Fedayeen crossing into Israel.

Meanwhile, the vitriolic war of words between Egypt and Jordan accelerated. Nasser called Hussein, "the whore of Jordan" in February, 1967. In response, Hussein recalled his ambassador to Egypt.

The spring of 1967 brought more terror and less hope to the Middle East. Tension pulled war's trigger tight. Palestinian Fedayeen escalated their attacks, verbal sparring became increasingly threatening, Syrians schemed, Egyptians planned, and the Russians maneuvered to increase their influence in the region. Hussein only sought to survive, but Samu pushed him from his previously chosen path. No longer would he rely on Israeli restraint if there was a future confrontation between Arabs and Jews. Instead, he would seek protection by looking for opportunities to reform his relationship with his Arab "brothers," the same Arab leaders who thirsted for him to disappear. It was a fateful decision by the Jordanian king that changed the region and the world forever.

CHAPTER TWO

April 7, 1967 — "Today they discovered they had made a small error."

On May 14, 1948, with the approval of the UN, Israel declared her Independence. It took just one day for her existence to be challenged; Egypt, Syria, Jordan, and Lebanon with the support of other Arab countries—attacked the new nation on May 15. The war ended with Syrian soldiers squatting on small strips of land claimed by Israel in the northern Galilee located southeast, east, and north of Lake Kinneret (the Sea of Galilee). Israel demanded that the Syrians pull back to the old international border, marked by the British and French in 1923, and recognized by the UN in 1947 when it voted in favor of Israel becoming an independent nation. Ten yards of contested land east of the lake was especially crucial. Without it, Israel would lose control of her most important water supply.

Syria refused to withdraw.

Tortuous ceasefire negotiations finally produced a tenuous interim solution in June, 1949. Israel and Syria agreed to create demilitarized zones (DMZ) on the disputed territory, but only after Israel accepted the inclusion within the DMZs of some additional land she held east of Lake Kinneret. Israel hoped that by making that concession that agreement would lead to a peace treaty. Those hopes did not reach fruition. The Syrians were finished with negotiations. Instead, they made clear that *their long-term policy goal was destruction of the Jewish State. And the DMZs, rather than being stepping stones to peace, became flashpoints for sparking a future war.*

The ceasefire agreement restricted military forces, formal or informal, from entering the DMZs, but allowed civilians to return to their villages and settlements. At the insistence of the Syrians, the agreement also included a provision that the Armistice Demarcation Line and the DMZs were created to separate the two opposing military forces, but could not be used by either side as a precedent in any subsequent negotiations.

After the ceasefire agreement with the Syrians was signed, Israeli farmers attempted, for the next eighteen years, to cultivate small noncontiguous agricultural fields within the DMZs. When they did so Syrian gunners routinely fired at them with small arms and artillery from the Golan Heights above, hoping to turn the tractors back. When Israeli crops ripened, the Syrians destroyed them with targeted fire. David "Dado" Elazar, then the IDF Commander for Northern Israel, said, "We plow, and the field turns brown; then we plant, and it becomes green; and then they burn it, and it becomes black. And then we come back and plow, and the whole cycle starts all over again." The Syrians fought hard to prevent the farmers from working the land in the DMZs because they believed civilian use would lead to an Israeli claim of sovereignty—a claim Syria fervently opposed. And since the Syrians considered themselves still at war with Israel, they had no problem using force.

The fighting in the DMZs was but one segment of the low-intensity warfare instigated by the Syrians that played out on the canvas of northern Israel during February and March 1967. In addition to periodic Syrian shelling of Israeli settlements from their artillery emplacements high on the Golan Heights, Palestinian terrorist groups—encouraged, trained, and financed in part by Syria—attempted to sabotage Israeli infrastructure and to spread terror throughout the populace. Over the first three months of 1967, Israelis in northern Israel endured an average of two terrorist actions a week. Then, on April 1, 1967, Palestinian terrorists attempted, but failed, to blow up a water pump in the north. The randomness of the violence, as well as its frequency, profoundly disrupted everyday life.

Israel's government decided the time had come to respond.

Levi Eshkol

Israeli Prime Minister Levi Eshkol's birth name was Levi Skolnik. His journey to Prime Minister was a long one. He was born in 1895 in a Ukrainian village seething with violence from pogroms directed at the Jews living in the region. For many young Jews there, devotion to religion was their only sanctuary from their daily reality of being potential targets of violence motivated by hatred. However, some instead became attracted to Zionism, the new late nineteenth century nationalist movement that recognized Jews needed a state of their own in the land of Israel to escape oppression and survive. Eshkol was one of them, and at age nineteen he chose to immigrate to what was then known as Palestine. Although his first job upon arrival was as an agricultural laborer, he soon became a political activist.

During the World War I years Eshkol campaigned on behalf of farmers who suffered hardship as a result of the war and Ottoman rule. When the war ended, Eshkol joined a group that founded the settlement *Degania Beth* in 1920. After surviving malaria and repeated Bedouin attacks, he participated in founding the National Federation of Jewish Laborers in Israel (*Histadrut*) and subsequently joined its agricultural center. In 1930 he helped found the Workers' party, Mapai. When the Nazi nightmare first began in the 1930's he traveled extensively in Germany on behalf of Jewish interests and raised funds for Jewish settlements in Israel. In 1937, he worked with others to establish *Mekorot*, the nation's water utility. It was the achievement Eshkol was most proud of and where he was chief executive until 1951. Additionally, Eshkol was elected Secretary of the Laborers Council in Tel Aviv, at the end of 1944, and held that position until 1948.

Eshkol was also a member of Haganah's command structure from 1921-1923 and again from 1940-1948. The Jewish leadership in Palestine first established the Haganah to defend Jews from Arab marauders. It was the main forerunner of the IDF. Eshkol was responsible for purchasing equipment and organizing mobilization of its forces. After

Israel became a nation, Eshkol acted as her first Director General of the Ministry of Defense; his chief responsibility was procuring equipment for the Israeli army. During that period he changed his last name from Skolnik to Eshkol. At the end of 1948, Eshkol was appointed Director of the Settlement Department of the Jewish Agency and remained in that role until 1963. In his first four years at the agency he initiated the establishment of 400 new settlements. He also served from 1949-1952 as the Jewish Agency treasurer where he dealt with the significant financial burden caused by massive immigration to Israel during the first years of her existence.

Eshkol was not charismatic and had little ability to influence others through passionate discourse. Although he often used pithy witticisms to make a point, he possessed a practical mind that worked methodically to find solutions. He was a man that could get things done; however, in part because he lacked military experience, many had little respect for his opinions on defense issues. Agriculture was a different story. That was his passion. Eshkol had a dream to cultivate every inch of Israel that he could. Perhaps then, due to his background in agriculture and as a water engineer, the attempt by Fedayeen to destroy the water pump on April 1 motivated Eshkol to respond militarily in hope of influencing the Syrians to stop their aggressive behavior. Perhaps, also, it was his regret for striking the wrong nation at Samu.

The Day Begins

The weather was poor in the early hours of Friday, April 7, 1967. But clearing skies were forecast for the morning. That was important. Four days before, bad weather had forced Israel to postpone plans to send tractors into the demilitarized zones to enforce Israel's right to cultivate the land. Israeli soldiers would need clear weather to ward off any interference posed by the Syrian army. The Israeli government expected that the Syrians would react violently, as they had in the past, to any

Israeli attempt to farm in a DMZ. Officers positioned their armor and prepared the Israeli Air Force (IAF) in anticipation of an opportunity to strike back. Their trap was set. At last, the Syrians would be taught a lesson

At 9:00 a.m. the weather cleared sufficiently for the operation to begin. Two Israeli armored tractors trundled onto a fifteen acre agricultural plot at the Southern tip of Lake Kinneret. The land was part of one of the DMZs. Above, to the east, the Golan Heights loomed, an imposing set of mountains and ridges controlled by Syria that towered over the irrigated fields and multiple villages, settlements, and towns in northern Israel. Syrian artillery emplacements and fortifications dotted its hillsides and plateau.

Syrian and Israeli observers, separated by geography and ideology, intently measured the tractors' progress. Syrian soldiers, with fingers pulsating on triggers, waited for their officers to order them to fire. The Israelis, including Chief of Staff Yitzhak Rabin, pensively waited for what they knew would come. Rabin's goal was to enforce Israel's right to farm the DMZs and to retaliate for Syria's hostile activity directed against Israeli civilians. He knew Syria would try to stop the tractors and might one day even try to grab the land for her own agricultural use. Rabin expected the Syrians to react violently. If they did it would provide the IDF the excuse to teach them a lesson.

From their fortified bunkers dug into the Golan hillsides, Syrian soldiers had no idea that orders to fire on seemingly helpless Israeli farmers would touch off a devastating response. The Israeli operators of the two armored tractors crawling into the demilitarized zone surely were aware of the danger to them. But they, like the Arabs, had no inkling of the dramatic geopolitical events their actions would unleash.

True to form, Syrian soldiers fired shells from their tanks, artillery, and mortars at the tractors. Both were hit almost immediately. The Israelis sent more tractors into harm's way. The Syrians responded by shelling Israeli villages north and south of the disputed DMZ. One of the villages was Kibbutz Gadot, a farming community established by holocaust survivors in 1949. The IDF, per the plan, fired back furiously. Late in the morning the Syrians agreed to a ceasefire, but only if Israel withdrew the tractors. Israel refused, and responded that the IDF would only stop shooting if the Syrians stopped firing. Israel's leaders believed to do otherwise would be an abdication of Israel's sovereignty over the land. The tractors continued to plow the fields; the fighting continued.

The Syrians had placed their artillery high up on the hills and set back from the cliff sides. The clever positioning made it difficult for land based weapons to destroy the guns. It became clear after several hours of trying to take out the Syrian weapons with tank fire that airpower would be needed to destroy them. Rabin pressured Eshkol to permit the IAF to join the fight. Eshkol agreed. Shortly after 1:30 p.m. the first bombs fell.

The fight intensified when Syrian planes took to the sky to intercept the Israeli fighter jets. By sunset, Israeli pilots had shot down six Syrian planes. At least one of them crashed in full view of Syrian civilians in Damascus. Exacerbating the already charged atmosphere, an Israeli pilot, Yiftah Spector, flew a victory lap around the Syrian capital. It was the Arab world's first introduction to Spector. He would become one of Israel's most celebrated ace fighter pilots, and a leader of the bombing raid that destroyed the Iraqi nuclear reactor in the 1980's.

At the end of the day, Yitzhak Rabin said," Today they discovered they had made a small error."

Bruised by Egypt's propaganda war against him, Hussein taunted Nasser for failing to come to Syria's aid on April 7, and for continuing to permit Israeli shipping to pass through the Straits of Tiran to Eilat, Israel's port at the tip of the Negev. Jordan's propaganda machine also accused Nasser of hiding from Israel behind the UN peacekeeping forces stationed in the Sinai. But behind the scenes, King Hussein warned Nasser that Syria was laying a trap that would ensnare Jordan and Egypt in a war with Israel before they were ready.

Nasser hoped to shield himself from criticism by sending his Prime Minister and Egypt's Air Force Commander to Syria three days after the Syrian battle with the Israelis and by supporting the Syrians publicly. Privately, they attempted to convince Syria, without success, to stop supporting Palestinian terrorists. Syria also refused Egypt's request to station its war planes at airports near the Syrian capital but extracted a pledge that Egypt would come to Syria's aid in the event of war.

The Egyptians did not want war, but the Syrians had different ideas. They were determined to continue their low intensity confrontation with Israel, unwilling to permit Israeli cultivation of the DMZs, and were unwavering with their support of Palestinian terrorists. The Syrians thought their actions would goad the Egyptians into confronting the Israelis on the battlefield, or shame them publicly. They believed either path would enhance Syria's leadership role in the Arab world. But the Syrians were also pragmatic; they knew they could not fight Israel alone without Egypt's assistance.

The April 7 fight, like the raid on Samu, did little to suppress Syria's support of terrorism or quell the Syrian indiscriminate attacks on Israeli civilians. Israeli public opinion demanded that something more be done.

A powder keg was building. It would only take one well-placed match to light a conflagration. In the tense atmosphere that prevailed, it did not take long for that to happen.

CHAPTER THREE
Russia Stirs and Nasser Cooks

The confrontation on April 7 ended any thought in the Arab world that Israel was intimidated by the Syrian-Egyptian Defense Pact or by the Russians. But the message sent to the Syrians did not stop Palestinian gunmen from ramping up their terrorist activities. Their goal was to create a nation of their own on the ruins of Israel. Arafat's Fatah knew they could not achieve it alone, but they hoped to incite a general war between Israel and the Arab nations that would end with Arab victory and an opportunity to create a Palestinian State. Over the next month, Fatah mounted fourteen terrorist operations into Israel while the Syrians continued to fling artillery shells at Israeli civilians.

Egyptian President Abdul Nasser

Nasser had a problem. The Syrian debacle on April 7 rallied both Arab states and the Palestinians to pressure him to confront Israel with military action. Nasser was not opposed to the idea of a war with Israel in the future, but not yet. Egypt was not ready.

President Nasser, forty-nine years old in April of 1967, was at the height of his domestic popularity and worldwide prestige. His path to power began shortly after the 1948 war with Israel in which he commanded an Egyptian battalion that was cut-off and surrounded by the Israelis, but never surrendered. Afterwards, Nasser became disillusioned with the corruption of King Farouk and the Royal Family who had a stranglehold on Egypt. His political convictions led him to take a leading role in the Association of Free Officers, a group composed of mostly young, activist officers in Egypt's armed forces. On July 22, 1952, the Free Officers launched their revolution. By the next day they succeeded in bloodlessly deposing Farouk. The Egyptian people first learned of the coup from a broadcast by Anwar Sadat, Nasser's future Vice President. Nasser, concerned the public might reject him as their new ruler because he held the low rank of lieutenant colonel, decided to install General Naguib as a figurehead president. But in 1954, after surviving an assassination attempt by the Muslim Brotherhood, Nasser removed Naguib and declared himself Prime Minister. Two years later he became President after receiving an alleged 99.5 percent of the vote.

It did not take long for Nasser's mystique to assume mythical proportions throughout the Muslim world. Within the Arab nations, nationalism was on the rise. Nasser embodied the aspirations of the "Arab street" even though a few leaders of other Arab countries loathed him. But his plans and machinations came at a cost. Egypt, despite being the most powerful Arab country, could not financially support Nasser's promises to his people nor serve as protector to Arab governments of his choosing. One of his attempts to do so led him into a disastrous war in North Yemen that pitted his country against the traditional rulers of Yemen and the Saudi Royal family. That war began in 1962 and was still going on in 1967. Up to 70,000 Egyptian troops were stationed in Yemen at one time. The Egyptians even used poison gas in a failed attempt to achieve victory. As the years passed many within Egypt began to characterize Nasser's Yemen war as Egypt's Vietnam. As a result, for the first time, cracks began to appear in Nasser's hold on the Arab world.

The Russians Tell a Lie

The Russians could not resist exploiting an opportunity to stir the pot. Syria was an important client of the Soviet Union, but Egypt was the prize they coveted. Even though Nasser championed neutrality and independence from the superpowers, he had become increasingly dependent on the Russians for military arms and limited economic support.

All over the world the United States and the Soviet Union were actively engaged in a cold war that included maneuvering for the political and military support of Arab nations. Anything was fair game for the Russians as long as it did not result in a nuclear confrontation with the Americans. Israel was a western nation supported by the United States. The Arab-Israeli confrontation served Russian interests because it highlighted for the Arabs the incongruity of them maintaining a friendship with the United States at the same time America that supported Israel.

On April 20, 1967, the United States upped the ante in a different region of the world. American planes began bombing Haiphong Harbor in North Vietnam to stop Russian arms from reaching the North Vietnamese. Russian leaders would not lose any sleep if they caused trouble for an American ally in a different part of the globe.

Then, on April 21, the Russians summoned the Israeli Ambassador in Moscow to the Russian Foreign Ministry. Ministry officials warned the Ambassador that Israel was playing with fire and that further actions and threats would result in serious consequences. In a thinly veiled reference to Israel's American friends the Russian official told the Ambassador, "The forces responsible for the situation in Vietnam are also responsible for the provocations in the Middle East…"

On April 25, the Soviet Foreign Ministry again summoned the Israeli Ambassador. This time the Russians warned him they were aware that Israel was massing troops on the Syrian border. Two days later the Russians, as an expression of solidarity with the Arabs, published an account of their April 21 meeting with the Israeli Ambassador but omitted any reference to the April 25 meeting. On May 1, Russian Premier Alexei Kosygin told Egypt's Vice President, Anwar Sadat, who had stopped in Russia as part of his trip to Mongolia and North Korea, that Israel had massed troops on the Syrian border and that war was about to break out.

Russia's allegation of an Israeli mobilization was false—the Russians knew it but did not care. Their accusations, coupled with the earlier warnings, were part of their deliberate policy decision. Truth became a casualty to Russia's plan to enhance Soviet ties with the Arab world to the detriment of the United States. That plan required careful calibration that would raise tensions but not cause a full-fledged war. They had made similar, false allegations eight times before; each time, despite increased tension, war did not break out.

This time, however, it would be different.

Because of the fighting on April 7, increasing terrorism, and Syrian intransigence, the Israeli public clamored for action. Israel's press was filled with bellicose statements threatening Syria with further military action if she continued to launch attacks. Thus, Israel's frustration with Syria's unrelenting assault, just short of war, cast off embers that created a dangerous environment for all.

Russia fanned them until they eventually burst into flames.

King Hussein

Hussein read the tea leaves wrong. Rather than distancing himself from Syria and Egypt he mistakenly changed horses. Hussein fired Prime Minister Tal, his assertive advisor who had insisted Jordan should avoid allying herself with Egypt and should stamp out any ability of the PLO to operate independent of Jordanian rule. Otherwise, Tal believed, an alliance with Egypt would inevitably drag Jordan into a ruinous war with Israel. Hussein disagreed. Memory of the Samu attack was still too fresh.

To defend Jordan, Hussein felt it imperative that he align with other Arab countries. He also needed a bulwark to gird himself against domestic agitation and external provocation. And he no longer saw any advantage in aligning himself privately with Israel. To achieve his goals, Hussein appointed a more malleable Foreign minister.

It was a fateful decision.

On April 28, despite the ongoing war of words between Jordan and Egypt, Hussein invited Egyptian Foreign Minister Riad to Jordan. Nasser accepted the invitation. When Riad arrived, Hussein warned him that Syria, by provoking a war, was laying a trap that would ensnare Egypt. Hussein also conveyed his fears that Jordan would suffer grievous damage in the looming confrontation. Riad responded that the danger would be less if Iraqi and Saudi troops were permitted to base themselves on Jordanian soil. Hussein refused. He said he would only permit their entry if Egypt ordered the United Nations Emergency Force (UNEF) peacekeepers out of Egypt. After Riad left Jordan, the propaganda war between Egypt and Jordan resumed. Riad's visit did little to stem the accusations of cowardice and lack of support for Arab causes both nations hurled at each other.

Israel's Reaction

Prime Minister Eshkol did not ignore the increasing level of terrorism. On May 11 he said, "In view of the fourteen incidents of the past month alone, we may have to adopt measures no less drastic than those of April 7." Even the UN's Secretary-General, U Thant, rebuked Syria at a press conference when he called the continued guerilla attacks supported by Syria "deplorable" and "menaces to peace." Then, Rabin turned up the heat in an interview on May 12, when he threatened overthrow of the Syrian regime. That, however, was too much for Eshkol. The Prime Minister reprimanded Rabin for straying from Israel's official line that she would only react to aggression. Even so, the impression lingered that

Israel was willing to resort to military action if Syrian provocations continued.

However, the Israelis were genuinely concerned about the false Russian accusation that they had mobilized their forces for an attack into Syria. On May 12, Israeli officials offered to take the Soviet Ambassador on a tour of northern Israel so he could see for himself that the IDF was not mobilizing. The Ambassador refused. He said his job was to communicate Soviet truths, not to test them. The Ambassador would have two more opportunities in the coming days to investigate whether the Russian allegations were false. Twice more he refused.

Israel had four red lines that, if crossed, would cause her to go to war. The **first** was a massive deployment of Egyptian troops in the Sinai. Since Israel depended on her reserves to fight her wars, a large Egyptian force in the Sinai would require Israel to respond by fully mobilizing her citizen army. But Israel could not sustain such a mobilization for long without destroying her economy. The **second** red line was if the Arab nations coalesced into a threatening mass. The **third** was if Egypt closed the Straits of Tiran to shipping bound for Eilat. The **fourth** red line would be crossed if Egypt ordered UNEF, the UN peacekeeping force, out. Violation of the third or fourth red lines would be especially troublesome for future peace negotiations. Without UN pushback it would negate international guarantees Israel received in return for pulling back from the Sinai after its victory in 1956. It would also cast doubt on any future UN guarantees.

Israeli leaders did not foresee, in April of 1967 that any of their red lines would soon be crossed. The IDF estimated Egypt's army was three to five years away from being in shape for war and believed that as long as the conflict in Yemen continued it would distract and prevent Egypt from attacking Israel. Since the Straits were open, the UNEF force was in place, and no other Arab nations were mobilizing, the IDF felt confident its assessment was correct. But facts on the ground were about to change quickly and without warning.

Nasser Cooks

Pressure from many Arab countries mounted on Egypt to come to the aid of Syria. Syrian aggressiveness, Russian lies, Palestinian terrorism, and Israel's aggressive statements created an inflammable mixture of bloodlust, fear, and uncertainty. Nasser felt compelled to take the lead when the moment was right.

When the Russians doubled down on their lies on May 13, they provided the excuse Nasser required. They sent another report, this time to the Egyptian President, that Israel's troops were concentrating on the Syrian border and planning to attack. Nasser suspected it was not true. He also knew it was not the right time to confront Israel. Almost a third of his forces were engaged in combat far away in Yemen. But the pressure on him was immense. His failure to aid Jordan during the Samu incident had weakened his political stature. His failure to come to Syria's aid on April 7, despite a defense pact negotiated with Syria six months earlier, had made his continued leadership role in the Arab world more precarious even though he was at the height of his power. Nasser felt he had no choice but to make a display of solidarity. He ordered Egyptian troops to move into the Sinai and head for Israel's border.

The next day, May 14, Nasser sent his chief foreign affairs advisor, Dr. Mahmoud Fawzi, to Syria to verify the Russian reports that Israel was mobilizing. Fawzi reported, "There was no sign of Israeli troop concentrations and the Russians must have been having hallucinations." Nevertheless, Nasser activated Egypt's defense pact with Syria and mobilized the armed forces. Thousands of Egyptian troops passed in review at a military parade in Cairo and then kept going. Instead of stopping they streamed into the Sinai.

The countdown to war began.

Nasser may only have intended to intimidate Israel with a public display of force. In 1960, he moved troops secretly into the Sinai, without Israel's knowledge and without any warning to the UN peacekeeping force. Nasser then ordered his army to enter the Sinai because of a misplaced fear that Israel would attack Syria—an eerie echo of events that would transpire seven years later in 1967. The IDF's belated discovery of the Egyptians in the Sinai in 1960 shocked both the IDF and Israel's government. For the twenty-four hours before Israel could mobilize her reserve forces, only the IAF stood between the Egyptian army and Israeli soil. Israel's subsequent complaint to the UN fell on deaf ears—the UN Secretary General refused to respond expeditiously to resolve the crisis. Fortunately, just as Israel completed her mobilization, Nasser began to withdraw his forces.

The Egyptians may have believed their aggressive movement of military forces into the Sinai in 1960 had deterred the Israelis from attacking Syria. On the other hand, what the Israelis learned from the 1960 embarrassment confirmed what they already knew; the UN would offer little help in a crisis. That time, even though Egypt crossed an Israeli red line, Egypt's expeditious, unilateral de-escalation avoided a war. But in 1960 the Egyptian military movements were not publicly known. Nasser had political room to back down. In 1967 it was different.

CHAPTER FOUR
The Independence Day Party Ends on a Bad Note

On May 15, 1967, Israel celebrated her Independence. The annual holiday commemorates Israel's proclamation of statehood in 1948. A huge military parade in Jerusalem usually marks the celebration. Not in 1967. Because of increased tension in the region, Prime Minister Eshkol pared it down to only 1,600 soldiers and a few vehicles. Even so, 200,000 rejoicing Israelis thronged the streets to watch the soldiers pass by. But despite his outward display of calm, Eshkol felt great concern. Near the end of the proceedings he leaned over and whispered into General Rabin's ear that they should meet afterwards to discuss new developments. Eshkol had reason to be worried. His hope to reduce tensions with the Arabs by limiting the size of the military parade had failed. Even worse, some Arab analysts saw the reduced number of celebratory troops passing through the streets of Jerusalem as evidence that Israel, as the Russians nefariously claimed, was mobilizing the IDF along the Syrian border.

Egypt Makes the First Move

During the evening of May 14, Prime Minister Eshkol and General Rabin headed to the sports stadium in Jerusalem to hear the debut of a new song, *Jerusalem of Gold*. Written by Naomi Shemer, it was a ballad about two lovers—Jews and Jerusalem. Shemer's inspiration for the title came from the Hebrew words for the tiara worn by the bride of a wealthy man.

The song speaks of a love delayed and then fulfilled. But Eshkol and Rabin were not feeling so carefree. They had learned earlier in the day that Egyptian troops were pouring into the Sinai but had decided not to react—yet.

As the night wore on, their concern mounted. Reports arrived that Egyptian General Muhammad (not to be confused with Mahmoud) Fawzi had flown to Syria. Given the defense pact between Egypt and Syria it seemed quite possible Egypt was coordinating her troop movements with the Syrians. Meanwhile, the number of Egyptian troops moving closer to the Sinai border with Israel continued to increase. Even more troubling, the soldiers settled into positions consistent with *Conqueror*, a known Egyptian plan for attacking Israel.

The threat to Israel increased on May 15. Two Egyptian divisions took up strategic positions in the Sinai that were consistent with their plan for war. The only good news was that Egypt's Fourth Armored Division, the army's best unit, was still stationed in Cairo. Rabin hoped and believed, that the troop maneuvers were for show. When Egypt had surprised Israel by moving its army into the Sinai, they retreated without fanfare a couple of weeks later. Perhaps, Rabin thought, Egypt was merely replaying her 1960 show of force.

Nevertheless, Rabin worried. He was a general: Diplomacy was for the civilian authorities. Israel's small standing army could deal with minor border incursions, but not an invasion. The IDF required a minimum of forty-eight hours advance notice to complete mobilization of the reserve forces necessary to defend against a determined Arab attack. Rabin feared that, if Israel failed to react to the huge Egyptian military force streaming towards its border, Egypt might be emboldened to invade. It might also encourage Syria to send more terrorists into northern Israel. However, Rabin knew he needed to balance his concern with restraint. He recognized that if Israel over reacted it could precipitate the war he hoped to avoid.

Eshkol's first instinct was to resolve the crisis through diplomacy. But he had no means to communicate with the Arabs directly because they refused, as a matter of policy, to have any contact with Israel. Therefore, he ordered Israeli diplomats to work through the auspices of the UN, England, and the United States to convince Nasser that Syria and Russia were making false, provocative allegations; and that Israel had no intention to attack Syria or anyone else. However, Eshkol knew he could not afford to completely ignore the presence of mounting numbers of Egyptian troops on Israel's border. Nor did Nasser's statement on May 15, "Brothers, it is our duty to prepare for the final battle of Palestine," provide any solace. Furthermore, Eshkol and his cabinet worried that Egypt's troop movements would motivate other Arab nations such as Jordan and Iraq to mobilize their armies. If that happened it was quite possible that Arab domestic politics, whipped into a frenzy by the rhetoric, would force Nasser and the other Arab nations to attack, even if that was not their present intention. Still, Eshkol resisted the temptation to order a general mobilization.

The danger to Israel increased during the night of May 15. Egyptian forces within Sinai tripled, and many moved to more threatening positions. Tanks, artillery, and vast quantities of ammunition, far beyond what was needed for normal defensive measures accompanied the troops. Egyptian bombers were transferred to forward bases near Israel's border putting them in range of Israel's nuclear reactor at Dimona. And the powerful, military unit that many in the IDF regarded as the canary in the coal mine, the Fourth Armored Division, moved into the Sinai.

Egyptian news media shrieked to the world that, if Israel sets the region on fire, then it, "will be completely destroyed in this fire, thus bringing about the end of this aggressive racist base." Government-controlled radio in Damascus joined the chorus with comments such as, "The war of liberation will not end except by Israel's abolition." Reports of Syrian troops massing on the Golan also arrived at IDF headquarters.

The Israelis knew that very soon, if not already, Egypt would be capable of launching an offensive into the Negev that might imperil their very existence.

In the North, Syria's military buildup worried the Israelis too. The Syrians had demonstrated by deed for two decades that inflicting Israeli civilian casualties was part of their plan, not an unfortunate byproduct of their actions. Since numerous Israeli settlements and towns lay close to the border with Syria, the IDF knew that any Syrian military success, however fleeting, would be devastating.

Eshkol pondered how to respond. If the IDF matched the Syrian buildup they would risk validating, after the fact, Russian accusations of mobilization. If Israel did not mobilize her forces immediately to meet the Egyptian threat, it might be too late to do so later. But at least the UN peacekeeping force, a porous line of observers based on Egyptian territory, remained in place along Egypt's border with Israel. For Egypt to attack Israel, Egyptian soldiers would have to surge through them first. Politically, Nasser would find it difficult to cross that peacekeeping tripwire.

The United Nations Fails

The hammer blow fell on May 16 at 10 p.m. An Egyptian envoy delivered an order from Nasser to General Indar Jit Rikye, the Indian commander of the UN peacekeeping forces stationed in the Sinai along the Israeli border. The message from Nasser demanded that all 3,400 blue-helmeted UN soldiers evacuate their observation posts and leave the area.

The final draft of the message was not what Nasser wished. Just before it was delivered he attempted to weaken it to a demand that the UN troops "redeploy" rather than "leave." Nasser also wanted to eliminate the word "all" because he did not want the UNEF troops to withdraw from Gaza or Sharm el-Sheikh. But Nasser was too late. The earlier draft was delivered instead. Nasser was not pleased but took no further action to rectify the error. He assumed the matter could be clarified in direct consultations with Secretary General of the UN, U Thant.

The UN peace keepers were in the Sinai as part of a ten-year old ceasefire agreement between Israel and Egypt. Their decade-long presence, along with guarantees of Israeli access to the Straits of Tiran, was one of the main reasons Israel agreed to withdraw from the Sinai in 1957. Nasser's demand shocked the Israelis and surprised the Russians. However, Rikye refused to submit to Nasser's will without direction from the UN. He forwarded the demand to U Thant in New York.

The next day, rather than refusing the request, U Thant responded that, if ordered to withdraw from the Sinai, the UN peacekeepers would withdraw from Gaza and Sharm el-Sheikh too. Gaza stretched deep into Israel's heartland. An Egyptian army presence in the Gaza Strip would significantly complicate Israel's ability to defend herself. Sharm el-Sheikh was a strategic spot due to its location at the southern tip of the Sinai on the Red Sea. To reach Eilat, Israel's southern port city, all cargo had to pass through the Straits of Tiran. From Sharm el-Sheikh, Egyptian artillery had the range to shut down the Straits. By doing so, Israel's economy would be devastated if cargo ships were unable to reach Eilat. U Thant's response taught Israel an important lesson that would complicate Mideast peace negotiations to the present day—UN guarantees are meaningless.

On May 17, Eshkol met with his cabinet. He told them, "We are not heading for war, we do not want war ... we do not want from any of our neighbors anything, except the status quo." While they were meeting, an aide interrupted them with startling news. Two MiG fighter jets had entered Israeli airspace from Jordan, at high altitude, and flown over the Dimona reactor site. The Israeli Air Force (IAF) scrambled interceptors, but they were too late and could not reach the altitude of the intruding jets.

The ministers knew that Dimona was the center of Israel's nuclear arms program. The reactor was built based on designs provided by the French in 1956 in exchange for Israel's co-operation with British and French plans to retake the Suez Canal that same year. Israel's nuclear program was a constant source of concern for the Arabs and also an issue between the United States and Israel. By 1967, Israel probably had the capability to build a nuclear weapon quickly, but had yet to do so. Even so, the Dimona reactor was a strategic asset of the highest priority. As a result, a new factor entered into the cabinet's deliberations. Were the Arabs planning to launch a pre-emptive war to destroy the Israeli reactor? Nasser had threatened to do so on three separate occasions. Now, his military had moved into place, his bombers were in range, and the UN was on the way out.

At noon on May 18, the Egyptians formally responded to U Thant's warning that he would only order a complete withdrawal of the peacekeepers, not a partial or temporary one. U Thant's attempt to intimidate Nasser by ratcheting up the stakes had failed. Nasser's response demanded that U Thant withdraw the peacekeepers, but he gave the UN an extension for leaving Sharm el-Sheikh until May 22. Nasser had already secretly decided that was when he would announce closure of the Straits to Israeli shipping and to freighters from foreign nations carrying oil to Eilat.

U Thant had legal grounds to delay or refuse the Egyptian request but chose not to do so. The peacekeepers were on Egyptian soil as part of the international agreement that was the quid pro quo for Israel pulling back from the Sinai after the 1956 war. The language of the agreement stated that Egypt would be guided by "good faith" before asking that the troops be withdrawn. The agreement's drafters interpreted the "good faith" clause as foreclosing the Egyptians from requesting a withdrawal until the peacekeepers' tasks were completed. Since the enabling resolution also included within its language a goal "to secure and supervise the cessation of hostilities," at worst there existed an ambiguity. Certainly, it was not the intent of the UN, Israel, or even Egypt at the time of the agreement in 1957, that the peacekeepers could be withdrawn to enable a war. They were there to prevent an outbreak of hostilities. But rather than requesting an emergency Security Council or General Assembly meeting to debate the issue, U Thant acquiesced.

While caving in to Nasser's demand, U Thant did make one attempt to resurrect the peacekeepers' mission. He asked Israel to permit the UN troops to move to Israeli territory along the border. But U Thant knew Israel would reject that idea; Israel had already done so in 1957, and had no reason to change her position. Given the international makeup of the UN, there was no guarantee the UN troops would be friendly to Israel, and, even if they were neutral, Israel feared that their mere presence would only interfere with the defense of Israel's border. As expected, Eshkol refused U Thant's request.

But Eshkol knew that international support might be useful to ward off an Arab attack. Therefore, Israel's Foreign Minister, Abba Eban, sent a message to President Johnson that requested a public expression of support. Eban argued that if Johnson publicly supported Israel there was less chance the Arabs would be emboldened by assistance received from the Soviet Union. As a precaution, however, Israel hastened preparation of her first nuclear weapon.

Israel Responds

On May 18, Eshkol and Rabin met twice—once in the morning and again in the evening. Their daily intelligence briefing still predicted that the possibility of war was remote. Even so, they decided they could no longer put off preparing for the worst. They agreed to mobilize more reserve soldiers and, quite ominously, to acquire gas masks in sufficient quantities to protect Israel's armed forces and civilian population.

Eshkol also received a message from President Johnson warning against military action without consulting the United States first. Johnson recommended that Israel take no action that might increase tension in the region. Eshkol responded that, given the massive Egyptian buildup on Israel's southern border, Israel needed a public expression of American support. He asked the same of France and England. All three countries ignored the request. Israel's sense of peril and isolation grew.

By May 20, six Egyptian divisions were in the Sinai, Syria was mobilizing her army, and Iraqi troops began moving towards Jordan's border with Israel. Egypt's ministry of religious affairs declared that a state of holy war existed to free Palestine. Syrian Defense Minister Assad said from Damascus it "was high time … to take the initiative in destroying the Zionist presence in the Arab homeland." Meanwhile, the "Arab street" whipped itself into a frenzy that propelled Arab leaders towards further confrontation.

After six days of increasing tension, the crisis began having a profound effect on Israeli citizens. The economy suffered from the loss of 80,000 troops mobilized into active duty, and public opinion was critical of the government's hesitancy to act decisively. David Ben-Gurion, Israel's founding father, was an old comrade of Eshkol's turned political opponent. Ben-Gurion strongly criticized Eshkol for failing to obtain international support and making needlessly belligerent statements that only exacerbated the crisis. Overcome by emotional stress, Eshkol began to deteriorate physically.

Rabin felt the pressure even more than Eshkol. Rabin's stoicism concealed a sensitive person highly attuned to his country's predicament. His attempt to hide the inner pressures he was enduring began taking its toll. Rabin's military philosophy had always been to seize the initiative and take the fight to the enemy on their territory. He preferred shaping events rather than reacting to them. The precipitous Egyptian move into the Sinai robbed him of that opportunity. As long as the civilian leadership restrained him, the Egyptians had control of what happened next, not he. Rabin feared that if Israel did not respond to the Egyptians immediately, with force, Israel's ability to deter future aggression would be diminished.

Rabin's impression that Eshkol had failed to lead decisively magnified his concerns. Eshkol was not only the Prime Minister, he also had kept for himself the role of Defense Minister even though he had never served in the army. Whether Eshkol was suited to be Prime Minister was debated by many, but within the military there was a broadly held view, increasingly shared by Rabin, that Eshkol lacked understanding of the IDF's needs. Eshkol's refusal to follow a defense policy that he had helped shape, and the likelihood that the IDF would incur many needless casualties because of that, weighed heavily on Rabin. At the same time, Rabin's cigarette smoking increased to a worrisome degree, and he began relying on black coffee for sustenance. Soon he began to stammer occasionally in an incoherent manner and, at times, walk about in an apparent daze.

Eshkol sensed the increasing fear felt by Israel's citizens. On May 21, he tried to calm the burgeoning crisis by publicly stating, " I wish to repeat … especially to Egypt and Syria, that we do not contemplate any military action … or intervention in their internal affairs…. We ask only from these states the application of these same principles toward us as an act of reciprocity." His statements didn't help. Rather than provide assurances to the Arabs his words reinforced his reputation, in some circles, as weak and timid.

Ben-Gurion summoned Rabin to his home for a meeting on the night of May 21. Rabin hoped to receive Ben-Gurion's blessing and support. Instead, Ben-Gurion loudly scolded him. He accused Rabin of failing the country with his provocative statements and massive mobilization of the army. He also wrongly accused Eshkol of leaving matters of war to the army, and charged both Rabin and Eshkol with risking the existence of

Israel by failing to obtain public support from at least one Great Power nation.

Rabin next met with Moshe Dayan, the former IDF Chief of Staff who had led the nation to victory in the 1956 war with Egypt. In 1967, Dayan was a heroic figure worshipped by Israel's citizens. He also was politically aligned with Ben-Gurion as a leading member of the Rafi party that opposed Eshkol. Dayan was not supportive of Rabin's actions, either. Shaken and upset, Rabin returned home at 8 p.m. His stress led him to convince himself that he was personally inadequate for the tasks ahead. He called Ezer Weizman, his second in command, and asked him to come over. When Weizman arrived Rabin suggested that it would be best if he took over. Weizman refused. He told Rabin to pull himself together.

Nasser Blockades the Straits of Tiran

On May 22, Nasser, still smarting from criticism by other Arab nations that Egypt was not sufficiently confronting Israel, announced imposition of a blockade of the Straits of Tiran. No Israeli ships would be permitted to pass through. Nasser knew his declaration could cause a war with Israel since a similar blockade had been one of the reasons Israel agreed with France and England to move into the Sinai in 1956. Sadat later recalled Nasser saying that same day that the blockade would make war with Israel 100 percent certain. Another person remembered Nasser stating that the blockade would make the chances of war more than 50%. King Hussein also knew trouble was brewing. He confided to the British Ambassador that Nasser's decision made war likely and endangered Jordan as a result.

A day later Nasser expanded the blockade to include all nations' ships that were carrying strategic materials to Israel. But he never revealed that he did not intend to completely follow through if challenged. His plan was to order his military to shoot across the bow and stern of Israeli ships, but not to use mines or attempt to sink them. As for ships of other nations escorted by warships, it was all bellicose words, nothing more. If anyone dared to challenge the blockade, they would be left alone. Words, however, matter. Nasser was fully prepared to back down, but who knew? Israel could not risk challenging the blockade. If Egyptian guns were to sink one of her ships, Israel would have to go to war immediately. However, if other countries had confronted the Egyptians, the crisis might have been defused. There was still time for noble deeds, but international will was lacking, and time was running out.

For Israel, the Egyptian blockade was the final straw. All four Israeli red lines had been crossed: the Straits of Tiran were blockaded by Egypt, the UN peacekeeping forces were gone, Egyptian troops were massed in the Sinai, and the Arab world was mobilizing. For ten years Israeli leaders had made clear that any one of those threatening developments would be met by force. War was inevitable unless Egypt and the rest of the Arab world would quickly reverse course.

News of the closure of the Straits of Tiran reached Rabin near 4:30 a.m. on May 23. He immediately called Eshkol. Four hours later the IDF General Staff met, and Eshkol called a Defense Ministerial Committee (DMC) meeting for 9:30 a.m. War was in the air. Rabin told his generals, "It is now a question of our national survival, of to be or not to be." Eshkol asserted that the Egyptian challenge could not go unanswered. But first Israel needed to ensure she would have diplomatic support once the war ended. Eshkol well remembered how intense American political pressure had forced Israel to relinquish the fruits of her victory over Egypt in 1956. Other DMC members' opinions split; some recommended patience while others advocated for immediate military action. Eban read to them a cable sent by the United States that requested Israel to abstain from any military action for forty-eight hours. During that time the Americans suggested that a multinational convoy could be gathered to escort Israeli ships through the Straits. The DMC unanimously saw Egypt's blockade as an act of aggression but did not want to anger the Americans. After considering the issue, the DMC agreed to wait forty-eight hours before responding with military force and to send Eban to the United States for consultations.

Later in the day, Eshkol, made a speech to the Knesset and said, "The Knesset knows that any interference with freedom of shipping in the Gulf and in the Straits constitutes a flagrant violation of international law ... it constitutes an aggression against Israel." He also ordered full mobilization of Israel's army. Eshkol had no choice. With Egyptian troops pouring into the Sinai and no sign that the crisis would soon end, Israel needed to ensure that a surprise attack would not take large swaths of territory and threaten population centers.

Israel's standing army was small. It depended on a massive influx of reserves to bring it to full strength. When full mobilization was ordered, almost every able-bodied man up to fifty years of age left his occupation and reported to his military unit. As a result, the economy shut down. Even grocery stores emptied until the government opened up warehouses to tide over the citizenry. But the mobilization could not be sustained for long. Duress set the clock ticking.

At IDF headquarters Rabin worried that delaying action for forty-eight hours was a grave mistake. He didn't believe Eban's mission would only take two days. Meanwhile, the number of Egyptian troops in the Sinai was rapidly increasing and every day they improved their positions. That meant more IDF casualties when the war, which he thought inevitable, would begin. Rabin felt a profound guilt for leading Israel into the crisis. The pressure became unbearable for him. Suddenly, he felt faint. Aides took him home to rest. For thirty hours he was on enforced bedrest. Rabin's collapse was kept secret from the public. The cover story claimed nicotine poisoning was the culprit, but it was the weight of his responsibilities. Rabin's second in command, Ezer Weizman, temporarily took over his duties.

On May 14, "the waiting" ("Ha-Hamtana" in Hebrew) began for Israel. The term describes a period when tensions escalated. The Israeli public descended into a gloomy psychosis. Their collective memory of the Holocaust, coupled with Israel's apparent international isolation, made the moment more about personal survival than about the Straits of Tiran. In the days to come the psychological pressure intensified and Israeli fears escalated.

At sea the U.S.S. Liberty, an American spy ship, left its station off the coast of West Africa and steamed for Israel. Whether the reason was concerns raised by the MiGs that overflew Israel's nuclear facility or just a general American desire to monitor the situation, the Liberty headed for a rendezvous with its own destiny.

CHAPTER FIVE
Israel Will Not Be Alone Unless She Decides to Go Alone

When Hussein mobilized Jordan's army on May 24 and declared his support for Egypt's President Nasser, Israel's sense of encirclement increased, and the pace of diplomacy quickened. The king agonized over his decision because Nasser avidly supported the PLO. He knew aligning with Egypt meant reaching a compromise with the PLO that would inevitably increase its power. Since the PLO's primary goal was a Palestinian State composed of the West Bank, Gaza, and Israel, strengthening them would create a direct threat to Hussein's continued control of the West Bank, and jeopardize his rule over Jordan. Equally worrisome, Hussein knew that by supporting the Egyptians he risked embroilment in a general war with Israel that also could cost him control of the West Bank. For years he had tried to prevent the PLO from upsetting the delicate political balance within Jordan while trading venomous barbs with Cairo in a propaganda war. So why did he decide to support Nasser, his arch enemy for so many years?

The answer lay with the potent "Arab street." Hussein could not ignore the emotions birthed by the Arab world's confrontation with Israel any longer. He worried that if he maintained his neutral stance that might cause the Palestinians in the West Bank, along with those living east of the Jordan River, to react violently. And he feared that his normally loyal Bedouin subjects and army might join with them. Previously, Hussein had hoped to maintain an unwritten peaceful, yet distant, relationship with

Israel. But after "Samu," Hussein wrongly concluded that Israel planned to conquer the West Bank at her first opportunity. As a result, the risk of an Israeli invasion became his primary concern. Therefore, Hussein decided that Jordan needed to ally with other Arab powers to ward off Israeli aggression. It was a damned if you do and damned if you don't moment. Hussein chose wrong. He cast his lot with the Egyptians.

U Thant chose wrong too when he agreed to withdraw the UNEF peacekeepers. Rather than speak out publicly against Egypt's provocative actions and demands, he decided to go to Cairo on May 23 in hopes of putting the genie of war back into the bottle he uncorked. But U Thant's sense of urgency did not match what was brewing. When he arrived in the Egyptian capital, the Secretary General declared he was too tired to meet with the Egyptians until the next day.

Cairo's streets were festive, its citizens eager for war. Posters of Arab soldiers killing and dismembering caricatures of Jews complete with hooked noses were prominent amidst the colorful celebratory atmosphere. Behind closed doors, Egyptian Field Marshal Amer finalized his plans for an attack. He confided to a fellow general, "This time we will be the ones to start the war." He issued orders for Operation Dawn, an attack into Israel. Operation Dawn was a clear departure from Egypt's original plan, codenamed Conqueror. Conqueror envisioned luring the IDF into starting the war, and then drawing the IDF deep into the Sinai wastes where it would be destroyed in a designated kill zone. Implementation of the new plan wreaked havoc on Egypt's army. Her units were deployed for defensive operations consistent with Conqueror, but suddenly they needed to move to new positions consistent with Operation Dawn. Nasser almost certainly knew of the changes even though he may not have formally approved them.

*In Israel, while Rabin was recuperating from his breakdown, Prime Minister Eshkol met with General Weizman. Weizman told Eshkol the IDF could be ready for war the next day, and there were three strategic options for him to consider. The **first** was to occupy the entire Sinai, the **second** to conquer half of the Sinai up to El Arish, and the **third** to only occupy Gaza. There was no talk of taking any territory in Jordan or Syria. Eshkol approved the second alternative; the IDF would occupy part of the Sinai if war broke out. He then said that he would relinquish the* territory gained only if Egypt agreed to end its blockade of the Straits of Tiran. While the discussions were ongoing, the IDF ordered Israeli tanks to move towards the border with Egypt; and a Kuwaiti armored brigade arrived in Cairo.

When U Thant met with Nasser on May 24, he failed to convince the Egyptian President to take steps to reduce pressure on Israel to react to his provocative moves. Nasser would only verbally agree that Egypt would not fire the first shot. The commitment was nothing more than a murderer agreeing not to shoot a victim he is already choking. Nevertheless, U Thant left Egypt encouraged. He believed Nasser had agreed to a "breathing space" if Israel would only follow suit. But his companion, the former UNEF Commander Rikhye, disagreed. Rikhye told him, "I think you're going to have a major Middle East war, and I think we will still be sorting it out fifty years from now."

Eban Takes a Trip

Israeli Foreign Minister, Abba Eban, left Israel at 3:30 a.m. on May 24 for a crucial four-day trip. The first stop on his whirlwind tour of the western powers was Paris. His last stop would be the most important—Washington, D.C. Many of the hawkish members of Eshkol's cabinet were clamoring for war. Eban's mission was to gauge the level of support for a peaceful international solution to Nasser's aggression, an aggression that if not reversed would leave Israel with no choice but to fight.

France and Israel, along with England, were allies in the 1956 Suez war. Afterwards, France played a large role in securing Israel's reluctant agreement to withdraw from the Sinai. France advocated then for Israel's unencumbered access to the Straits of Tiran and supported the deployment of UN peacekeeping forces to Egyptian soil along its border with Israel. The French also helped Israel build a nuclear reactor, a project that was instrumental to the development of Israel's nuclear weapons program. In addition, French sales of weapons and spare parts to Israel were a vital component of Israel's military strength. In short, for more than ten years France had been Israel's close friend.

Eban met with French President de Gaulle at noon. De Gaulle immediately declared that Israel must not shoot first. Instead, spewing Gallic pride that far exceeded Gallic capabilities, he assured Eban that the four powers—France, England, the United States, and the Soviet Union—would resolve the dispute.

Eban responded that he had come to consult with France because she was a great friend of Israel, and, "Israel was faced with Syrian terrorism, Egyptian troop concentrations, and the blockade of the Straits." He then reminded de Gaulle that France had guaranteed Israel passage in the Straits of Tiran as part of the 1957 withdrawal agreement.

"That was 1957," de Gaulle answered coldly, "This is 1967." De Gaulle then inquired, "What are you going to do?"

"If the choice lies between surrender and resistance, Israel will resist," Eban replied. "Our decision has been taken." But Eban assured de Gaulle that Israel would not act immediately. She would first explore the possibility of resolving the dispute short of war with the help of the international community.

During their conversation, de Gaulle's responses regarding Israel's plight failed to refer to Egypt's provocative actions which were, in effect, a declaration of war. Instead, he repeatedly emphasized that Israel must not declare war or fire the first shot and downplayed the significance of the blockade imposed by the Egyptians. Nor did he think that a naval flotilla, comprised of ships from the maritime powers, would resolve the problem if it entered the Straits for a demonstration that those waters were free to international navigation. Then he insisted that the Soviet Union must be enlisted to help find a solution and warned, "The more Israel looks to the West, the less will be the readiness of the Soviet Union to cooperate."

Eban concluded his meeting with de Gaulle by telling him Israel greatly appreciated the arms and military support had France had provided in the past. Eban saw that further discussion was unnecessary;

nothing would be gained by it. It was clear, France would not be part of a solution satisfactory to the Israelis. The meeting closed rather ominously with de Gaulle advising, "Israel was not sufficiently established to solve all of her problems herself." It was a warning to Eban that there would be consequences if Israel acted unilaterally.

Reflecting on the discussion much later, Eban said, "I had been an eye-witness to the death of solemn commitments," and "Expressions of support were vague, advice to abstain from resistance direct and specific."

Eban left Paris for London where he met with British Prime Minister Harold Wilson. To Eban's surprise, he received a much warmer reception there than in France. Eban told Wilson, "Israel would not live without access to Eilat or under the threat of Egyptian encirclement. Israel's choice was either to fight alone or to join with others in an international effort to force Nasser's withdrawal."

Wilson assured Eban that England considered the Straits of Tiran international waters. When de Gaulle's four-power solution came up for discussion Wilson was neither enthusiastic nor optimistic, but he was willing to participate. Wilson also indicated willingness to support an international flotilla that would assert the right of freedom of navigation by traveling through the Straits to Eilat. And he added that although he preferred to act with the cover of a UN directive, he would be willing to do so without UN approval if necessary.

Nevertheless, Eban, already exhausted by his travels, was worried. Wilson had not agreed to lead the effort, only to follow the paths of others. He knew the next leg of his journey, his visit to the United States, would be critical. Empty promises would not be enough for Israel to remain patient. If the Straits stayed closed for much longer, there would be war.

While Eban was in France and England, Abraham Harmon, Israel's Ambassador to the UN, flew to Gettysburg to meet with former

President Eisenhower. Since Eisenhower had been President in 1957 when the United States guaranteed Israeli passage through the Straits of Tiran, Harmon believed it important to solicit Eisenhower's views. Eisenhower told Harmon what he wanted to hear. The former president confirmed that the Straits were an international waterway, and that he believed the Egyptian blockade was illegal.

Eban flew to New York on May 25. The same day more Egyptian armored units crossed into the Sinai, and the IDF increased its pressure on Eshkol to immediately go to war in response. The army was ready. Mobilization was complete. General Ariel Sharon, commander of a division in the Sinai, told Eshkol war was unavoidable: The sooner it started with an Israeli first strike, he said, the easier it would be to achieve Israel's goals.

Later, more alarming information arrived during a contentious ministerial meeting in Eshkol's office. Israeli intelligence reported that the Egyptians and Syrians intended to launch a coordinated attack on May 27. Once again opinion was divided as to whether Israel should launch a pre-emptive strike. Rabin, who was at the meeting but not yet at full strength, offered to resign in light of his physical and emotional condition. Eshkol swiftly rejected the offer. After further discussion, Rabin suggested Israel should seek a declaration from the Americans that an attack on Israel was an attack on the United States. If President Johnson agreed to publicly state that, Israel would wait. Otherwise, Israel would strike pre-emptively. The cabinet approved Rabin's suggestion.

Soon after Eban arrived in New York, he received two cables from Eshkol that altered his diplomatic strategy. Eban later said their contents were, "one of the severest shocks of my life." The cables Eshkol sent warned, "The Arabs are planning a large-scale offensive ... The question is no longer the Straits of Tiran but Israel's very existence." Eshkol ordered Eban to push President Johnson to clarify "concrete measures ... he is willing to take to avert the impending explosion." The instructions also ordered Eban to convey to President Johnson the request for him to declare that an attack on Israel was an attack on the United States. Eban was infuriated. He did not believe the Arabs intended to attack. He also believed it a mistake to change focus from lifting the blockade to a confrontation over Egyptian troops in the Sinai. And he did not think the Americans could, or would, give the assurances Eshkol demanded. But he had no choice. An order was an order. Eban responded he would attempt to achieve what was asked of him.

Eban's assessment was correct on the politics but wrong on the facts. Jerusalem's fears were not unfounded. Egypt had completed her preparations for Operation Dawn. Families of Egyptian officers had been evacuated from Gaza. In their stead arrived civilian managers, engineers, and physicians that would be required after Israel's Negev was conquered. The commander of Egypt's land forces had already gathered the army's senior generals and told them their attack would begin at first light in two days. The Egyptian army was preparing to march.

Eban was scheduled to meet with American Secretary of State Dean Rusk at 6:00 p.m. (midnight in Israel), but the meeting was pushed up an hour at Eban's urgent request. Eban told Rusk what was in the cables he had just received. Rusk responded that a public declaration of support presented constitutional problems because it was a contingent declaration of war without Congressional approval. Rusk ended the meeting quickly so he could advise President Johnson of the new developments.

After Rusk left to see Johnson, Eban attended a working dinner at the State Department. There he discussed with the American diplomats their plan for reopening the Straits of Tiran. Through the auspices of the UN Security Council, the Americans wanted to co-ordinate a declaration by maritime powers regarding the right to passage through the Straits. Then, a naval force composed of ships from many nations would move through the Straits to assert that freedom. But as the evening wore on,

Eban grew concerned that their proposed solution might include some form of limitation of Israeli movement in the disputed waterway. Such a concession would never be acceptable to Jerusalem.

Later that night Eban met with Rusk a second time. Eban's warning of an imminent Egyptian attack was the second one the United States received that day. Earlier, the American Ambassador in Israel communicated a similar concern based on information he received from Israeli government sources. But Rusk also knew that the American intelligence community, after checking with the UN, Britain, and its own sources, did not believe Egypt planned to attack. The intelligence advisors thought that the Egyptian deployment was defensive in nature. Therefore, Rusk told Eban the United States did not think an attack on Israel was imminent. He added that, without approval of Congress, Johnson could not provide the public, verbal assurances Eshkol had asked for. Then he tried to reassure Eban. Rusk told Eban the United States would pressure Arab countries to resolve the matter. However, he warned, Israel should not engage in any pre-emptive actions. Eban communicated the American views to his government at 1:30 a.m. EST time on May 26 (7:30 a.m. in Israel).

Despite believing that Israel's fears were unfounded, in an abundance of caution, the Americans cabled the Russians to advise them they had received information from Israel that Egypt was planning to attack. The contents of the cable cautioned that Israel's warning could not be verified, but the United States expected the Russians to discourage the Egyptians from taking any warlike acts. That message set in motion a swirl of Russian diplomatic activity culminating in a visit with Nasser in the early morning hours of May 27 that may have changed the course of history.

While the diplomatic discussions in the United States continued, Arab verbal threats intensified. Radio Cairo said, "The Arab nation is determined to wipe Israel off the face of the earth and restore Palestinian

Arab honor." And in response to a question about the fate of Jews born in Israel, Ahmad Shuqayri, head of the PLO, said, "Those who survive will remain in Palestine. I estimate that none will survive."

By May 26, relentless and escalating Arab threats of destruction and extermination in the media and by public statement, coupled with mobilization of Israel's citizen army that brought the economy to a halt, caused many Israeli citizens to suffer from an increasing sense of doom. Even though their generals were confident of victory, military censorship kept that from them. And some of the preparatory measures observed by the public magnified the hysteria. The government ordered thousands of coffins, and Rabbis consecrated parks for emergency burials. Children delivered the mail and newspapers. Miles of trenches were dug. Frequent air raid drills interrupted daily life. Those not called to military service worked extended hours to make up for the loss of reservists' labor. Private vehicles and busses were called into national service. Dreading a coming confrontation with the Arabs, Israelis found optimism in short supply.

Adding fuel to the fire, Nasser delivered a speech to Arab trade unionists on May 26. In reference to closing the Straits of Tiran, he said:

> Taking such action also meant we were ready for general war with Israel. It is not a separate operation … if Israel embarks against Syria or Egypt, the battle against Israel will be a general one … and our basic objective will be to destroy Israel.

Nasser's close friend Mohamed Heikal, a reporter and reliable mouthpiece for Nasser's thoughts, wrote that morning in a weekly newspaper column that Israel had no choice but to go to war, and that he expected hostilities to start at any moment. Nasser's speech and Heikal's column combined left little doubt of Egypt's intentions.

Eshkol convened a ministerial meeting on May 26 that lasted six hours. Rabin was present and by then fully recovered from his breakdown. The atmosphere was tense. The doves within the cabinet expressed their concerns about going to war. They emphasized that all factions within the government should participate in the decision. The hawks argued strenuously that further delay could be disastrous. Eshkol stressed that they must respond immediately to the Egyptian build-up; the blockade, he said, could continue for a while without their taking any action in order to give the international community an opportunity to resolve the problem. Yigal Allon, a former hero of the IDF present at the meeting, said to Eshkol, "This is one of the great issues in Jewish history. I believe you can go down in Jewish history as another King David—if you decide to act now." But rather than order war, Eshkol sent another cable to Eban instructing him to emphasize to President Johnson that the Egyptian build-up in Sinai was the most important immediate threat—not the blockade.

During the day an Egyptian MiG fighter jet, possibly operated by a Russian pilot, again overflew at high altitude Israel's nuclear facilities at Dimona. The presence of the plane above the most sensitive military site in Israel intensified concerns of Israel's political and military leaders regarding Egypt's plans. Those fears were not unfounded. Egypt's planned attack on Israel the next day included bombing Dimona.

In Washington D.C., Rusk asked Eban to stay an extra day so the outcome of U Thant's visit to Egypt could be evaluated. Eban refused. He told Rusk that he had to be present at the cabinet meeting scheduled for the next day because the ministers would be much influenced by what President Johnson would tell him.

After his meeting with Rusk, Eban went to the Pentagon to see the American military Chief of Staff, General Wheeler, and Robert McNamara, the Secretary of Defense. Eban stressed to them that the Egyptian build-up in the Sinai was Jerusalem's primary concern. Wheeler responded that in his view Israel would win no matter who started the war but that he opposed using a flotilla of ships to break the blockade. McNamara agreed with Wheeler's assessment.

Later that evening at 7:15 p.m., Eban met with President Johnson. Eban told Johnson, "The question to which I have to bring the answer is, do you have the will and determination to open the Straits. Do we fight alone, or are you with us?"

Johnson was a stalwart supporter of Israel, but he would not commit to a public expression of coordination of military support. He responded to Eban that he understood "you are the victims of aggression," but he could not commit the United States to intervene without permission of Congress. Johnson pledged, however, to help create an international force that would sail through the Straits, and was more optimistic regarding its success than the other leaders Eban had spoken with. Johnson then emphasized that Israel could depend on him. He recognized that Israel would do what she wanted, but advised that the United States would take no responsibility for any consequences which might ensue if Israel attacked. He further told Eban that he did not think the Arabs would launch a surprise attack and that Israel should not hold to any arbitrary deadlines. What Johnson did not say, however, was something a few members of his administration already knew—international support for an international force had already waned, largely due to fears that Arab nations would retaliate with an oil embargo.

Johnson concluded the meeting by handing an aide-memoire to Eban that said, "I must emphasize the necessity for Israel not to make itself responsible for the initiation of hostilities. Israel will not be alone unless it decides to go alone."

"Israel will not be alone unless it decides to go alone." Johnson repeated it three times.

When the meeting with the president ended, Eban left for Israel by way of New York, There he received news that U Thant's mission to Egypt had been unsuccessful. Eban left New York for Israel at midnight feeling hopeful despite his failure to win from

President Johnson the assurances Eshkol had requested. Eban believed that, even if international efforts to break the blockade failed, Israel's willingness to remain patient for a while would reap her benefits if, and when, she would have to act alone.

CHAPTER SIX
The Speech

The cable that warned the Soviet Union that Egypt planned to attack Israel on May 27 also included a related warning from President Johnson: If Egypt were to attack Israel, the United States would not exercise restraint. The news galvanized the Russians into a diplomatic frenzy. After instigating the crisis by making false allegations of Israel mobilizing along the Syrian border, they would have to work fast in both Tel Aviv and Cairo to avert a war their intrigues had set in motion.

Russian Warnings

Soviet Embassy personnel in Tel Aviv contacted the Israeli government at 2:00 a.m. on May 27. The Russians insisted that Ambassador Chuvakhin must meet with Eshkol immediately. Eshkol and his wife were spending the night at the Dan Hotel along the Tel Aviv Mediterranean shoreline. Aides woke Eshkol at 2:30 a.m. with news that the Russian Ambassador was in the lobby urgently demanding to see him. Eshkol asked his wife for advice how he should respond. She answered that, if the ambassador wanted to see him in pajamas, he should be permit the ambassador to come up.

When Chuvakhin entered the room he handed Eshkol a prepared note. The message accused Israel of colluding with western powers and having plans to attack Syria and Egypt. The dispatch warned Israel against attacking and concluded ominously, "it is easy to ignite a fire but putting out its flames may not be as simple as those pushing Israel to the brink of war imagine." Chuvakhon then insisted four times that Israel refrain from firing the first shot even though both men knew that Egypt's blockade of the Straits of Tiran, the massive movement of its army into the Sinai, and the overflight of the Negev by Egyptian planes constituted acts of war.

Rather than back down, Eshkol angrily responded, "The Egyptians, sir, have already fired the first shot in this war." Still, Eshkol hoped to avoid bloodshed. Therefore, he also said he would be willing to travel to the Soviet Union to resolve the issues between their two countries. But Chuvakhin did not come to negotiate. He explained that his superiors instructed him to deliver the note, nothing more.

Dimitri Pojidaev, the Russian Ambassador in Cairo, delivered a stronger message to Nasser than the one delivered by Chuvakhin to Eshkol. Pojidaev's message demanded that Egypt refrain from taking offensive action against Israel. The ambassador's visit was timely, but only barely. Unbeknownst to him, the Egyptians were counting down the few remaining hours to sunrise when "Operation Dawn," their attack on Israel, would commence. The Egyptians planned to begin with air strikes on Israeli airfields. Next, General Shazli's armored strike force would cross Israel's border, punch through the Southern Negev and occupy Eilat, only a scant few miles from the Egyptian and Jordanian borders at the southern tip of Israel.

At first, Nasser hesitated after receiving the Russian note. He then hurried to his Supreme Headquarters where he met with Field Marshal Abdel Amer, his powerful rival and the commander of Egypt's military forces. Nasser ordered Amer to call off the attack. He had realized there were too many unknowns that could cause negative consequences, including: The possibility of American intervention,

Israel's readiness, and whether the Russians would come to Egypt's aid if needed. Amer disagreed and delayed implementing Nasser's order. Amer wanted war, but within an hour he acquiesced to his superior's command and canceled the attack. Many weeks later, Nasser told the Russians, "You prevented us from inflicting the first blow. You deprived us of the initiative. It was none other than a conspiracy."

Israel on Edge

History did not record whether Eshkol went back to sleep after meeting with the Russian Ambassador, but by 9:30 a.m. he was in a high-level government meeting that included Rabin and Golda Meir. He told them about the "pajama" meeting hours before. When their discussion ended, Rabin thought Eshkol had decided to go to war. Israel could not endure much longer the economic, political, and emotional pressure of waiting—especially when waiting exposed the IDF and the nation to the likelihood of greater casualties and even defeat.

Later, Eshkol chaired another cabinet meeting that began at 10:30 p.m. By then, he had been awake for as much as twenty hours. Stress-induced fatigue, combined with lack of sleep, dulled his senses. Nor could his health have been enhanced by stagnant cigarette smoke swirling throughout the room or the nondescript cups containing stale coffee residue littering the table. The ministers debated whether to launch a pre-emptive war or to give the Western powers further opportunity to resolve the crisis. Their collective mood leaned precipitously towards war, but Eban's dramatic return from the United States swung the pendulum back. Eban told them that the United States had requested Israel to demonstrate restraint. The news deadlocked the cabinet nine to nine on the question of war versus more diplomacy. Eshkol, despite having appeared to favor a military solution to the crisis, suggested adjourning to give everybody an opportunity to rest before reaching a final decision. The inconclusive meeting ended between 4 and 5 a.m. on May 28.

Eshkol scheduled a follow up meeting at 3p.m. When they started anew he had been awake and active for close to thirty-seven hours; the beleaguered 72 year old Prime Minister had had no time to rest. Tension, responsibility, a bombardment of telephone calls, and the need for political and military consultations before the afternoon meeting did not leave room for needed sleep.

Meantime, while the Government dithered, Israel's economy ground to a stop. Industrial output came to a virtual halt. Committees formed that were charged with finding short-term solutions for the loss of key infrastructure workers called to the front. Since the IDF had requisitioned virtually all busses and taxis for military use, public transportation fell apart. The economic vitality and social fabric of the country was unraveling due to the massive mobilization required to defend her existence.

And Israeli civilians were exposed to constant reminders of their imminent danger in addition to the economic disruption. Many still remembered desperate moments in 1948 when Jewish civilians were terrorized by Arabs living within the new nation's borders and threatened by Arabs from without who tried to overrun the fledgling country. Those memories magnified the impact of the statements issued by their Arab neighbors threatening destruction of the Jewish State. None felt safe. Israelis in the north lived with the constant menacing reminder of the looming Golan Heights—lined with a deadly arsenal trained on the Jewish settlements below. In the populous central regions thousands knew they and their children lived within range of Jordanian rifles. Even those outside of rifle range understood that Jordanian troops stationed along the border at Israel's narrowest point were only a few minute drive from cutting Israel in two. Nor did Jews living in the populous cities of

Tel Aviv, Beersheba, or Eilat feel any sense of comfort. An Egyptian army in the south was poised to strike towards them.

The Israeli military was confident it would defeat the Arabs. But the reasons for their confidence could not be made public without giving away their plans, and despite the IDF's philosophy of carrying the fight to the enemy's territory the need to take precautions still remained. Therefore, civilians practiced daily for air raids, schools were outfitted with bomb shelters, and parents planned for emergency evacuations of their children to European destinations. Public-minded civilians collected and organized basic food items and gathered antidotes for poison gas. Ten thousand graves were prepared for imminent use. Teenage boys filled countless sandbags and helped dig thousands of trenches. Fear and trepidation for what might come soon pervaded the everyday consciousness of Israeli adults and children on the home front. When would the Arabs attack, how would they survive? Jews faced their mortality again only twenty-five years after Hitler instituted his "Final Solution."

Amid the hysteria, Israel's atomic scientists in the southern Negev were busy. One source reports that Eshkol had ordered them to expedite assembly of Israel's first two nuclear weapons. Since receiving a nuclear reactor from France as part of their agreement in 1956, Israel's nuclear program had made significant progress towards developing an atomic bomb. The bomb design was crude, but the weapons were mobile. If Egyptian forces overwhelmed the army, the IDF planned to deploy the atomic weapons by truck to the battlefield.

The Speech

On May 28, Eshkol's office issued a statement that he would address the nation that night at 8:30 p.m. Expectations ran rampant since it was well known that Eban had returned the night before from his diplomatic effort in Paris, London, and Washington D.C. The homeland, struggling to avert a collective hysteria, held its breath.

Before the cabinet reconvened at 3:00 p.m., Israel received three new important messages. **One**, from England's Prime Minister, urged restraint as long as diplomatic efforts were underway. The **second** was from de Gaulle. He doggedly insisted that Israel wait while the four powers—France, England, the Soviet Union, and the United States—find a solution. De Gaulle's proposal was unpalatable. Israel had no interest in depending on Russia and France, nations that did not place her welfare high on their priority list. The **third**, and most important, message was from the United States. The Americans advised that the United States would advocate for a solution in the UN. More importantly, the United States committed herself to uniting the maritime powers for a declaration on behalf of freedom of navigation in the Straits of Tiran and for a forceful demonstration of that principle by sending American ships, along with those of other countries, through the Egyptian blockade.

The American message had a decisive impact. The cabinet decided, after five more caffeine and nicotine-fueled hours, to wait two more weeks before going to war in order to give diplomacy a chance. The decision was not unanimous. Rabin was especially embittered. He insisted that Eshkol must speak to the IDF's leading generals to explain the decision and its rationale. It was 8 p.m.

Almost as an afterthought, Eshkol looked at the speech he was to deliver to the nation by radio address at 8:30 p.m. Prepared by his aides, it was more of a statement than a speech. The document contained handwritten changes to the typed text. He had planned to pre-record delivery of the address in a private room. Never an inspirational speaker, Eshkol was burdened by a heavy cold which, coupled with his fatigue, had left him weakened. Glancing at the text, he quickly made indecipherable handwritten changes. Not enough time remained to retype them. There was no time to record the speech. There was no time for anything other than racing to the radio studio to deliver the words a frightened nation waited to hear.

Around the country hundreds of thousands tuned to the radio. Soldiers in the field facing their enemies and civilians burdened by fear waited pensively. It is hard to imagine today the power and weakness a single voice alone can convey. In the twenty-first century, video images on television and the internet often overpower the spoken word. But in 1967, in Israel, radio broadcasts coupled with printed media were the main means for mass communication. On May 28, families gathered around their radios throughout the country to hear Eshkol's words. Children intermingled with the elderly, their mothers, and the infirm. They took seats within earshot of the central focus of their lives at that moment—a small box emanating crackling sounds and a voice. Few of those listening had been left untouched by Arab violence in the past. Most felt threatened again from the Arab armies stationed nearby.

The nation stood on a precipice.

Eshkol arrived at the radio studio in a flurry. He moved quickly into position to speak. He felt rushed because, after the radio address, he had to confront the IDF's military leaders and explain the cabinet's reasons for delaying a forceful response to Arab aggression. Eshkol's vision was impaired; one eye had an artificial lens implanted in the aftermath of a recent cataract surgery. His cold caused his eyes to tear. His mounting fatigue had dissipated whatever reservoirs of strength he once possessed.

He began.

Eshkol's first words were gravelly, and his breathing was labored. Then he stammered. He repeatedly added an unsteady "err" to his comments. The hundreds of thousands of Israelis expecting encouragement and guidance quickly lost any confidence they had tenuously been clinging to. Concern mounted among the shocked listeners as Eshkol audibly shuffled his papers and cleared his throat. The handwritten changes, written less than hour earlier, confused him. When he could not decipher the hastily written amendments he attempted to ad lib, but his improvisation failed. In the midst of his speech, Eshkol paused in confusion over the written changes after he referenced the Egyptian military mobilization.

It was the worst possible moment for a verbal stumble.

The pregnant pause heightened most listeners' fears of what they faced. Eshkol tried signaling to an assistant that he wanted to halt the speech because of his confusion, but that was no longer possible.

He struggled on.

Eshkol stated that Israel would rely on an American led initiative to prevent the outbreak of war. He tried to finish strongly by stating that Israel would defend herself from all aggressors. However, a nation that prided herself on thwarting the designs of its enemies focused on what he had said earlier in his comments. Was Eshkol depending on the United States and other nations for Israel's survival? Was that a signal that Israel did not have the means to defend herself?

Six minutes of halting words—delivered by an elderly, exhausted man with a cold—stunned the nation. A universal sense of foreboding instantaneously spread throughout the country. Tears streamed down the faces of soldiers in the Negev. Eshkol's wife sensed disaster while listening to the speech from her car. She rushed to the radio studio only to find her husband had already left to face the generals.

Eshkol, too, must have sensed his failure. And any remaining illusions that his radio address had conveyed his message convincingly were quickly dispelled by his subsequent meeting with the IDF generals in the "Pit", the deep underground military headquarters of the IDF. To some, Eshkol appeared depressed, but it may only have been fatigue laid roughly upon tension long endured. The meeting was tense, the air inflammatory from barely restrained rage. The generals were united. Any further delay in attacking their enemies would cost thousands of lives and carried the risk of defeat.

Eshkol began the meeting by telling the officers that his radio address might not have properly explained the basis for his decision to rely on others for Israel's security. He said that politics and international pressure delayed a cabinet decision to attack, a decision that only a day before the cabinet had been prepared to make.

But the generals were not persuaded. They were convinced that only a pre-emptive strike guaranteed success. They argued that further delays would only aid the Arab cause. They feared that instead of the IDF grabbing the initiative, the delays would leave Israel the victim of an Arab first strike. Ariel Sharon said, "Today we have ourselves chopped off the IDF's deterrence capability. We have chopped up our main weapon—the fear of us". He continued that further delay would cost thousands of deaths and then analogized the loss of deterrence to a thin electric wire that was used to keep cows within a pasture. Once a cow touched a wire that was no longer charged; all fear was lost. It would not hesitate to trample it and break out to the fields beyond.

Rabin forcefully told Eshkol that the only strength the country could count on was the army. General Yoffee added, "If you go on begging protection from Paris and Washington we shall be lost." Others said that in two weeks the Straits of Tiran would still be blockaded but their chances for success would be reduced. Some worried that Israel's plan of attack would leak. A few warned of the growing economic catastrophe caused by the mobilization.

Eshkol resisted his temptation to relieve the immense pressure they were placing on him by honestly conveying that he too leaned towards war. Instead, he argued the diplomatic basis for the decision: The Egyptians could always rebuild if their army was destroyed, but Israel could not exist without outside help. Therefore, since their potential allies were pressuring Israel to stay her hand; Israel needed to give diplomacy a chance. He then questioned whether they could "live forever by the sword."

No one suggested mutiny, but, when the meeting drew to a close, a hint of it lingered. Eshkol left angry and depressed, perhaps especially by the taunt, "Why are we always begging protection from others?" Although many of the generals believed the government had the "right and obligation..." to make the decision, they vociferously argued that the government's chosen path risked the existence of the State. One general summarized the overall mood of the younger officers when he privately said in reference to the tentative, aging politicians leading the country who had immigrated to Palestine long before, "Our main enemy is not Nasser, but the second Aliya." Rabin concurred. When he referred to the cabinet, while conversing with his generals, as "the Jews," it was a clear reference to the cabinet's cautious nature.

Some officers expressed concern about how the troops in the field would react to more delay. After Eshkol left, the generals remained behind. They discussed how to deal with the flagging morale of soldiers coiled tight into a spring, straining to pounce, who had no choice but to wait tensely without release. Rabin said, "There's only one element that can stand now, and that is the army. That's why our responsibility is so grave. It all depends on us now, all of it."

News of Eshkol's clash with the generals leaked. Editorialists and reporters called for Eshkol to step down in favor of Ben-Gurion or Moshe Dayan, the former IDF Chief of Staff and architect of the 1956 victory over Egypt. Letters to the editor printed in newspapers accused Eshkol of appeasement. One titled "Chamberlain is still remembered," compared Eshkol to British Prime Minister Chamberlain who gave up Czechoslovakia in 1938 to the Germans in return for Hitler's empty promises of peace. Still, nobody thought a military coup was imminent. Though, when word of a possible military revolt spread, Ben-Gurion, Israel's first Prime Minister and revered founder of the country, called a news conference in the Knesset. He read from a written statement, "An army in a democratic country does not act by its own option and not by the opinions of its military commanders, but by the opinion of the civil government and its orders."

Thus, just when Israel needed to band together, Eshkol's failure to respond decisively to Egyptian provocations was having a devastating impact on civilians and the military. A few more weeks without resolution might have caused the military to take matters into its own hands. Fortunately, matters took a different course.

Meanwhile, rather than taking steps to end the crisis, Nasser fanned the flames. Domestically and internationally his prestige in the Arab world had never been higher. On May 28, he told Arab journalists that Israel's existence was the problem, not his closure of the Straits of Tiran. He said that Egypt would not agree to co-exist with the Jewish nation, and, in a radio address, he threatened inflicting unimaginable damage to any nation that touched the rights of Egyptian Sovereignty (a reference to Israel). On May 29, he told the Egyptian National Assembly he was prepared to, "restore the situation to what was in 1948," and that "we shall certainly, with God's help, be able to restore the pre-1948 situation ... we want the full and undiminished rights of the people of Palestine."

The three branches of Egypt's armed forces matched Nasser's rhetoric with increased military pressure. When a tanker, captained by an American and registered in Liberia, attempted to run the Egyptian blockade of the Straits of Tiran, an Egyptian naval vessel fired a warning shot that caused the ship to turn away. Nasser no longer was willing to back-off if challenged. Egypt's Air Force flew reconnaissance missions over Israeli airspace. And an Egyptian army patrol moved into Israel. When an Israeli unit tried to intercept it, Egyptian artillery fire pinned the Israelis down.

Still, Israel did not respond.

And Eshkol knew that neither his speech nor his meeting with the IDF generals had been his finest hours. He tried to clarify his position by issuing a statement that Israel would permit more time for diplomatic efforts, but she would not make any concessions related to her right to freedom of navigation in the Straits of Tiran.

However, the diplomatic process, up to then, was not reassuring. The UN Security Council was unable to reach agreement on how to proceed. The United States was still trying to mobilize international support for a flotilla to run the blockade but did not appear to be succeeding. And the French told Israel that the Russians turned down their Four Power idea. With the Vietnam War still raging, and the Cold War between Russia and the United States very much ongoing, the Russians had little motivation to work with the west to find a solution to a problem they had instigated and that only brought them closer to their Arab allies.

The clock ticked faster.

King Hussein understood what was happening. He knew Nasser's actions meant war. He also knew that his Palestinian and native Jordanian citizens were being swept along by their heightened expectations that Palestine would be liberated. Nasser's popularity was soaring among Hussein's subjects. If he didn't align himself with the prevailing sentiment his rule would be threatened.

Hussein's survival strategy since the Israeli attack on Samu was to ally with stronger Arab powers. The events of the previous few days provided an opportunity. Syria was not an option. There was too much troubled history between Syria's leadership and himself. But Egypt was a possibility. Hussein arranged to meet the Egyptian Ambassador at the house of a friend of his. Hussein told the ambassador he thought Israel was about to attack Egypt, and that he wanted to go to Cairo to see Nasser to coordinate a response.

The next day Hussein received Cairo's answer. Come as soon as you can.

CHAPTER SEVEN
Hussein and Nasser

The fragile emotions of Israeli civilians absorbed yet another blow on May 30 when they learned King Hussein had gone to Egypt for an unannounced visit and reached an agreement with the Egyptians. Until then, Jordan's and Egypt's propaganda machines had hurled accusations and insults directed towards each other's leaders. When Syria learned Hussein had gone to Egypt, a shocked Syrian leadership demanded an explanation from Nasser why he was seemingly reneging on their agreement to isolate Hussein. Nasser replied that the Syrians should calm down. He had something in mind.

For Israel, Hussein's arrival in Cairo signaled something more ominous than thawing relations between Jordan and Egypt. A second front, much longer and much more difficult to defend than the border with Egypt, appeared to be opening. Even though Jordan's army was small, suddenly the possibility existed that Hussein would change his policy and permit Iraqi, Saudi, and Egyptian forces into his country. From the perspective of Israel's public and the IDF, a bad situation rapidly was growing worse.

Hussein and Nasser — May 30

Hussein, clad in a khaki combat uniform and wearing Field Marshal insignia, personally piloted his French built Caravelle plane to an

Egyptian air force base near Cairo. A small group of advisors accompanied him. Nasser waited on the tarmac for his arrival. When Hussein strode towards the Egyptian, Nasser greeted him with a question, "Since your visit is secret, what would happen if we arrested you?"

Hussein responded with a feeble smile, "The possibility never crossed my mind."

The two Arab leaders headed to the Kubbah Palace to talk. Hussein opened their discussions with a suggestion that the United Arab Command be re-instituted. Nasser rejected Hussein's Pan-Arab approach. Instead, he suggested a direct pact between Egypt and Jordan. Hussein agreed.

Hussein quickly made further concessions at Nasser's request. The Jordanian King was so eager to close the deal that to save time he suggested their pact be modeled after the one Egypt had signed with Syria the year before. When the Egyptians brought the document to Hussein for his review he skimmed it quickly and impulsively said, "Give me another copy. Put Jordan instead of Syria, and the matter is settled."

The new treaty bound each country to aid the other if attacked. But detailed, additional provisions that fleshed out the agreement's framework gave Nasser everything else he wanted. The two leaders agreed that Egyptian General Riad would command Jordan's military. Hussein also consented to what he had never accepted previously for fear of being overthrown by foreign soldiers—entry of Egyptian, Syrian, Iraqi, and Saudi Arabian troops into his country. He also agreed to release Fatah and PLO prisoners and permit the PLO to re-open its offices in Amman even though he knew it might destabilize his rule. And in a further abdication of his previous stance, in order to curry favor with Nasser, Hussein humiliatingly agreed to not only reconcile with his enemy, PLO leader Ahmad Shuqayri, but also to return him to Jordan in the plane he had himself piloted to Egypt.

Hussein did warn Nasser that the Israelis would begin a war with a surprise air attack designed to destroy Egypt's air power. However, Nasser assured him that he and the Egyptian military were expecting such a strike and prepared for it. Nasser told the Jordanian monarch that Jordan's role was to tie down Israel's military to prevent Israel from concentrating on one Arab state at a time. In return, Egypt and Iraq would defend Jordan's airspace. Then, to reassure Hussein, Nasser took him into another room where Hussein viewed a map with the location and number of Egyptian air squadrons ready for war. Afterwards, Egyptian military leaders took Hussein to an air force base so he could personally verify the Egyptian Air Force's readiness.

Hussein sat next to Shuqayri during the signing ceremony broadcast live that same day on Radio Cairo at 3:30 p.m. The broadcast marked the end, for the moment, of Egypt's propaganda war with Jordan. Within the course of a single, day years of enmity between Nasser and Hussein evaporated. Shortly after, Hussein flew back to Jordan. Shuqayri stepped off the plane onto the runway alongside Hussein and immediately headed for the West Bank. Hussein's motorcade made its way to his hilltop palace. Along the road jubilant crowds cheered his decision to join his Arab brethren in confronting Israel.

Later during that fateful day, Hussein reviewed one of his military units. He told some of its officers, "I am convinced that we are not going to win this war. I hope we do not get involved in this war but if we do, all I ask you to do is your best, respect your traditions, and remember that you are fighting for your country."

Hussein felt satisfied, if not happy. He knew that if he remained on the sidelines he would be vilified and probably deposed if the Arabs won the war he saw coming. But if the Arabs lost, as he thought would happen, Hussein rationalized that the Israelis would probably take the West Bank but he would survive. Years later Hussein remarked, "We knew what the results would be. But, it was the only way and we did our best and the results were the disaster we have lived with ever since."

In hindsight it is clear Hussein erred. The Syrian leadership had a pact with Egypt, but, unlike Jordan, did not give up control of her forces nor permit military units from other nations on Syrian soil. Hussein's decision served to increase regional tensions and enhance the influence of those in Israel clamoring for war. The consequences would almost be more than he and his Kingdom could bear.

Politics in Israel — Green Lights in America

Not surprisingly, the Egyptian-Jordanian pact alarmed Israelis because it strengthened the ring of steel surrounding them. If Arab troops from other countries were to enter Jordan, yet another Israeli red line would be crossed. The noose was tightening.

At Eshkol's request, Eban drafted a response to Johnson's plea for Israeli restraint. Eban wrote that the proposed international naval force must move through the Straits within a week or two. He also reminded the President that, in 1957, America had committed to Israel that Israeli shipping would be able to pass freely through the Straits. In addition, Eban's message opined that an "aggressive dictator" cannot be appeased. However, Eban was not willing to just rely on the written word to communicate his message. He held a press conference at noon during which he warned that Israel would not wait too long for the crisis to resolve. He also criticized the UN and U Thant for acquiescing to Nasser's demand to remove the UN peacekeepers.

But Eshkol needed more than Eban's counsel. He sent the head of Israel's intelligence services, Meir Amit, to the United States to learn more about America's intentions. Time was running out for a peaceful solution.

Up until then, Eshkol stubbornly had kept two jobs for himself— that of Prime Minister and also Defense Minister. His capacity for leadership, much questioned since his speech to the nation two days earlier, came under even more scrutiny after the Egyptian-Jordanian pact became public. Since Eshkol had never served in the IDF, had no military training, and had never been personally exposed to the dangers of war, the hole in Eshkol's resume was enormous for a country that placed a premium on military service. Thus, that Tuesday, the same day Hussein's pact with Cairo was announced, Eshkol faced enormous pressure, from the IDF, from his political enemies, from civilians, and even from members of his own political party, to give up the Defense Minister portfolio to someone with military experience.

Eshkol, exhausted but in a good mood, attended a meeting of his political party during the evening. What he heard could not have been uplifting. One speaker after another stridently demanded that he relinquish his hold on the Defense Ministry. Some suggested he should appoint Yigal Allon to the position. Allon, the forty-nine-year-old Minister of Labor, had two decades of military experience dating back to 1945 when he was a Palmach commander.

But the clear favorite was Moshe Dayan. Israel's public revered Dayan, the fifty-two-year-old former Chief of Staff who had commanded the victorious IDF during the Sinai war in 1956. Most thought him to have tremendous fighting spirit. But some who knew him well saw another side. They did not doubt his courage or intelligence; they feared his independence. They viewed him as a "lone wolf" who might act more in accordance with his own whims than as part of a team. Nevertheless, most at the meeting recognized that Dayan exuded strength and Eshkol did not. Thus, they thought Dayan would give the country a well-needed psychological boost.

Eshkol was shocked by the sentiments expressed by many he had regarded his supporters. Well after midnight he left the meeting, slammed the door behind him, and contemplated resignation.

The next day, Amit discussed Israel's plight with American governmental leaders in Washington. He first met with James Angleton, the head of the CIA's counterespionage department. Angleton was always preoccupied with threats posed by the Soviet Union; he was also strongly supportive of Israel taking whatever action she deemed necessary. Amit next met with Richard Helms, the Director of the CIA. Amit and Helms were personal friends. In the past, they had visited each other's homes. To his surprise, Amit learned from Helms that no multinational naval force existed that would break the blockade of the Straits. And there were no concrete plans to create one.

Amit then met with Defense Secretary Robert McNamara. McNamara echoed Helms when he expressed his skepticism that the United States would create an international fleet to run the blockade. During their conversation, Amit told McNamara that Israel only needed two things: American weaponry to fight the Arabs and political support to prevent the Russians from interfering. But the longer Israel delayed an attack on the Egyptian army in the Sinai, the greater the likelihood that Israel would have to ask the United States to help with her own military forces. Amit added that the delay till then had already probably increased the number of casualties Israel would suffer once war broke out, and that mobilization of the IDF was crushing the economy. He also warned that Israel's inaction benefited Nasser and Russia because the other Arab nations were increasingly falling under their sway. At the end of their meeting Amit said he was going to recommend to his government that Israel attack, but that McNamara need not respond so there could be no charge of collusion.

McNamara's silence was the green light Amit hoped for.

The only government official who left Amit unsatisfied was Secretary of State Dean Rusk. Rusk was not buying Israel's need to pre-empt. Amit was so exasperated he blurted to Rusk, "Must Israel have to accept ten thousand casualties before the U.S. will agree that aggression has occurred."

Later that night Undersecretary of Political Affairs, Eugene Rostow, told President Johnson, "Those boys are going to be hard to hold a week from now," and advised Johnson to "unleash the Israelis like a sheriff at high noon." Rostow thought that if Nasser lost power new opportunities for America would arise.

On the same day Amit was meeting with the Americans, Eshkol met with leaders of his party at 11:00 a.m. to address the growing political crisis at hand. He decided to offer Yigal Allon the Defense Minister job and Dayan the position of Deputy Prime Minister. But when Eshkol met with Dayan at 4:30 p.m., Dayan refused. He told Eshkol he would only accept a political position with clear authority or a military command. Eshkol responded to Dayan that he could replace the current Southern Front Commander and serve under Rabin. However, when Rabin learned of the proposal he resisted the idea as did many other generals. Their disapproval forced Eshkol and his advisors to search for a solution to the political storm engulfing him, a solution that did not include appointing Dayan as Defense Minister; but they found none. One said, "I am deeply upset; instead of preparing for war we're busy with civil war." Their discussions ended without reaching a final decision on who would be offered the Minister of Defense position. Eshkol said afterwards, "[I]t breaks my heart the defense portfolio being taken from me."

Eshkol Gives In

For almost twenty years Israeli and Jordanian soldiers had stood toe to toe along the green line. The green line was the name coined for an armistice boundary dating from the end of the 1948 war. Its naming was inspired by the green ink used on a map in 1949 to delineate the border between Israel and her Arab neighbors. Israel's legislative body, the

Knesset, was housed in a building one mile from the border. The Prime Minister's residence was even closer.

On June 1, Egyptian General Riad flew into Jordan to command the Jordanian army. In Israel, high school students still dug trenches in public parks; and volunteers still filled sandbags, cleaned out bomb shelters, and taped windows to protect against explosions. The threat of war was very real. Five years earlier, more than 100 witnesses testifying at the Eichmann trial riveted the nation with their testimony of the horrors of the Holocaust. As the country prepared for a climactic clash those memories became very real and very vivid once again

By midday on June 1, Eshkol abandoned his hope to keep the Defense Minister portfolio for himself. Earlier in the day, Rabin had told Eshkol that his plan to make Dayan Southern Front Commander had met too much resistance from other high-ranking officers to ignore. While Eshkol sat in his office contemplating his next move, Ezer Weizman, the Deputy Chief of the General Staff, burst into the room after having visited with the troops stationed along the border with Egypt. He half-yelled, half-cried to Eshkol,

> *The state is being destroyed, everything is being destroyed. Give an order and [the IDF] will go to war. Why do you need Moshe Dayan? Who needs Yigal Allon? You have a strong army and it is only waiting for your order. Give us the order to go to war and we'll win. We will win and you'll be the head of government of the victory.*

Weizman then tore his general's insignia from his shirt and stormed out of the room.

Despite Weizman's impassioned plea, Eshkol knew he needed to do what he least desired. Later in the day he offered Dayan the Defense Minister position and Allon withdrew his candidacy. Dayan accepted at 4:15 p.m. But Eshkol instinctively felt that Dayan's appointment would not be enough to quiet divisive criticism of his leadership. Therefore, he also announced that Menachem Begin, leader of the opposition party, would join his cabinet. Eshkol practiced the dictum of holding your friends close, but keeping your enemies closer. And so, Israel's unity government sprang into being.

News of Dayan's appointment spread quickly. Soldiers and civilians alike felt immediate relief. Troops keeping warm at bonfires in the desert joyously sang "Jerusalem of Gold." Israelis everywhere toasted the appointment. Coincidently, General Chaim Herzog began broadcasting to the Israeli people that same day with his famous reassuring statement:

> Knowing the facts, I can say that if I had a choice between sitting in an Egyptian aircraft sent to bomb Tel Aviv and sitting in a house in Tel Aviv, then I would prefer for the good of my health to sit in Tel Aviv.

Public morale soared.

The first cabinet meeting after Dayan's appointment began shortly after 10:00 p.m. that night. The news was dire. The Security Council once again had failed to act, de Gaulle reiterated that France would remain neutral, and Iraqi troops were on their way to Jordan. Amit's report from the United States had also arrived. In it he stated, "From hints and scattered facts that I have heard, I get the impression that the maritime force project is running into heavier water every hour." Eshkol looked pale and tired, but Rabin appeared invigorated by Dayan's appointment. Dayan told the ministers they needed to decide whether to attack, and if so, do it immediately. If not, then they had to prepare for defense. Still no decision was made. After further discussion they adjourned until morning.

While the political crisis festered in Israel, the United States made a last attempt to diffuse the problem before it flamed out of control. President Johnson sent a secret envoy to Nasser. His name was Robert Anderson. Anderson's background was in the oil business. On June 1, Anderson found Nasser confident and relaxed. Nasser told him that Egypt was strong enough to resist anything that Israel did but agreed to send an envoy to Washington to discuss resolution of the crisis. Anderson's clandestine trip required him to leave Egypt for a secure location where the message he wanted to send to Washington could be encrypted. By the time Anderson was able to inform Washington of Nasser's willingness to send a representative to Washington, it was too late to schedule a meeting before the outbreak of war.

Nasser spoke with his military leaders after meeting with Anderson. He told them he believed a war would break out on June 4 or June 5 because that was when he thought Iraqi forces would arrive in Jordan. He predicted that the Israelis would not sit idly by and permit that to happen. Nevertheless, over their objections, he declared that he would heed Russian and American warnings. There would be no Egyptian first strike. However, he also insisted that he would do nothing to reduce tensions. He would force Israel to strike first.

CHAPTER EIGHT
Israel Decides

June 2, 1967

Eshkol, Dayan, and Begin met with top officers of the IDF during the morning of Friday, June 2. The IDF officers pushed hard for an immediate decision to attack Egypt. Once again, a dejected and downcast Eshkol resisted.

Rabin admitted during the meeting that the Egyptian army was "perhaps in a defensive orientation only," but said:

> I think we might find ourselves in a situation where we'll lose much of our advantage and we might reach a situation that I don't want to describe too clearly, but it will pose a threat to Israel's existence, and the war will be difficult and savage." Rabin continued, "Now that we've waited, and the Arabs have defined their political goal as a return to 1948, and this is clearly defined, we must not wait until there's a situation that makes things difficult, if not worse....

Rabin added that every day they delayed the Egyptians improved their positions and their confidence increased. The other generals strongly agreed with their Chief of Staff.

Eshkol responded that he was not asking for another three or four weeks, but just one.

Rabin answered, "I'm saying that every day is more of a burden, making operations more difficult and more costly."

However, the impassioned arguments by the Generals failed to persuade the Prime Minister. Eshkol also took one final stab at making them understand that he had to take into account the opinion of President Johnson:

> "I want to drill it into Johnson so he doesn't say we cheated him. We may still need him. I hope we don't need him in the middle of the war.... Military victory will end nothing. Because the Arabs are here to stay."

After the meeting ended Eshkol, took Rabin, Dayan, Eban, and Allon aside. The cabinet, he said, would not make a final decision whether to attack or continue to wait until after Amit returned from Washington. Eshkol then asked for their opinions. Dayan said they should decide to go to war on June 4 and attack on June 5. On a tactical level, he suggested they should avoid moving into Gaza and refrain from going all the way to the Suez Canal. Allon agreed that Israel should attack Egypt, but, contrary to Dayan, he recommended that Israel approach the canal with the implicit threat of closing it and also threaten to move Gaza's residents across the canal and into Egypt. Dayan responded that Allon's plan was inhumane.

Later on June 2, Dayan permitted a reporter from *Time* magazine, Winston Churchill's grandson, to interview him. When asked by Churchill if war was imminent, and, if not, could he go home without fear of missing anything; Dayan replied disingenuously that he should go home.

Late that night, Dayan met with Rabin and other high-ranking officers of the IDF. General Gavish, the Southern Front Commander, presented two plans. The opening act for both was the destruction of

Egypt's air force. One plan included conquering Gaza. The other did not. Dayan selected the plan that left Gaza alone but added to it a mission to take Sharm el-Sheikh in order to end Egypt's blockade of the Straits of Tiran. Dayan's goal was to destroy the Egyptian forces in the Sinai while staying clear of the Suez Canal. He did not want to advance to the canal because he thought it would inevitably result in a confrontation with Russia and a war without an end. It was Dayan's decision alone. He chose and changed the plan without cabinet approval.

While Dayan pushed Eshkol to order an attack, the Russians and French increased their pressure on Israel to back down. The Soviet Union sent a note to the Israeli government that she would do what she could to prevent war, "but if the Government of Israel should decide to take upon [herself] the responsibility for the outbreak of war, [she] will have to pay the price in full."

The French clamored that any nation that initiated hostilities would not have her "approval or acclaim." They also announced an embargo of arms to the Middle East effective June 5, but for some selected items the embargo would begin immediately. The embargo was not an even-handed declaration. None of the Arab nations depended on access to French arms, only Israel.

June 3, 1967

On Saturday, June 3, the IDF gave thousands of soldiers the weekend off. Many went to the beach. The sight of young men crowding together on the sand seemed to signal that tensions were easing. Dayan did his best to give a similar impression. At 4 p.m. he held the first of two press conferences. Dayan used them to mislead the Egyptians. When asked by correspondents if war was coming soon, he responded, "a month, two months, six months. War [is] not imminent." When asked "until when" Israel would give diplomacy a chance, he responded, "Until the Government decides." In an attempt to reassure the United States, he also stated that he didn't want American boys to fight for Israel and didn't think they were needed. But, even while Dayan hid his hand, three battalions of Egyptian commandos arrived in Jordan to join General Riad; and Iraqi troops moved closer to the Jordanian border. A red line was massively crossed.

That evening, Amit returned to Israel on a jumbo jet from his mission in the United States, bringing with him a full load of gas masks and other equipment. Amit told Eshkol, "The United States won't go into mourning if Israel attacks Egypt."

Amit's official report was somewhat different. It stated, "The Americans will hesitate to act against us and there is reason to hope that they will even support us." However, Amit did caution that American support for Israel taking immediate action was not unanimous. Therefore, he suggested that, rather than attacking immediately, they should send an Israeli ship through the Straits to force Egypt to fire the first shot. Amit added that he believed the Americans would be happy to be released from their promise to form an international force to break the blockade.

Allon did not like Amit's idea. He argued that sending an Israeli ship through the Straits would alert Egypt that war was imminent. Dayan and Rabin did not like the proposal either because it meant more delay. They repeated that the longer Israel would wait the more casualties the IDF would incur.

Eshkol had heard enough. He had just received a letter from President Johnson that acknowledged Israel's right to freedom of passage in the Straits, but it did not include a commitment for immediate American action. It also did not include a warning against initiating hostilities. The letter made Eshkol comfortable that America's position had changed: Johnson would no longer react angrily if Israel initiated hostilities. Eshkol decided that, whether Israel waited two days or another week, American reaction would be the same. It was the bright, green light Eshkol had hoped for after glimpsing McNamara's dimmer one.

Eshkol's high-level advisors ended their meeting with a decision to recommend to the cabinet that Israel should attack Egypt. In the north, the IDF would remain in defensive positions along the border with Syria. The IDF would only do what was necessary to ensure that Syrian forces did not take any Israeli territory.

And they agreed—Jordan would not be touched—unless Jordan attacked first.

June 4 & 5, 1967

Israel's Ministerial Committee for Defense met at 8:30 a.m. on Saturday June 4. By 11:00 a.m. the other cabinet ministers joined them.

Dayan reviewed the military situation. He reported that Egypt had 100,000 troops in the Sinai backed by another 60,000 in reserve. Their equipment included 1,000 tanks and 400 warplanes. Dayan stated that the Syrians had massed 50,000 troops in the Golan Heights accompanied by 200 tanks, and supported by 100 warplanes. Dayan then turned his attention to the Jordanians. He told the ministers that Hussein had mobilized another fifty to sixty thousand soldiers along with 250 tanks plus a few warplanes. Dayan also revealed that Egyptian commando battalions had already joined the Jordanians, and Iraqi soldiers were on the way. Even those ministers who had counseled patience were struck by the growing military threat.

Eban advised that he did not think the United States would force Israel to withdraw from any newly-conquered lands, as happened after the 1956 war. Eshkol then emphasized that Israel had to act soon. If they did not order the attack immediately they could expect a "slaughter" later. He also added, perhaps, the most crucial new factor for their consideration: The United States no longer required Israel to wait, and he felt certain that the United States would provide political support.

One minister suggested that Israel should not act until she could find another ally to fight with her. Dayan responded that by the time that happened, Israel might no longer exist.

Dayan pushed hard for an immediate decision to initiate a preemptive war against the Egyptians. The meeting ended at 3:00 p.m. with eighteen of the twenty cabinet members present voting to authorize war. The two holdouts subsequently agreed to vote in favor after further deliberation. Israel's government was unanimous. The ministers left it to Eshkol and Dayan to decide when Israel would launch the strike against Egypt. The status quo was about to end.

After the cabinet meeting, Dayan returned to military Headquarters. He made clear to Central Commander, Uri Narkiss, and Northern Commander, David Elazar, that they must remain in defensive positions and were only authorized to make limited tactical advances into Jordanian and Syrian territory if attacked. Dayan also specifically warned General Elazar that he would have to make do with the forces he had. Dayan was anticipating a tough fight in the Sinai and could not spare reinforcements for the north.

In Jerusalem, intermittent shooting had already broken out between Jordanian and Israeli troops at the Mandelbaum Gate that separated Jewish-held Jerusalem from Jordanian territory. Even so, the Israelis intended to tolerate those, and any other minor Jordanian provocations, because, as Eshkol later said, "There was nothing here of the inhuman virulence which marked the attitude of other Arab nationalists towards Israel's existence."

In Cairo, Nasser declared that he expected an Israeli attack and was ready. However, it was an empty boast. Made even more vacuous by the fact that Hussein had tried twice to warn him that Israel would attack the following morning day.

Hussein sent his **first** warning after the Turkish ambassador told him that Israel would begin her attack the next day, or the day after, by bombing Egyptian air bases. Then, the Iraqi Ambassador corroborated the information received from the Turkish ambassador. He told the king that Iraq had information Israel would attack during the morning of the following day. Hussein made sure General Riad was informed. Riad relayed the information to his superiors in Cairo. They replied they knew and were ready.

Hussein's **second** warning came after he received information from Jack O'Connell, an American CIA liaison stationed in Jordan. Quite possibly without knowledge of President Johnson or his advisors, O'Connell frantically interrupted Hussein at a dinner party at 7:00 p.m. on June 4. The CIA officer shared with the king information that Israel would attack Egyptian airfields, but not those of Jordan or Syria, the next morning at 8:00 a.m. O'Connell had received his information from an American military attaché in Tel Aviv. Once again, Hussein made sure the warning was relayed to Cairo. After the war ended, Nasser confessed to Hussein that he did not believe the warnings.

Late Sunday evening, Israel's forces made their final preparations. Since being mobilized two weeks earlier, ground troops had been living in temporary shelters in barren deserts. Now they had their orders; they made ready. Egyptians in the southern end of the Gaza strip observed Israeli preparations, but the Egyptian high command ignored their warning to expect an attack at dawn. Commanders of the Israeli air squadrons that would lead the attack tried to catch a few fitful hours of sleep. For security reasons, the pilots were not told they would be attacking into the heart of Egypt the next day. In the Port of Alexandria, IDF navy frogmen slipped into the water. Their mission was to interdict Egyptian naval operations with explosives stuck to the hulls of Egyptian ships.

In the United States, newspaper columnist, Joseph Alsop, presciently penned a column for publication the next day. It was titled "The Meaning of Moshe Dayan." Alsop compared the importance of Dayan's appointment as Defense Minister to Winston Churchill joining Britain's Cabinet in 1939 because of the threat posed by Hitler. Alsop argued that Dayan's appointment meant Israel could not wait any longer and "[that] Israel, it must be understood, is now struggling for [her] very survival."

In Baghdad, Iraq's President opened a conference of Arab oil producing nations on June 4 by threatening the oil companies that their property would be "seized" and "liquidated" if they supplied oil to Israel.

CHAPTER NINE
The War Plans

Control of the air is the most important condition required for victory in a war between two traditional armies. Planes loaded with bombs, and equipped with cannons and machine guns, do not suffer from the same range and topography restrictions that hamper artillery and direct gunfire. The air force that achieves dominance can freely fly over the battlefield and, especially in a desert environment where nothing can move without being observed from above, wreak havoc on an opposing army below. The armies of Israel and Egypt required an enormous amount of supplies on a daily basis to refuel their vehicles, replenish ammunition, and restock food and water. The thin-skinned trucks that carried the supplies were fat targets for fighter-bombers, and even tanks lacked sufficient armor to protect them from weapons fired from planes. But most exposed to aerial attack were ground troops. No matter how brave, they could not alone withstand jets raining bullets and explosives from the heavens. Total control of the skies may not guarantee victory, but rarely can victory be achieved without it.

Israel

The IAF knew Israel had to win every major confrontation with the Arab world and to minimize Israeli civilian and military casualties while doing so. To achieve both goals, owning the sky was necessary. IAF experts began developing a new plan for destroying Egypt's air force in the early sixties. It was codenamed *Operation Moked*. Until then, IAF plans had relied on air-to-air engagements and uncoordinated attacks on Arab air bases to attain command of the skies. But Israel did not possess enough planes to ensure quick success, and the longer it took to achieve air dominance the more exposed the IDF ground forces would be.

New thinking focused on runways. If bomb blasts could render runways unusable: Arab planes aloft would not be able to find a safe place to land, planes based out of range would be unable to transfer to the frontline airfields, and aircraft on the ground would not be able to take off. Those planes could then be destroyed in their revetments over time. Three problems, however, bedeviled IDF planning. The **first** was how to damage the runways so severely that the Egyptians could not repair them quickly. The **second** difficulty involved getting IAF planes over the airfields undetected, and how to make sure that each target was attacked in unison. If any airbase received advance warning of an imminent attack some or all of their warplanes might be able to takeoff and disrupt the Israeli strike. The **third** problem was to convince Israel's leaders that the new plan, which left the homeland exposed because only twelve planes would be left behind during the first few hours to provide air defense over Israel, would not result in massive destruction of military and civilian sites in Israel.

At first, *Operation Moked* planners did not have a method for destroying the Egyptian runways for an extended period. They tested traditional, cast-iron bombs on concrete tarmacs, but the explosives rolled off without creating more than superficial damage. Rockets and shells fired from attacking planes could only create small holes in runway concrete that were easy to fix. The *Moked* planners finally found an answer in the mid 1960's. They coupled bombs with rockets that drove the explosives into the concrete before blowing up. Tests showed that the new weapon created holes more than fifteen feet wide and four and a half feet deep.

The planners solved the problem of arriving undetected over the airfields by closely coordinating the flight path of each pilot to his target. However, the IAF knew it could not hope to fly over Egyptian territory undetected by observers on the ground. The IAF's solution was to fly very low from the moment the planes took off in Israel so that Arab radar could not detect them, and then to chart a course for each plane over the Mediterranean to avoid ground surveillance. Once over the ocean the attacking planes would turn south, and then proceed over water for a specified time until a precise moment when they would turn again to reach their targets over the Sinai, Suez Canal, and the Nile Delta.

The degree of difficulty imposed on the young pilots was unprecedented. Nearly 200 planes had to take off from several airfields, only a few at a time because of the limited number of runways available, and then form up into more than a dozen attack groups. To avoid detection the planes had to stay within thirty feet of the surface while hurtling through the air at hundreds of miles per hour for a long time. Each attack group had to keep track of its speed, direction, and the amount of elapsed time. Then, at the exact, pre-planned moment, calculated to ensure that multiple Egyptian airbases would be attacked simultaneously, the attack groups had to turn away from the ocean to head overland to their destination. Only when they reached their targets could the pilots increase their altitude to start their bombing runs. And to ensure surprise they had to maintain radio silence for the entire flight from Israel to their targets. If a pilot's plane malfunctioned, he would have to crash without saying a word to his fellow pilots or controllers.

Once the *Moked* plan took form, the IAF implemented extensive, exhaustive training for the mission. For several years large flights of planes took off from their bases almost every day and flew over the Mediterranean to hone the skills necessary to complete the mission. The daily, repetitive activity eventually lulled the Egyptians into complacency. By June 5, 1967, even though Egyptian radar detected numerous IAF planes taking off from their bases and heading over the Mediterranean, the Egyptians no longer saw that habitual behavior as a threat.

The IAF plan designated planes with short operational ranges to bomb the closer Egyptian bases and longer range aircraft to strike the more distant ones. But the planners recognized they had a problem that jeopardized the meticulous planning. They knew how far each plane in their inventory could travel in ideal conditions but were not confident the same metrics applied under battle conditions. Large and heavy bomb loads increase aircraft weight and air friction, as does flying at low altitudes for long distances. Those factors affect airspeed and range. The only way to find the answers they needed was to simulate in different weather and atmospheric conditions the configuration and flight paths that the plan required. Therefore, Israeli citizens grew used to seeing their air force flying the length of the country at altitudes no more than three stories high.

On paper, *Operation Moked* promised success. But could Rabin and Eshkol be convinced? The plan called for thirteen Egyptian airfields set in locations far apart, each with three or more runways, to be attacked simultaneously and without warning. In order to prevent the Egyptian air force planes from taking off or landing, the first wave of IAF planes needed to deliver several of the specially designed bombs to multiple locations on the runways. Since the IAF did not have enough planes to do everything at once, the first wave of attackers was responsible for runway destruction. But, if the Egyptians were not surprised, large numbers of Arab planes would take off and intercept their attackers before the runways could be incapacitated. The resulting melee would upset mission timing and reduce the chance of success.

A second wave of warplanes was supposed to arrive over the airfields ten minutes after the first wave. Their mission was to use their missiles and guns to destroy Egyptian planes trapped by runways damaged by the first wave. Succeeding waves would destroy any aircraft that escaped the second wave. To ensure that each IAF plane performed its mission as efficiently as possible, the pilots learned to seesaw back and forth over the airfields to make it easier to line up their guns with Egyptian planes that were not parked in orderly rows. It was also vital that the location of the planes and the configuration of the runways be pre-determined so that each Israeli plane could destroy the maximum number of Egyptian aircraft during the short window of time available to them before fuel constraints forced them to head for home.

Israeli intelligence agents fanned out all over Egypt to obtain the targeting information. They mapped the airfields, learned where the planes were parked, and even identified the names and habits of the Egyptian pilots and their commanders. But there still was a problem. Israel did not have enough aircraft to accomplish the mission. At best, the IAF had 180 modern jets capable of attacking the airfields. The Egyptians alone had more than 400 aircraft. Even when low performance training planes were added to the mix it was not enough.

The IAF's answer to the numbers conundrum was to accelerate the turnaround time of their jets. When a warplane returns from a combat mission it needs to be refueled, rearmed, and repaired. Other than in Israel, most military planners in 1967 assumed a plane could only be used twice in one day. The IAF learned to turn around planes in twenty minutes through constant, focused training that emphasized technical readiness of the aircraft. Ground crews competed between squadrons and bases for the honor of achieving the fastest turnarounds. They were timed to the tenth of a second. Pilots learned to notify ground crews by radio of any damage or problems they were experiencing while the plane was still in the air. When their plane landed the appropriate expert would be standing by. As a result, IAF planners thought that every plane in their inventory could carry out four to five missions in a day. As a result of the fast turnaround, as long as the planes were not shot down, the IAF could accomplish what otherwise would have required hundreds more planes.

It was a force multiplier of monumental significance. Even though the IAF only had 180 planes, they would fly the same number of sorties that 400 or more would fly in other air forces.

The *Moked* plan called for IAF planes to arrive over their targets at 7:45 a.m. (8:45 a.m. Egyptian time). By then, IAF intelligence had learned that Egypt's dawn patrols always landed, the Egyptian pilots were on the way to breakfast, and their commanding officers were still commuting to work. The time was also perfect from the perspective of visibility; the rising sun could be expected to have burned off any early mist. Blue skies, no opposition, complete surprise—it was the perfect recipe to destroy the enemy from the air.

But Eshkol and Rabin were not easily convinced the IAF's proposed plan would work. Eshkol demanded assurances that no Arab bombs would hit Tel Aviv. Rabin was skeptical because the plan called for concentrating the entire strength of the Israeli air force against Egypt. What would happen if Syria and Jordan chose that moment to strike? What would happen if the Egyptians were ready and disrupted the attack? Rabin also disliked that the IAF's insistence on surprise meant that Israel's ground forces could not move until the first bombs dropped on the runways. As a result, the IDF would lose its opportunity to surprise the Egyptian army and would have to operate without air support for a while. However, Dayan got it. He saw, in the complexity of the idea, a simplicity of purpose. Planes that left at different times from different bases would arrive all at one time with one purpose: Trap and then destroy Egypt's air force.

The IAF commander, General Hod, assured Eshkol that Tel Aviv would not suffer significant damage; he neglected, however, to tell the Prime Minister that only twelve planes would be held back to defend Israel's heartland. In reality, Hod's homeland defense plan depended on surprising the Egyptians and on Syrian lethargy. He knew that once the

Egyptian planes were destroyed, the IAF could turn on Syria's air force if necessary, and Jordan's, too, if Hussein entered the war.

On the ground, the IDF concentrated most of its forces facing Egypt into three divisions that each consisted of about 15,000 men plus varying numbers of tanks. Generals Tal, Sharon, and Yoffee were the division commanders. In addition, several independent brigades and paratroop units had defined missions. In all, 70,000 Israeli soldiers were assigned to the Southern front along with nearly 800 tanks. The IDF concentrated its strength along the northern and central portions of the Sinai. Farther south only light screening forces guarded Eilat from a powerful Egyptian unit commanded by General Shazly.

The IDF hoped to exploit its superior mobility to encircle and destroy the Egyptian forces close to the border, and then penetrate deep into the Sinai. To maximize destruction and confusion among the Egyptians, the IDF's plan concentrated overwhelming force against a few key points. It was fully consistent with IDF doctrine that relied on maintaining the initiative, whether on the ground or in the air. As long as the Arabs were off-balance and reeling from the blows, the IDF felt it could take calculated risks because it could dictate where and when the battle would be joined. That would make victory theirs for the taking.

The Arabs

Despite failing to perform with distinction in the 1956 Sinai war, Field Marshal Amer led the Egyptian ground forces stationed in the Sinai. The Egyptian army in the Sinai consisted of six divisions, an additional armored task force, and to defend the Gaza strip a poorly trained Palestinian Liberation Army division. They totaled 100,000 men and over 900 tanks. It was a formidable army even though another 50,000 Egyptian troops and many tanks were still in Yemen fighting Nasser's longstanding Middle East "Vietnam."

The Egyptians had developed their initial battle plan in 1966. It envisioned a mobile defense in depth and that the majority of the army would mass in the center of the Sinai with only screening forces on the border. The Egyptians schemed to draw the Israeli army into the Sinai and then to surround and snap off its leading elements as it advanced. If anything went awry, there would be a second line of defense based on the narrow mountain passes that Israeli divisions, bent on reaching the Suez Canal, would have to traverse.

However, on June 4, Amer did not have the Egyptian army in the positions mandated by the plan. Instead, he located the bulk of the army much closer to Israel's border. The army planners in 1966 did not account for political mandates that at the last minute forbade deploying in a manner that would relinquish any territory, however temporarily, in order to trick the Israelis. Nasser refused to give up any of Gaza and in the Sinai—Rafah, Kuntilah, El Arish, and Abu Ageila—to advancing Israeli forces without a fight. Then, the Egyptian decision to launch an offensive into Israel's interior in late May coupled with its cancellation at the last minute, contributed to further disorganization on the ground. Poorly led from the start, the Egyptian army had not finished building its defensive positions near the border when war broke out.

Along the Jordanian border, the IDF positioned six brigades under the command of Uri Narkiss. Narkiss did not plan to take the West Bank or the Old City of Jerusalem. He had been ordered by Rabin and Dayan to remain on the defensive even though the Jordanians held positions in the hills surrounding Jerusalem on three sides, and he was told to ignore any minor shooting that Hussein might feel the need to authorize as a face-saving gesture. However, if the intensity of attacks from the Jordanians suggested that Hussein was fully committed to going to war, Rabin gave Narkiss the green light to engage. Then, only if Israeli territory was endangered, Narkiss had permission to take the tactically important hills surrounding Jerusalem. He was also cautioned that, if heavy fighting broke out, he would only receive minimal reinforcements consisting of additional mechanized troops and a parachute brigade under the command of Mordechai Gur.

However, the Jordanians wrongly suspected Israel had designs on the West Bank. Hussein had held those concerns for more than a decade, but the attack on Samu made them acute. But neither Hussein nor General Riad thought the West Bank could be adequately defended from a determined Israeli offensive. The Jordanian army had identified thirty-three potential places that Israeli ground forces might initiate attacks. At many of those locations tall trees and dense orange groves along much of the Israeli side of the border helped conceal IDF troop movements, and Israel's modern road network made it possible to rapidly transfer troops from one spot to another. Those two advantages made it difficult for the Jordanians to know if, and where, Israel might attack.

Unfortunately for the Jordanian army, it did not enjoy the same opportunities for concealment the IDF had. Nor did it have access to developed transportation networks. The West Bank had mainly poor roads that snaked through mountainous terrain filled with choke points exposed to attack from the air. Arab troop movements would be plainly visible to the IDF. Their new Egyptian commander, General Riad, had to choose between disbursing his forces over hundreds of miles of border, or to concentrate on a few key areas. Widely spread army checkpoints with regular patrols in between might work to block lightly armed Arab terrorists from leaving Jordan to attack Israel, but they would be nothing more than a speed bump for an invading Israeli army. On the other hand, concentrating the army would have meant leaving many populous and fertile regions near the border defenseless against Israeli troops. Neither solution was promising.

Before Riad's arrival, Jordanian army strategists had decided to mount forward defenses that would challenge an invading Israeli force as it moved into the West Bank even though they knew the chances of stopping them were slim. Therefore, Jordanian defensive plans envisioned counterattacking with heavy forces concentrated near Jerusalem and the Jordan Valley. The Jordanians hoped to encircle and seize Jewish Jerusalem in order to trade it for land lost to Israel elsewhere. The Jordanians believed that their success required capturing lightly defended Mount Scopus, an area where the Hadassah hospital and Hebrew University were located. Jordanian territory encircled the area and the 1949 armistice limited Israel to maintaining a force of eighty-five police officers and light weapons on Mount Scopus. However, because of the obvious threat, the Israelis successfully had smuggled in some heavier weapons. The Jordanians also planned to heavily defend territory astride narrow stretches of land that ran past Latrun within which ran the main highway artery from central Israel to Jewish Jerusalem, and from there into the West Bank. General Riad made few changes to Jordanian dispositions other than to move heavy artillery closer to the front so it could shell Israeli airports and military bases.

Seven Syrian brigades sat tight astride the Golan Heights. They constituted almost the entirety of Syria's 70,000 man army. The army was trained for defense, not offense. It was also missing a competent command structure: After the 1966 coup, the new Syrian leadership feared a counter-coup. To ward it off they purged many experienced officers. The purges were still ongoing in June. However, the topography surrounding Syria's defensive positions gave them strength and made up for the lack of quality military leadership. The Heights ran almost fifty miles from snowcapped Mt. Hermon over 9,000 feet high in the north to the Yarmouk Valley in the south along the border with Jordan. The Western slopes of the Syrian Golan rose 1500 feet or more above Israel's Huleh valley and the Sea of Galilee below. The Golan plateau then extended east from Israel more than twenty miles before dropping down to the Damascus plain. On top of the Golan, volcanic cone shaped hills, known as Tels, eerily jutted from the rocky terrain. For the IDF to attack, it would have to move up a steep slope littered with large rocks and other natural defensive positions.

Syrian defense lines were in some places more than ten miles deep. Pillboxes and other prepared positions littered the area. The Syrians could send ten tons of shells a minute towards Israel from more than 250 guns poking out from concrete emplacements. In addition, Syrian soldiers had scattered mines that were augmented by heavier concentrations throughout the region in designated defensive zones.

Israeli Northern Commander, David "Dado" Elazar, faced the Syrians with seven brigades. His task was complicated by his responsibility to defend against any incursions from Lebanon in the northwest and Jordan to his south. Elazar had been the northern commander for three years. He had long endured Syrian provocations and shelling. He was itching to move up the Heights and evict the Syrians, but like with Narkiss opposite Jordan, Israel's high command restrained him.

Despite the long, Jordanian border and the imposing Golan Heights, the Israelis viewed the Egyptians as the most dangerous. The IDF believed it crucial to eliminate Egypt's threat to Israel's existence as quickly as possible. It did not want to fight on three fronts simultaneously. That is why the IDF's leaders knew they had to move quickly and decisively to weaken their main foe. If they succeeded, the war would end, and a peace treaty could be negotiated.

Or, so they thought.

CHAPTER TEN
JUNE 5

Morning

Forty warplanes roared off the tarmac of Israel's airfields shortly after 7:00 a.m. (8:00 a.m. in many parts of Egypt) on June 5, 1967. Forty more followed within a few minutes and forty more soon after that. Thereafter more planes took off every few minutes until only the twelve fighters held back to defend Israel's airspace remained. A Jordanian radar station spotted the activity and promptly informed General Riad. He immediately sent a warning to the Egyptian High Command.

Riad's message did not arrive.

Most of the pilots flew their planes west over the Mediterranean. Once over the ocean they dropped to the deck, no more than thirty feet off the sea, and then turned south, and raced parallel with, but beyond sight of the Sinai coast. After a few minutes they turned east in groups of four, each quartet headed for a different Egyptian airfield. The first wave's goal was to arrive at all but one of the airfields simultaneously. The average age of the pilots was twenty-three.

Every day the Egyptians had made ready for a surprise attack at dawn. Beginning at 4:00 a.m., pairs of Egyptian fighter planes would fly patrol patterns along the Sinai border with Israel. Other fighter pilots sat strapped into the cockpits of their planes at the end of their runways. They were on a five-minute alert to take off and intercept any Israeli planes spotted. But by 7:35 a.m. the last of the Egyptian patrol planes always landed, and the pilots on runway alert left their cockpits. Most headed to the dining halls to eat breakfast. The majority of the ranking Egyptian officers left their homes for work after 7:00 a.m. They did not usually arrive at the office until 9:00 a.m. Egypt had been ready for an Israeli surprise attack when the sun rose on June 5. A couple of hours later they no longer were.

And, in a stroke of luck for the Israelis, Field Marshall Amer and the Egyptian commander of the air force were in planes heading to a meeting in the Sinai when the IAF planes took off from their bases. To ensure their leaders would not be struck by friendly fire, the Egyptians turned off their air defense system while they were in the air.

The IAF planes, mostly *Mirage* and *Mystere* fighter bombers purchased from France, reached their targets at 8:45 a.m. Egyptian time. Their first pass over the airfields was a bombing run during which they dropped specially-made bombs with rockets to drive the explosives deep into the concrete before exploding. Only one airstrip was spared that form of attack, and only because the Israelis planned to overrun and use it. To maximize the effect they swooped high at the last moment and then dove to increase the depth the explosives would penetrate before exploding. To ensure maximum devastation, every bomb had a fuse that delayed detonation until after the runway surface was penetrated. After dropping their bombs each plane made three or four strafing runs that targeted Egyptian planes lined up on the runways without any concrete revetments to protect them. The Egyptian habit of grouping similar plane types at the same airports made it easier for the IAF aviators to destroy the most dangerous Egyptian planes first while they were still trapped on the ground due to the damage done to the runways. Also, to increase their accuracy, IAF pilots dropped their landing gear to slow their planes down while aiming their weapons at targets. Then, precisely seven minutes after initiating the attack, they broke off to return to Israel to refuel and replenish their armaments.

Three minutes after the first attacking group departed another wave of four planes bombed and strafed each airfield. The second wave was followed by another, each separated by a respite of exactly three minutes. Seven minutes over the target, three minutes of quiet, and then another wave. They kept coming—followed by quiet for an extended period. And then the carnage began again. More waves, each consisting of four jets over each target, rained terror on the hapless Egyptian air force below.

Mordechai Hod, Israel's Air Force Commander, said, "The first forty-five minutes felt like a day." How could it not have? The plan required numerous aircraft to take off from multiple locations, fly a hundred miles or more, and arrive at precisely the same time over multiple targets while maintaining radio silence. Then the pilots returned their planes to base, quickly rearmed and refueled, and returned to the fight. Within fifteen minutes of receiving confirmation that the Egyptians had been surprised, and that the runways had been disabled by the first wave, Hod knew that the IAF had won the air battle. Even so, he patiently waited until 10:35 a.m. to say to Rabin, "The Egyptian air force has ceased to exist."

When Dayan heard of the IAF's success he ordered, "Don't publish anything." Dayan did not want the Arabs to learn the extent of the calamity they had suffered. He feared that recognition of Israel's success would lead to increased international pressure for a ceasefire: The IDF still had to destroy the Egyptian army and end the blockade of the Straits of Tiran. As for the Israeli people—they would have to worry a little bit longer. It was a comparatively small price to pay.

Three hours after the war began, the air over Egypt was empty; the broken Egyptian airbases were in shock. During those 180 minutes, almost every plane in Israel's air force flew more than one sortie. By noon, Egypt's air force no longer functioned—300 planes lay burnt and twisted beyond repair; more than a quarter of Egypt's trained pilots lay dead, and the runways on Egyptian airbases were unusable. The IAF had achieved control of the skies over the Sinai at little cost.

Fifteen minutes after the first wave of IAF planes headed towards Egypt, Rabin called the IDF Southern Commander, General Gavish, and said, "The Knesset session is on." He then ordered Gavish to begin operation *"Red Sheet."* They were code words for ordering Gavish to begin army operations against Egypt. Within minutes the first Israeli troops entered the Sinai.

The IDF planned a three-pronged, concentrated attack. General Tal took the northern route through the Arab town of Rafah at the base of Gaza on its border with the Sinai and then along the Mediterranean coast. General Sharon moved from the center of Israel's Negev into the central northern part of the Sinai. Sharon's mission was to follow the road network to the road junction at Abu Ageila and then break through to the mountain passes of Mitla and Giddi almost one hundred miles beyond. General Yoffee's orders were to move his division between Tal and Sharon over trackless sand dunes the Egyptians thought impossible to traverse.

King Hussein strode into his military headquarters at 9:00 a.m. Aides gave the king a cable from General Amer that falsely boasted Egypt had destroyed 75% of Israel's attacking aircraft and that directed General Riad to order the Jordanian army to attack Israel. In addition, Hussein received promises from Syria and Iraq that they would provide troops and, most importantly, air cover if Jordan entered the war.

Hussein also received the first of three messages from Israel asking him not to get involved in the fighting and stating that Israel did not want a war with Jordan. But Hussein felt honor bound as a fellow Arab to help Egypt. By 9:30 a.m., Jordanian troops began firing bullets and then artillery shells at the Israelis.

Later in the morning, a second message arrived from Amer. The message repeated Egypt's false claim of destroying massive numbers of IAF aircraft, but conceded that Israel continued to mount air attacks. Amer also informed Hussein that Egyptian forces were pushing into the Negev. As the morning wore on, Jordan's artillery units intensified their fire despite Hussein's receipt of a second message from Israel through the UN that said, "We shall not initiate any action whatsoever against Jordan. However, should Jordan open hostilities, we shall react with all our might, and the king will have to bear the full responsibility for the consequences."

But Hussein didn't believe the Israelis. He still suffered from "Samu Syndrome". The king was certain that Israel's plan was to delay until she was ready. Then the IDF would strike with the goal of occupying the West Bank. He felt Jordan's only chance to survive intact was to ally with his Arab brethren. Therefore, he disregarded the message conveyed by the UN. Since the Jordanians continued to shoot, Israeli forces began returning fire.

After the Jordanians began shelling the Israelis, Narkiss, the IDF Central Commander, asked his superiors three times for permission to attack and occupy the hills surrounding Jerusalem. It was personal for Narkiss. In 1948, he led a relief force that broke into the Old City with the hopes of relieving many Jews trapped in the Jewish Quarter. The Jordanians threw him back after bitter fighting. Shortly afterwards, all of the surviving Jews in the Old City surrendered. For the next nineteen years the Old City, including the Jewish Quarter, remained under Jordanian control. It was a bitter memory Narkiss sought to assuage. But twice Rabin said no to Narkiss. Rabin's deputy denied his third request. It must have been difficult emotionally for Rabin to refuse permission. Rabin was the commander who had ordered Narkiss into the Old City in 1948.

Just before noon, Jordan's tiny air force attacked Israeli targets. The Jordanians had waited all morning in hope of coordinating with the Syrian and Iraqi air forces. The Syrians had first asked the Jordanians to wait thirty minutes. Then they requested another hour's delay before commencing air strikes. That request was followed by requests for further postponements. Finally, Hussein decided he could not wait any longer. At 11:00 a.m. he ordered his air force to attack on its own. The Jordanian air attack only caused minor damage, but it made a major statement: Jordan had joined the war against the Jews.

Meanwhile, Shuqayri's courage did not match his rhetoric. Only days earlier the PLO leader had called for the Arabs to destroy Israel. But rather than lead he fled. At the first sound of gunfire, Shuqayri jumped into a car and bolted from the West Bank to the safety of Damascus.

In the north, the morning was quiet. Despite being asked to launch airstrikes at 9:00 a.m by General Riad and the Jordanians, the Syrians did not begin operations until well after eleven. When the Syrian and Jordanian air forces, along with the Iraqis, finally attacked, the last waves of IAF planes were already returning from destroying the Egyptian air force. Those raids, though of little effect, were not forgotten by the IAF. Syria, Jordan, and Iraq would get their turn soon.

Afternoon

At 1:00 p.m., Israeli air strikes struck Syrian and Jordanian airfields. In addition, rockets from one jet crashed through Hussein's vacant office causing some to believe the Israelis had attempted to assassinate the king. By sundown, Jordan's and Syria's air forces were in ruins. IAF jets also attacked an Iraqi airfield near the Jordanian border, destroying the two Iraqi aircraft squadrons stationed there.

Despite the IAF's destruction of Jordan's air force, in the afternoon Jordanian troops were able to capture a UN position called the *"Government House,"* located in the demilitarized zone between Israel and

Jordan in Jerusalem. It was a strategic location that the Jordanians could use as a springboard to stretch armed tentacles around Jewish Jerusalem. Also, in the north, Jordanian artillery struck an Israeli airbase. In the early afternoon, Eshkol gave the IDF permission to respond. A limited counterattack by ground troops took the Government House back. Then the IDF moved north and east along the hills to begin its own encirclement of Arab Jerusalem. At 2:30 p.m., Colonel Mordechai Gur, who was born in the Old City of Jerusalem, received new orders. To support the assault into the Sinai, the parachute brigade he commanded had planned to drop from planes into the desert beyond Israel's border with Egypt. Instead, busses transported his soldiers to Jerusalem. Israel's hopes for quiet on the West Bank were dashed, but the opportunity to transform a dream into reality was at hand.

Nasser spoke with Hussein by telephone at 1:45 p.m. (Egyptian time). He told the king that Israel had attacked first, Egypt had retaliated, and that Egyptian forces were proceeding with their offensive into the Negev. Nasser urged Hussein to seize as much territory as possible. Nasser's exhortations and subsequent orders from General Amer changed Hussein's and General Riad's plans. Rather than encircle Jewish Jerusalem, Riad shifted his Jordanian forces south to join with what he thought were Egyptian troops advancing on Beersheba in the central Negev.

The change flabbergasted the leadership of the Jordanian army. No blueprint existed for a plan to capture any Israeli territory other than land surrounding Jerusalem. Jordan's military leaders knew their army was too weak to fight the Israelis along their entire frontier; to do that they would need help from other Arab countries, but, so far, none had come to their aid. They also that knew moving much of their army's strength south would significantly weaken defenses in the strategically critical center, invite air attacks on the units while they were on the road, and effectively end any hope of taking Jewish Jerusalem as a bargaining chip.

As the afternoon progressed, reports of Israeli advances paralyzed Egyptian command and control even though General Amer and other high-level Egyptian military commanders had returned by noon to their headquarters in Cairo. Their collective panic prevented them from responding to events rationally even though it might not have been too late to invoke Egypt's previous plan to lure the IDF into central Sinai where it could be destroyed. But, rather than calmly directing units to pull back to defensible lines, in the late afternoon Israeli intelligence heard Amer on the phone with his divisional commanders imploring them to send reinforcements to buttress their crumbling front lines. Thus, rather than instituting the Egyptian plan to cut off the Israelis, Amer sent his soldiers forward to their own funeral. The morning had brought one disaster from the skies. Another was in the making on the ground.

Amer also failed to warn the civilian leadership about the disaster that had befallen the Egyptian armed forces. Vice President Anwar Sadat felt that something was amiss when he entered the General Headquarters building in the afternoon and observed rampant panic and confusion. By many accounts, Nasser first learned of the disaster when he arrived at the headquarters at 4:00 p.m. and found Amer depressed and barely coherent in a building filled with confused and disorganized officers.

At 5:00 p.m., the vanguard of Sharon's division arrived in front of the fortifications at Abu Ageila, deep in northern Sinai. Along the Mediterranean, elements of Tal's division rolled down the road to El Arish. Colonel Gonen, an acclaimed and aggressive commander of the Seventh Brigade destined to become Southern Front Commander several years later, led their advance. Lt. Avigdor Kahalani commanded one of the lead tanks. Kahalani, born in Yemen, had a dark skin tone and an ivory smile. While his tank moved through the Jirardi Defile, the last obstacle before El Arish, it was struck by a shell. Severely burned as a result, Kahalani's survival was questionable. Six years later, during the

Yom Kippur War, his leadership and courage on the Golan saved Israel. And during those moments years in the future while Kahalani was standing fast against the Syrians during the Yom Kippur War, Gonen's command failures in the Sinai almost caused Israel's destruction.

By the end of the day Nasser knew he needed to find a scapegoat for Egypt's failure. He decided to falsely accuse the United States and England of launching airstrikes on behalf of the Israelis. He did it to preserve Egyptian honor and to draw Russia into the fight. He also asked Arab oil producers to suspend oil shipments to the United States and Britain. Iraq and Kuwait were the first to agree.

Meanwhile, Syria's army lingered while Egypt burned and Jordan smoldered. Rather than initiate *"Operation Victor,"* a bold thrust of their armored forces into northern Israel north of Lake Kinneret, Syria's generals would only launch much more modest border attacks. The Syrians also reneged on their promise to move soldiers into northern portions of the West Bank to protect Jordan's flank left naked when General Riad moved a Jordanian brigade to Jericho in compliance with Amer's orders. That left an undefended pathway into the West Bank for Elazar's northern command to exploit, if given the order.

Perhaps Syria's perfidy should have been expected. Before the war, amidst the propaganda salvos hurled back and forth with the Jordanians, Syria's leadership suspected Hussein of conspiring with renegades to overthrow their government. The war changed little regarding their feelings for the king. Unlike Hussein, who willingly came to Egypt's aid despite their previous antagonistic relationship, the Syrians had no interest in putting their hatred aside for the common good. Syria's failure to close ranks with Jordan was a betrayal that Hussein would never forget.

Israel's successes did not go unnoticed by the Kremlin. On August 30, 1963, a hotline had been established to facilitate communication between the superpowers in the event of an emergency. It was a Teletype link; messages had to be typed to be sent. Reliable international telephone technology did not yet exist. On June 5, for the first time since it was activated, Russian Chairman Kosygin used the "hotline" to send an emergency request to President Johnson to use his influence with the Jewish State to secure Israel's acceptance of a ceasefire. Johnson received the message shortly before 9:00 a.m. in Washington, D.C. (4:00 p.m. in Cairo).

During the day, while diplomatic activity picked up at the UN, little momentum built towards a broad-based international demand for a ceasefire. Israel's Ambassador to the UN sought to delay any resolution in order to give his country time to complete her victory. The Arab Ambassadors similarly sought to delay voting on a ceasefire resolution because, based on information given to them by their governments, they thought Israel was losing. Meanwhile, the Soviet Union tread water. The Russians still hoped the Arabs would win and threatened to veto any resolution that did not condemn Israel for attacking. The United States favored pushing for an early ceasefire resolution, but only one that required both Egypt and Israel to withdraw their forces from the Sinai. Therefore, the Americans and the British rejected an Indian proposal demanding an immediate ceasefire followed by all parties returning to the positions they had held on June 4. That proposal had no chance of acceptance by Israel or the Americans since it would have left Israel still facing the threat of an Egyptian attack without warning and still subject to Egypt's blockade of the Straits of Tiran. With all sides still jockeying for a resolution most beneficial to their interests, the conflict raged on as the burning, desert sun set on the fifth of June.

Night

Abu Ageila was a pivotal crossroad in the Sinai. Backed by artillery at Um-Katef, it was defended by three parallel lines of Egyptian soldiers. The IDF had failed to punch through the position during the 1956 war.

However, General Arik Sharon was confident that his division would break through that night. He had planned an ambitious assault consisting of a frontal attack by tanks charged with occupying the attention of the Egyptian defenders, combined with stealthy attacks from multiple other directions. Success required absolute precision.

Helicopters transported paratroopers to the rear of the Egyptian position, but, due to harassing fire from Egyptian soldiers who heard them coming, only half of the 300-member-unit was able to land. In addition, three IDF infantry battalions marched several hours through sand dunes to reach a point at the of the Egyptian trenches where each battalion targeted one of the trench lines dug into the sand. However, rather than attacking from the front, the battalions struck the flank of their assigned trench where it began. They then moved forward, parallel to their designated trench, marking the progress of their unit with different colored lights chosen specifically for each battalion before the attack. IDF tank and artillery observers fired explosive shells into the trenches ahead of the illuminated markers to support the advancing IDF soldiers. Meanwhile, the paratroopers attacked the Egyptian artillery based behind the trench lines to prevent them from interfering with the infantry battalions. By first light, Abu Ageila was taken. The road to the mountain passes, and the Suez Canal beyond them, was open.

Meanwhile, Israel's cabinet ministers gathered that evening in their wood-paneled room at the Knesset in Jerusalem while Jordanian artillery continued to hammer the city. They were excited, aware that momentous decisions awaited them. Eshkol banged his gavel to bring the meeting to order and then gave the floor to Menachem Begin. Begin had been leader of the Irgun in 1948. Now, in 1967, he was a leading member of the political opposition to Eshkol. In a demonstration of unity, the Prime Minster had asked him to join the government a few days before. He began, "Mr. Prime Minister, the question before us is of unprecedented historic consequence," but could not finish because the sergeant-at-arms flung the doors open and shouted, "Out, out, shells are falling again." Guards hurriedly escorted the ministers to a cluttered, basement room where their meeting began anew. Begin lost no time addressing the issue before them. He lamented that because the UN Security Council was currently in session; soon they would lose the priceless opportunity that Hussein's failure to heed their warnings had given them—an opportunity to take back the Old City.

The ministers knew the decision before them was a historic one. If they decided to take the Old City, no future Israeli government could ever give it up willingly. But Eshkol was hesitant. He also knew that Dayan, who was not present, was reluctant to conquer the Old City. Eshkol relayed Dayan's concerns that house-to-house fighting would be costly. The Prime Minister also worried that holy places of other faiths might be damaged in the fighting, a result that would cause the world to rally against Israel. And he reiterated Dayan's view that just encircling the Old City might cause it to fall. Allon, however, disagreed. He predicted that Jewish boots would have to enter the Old City to capture it, a move that he predicted would not cost many casualties. After further talk, the ministers agreed to defer a decision until Dayan and Rabin could be consulted. Eshkol expressed the thoughts of many at the end of the meeting when he said, "An opportunity has perhaps been created to capture the Old City." He then turned to Begin and quietly said, "If it comes to it, I'll overrule Dayan."

That night, Dayan and Rabin turned their thoughts to Syria. General Elazar pushed for permission to attack. The last thing he wanted was to leave the Golan in Syrian hands at war's end. Elazar argued that the defense of northern Israel required aggressive movement up the Heights and onto the Golan plain. Syria, however, had limited her engagement to mainly firing artillery intermittently at Israeli settlements, and, therefore, there did not appear to be any significant imminent danger. Rabin and Dayan granted Elazar authority to take the demilitarized zones—scenes of many skirmishes involving Israel's attempt to farm her own territory—but nothing more. Once again, it appeared that Syria would escape retribution.

During a press conference that day in Tel Aviv, Eban told reporters, "The pattern of aggression which is now unfolding, in a culminating stage, did not, of course, begin this morning.... In our view, the actual hostility began with the act of the blockade." Eban then continued, "Government policy includes no aims of conquest ... our single objective is to frustrate the attempts of the Arab armies to conquer our land and so to break this siege and ring around us."

As night descended on the Egyptian people, they still did not know about the disaster that had overtook their armed forces. Nasser announced that more than 100 Israeli planes had been shot down and dramatically said to his people, "Pack your bags! We will be in Tel Aviv by tomorrow night." Posters appeared throughout Cairo showing muscular Arab soldiers booting Jews with nooses around their necks out of Israel. And, by the end of the day, Egyptian police had arrested several hundred of the 3,000 Jews still living in Jewish quarters in Cairo and Alexandria.

The truth was that Israel's major ground goals in the Sinai had been fulfilled, if not surpassed, on the first day of battle. Only in Gaza, things had not gone as planned. Dayan had ruled out entering the Gaza strip. But, when Palestinian forces fired on Israeli settlements, Rabin had overruled Dayan and sent a brigade into the strip. By sunset the IDF had taken the strategic areas but Gaza City had not yet been subdued, and the IDF had suffered heavy casualties in the crowded environs.

However, one thing was clear to all of the combatants, and an Israeli general staff officer expressed it succinctly, "Israel is now the only air power in the Middle East."

CHAPTER ELEVEN
JUNE 6

Twenty-four hours after the war started it was clear Israel had won. IAF planes pounced on remaining targets without interference. The Egyptian and Jordanian armies were in disarray.

General Rabin spoke to the Israeli people at 1:00 a.m. Until then, Arab radio and TV media that spouted false boasts of Egypt's victories and advancing army were the only news sources for Israeli citizens. Rabin revealed the truth. He announced that IDF forces had moved deep into Sinai and that key positions surrounding Jerusalem had fallen to the IDF. Also, most importantly, he revealed the devastating blow delivered to the Arab air forces.

Morning

Colonel Gonen's Seventh Brigade took El Arish in northern Sinai early in the pre-dawn hours. From there, an Israeli column raced towards the Suez Canal as the sun began to rise. Meanwhile, Sharon's division recovered from its bruising fight to take Abu Ageila and the fortifications at Umm Qatef. In the afternoon, he, too, headed for the mountain passes and the canal beyond. The Israelis were exhausted and low on supplies.

Even so, the momentum gained from their success during the first twenty-four hours of war propelled them forward.

The Egyptian army lost thousands of military vehicles during the first day of fighting, sustained heavy casualties, and had no remaining defenses to ward off Israeli air strikes now wreaking havoc on the living. However, more than half of the Egyptian forces were still intact. Many Egyptian troops had not yet had a shot fired on them, and reinforcements and armaments were on the way to Cairo. Much was still left to salvage. The means to fight still existed. But the army lacked leadership.

The Egyptian high command did not learn the full extent of the Israeli breakthrough until the morning of June 6. When they did, General Amer panicked. Believing the situation more desperate than it really was, he ordered all Egyptian forces to abandon their heavy weapons and withdraw from the Sinai by no later than daybreak on June 7. Some speculate that Amer's memory of French and British landings along the canal during the 1956 war triggered his fear of an American amphibious assault on vital Egyptian areas. But there was no basis for such concern. Nor were Amer's orders to retreat cleared with President Nasser. Instead, his headquarters transmitted them immediately to the field commands.

Upon receiving Amer's order, some high-level officers told their subordinates to initiate the withdrawal but then did not wait to see their orders implemented. Instead, they jumped into their chauffeured cars and quickly sped across the Suez Canal out of harm's way. One division commander was later seen in Cairo's cafes before the unit he commanded reached safety. Egyptian troop morale plummeted, in large part due to the failures of their leaders.

Amer's orders shocked many officers serving on his General Staff. Egypt's basic war plan had called for drawing the Jews into the killing grounds of Sinai's barren central wasteland. The IDF was where the Egyptians wanted them. The officers thought that Israel could still be defeated. They implored Amer to change his mind, arguing that, if he did not revoke his order, the wholesale retreat would no doubt turn into a disaster. Amer agreed and issued new directives countermanding the withdrawal. But it was too late. The rout was on.

The Jordanian army fared no better than the Egyptians. After dark, the IDF closed in around Jerusalem. Shortly after two a.m. on June 6, Colonel Gur's paratroopers moved across the demilitarized zone near the Mandelbaum Gate. Their main target was Ammunition Hill, named after a British supply depot in World War I. It was a short distance north of the city and west of Mount Scopus. Ammunition Hill was the key to defending Jerusalem.

The paratroopers had little time to prepare after their bus ride from the south. They were trained for a parachute drop in the Sinai, not to take heavily defended trenches in unfamiliar terrain at night. However, they were some of Israel's best troops; they prevailed. When the battle was over thirty-seven dead Israelis and over one hundred dead Jordanians littered the battlefield. Even more were wounded. Those paratroopers who survived were dazed and exhausted. They required rest before they could again be an effective fighting force. But the desperate battle, on what became hallowed ground for Israelis, opened the path to Arab Jerusalem. To traverse it, all that was required was the political will to do so.

Ammunition Hill was not the only IDF success in the region. Soldiers cleared the ridges circling the city, and, by seven a.m., IDF troops arrived before the Damascus Gate entrance to the Old City. Only Moshe Dayan's hesitancy to order them into the Old City stopped them. Later that morning, the IDF took Latrun, a strategic choke point on the road to Jerusalem. Jewish blood had flowed copiously in front of its stone walls due to three failed attempts to take the position during the 1948 War. By midday, Jordanian commanders received a report that the Israelis had taken all of Arab Jerusalem—except the Old City. For the moment, that prize, one for which Jews yearned, still remained in Arab hands.

The punch to Jordan's solar plexus in the central West Bank near Jerusalem was joined by a roundhouse left delivered by General Elazar's northern command. Elazar's focus had always been Syria. When Rabin ordered him to move into the West Bank, it both surprised and disappointed him. For years Eshkol had refused to permit Elazar to deliver a harsh blow to the Syrians—the people who indiscriminately, from their high haunts on the Golan, killed Jewish citizens farming below. The onset of war seemed to provide an opportunity long overdue. But Elazar dutifully followed Rabin's orders rather than the dictates of his heart, and, by three a.m., many of his units moved into the West Bank rather than the Golan. Elazar planned to disembowel the West Bank by taking Jenin; General Riad's last-minute movement of powerful units of the Jordanian army to the south had cleared the way. Nevertheless, resistance from residual Jordanian forces was fierce, even if it was futile. When IAF airstrikes disrupted those Jordanian units that had achieved some success holding up the Israelis, Elazar's soldiers surged forward. Very quickly the most northern portions of the West Bank fell to the IDF.

King Hussein and General Riad spoke at 5:30 a.m. Riad told him the war on the West Bank was lost and the army "will be isolated and destroyed." Riad said there were two choices: Hussein should either try for an immediate ceasefire or withdraw his army to the East Bank of the Jordan River. He told Hussein he had twenty-four hours to decide. Any more, Riad added, "you can kiss your army and all of Jordan goodbye!" Hussein answered that, before deciding, he wanted to find out what Nasser thought.

Hussein felt caught between a rock and a hard place. Whether he retreated or called for a unilateral ceasefire, his rule was at risk. If his subjects—loyalists and rivals alike—perceived him forsaking Egypt during her desperate struggle, they would riot and call for his overthrow. The army might also revolt. But, whether he retreated or requested a ceasefire, it would mean the same thing—Jordan's exit from the war.

A half hour later, depressed and unsure, Hussein spoke to Nasser. They communicated through the public telephone network. Neither was aware that Israeli intelligence was listening to their conversation. They discussed the air disaster of the day before. Hussein told Nasser that Jordanian radar had detected sixteen planes arriving in Israel which he alleged came from an aircraft carrier. Nasser responded with a question: should they accuse both England and the United States of providing air support to the Israelis or just the United States? They agreed to accuse both. Hussein maintained to his death that he believed it true at the time. However, both were publicly shamed the next day when Israel made the transcript of the conversation public. Faced with denials from America and England, and without any evidence to support them, neither Nasser nor Hussein would recant their farcical claim.

While the IDF was on the march in Jordan and Egypt, the Syrians sat smug, snuggled into their defensive positions, even though they were the root cause of the war. It hardly seemed fair that the Syrians had remained unscathed. Over the years, Syria's refusal to recognize, negotiate, and/or peacefully co-exist with Israel had found expression in numerous firefights between the IDF and the Syrian army that had kept northern Israel on edge for years. Most of the fights were over Israel's right to farm in the DMZ. Not content to lob shells at civilians, the Syrians had also enthusiastically supported Palestinian terrorists. Their active support of the Fedayeen had triggered Israel's attack on Samu which led to Hussein's devastating decision to embroil Jordan in the current war. Then, in May, when Russia and Syria falsely accused Israel of mobilizing in the north that instigated the all-out war that was engulfing the region. Yet, other than two desultory air attacks and artillery bombardment of Israeli settlements the day before, the Syrians did nothing more. They were content to sit back in their mountain fortresses while Jordan and Egypt suffered. For the time being, the IDF did little to threaten them.

At 2:00 a.m., things changed. Syrian artillery units increased their shelling, especially near Kibbutz Dan. Eager to bounce back from the devastating air attacks of the day before, Syria's confidence swelled when the IDF chose not to respond. Syria's impression that Israel was in trouble was enhanced when a message from Egypt arrived bragging that the Egyptian army was advancing on Tel Aviv and that even went so far as to claim that much of Israel's air force had been destroyed. Defense Minister Assad announced, "At this crucial and historical hour our forces have begun to fight and to bomb the enemy's position along the entire front. These are just the first shots in the war of liberation."

Finally, the Syrian leadership ordered the army to institute *Operation Victor*. The first step was a feint towards Kibbutz Dan. The IDF drove them back easily. The second step, a large attack from the Southern Golan, never materialized. Perhaps it was due to poor communication, perhaps because the feint in the north was beaten back, and perhaps due to an increasingly active Israeli air force and artillery. Or perhaps because the Syrians had not thought to check the width of the bridges that crossed into Israel—they were too narrow to permit passage of Syria's armored vehicles.

Afternoon

At 12:30 p.m., Hussein's army was crumbling. Desperate, Hussein sent a personal telegram to Nasser. The king wrote that the situation in Jerusalem was critical, that every ten minutes Jordan lost another tank. He asked Nasser what he should do. Nasser did not respond. But coincidentally, within minutes of Hussein sending his telegram, General Amer answered General Riad's telegram earlier in the morning which had alerted his Egyptian superiors that Jordan's army was in danger of being destroyed. Amer told Riad he agreed with Riad's plan to retreat and to arm the civilian population.

While the king was attempting to communicate with Nasser, Dayan met with General Narkiss in Jerusalem. Narkiss again requested permission to take the Old City, and again Dayan refused, telling Narkiss to instead focus on the hills surrounding the city.

In the northern city of Jenin, Elazar's forces were able to subdue resistance by 1:00 p.m. But the arrival of the crack Jordanian 40th armored brigade from Jericho (where General Riad had sent it the previous day) kept the fight fierce in other areas of the northern West Bank. As a result, when the afternoon drew to an end, the Jordanians still possessed the crossroads necessary to exercise control over the region.

Hussein knew he needed a ceasefire but feared requesting one without permission from the other Arab nations. His solution was to ask America to arrange it. The king summoned the Ambassadors of the United States, England, France, and Russia. He told them he would accept a ceasefire but could not ask for one. The Americans passed the message to the Israelis, but asked them to keep Hussein's decision secret to avoid creating domestic instability within Jordan.

And, Hussein still debated whether to order his army to retreat behind the Jordan River. When he received word, however, that the Israelis would not agree to a unilateral and immediate cessation of hostilities in Jordan, his hopes of keeping control of the West Bank dwindled. The Israelis simply would not forgive his failure to stay out of the war the day before. During the course of the day they refused four separate requests from Hussein for a ceasefire that would freeze Israeli forces from advancing further.

Late in the afternoon, Hussein abruptly left his headquarters, jumped into a jeep, and crossed the Jordan River into the West Bank where he saw his retreating troops. Reflecting back on those moments, he later said:

"I will never forget the hallucinating sight of that defeat. Roads clogged with trucks, jeeps, and all kinds of vehicles twisted, disemboweled, dented, still smoking, giving off that particular smell of metal and paint burned by exploding bombs—a stink that only powder can make. In the midst of this charnel house were men. In groups of thirty or two, wounded, exhausted they were trying to clear a path under the monstrous coup de grace being dealt them by a horde of Israeli *Mirages* screaming in a cloudless blue sky seared by the sun."

At 6:40 a.m. in Washington D.C. (12:40 p.m. in Israel and Jordan), the Russians activated the hotline again. Kosygin sent Johnson a thinly-veiled threat to influence the Israelis to withdraw from the Sinai or face the prospect of Soviet intervention. Two hours later, the Russians received Johnson's reply: "The United States would not act unilaterally. The place to seek an end to the Arab-Israeli war was at the United Nations. The method was a UN ceasefire resolution."

Johnson also denied any involvement in the attack on Egypt, rebutting Hussein's and Nasser's accusations that American planes had helped the Israelis. He reminded Kosygin that, since Russian ships shadowed the American aircraft carriers, the Russians knew the American denials were true.

The accusations by Nasser and Jordan of western complicity with the Israelis, despite the emphatic denials by Washington and London, inflamed the passions of the "Arab street." Mobs attacked American embassies and consulates located throughout the Arab world, and Egypt and six other Arab nations, including Syria, severed diplomatic relations with the United States. In addition, Arab oil-producing nations cut off oil shipments to America. Nasser did not help matters. He issued a statement that implored "the Arab masses to destroy all imperialist interest." Americans who had lived for extended periods in Egypt were given a few minutes to pack their bags and leave the country. Many were searched at gunpoint, leading one *Life* magazine reporter to write, "This is how people felt on their way to Auschwitz."

At an Israeli Ministerial Defense Committee meeting, Begin argued, "This is the hour of our political test. We must attack the Old City." Dayan opposed him. He worried that heavy fighting in the narrow streets and alleyways would cause numerous casualties. Normally that fact might not have deterred him, but, because he thought the international community might not let Israel retain its conquest, he feared the lost lives of his soldiers would be for naught. Dayan also worried that, if the Christian, Muslim, and Jewish holy sites were damaged by the fighting, Israel would be blamed. Dayan proposed an alternative. He recommended that the IDF complete the encirclement of Jerusalem along the hills that overlooked it. Dayan argued the Old City would fall after a few days without the need to enter it by force. He also made two other suggestions: stop the IDF in the Sinai short of the Suez Canal, and end the IDF's advance in the West Bank at the eastern edge of the hills overlooking the Jordan River, several miles from the river's shoreline. Dayan feared that, if they failed to restrain the IDF, the Soviet Union would be tempted to intervene.

With regard to Syria, Eshkol proposed ordering General Elazar to take the source of the Banias River on the Golan and the fortification of Tel Azaziat that overlooked some of Israel's valley settlements. Rabin and Elazar wanted to move further into the Golan. Allon agreed with them, but again Dayan demurred. Dayan argued that the Syrians would never accept losing their territory. Therefore, the war would never end, and the Russians might intervene, just as he feared, if the IDF reached the shores of the Suez Canal or the Jordan River.

After leading the IDF to victory in the 1956 war, Dayan's public support was strong. As Defense Minister, he reported to Eshkol, but politically and emotionally he remained the people's number one hero. Therefore, his actual power exceeded his legal authority, making his recommendations difficult to challenge. As a result, on issues involving how far the IDF should go, Dayan's views prevailed. Thanks to Dayan, the Syrian army was safe for a little longer.

Night

General Gavish, the IDF's Southern Front Commander, recognized the opportunity provided by the Egyptian retreat. He was determined to overtake the Egyptians before they reached the narrow mountain passes that led to safety. Gavish ordered small units to sprint forward, pass through the Egyptian army, and then stop, turn, and set up blocking positions. He ordered the rest of the army to follow behind and to destroy the desperate Egyptian forces which were prevented from escaping by the Israelis in front of them. Jewish soldiers in their armored vehicles cut through the Arab columns. The Arab rank and file, mostly abandoned by their highest echelons of leadership, had lost the capacity or inclination for combat because of their panicked retreat. Above, in the skies, Israeli jets prowled like birds of prey, swooping down on any Arab targets worthy of their effort. But, even in the midst of defeat, some brave Egyptians fought back. The Egyptian 4th armored division attempted a counterattack during the night but was unsuccessful. The rout of the Egyptians continued unabated.

In New York, the UN Security Council met. Abba Eban had been in transit from Israel since the day before. His journey began with a fright. He was almost struck by shrapnel from a Jordanian artillery shell in the front yard of his home. After a several hour delay waiting for his plane, following stops in Athens and Amsterdam, he arrived in New York. Eban first met briefly with the Israeli and American UN Ambassadors, then went to the UN to address the Security Council. Despite having not slept in over a day, many believe Eban's speech was his finest hour.

"I have just come from Jerusalem," he said, "to tell the Security Council that Israel, by its independent effort and sacrifice, has passed from serious danger to successful resistance." He then spoke of Nasser's intent: "Here was a clear design to cut the southern Negev off from the main body of our State ... [after which he] predicted that Israel itself would soon expire." Eban explained that Israel had been confronted by "an alarming plan of encirclement" that included being "suddenly and arbitrarily choked" from losing the freedom to navigate the Straits of Tiran.

Eban continued by describing the tension Israel's citizens felt before June 6 as "an apocalyptic air of an approaching peril and [that] Israel faced this danger alone." Eban followed, "Here, then, was a systematic, overt, proclaimed design at politicide, the murder of a State ... and the State thus threatened with collective assassination was itself the last sanctuary of a people which had seen six million of its sons exterminated ... two decades before." Nearing the end of his speech, Eban then asked a question that haunts to this day when Israel is asked to take existential risks in return for mere guarantees, "What is the use of a United Nations presence if it is, in effect, an umbrella which is taken away as it begins to rain?"

Eban opposed a ceasefire because Israel needed more time to reach all of her goals. The Israelis argued that only after a clear-cut Israeli victory would a historic opportunity for regional peace present itself. The Americans floated a ceasefire proposal that included a withdrawal behind the armistice lines and, according to American Ambassador Goldberg, would end the blockade in the Straits of Tiran and be a vehicle for talks on separation of forces and territorial changes.

Russian Ambassador Fedorenko, at 10:00 a.m. in New York (4:00 p.m. in Israel), rejected the American proposal because it included an end to the blockade of the Straits. Fifteen minutes later, his instructions changed. He received orders from Moscow to seek a ceasefire in place because of the Arab military disaster, the dimensions of which were getting worse by the minute. After receiving the new orders, Fedorenko called Goldberg to inform him.

The Israelis were not pleased with the American ceasefire proposal, despite Goldberg's assurances that withdrawal from the newly-won territories could take at least four months, thereby providing ample time for further diplomacy. However, for the Israelis, any mention of a withdrawal to the armistice lines was anathema. Israel's leaders launched their pre-emptive attack because of the threats the country faced. Any agreement to withdraw to the starting line without a substantial change to the status quo as it existed before the war risked creating a perception that the war had been for reasons other than defensive ones. Nevertheless, Eban grudgingly accepted the American proposal. At 4:30 p.m. in New York, the resolution passed. It was to go into effect at midnight in Israel and Jordan. Then it hit a fatal snag. Egypt's Ambassador rose, based on orders from Cairo, and told the Security Council that Egypt would not accept the ceasefire proposal. Egypt would only agree to a ceasefire that included an unconditional Israeli withdrawal.

Egyptian insistence on what could not be obtained sealed Egypt's fate, along with that of Jordan and Syria.

Hussein's long afternoon continued into the night. He still had not received a response from Nasser. At 7:00 p.m., General Riad ordered Jordanian forces to withdraw from the West Bank. At 11:00 p.m., Riad received word that the UN Security Council had issued its call for an unconditional ceasefire. The surprising news led Hussein and Riad to realize that the seemingly imminent ceasefire might mean that Jordan could hold onto significant portions of the West Bank. They countermanded the retreat order; but, like Amer's order in the Sinai, it was too late. The reversal caused confusion. Jordanian soldiers who tried to regain their previous positions, could not. IDF forces, aware of the looming ceasefire, had moved forward aggressively. They prevented the Jordanians from returning.

At 11:30 p.m., Nasser finally responded to Hussein's cable from much earlier in the day. By then Hussein had learned from other sources of the destruction of Egypt's air force. "We have been purely and simply crushed by the enemy," Nasser admitted. His recommendation to Hussein was to evacuate his army from the West Bank, hope for a ceasefire, and to maintain relations with the United States and England.

CHAPTER TWELVE
JUNE 7

On June 7, during their morning meeting, the Israeli cabinet granted the IDF permission to enter the Old City. They also discussed whether the IDF should be given instructions to advance all the way to the Suez Canal in the Sinai. Dayan told the ministers he had ordered the IDF to stop before reaching the canal because:

> "If [the IDF] will reach the [c]anal, the war will never finish. The Egyptians will not be able to allow themselves the occupation of the bank by [the IDF], neither will the Soviets acquiesce with this. It is possible they will intervene, maybe by indirect military means …. If we reach the [c]anal, Nasser will refuse a cease-fire and the war will continue for years."

Dayan's fears were not misplaced. Chuvakhin, the Russian Ambassador to Israel, had delivered a menacing note to the government earlier in the morning. The note condemned Israel's attack and accused her leaders of being "willing to gamble with their whole destiny." The note also contained a threat to break diplomatic relations with the Jewish State if Israel did not immediately comply with the UN ceasefire resolution (despite Egypt's refusal). And then, rather ominously, the Russians threatened to "examine [their] position and take other necessary steps resulting from the aggressive policy of Israel." The day before, the West German ambassador to Israel had passed on to Israel's government Chuvakhin's comment that, if Israel did not stop its attacks "the future of this little country will be a very sad one."

The Russian Politburo met early that morning too. They debated whether the Soviet Union could do anything to stabilize the Egyptians. One possibility was to rush more military equipment to Egypt, but they decided it probably was too late to make a difference. Another option was to send Soviet military personnel to defend the Egyptians. But, when Turkey refused to permit the Russians to fly over their airspace, that option faded away. Therefore, despite the threatening note delivered to the Israeli government, the Russians knew they could do nothing to save their Arab clients.

The Old City

In order to avoid complete destruction of the Jordanian army, at 2:30 a.m. General Riad ordered the soldiers under his command to retreat across the Jordan River. That order left the entire West Bank open to the IDF. The day before, Amer's withdrawal order had disheartened Egyptian soldiers. Likewise, Riad's order caused Jordanian army morale to crumble. As a result, some soldiers deserted rather than engage in an orderly withdrawal. In Jerusalem, officers, together with rank and file, fled their posts. And soldiers were not the only ones to flee. Police officers and armed civilians joined them racing to the rear. But the new instructions came too late for a Jordanian brigade traveling in the opposite direction along the uphill route from Jericho to Jerusalem. IDF tanks, artillery, and air strikes took advantage of the brigade's trek while it was strung out along the road, destroying it shortly after sunrise.

After Riad's order, Hussein desperately maneuvered for a deal that would stop the fighting immediately; at least then he could salvage a small portion of the West Bank that would remain under his control. He knew that he could not expect any help from the Syrians who had betrayed him the day before by failing to protect the northern portions of the West Bank while the Jordanian army headed south. Already, Hussein had sent four frantic messages to the Americans asking that they influence the Israelis to agree to an immediate ceasefire in place. The messages contained warnings that he was in danger of losing control and, if the fighting continued, being overthrown. Desperately, Hussein restrained the few still intact units in his army from fighting back aggressively. His aim was to avoid further provoking the Israelis while projecting an image to the Arab world that Jordan was still fighting. Then, once the Egyptians agreed to a ceasefire, he could too; but with honor.

The Israelis, however, were not so eager to restrain their military short of conquering the West Bank, nor were they sympathetic to Hussein's fear of losing his throne. Jordanian bombardments of Jerusalem and other Jewish civilian settlements on the first day of the war had hardened Israeli attitudes towards the Jordanian monarchy. What's more, the Israelis had recognized that they had a fortuitous opportunity: Jerusalem could be united under Israel's control. It was a dream they had sacrificed in the interest of peace in 1949 but never forgot.

Dayan's response to press reports that the Jordanians were ready to negotiate a ceasefire with Israel was indicative of the prevailing attitude: "We have been offering the king an opportunity to cut his losses ever since Monday morning. Now we have 500 dead and wounded in Jerusalem. So tell him that from now on, I'll talk to him only with the gunsights of our tanks."

At 4:00 a.m., while Hussein wrestled with his dismal alternatives, Menachem Begin lay awake in bed. His growing excitement made it too difficult to sleep. For the first time he had the opportunity to directly influence the highest ranking ministers in the Israeli government. As a member of the political opposition, Begin had never enjoyed such access and such sway. The majority political party had always viewed him a radical—a radical with political and moral roots extending back to his days as leader of the Irgun, an extremist Jewish group viewed by some as terrorists for actively engaging British occupiers and Arab opponents before 1948. Therefore, they discounted or ignored him. But it was Begin who saw from the first moments of the war the opportunity to regain control of the Old City of Jerusalem. He saw in Israel's success a golden opportunity.

Rather than sleep, Begin turned on the radio and heard media reports that the UN Security Council was about to vote on a ceasefire resolution. The news galvanized him. He called Eshkol and pleaded with the Prime Minister to order the IDF into the Old City before it was too late. Eshkol sleepily responded that Begin should call Dayan and see what he thinks. Dayan agreed to arrange an early morning cabinet meeting to discuss the issue.

The cabinet's decision was unanimous; it ordered the IDF into the Old City.

Shortly after receiving word of the cabinet's decision, Deputy Chief of Staff Bar-Lev told Central Front Commander Narkiss, "We are already being pressed for a ceasefire. We are at the [c]anal. The Egyptians have been carved up—don't let the Old City remain an enclave." It was music to Narkiss's ears. He ordered Gur's paratroops into the Old City. From the heights of Mount Scopus, Gur was enraptured. He could see his objective—a narrow lane called the al-Buraq road that lay a short distance from the gleaming Dome of the Rock on top of the Temple Mount, the third holiest site in Islam where, Muslims believe, Muhammad ascended to heaven. The road, shaded by a high stone wall, was located in the Moroccan quarter. After the war, Gur admitted, "It was difficult to move [my] eyes away from the breathtaking vision."

Only 100 armed Arab combatants, mostly civilians, remained to impede the paratroopers advancing on the Old City. Shortly after they moved past the ancient walls that surrounded their objective, the regional

Arab governor, mayor, and other city officials met them with a message—they would offer no resistance.

The IDF secured the Old City between 10:00 a.m. and noon. Once again, that high, stone wall, known as the Western or "Wailing" Wall, was in Jewish hands. The Western Wall may have more significance to many Jews than any other location on earth. If one honors Mecca as the holiest spot in the Muslim world and understands the feelings Christians have for the Church of the Holy Sepulchre which stands over the spot many believe Christ was crucified, it is easier to comprehend the attachment Jews have to the Western Wall. It is the last remaining remnant of the Second Temple, destroyed by the Romans two thousand years ago. It is also part of the retaining wall of the Temple Mount and where, before God intervened, Abraham was about to sacrifice Isaac from the same stone the Dome of the Rock now covers. For many Jews, the Wall is a visible testament to Jewish survival through exile, suffering, the Holocaust, and other deprivations. It has also always been the holiest spot where Jews have been permitted to pray by their rabbinic leaders. In June of 1967, the exposed portion of the wall was about 187 feet long. Another 1,400 feet of the wall's length was underground (350 feet of that was dug out by the Israelis after the war ended). Touching it and pausing along its roughened surface connects Jews to their souls, often bringing forth euphoric emotions that normally lay dormant or non-existent. But, for centuries, the Arabs who lived in the shadow of the wall dumped garbage at its base. And after 1948, the Jordanians prevented Jews from entering the Old City to pray there. For nineteen years the wall had not seen a Jewish presence. That was about to change.

When the first paratroopers reached the Wall, they saw a narrow alley adjacent to the slum dwellings of the Moroccan quarter that butted up to the craggy stone edifice towering above them. Vegetation sprouted from its highest reaches. The homes, crowded and filthy, stretched from a passageway up to the western edge of the rise where, before Arab occupiers desecrated it during the 1948 war, the homes and synagogues of the Jewish quarter once were.

Many of the elated soldiers were dazed, overcome by the significance of the moment. Very soon more paratroopers in their uniforms caked with dust and grime arrived and crowded into the cramped area before the ancient landmark. Some, with guns slung over their shoulders and Kippahs on their heads, chanted prayers while bending repeatedly before it. General Gur radioed Narkiss at 10:00 a.m. and told him, "The Temple Mount is ours! I repeat, the Temple Mount is ours. I'm standing next to the Mosque of Omar now. The Wailing Wall is a minute away."

As soon as Narkiss heard Gur's words he clambered over a tank stuck in the Lion's Gate, and, along with General Bar-Lev, entered the Old City. A haunting wail enveloped the enraptured men on the battlefield as Rabbi Goren made his way forward while blowing into a ram's horn—what Jews call a *shofar which is* typically only used in synagogues during the Jewish High Holidays and the month leading up to them. As the Wall came into view, soldiers of all ages and from all walks of life started to run. Paratroopers, who for the previous twenty-four hours had faced down death, felt their exhaustion evaporate as their exhilaration erupted into song. Many sang "Jerusalem of Gold," the new musical symbol of hope unveiled less than a month earlier as part of Israel's Independence Day celebrations. Others wept with religious fervor, with recognition of their respite from the anxieties of war, with the pure unadulterated emotion of sharing a profoundly moving, historical moment with comrades.

In the midst of the enthusiasm, Rabbi Goren approached General Narkiss. Earlier, when he arrived before the Wall, he had spoken in a loud and confident voice while facing it and holding a *shofar* in one hand and a Torah scroll in the other: "I, General Shlomo Goren, chief rabbi of the Israeli Defense Forces, have come to this place never to leave it again." When Goren reached General Narkiss he said, "This is the time to put a hundred kilograms of explosives in the Mosque of Omar, that's it, we'll get rid of it once and for all." Narkiss, probably realizing Goren really meant the Dome of the Rock, cut him off, "Rabbi, stop it." Goren was persistent. "Uzi, you'll enter the history books by virtue of this deed." Narkiss would not budge. He answered, "I have already recorded my name in the pages of the history of Jerusalem." Rabbi Goren walked away without another word.

Israel's aristocracy visited the Wall in the afternoon. Rabin, Ben Gurion, and Dayan arrived about 1:00 p.m. Concerned for his safety, the army asked Eshkol to delay his visit. That made Dayan appear the sole victorious conqueror. Video of that moment captured a charismatic Dayan wearing his customary black eye patch while confidently striding towards the wall. After touching the ancient stone with his outstretched hands, Dayan said:

> We have returned to the holiest of our places, we have returned never to be parted from them again. To our Arab neighbors we extend at this hour ... the hand of peace.... We have not come to Jerusalem to conquer the holy places of others or to constrict the freedom of other religions, but to assure its unity and to live here with others in understanding.

Rabin, called that day the "Peak of my life." Many years later he said,

> I think, if there can be something for a human being that can be called the fulfillment of a dream, that is what I felt when I neared the Wall then. And to a Jewish boy who was born in Jerusalem, grew up in Palestine, managed to see the creation of a Jewish State, commanded a brigade in '48 and failed to liberate the Wall, who became, nineteen years later, Chief of Staff, and then as Chief of Staff to be able to bring about the liberation of the Wall, who can achieve more than that?

However, despite his elation, Dayan had understanding for how others would view Israel's accomplishments. An Israeli flag placed by a soldier on the Dome of the Rock flew for several days until Dayan ordered it taken down. Later, Dayan pulled all Israeli troops from the Haram al-Sharif compound within which the Dome of the Rock sat. He sensed it was one thing to take the land, another to hold onto it. Dayan hoped to avoid further provoking an already furious Muslim world. His sensitivity to Muslim beliefs was in sharp contrast to Jordanian and Palestinian desecration of everything Jews held dear during the nineteen years they controlled the land.

Elsewhere

Throughout the West Bank, fighting tapered off as the Jordanian army withdrew. However, most Arab civilians still believed the outcome was in doubt. When Israeli troops approached the town of Nablus they found an Arab crowd outside the city waiting to greet them. The Arabs thought the Israelis were Iraqi reinforcements.

During the night, Egyptian soldiers and vehicles streamed towards the bridges over the Suez Canal to safety. Many were leaderless. For some, their route required navigating the Mitla and Giddi mountain passes. Israeli soldiers who had fought through the Egyptians to the eastern side of those passes set up blocking positions. There was nowhere safe for the Egyptians to go, and during that night, Egyptian tanks, trucks, and other military vehicles became ensnarled within the Mitla pass in a logjam more than four miles long. They were stuck while parked nose to tail, and in places, two or three across.

At dawn, IAF warplanes swooped down among the sitting ducks. One vehicle after another burst into flames. Soon, nothing remained but scorched, twisted, metal carcasses laden with the stench of death from bloated flesh often charred and shredded beyond recognition. As the sun rose, plumes of black smoke marked the slaughter below.

Some stray IDF ground forces reached the Suez Canal early that morning. Dayan ordered them to pull back a little more than twelve miles, for he had something new to worry about. He feared that, in addition to inviting a Soviet reaction, photographs of Jewish soldiers soaking their tired feet in the canal would hasten imposition of a ceasefire before all of his goals had been fulfilled.

One main reason Israel launched her pre-emptive strike was to relieve the Egyptian blockade of the Straits of Tiran. From the town of Sharm el-Sheikh in southern Sinai, Egyptian artillery commanded the approaches to the Straits. The IDF had planned to drop paratroops to take the strategic spot. But at 3:00 a.m., three torpedo boats sped to the shore adjacent to the city. Their crews found the city deserted. Soon after, rather than continue with a planned, risky paratroop drop into the desert nearby, the paratroopers landed at a small, nearby airstrip. Sharm el-Sheikh was secured.

During the rest of the day on the West Bank, IDF forces continued their advance. The army occupied Bethlehem without a fight. When one brigade reached the outskirts of Jericho near the Dead Sea and the Jordan River, Dayan ordered it to pull back. But after Dayan learned of Hussein's decision to abandon the West Bank, he permitted the brigade along with other units to surge forward. By nightfall, the IDF had taken control of the entire West Bank, including Hebron and the Etzion Bloc where Arabs had massacred Jews decades before. Before them, Jordanian troops mixed with thousands of Arab civilian refugees as they streamed across the bridges spanning the Jordan River. Jordan could not afford to support the fleeing Palestinians (who would only further upset the political balance in Jordan in future years), but did nothing to stop them. After the last of them crossed, the IDF destroyed the bridges.

The sun set on June 7 over 700 dead Jordanian soldiers killed during the fighting and thousands more wounded. The IDF suffered

300 dead during the campaign on the West Bank and another 1,400 wounded. More than 200 Israeli soldiers died battling the Egyptians, but the Egyptians lost thousands, many of whom had perished while wandering lost in the Sinai desert, parched and delirious, exposed to a relentless sun that bore down on them.

And, despite Dayan's orders, momentum more than design propelled the IDF forward until it was stopped by the Suez Canal. Egyptian soldiers, joking about their defeat, said, "It was the Russian military strategy manual; first, draw the enemy into your own territory. Second, wait for winter." In the desert climate of the Sinai, it would be a long and bloody wait.

That night, Hussein spoke to his people over the radio. He admitted defeat and told them the fighting on the West Bank was over.

The Israelis saw a miracle in the Arab nightmare: Jews once again ruled the ancient West Bank lands of Judea and Samaria that had been part of Israel 2,000 years before. Dayan triumphantly told the world at a press conference that night that Israel had "attained its political and military objectives", and then said somewhat tongue-in-cheek, "The Straits of Tiran has been opened to international navigation, and every country has a right to use it—including Egypt." When Begin reached the Wall that evening he said:

"When I touched the [W]all I cried. I suppose everyone had tears in their eyes. Nobody need be ashamed. They are men's tears. For the momentous truth is that on this day we Jews, for the first time since the Roman conquest of 70 C.E., have regained ownership of the last remaining remnant of our Temple site, and have won for ourselves free and unfettered access to pray there."

But Rabin understood that Israel's victory had sown the seeds of a dilemma. "How do we control a million Arabs?" he asked Dayan. A staff officer corrected him, "One million, and two hundred and fifty thousand." And, when Dayan was asked by another how Israel would control the population on the West Bank, he responded that the Arabs should be permitted to rule themselves; but they should know who the boss is.

With matters on the Egyptian and Jordanian fronts settling down, Eshkol's gaze turned to the Syrians. He broached the idea of attacking them with Allon, Rabin, and Elazar. Eshkol suggested capturing the Banias, a source of water for the River Jordan, and a Syrian fortified position on the Golan Heights used by them to attack the settlements below. Allon and Elazar wanted to do even more. But, other than moving into Israeli territory that comprised the DMZs, and perhaps up to three miles beyond, Dayan persistently resisted attempts to convince him to launch other attacks against the Syrians. Rabin, however, argued against taking small steps rather than large leaps. He said that the casualties the IDF would suffer achieving limited goals would not be worth modest gains. Eshkol's probing ended in a stalemate. Most wanted to move deep into the Golan, but Dayan continued to resist out of fear of the Russians. At a meeting at the Knesset later in the day, Dayan again objected to launching a major attack against the Syrians, yet did so in a passive-aggressive manner that made clear if ordered by the cabinet, he would acquiesce to its demands and take the Golan.

At 1:00 p.m. in New York (7:00 p.m. in Israel), the Security Council reconvened at the request of the Soviet Union. The Russians realized that Egypt's plight was desperate and that Russian prestige would suffer from the massive defeat of Soviet arms at the hands of an ally of America. They also knew it was no longer possible to reach a ceasefire that satisfied Arab prewar goals. Their only thought was to stop the fighting immediately before the situation worsened. Therefore, the Russians pressed for an immediate Security Council vote on a resolution demanding a ceasefire in place. For once, now that Arab, rather than Israeli, interests were at stake; the Security Council moved quickly. It approved a resolution demanding a ceasefire in the region scheduled to take effect three hours later. The Jordanians immediately accepted, but the Egyptians equivocated. The Egyptians argued that the resolution required the Israelis to stop shooting and withdraw, but even the Russians, in conjunction with others, disputed the Egyptian interpretation. Eban accepted the ceasefire on behalf of Israel but noted he had yet to hear from Egypt, Syria, or Iraq. Eban further indicated that he welcomed Jordan's agreement but reminded the world that an Egyptian general commanded Jordan's military. Therefore, even Jordan's acceptance of the resolution had no effect. Later, Eban's warning seemed prescient; Cairo radio declared that Egypt rejected the ceasefire proposal.

The war was not over yet.

CHAPTER THIRTEEN
JUNE 8

Teddy Kolleck, the Mayor of Jerusalem, was having lunch with former Prime Minster David Ben Gurion when Ben Gurion told him, "This is not the end of the war.... The Arabs cannot take such a defeat and such humiliation. They will never accept it." Even so, Ben Gurion encouraged Kolleck to knock down the ancient walls of the Old City. He feared that as long as those walls remained standing, as long as the old City remained separate from Jewish Jerusalem surrounding it, the Palestinians would continue to believe they could regain control of what they had lost.

King Hussein addressed his people again in a radio broadcast during the early hours of Thursday, June 8. He was exhausted. His voice betrayed his turmoil when he revealed that he had accepted the UN Security Council's unconditional demand of a ceasefire. He then said:

> My brothers, I seem to belong to a family which, according to the will of Allah, must suffer and make sacrifices for its country without end. Our calamity is greater than anyone could have imagined. But, whatever its size, we must not let it weaken our resolve to regain what we have lost.

Later, Hussein spoke at a press conference attended by some fifty foreign and domestic correspondents. The past few days had taken their toll. The strain was evident on his unshaven face, and he appeared shaken and dispirited by what he had endured. Three days of little sleep while relying on tea and cigarettes for sustenance had only made it worse for him. Fighting back tears he bravely faced the journalists while his self-inflicted grief gnawed at his stability. He could not block the pain caused by loss of the lives of his men who had fallen fighting the Israelis and the loss of the holy places he had felt honor bound to defend.

Jordan was defenseless. The IDF had destroyed Hussein's air force along with eighty percent of Jordan's tanks. Surviving soldiers were dispirited. At least, however, Jordan no longer had to fear the IDF because Israel had no interest in conquering Jordan. But the same could not be said for Hussein's Arab neighbors. Jordan floated in a stormy sea of shifting Arab attitudes. Without a strong army to fend off Arab sharks that sometimes circled his throne, Hussein knew his days might well be numbered.

And, even more devastating for Jordan than the military calamity, was the economic impact. A significant percentage of Jordan's tourism revenue came from tourists visiting the Old City and other towns in the West Bank. Half of Jordan's inhabitable territory was in the West Bank along with half of Jordan's industrial capacity and a quarter of her water resources. As a result, in just three days, Jordan had lost the means to produce forty percent of her GDP. Compounding the economic misery and Hussein's political problems were the swelling numbers of Palestinian refugees east of the Jordan River. They numbered 500,000 before the war; within days of its outbreak another 250,000 fled their homes on the West Bank to join them.

But the disaster brought Hussein one bit of relief—for the time being Jordan was back in the Arab fold and no longer challenged by other Arab nations. And Nasser was grateful that Hussein stood shoulder to shoulder with him. He later told Hussein, "We have entered this war together, lost it together, and we must win it together." Thus, for that fleeting moment, all Arab nations, whatever their political or religious persuasion, united in their grief and despair at their defeat at the hands of the Jews. Even so, thirty years later, Hussein said in a candid moment, "In reality it was probably our duty to try to prevent this country from being part of the battle."

Encouraged by Nasser, Hussein also worked to maintain diplomatic relations with the United States. Through the offices of the king, Nasser hoped to enlist the Americans to help force a negotiated return of the West Bank without any reciprocal requirement for Egypt to agree to a peace treaty with the Jewish State. But, for Hussein, his relationship with America also offered him a sense of protection from an alliance with a friendly United States eager to retain her only remaining strong tie with the Arab world.

Throughout the morning, and into the afternoon, more Israeli troops approached the canal. In some places fighting remained intense while in others the Egyptians did not put up any resistance. Dayan's order for the IDF to stay several miles from the canal still stood, though loosely obeyed. One report even has Dayan ignoring his own directive by soaking his feet in the canal's waters. With such an inviting goal in sight, it was nearly impossible to restrain soldiers, surging forward and jockeying for position in the midst of fire fights, to halt short of such a visible landmark of victory.

During the day, Sharon's division encountered an entire brigade of abandoned Egyptian tanks and self-propelled guns. When the Egyptian commander had received orders to withdraw, he ordered his men to escape without taking the heavy equipment. In his haste, when his unit encountered Sharon's soldiers, the commander abandoned his troops and set off on foot for the Suez Canal. When captured, he said he didn't destroy the equipment because nobody ordered him to do so and he feared the noise would alert the Israelis. It is no surprise that, after the war, Sharon reflected that the Egyptian soldiers had the heart to fight but their officers had failed them.

However, not all Egyptian officers were cowardly. General Shazly commanded a small, elite force in the southern Sinai along the border with Israel. When war broke out, he advanced a short way into Israel where he established an L-shaped blocking position. When he received the order to retreat, he refused to move until after dark on June 7. Shazly managed to keep his force intact despite attacks by Israeli warplanes. On June 8 he led his unit across the canal during the evening with little loss of men or equipment. His leadership reaped him recognition that would, four years later, propel him to the highest post in the Egyptian military. From there he played a crucial role.

By the end of the day, Nasser knew he had no choice. Near midnight, Nasser told his foreign minister to inform the UN that Egypt would accept an immediate ceasefire. The fight in the Sinai was over. Egypt suffered more than 11,000 casualties, half of which were fatalities. Much of the Egyptian army's equipment, including 700 tanks and 10,000 trucks, was destroyed. For the moment, Egypt no longer possessed the means to wage war effectively.

The Liberty Tragedy

Perhaps the event most shrouded in mystery during the Six-Day War was Israel's attack on the American spy ship, the *USS Liberty*. At 12:30 p.m on June 8, the *Liberty* cruised in international waters about twenty miles from the Sinai coast. But, the night before, the *Liberty* was only twelve and a half nautical miles from Egypt and six and a half miles from Israel—just outside of Egypt's and Israel's claimed territorial waters. While cruising so close to shore, where fighting still raged, crewman on the ship heard the American Ambassador to the UN, Arthur Goldberg, proclaim that no American ship was within 300 miles of the coast. Perhaps that is why corrective orders were issued that morning for the

Liberty to move further out to sea. Tragically, a transmission error prevented the *Liberty* from receiving the order.

In the light of day, the minarets of the mosques in El Arish could be seen from the bridge of the ship. The *Liberty* had arrived, direct from its previous station off the coast of West Africa, teeming with antenna and other equipment for electronic snooping. Accompanying the sailors manning the ship were technicians from the NSA, America's pre-eminent, electronic spy agency. The vessel was on its own in the event of a threat, and not well armed at that; its complement of weapons primarily consisted of only four machine guns. The closest American naval warships were 500 miles away.

About 5:00 a.m., IAF planes flew over the *Liberty's* deck several times and, at least once at an altitude of less than 200 feet. Shortly after 1:00 p.m., the ship sounded general quarters. That was a drill. Less than hour later, all hell broke loose.

Near 1:50 p.m., the chief Israeli air controller, Colonel Kislev, ordered a pair of IAF *Mirage* fighter planes to head toward a ship in "Location 26." If it was a warship, he ordered the *Mirage* pilots to destroy it. Three minutes later, another weapons controller said with concern, "What is it? An American?" That officer questioned the identity of the mysterious ship because he thought the Egyptians would not dare send a single vessel without support into the region. Kislev, in apparent recognition of that concern, contacted his superior. Voice recordings picked up Kislev saying, "What do you say?" and then "I don't say." At least one Israeli historian who has listened to the tape recording believes that Kislev's tone indicated he didn't want to know the answer.

Three minutes later, Kislev repeated his order to attack the unknown ship if it was a warship. He did not add that, before attacking, the pilots should first establish the ship's identity or nationality.

The *USS Liberty* was clearly marked as an American ship. It flew an American flag eight feet wide and five feet high. But the markings didn't protect her. IAF *Mirages* swooped down and attacked. *Liberty's* crewman tried to send an SOS signal to the American Sixth Fleet hundreds of miles away, but Israeli electronic countermeasures jammed the signal, already weakened by rocket fire which had blasted away the onboard antennas.

The *Mirage* pilots reported to their air controller that their ammunition was used up, but that they had hit the ship hard and it was burning. The air controller ordered two more warplanes to press home the attack. They dropped napalm, and their machine gun fire raked the top decks. At 2:14 p.m., one of the attacking pilots questioned the identity of the ship because its identifying numbers were not Arabic, but western. Kislev, the chief controller, responded twice that the ship was probably American. But that did not stop the onslaught. At 2:26 p.m. Israeli torpedo boats arrived and attacked. They launched five torpedoes. One struck the American ship.

News that the *Liberty* had been attacked reached the United States, Israel, and Egypt thirty minutes later. In Egypt, the American embassy feared that public knowledge of the *Liberty's* presence nearby would endanger every American in Egypt. Embassy officials thought the "Arab street" would assume that the *Liberty* had been feeding intelligence to Israel, and that mobs might form that intended to kill Americans and destroy their property.

Israel immediately apologized and accepted full responsibility. The Israelis explained to the Americans that the incident had started with false reports that troops in El-Arish were being shelled from the sea. The confusion was then compounded when the Israelis lost track of the *Liberty* which they had identified earlier and which they thought to be traveling at a much higher rate of speed than it was.

American Secretary of State, Dean Rusk, demanded reparations and punishment for those responsible. He believed that the attack was made with full knowledge of the ship's true identity. Israel paid compensation, but, a month afterwards, an IDF military judge decided there were no grounds for disciplinary action. To this day, opposing views are strongly held whether the thirty-four American soldiers and citizens who paid with their lives, along with another 171 that were wounded, were unintended victims of the fog of war or casualties of an intentional Israeli attack launched to prevent the United States from obtaining intelligence concerning IDF activity.

The United States chose to accept Israel's apology without any retribution, and the incident did not impact future American-Israeli relations. Israel was fortunate the ship was American, not Soviet. An inadvertent attack on a Russian ship might have brought a harsh response that could have jeopardized the nation's existence.

Syria

Throughout the day, the question of whether to eliminate Syria's ability to bombard Israeli settlements plagued Israel's leadership. Rabin continued to believe that the benefit of moving into the DMZ, and perhaps a small distance beyond, did not justify the casualties the IDF would suffer. Yet, how could it be that the country that played such a large role in instigating the war, that was Israel's most implacable and unpredictable enemy, and that held positions that allowed Syrian soldiers to kill and maim Israeli farmers with relative impunity, remained unscathed?

But Dayan feared overextending the army and still worried how the Soviets would react if the IDF attacked the Golan Heights. "We started this war," he said:

> in order to destroy the Egyptian force and open the Straits of Tiran. On the way we took the West Bank. I do not think it is possible to open another campaign against Syria. If the idea is to go into Syria and change the border in order to make life easier for the settlements, I am against it.

Dayan also believed that if the Syrians lost territory they would never agree to a peaceful end of the conflict. He even went so far as to suggest that, rather than attacking Syria, Israeli settlements should move ten miles from the border. Eshkol and Allon were outraged by the suggestion. The northern panhandle of Israel was little more than ten miles wide in many places. The settlements had nowhere to move to even if they should want to. Eshkol commented that the Syrians could hardly hope for a greater victory. But Dayan's prestige—at its zenith after four days that brought Israel from despair to euphoria—was enough to overcome the inclination of many to send the IDF into Syria. Eshkol decided to defer the decision for a couple days, and to ask Rabin to develop an operational plan.

That night, the Defense Ministerial Committee invited representatives of the thirty-one Kibbutzim and other farming settlements in the northern Galilee to meet with them at 7:00 p.m. General Elazar, a strong advocate of attacking Syria, was present as well. The farmers pled to not be left to the dubious mercy of Syrian guns. Their emotional presentation moved all those present except, for Dayan. Dayan sat in the back of the room with his feet casually resting on a desk. He pretended to be asleep. Later, he declared the farmers were only interested in obtaining new farmland on the Golan.

General Elazar left the meeting dismayed. He believed that an attack would not be ordered. Late in the evening, he called General Peled, commander of a powerful unit assigned to Northern Command. Elazar told him to sleep at his headquarters in Nablus on the West Bank; an attack on Syria was not in the cards, and the war would soon be over.

At the UN, during the mid-afternoon in New York (8:50 p.m. in Israel), the Security Council reconvened. News arrived that Egypt had finally accepted the ceasefire, but no word had been received from Iraq and Kuwait, who, despite having only small contingents of troops involved, had previously refused to end the fighting. Israel responded by affirming her commitment to the ceasefire on the Egyptian front. The war was over in Egypt and Jordan.

Conspicuous by her absence, Syria also had not yet accepted the ceasefire resolution. While the Russians sought another resolution condemning Israel and demanding the Jewish State's withdrawal from the territories take (as reported by Foreign Minister Eban) the Americans quietly hinted to Israel they would not oppose an IDF attack on Syria as long as Damascus was not taken.

Meanwhile, along the forty-mile long border with Israel, 70,000 Syrian soldiers waited in their Golan Heights fortifications that ran in some places to a depth of fifteen miles. At some points the escarpment was only 130 yards high. At other locations, the Heights towered more than 3,000 feet above the valley floor. The Syrians supported the emplacements with more than 200 artillery tubes, mortars, and dug in tanks. Towering 9,230-foot-high, Mount Hermon protected their northern flank; their southern flank had Lake Kinneret and the Yarmouk River to boost its defensive strength. For twenty years the Syrians, with the help of their Russian advisors, had put much effort into registering the approaches to their defensive positions to ensure accurate weapon fire. As a result, the defenses seemed impregnable. But there was one weakness—the soldiers. The Syrian rank and file had received marginal training; their equipment was poorly maintained, and their morale was low, principally due to repeated coups that robbed them of consistent leadership. But they thought they had little cause for concern. Their superiors had been smart to keep them out of the war. The confrontation would soon be over. They would be safe.

Or, would they?

Israeli troops consolidated their hold on the entire Sinai during the day. At 9:35 p.m. EST on June 8, Egypt unconditionally accepted a ceasefire with Israel. By then, eighty percent of the Egyptian military equipment committed to battle in the Sinai had been left in ruins, or abandoned, in the sands of the Sinai. Several years after the battle ended, stories arose that some Egyptian troops and Palestinian Fedayeen were massacred by Israelis after they surrendered. One Israeli historian alleges at least 900 were killed. Other rumors have surfaced that many captives were killed in anger when Egyptian prisoners opened fire after giving up, killing two Israeli soldiers. However, there are also many accounts of numerous acts of kindness by Israeli soldiers directed towards Egyptians who had surrendered. What is certain is that there was no official IDF policy to abuse prisoners. But equally certain, as is often the case in war, emotion, fear, and command failures led to sporadic, individual acts of vengeance wrongfully inflicted on the hapless Egyptians in IDF charge.

CHAPTER FOURTEEN
JUNE 9

Syria

During the early hours of June 9, Nasser warned Syrian President al-Atassi that Israel would soon concentrate her forces for an attack against Syria. He advised al-Atassi to immediately notify the UN that Syria would accept a ceasefire. Israeli intelligence intercepted the message, and brought the information to Dayan along with other information that indicated the Syrian army was collapsing. Nothing else had changed in the few hours since Dayan had adamantly refused to attack Syria. The Russian threat remained, and it was still likely that the Syrians would never accept their permanent loss of the Golan Heights.

Abruptly, Dayan changed his mind regarding Syria. It was the likelihood that the Syrians would soon accept the ceasefire that probably swayed him. Within moments he had changed from an obstructive warrior to a decisive advocate. In the margins of the intercepted message he wrote a handwritten note to Eshkol which read:

"Eshkol, 1. In my opinion this cable obliges us to capture the maximal military lines. 2. Yesterday I did not think that Egypt and Syria (their political leadership) would collapse in this way and give up the continuation of the campaign. But since this is the situation, it must be exploited to the full. A great day. Moshe Dayan."

Dayan then called General Elazar and asked if he could attack immediately. When Elazar responded affirmatively, Elazar then heard the words he had hoped would be said but despaired of ever hearing. "Do whatever can be done," Dayan told him. That statement galvanized Elazar to try to take the entire Golan with the few brigades at his disposal—much less than the ten to thirteen brigades the Russians had falsely warned of in the middle of May.

Dayan's order to Elazar bypassed both Eshkol and Rabin. But neither was overly upset over Dayan overstepping his authority because they supported punishing the Syrians. Rabin first learned of the attack on Syria when he was awakened at about 7:00 a.m. while sleeping at home for the first time since the war started. "[I] had no desire to quibble when the Syrians were about to get their just desert for malicious aggressiveness and arrogance," Rabin would later reflect. Eshkol too first found out about the attack at 7:00 a.m. Dayan's arrogant, unilateral assumption of authority angered him. He viewed Dayan to be a glory seeker and "a vile man." But he agreed with Dayan's decision and did not try to reverse it. At the Defense Ministerial meeting, urgently called for 9:30 a.m., many ministers expressed anger over Dayan usurping the powers of the government by unilaterally ordering the attack. However, since most supported the idea of attacking Syria, they dropped the issue.

At 9:40 a.m., Israeli airplanes pounded Syrian positions in the Golan. Since the IAF was no longer needed in the skies over Egypt, the full power of the air force was brought to bear on Syria. Nearly two hours later, IDF ground forces began tortuously moving up the narrow roads cut from the hillsides and into the teeth of the Syrian fortifications. The fact that Syria had accepted the ceasefire a few hours before the operation started did not matter to the Israelis—the Syrians were too late. The Israelis told the Security Council that, despite Syria's agreement to stop fighting, they had continued to bombard Israeli civilian settlements. The Soviet Union and her allies responded with a demand for Israel to stop and released a statement pledging their assistance to the Arabs. The declaration fell short of threatening Russian military intervention, but it did provide an unambiguous indication of political solidarity and intent to provide military equipment.

The Israelis made their major effort in the northern Golan. After breaking through, they planned to move along an old road to the foot of Mount Hermon and then head south to take Kuneitra, the major Syrian city on the Golan. Near the border with Jordan, in southern Golan, secondary attacks simultaneously engaged the Syrians. Eight bulldozers led the soldiers through Syrian blocking formations and minefields that could not be avoided. Using five different axes, the Israelis hoped to obfuscate where their main effort was. Aerial photographs previously taken of Arab farmers in the fields, coupled with careful observation, identified terrain free of mines where it was safe for the attacking troops to traverse. The IDF was on its way up to the Golan plateau.

The offensive proceeded slowly. Over 1,000 bombing missions flown by IAF planes softened up the defenders. But the Syrian concrete bunkers were deep. They had grooves to funnel away the jelly-like, burning napalm dropped on them from aircraft. It took three hours, a painstaking advance up and over rocky cliffs, and heavy losses, before Elazar's soldiers took their first objectives. In the southern Golan, however, IDF tanks moved ahead of the infantry. They made rapid progress. When Syrian commanders attempted to move reinforcements to the region, IAF airplanes blocked their progress and destroyed them.

After reaching the crest of the Heights, many IDF units took a wrong turn that delayed their progress. Still, by late afternoon, Israeli troops had reached the outskirts of Kuneitra. By the end of the first day, all of Elazar's most important objectives had been achieved, along with many secondary ones. Elazar was pleased. Progress had been faster than anticipated.

Jordan and Egypt

The American Ambassador in Jordan was relieved when Hussein assured him that Jordan would not break relations with the United States. The ambassador had worried during the day about how the king would react to Arab allegations that the United States was actively assisting Israel. But Hussein had more pressing matters to be concerned with. The war had created a new wave of refugees pouring over the Jordan River.

For residents of the West Bank, the Deir Yassin massacre—a village where over one hundred Arab civilians were killed by Israeli combatants during the 1948 war—remained fresh in their memories thanks to the efforts of Arab propagandists. Thus, the specter of armed Israelis swarming through town and city squares gave sufficient impetus for fearful West bank residents to flee. Hussein knew that those frightened men, women, and children might soon turn into a new wave of angry refugees hostile to his continued rule. Thus, a healthy continued relationship with America was becoming more important than ever.

At 7:43 p.m. in Egypt, Nasser began speaking on Egyptian television. Nasser had ordered that his name not be mentioned in any earlier broadcasts that day. Until a few hours earlier, the radio had been filled with fictitious news of Egyptian victories. Nasser was fatigued and depressed as he began to speak. Uncharacteristically, he stumbled over his words while reading from a prepared text. Despair overwhelmed him. His natural charisma was no longer evident. He said there had been a "*naksa*" (setback). Interestingly, he did not use the term '*nakba*' (catastrophe), which is the term commonly used by Arabs to refer to their loss in the 1948 war. Instead, he was subliminally signaling that the most recent disaster would eventually be reversed. Nasser blamed Western powers for the debacle. He declared that Israel's air force had been operating at three times its normal strength, leaving a false inference of Western involvement. Nevertheless, he declared that he was prepared to take responsibility, and as a result, would give up his official posts and return to civilian life.

After Nasser finished speaking, the voice of the news anchor quivered and broke. In the streets, there was stunned silence. Then, the voices tens of thousands could be heard, then hundreds of thousands. Weeping citizens poured outside their homes, others pressed against the windows of buildings. All loudly implored Nasser not to leave and reaffirmed their need for him. Egyptian officials rounded up Americans in the country, placed them on a train to Alexandria, and then on a Greek ferry that took them out of the country. Along the way, small crowds of Arabs gathered and demonstrated their scorn for America by waving the soles of their shoes at them to indicate that the Americans occupy a station in life lower than the soles of their shoes.

But Nasser's speech had one unintended effect. Syrian political leaders panicked when they heard the Egyptian president's broadcast. Nasser's words drove home to them the realization that they then faced a vengeful Israel alone. The Golan was in flames. Israeli soldiers were fifteen miles into Syria and only forty miles from Damascus. No other country remained in the fight. Suddenly, the Syrians no longer just feared losing the Golan; they feared losing their capital. Syrian military headquarters frantically ordered the army to withdraw towards Damascus. Onrushing Israeli forces filled the void left by the Syrian army vacating the Golan plateau.

It is still debated today whether the public expressions of support for Nasser were mostly spontaneous or arranged. Prior to Nasser's speech, Egypt's ruling political party, the Arab Socialist Union had informed up to 20,000 hard-core supporters to expect instructions when the speech was over. Whether they provided the impetus for the euphoric, public display of support will probably never be known. But the president's power was no longer at risk. The "Arab street" had voted. He would continue to rule.

Meanwhile, a sullen peace partly enveloped the newly-won territories. In Jerusalem, the IDF was able to protect Muslim holy places, but some looting in the Old City and Gaza by follow-on Jewish forces did occur. Israeli commanders ordered an end to further destructive activity, but, at times some individuals ignored the edicts. While few Arab suffered violent acts or improprieties, their unease lingered. A new sheriff was in town.

CHAPTER FIFTEEN
JUNE 10

During the night, Damascus radio reported that the Israelis had taken Kuneitra. Syrian troops on the western side of town facing Israel panicked upon hearing the report. Believing they would soon be trapped, they hastily withdrew from their defensive positions. But Kuneitra had not fallen. Two hours after the radio broadcast, Defense Minister Hafez al-Assad issued a correction that was too late to reverse Syrian fortunes. Instead of standing fast, Syrian troops streamed out of the Golan onto the Damascus plain below while their commander escaped on horseback.

Syria

In the early morning hours of June 10, Eshkol held a meeting to discuss how far the IDF should advance into Syria. They did not reach a final conclusion. Everyone knew the diplomatic clock was ticking, and Israel would soon have to stop. While they spoke, IDF units in the northern Golan pressed north towards the Lebanese border and south and east towards Kuneitra. In the southern Golan, Israeli forces were moving north and also east towards Kuneitra.

Dayan and Eshkol flew by helicopter to the battle areas at 10:30 a.m. Dayan wanted to stop the IDF's advance much closer to the western crest of the Golan, and nearer the Israeli border than Eshkol did; but the

Prime Minister insisted on taking enough territory to prevent future Syrian artillery attacks from reaching Israeli settlements in the Huleh valley. While the government dithered, General Elazar, with Rabin's agreement, did all he could to push further into Syria. Paratroopers sometimes landed in advance of the ground forces. In the end the civilian leadership decided that the IDF could determine where to stop based on military considerations—not diplomatic ones. That made the decision easy. If the IDF possessed the strategic crossroads and elevated points along the ridgeline overlooking the Damascus plain, it would give Israeli soldiers manning defensive positions a tremendous advantage should the Syrians attack in the future. Instead of Syrians looking down on Israel, soon Israelis might be looking down on Syria. In the short time remaining, Elazar drove his commanders to accomplish that goal.

The fighting on the Golan caused consternation in the UN and between the superpowers. Kosygin sent another message on the hotline at 8:00 a.m. in Washington (2:00 p.m. in Israel) in which he warned that it was a "very crucial moment," that there was the possibility of an imminent "independent decision" by Moscow, and that, if Israel did not halt within a few hours, the Russians would take "necessary actions including military." Meanwhile, Russian ships began moving ominously towards the Syrian-Israeli coastline. Some historians believe that Russian troops were on board, with the mission of attacking Haifa, and/or instigating an attack on them by Israeli forces that would give the Soviet Union an excuse to use more military force against Israel. Additionally, there is some evidence that the Russian air force prepared to bomb Israeli targets but was restrained by the Kremlin.

President Johnson assured Kosygin that he would pressure Israel to stop her advance on the Golan. But he also ordered the Sixth Fleet to cut its 300 mile distance from the Syrian coast to fifty miles. He wanted to send a clear signal to the Russians that the United States would resist any Soviet military moves in the region.

Kuneitra fell to Israeli troops at 2:30 p.m. The road to Damascus was open, but Elazar had no desire to advance further. To ensure that the Israelis would not be tempted, the British and French began to exert considerable political pressure. They asserted that the Israeli decision to take Kuneitra, the regional capital of the Golan, constituted an unjustified land grab. The Americans weighed in as well. They told the Israelis they must announce their willingness to stop the fighting. Otherwise, the Russians would issue an ultimatum and take political credit for ending the war, which was going to end shortly anyway. The Israelis agreed it would be a mistake to risk increasing Russian prestige. A ceasefire on the Golan took effect at 6:30 p.m.

The threat of Russian intervention had ended, but Israel's diplomatic fallout with the Soviet Union continued. Twenty years earlier, Russia had been one of the main proponents of creating the Jewish State. Russia had voted on behalf of Israel's independence in the hopes that Israel would become its ally. When those hopes were dashed, the Russians quickly recalibrated towards the Arabs. For them it was about self-interest, nothing more. The Arabs would need their help to rebuild. In return the Russians calculated that they would be able to influence Arab oil diplomacy, obtain military bases, and receive political support for their ongoing conflict with the West. That would be a good deal for the Soviet Union. Opposing Israel increased their likelihood of achieving those goals. Therefore, with Arab emotions running high, the Kremlin saw an opportunity to further cement its relationship with the Arab nations: Russia and her communist allies severed relations with the Jewish State.

Egypt

Egypt's hot war with Israel had ended, but the repercussions led to another momentous day in Cairo. Military officers feared for their future because of their failures in the war, and with Nasser's resignation, they also felt deep concern for what the leadership vacuum would bring. But resignation was not to be. Whether planned or spontaneous, the public demonstrations in Egypt following Nasser's speech had an impact. The Vice President refused to accept Nasser's resignation. Neither did the National Assembly which voted 360 to 0 against permitting Nasser to leave office. Nasser then withdrew his resignation. He told the National Assembly, "I feel that the peoples' will cannot be refused. Therefore, I have decided to stay where people want me to stay until all traces of aggression are erased."

Nasser's personal decision did not mean he would keep all of his military officers. He struck hard at those who had been disloyal, cowardly, or who had failed. At 2:30 p.m. a radio announcer read the names of a dozen officers who had been forcibly retired. Included in the list was Nasser's former friend and current rival, Field Marshal Amer. More names were announced later. It was a precarious moment for the government—most of the army was destroyed, still in Yemen, or streaming back from the Sinai disorganized and dazed. A coup was certainly possible, but nobody at that time possessed the stature necessary to overthrow Nasser. He lived within an impervious bubble of his own self-created aura.

Once it became clear that the ceasefire along the Suez Canal would hold, soldiers of both sides began to engage in their own improvised forms of communication. A primitive barter system emerged; Israeli soldiers swapped the freedom of Egyptian prisoners of war for watermelons floated by the Egyptians across the canal to the Israelis. For those Egyptians who could not swim across the canal, ropes were stretched across its width for them to use to pull themselves to freedom.

If only all negotiations between Arab and Jew were so simple.

Jerusalem

June 10 was a Saturday, the Jewish Sabbath. In the Old City of Jerusalem, Israelis removed a urinal disdainfully located alongside the Western Wall years before by the city's Arab inhabitants. Abutting the Wall, across a narrow alley, was the Moroccan (Mughrabi) quarter where 1,000 Arabs lived in a dense collection of homes. The ancient dwellings were sandwiched between the Wall and the former Jewish Quarter on a rise behind them. The following Wednesday was the Jewish Festival of Shavuot. Tens of thousands of Jews were going to flock to the area.

General Narkiss and Chaim Herzog knew the war presented them with a historic opportunity that, if not seized, might never exist again. They ordered bulldozers to clear the dwellings in order to create a huge open courtyard in front of the Wall. Whether the idea was their own, or stemmed from the mayor of Jerusalem, Teddy Kollek (as he asserts), Narkiss and Herzog decided that the operation would begin at sundown. The Arab residents were only given a few minutes warning to leave. Busses arrived to take them to homes that had been abandoned by Arabs in East Jerusalem. Residents in one dwelling refused to leave. When the walls crashed in on them, medics came to care for the injured. Meanwhile, Kollek met with Eshkol. The energetic Kollek was eager to unite East and West Jerusalem into one city.

When cabinet ministers and Kollek visited the cleared site the next day, they were pleased. The former Arab residents of the Mughrabi quarter, as would be expected, were not. A year later, half of the evacuated families accepted an Israeli Government offer of one hundred Jordanian Dinars as compensation. The other half refused.

The war in the north was over for all practical purposes—other than when the IDF two days later took possession of the abandoned, strategic heights of Mount Hermon. From that lonely windswept mountaintop that towered over the northern Golan, the IDF could gaze far into the Syrian heartland and observe Damascus. With the IDF in possession of that spot, the Syrians would not be able to launch a surprise attack—or so the IDF thought.

And once again, Arabs fled out of misplaced fear; 120,000 Syrian civilians left the Golan for makeshift camps below in Syria. Only 7,000 Druze civilians remained.

For the most part, Western Europe and the United States reacted positively to the outcome of the war. David had beaten Goliath. And—Israel's decision to delay her preemptive strike to give the United States an opportunity to challenge and end the blockade, Nasser's demand that the UN evacuate its peace keeping forces, and the massing of Egyptian troops in close proximity to Israel's border—collectively convinced the western world that Israel held the moral high ground.

Some argue that Israel was never in jeopardy of suffering defeat. While that may have been true, to a degree, Israel could not have endured for much longer the cost of sustained mobilization which the massive Arab military presence on her borders necessitated. And the consequences of the Egyptian blockade's continuing would have been devastating—economically, politically, and emotionally. Furthermore, if the situation Israel found herself in had continued much longer, the growing coalescence of the Arab world would have strengthened the Arabs and dissipated Israel's morale beyond its breaking point. Thus, whether Nasser intended to attack or just to wait, they both amounted to the same. Further delay would have destroyed the Jewish nation. Civilians cannot sit on a razor's edge for long without taking action. To do so risks dissolution of their society; economies do not always return with vigor from a massive disruption, and the failure of deterrence would have inevitably brought more enemies to the front. In short, Israel had no choice.

The run-up to war also emphasized that, from Israel's perspective, Israelis could not count on the UN. UN Resolutions were one sided. UN agreements to enforce freedom of navigation and to maintain peacekeeping forces had proven hollow. Israel learned that she could only depend on her own strength for her security. The words and acronym former Prime Minister David Ben-Gurion used to refer to the United Nations Organization say it best, "UNO, Shmuno."

But the question remained: what should Israel do with its success? "The war is over," said Dayan, "Now the trouble begins."

CHAPTER SIXTEEN
June 11 — The Day After

The magnitude of their victory stunned the Israelis and alleviated their fears. After fighting with Egypt had begun, Eshkol had hoped to avoid conflict with Jordan, but Hussein initiated hostilities. Even after the first Jordanian shells landed, Israel had remained hesitant until it was obvious that Hussein intended to continue. That is why the Israeli advance into the West Bank did not evolve per a preplanned schedule, but instead per the unpredictable currents of a battle not expected. The hurricane winds of war that blew through the Middle East in May caught Israel as unaware as the IAF's planes had caught the Arab air forces on the ground. Managing the aftermath proved even more daunting.

  Because Israel's government never intended to enter into a war of conquest, no plans existed to administer the territories or manage the huge unfriendly populations in the West Bank and Gaza. Suddenly, without forethought, the fates of Israelis and Palestinians were entwined. Many of the Arabs in the conquered territories lived in crowded and squalid conditions. Their survival depended on food production and its uninterrupted distribution, along with easy access to water and electricity. Also, amid the chaos, a security void needed to be filled. There was no time for the Israelis to contemplate; immediate action was required. Overnight, the administrative sinews of the occupation had to be created and implemented.

For most Arabs, despair would be too weak a word to describe their mental state. Arabs, in general, began referring to the war as al-Naksa, "the setback." Perhaps the reference was not as dire as al-Nakba, "the catastrophe," the term Arabs used to describe Israel's victory in her war for independence; but the consequences for some Arab regimes were potentially far more destabilizing. Many Egyptians not only viewed the defeat as a naksa, but also as a moral judgment of their society. The festive atmosphere in Egypt on June 4, complete with signs prominently displaying slogans such as "On to Tel Aviv," had vanished. An Arab Nobel Prize laureate said, "Never before or after in my life had I ever experienced such a shattering of consciousness as I felt at that moment." One popular poet and former ardent supporter of President Nasser called on a "new generation …, not tainted by corruption or power, to smash the existing order and overcome defeat."

In Jordan, Egypt, and Syria the loss of territory, the casualties they sustained, and the damage to their military crushed the spirit of their civilian leaders and shifted their focus. They became less concerned with helping Palestinians "throw the Jews into the sea" and more concerned with recovering their own lost lands. Egyptian, Jordanian, and Syrian civilians were shocked and bewildered by the magnitude of their defeat. And, especially in Egypt and Jordan, they had to face the grim, economic realities of the changed landscape. Meanwhile, Arabs on the West Bank and in Gaza awakened to their new status—a conquered people. The newly-occupied lands teemed with hostile Arabs who saw, in a few short days, their dreams dashed—their dreams of an Arab victory that would permit them to return to their former homes on Jewish-held land that they called "Palestine."

Soon, the war came to be known in the West as the "Six-Day War." Throughout the world, for most who care about such things, the outcome aroused strong emotions. Those living in Muslim nations felt humiliated. The majority of the civilian populations in the western democratic nations admired Israel's stunning victory. But, as with glaciers that, after receding, reveal a newly scoured topography; the war's aftermath exposed new forces, empowered old ones, and weakened regimes that needed to alter course, or else disappear forever.

Israel

Israelis exhaled on what some called "the seventh day." For many, deliverance from Arab threats of extermination was enough. But, for other Israelis, the seventh day was an opportunity to explore Arab Jerusalem. Israeli authorities removed concrete baffles and concertina barbed wire from the alleyways marking the Green Line boundary that, before the war, had divided the city. Jews, driven by insatiable curiosity, headed for the Old City of Jerusalem, those few, cherished acres that since 1948 the Jordanians had barred them from entering. They crossed through checkpoints, and traversed formerly forbidden routes, routes that just a week earlier would have made them targets for Jordanian soldiers. They returned to the Wailing Wall and the rubble that remained of the Jewish Quarter, desecrated and demolished by Arabs when it fell in 1948. They walked the streets freely, stopped at Arab shops to purchase goods, and intermingled with the Arabs who lived there.

For a short time, wonder had replaced fear. It would not last long.

The byproduct of victory was that Israeli-controlled territory had quadrupled in size, increasing from little more than 20,000 square miles to nearly 90,000. The territorial acquisitions were extensive, but now they had to be defended. Fortunately, the Sinai gave Israel strategic depth and a border frontier twenty-five percent shorter than before which was also easier to defend. As a result, the dagger-like Gaza strip that ripped deep into Israel's innards no longer presented a danger. The same advantages held true opposite Jordan. Israeli control of the West Bank brought a border with Jordan shortened by half and protection for the narrow waist of Israel that was only ten miles wide. The new border also was much easier to defend because of the opportunity it provided to establish defensive positions along the Jordan River and the steep hills that loomed only a few miles back. In the north, the Golan Heights brought relief as well. It was relief from Syria's ability to shell the farming villages below, relief from infiltration of terrorists, and relief from Syria's never-ending attempts to impact, and interfere with, Israel's daily life. Suddenly, instead of Syrians peering down into Israel's northern Galilee, it was the Israelis who kept watch on the Damascus plain below.

But should Israel keep the new lands, or should she give them back? If the decision was to return some or all of the newly-conquered territories, what would the conditions be for a withdrawal? Who would take over if Israel withdrew? In the Sinai and the Golan the issues were easier and cleaner. The Sinai was undisputed Egyptian territory. The Golan was Syrian land. Israel would withdraw if, and when, it was safe to do so.

But the lands containing Palestinian Arabs presented much thornier problems. The Gaza strip was occupied by Egypt in 1948. It never was a country, and its geographic location posed a security threat to Israel. Much of its population consisted of Palestinian refugees from the 1948 war. The West Bank presented similar issues, but had many more Arabs who had lived there for decades, if not centuries, and who were intermingled with newly-arrived refugees from the 1948 War. And, like Gaza, the West Bank had never been an independent Arab nation, even though, after Hussein's grandfather annexed it in 1950, it had been part of Jordan for nearly three decades.

And then, of course, there was the issue of Jerusalem. It was the third-most holy site in Islam; and, for Jews, it was the fulfillment of a dream, the epicenter of their religion, their ancient capital.

One Israeli soldier, a son of Kfar Etzion, yearned to return to his home. The village of his birth was part of the Etzion Bloc. In 1948, Jordanian troops had destroyed the four villages in the bloc and massacred most of Kfar Etzion's Jewish inhabitants. His journey only required traveling a few short miles south of Jerusalem. The young man hitched a ride on an army jeep. When the vehicle passed through a military checkpoint an Israeli standing guard admonished him that only soldiers on duty could travel in the occupied lands. The soldier replied that his duty was to "go home."

The soldier's route passed through Bethlehem where images of King David from the ancient past filled his mind—not the plight of Arab townspeople he passed by. He traveled through hills where the ancient Jewish Maccabees, memorialized by the Hanukkah holiday, fought for their freedom against the Seleucid Empire centered in Syria. He traveled desolate roads where, less than twenty years earlier, Arab villagers slaughtered and mutilated Jewish men and women that tried to resupply the isolated defenders of the Etzion Bloc before it fell. When the soldier reached the Etzion site, he didn't see his former home. He didn't see any remnants of the villages that once stood there. He saw Jordanian army buildings and a Jordanian army mosque. He saw no reminders of the Jews who had built their homes there, toiled on its land, and died defending it.

That one soldier was not yet part of a movement. For two decades since 1948, few had shared his dream. Most Israelis had neither the time nor the strength for such thoughts. They were struggling to survive in an isolated, threadbare land surrounded by people filled with hatred and who never accepted Israel's legitimacy or existence. But on June 11, 1967, circumstances changed. One man engaged in a personal journey. He followed his vision. But it was a vision others soon shared—a vision that would coalesce and take shape. It was a vision that would help spawn the settler movement based on both secular and religious dreams that would inspire many and infuriate far more.

Who was primarily responsible for Israel's victory? Prime Minister Eshkol was Israel's nominal leader; Rabin was the IDF's Chief of Staff, but everyone's hearts and minds belonged to Moshe Dayan. The architect of Israel's victory in 1956, overnight, became the hero of 1967. Eshkol's halting speech to the nation on May 28 had filled Israel with fearful uncertainty. Dayan's appointment as defense minister on June 1 was the inspirational antidote that changed the mood of the country. For the people, Dayan won the war, not Rabin nor Eshkol nor all the other leaders who contributed so much to victory. However, those feelings, although understandable, were not grounded in reality. The war was won at such minimal cost due to the courage of Israel's soldiers, the careful planning and leadership of her officers, and the patience of the political leadership. But, on June 11, Dayan was thought to be a superman by Israel and the world.

Eshkol, ever practical even with his humor, joked, "Israel had received a good dowry, but that it came with a bride it doesn't like." The cabinet met on June 11 to decide what direction to take in the future. None had forgotten how, after the 1956 war, Israel had pulled back after taking the Sinai in return for empty promises from the international community and the UN. When those promises were not kept, the most recent ordeal had begun, an ordeal that they had just survived at the cost of hundreds of Israeli lives.

Overnight the Israeli government had to agree upon and implement policy amidst unforeseen challenges that changed with each new day. But it was not a normal government, selected by popular vote and led by a cabinet chosen by the Prime Minister in order to construct a ruling coalition. Instead it was a unity government appointed to demonstrate solidarity during the difficult days leading up to the war. The cabinet included twenty-one ministers from seven different political parties that all embraced a wide spectrum of views. It was a coalition that would last until Eshkol died two years later and would, due to its divisive structure, hamper decision-making. This diverse set of ministers had to decide what Israel's policy would be for the future—and decide quickly.

What to do with the newly-won territories divided them. They faced a new reality that Israel now ruled more than a million Arabs in the occupied lands. They all felt anger towards King Hussein, not just because of his decision to attack Israeli military sites and shell civilian centers, but, even more so, because Israel had given Hussein a final chance after the fighting started to avoid conflict, a chance he rejected. As a result many Jewish lives were lost in Jerusalem and the West Bank.

Should their sacrifices be in vain, especially with regard to Jerusalem? For some, the issue was emotional; for others, religious or practical. Their perspectives took them in many directions—except one. They all agreed that the Old City of Jerusalem would never be handed back to Arab rule.

Prime Minister Eshkol led the cabinet meeting that convened on June 11. Eshkol felt conflicted. He could envision giving up Israel's hold on the Sinai and the Golan within the context of ironclad, security guarantees and peace treaties (as opposed to promises that could easily be forgotten as were those made after the war in 1956). But Gaza and the West Bank presented an entirely different problem. Possession of the land meant that Israel would be responsible for the lives of more than one million Arabs. But those lands were tied to Jewish historical claims and inextricably intertwined with Israel's security needs. Eshkol referred to Gaza as the "Egyptian finger" that stretched into Israel and pointed towards Tel Aviv less than fifty miles beyond. In another breath he referred to Gaza as, "A rose with a lot of thorns." As for the West Bank, he stated that he, like others, had considered how to live with so many non-Jews without giving up the conquered territory. But he did not articulate how it could, or should, be done.

Eshkol supported maintaining Israel's hold on the Arab districts of Jerusalem and the Old City but did not minimize the difficulty of continued control. Jerusalem, especially, he knew, would present difficult legal and political problems. It was a problem that needed a resolution, but it had not been the subject of prior study. On June 10, Eshkol did, however, receive a written memorandum filled with advice from a Professor from the Hebrew University.

The Professor said that Christians would not oppose Israel maintaining control of the Old City but predicted that the Muslim world would cause problems, and that Jewish extremists might push to rebuild the Temple. Even so, the professor recommended bringing all of Jerusalem under Israeli sovereignty, but to treat East Jerusalem, where many Arabs resided, differently from the Old City, which held significance for many religions. He suggested that East Jerusalem should be ruled by the military government for the captured territories, that the Muslim and Christian areas of the Old City should be ruled by Israel's Ministry for Religious Affairs with input from Muslim and international Christian Councils, and that the Jewish Quarter should be ruled by Jerusalem's Jewish government.

The cabinet discussion then addressed how best to incorporate newly-conquered portions of Jerusalem into Israel. Begin pushed for claiming all of Jerusalem as Israel's capital. Some advocated direct annexation. But such steps violated international law, which clearly did not permit annexation of newly-conquered territory. However, many wondered whether international law was applicable and if it should be the guiding principle, especially since the West Bank and Arab Jerusalem had not been part of a recognized state for two thousand years since Israel was taken by the Romans. And, historically, many nations annexed territory they took in a war, a legacy that included Jordan's annexation of Arab Jerusalem in 1950. Also, international law neglected to address many factors: **foremost** among them were the dangers Israel had faced since her inception; and, **in addition,** that in 1948 Jordan had taken the Jewish Quarter of the Old City during the War for Independence, evicting all of its Jewish residents in the process. Nevertheless, the ministers knew any attempt to annex was sure to gain international attention and probable opprobrium.

Some cabinet members proposed a compromise to avoid some of the legal complexities. What if Israel merely extended the city boundaries of Jewish Jerusalem to incorporate East Jerusalem and the Old City? The idea gained momentum. The proponents then suggested guidelines. The boundaries would be redrawn to include not only all of Jerusalem but also contiguous areas formerly held by Jewish communities in 1948, along with land that had historical significance, strategic ridgelines required for defense, and areas designated for future growth. The proponents continued that care should be taken to draw the new boundaries with regard to excluding from the enlarged Jerusalem boundaries, as much as possible, regions with significant Arab populations. Within a few days the cabinet agreed upon a new boundary for Jerusalem that included 70,000 Arabs outside of the former green line, in addition to uninhabited new land to the north, east, and south of the city. It was an Israeli version of what is often done in the United States—drawing new electoral boundaries within a state to accomplish political goals. However, it needed to be finalized quickly before international pressure forced an unwanted alternative solution. The government went to work to make the cabinet directive a reality.

An announcement would come in two weeks.

American special counsel, Harry McPherson, cabled back to the White House that same day that Israel was unlikely to pull back voluntarily from the newly-won lands. He advised that, this time, the same paper guarantees provided after the 1956 Sinai War would not suffice, nor would threats of cutting off assistance from the United States.

Earlier in the day Moshe Dayan was interviewed for *Meet the Press*, the American public affairs weekly news television broadcast. Dayan said that Israel should keep Gaza and the West Bank. Arabs there should be given autonomy but not citizenship. As for the other territories, he said that Israel was willing to negotiate a peace treaty directly with Arab countries. But, in the absence of a treaty, Israel would remain where it was, and there would be a new Israel. Dayan displayed bravado. He did not consider the impact that Arab pride and humiliation would have.

Palestinians

Palestinians anguished over their new status. The 1947 UN plan they should have accepted, but had not, set aside nearly 8,500 square miles of land for an independent Palestinian nation. After the Arabs had attacked but failed to defeat the Israelis in 1948, land under Palestinian control in the West Bank was reduced to a 2,300-square-mile enclave under Jordanian domination. The Gaza Strip, ruled by Egypt, was much smaller. The impact on the Palestinians of the 1967 War was to swap a much-hated Arab monarch and an Egyptian president for a Jewish military government often short on compassion and long on decrees.

Living under the IDF's thumb was understandably difficult for many and a nightmare for some. As a result, within days of the war's end, many Palestinians made poor choices for their future. During and after the Six-Day War, the Israeli government did not have a policy for forcibly evicting West Bank citizens encountered by the army. But Israel shed no tears over those Arabs who wished to depart. In fact, Israel provided free transportation by bus for any who wanted to leave their homes and evacuate to Jordan. Tens of thousands accepted the free ride because of their misguided fears that the Israelis would otherwise visit the harm on them that they had fully intended to inflict on Israelis if the Arabs had instead been victorious. The buses deposited them on the side of the Jordan River controlled by the IDF. Most then crossed by way of the partially destroyed Allenby Bridge. To do so required sliding into the shallow, muddy river and wading through the current to the other side. There, Jordan had no established facilities to receive them. Those Palesitnians that chose to leave quickly learned that by escaping the frying pan of their misguided fears, they had walked into the fire of physical suffering caused by intense desert heat and privation—far worse than what they would have experienced with the Israelis.

And it was a one-way ticket. Once gone, there was no option to return.

It is also true, however, that some local Jewish commanders went a step too far and took matters into their own hands. In a small minority of Arab villages and cities, Israeli soldiers equipped with loudspeakers strongly encouraged and occasionally ordered Arab inhabitants to leave. General Narkiss went one step further. Near the fortress of Latrun, Narkiss unilaterally changed facts on the ground. During the 1948 war, Jordanians based at the fortress prevented Jewish convoys from using the road that went past it to take supplies to Jewish-held parts of Jerusalem. For the next twenty years, it was a thorn in Israel's side despite construction of what, at first, was a precarious alternate route until it was improved after the 1948 war ended. On Narkiss's orders, bulldozers razed three Arab villages near the road that had been the home to some of the Arab irregulars who had slaughtered Jews in convoys attempting to navigate past the Latrun salient twenty years earlier. The inhabitants had no choice but to leave. Narkiss was determined that Jerusalem would never again face strangulation. After the bulldozers finished their work, the IDF denied residents of the demolished homes permission to return.

However, one group of Palestinians was neither infected nor paralyzed by the shock and grief coursing through the "Arab street." Fatah, the largest and most cohesive group within the Palestinian National Liberation movement, saw opportunity rather than despair. A small, cohesive group that had worked together for more than a decade ran the organization. They had studiously avoided inter-Arab disputes so that Fatah could recruit from all ideologies. The organization really only had one goal—a goal represented by its name, an acronym formed by reversing the letters that stood for the Palestinian liberation movement. When reversed, they meant "conquest".

Before the war, Arab governments had permitted the various Palestinian factions to operate under strict guidelines, so long as it benefitted their national goals. But when they strayed, Arab governments made sure to rein them in. After the war, however, restraining the Fedayeen was not so easy. Arab military forces, especially those of Egypt, were exposed as hollow shells. And, after the defeat, Egypt and Jordan cared more about recovering their lost lands than destroying Israel.

Therefore, Palestinian activists outside of the conquered territories made plans to increase their power and influence. They scheduled a conference for June 12 in Damascus to discuss new strategies for confronting Israel.

The PLO saw that it had an opportunity to fill the political void left by Egypt's eviction from Gaza. Before the recent conflict, any attempt by inhabitants in Gaza to rule themselves were ruthlessly suppressed by Egyptian internal security. More than half of the 350,000 residents still lived in filthy refugee camps created after the 1948 war. They comprised one of the highest population densities in the world and possessed little wealth with which to support themselves. As a result, hatred went hand in hand with helplessness. It was a fertile ground for PLO recruitment.

However, on the West Bank, the PLO and Fatah had their work cut out for them. Before Israel evicted the Jordanian army, the West Bank had had an active leadership composed mainly of notables from wealthy and powerful families with status, almost all of whom were tied to King Hussein by inclination or bribery. The king cultivated them after assuming the throne in 1953, three years after his grandfather annexed the territory in 1950. They flourished despite the presence of many young, more radical, leaders who had studied in Cairo's universities and who were not so enamored with the king's autocratic rule. But after the Six-Day War, political conditions in the West Bank were in flux. Some inhabitants saw that the chaos might yield new opportunities. The PLO was only one of many choices. And Israel recognized that it was in her best interest to maintain a counterweight to more radical organizations. Therefore, after the fighting ended, Israel permitted individuals in the local governing bodies to keep their positions and allowed Jordan to continue paying their salaries and to funnel money to supporters and former civil servants. It was a quiet agreement that Hussein was only too happy to take advantage of in order to maintain his influence on the West Bank.

Rather than insurrection, many West Bank leaders mulled over two other options. **One** was to work for a return to Jordanian rule. **The other** was to create an independent separate entity with boundaries defined by the 1947 UN partition plan. Fatah, which believed that King Hussein's primary interest was to regain power in the West Bank, did not support either of those plans; it also knew that the Israelis would never voluntarily agree to anything that not only required relinquishing their newly won gains, but that would also require further withdrawal from lands they had controlled since 1948.

However, when two Arab notables approached Israeli officers on June 11 to seek permission for fifty West Bank leaders to hold a meeting in Ramallah, the officers refused. Israel had no interest in creating an assembly with whom it could negotiate. Neither did King Hussein, nor did Fatah.

Jordan

King Hussein felt the loss of the West Bank and Jerusalem profoundly. For him, it was an issue of honor—as well as economics. The Jews had taken what his grandfather, King Abdullah, had gained—the third-most holy site in Islam.

The West Bank comprised a quarter of Jordan's arable land, half of her inhabitable areas, half of its industry, and much of her water resources. By losing Jerusalem and Bethlehem, Hussein also lost crucial sources of tourist revenue for his already impoverished country. Instead of international tourists swelling his coffers, Hussein faced the burden of caring for 175,000 new refugees streaming into his country from the West Bank, to say nothing of the hundreds of thousands of Palestinians already housed within Jordan for two decades in makeshift camps. (The Arab world had callously made no effort to assimilate the refugees — a stark difference from Israel's priority to uplift living standards for Jewish refugees that had fled persecution in Arab and other nations.) The influx overwhelmed the Jordanians and further upset a teetering, demographic balance between unfriendly Palestinians and Bedouin loyal to the king.

Hussein's woes did not stop with economics. His survival was at stake. His military was shattered. Up to eighty percent of Jordan's tanks and other equipment had been destroyed. Her air force had been eliminated by Israeli strikes on the first day of the war. More than 700 soldiers had been killed, almost ten times more were injured. On June 11, Hussein's army was virtually powerless. But the same statement could not be made for the Iraqi army which had entered his country and still remained. They arrived too late to take part in the fighting, but not too late to potentially topple his regime. Likewise, the Syrian army was battered and bruised but still relatively intact and still a threat to the king. Hussein feared what might happen if the Iraqis remained, but he was equally worried about Syrian and Palestinian intrigues if the Iraqis left. His path forward was unclear. To survive required a deft balancing act, maneuvering between and among a far more confident Israel, a disillusioned population, and unpredictable Arab leaders in search of their own solutions for threats to their survival.

It was, for the young king, a precarious moment.

Egypt

Nasser was devastated. The Suez Canal was closed for two main reasons; **one** was because he had ordered ships sunk within its waters to bar its usage by the West. The **second** was because of sporadic fighting that continued between his army and the IDF. Egypt's loss of significant revenue as a result was a tremendous economic blow. That meant Nasser had to shift his focus from leading the Muslim world to concentrating more on restoring Egyptian power and pride. But, because of Egypt's financial hardships, he was forced to become more dependent on Arab oil producers, economically, and the Soviet Union, militarily. Egypt's ability to act strictly in her own interests was now severely diminished.

Nasser's fall from his prestigious position in the Muslim world was precipitous. And the futility of his army should not have come as a surprise to him, either. Army officers came from privileged sectors of society. They received their commands based on their influence, not their abilities. The rank and file soldiers did not make up for their leaders' shortcomings. They came mostly from low levels of Egyptian society and had little education. Their training did little to improve their lot. As a result, there was no cohesion, little professionalism, and scant pride. Nasser's rash move into the Sinai while he was embroiled in another war in Yemen had, not surprisingly, proved unsustainable. As opposed to Israel, who used the three weeks between mobilization and war to fine-tune her army; the Egyptians struggled to provide adequate food, water, fuel, and ammunition to their forces in the Sinai. Whereas the Israelis were able to stay in place, train for, and study their plan of attack; the Egyptian high command shifted their forces from one position to another. Even though some strong defensive positions were occupied, the troops had little time to familiarize themselves with them. All told, it was a failure of leadership at all levels, more than anything else, that caused Egypt's calamity.

After the war, a profound depression descended upon the Egyptians. Only a week earlier there had been a festive atmosphere in the streets when the war started. Signs, such as ones that read, "On to Tel Aviv" had proliferated. Many believed that Tel Aviv would feel the trampling of Egyptian boots by the end of the first day. Propaganda for many years that overestimated Egyptian strength and devalued Israel's had only encouraged those beliefs. Suddenly, instead of liberating Palestine, the Egyptians had to face the reality of the rout.

Not only did Egypt lose the Sinai; she lost the economic engine of the Suez Canal. As long as opposing armies sat on opposite shores trading fire, whether purposively or haphazardly, the canal could not be cleared of the ships sunk within. Every month that shipping did not move through the canal cost Egypt more than thirty million in lost fees. In 2015, that amount would have equaled nearly two hundred million per month—a staggering sum for a poor nation with few other resources.

Many Egyptians saw their loss as a moral judgment of their society. One Nasser supporter called on a new generation, untainted by corruption, to replace the existing regime and reverse Egypt's fortunes. Nationalists, Marxists, and liberals began to doubt their ideologies. The Muslim Brotherhood, brutally suppressed in pre-war days by Nasser for challenging his control of the nation, saw an opportunity provided by nationalism's diminished appeal. They trumpeted the tenets of Islam over the prerogatives of the State. Nasser would not live to see the Brotherhood's power grow, but its outstretched hand would assassinate his successor in 1981. Later, after the turn of the century, Muslim extremism that owed much of its roots to the Muslim Brotherhood would assert itself in chilling fashion.

Nasser's focus changed as a result. He became less interested in leading the Arab world and more determined to rebuild Egypt's military strength. He became more interested in achieving the return of the Sinai and less concerned with the Palestinian goal of occupying Israel. As part of his philosophical change he began using the phrase "erasing the traces of aggression." His main objective was to restore Egyptian sovereignty in the Sinai. To achieve that, he felt it absolutely necessary to prevent Israel from consolidating her gains. His strategy was to avoid admitting defeat by refusing to enter into any agreement with Israel that resulted in the loss of even an inch of territory. To recover the Sinai he was willing to agree to non-belligerency, freedom of navigation in the Straits of Tiran, and perhaps even Israeli usage of the Suez Canal. But on one thing he was clear and resolute: Egypt would not talk directly with Israel, nor would she agree to a peace treaty. Doing so, from Nasser's perspective, would be tantamount to surrender.

Syria

Of all the Arab nations that were heavily involved in the war, Syria was the least impacted by it but remained the most virulent. Though her air force was destroyed and the Golan Heights lost, much of Syria's army remained intact. Still, Syrian civilians blamed the debacle on what they believed was Syria's incompetent army. The army, of course, felt differently. It blamed the civilian leadership for improvidently initiating the conflict.

Fortunately for Israel, the Golan did not present the same demographic problems that existed in the much-more densely, populated West Bank and Gaza. Of the more than 100,000 Arabs and Druze who had lived before the war on the Golan's rocky lands, only 7,000 Druze remained. The rest fled. On June 5, Kuneitra, the most important Syrian city on the high mountain plateau, had a population of 17,000. On June 11, the city was deserted, with most of its citizens having decamped to Damascus.

Defense Minister Assad was by no means sanguine in the wake of Syria's defeat. Damascus was teeming with new refugees who served as a constant reminder of the army's humiliation. And the military was Assad's responsibility. Despite holding defensive positions that had seemed impervious to attack, the army had failed. Assad tried to maintain a normal schedule after the war ended, but he could not. He was depressed and had difficulty sleeping. Finally, it was too much. He fainted from fatigue; after that he went home for three days and refused to see anybody while he brooded over the Arab failures. Meanwhile, Ba'ath party malcontents fell one vote short of forcing him to resign.

However, rather than slide into obscurity, Assad's self-reflection motivated him to seek power. Before the fighting with Israel started, he had been content supporting Syria's strongmen. But Assad decided that Jadid, the real power in Syria rather than President Al-Atassi, was too aggressive. Assad also felt that the Fedayeen had not been sufficiently controlled. If the Palestinians were not managed by a stronger hand in the future, he believed they might lead Syria into another war it was not yet ready for. In addition, Assad saw advantage in entering into alliances with other Arab nations—even if their ideologies and goals did not coincide completely with Syria's. Assad's primary goal became recovering Syria's lands lost in the war. He wanted to advance Palestinian causes, but on his terms and nobody else's. So, Assad methodically began to build his power base among the Syrian military, distributing favors to cultivate important friendships within the ranks. From Assad's perspective, he already was receiving much of the blame for the failures of Syrian leadership, so he might as well be the leader, too.

America

Although President Johnson was fond of the Israelis, he did not hate the Arabs. He was, however, certainly displeased with Egypt's and Syria's support and friendship with the Soviet Union. Nor did the radical tendencies among Arab nationalists make him happy. This was especially true given the turmoil the Vietnam War caused, along with the global Cold War confrontation with the Russians. Also, ever the political animal, Johnson was aware that public opinion was strongly in favor of Israel. Therefore, Johnson was determined to make sure that Israel maintained her military superiority. His goal, then, was to create a diplomatic framework within which Israel could trade land for peace.

President Johnson also decided that the United States would not pressure Israel to pull back from the territories taken during the war. However, although he did not blame Israel for starting the war, he was pessimistic that any of the region's problems would be solved by the way it ended. But Johnson was equally leery of forcing Israel to pull back based on empty guarantees. He was fully aware that, after the 1956 war, President Eisenhower had forced Israel to withdraw from the Sinai in return for empty promises from the international community. The 1967 war was unavoidable, he knew, because of the failure to honor those guarantees.

Russia

What was with the Russians? Why did they knowingly spread false news of Israel's mobilization in the North? Why did they instigate a political crisis they must have known might end in the defeat of their Arab clients? And it was not the first time. Russia had issued false warnings about purported Israeli plans several times before. Each time those warnings were as false as the warning in May 1967.

Most scholars believe the Russians did not intend for a war to start. They argue that Russia hoped for an Israeli reaction, short of war, that would inflame international opinion, diminish the West's standing in Muslim eyes, and bring Syria and Egypt closer to the Soviet orbit. Others believe that Russia wanted to make sure Syria was protected from Israel, and to strengthen Soviet ties with the Baathist regime by forcing Egypt to help deter Israeli aggression. Although a few argue that Russia wanted a war in order to destroy, or at least delay, Israel's blossoming nuclear option (the Dimona nuclear reactor), it is hard to imagine that the Russians would risk a confrontation with the United States over that issue—at least not without first unleashing an unrelenting propaganda campaign to increase international pressure on the Israelis to give up their budding nuclear option.

What is clear is that the Russians knew that their false accusations would increase Russian influence in the region. The more the Arabs depended on the Soviets, the more isolated America would become. Russia coveted a base in the region for her navy. Russia also hoped to exert influence on the terms and conditions for the export of Arab oil. If successful, she could then employ that economic control to damage western interests in the future.

In the short term, Russian plans to increase Soviet influence in the Arab world worked. However, the Soviet Union did not anticipate that Nasser would evict the UN peacekeepers and close the Straits of Tiran. As a result, events spiraled out of Russia's control. But before the war ended, the Russians took steps to increase their sway with the Arabs. They started an airlift to Egypt to provide replacement weapons; and, in addition, shortly thereafter, massive quantities of Russian arms arrived in Egypt, Syria, and Iraq by sea.

The Russians were also pleased to see American influence in the Arab world wane when many Arab countries severed their diplomatic relations with the United States. The only diplomatic cost for isolating the Americans from the Arabs was that Russia felt bound to sever diplomatic relations with Israel. It was a step the Soviet Union felt was needed to maintain solidarity with the Arabs, but, in the long run, it would serve to reduce Russia's ability to influence future events in the region. It was a diplomatic void that the United States would seek to fill.

It is certain that without Russian intrigues the war in 1967 would not have occurred. Whether for internal purposes, Cold War intrigue, the reasons previously mentioned, or some inscrutable motive yet to see the light of day, the Russians set in motion the events that caused the 1967 war to break out. Until the covers are torn off all the Russian archives, we will never be certain why; but all inhabitants of the region, along with the rest of the world, will live with the results.

CHAPTER SEVENTEEN
The West Bank — June 12 to June 19

The number of Israelis visiting the Old City of Jerusalem and the Wailing Wall continued to increase. Within a few days it became a ceaseless torrent. What had been off-limits less than two weeks before was open for peaceful exploration.

Peace was not on the agenda for Fatah's leaders at their meeting in Damascus on June 12. Out of the devastating Arab loss, Fatah saw opportunity. Yasser Arafat argued, "This is not the end. It is the beginning." He then pronounced, "We are going to resume military actions." Some of the attendees expressed concern that they would be sold out by Arab nations more interested in recovering their lost territory than in helping the Palestinians retake the West Bank and conquer Israel. Their concerns had validity and needed to be addressed. Therefore, the participants decided that, in addition to targeting military operations against Israel, political efforts to further Palestinian causes would be directed towards Arab governments. After the conference ended, Fatah representatives visited several Arab capitals to raise financial and political assistance. Simultaneously, Arafat and others made plans to slip into the West Bank to gauge support there for a revolt against the Israeli occupation.

Fatah recognized it could potentially emerge a winner in the wake of Israel's massive victory. It was the only Arab institution in the region left intact after the war; and it was independent, financially viable, and not aligned with any Arab government. The Arab states bordering Israel were smashed—militarily and psychologically. And the Palestinian Liberation Organization, created by Nasser and believed by many Palestinians to be a puppet of Arab governments, had been discredited by its failure to offer any resistance during the war in which much of its infrastructure was destroyed. For a few militants, it was Islam, not the more secular philosophy of Fatah, that provided answers for their present dilemma; but that was a path which would take years to germinate among the mainstream. Therefore, Fatah's leaders felt certain that for Palestinians hoping to strike back in their despair, they were the only outlet for their vengeance. Fatah had only one major goal—emergence of a Palestinian State on Israel's ruins.

In Israel, one politician organized a trip to the Etzion Bloc. He included in the group a survivor from each of the four villages that once stood there. Upon arrival they saw that no building present in 1948 had survived; all of the orchards were gone, and a Jordanian army base stood on the grounds where Kfar Etzion had once stood. It was the first, organized trip to the Etzion Bloc. It would not be the last. The idea of re-settlement was just beginning. Etzion was one of the incipient movement's emotional epicenters. Thus, while Fatah dreamt of returning Palestinians to Israel, some Israelis dreamt of resettling lands held by Jews in both ancient times and also fewer than twenty years before.

On June 15, 200,000 Israelis journeyed to the Wailing Wall to celebrate Shavuot. Shavuot is a Jewish holiday that celebrates God's gift of the Torah to the Jewish people. The Torah is the Jewish religion's most sacred document because it contains the fundamental laws which guide the faith. Before the day was done, the open plaza below the wall, so recently crammed tight with the shanties of the Moroccan quarter, filled with a euphoric throng. If ever there was a thought that Israel would return the Old City to Arab hands, the presence of so many Jews emphasized the growing reality: Permanent Jewish control of the Old City was non-negotiable for many. Against the backdrop of those joyous citizens rejoicing before the Wall, the Ministerial Committee of Israel's cabinet began formal meetings to develop Israel's policy with regard to the conquered territories.

But while Jews celebrated, the exodus of West Bank Palestinian refugees which had slowed, gained steam. UN sources estimated that 200,000 refugees crossed the Jordan within days of the end of the war. Of them, 93,000 were second-time refugees, having fled Israel in 1948.

Some of the Palestinians left due to ongoing psychological pressure, whether they had just cause or not. Others departed because they wanted to, and others still were leaving because Israel made it easier for them by providing free transportation to do so. The same day Jews thronged to the Wailing Wall, Chaim Herzog, the Military Governor appointed to administer the West Bank, issued an exit order: Those Jordanian citizens wishing to leave the West Bank were provided transportation from Nablus to Jericho. From that point, they had to proceed on foot across the Jordan River.

General Narkiss, Israel's Central Front Commander in the region, had a long memory of what Jews had endured twenty years before and was haunted by his personal failure in 1949 to relieve the Jews living in the Old City before they surrendered. Therefore, the sight of Arab civilians fleeing did not bother him. Even though Israel had no formal policy to evict Palestinians, from his perspective and that of many others, the fewer who remained behind, the smaller the problem for Israel. Other than in military sensitive areas, such as Latrun, the soldiers under his command did not forcibly remove civilians. But, in numerous instances, they certainly attempted to persuade Palestinians to leave, especially those near the pre-war border with Israel. In addition, Central Command soldiers razed a few Arab villages to the ground: the three previously-mentioned ones near Latrun and another close to the Etzion Bloc. When Rabin heard of the destruction, he put a quick stop to any further wrongful activity. Shortly before his death, Narkiss admitted he had ordered the destruction of the villages, more out of retribution than military necessity. It was not something for him or his country to be proud of.

After they crossed the Jordan River, the refugees did not find any preparations for their arrival. The Jordan valley is a desert region with little cover from the scorching sun. There was no natural shade, water, or tents. Latrines were relatively non-existent and garbage accumulated. The United Nations Relief and Works Agency (UNWRA) was overwhelmed. Tents, some composed of sticks covered by blankets buffeted by desert winds bearing grains of coarse sand, slowly coalesced into veritable cities. Bitterness grew among the adults. Even more so it grew among the older children. For those Palestinians who had a change of heart, and sought to return to the West Bank, the Israelis refused them re-entry. It should come as no surprise that the seeds of many future terrorists were sown in those crowded camps.

It was not a pleasant time to be an Arab resident of the West Bank. But Palestinians were not the only people to suffer as a result of the war. In Egypt, authorities arrested 800 Jews and confiscated their property. Jewish citizens of Yemen, Lebanon, Tunisia, Libya, and Morocco were attacked and their synagogues burned. The physical violence directed at Jewish citizens by the local populations of many Arab nations, the confiscation of their property, and the subsequent, forced expulsion of Jews from Arab lands was far more widespread than the difficulties that befell Palestinian West Bank residents. But the suffering of those Jews, as undeniable as the suffering of many Palestinians, was much less reported. And Israel opened her arms to those Jews that had lost their homes as opposed to the Arab nations that were content to leave the Palestinians living in squalor for their own political purposes.

Moshe Dayan visited the West Bank, including the populous cities of Nablus and Jenin, the day after the war ended. Israel's government had not yet decided what it would do with the new territories, but arrangements for governing the West Bank were moving ahead at full speed. While in Nablus, Dayan met with local leaders. Afterward, he ordered the provisional military-government to weaken the curfew restrictions it had imposed on Arab residents.

Dayan was literally the man behind the curtain for all West Bank policy. His philosophy was that consideration should be given to the plight of the Arab populace by giving them a greater say in their own affairs. He also insisted on selecting the military officers who would govern each district that the IDF had so recently created in the West Bank. Dayan wanted governors who were, "admired but still respected by the Arabs." He did not want good soldiers who were only trained to take the objective. His philosophy was to extend one helping hand, but to use the other to beat down any opposition. He never forgot the old Arab proverb, "If you can see the lion's teeth, don't be tempted into believing he is smiling."

During those first few days, Dayan only had time to give General Herzog broad guidelines for his mission to govern the West Bank. Herzog was to focus on returning basic services as soon as possible, especially to Jerusalem. Dayan also made clear that the Temple Mount must remain under local Arab control, and that Muslims should be permitted to pray there. It was a courtesy which had not been provided by Arabs to Jews for the previous nineteen years at Jewish holy sites in Jerusalem and the West Bank. Herzog successfully put an end to some ongoing looting of Arab homes and businesses. But he was hampered by administrative disorganization, no clear lines of authority, communication difficulties, and the general lack of decision-making within the government and the IDF.

On the West Bank, Arab notables attempted to take their own first steps towards determining their fate. On June 18, Israeli authorities gave passes to nearly twenty Arab leaders to travel to a meeting to discuss the future of the West Bank. But their discussions centered on unrealistic options. **One** was to obtain Israeli agreement to withdraw well past the June 4, 1967 boundaries to the boundaries designated in the 1947 partition plan. Those boundaries were supported by the UN and approved by the Jews that declared Israel's independence (but not the Palestinians) before the outbreak of the 1948 war. They went by the wayside when the fledgling state was attacked on all sides, and from within, by Arab nations and the Palestinians. **Another** idea was to create a bi-national state encompassing both Israel and the West Bank. That idea, if implemented, would have ended the Jewish State. Those alternatives, and all other variants discussed, required Israel to give up control of the newly-won parts of Jerusalem. Nothing those leaders discussed had a remote chance of being acceptable to Israel. As such, the Palestinians lost an opportunity to begin a meaningful dialogue.

Even so, news of their meeting did not make King Hussein happy. Nor did his Arab "brethren" receive it with enthusiasm in Syria. Syria and Jordan almost never saw eye-to-eye, but the thought of Palestinians solving their own problems without being controlled or beholden to Jordan and Syria was too much for either nation to bear. Syrian and Jordanian propaganda outlets denounced the West Bank leaders for even trying. And for those West Bank leaders willing to reach a compromise with Israel that excluded Jordan, fear of Hussein's retribution (should the West Bank ever reunify with Jordan) muted their voices. Israel's silence regarding their future safety if they would come forward did nothing to alleviate the apprehension of the notables. Thus, the newly-conquered were too intimidated, too fearful for their personal wellbeing, to offer any solutions for the situation they were now in that took into account Israel's core needs. That was a dynamic that exists to this day, and that is a dynamic that has bedeviled negotiations with some Palestinians that otherwise might be willing to consider an accommodation with any chance of acceptance by Israel since then.

CHAPTER EIGHTEEN
Politics, June 12 — June 19

June 12 was a day filled with speeches and conversations, but was not without action. Eshkol spoke to the Knesset, Israel's legislative body. He assured the ministers that Israel would protect Christian and Muslim holy sites, a courtesy not provided by the Jordanians who, under their stewardship, had done nothing to protect Jewish holy sites from desecration. Eshkol then declared, "Let this be said—there should be no illusion that Israel is prepared to return to the conditions that existed a week ago.... No more will land of Israel be no man's land, violated by acts of sabotage and murder..." And then in a message to the Muslim world he continued, "To the Arab nations ... we were not glad we had to go to war. We acted in the absence of any other choice, to protect our lives and our rights." Dayan amplified Eshkol's remarks in a BBC interview, "We are awaiting the Arabs' phone call. We ourselves won't make a move. We are quite happy with the current situation. If anything bothers the Arabs they know where to find us."

Israel's leaders knew it was imperative for them to establish their policy for finding a path to sustained peace with their Arab neighbors. But each politician had distinct ideas how to do that, concepts shaped in part by their varied, personal background and experiences. During their discussions, a broad range of ideas were expressed in a manner akin to half-baked utterances at whiteboard sessions which identify options without much analysis or thought given to any one suggestion when first proposed. Therefore, it is dangerous for historians to draw any conclusions from those informal utterances. The first coherent step towards planning Israel's path forward was an informal meeting held at Eshkol's home on June 13. Eshkol only invited the most influential members of the government, including Dayan and Allon. They agreed that Israel should be willing to withdraw from Egyptian and Syrian land to the recognized international borders that existed before the Six-Day War in return for recognition and peace. They also preliminarily agreed that Israel should be prepared to withdraw from heavily populated areas of the West Bank.

At the United Nations

The Russians were unwilling to wait for Israel to develop her policy. The Soviet Union demanded that the Security Council meet again on June 14. That day Fedorenko, the Russian Ambassador to the UN, introduced a resolution that condemned Israel and called her territorial conquests "unacceptable and unlawful." The Russians also proposed a second resolution that demanded an immediate Israeli withdrawal without any pre-conditions. Only six of the fifteen nations on the Council voted in favor of that proposal, three short of the number needed for it to pass unless one of the five permanent members of the Security Council exercised its right to veto. The resolution sponsored by the Soviets condemning Israeli aggression fared even worse, receiving only four votes. The outcome taught the Russians that their political agenda stood a better chance in the General Assembly than in the Security Council.

The General Assembly reconvened at the Soviet Union's request on June 17. The Russians tried to turn the meeting into a summit conference on the Middle East. It was clear what the Arabs and their Russian allies wanted, a complete withdrawal of Israeli forces to the June 4 pre-war boundaries. But the Americans pushed back, insisting that all proposals be considered, not just the Russian one for withdrawal.

The confrontation between the Soviets and Israelis reached a crescendo on June 19 in the UN General Assembly. Many American television stations and radio broadcasts canceled their normal programming to carry the debate. Its highlight was a lively, oratorical duel between Russian Prime Minister Alexei Kosygin and Israeli Foreign Minister Abba Eban.

Kosygin led off. He introduced a draft resolution which condemned Israel for her aggression, demanded that Israel unconditionally withdraw to the original armistice lines, and insisted that Israel pay compensation for damage suffered by the Arabs during the war. For many listeners, his words fell flat. In effect the Russians were demanding a "do over" financed by Israel.

Eban responded with a long, eloquent speech. He began by summarizing what caused the confrontation:

> [I]n recent weeks the Middle East has passed through a crisis whose shadows darken the world. This crisis has many consequences but only one cause: Israel's right to peace, security, sovereignty, economic development, and maritime borders—indeed its very right to exist—has been forcibly denied and aggressively attacked.

Eban then made clear who was responsible:

> *The threat to Israel's existence has been directed against her in the first instance by the neighboring Arab states. But all the conditions of tension and all the impulses of aggression in the Middle East have been aggravated by the policy of the Soviet Union. The burden of responsibility lies heavily upon it.*

Eban followed by explaining the decision Israel made:

> On the morning of June 5, our country's choice was plain: the choice was to live or perish; to defend the national existence or forfeit it for all time. What should be condemned is not Israel's

action but the attempt to condemn it. Never have freedom, honor, justice, national interest, and international morality been so righteously protected.

Eban then struck at the heart of Kosygin's accusations:

> So long as men cherish freedom, so long as small states strive for the dignity of survival, the exploits of Israel's armies will be told from one generation to another with the deepest pride. The Soviet Union has described our resistance as aggression and sought to have it condemned. We reject this accusation with all our might. Here was armed forces employed in a just and righteous cause, as righteous as the defense of freedom at Valley Forge; as the expulsion of Hitler's bombers from British skies; as noble as the protection of Stalingrad against Nazi hordes, so was the defense of Israel's security and existence against those who sought our nation's destruction. Never have freedom, honor, justice, national interest, and international morality been so righteously protected.

Near the end of his statement, Eban verbally confronted Kosygin and the U.S.S.R.:

> In a letter to the Israeli Government, and in the words of Prime Minister Kosygin, the U.S.S.R. has formulated an obscene comparison between the Israel defense forces and the Hitlerite hordes which overran Europe in the Second World War. There is a flagrant breach of elementary human decency and of international morality in this odious comparison. Israel with Nazi Germany. We never signed a pact as you did with Hitler in 1939.

Finally, Eban neatly summarized Israel's position from that day to the present:

> The Arab states can no longer be permitted to recognize Israel's existence only for the purpose of plotting its elimination. They have come face to face with us in conflict; let them now come face to face with us in peace.

The United States

The same day the debate raged at the UN, President Johnson gave a speech in Washington, D.C. which laid out the principles that he believed should guide future resolution of the crisis. The **first** was the right of every nation in the region to live and be accepted by its neighbors. His **second** and **third** points outlined the need to find a solution for the refugee problem and to respect the maritime rights of all nations. The **fourth** called for an end to the arms race in the region, but Johnson tied that into maintenance of the independence and territorial integrity of all states through peace. **Fifth**, he called for troops to withdraw, but only when the conditions and solutions delineated in his first four points had been achieved.

President Johnson believed the onus for making peace was on the parties involved, not the United States or the UN. He also clearly blamed Egypt for the war by referring to the closure of the Straits of Tiran as an "act of folly." Johnson's speech proved that Israel's restraint before June 5 was appreciated. Further, the president recognized that an Israeli return to the June 4 borders, and the status quo, was a recipe for future war.

But, behind the scenes, the Americans pressured Israel for an answer to an important question: What would Israel's future policy be?

Israeli Policy

Israel's cabinet ministers agreed on an answer to America's question the same day that Johnson and Eban spoke—sort of. The cabinet was united on three key principles. **First** and foremost, direct negotiations between Israel and each affected Arab country was a pre-condition for any withdrawal from the Sinai and the Golan. The depth of the withdrawal would then be based on Israel's security needs. Furthermore, the cabinet agreed that a full withdrawal to the internationally recognized border would only happen in conjunction with a full, written, peace treaty. **Second**, as part of any agreement with Egypt, Israeli shipping had to have free and full access to the Straits of Tiran and the Suez Canal, and Israel's civilian aircraft had to enjoy the same overflight privileges that air carriers from other countries had. The **third** principle involved land. Israel would never withdraw from Jerusalem for reasons that went to the core of the souls of her citizens. Nor would Israel withdraw from Gaza for security reasons. The Golan and the Sinai would have to be permanently demilitarized, and Israel would have to receive guaranteed access to water flowing into the Jordan from Syria so that the water crisis instigated by the Syrians in 1965 would not happen again.

Determining future policy for the West Bank was much more difficult for the cabinet; unanimous disagreement displaced unanimity. And there was no love lost for King Hussein; after all, it was Hussein who had attacked Israel when the war started. Months later, Minister Allon expressed the views of many when he said, "In his attack on us, Hussein acted like Mussolini when he stabbed France in the back shortly after the German invasion. He showed that he was not trustworthy."

> The ministers understood that they had three main options, each with multiple variants, for future policy regarding the West Bank: do nothing, try to reach an agreement with King Hussein (directly or with the help of the West Bank leadership), or try to reach an agreement with local Palestinians towards establishing a new entity. Most of the variants concerned how much control Israel would keep: whether it would be total governance of the territory, partial control with Jordan receiving back much of the West Bank

(other than areas required for Israeli security), or Palestinian political autonomy independent of Jordan under an Israeli military umbrella.

The cabinet discussions regarding the West Bank raged back and forth. Other proposals from lower levels of Israel's government also surfaced. Some suggestions were comprehensive and realistic; others were outlandish and impossible to implement. Eshkol wanted Israel to maintain military control up to the Jordan River but did not want to grant the Arab population Israeli citizenship. A few favored creating a new Palestinian State separate from Jordan. Menachem Begin and a small number of other ministers wanted to annex all of the West Bank because of its historic and religious link to the Jewish people. But none who wanted to maintain control of the West Bank offered realistic solutions for the demographic time bomb—the Arab birth rate—that many thought would eventually overwhelm the Jewish nature of Israel (future immigration of massive numbers of Russian Jews and an increasing birthrate of Israeli Jews was not yet a fact). Therefore, some thought it best to return the land to Hussein—with some exceptions.

The ministers also had varying opinions regarding which portions of the West Bank were vital strategically. Allon thought much could be left to the Palestinians except for the river valley abutting the Jordan River. Dayan felt the ridgeline several miles back from the river was the most strategically important terrain. There was too little time, and the cabinet was too disparate a group, to reach a consensus. So, they took the time-honored way out of deciding that has served politicians throughout history—they agreed to defer their decision for further study. Their failure was no more lamentable, but equally impactful, than the failure of the Arab notables to find a path to a peaceful future that held realistic promise for a peaceful future for the West Bank and its bevy of issues. Everyone, Arabs and Jews alike, wanted too much for the little they were willing to give.

Israel conveyed to the Americans the June 19 cabinet decision regarding future policy, for delivery to the Arabs; but did not publicly announce it because the cabinet well understood that no Arab leader would talk to them. The Israelis were not optimistic. Perhaps Foreign Minister Eban best summarized the prevailing Jewish view when he suggested that the Arabs want one hundred percent of the land and zero percent of the peace. That was most certainly true of Syria, probably true of Egypt, but not necessarily true of King Hussein in Jordan.

The common wisdom is that the Americans informed the Syrians and the Egyptians, who rejected the proposal, a few days later. But some historians question whether the Syrians and Egyptians were ever told about the offer at all. If not, it was the fault of the Americans, not the Israelis. However, given the political environment within Syria and Egypt, there is little doubt that no harm was done if the offer was not communicated. It would have been summarily rejected.

And if the Arab countries were truly interested in "land for peace," it would have been easy for the Arabs to infer from Israel's public statements Israel's intent. A deal could have been made if any Arab leader would have been willing to publicly accept Israel's existence as a partner in the region. None did. The Arab world had neither the will, nor the interest.

Israel won the battle of the General Assembly. When a vote occurred on July 4, the Russians failed to obtain passage of any resolution that demanded Israeli withdrawal or censure. David beat Goliath in the UN, but Goliath was getting stronger. Things would soon change.

CHAPTER NINETEEN
And so it Began

Internationally, the first rumblings of Western discontent with Israel emerged just weeks after the war had ended. French President de Gaulle declared, "France condemns the opening of hostilities by ... Israel. France accepts as final none of the changes affected on the terrain through military action." De Gaulle's policy had serious implications for Israel's air force which had primarily used planes supplied by the French to win the Six-Day War. Later, de Gaulle refused to deliver fifty, advanced Mirage fighter planes manufactured in France that Israel had already contracted for. He also blocked delivery of spare parts for French planes in Israel's possession. The Jewish State needed to find a new friend and arms supplier.

That friend and supplier became the United States. Eban recorded that Secretary of State Dean Rusk was impressed that, after such an overwhelming victory, Israel was willing to give up most of her gains so quickly in return for a lasting peace. Also, Rusk worked for an American President who empathized with Israel's struggle to survive and who had decided not to force Israel to "accept a puny settlement." In addition, Israel's victory persuaded many members of Congress that, despite Israel's modest size, she could be a muscular ally in the Cold War. What's more, millions of American Evangelicals saw Israel's triumph as a pivotal moment. Some fervently believed that the Jewish State's victory was an act of divine intervention heralding the arrival of the messianic age. Others supported Israel for a variety of philosophical and religious reasons. As a result, America very quickly filled the political and military void left by France's change of attitude.

June 21 Visitors

Richard Nixon arrived in Tel Aviv on June 21, 1967 as a private citizen, but one with outsized ambitions. He had been a powerless vice president under President Eisenhower in the 1950's and a failed gubernatorial candidate in California in 1962. But in 1967 he was planning his presidential campaign for election in 1968.

While in Tel Aviv, Nixon met with Egyptian prisoners of war. An Egyptian tank commander told Nixon, "Russia is to blame ... they furnished the arms. We did the dying." Nixon understood that Nasser had been the aggressor in the 1967 war, but he thought the Russians largely responsible for the hostilities because they supplied the Arabs with arms and incited them. And Nixon did not think Israel should withdraw until peace was achieved but thought it would probably require the United States and Russia to guarantee it. On the other hand, Nixon had little concern for Israel independent of American interests—especially if turmoil in the Middle East impacted America's relationship with the Russians.

The same day Nixon arrived in Israel, Nasser welcomed President Nikolai Podgorny in Cairo. Podgorny was one of three leaders who then held power in the Soviet Union. The other two were Alexei Kosygin, the titular head of government, and Leonid Brezhnev, the First Secretary. In the early 1970's, both Kosygin and Podgorny lost a power struggle to Brezhnev for control of the Soviet Union. But in 1967, Podgorny was first in rank. In May he had played a role in initiating the 1967 war by falsely warning Egyptian Vice President Sadat that the Israelis were mobilizing on the Syrian border. Podgorny promised the Egyptians assistance to develop an air defense system, weapons to rearm Egyptian military forces, and military advisors to provide training. Nasser eagerly accepted. The Russian hook was set. Within months Russian advisors permeated the Egyptian army; their naval vessels were given access to ports in both Egypt and Syria, and Russian weapons poured into the country. A few weeks later, Podgorny promised the same to the Syrians. Once set, no matter how much the Arabs wriggled, the Russians knew their hook would be difficult to dislodge.

Within a week of Podgorny's visit, Russia delivered 130 new combat aircraft to partially offset Egypt's losses in the war. Within a year, virtually all of Egypt's losses were restored. In addition, thousands of Soviet instructors poured into the country. What had been a trickle became a virtual invasion. Russians became embedded in the Egyptian military throughout Egypt, and Russian ships were granted access to Egypt's ports—Russia's geopolitical desire for naval bases along the Mediterranean was fulfilled. Nasser's only setback was that the Russians refused his request to enter into a mutual defense pact.

And that same June 21, Yasser Arafat snuck from Jordan into the West Bank. It was three days before his thirty-eighth birthday. When Arafat was younger he worked and studied in Egypt. While in Egypt, he helped found the political and paramilitary group, Fatah, in 1959 when he was twenty-seven. Before coming to Egypt, he lived for a time in Jerusalem. In fact, his uncle's home where he had stayed as a child was in the same Moroccan quarter cleared by the Israelis on the evening of June 10 to make room for a plaza before the Wailing Wall.

Arafat was an unheralded beneficiary of the 1967 war. Initially, few knew him, but those that did whispered their admiration. As a result his reputation built. And he electrified with excitement many who came to know him, especially those not previously tied to the Hussein regime by allegiance or graft. The paths he traveled that year throughout the West Bank were his first steps on the road to international recognition.

After arriving in the West Bank, Arafat divided the region for organizational purposes into three sections: south (Hebron), central (Jerusalem), and north (Nablus). He also made contact with the few Fatah supporters not intimidated by events and encouraged them to recruit and build terrorist cells. Arafat used disguises to mask his movements as he laid groundwork for an eventual insurrection. His message was clear: Arab countries had failed the Palestinian people, and therefore, they could only depend on themselves. The PLO set up a rival council to counter Arafat's increasing influence. George Habash, another terrorist leader of a smaller faction, did so too. But Arafat's power continued to grow, even if his operational prowess did not.

That is not to say the path was clear and easy for Arafat. Despite the squalid and hate-filled refugee camps on the East Bank that were fertile grounds for Fatah to find recruits, most inhabitants of the West Bank were hesitant, at first, to follow him. Many thought that Israeli police treated them better than the Jordanians had and hoped that economic conditions would be better than before. Also, the tribal-elder system resisted Arafat's influence because the elders wanted to maintain the respect and power they had commanded under Jordanian rule. In addition, Israeli informants were busy bedeviling Arafat's recruiting and stifling his operations.

Settlers

While Arafat sought to raise support in the West Bank, an extraordinary meeting took place at Dafnah, a kibbutz situated at the northern tip of Israel in the shadow of the newly-won Golan Heights. It was a meeting only made possible by Israel's victory that stirred powerful forces within Israel's soul that would soon emerge. It was the dream and yearning to resettle Judea and Samaria, known otherwise as the West Bank. It was also the hope to place Jewish settlements on the Golan, in Gaza, and the Sinai. It was a dream that many did not even know they possessed until it was unlocked by Hussein's decision to go to war and by the IDF's success taking coveted land held by the Arabs. It was the beginning of the Jewish settler movement that, along with Yasser Arafat, rose to prominence as a result of emotions and desires unleashed by the 1967 war.

A week later some of those who attended the meeting drove east and across a narrow bridge that spanned the Jordan River. They headed for Naffakh on the Golan, where a Syrian army base was once located. A few buildings were scattered throughout the area. The land was poor. But it did not matter. It seemed the perfect place to start a new, Jewish settlement. The pioneering spirit of Israel's founders in the late nineteenth and early twentieth centuries was reborn. That spirit had a powerful political ally—Yigal Allon.

King Hussein

King Hussein was determined to recover the West Bank and Arab Jerusalem. He did not realize at that early date he was in a race against time with a settler movement within Israel. Hussein was plagued by his loss of what King Abdullah, his grandfather, had gained. But Hussein knew he required both Egypt's and America's assistance to succeed. From Egypt, Hussein needed political cover to shield him from Arab regimes that otherwise would criticize him for negotiating with Israel. Without Nasser's support he feared that Arabs within Jordan, along with Arabs worldwide, would turn on him. He also needed the Americans to put pressure on Israel to reach an agreement and to provide the economic and military support that would permit him to secure his throne.

When Nasser wrote to Hussein saying they must "put all we have in the service of the common destiny of our two peoples," it was clear evidence that the poisonous relationship between Egypt and Jordan that had existed before Hussein's visit on June 1 had changed. Nasser made the existence of their new bond crystal clear when he later told Hussein in Cairo, "We have entered this war together, lost it together and we must win it together." As a result of their meeting, Nasser gave Hussein the green light to negotiate with the United States to obtain the return of the lands he had lost—as long as he did not sign a peace treaty with Israel.

On June 26, King Hussein addressed the UN General Assembly. Ostensibly he was speaking on behalf of the Arab nations. However, it was unclear whether he had permission to do so from the more strident countries such as Syria. Hussein offered peace in return for all of the lost Arab territory but did not offer direct negotiations or a written peace treaty. In effect, all he offered was a return to the uncertainties that existed before the war. Nothing more tangible was offered by the king to prevent the same, or some future, Arab leadership, from threatening Israel's existence again.

Hussein had an opportunity to act courageously and directly. If he had, he might well have negotiated an agreement with Israel that satisfied core needs of both nations. But he failed to do so. Rather than publicly and unambiguously offer the same peaceful relations enjoyed and expected by most nations in the world, he only offered words that risked, for Israel, a return to a status quo that had previously had failed.

Jerusalem

During the evening of June 28, Jerusalem's Mayor, Teddy Kollek, and Moshe Dayan met on the terrace of the King David Hotel, a swanky hotel built by a wealthy Jewish Egyptian. Dating back to when the King David first opened its doors in 1931, it was the first choice for royalty visiting the area. Three different heads of state had set up within the King David's confines after they were deposed. Following the end of World War II, the British converted part of it into a military headquarters from which they administered Palestine before Israel declared statehood. While hosting the British, the hotel was targeted by Jewish extremists seeking to end Britain's oppressive rule in Palestine. Its southwestern corner, which housed the British offices, was destroyed in 1946 by a bomb placed by a branch of the Irgun, a militant Jewish extremist group. Also, the movie *Exodus*, filmed in 1960, contains an iconic scene shot from the hotel's rear balcony. To this day it remains not only a desired place to stay when visiting Jerusalem but a location steeped in history still being made. Its more recent guests have included Presidents Nixon, Ford, Carter, Clinton, and Bush as well as famous entertainment figures ranging from Elizabeth Taylor to Madonna.

The hotel is located in the center of Jerusalem and is situated along the armistice line that divided Jordan and Israel from 1948 to 1967. From its terrace there is a mesmerizing view of the minarets and stone walls of the Old City which carry so much religious and historical significance.

Dayan and Kollek, old acquaintances, met at the hotel to discuss the future of Jerusalem. Kollek was fifty-six years old. He was in the midst of serving the first of what would be six terms as Jerusalem's mayor. When Kollek was twenty-four he escaped Austria in 1937, three years before the Nazis seized power, and immigrated to Palestine. Years later he expressed his understanding of the responsibility he felt after the war ended:

> "When the city was united, I saw this as an historic occasion. To take care of it and show better care than anyone else has … I think Jerusalem is the one essential element in Jewish history. A body can live without an arm or a leg, not without the heart. This is the heart and soul of it."

Kollek was cautious. He wanted to reunify the city slowly, citing the danger of precipitously removing all restraints in one fell swoop. Kollek feared that if the authorities did not tread carefully, violence would burst forth due to latent resentments carried by both Arabs and Jews. He suggested to Dayan that, at first, they only open the new and old city for no more than two hours each day. During that time, citizens of Jewish Jerusalem and Arab Jerusalem could mix together. Then, over time, if all went well smoothly, security could be further relaxed.

Dayan sat back with his feet comfortably elevated on the table. He relished his new role as the de-facto "King of the Jews." Dayan saw himself as a man of action and displayed the casual air of a man comfortable with his self-created destiny. His career had been one of success built from decisiveness. Therefore, he disagreed with Kollek. Dayan sensed that Arabs and Jews would react positively to a *fait accompli*.

And he insisted on moving swiftly.

Dayan demanded that the fences delineating the old boundaries must come down as soon as possible. Previously, Dayan had been given estimates that it would take two months to remove the barriers and checkpoints that prevented free movement. Dayan responded then that he would only give two weeks for the government to finish the job. But, by the end of the evening on the terrace, he changed his mind. Dayan told Kollek all of the obstacles preventing exit and entry between the Arab and Jewish Jerusalem must be removed by the next morning. The cities would be integrated immediately.

Dayan's insistence on immediate integration was influenced by decisions made by the cabinet that had been publicized the day before. The cabinet planned to request Israel's legislative body, the Knesset, to pass three laws that collectively would amount to de facto annexation of all of the newly-occupied Jerusalem without saying so. The **first** law legitimized extending Israeli law into any part of Israel by administrative decree. The **second** authorized Kollek to alter the boundary of Jerusalem's city limits at his discretion. The **third** law guaranteed freedom of access to holy places of all religions. The third law was a significant declaration. Under the Old City's prior rulers, the Jordanians, religious freedom did not exist. Christianity was tolerated, but Jews were refused access to their religious sites and their most holy spots, including the Western Wall. Instead, the Jordanians permitted, if not countenanced, the desecration of Jewish synagogues and cemeteries.

The cabinet fully understood what the new laws would condone. The new land that Kollek would immediately incorporate within the city limits of Jerusalem would increase the size of the city twelvefold. The plan prioritized taking control of strategic hilltops and ridges and left room for significant construction of new homes for Jewish settlers. It also sought to avoid, as much as possible, bringing Arab villages into the newly-enlarged Jerusalem. Even so, 66,000 Arabs were added to the 200,000 Jewish residents of the City. Those Arabs, despite their status as residents in a Jewish-run city, would be permitted to choose whether or not they would accept Israeli citizenship.

The cabinet ministers hoped that, by not declaring Israel's annexation of Arab Jerusalem, their intent would be obscured and international uproar would be minimized. However, the announcement did not fool anybody. Its intent was clear, and so was its impact. The cabinet's decision was Israel's first assertion of her sovereignty over Israel's ancient homeland. Over time, the declaration contributed to Israel's loss of international support and forced Israel to rely more and more on America's friendship. But it also succeeded—Jerusalem would remain firmly in Israel's grasp.

By the morning after the Kollek-Dayan meeting, Israeli soldiers and government employees finished dismantling checkpoints, destroying sniper nests, removing landmines, and unraveling barbed wire that impeded freedom of movement. Within hours, huge numbers of Israelis freely crossed into the Old City. Many Arabs crossed peacefully into Jewish Jerusalem as well, thus relegating to the trash bin the fears of some that the Arabs would instigate violent acts. Both groups displayed curiosity rather than hatred: They freely examined each other's homes and shops, relished touring the newly-accessible sights, and despite the presence of women showing their bare arms and soldiers carrying their guns prominently, Arab storekeepers reveled in their many sales to Jewish customers.

Within days, technicians integrated the electrical, water, and telephone systems of Jewish and Arab Jerusalem. Soon, the Israeli government began to collect taxes in the newly-incorporated areas. Israeli banks replaced Jordanian ones, and ID cards with each person's name, age, and religion printed on them were distributed to the Arab residents. For a short while an atmosphere of friendship and peace prevailed.

The government's rush to eliminate the boundaries between pre-war Israel and Jerusalem mirrored the attitudes of Israeli citizens. Polls conducted in July of 1967 indicated that 91 percent of Israelis wanted to keep East Jerusalem permanently, 85 percent felt the same about the

Golan, and 71 percent wanted to hold onto the West Bank in its entirety. Only in the Sinai did polls indicate a roughly even division between those who wanted to retain it and those willing to return it to Egypt. One Israeli poet said, "The State and the land are henceforth one essence." That poet believed the bible obligated Jews to keep the newly won lands. But other intellectuals, such as Amoz Oz, were opposed to what was happening. His book, *Soldiers Talk*, contained a prescient prediction that would increasingly come to pass: "The feeling of [being in] an occupying army is an extraordinarily filthy feeling."

Just because Arabs and Jews were mingling without incident in and around Jerusalem did not mean all was normal on the West Bank. In order for the military government to better control the region, Israel administratively divided the West Bank into smaller districts. But Israeli soldiers in charge were trained to fight wars—not police the land. Physical confrontations increased, and concern mounted over the need to recover the many weapons and mounds of ammunition the Jordanians had left in their hasty retreat. The Israelis tried to confiscate what they could but were unable to discover all of the secret stashes of lethal items created by local Arabs. As a result, the tools for an insurgency remained; ready for use by those who would not accept the status quo. Soon the twin forces of Jewish administration and Arab terror would germinate hatred for the occupation within the hearts and minds of the local populace. Then, the desire and success of some Jews to return to lands that had religious significance or that were once controlled by Jews, would also fuel Palestinian rage. And sadly, any chance of dousing those angry flames was lost because many Palestinian leaders failed to grab the opportunity present during those early days to effect meaningful changes that would enhance the lives of their fellow Arabs. Instead, they stubbornly insisted on solutions that required Israel to relinquish newly-gained Jerusalem, a demand that would never be met for both political and emotional reasons.

Perhaps a moment should be taken to consider why Jerusalem was, and is, so important to most Jews. It was the capital of a vibrant Jewish nation 2,000 years ago under the leadership of King David. It was also home to the Second Temple, the last remaining remnant of the most religiously significant spot in Judaism; and during the 2,000 year diaspora when Jews were spread throughout the world without a land of their own, it served as a focal point for Jewish prayer and Jewish survival. The essence of Judaism points to Jerusalem as the one true home. The experience of Judaism: the suffering, torture and turmoil inflicted on its adherents when Jews lost their welcome in the many countries where they lived created recognition of a lasting need for a land where being Jewish was a blessing, not a sin. As such, Jerusalem is a symbol of freedom and its possession a harbinger of peace to Jews. To return Jerusalem to those who had defiled it, to those who had barred Jews from returning to their sacred religious sites, and to those that preached the extermination of Jews, would have rendered much of Jewish thought meaningless and would have rendered the sacrifices of so many useless and without meaning. No Jewish government, no Jewish leader could betray in such a way those who had voted them to power. It could not be, nor would it ever be.

That is not to say that Jerusalem is not important to others; in fact, it is crucial and vital to many. It contains religious sites that arouse passion for people of many faiths. The Dome of the Rock is the third-most important spot in Islam. King Hussein believed that he was a descendent of the Prophet Muhammad, who ascended to heaven from the Rock. The streets and hills of the Old City contain numerous sites where Christians believe Jesus walked, was persecuted, and died. The various religious sites should remain under the supervision of those who feel their calling. But Jews have no doubt the land belongs to them. It was once their home; it became their home again, and if they had gave it up, nowhere else on earth would mean the same. Thus, to re-take and then voluntarily return Jerusalem would have threatened the continued existence of Judaism and the nation.

But no matter how righteous Israel's claim to Jerusalem might have been, and still is, in the minds of those sympathetic toward suffering of any kind, Israel's argument unraveled. Within two weeks after the war ended, media outlets worldwide began reporting on the conditions endured by Arab refugees. Jordan was unable to cope with the influx of people. Older refugee camps in existence since the end of the 1948 war provided a threadbare existence to their present inhabitants. They lacked the capacity to shelter newcomers. New camps simply did not exist. When some refugees changed their minds and tried to return to the West Bank they found they had traveled a one-way street. Israeli soldiers did not permit them to return. Some were shot when they tried to sneak back in. Soon, heartbreaking pictures of refugees' suffering flooded the international news.

Moshe Dayan explained Israel's policy of refusing readmission into the West Bank by reminding reporters that only twenty days previously many of those same refugees had hoped for the extermination of Jews in Israel. Nevertheless, the international sympathy Israel had enjoyed less than a month earlier because of mounting Arab threats began to dissipate.

CHAPTER TWENTY
Two Months on the West Bank

The General Assembly ended its meeting on the Middle East crisis on July 4, 1967. For over two weeks they had debated resolutions criticizing Israel or that insisted that, under certain conditions, Israel withdraw from the newly, won territories. Some nations friendly to the Arab cause fought, without success, for a resolution that demanded unilateral Israeli withdrawal from the territories. Other nations argued that the Arab countries involved, as a pre-condition for Israeli withdrawal, should promise there would not be any further military confrontations.

*After a marathon, voting session where multiple formulations were rejected by enough nations to prevent passage, only two resolutions passed—both without dissent. **One** was purely humanitarian. It passed unanimously. The subject of the **second** was the status of Jerusalem. It passed 99 to 0 with twenty abstentions (including the United States). That resolution called on Israel to rescind the new laws passed regarding the city and declared them invalid. The resolution also demanded that Israel take no new measures to change the status of Jerusalem. Recognizing he was in a race against time, Prime Minister Eshkol reacted within days by ordering that Jewish neighborhoods be built in East Jerusalem as quickly as possible. Israel's cabinet responded by making it clear that Israel did not "claim unilateral control or exclusive jurisdiction in the holy places of Christianity and Islam," and then added, "In the peace settlement, we would be ready to give appropriate expression to this principle."*

On July 8, the UN Security Council reconvened; fighting had again broken out along the Suez Canal. What was unusual was that the meeting was requested by both Egypt and Israel. The Israelis accused the Egyptians of sending troops across the canal and shelling Israeli positions. Two days later, the Security Council decided to place observers on both sides of the canal to monitor and prevent further ceasefire violations.

And, despite supporting Israel in the UN, the United States pressured the Jewish State to develop a policy for the West Bank. The Americans hoped to arrange a secret meeting between Israel and Hussein. They were unaware that a meeting (discussed below) had already occurred. Israel responded by playing for time, hoping for a favorable outcome of their covert conversations with Hussein, and for a positive outcome from the Arab Summit scheduled for the beginning of September. The last thing the Israelis wanted was American pressure at that delicate moment, but they knew it would be difficult to hold off the United States much longer. So, on July 18, they told American diplomats that they would have a response in approximately two weeks.

But the Americans were unwilling to wait. Two days later, when Foreign Minister Eban arrived in New York, he learned that the United States had reached agreement with Russia on a resolution which stated:

> The General Assembly affirms the principle that conquest of territory by war is inadmissible under the UN Charter and calls on all parties to the conflict to withdraw, without delay, their forces from the territories occupied by them after June 4, 1967." The resolution also affirmed "likewise the principle of acknowledgement, without delay, by all member states in the area, that each of them enjoys the right to maintain an independent national state, and to live in peace and security, as well as to renounce all claims and all acts inconsistent therewith.

Eban was apoplectic. The proposed resolution would demand that Israel relinquish all of her gains with little recompense. It was also inconsistent with Johnson's speech of June 19 in which he clearly stated that a return to the conditions of June 4th was a prescription for a renewal of war. The word "Israel" did not even appear in the *new Resolution. Eban was angry, inconsolable, and later complained vehemently to Arthur Goldberg, America's UN Ambassador. Goldberg refused to compromise.*

But good fortune intervened in the form of a message that arrived just when Eban's conversation with Ambassador Goldberg was ending—The Egyptians and Libyans had rejected the proposed resolution. They refused to acknowledge, in any fashion, Israel's rights in return for an IDF withdrawal. The opportunity for an agreement between the superpowers was gone.

Secret Meeting

King Hussein furtively tried to gauge how willing Israel was to return his lands. On July 2, he visited Jordanian war wounded being treated in British hospitals in London. But that was not the real reason for his presence. Instead, he had arranged, once again, a secret meeting with Yaacov Herzog.

Hussein appeared sad and resigned, but not bitter or angry. Despite his depression, he also was in some ways relieved because his stature in Arab eyes had grown due to Jordan's sacrifices. His motives were no longer doubted, nor was his loyalty to Muslim causes.

Herzog asked Hussein for his thoughts regarding the war.

"In your place I would have acted the same way," answered the king.

Hussein told Herzog that the Arabs had made great mistakes; and, by failing to caution his Arab brethren about the path they were heading down, he, too, had made a mistake. Hussein admitted to Herzog that, in 1965, there was an Arab resolution at a meeting in Morocco to go to war within three years, before Israel would have nuclear weapons. But he denied that Egypt and Syria had intended to start a war with Israel in June. As Hussein put it, "One of the great failures of the Arabs is the confusion between words and deeds."

Herzog asked Hussein whether he thought there would be peace in the future—or more war. Hussein resolutely told him that there could only be peace if it was "peace with honor and nobility," but he admitted that extremists wanted a much different path. Hussein explained, "Not only you have rights. We also have rights. Do not push us into a corner.... So much depends in the coming weeks on how you behave and how we behave. Be careful of our emotions. Treat them with respect and understanding."

Hussein assured Herzog that he was pushing for a productive, Arab summit, but if the other Arab nations could not agree on how to address their issues with Israel, he would feel free to act as he wished. Herzog answered that it was important that Hussein understood that an attack on any Jew in Israel, whether a farmer or a random individual, was an attack on all Israelis. He further explained that Israelis felt joined to the land. They were not refugees living in a strange place. They were a people with a historical, eternal link to the land of Israel.

Hussein then told Herzog how the Samu attack had devastated him personally. He explained that, for him, it was vivid proof that, in Israel's eyes, there was no difference between Jordan and Syria. No difference at all, even though Jordan had tried to curb terrorist activity (as acknowledged by Israel before Samu) while, at the same time, Syria had continued to encourage and support the Fedayeen.

Hussein also told Herzog that he would enter into direct negotiations with Israel if he knew in advance that all substantive issues, including his lost territory, were open to discussion. In essence he wanted some form of assurance before risking his neck. But in keeping with Israel's policy, Herzog could only respond that Israel would not discuss what the negotiations might achieve until the king stated formally, and publicly, that he would enter into direct peace negotiations with Israel. Israel had no interest in making painful concessions to an Arab leader who required that the mere fact that they were speaking be kept quiet. Thus, without a public gesture that demonstrated Jordan's recognition of the Jewish State, and commitment to live in peace with it, little progress could be made.

Even though it was a private meeting, Hussein placed himself in great political and physical danger when he agreed to meet with Herzog again. But he was desperate to recover his lost lands and knew, for that to occur, he would have to establish a relationship of some kind with Israel. They parted ways with the understanding that Hussein would push for a unified Arab agreement to move towards peace at a summit meeting he planned to promote. If that failed, Hussein would move unilaterally towards peace. In the interim, Israel would wait.

Nevertheless, the Israelis had little faith in Hussein. They still felt betrayed by Hussein's decision to join with Egypt by opening a second front against Israel a month earlier. In part, because of that, they were not willing to pay the price that Hussein demanded. And they were right to be concerned about the price. Hussein subsequently said, "I'll make peace, and I'll do it alone, but I have to get everything back to do it."

A few days later Nasser bestowed upon Hussein a partial green light to pursue peace talks. Nasser told him that it would be all right for the king to speak indirectly to Israel, but there could be no direct negotiations and no formal peace treaty. Nasser, however, was determined to follow a different path. He made no effort to approach the Israelis. Instead, he closed the canal to shipping, sank the ships trapped within it to further block international usage of the waterway, and Egyptian military units precipitated firefights with Israeli soldiers. Even though Hussein had a green light, Nasser kept his red.

West Bank Policies

The same day Hussein met with Herzog in London, Israel's cabinet met to discuss the growing humanitarian crisis ensnaring Palestinian refugees who had fled to Jordan after the war. International pressure was mounting to address the plight of those who left the West Bank, changed their minds, and wanted to return. Eleven cabinet ministers overrode opposition from Eshkol and six others when they voted to permit

Palestinians who had left the West Bank between June 7 and July 4 to return by August 10, so long as they posed no threat to Israel.

In addition, throughout July, Israeli Government representatives met more than twenty times with twenty-five different, mostly pro-Hussein, Palestinian leaders. But those talks failed to progress because the Palestinians insisted that Israel must agree to relinquish the parts of Jerusalem previously controlled by Jordan. Perhaps the international backlash to Israel's de-facto annexation of Jerusalem influenced them not to moderate their demands. In the midst of those meetings the Palestinians requested permission from the Israeli military government to convene a meeting of eighty-three notables to discuss the political future of the West Bank. The Israelis refused, concerned the meeting would only help facilitate creation of a more-organized, political voice that would disrupt the occupation, a voice that extremists would eventually co-opt. But Israel's denial had a long term cost. By impeding the Palestinian political process, it only increased the likelihood that the Palestinian's would eventually choose a more violent path.

Dayan, however, hoped to reduce conflict by instituting policies that would increase the likelihood that Arabs on the West Bank would be born, live, and die without having to deal with any Israelis. And in order to promote the region's economy he instituted an "open bridges" policy over the Jordan River that permitted trade between the West Bank and Jordan. The Israelis also selectively rewarded some Palestinian leaders who seemed more inclined to promote peace by lifting some restrictions that impacted them. However, Israel's "cooperation" incentives did not convince Palestinian leaders to join the expanded Jerusalem Municipal Council. Most refused to cooperate with the Israelis because of leaflets warning of reprisals against collaborators distributed by Fatah terrorists. In the fall, Israel ended the failed reward program because those that received the favorable treatment were viewed by other Palestinians as "Quislings." Once labeled, even if they survived retribution, the

"Quislings" influence among fellow Arabs would then be severely diminished.

Little more than six weeks after the end of the war, opposition to Israel's occupation notably increased throughout the West Bank. On July 24, twenty-four Muslim notables met on the *al-Haram al-Sharif* (the Temple Mount). They included both religious and secular leaders, such as the former Arab Mayor of Jerusalem. The notables publicly refused to cooperate with Israel's virtual annexation of land into greater Jerusalem's new boundary. They also refused to submit their Friday religious sermons to the Israelis for review, as was required by the occupying authorities. They called themselves the Islamic Council, which, they declared, would be responsible for Islamic affairs in Jerusalem and the West bank. The Council's statement contained one interesting reference and one equally important omission: They acknowledged that Arab Jerusalem was part of Jordan, they did not make reference to a Palestinian entity.

The Israelis tried to muzzle the Council members by exiling some of them to towns in the West Bank or Israel. The Israelis hoped, as stated in an old Arab proverb, to, "Extract the tooth and extract the pain with it." It didn't work. The deportations only hardened the attitudes of local leaders; acts of civil disobedience began to occur.

However, some Arabs on the West Bank were not eager to return to Jordanian rule. Chief among them were Palestinian Fatah terrorists filtering back into the area. In addition, many leaders were open to exploring self-rule rather than returning to Jordanian domination. They had not forgotten Jordan's repressive policies. Their lack of consensus with other Palestinians undercut some Israeli leaders who had called for creating a new Palestinian State federated with Jordan.

Israel's cabinet was aware of the problems. The ministers knew they needed to develop a policy that addressed the future of the West Bank. Allon was the first to submit a plan to the cabinet for consideration. He argued that, to maintain Israel's security, the IDF must retain control of a strip of land about six to nine miles wide that stretched along the entire border with the Jordan River. That land is hot, flat, and dusty. It separates the Judean hills to the west from the narrow Jordan River. Few people lived there in the mostly forlorn desert. Allon argued that, by holding this narrow strip, the IDF would retain a defensive advantage over Jordanian, Iraqi, and other Arab troops, who would have to engage in a costly river crossing under heavy fire before being able to attack. In addition, Allon said that Israel needed to retain a band of territory around the Latrun salient to prevent Jerusalem from being cut off from the rest of Israel, as happened in 1948. In order to hold the territory he deemed crucial, Allon suggested building permanent settlements and military bases there.

Everywhere else, other than in the newly-incorporated areas around Jerusalem, Allon advocated negotiating with the Palestinians to turn the West Bank into an autonomous region. He also supported construction of two roads. The **first** would be a narrow road that led through Jericho to connect Palestinians to Jordan. The **second** was a north-south road to join the northern Palestinian enclave he envisioned on the West Bank to a southern one.

Moshe Dayan did like Allon's idea. Dayan proposed a "four fists" approach. He wanted to construct each fist on the ridge of the Judean hills that overlooked the desert stretch along the Jordan River. They would be built near the large Arab cities of Jenin, Nablus, Ramallah, and Hebron. Within each fist he suggested establishing an army base surrounded by civilian settlements. In essence, Dayan wanted to defend the interior of Israel from the ridgelines, not the water's edge of the Jordan. Dayan's political solution was that Israel would continue her rule over the Arabs on the West Bank, but the Palestinians would remain Jordanian citizens. That was his solution even though it would comingle citizens of two nationalities within one area under Israeli control.

Some of Prime Minister Eshkol's angst arose from the historical link between Israelis and Jews in general with portions of the West Bank. The anguish and pain of 1948, after all, was not so distant a memory; if he failed to approve construction of a permanent settlement on the hallowed ground of the former Etzion Bloc, Eshkol knew his guilt would be unbearable. The same was true for Beit HaAraveh, a Kibbutz along the northern tip of the Dead Sea abandoned in 1948. Eshkol wanted to repopulate it with Jews. He also could not forget Hebron, home of the Tomb of the Patriarchs. Hebron was the burial place of Abraham, Sarah, Isaac, Rebecca, Jacob, and Leah. It was a location linked to the foundation of Judaism, and also the site of Jewish suffering at the hands of Arab rioters before World War II. Setting aside his dreams to redress those memories was something that did not come easily to Eshkol.

Faced with the competing visions of its leaders, the cabinet once again was unable to agree. Nor were they pushed, or given any incentive, by the Arab world to end the conflict. Since the Syrians and Egyptians would neither demonstrate nor enunciate peaceful intent, Hussein was the only hope for breaking the political logjam. But Hussein would not publicly offer peace without first receiving Israeli assurances that Arab Jerusalem and the entire West Bank would be returned to his control. Of course, that was an assurance Israel would never give ahead of a negotiation to iron out the details of a lasting peace. In the absence of public announcements by Arab governments of their willingness to talk peace with Israel, American pressure on Israel to clarify her position on Jerusalem soon dissipated. And in the absence of international pressure, no domestic pressure could build to take security risks that required the cabinet to make painful decisions. It simply would not have made sense for the cabinet to unilaterally adopt a risky stance without an Arab partner proving their willingness to do so as well. It was not the first time, nor would it be the last, that lack of courageous Arab leadership doomed the region to a violent future.

By late summer the cabinet decided to build five Israeli army bases along the West Bank ridgeline. But they never formally agreed to adopt either Dayan's plan or Allon's. And the ministers shied away from permitting Israeli citizens to establish settlements. They did so because the majority hoped to avoid being condemned by the international community for approving permanent resettlement of the occupied territories (as they had experienced after effectively annexing territory surrounding Jerusalem).

Fortunately, although Jewish and Arab leaders could not agree on a political plan for the West Bank, in early August Dayan was able to lessen the economic burden weighing on its inhabitants. When he went to Damia, where the Jordan River was especially shallow, Dayan witnessed hundreds of Arab trucks crossing from the West Bank to the eastern (Jordanian) side of the Jordan River loaded with tomatoes, potatoes, peaches, and apples. The rudimentary commerce that required crossing and re-crossing the river was against Israeli policy because it made it easier for terrorists to infiltrate and for refugees to return. But it was good for the Palestinian economy. Dayan said, "There'll be a lot of pressure building up on the West Bank and this opening will be a valve." Consequently, he sought Hussein's approval to rebuild the Allenby and Adam bridges that had spanned the Jordan before the Israelis destroyed them during the war. The king agreed, but only under the condition that Jordan rebuild them. Within months those new spans were used to facilitate movement between Palestinians on the West Bank and Arabs to the east of the Jordan River. Eventually, the Israelis permitted Palestinians to sell and transport to Jordan industrial equipment built on the West Bank, along with fresh fruit and produce. Thus, even though Israelis and Jordanians could not find their way to a political settlement, and because of Hussein's fears, did not communicate directly at the highest levels, they did find a way to cooperate to the benefit of West Bank inhabitants and the people of Jordan. Nevertheless, trouble was always just around the corner. Dayan admitted, "We've held the territories for over two months and we still can't see the end."

Then, as was inevitable—political, religious, and historical forces coalesced around the desire of increasing numbers of Jews to build settlements and live in the West Bank. On August 2, in Jerusalem on the Mount of Olives, Dayan gave voice to the dreams of many when he said in a ceremony commemorating the re-interment of Israeli soldiers who had died fighting to save Jerusalem during the 1948 war:

> We have not abandoned your dream [of those who fell] and we have not forgotten your lesson. We have returned to the mountain [the hill country of the West Bank], to the cradle of our people, to the inheritance of the Patriarchs, the land of the judges and the fortress of the Kingdom of the House of David. We have returned to Hebron and [Nablus}, to Bethlehem and Anatot, to Jericho and the fords of the Jordan at Adam Ha'air.

Dayan could not have been more transparent. Israel was not leaving the new territories; instead, some Israelis were coming to them. Then, in early August, the Land of Israel Movement was founded by Rabbi Moshe Levinger. The trickle of Israelis yearning to live in the ancient Jewish lands of Judea and Samaria (biblical names for the southern and northern portions of the West Bank) eventually turned into a torrent. Israel would never be the same.

But, even though economic conditions had improved on the West Bank, the plight of those Arabs who had left and wanted to return grew worse. Israel was not eager to repatriate from Jordan 100,000 or more displaced Arabs. Israel's bureaucracy, fueled by a deep-seated reluctance to facilitate the desires of Palestinians that fled, delayed two weeks before establishing a process, consistent with the cabinet's July 2nd decision, to manage their return.

Then, another three weeks were lost over an application drafted by Israel that Arabs wishing to return would have to fill out. When the Jordanians received the proposed document on July 17, they rejected it.

The Jordanians were apoplectic because it contained a caption on Israeli letterhead that read, "State of Israel, Ministry of Interior, Application for Permit to Return to the West Bank." The Jordanians thought it implied that the West Bank was part of Israel. And they were not willing to countenance joint use of any document which contained a suggestion that the Jordanian government was working directly with Israel. Negotiations ensued. Finally, the Jordanians and Israelis agreed that there would be a triple header at the top of the page that contained reference to Jordan, Israel, and the Red Cross. But another snag then developed when Israel demanded direct contact between high-level representatives of Israel and Jordan to work out final details. Israel backed down, but only after the United States applied pressure on her to do so. Finally, on August 6, an agreement was reached.

Israel's cabinet agreed, due to the delays, to extend the August 10 return deadline to August 31. Beginning on August 12, applications were distributed, and people started returning six days later. Tens of thousands of families submitted applications that listed the names of substantially more than a 100,000 Arabs. But Israel only permitted up to 3,000 per day to re-enter the West Bank and did not allow any Arabs to return on Saturdays due to the Jewish Shabbat. Probably, the Israeli restrictions were based on obstinacy coupled with the logistical difficulty of processing thousands of people each day. But, whatever the reason, the new arrangements left room for only 36,000 Arabs to return, in addition to 150 designated hardship cases, during the remaining days left under the deadline.

However, the number of Palestinians that managed to cross back to the West Bank turned out to be far less than 36,150. Organizational difficulties interfered. The Israelis would only approve applications the day before entry was permitted. But the refugees were scattered in many camps. The difficulty of finding and transporting the chosen few was great. Jordan charged that Israel needlessly created too many hurdles for them to overcome. Israel countered that it was Jordan's intentional inefficiency, designed to keep the refugee problem on the world center stage that was the real problem—a problem that could only be alleviated by direct face-to-face negotiations—something that Jordan routinely refused to do. In the end, approximately 14,000 were legally able to return.

The snafus and delays were not all due to Israel. Israeli suspicions and fears were raised by foolish statements such as one by a Jordanian minister on August 7 that said, "Every refugee should return to help his brothers to continue their political actions and remain a thorn in the flesh of the aggressor until the crisis has been resolved." It was no wonder that Israel was being exceedingly careful of who they allowed back into the West Bank.

Nor was King Hussein providing any help in cutting through the red tape at that pivotal moment. The weekend before the final negotiations with Israel regarding the refugees, Hussein hosted a party in his holiday home in Aqaba, a town along the Red Sea adjacent to the Israeli port of Eilat. One of the guests was Linda Christian and her attractive daughter. Christian, a faded Hollywood actress, had an unsavory reputation. Two of her most important claims to fame were being the first "Bond" girl in the 1954 television adaptation of *Casino Royale* and her seven year marriage with movie star Tyrone Power in the 1950's. Perhaps Hussein's reputation or proclivity as a playboy overtook him. Christian laced his food and drink, along with the refreshments of the other guests, with LSD. The king did not eat the food, but the same cannot be said for the drink. Hussein became violently ill. He had trouble understanding where his body ended and the chair he sat on began. An American summoned to help the king found him catatonic. Two American doctors were brought from Athens to treat him.

By the middle of August, the seeds of unrest on the West Bank germinated. Some Palestinians called for a general strike. Palestinians began joining various groups from which they coordinated opposition activities. The Israelis responded vigorously with shop closures, license revocations of the Arab bus line, and arrests. But Israel's response more impacted shop owners and Arab notables than the terrorists whose activities they were designed to disrupt. The Israelis also tried to rid Palestinian school curricula of anti-Israeli propaganda. In the end, their efforts, rather than obscuring the occupation as Dayan hoped, emphasized to West Bank residents the pervasive sweep of Israeli control.

On August 20, Fatah leadership decided to take advantage of the increasing discontent by resuming their guerilla campaign before the end of the month. They did so, even though Fatah's sway had plateaued on the West Bank. Hussein's policy of continuing to pay the salaries of civil servants served to maintain his influence, much to the dismay of Fatah recruiters.

Arafat established his base in Nablus and began rudimentary training for recruits in clandestine locations. He also hoped to organize acts of civil disobedience to supplement terrorist activity. Eventually, he hoped to merge the two into a revolution. While traveling in disguise throughout the West Bank, Arafat once reportedly returned to his childhood home in Jerusalem where he saw his brother in a doorway but could not call out to him for fear of being recognized.

Arafat's chosen path was made difficult because Israel had confiscated Jordanian security service files after overrunning the West Bank. Those files were valuable because of the effectiveness of Jordanian and Egyptian domestic security agencies before the war. Also important, the Israelis secured the cooperation of one of Jordan's former intelligence officers who facilitated use of the West Bank files. As a result, Fatah infrastructure on the West Bank was shattered. Nevertheless, despite the intelligence coup, Arab terrorists stayed focused on the West Bank rather than Gaza. The long border with the West Bank was much easier to traverse than a dangerous journey to isolated Gaza.

Israel responded by ramping up her response to the terrorist threat. The Israelis demolished homes of suspected sympathizers and established inflexible curfews that impaired economic activity. They also searched caves and other hideouts within the region. Hundreds of suspected Fedayeen were rounded up and held without trial.

In the end, Arafat's first attempt to organize on the West Bank failed. He had no infrastructure from which he could build an indigenous terrorist organization. He also failed to win over many new adherents to his cause; Palestinian leaders and many others were too financially dependent on Jordan. In addition, those leaders expected there would be a political settlement that would return the West Bank to King Hussein's control, and, therefore, they feared his retribution if they threw their lot in with Fatah.

On August 27, Israel's cabinet met again. It was only a few days before the start of an Arab Summit meeting in Khartoum. International pressure was mounting to permit more of the Arabs that had fled to return to the West Bank. Israel responded by approving another 6,000 potential returnees. But, like before, few successfully navigated the hurdles to return. Eshkol was not too concerned. He believed the plight of those who had left and were unable to return should be resolved within the context of an overall resolution of the West Bank issue.

On July 3rd the Israeli cabinet considered Yigal Allon's proposal to establish two or three temporary, work camps on the Golan. Their purported purpose was to house laborers who would work the land. He suggested calling the camps "experimental farms" rather than settlements in order to more easily pass muster with the international community, and he suggested populating them with reservists so their civilian purpose could be disguised as a military one. Since Allon was Labor Minister, he had access to the money required to fund the program if the cabinet approved. However, the cabinet could not reach a final decision on the issue. Their failure to authorize the Allon plan left a policy void. On July 16, facts on the Golan filled the void. A settler exited his jeep at a former Syrian military base. Within days others straggled in. A new settlement was born.

Almost two months later, on August 27, the cabinet approved Allon's proposal to permit establishment of a work camp on the Golan, with the goal of working the land. Eshkol would not go so far as to approve the establishment of permanent settlements, but he agreed that workers could use buildings already present and maintain preexisting orchards. Anything more would have to wait. In addition, the cabinet approved a proposal to operate experimental, agricultural stations which had been built by Egypt in the northern Sinai, near El-Arish.

The door for settlement activity was ajar.

CHAPTER TWENTY-ONE
Khartoum

King Hussein had vivid memories of coping with the vicious propaganda Cairo and Damascus spewed before the war that inflamed his Palestinian subjects. He also knew the influx of Palestinian refugees into Jordan from the West Bank, still living in terrible conditions near the eastern bank of the Jordan River, was the source of much potential instability. To make matters worse, the war had taken a heavy toll on his still-loyal army. As a result, it was much less able to handle domestic unrest. Therefore, Hussein was determined to ensure he had the support of other Arab nations before negotiating with Israel. Without it, he feared that external criticism would fuel internal unrest which could topple him from power. In addition, Jordan's financial predicament was an urgent problem. Losing the West Bank had dealt a heavy blow to the Jordanian economy, and the needs of the refugees increased his burden. Hussein knew that, in addition to their political support, he would need financial assistance from the oil-producing Arab nations

Fortunately for the king, Nasser's agenda aligned with his. Egypt also required financial assistance. The Egyptian army needed rebuilding, but Nasser lacked the resources to do so. The Suez Canal, a major source of revenue, was no longer operational. Tourism had dwindled. The only practical answer to Egypt's economic problems was to solicit help from the Arab oil producing nations.

Therefore, both Egypt and Jordan had much more pressing needs than fighting Israel. Hussein wanted the West Bank back but did not want to have to fight for it. Nasser needed time to rebuild his army before confronting the Jewish State again. The Russians were willing to supply the weapons to the Egyptians, but not for free. Nasser needed money to buy them. Both Nasser and Hussein hoped that the upcoming Khartoum summit, scheduled to begin on August 29, would bring relief.

However, Nasser's problems were not limited to money and prestige.

Two days before the Khartoum summit, Nasser received warnings that members of the military were planning a coup to remove him from power. They were led by Nasser's former friend and partner, General Amer. Amer had been in control of Egypt's armed forces from 1962 until Nasser fired him shortly after the Six-Day War ended. Nevertheless, even though he bore heavy responsibility for Egypt's defeat, Amer remained popular within the military. Nasser responded to the information decisively. He ordered Amer detained and placed under house arrest, along with the generals who supported him. Two weeks later, Amer committed suicide. Nasser's complicity in that supposed voluntary act remains a mystery.

With his political flanks protected, Nasser headed to Khartoum for the Arab summit.

The Conference

On August 29, the heads of state of eight Arab league members and ministers from four other Arab nations gathered in Khartoum for a summit meeting. In addition, Shuqayri was present in his capacity as Chairman of the PLO. Their agreement to meet caused controversy in the Arab world. Syria refused to attend because the Syrian leadership feared the conference would be used by moderate leaders, such as Hussein, as cover for caving into Israeli demands. Perhaps in recognition of the extraordinary nature of the conference, and the risks to participants if information leaked regarding what was said, each leader was only permitted to bring one aide into the meeting room. Note-taking was barred.

The first item on the agenda was whether to resume the war with Israel. The heat of the rhetoric within the room must have matched the hot air outside. The president of Iraq, the Algerian representative, and PLO Chairman Shuqayri castigated Nasser for agreeing to a ceasefire. Shuqayri pressured the Egyptian leader to resume the fighting. He accused Egypt and Jordan of betraying the Palestinian cause and adamantly declared that the military struggle against Israel must continue without pause—without regard for the cost. He labeled anyone who refused a traitor. Nasser inwardly seethed at the suggestion that Egypt had failed in her duty to the Arab cause. Palestinian provocation was one of the root causes of the war, but thousands of Egyptians, not Palestinians, died as a result. Everyone in the room knew, leading up to the war, that Shuqayri played politics and had made stirring, provocative speeches predicting doom for the Jews, but he had never created an effective resistance movement. However, even though the Palestinians had shed little blood for a war that supported their cause, Nasser still felt obligated to respond.

Nasser bluntly stated that Egypt was not in a position to fight at the moment. He added that Egypt and Jordan had borne the brunt of the devastating losses; as a result, there was no chance that the Arabs could win a military confrontation with Israel in the near future. Further, he said, that although the Russians were willing to provide new armaments, they were reluctant to give the Arabs offensive weapons. Therefore, the lost territories would have to be regained by political means, not force. He also warned that the longer the Arabs took to find a way to push the Israelis to leave, the more difficult it would be to dislodge them. To amass sufficient political pressure, he pronounced, it would require pressuring Israel in the UN and the assistance of both Russia and the West. Hussein strongly supported Nasser's comments. Surprisingly, King Faisal of Saudi Arabia supported Nasser, as well, even though he and Nasser actively supported opposing sides in the war in Yemen.

To pressure the West, Iraq suggested continuing the Arab oil boycott. But that presented economic problems for those Arab nations that depended on the money oil exports provided. In addition, Egypt and Jordan needed financial assistance. If there was a boycott they could hardly request help from the same nations that were being asked by the conferees to take steps that would reduce their own oil revenues. Saudi Arabia and Kuwait opposed Iraq's suggestion. They decided helping Egypt and Jordan financially would be better than refusing to sell oil to nations that were friendly to Israel. However, their assistance came at a price. Egypt had to agree to withdraw her troops from Yemen and work towards settling the dispute there.

All that remained when the conference ended was to issue a joint resolution from the nations present. This was done on September 1. The first sentence gave lip service to Hussein's goal of obtaining political cover for him to work in a peaceful manner towards withdrawal of Israeli forces from the West Bank. It read:

> The Arab Monarchs and heads of state agreed on unifying their efforts to political action on the international and diplomatic level to remove the traces of aggression, and to ensure the withdrawal of Israeli forces from the Arab territories that have been occupied since June 5.

If that was all that had been said, it might have provided a framework from which fruitful negotiations would have ensued. But Iraq, Algeria, and the PLO charged that the language amounted to surrender. As a result of their emphatic objections, another sentence was added. That sentence was to have lasting impact and shutdown any hope of resolving the dispute with Israel for years to come. In reference to the first sentence calling for a political process, it clarified:

> This is within the framework of the basic principles by which the Arab states abide, namely: <u>no peace with Israel, or recognition of</u>

<u>her, no negotiations with her</u>, and the upholding of the Palestinian people in their homeland." [Underlining added by the author]

Hussein fought hard against including what amounted to, "the three no's"—no peace, no recognition, and no negotiation with Israel—within the resolution. He knew that, despite the absence of any language calling for the destruction of Israel, it was a recipe for gridlock not negotiation. Even though Arab nations with a more moderate perspective interpreted the resolution as only requiring prior consultation and pan-Arab approval before any nation entered into a separate peace with Israel, they were bound to keep the basis of their interpretation (what had been said during the meeting) private. Therefore, they remained silent. And, by constantly referring to the plain meaning of "the three no's" in press conferences, the PLO ensured that the resolution would be interpreted in its most negative construction possible by Israel.

Nevertheless, Nasser did give Hussein his blessing to try negotiating his own deal with Israel in private, as long as he did not engage in direct talks and/or enter into a peace treaty. Nasser also did not explicitly call for Israel to withdraw from the Sinai. He accepted that recovering the West Bank came first.

Not surprisingly, Israel took a dim view of the Khartoum resolution. The Israelis interpreted "the three no's" as it was written; a sign that the Arabs were not willing to compromise. Some historians, however, have subsequently argued that moderate Arabs had a different (tortured) slant. They say that moderate Arabs thought the "the three no's" meant:
- No refusal to talk through third parties;
- No rejection of peace just of a formal treaty, and
- No Acceptance of Israel's existence by policy, but realization she existed in fact.

But Israel had been clear from the end of the Six-Day War there would be no withdrawal without direct negotiations and a peace treaty.

The resolution defiantly declared that there would be neither. Nor could any other meaning have been gleaned from its words absent a convoluted interpretation with no basis other than naïve hope.

One historian has suggested that because Israel possessed a secret tape recording of the Summit meeting obtained by the CIA, that Israel knew, despite the wording of the resolution, the Arabs were prepared to negotiate. However, even if that were true, there is a vast difference between private conversations and public statements. What is said in private often remains private and never becomes publicly acknowledged. Much of the difficulty resolving issues between Arabs and Jews in the Middle East was because Arab leaders failed to publicly recognize Israel's right to exist. After having fought a war of national survival and won, Israel would never agree to return to the previous status quo. The Israeli government saw the Khartoum resolution as a public rejection of Israel's June 19 offer to return to the prior borders with Egypt and Syria, subject to possible adjustments for Israel's security needs, in return for recognition and peace. If Khartoum is their position, Prime Minister Eshkol said, "We stay here." He made clear the Arabs were only, "Playing chess with oneself."

Despite "the three no's" Hussein believed the moderates had won in Khartoum. But West Bank Palestinians were displeased. If it was a "win," West Bank Palestinians were not aware of it. Even though Hussein convinced the attendees to focus on West Bank issues, the Palestinians felt he, and the other Arab nations, had abandoned them. They also thought the resolution lacked urgency and resolve. It would not be long before they began to explore, with increased fervor, the notion of negotiating directly with the Israelis.

So goes the byzantine world of the Middle East where both Palestinians and Israelis interpreted the same resolution in completely different ways. The Palestinians felt it was not strong enough, and the Israelis understandably were unable to find any solace from "the three no's" that some Arabs thought should have somehow been intuitively interpreted by Israel as three yes's.

Nor did Fatah feel restrained by the conference proceedings. While the Arab leaders deliberated in Khartoum, Fatah launched its first terrorist attacks on Israel since the end of the war. On a farm, a bomb killed a Jewish boy and wounded his parents. Fedayeen blew up a kibbutz factory too. Terrorists also derailed a freight train, and a bomb was discovered at a Tel Aviv movie theater. Fatah hoped to force the Israelis to respond in an indiscriminate fashion that would further inflame the Arab world and motivate more Arabs to take up the sword by joining their organization.

The Syrians also tried stirring the pot. A Ba'ath party conference convened in Damascus in early September. While it was in session, a Syrian-controlled, Damascus radio broadcast announced:

> By means of a Fedayeen struggle we will retrieve Palestine and tear the Zionist settlement out by the roots. Fedayeen war will bring us Tel Aviv today, and tomorrow to Haifa. Because of the Fedayeen, Israelis will swarm to the sea and airports to flee Israel.

Cleary the Syrians had something violent in mind. There was no other justification for reopening army bases for Fedayeen training, two of which were located near Damascus. Syria was not yet ready to permit Fedayeen raids from Syrian territory into Israel, but Syrian drums were once again beginning to pound.

Neither did the Egyptians cease their aggressive tactics in the days after the conference. On September 4, two Israeli patrol boats were in international waters near the Egyptian Port Tewfik, at the southern end of the Suez Canal. The Egyptians warned them that if they continued moving northwest towards the port they would be fired on. The vessels, however, did not stop, and the Egyptians began shooting. The IDF responded, and artillery shelling spread along the entire 101-mile-long

Suez Canal. After that day, Egyptian shells soared almost daily through the air over the canal towards IDF positions. The IDF responded vigorously. Soldiers of both armies huddled in shelters and endured the concussion of artillery shells exploding. The ceasefire, supposedly agreed to by Egypt and Israel, continued to exist in name, but not in deed.

The Aftermath

On September 10, just ten days after the Khartoum Resolution shattered any hope of an imminent, peaceful resolution to the conflict, Israel's cabinet met and once again discussed settling the newly-won lands. One view expressed, applicable to the West Bank and Gaza, was that the occupied lands were stateless prior to the war. Therefore, Israel's present possession was legal because of Jewish historical roots dating back more two millenniums when a Jewish State then existed that had sovereignty over the disputed territory. It was an argument that Jordan and Egypt could not make when they controlled those territories. Nevertheless, legal counsel from the Foreign Ministry told the cabinet that, if they were to establish settlements in the conquered lands, many nations would consider that a violation of international law. But it was only ten days after the Arab summit. Legal arguments held little weight when compared to the stinging disappointment of "the three no's" from Khartoum. Pressure was mounting within Israel to approve new settlements. The fledgling, unofficial Golan settlement already existed. The cabinet's resolve to maintain the status quo, in hopes of promoting the chances of peace, was weakening in light of Khartoum's clear signal of continued conflict. The ministers approved plans for more settlements in the northern Sinai and the Golan. Approvals for West Bank settlements would soon follow.

In a subsequent meeting, the cabinet attempted to avoid any questions regarding the legality of the settlements by placing them within the jurisdiction of Nahal, an acronym for Fighting Pioneer Youth. Nahal was organized within the framework of the military. Its members divided their time between military duties and civilian service in newly-founded, agricultural settlements. The cabinet stated they approved of the new settlements because the settlements had a military purpose—to hold and defend the land. It was an excuse that resonated. Israel owed her existence to the hardy pioneers who came to the area in the late nineteenth and early twentieth century. Without their efforts which established facts on the ground, the nation would not have been created. Pioneering and settlements were in the DNA of the cabinet ministers. Nevertheless, the military purposes excuse was a thin argument that did not always ring true. Not all of the volunteers were from Nahal, and not all settlements had a clear, military purpose.

The positions of cabinet members in favor of establishing new settlements in the occupied territories mirrored the opinions of some Israeli citizens. The Movement for the Whole Land publicly debuted its organization for the first time on September 22. It ran large ads in the newspapers which said, "We are faithfully obligated to the wholeness of our land…. No government in Israel has the right to give up this wholeness." It was not only a statement of their philosophy; it was a subtle threat to the legitimacy of any government that might seek to limit settlement activity.

The same day the Movement for the Whole Land ad appeared, Eshkol met with a leading member of a group dedicated to establishing a new settlement on the foundations of the Etzion Bloc, destroyed by the Jordanians and Palestinian irregulars almost twenty years before. The group's request was not to establish something new; instead, it was to rebuild something old. Within days the group received approval of its plan for Etzion. On September 27, a handful of men and women moved into an intact Jordanian army building at the Etzion site. They were accompanied by survivors of the massacre a generation earlier, reporters, and a vintage 1948 *Egged* bus with plywood painted grey to emulate the metal-plated busses that had provided protection from Arab bullets before the Etzion Bloc was overrun.

During the second week of October, another settlement started in the Golan. It was located in Kuneitra, the former Syrian administrative hub of the Golan. For living space, the new kibbutz used three-room houses, formerly occupied by Syrian army officers and their families or by Russian advisors. They had beds and furniture but no electricity. The interior walls of a larger house were knocked down to create a community room that would fit at one time the more than eighty people already there. Soon Israeli government officials arrived. They tried to persuade the settlers to become a Nahal outpost and to wear uniforms to give the appearance of conforming to Government policy. At first the settlers refused, but Allon eventually convinced them to compromise by flying a Nahal flag. However, they would not wear uniforms. From its inception, Israel's pretext for creating settlements had quickly evaporated.

The joyful relief Israel experienced in June after the war ended dissipated over the following four months. By October, Israelis became increasingly resigned to a long, difficult struggle. Russian influence was gaining in the Arab world, especially in Egypt where the loss of income and relationships with the western world made Nasser increasingly dependent on Russian handouts to rebuild his military forces. For the Israelis, administration of the territories was becoming increasingly difficult and complicated. The number of Arabs remaining in the occupied territories, along with their prolific birth rate compared to that of Israeli citizens, clouded the political horizon. Firefights raged along the canal that sapped the lives of Jewish soldiers; Syria retained her unyielding stance, and the pinpricks delivered by Palestinian terrorists, mainly led by Arafat, were becoming increasingly painful.

On October 1, four terrorists crossed the Jordan River, blew up a building and killed an Israeli soldier. Terrorism emanating from Fatah bases in Jordan was becoming problematic for the Israelis who, with the assistance of many West Bank Arabs, had successfully prevented terrorists from establishing bases within the West Bank. As October eased into November, the frequency of terrorist acts in Israel emanating from Jordan increased. It was not just the number of deaths, injuries, and property damage the attacks meted out. It was the uncertainty of when, where, and how they would occur.

Israel responded in several ways. The IDF increased its border vigilance, and Israeli officials exiled or deported those they identified as aiding the terrorists within the West Bank. The Israelis also destroyed the homes of terrorists living on the West Bank, even if owned by others, despite the proscription of the Geneva Convention that says, "No protected person may be punished for an offense he or she has not personally committed.... Reprisals against protected persons and their property are prohibited." Increasingly, it became a desperate struggle to save the lives of innocent civilians. Israeli attitude was perhaps best described by General Narkiss who said: "If you know the Arab mentality, you know this toughness is probably good, I don't think they really understand any other language."

Dayan defended his country's anti-terrorist policies. He stated that, especially when compared to occupations by other countries throughout history, Israel's policies were necessary, humane, and relatively "benign." He later added that, for the most part, relations between Arabs and the military administration in the occupied territories were good. Dayan also pointed out that the Palestinians living in the occupied territories were experiencing an increase in their standard of living and that Israel was making a significant effort to stay out of the affairs of their daily lives. But the longer the occupation continued, the more friction there would be between the occupiers and the occupied.

From the vantage point of an outside observer almost fifty years later, the Israeli response may seem harsh and in violation of international law.

However, there is no doubt that great effort was expended to avoid unnecessary loss of life. Property destruction in response to terrorist acts was, with few exceptions, selective. Critics can find much to criticize now, but they offer no alternatives for the decisions made in 1967—save, of course, Israel's withdrawing without any guarantee of a peaceful future. However, even if Israel had withdrawn from the occupied territories, it is likely that the terrorists would not have been satisfied and probably would have been encouraged. Whether an Israeli withdrawal would have spurred recruitment for terrorist causes or reduced the incentive for joining the terrorists, is speculative. What is not speculative is that it would not have been long before the terrorists carried their fight from the West Bank into the length and breadth of Israel, as they had begun to do before the 1967 war. For Israel, there simply was no choice other than to respond by targeting those who delivered the violence, as well as those who aided them.

But, from the perspective of many Israelis, there was at least one positive development in October: Jews began to settle in the Jewish quarter of the Old City. The Jewish quarter was located near the Wailing Wall. In 1948, its 2,000 residents were besieged and forced by Jordanian soldiers to surrender and evacuate. Before then, the Jewish quarter had had a nearly-continuous Jewish presence dating back more than two millennia. Over the years following the end of the 1948 war, more than a third of the buildings formerly owned by Jews were destroyed, thirty-four of the thirty-five synagogues were demolished, and some of the remaining structures were used by Arabs to shelter animals. Jews were coming home to rebuild what once was theirs.

For King Hussein, however, October was not a happy month. His nation was the only Arab confrontation-state to maintain good relations with the United States, but Hussein had become increasingly unhappy with the Americans. On October 7, he wrote a letter to President Johnson expressing his anger that stemmed from America's pro-Israeli stance. Hussein had a valid basis for concern. Israel was not interested in negotiating with him in the shadows, out of the public eye. But secretive talks were the only avenue Hussein could explore after Khartoum. In addition, West Bank residents, despite the fact that many of them were former Jordanian civil servants still being paid by Hussein, increasingly questioned whether they should remain loyal to him. Jordan's economy was in ruins, and his rule was being jeopardized by the influx of Palestinians who had no love for him and who supported terrorist organizations in Jordan that were arming and becoming increasingly bold. Hussein could do little to escape his predicament without American help. He needed America to pressure Israel.

Within the West Bank, pro-Hussein and pro-Palestinian-independence forces held a stormy meeting. The independence movement opposed King Hussein's return to power on the West Bank; an event that they perceived would only amount to an alternative Jordanian occupation. They wanted an independent state. And they feared retribution if Hussein returned. On the flip side, pro-Hussein leaders wanted a return to the old ways during which many of them benefited financially or otherwise. The two groups did not come to an agreement, but Hussein believed Israel was at least somewhat complicit by attempting to turn the West Bank residents away from him. However, Israel never supported either camp—Israel just listened. And, since there was no pressure on Palestinians as a whole to make a decision as to which path to take, the stalemate continued.

On October 17, Israel's cabinet rescinded its decision of June 19 concerning how to end the conflict with Syria and Egypt. After Khartoum, Eshkol said in the Knesset:

> The Government notes with regret the fact that the Arab states adhere to their position of not recognizing, not negotiating, and not concluding peace treaties with Israel. Faced with this position of the Arab states, Israel will maintain the situation fixed by the

ceasefire agreements and reinforce its position by taking into account its security and development needs.

Thereafter, Israeli security would trump any urge to rush withdrawal, and if a decision to withdraw were made, security needs would dictate how far.

By the end of October, no plan existed for future negotiations. Nor had a framework been put forth by any international body that set principles for future resolution of the dispute. And for their part, the Arab nations had displayed no interest in living in harmony with Israel. Not surprisingly, given her experience during the first two decades of her existence, Israel had no interest in returning to the uncertainties of the past. In short, there was an impasse. No movement, much suffering, much frustration. Nasser's warning that delay would harden resolve had come to fruition.

CHAPTER TWENTY-TWO
October 21 to Early November

On October 21, as is so often the case in the Middle East, violence reshuffled the diplomatic deck.

Fighting Flares Anew

The flagship of Israel's navy, the destroyer *Eilat*, was patrolling off the shores of Egypt's Port Said. Later, Israel announced it was cruising in international waters approximately thirteen-and-a-half miles from shore. The Egyptians said that the *Eilat* was less than twelve miles from shore, well within Egyptian territorial waters. For those who died, the dispute over a couple of miles did not matter. Egyptian naval vessels moored in Port Said's harbor fired three missiles towards the destroyer. The first struck the *Eilat* amidships and exploded. The second, launched a few minutes later, hit the engine room. The third missile also hit home and finished the job. An hour-and-a-half after the first missile was fired—the *Eilat* slipped below the ocean's surface and sank to the sea floor. Forty-seven Israeli sailors died, ninety-one were injured.

Three days later, IDF artillery and warplanes struck Egyptian oil refineries in Suez City. They destroyed eighty percent of Egypt's refinery capacity and left many oil storage tanks in flames. Egypt's already-reeling economy suffered a devastating blow.

Both Israel and Egypt asked the Security Council to take action. Judging from the UN's past failures, it was unlikely that another meeting which invariably would include speeches filled with vindictive accusations would achieve anything. Even so, both sides wanted to grab diplomatic initiative to take the sting out of any international response.

The Security Council met to address the issue on October 24. Two days of speeches followed, during which all of the Council members, except China and Mali, addressed the room. Lord Caradon, the sixty-year old UN Ambassador for Britain spoke first. His given name was Hugh Mackintosh Foot, but he went by the name Lord Caradon after receiving his title in 1964. Before being posted to the UN, he served for more than twenty years in England's diplomatic service. Caradon alluded to the UN's failure to agree on a set of principles to resolve the Middle East crisis when he said, "Surely no one can claim that we should hesitate any longer." The Russians ignored Caradon's implicit, clarion call for compromise. Instead, Fedorenko, Russia's UN Ambassador, introduced a draft resolution condemning Israel. He rubbed salt into the wound when he demanded that Israel compensate Egypt for her losses. American Ambassador, Arthur Goldberg, advocated a more even-handed response. He called for a resolution that condemned any nation violating the ceasefire and insisted that all parties strictly observe it in the future.

The Security Council reconvened during the afternoon of October 25 and approved a resolution that closely modeled the American suggestion. However, the Security Council was not satisfied with only doing that. The Council attempted to agree on another resolution that would delineate a path towards ending the ongoing crisis. All agreed that Israel had to withdraw—how far, and even more controversial, under what conditions, were the sticking points. The Council members also attempted to propose a solution for the growing Palestinian refugee problem and to address Israel's right to freely navigate the Suez Canal and the Straits of Tiran. They were unsuccessful. But, after further deliberations in private, everyone understood they would soon reconvene.

Eshkol spoke to the Knesset on October 30, five days after the Security Council meeting. Three days before, Russian military ships had docked at Egyptian ports in a show of strength designed to send Israel a message to tread lightly. However, Eshkol refused to be deterred. He told the assembled legislators:

> Regarding the Golan Heights we will not allow a return to the status quo ... which brought destruction and ruin to our settlements in the valley. The status quo ante in the Sinai ... and the Suez Canal will also not return ... we must now seek to set agreed national boundaries based on peace accords.

Eshkol also said that the Jewish quarter would be rebuilt in the Old City of Jerusalem and that the government would construct a new neighborhood which would house 1,500 families on the northern side of East Jerusalem. With regard to the Golan, he made clear that he believed Israel should leave the border as it stood but that he was "not rushing to decide." Nor did he express any interest in relinquishing control of any portion of the West Bank. Eshkol saw the Jordan River as a national border but recognized the problem with that policy; in Nablus and Jenin he said the Arabs "are as numerous as olives." Eshkol's remarks suggested that he leaned towards Allon's plan of giving up control of the cities while maintaining a strong presence on the border. However, he knew he had to be careful—taking a definitive stance would have divided his cabinet and inhibited his ability to govern effectively. With nobody on the Arab side willing to negotiate openly, Eshkol had no reason to incur the political risk of stating his own government's goals with any clarity.

However, there may have been at least some contacts between Israel and Egypt despite Nasser's strident words and professed refusal to permit direct negotiations with Israel. One historian writes that Nasser told Hussein that the Israelis had reached out to him with an offer of full withdrawal from the Sinai in return for a peace treaty. Nasser is said to have refused because it would leave Israel in a commanding position with Syria and Jordan, and then Israel would never give up the West Bank. It is unclear if Israel actually made such an offer, but if so, the deal purportedly offered was almost identical to the deal Egyptian President Sadat would agree to little more than ten years later.

One thing, however, was clear. Israel would not withdraw and then negotiate; she would negotiate first, and only then withdraw.

Eshkol and his cabinet knew another meeting of the Security Council was imminent. Their diplomatic priority was to block any resolution that demanded Israel's complete withdrawal from the occupied territories. They would have preferred no resolution at all, but, failing that, they hoped for a resolution that provided procedural guidelines without detailed substance. If a resolution couldn't be kept to that level of fuzzy detail, the Israeli fallback position was a resolution that consisted of obscure principles.

Israel's government also agreed it was important to ensure that the United States remained sympathetic to Israel's needs. Therefore, to placate the Americans, Eban told them that minor, land adjustments could resolve Jordanian issues. Whether that was still true in late October is debatable. However, it is clear that if Hussein had mustered the courage to step forward publicly with his acknowledgement of Israel's right to exist and expressed his willingness to negotiate, much might have been accomplished to resolve the increasingly-intractable dispute between the two countries. That is so even though some members of Israel's cabinet questioned the wisdom of dealing with Hussein at all. They did not think that he would remain in power for long, and they also thought Israel had another potential suitor—Palestinian leaders on the West Bank who might be willing to negotiate with Israel, independent of Jordan.

Unfortunately, Hussein failed to grasp the moment. He dithered in hopes of first receiving private assurances from Eshkol of the shape of a deal envisioned by the Israelis. But Israel's divided "unity" cabinet made it impossible for Eshkol to privately commit to anything. Without the public pressuring it do so, it was politically impossible for the cabinet to reach an internal consensus. Meanwhile, making the diplomatic challenge more difficult, a Jewish settler movement bent on living in the West Bank, and incorporating the West Bank into Israel, had emerged. The settler movement did not yet have sufficient, political traction to block or impede negotiations with an Arab nation if the appropriate opportunity presented itself. But its power and allure were growing. It would not be long before those who wished to settle in the newly-conquered lands would become powerful voices within Israel's electorate. Hussein should not have waited. Time was running out.

On November 1, rather than reading the tea leaves correctly, Hussein doubled down on his refusal to negotiate directly with Israel. On the *David Frost Show* he rejected Eshkol's proposal for them to meet. After "the three no's" it was impossible for any Arab leaders to publicly support direct and open negotiations. The influence of an increasingly powerful Arafat, who virulently opposed direct negotiations with Israel, also served to intimidate any Arabs living on the West Bank who otherwise might have spoken out. Hussein's rejection of Eshkol's request, coupled with the fear Arabs living in the occupied territories had of Arafat, meant Israel had no partner. Without a partner, Israel was not motivated to consider making hard choices—hard choices that would have been much easier to implement then, than would be the case decades later.

During the first week of November, Hussein visited the United States. He told the Americans that he and Nasser had agreed that if Israel withdrew totally from all of the occupied territories, including Jerusalem, accepted an end to belligerency, and cooperated on finding a permanent home for Palestinian refugees, then Egypt and Jordan would do the following:

- End their belligerency with Israel.
- Agree that all states in the region have the right to live in peace and security.
- Open the Suez and other international waterways to Israeli shipping.

The news may have been new to the Americans, but it was not to Israel. Israeli intelligence had previously learned of the conversation between Hussein and Nasser and reported it to Eshkol.

Hussein's diplomatic offensive continued on the American television program, *Face the Nation*. He said the Arab offer "would mean that we recognize the right of all to live in peace and security," and that it included free passage of Israeli shipping in the Suez Canal and the Straits of Tiran. Hussein told reporters that Nasser shared his views. Two days later, Egyptian government officials confirmed Hussein's statement.

The catch was what they were not saying.

For Hussein and Nasser, explicitly recognizing Israel's existence, in any manner, was out of the question. They also continued to refuse to negotiate directly with the Jewish State. The net effect of what they said was that Israel should give back their lands, as she had after the 1956 war, and trust that there would be no war in the future. That approach had not worked for Israel. After returning the Sinai, Israel continued to face unrelenting threats to its existence, terrorism emanating from all four of its borders with Arab nations, and an Arab mobilization that culminated in the Six-Day War. Thus, the promises Hussein and Nasser might have now been willing to make were little different from the implicit ones made by Nasser a decade earlier because they came with no guarantee for future compliance. Israel's leadership was determined to accept nothing less than real peace and real recognition. Anything short of that they viewed as a subterfuge. Israel had gone down the wrong road before; she would not travel that path again.

Towards the end of the week, the United States declared support for Israeli withdrawals coupled with minor adjustments of the armistice lines, as they existed on June 4, but only in exchange for peace. If the Arabs agreed to the American suggestion, President Johnson assured Hussein that the United States would pressure Israel to relinquish her hold on most of the West Bank.

Hussein did not indicate any interest.

CHAPTER TWENTY-THREE
Resolution 242

In early November, while the United States engaged in talks with King Hussein, three nations collaborated on a proposed resolution to end the Middle East impasse. India, Mali, and Nigeria presented a draft resolution to the UN Security Council that said in part:

> *"Israel's armed forces should withdraw from all the territories occupied as a result of the recent conflict ... [and receive a guarantee of freedom of navigation in the Straits of Tiran] in accordance with international law."*

But the guarantee was not as sweeping as it sounded. Egypt claimed that the Straits were part of her territorial waterways. Therefore, the proposed resolution left the Egyptians free to argue that it did not require them to permit Israeli shipping through the Straits because international law does not require a country to let other nations' shipping enter their territorial waters.

But Egypt urgently needed relief. Her economy was in shambles, and her people restless. The fighting that destroyed refineries in Suez City also displaced hundreds of thousands of her citizens. The confrontation with Israel was raising havoc with Egypt internally, and Nasser was desperate to find a solution. Therefore, the Egyptians requested an urgent Security Council meeting to address the crisis.

Egypt's urgent request, and the resolution proposed by the three nations led by India, took the United States by surprise. The Americans had hoped to build a consensus for their own draft before presenting it to the UN. But the American formulation was as objectionable to the Arabs as the three nations' resolution was to Israel. The language in the American proposal called for a withdrawal of "armed forces from occupied territory." The Arabs were concerned that the term "occupied territory" would permit Israel to argue that, since Jordan occupied the West Bank, and Egypt occupied Gaza before the war, they were barred from administering those territories after an Israeli withdrawal because they too had been "occupying powers." Or, alternatively, Israel might argue that she would not have to completely withdraw under the terms of the resolution because the West Bank and Gaza did not meet the definition of "occupied territory." In addition, the Arabs refused to accept the term "occupied territory" without further explanation because it did not explicitly call for withdrawal from all of the territories. Finally, Egypt rejected language in the American draft specifically referencing, "freedom of navigation through international waterways in the area" because it did not confirm Egypt's territorial claim to all of the Straits of Tiran.

However, the American draft did meet the Arabs' refusal to engage in direct negotiations halfway by recommending that the Secretary General of the UN appoint a special representative to assist the parties. Therefore, direct negotiations were neither required nor rejected.

The same day that Egypt requested an emergency meeting of the Security Council, Israel's cabinet met again. The cabinet failed to reach agreement on substance, but succeeded on procedure. Israel told the United States she would only accept boundary changes from the present lines as part of a peace treaty directly negotiated between Israel and the Arab nations involved.

For a resolution to pass the Security Council, nine of its fifteen members must approve it. However, any one of the five permanent members of the Security Council (at that time the United States, the Soviet Union, England, France, and Nationalist China [Communist mainland China was not awarded the seat held by the Nationalist Chinese in Taiwan until 1971]) had veto power. Neither the American nor the

Indian resolution had any prospect of receiving support from nine members of the Council, let alone any likelihood of avoiding a veto from one of the five permanent members. Something new was required.

Crafting a Resolution — Part One

The opening session of the Security Council, on November 9, 1967, did not augur well. The delegates spent four hours haggling over the order in which they would speak. After that minor detail was finally resolved, the Egyptian delegate opened the proceedings. He declared that Israel must withdraw unconditionally, and he disingenuously said that the attendees at the Arab Summit in Khartoum in late August had agreed to seek a political solution. He failed to explain how "the three no's" were consistent with his statement. Nor did he expound on whether Khartoum's supposed political solution was a first step towards a more violent, final Arab solution. He then added that nobody in the region benefited from war, but that the UN should force Israel to withdraw if she refused.

The Egyptian representative also called for Palestinian self-determination. That was a curious demand given Hussein's fervent desire to take back administrative control of the West Bank and Egypt's domination of Palestinians in Gaza before the war. Was Egypt suggesting that Palestinians should have their own state in Gaza and the West Bank? Or was it really a demand for a Palestinian State in Israel that would put an end to Israel as a Jewish nation?

The Indian spokesman next presented India's, Mali's, and Nigeria's joint proposal. He said they were willing to re-word their draft with regard to freedom of navigation. He also said their draft did not rule out direct negotiations, if they were feasible. However, it was clear to many that the practical effect of a proposal that did not rule out direct negotiations, as opposed to requiring them, was that direct negotiations would not happen.

Goldberg spoke next on behalf of the United States. He said the United States thought that the Security Council meeting was premature because more time was required for diplomatic consultation before proposal of a resolution. Nevertheless, he stated that the American draft-resolution accommodated the positions of all parties to the dispute.

Lord Caradon then rose on behalf England. He said that neither proposal met the needs of the situation. "Consequently," he continued, "I would earnestly put to the Council the suggestion that when we have heard the opening statements in this debate, we should allow a short period for further urgent consultations among ourselves." The Japanese member agreed with Lord Caradon. The Russian member then told the Council that the Soviet Union did not favor either draft. He criticized the American resolution for its ambiguous treatment of the term *withdrawal* but suggested that he could support the Indian draft language. The meeting then adjourned.

Four days later, the Security Council reconvened. Israel's foreign Minister Eban presented Israel's position. He quoted from statements made by Nasser and Radio Cairo in May of 1967, just before the war started, which clearly demonstrated Nasser's intent to destroy Israel. He told the members of the Council that Arab intent was the foundation for Israel's approach and then advised, "After the ceasefire lines a permanent and mutually recognized international boundary is our only possible destination," Eban contrasted Israel's present policy with that of the Arabs by saying, "Against the Khartoum policy of no recognition, no negotiation, and no peace, Israel presents its policy: recognition, negotiation, peace."

Eban also cautioned the UN with regard to the Arab position. "This is the most extraordinary of all recent developments," he said. "The United Nations jurisprudence on the problem of negotiation has been in constant retreat for many years." It was a courageous challenge to the UN members who were considering supporting a position that differed from their past preference for negotiations. To buttress his point, Eban refuted a French statement that it would be "unrealistic to have negotiations without withdrawal" by commenting, "I only invite the Council to believe that it is unrealistic to believe that there can be withdrawal without negotiations." Eban also could not resist taking a shot at the irony of the Egyptian and Jordanian commitment to the Palestinians. He highlighted correctly that, prior to Israel occupying Gaza and the West Bank, Egypt and Jordan had occupied the same territory.

Jordan's Ambassador spoke next. Eban's tutorial did not sway him. He accused Israel of twenty years of aggressive behavior, conveniently failing to mention that Jordan had sent her army into the West Bank in 1948, had annexed it in 1950, and then had attacked Israel first in 1967. The Ambassador focused on Israeli withdrawal, not negotiation; border modification of any kind was unacceptable to him.

The meeting subsequently adjourned. Another was scheduled for two days later. Meanwhile, behind the scenes, diplomatic activity continued. Lord Caradon met with the Indian Ambassador to explore a compromise between the American and Indian-led drafts. Caradon pointed out that the two resolutions were relatively similar and that common ground should be found. The Indian representative was open to change, even as a Latin American member of the Council circulated another draft resolution that failed to gain any support. As the new Security Council meeting date approached, the diplomats continued maneuvering, but no common ground was found.

Many Security Council members felt gloomy when they met again on November 15. Their spirits were certainly not raised when the Syrian representative declared that his country would only support the Russian draft resolution from July that condemned Israeli aggression, ordered Israel to withdraw to the June 4 lines, and demanded that she compensate the Arabs for damages they suffered from the war. The Syrian delegate ignored the inconvenient fact that the Russian proposal had failed to pass when it was presented.

Caradon then spoke to the Council again. He calmly said that the Arab and Israeli positions were not that far apart. The Arabs wanted attention directed towards recovery of their lost territory. Withdrawal was their top priority. He continued, "The Arabs want not charity but justice. They seek a just settlement to end the long and bitter suffering of the refugees." Caradon then summarized his view of Israel's position that, "withdrawal must never be to the same precarious truce; that it must be a permanent peace, to secure boundaries, to a new era of freedom from the use or the threat or the fear of hostility and force."

Caradon continued, "Both are right. The aims of the two sides do not conflict. They converge.... They are of equal validity and equal necessity." His summation cast both sides' positions in their best light. One side could not credibly deny the other. Caradon's comments reflected his mastery of political dynamics within the Security Council. He then asked for another short adjournment so that he could finish consulting with the member nations on a new resolution.

Lord Caradon presented his new draft-resolution to the Security Council the next day. It was a product of back and forth meetings with the Arab delegations and the Israelis. It differed from the American draft in that it called for withdrawal of Israeli forces, as opposed to "armed forces." For the Arabs, this alleviated their concern that Israel would argue that the resolution did not apply to her soldiers. It also clarified that it was a withdrawal from "territories occupied in the recent conflict," as opposed to the American draft which just mentioned "occupied territories." The Caradon resolution added that the acquisition of territory by war was inadmissible. On that score, it tacked closer to the Indian draft than the American one. However, Caradon copied the American draft language word-for-word with regard to freedom of navigation, the issue of refugees, territorial viability, and political independence.

The Caradon proposal had a profound impact on the Security Council members. Neither the Egyptian representative nor the Israeli representative rejected Caradon's draft-resolution during their short statements in response. But, after the meeting adjourned, the Arab delegates told the Russians that the omission of a phrase clearly stating that Israel must withdraw from all the territories would leave Israel able to argue she only needed to partially, rather than fully, withdraw. Their criticisms were primarily directed towards omission of the article "the" before the word "territories" in the draft resolution.

The next morning, the Arab delegates met. They decided that, even though the Caradon resolution was not perfect, it was better than the American one. Although they preferred India's version, they pragmatically recognized that it would never gain the support required in the Security Council. Therefore, rather than risk that the Security Council would fail to agree to any resolution, they chose to support Caradon's proposal because it would get the support of all fifteen members of the Security Council. It was the best they could expect the Council to approve.

When the Security Council reconvened in the afternoon, the Russian Ambassador had not yet received voting instructions from Moscow. Russia's leaders purposely delayed responding because they wanted to check directly with the major Arab capitals before giving their UN Ambassador direction. Therefore, the Russians asked the Bulgarian delegate to take the heat for requesting a three-day postponement of the vote until Monday, November 20. The delegates were not naïve. The politics were fluid, and the antagonists involved were combustible. They knew a postponement would endanger passage of the resolution. But Russia had veto power. They had no choice. The meeting adjourned.

An Interlude in London

Over the weekend, King Hussein met again with Herzog in London at the home of former British Minister Avery, who had arranged the meeting. To maintain the fiction of having had no prior direct contact between Jordan and Israel, the two men pretended, in Avery's presence, to have never met. But Hussein slipped when he asked Herzog if he had stopped smoking.

Herzog told the king that Israel had waited several months without hearing anything new from Jordan. Therefore, his superiors had instructed him to ask if Jordan was ready for direct talks and a peace treaty. Hussein responded that he had tried to get the attendees at the Khartoum conference to agree to settle the conflict with Israel, but that they had only "adopted general directives to search for a political solution." Hussein then revealed that he had talked with Nasser afterwards. He said they had agreed they would, as had been previously communicated to the Americans, end the fighting and recognize Israel's existence and freedom of navigation, in return for Israel's withdrawal from all occupied territories and a solution to the refugee problem. However, Hussein told Herzog that direct negotiations were not possible. Jordan could not act separately but only as part of an all-Arab agreement. Herzog bluntly responded that, without direct negotiations and a peace treaty, Israel had no interest in moving forward.

Herzog then asked Hussein whether Jordan would break from the pack and negotiate directly with Israel if the other Arab countries continued to refuse to do so. Hussein answered that he was thinking about it, but he needed to know if Israel would return the West Bank as part of a negotiated resolution. Herzog answered that he was only authorized to listen, not to speak about Israeli policy. He did, however, volunteer that there were different schools of thought whether or not to deal with the king. But, until Hussein indicated his willingness to sign a peace treaty upon a successful conclusion of negotiations, Herzog said, there was nothing for the Israeli government to decide.

Hussein then said he had made it clear to other Arab leaders that, if asked by the inhabitants of the West Bank to negotiate on their behalf, he would. In effect, Hussein was suggesting an alternate path to direct negotiations.

Herzog then inquired whether Hussein's boundary requirements were rigid, or flexible. Hussein responded that they were flexible.

At the end of the meeting, Herzog asked if he could report "that the king is willing to consider harmonization of what he describes as his right to the West Bank with Israel's security requirements and her historical association with it?" Hussein hesitated, and then answered yes. Hussein told Herzog, almost as an aside, "I urge you not to recognize a Palestinian entity."

The next day they met again at a location arranged by Hussein's doctor, the same person who had been instrumental in arranging their meetings before Minister Avery's involvement. Their avowed purpose was to discuss terrorist incidents perpetrated by Fedayeen in the Beth She'an area of Israel, near the Jordanian border. But their real motive was to cut Avery out of the loop for future meetings.

Crafting a Resolution — Part Two

The same weekend Hussein and Herzog met, an unforeseen development occurred in New York. On Sunday, Russian Ambassador Kuznetsov received a new draft-resolution from Moscow to present the next day. Moscow sent a copy to President Johnson, as well. The Russians had high hopes for their alternative proposal because it reflected the abortive agreement, privately reached in July, between their UN Ambassador and Goldberg. The Russians also gave copies of their newly, proposed resolution to the Indian and Arab delegations that same day.

They waited until Monday morning to give a copy to Caradon. It was literally a last-second bolt from the blue.

When the Council reconvened during the afternoon of November 20, Kuznetsov presented Russia's proposal for a resolution. He warned Israel that, if she continued to occupy Arab territory, unforeseen and dangerous consequences awaited that could have broad international impact. It was a thinly-concealed reference to a potential military confrontation in the Middle East—a confrontation that might involve both the United States and the Soviet Union. Kuznetsov added that the Arabs had demonstrated clear interest in achieving a political settlement, and that the Russians wanted peace in the Middle East. He then made a tepid attempt to demonstrate evenhandedness by declaring that the Russians favored the independent existence of all nations in the Middle East. But he could not bring himself to specifically mention Israel. His failure to do so spoke volumes.

Kuznetsov then introduced the new Russian proposal. It was much less strident than the Soviet proposal in July. It included language requiring:

- Immediate recognition of all states in the region.
- Renunciation of the use of force and threats of it.
- An end to belligerency.
- An end to the arms race in the region (perhaps a reference to Israel's nuclear program).
- Settlement of the refugee issue.
- "Innocent passage through international waterways."

The proposed resolution also demanded that Israel withdraw to the June 4 lines. That requirement was not specified in the Caradon proposal. The Russian proposal also lacked clarity on whether Israel would be guaranteed freedom of navigation in the Straits of Tiran and use of the Suez Canal. Kuznetsov then asked that a decision on which resolution to approve be delayed so the Russian draft could receive consideration.

Caradon spoke to the Council in response. He stressed that a decision should be made "without delay." But, after speeches by Eban and Goldberg in favor of the Caradon proposal, the Bulgarian delegate then dutifully requested a two-day postponement. Once again, perhaps in deference to Russian veto power, the Security Council agreed to the postponement request.

During the two-day interval between the Russian presentation and the final vote, diplomatic activity feverishly continued. Even though they were not enamored with it, the Arabs supported the Russian draft. But Caradon stood firm. He refused to amend the text of his own proposed resolution and argued that his text had the widest support. As the hours ticked away, Caradon's proposed resolution gained momentum towards approval. Then another problem arose. Some nations put forth their interpretation of the Caradon draft. The Indian delegate stated that it was his understanding that the draft called for Israeli withdrawal from all of the territories, and that India would vote for it on that basis.

On the afternoon of November 22, shortly before the Security Council was scheduled to meet again, the consensus of those supporting the Caradon agreement almost collapsed. Caradon told the Indian delegate he would declare to the Security Council that, although every delegate was entitled to their own interpretation of whether the resolution called for Israeli withdrawal from all of the territories, their individual interpretation would not bind the Council. But, when the Russian Ambassador caught wind of Caradon's conversation with the Indian Ambassador, he said that, if Caradon said to the Council what he had told the Indian delegate, he would veto Caradon's proposal.

Caradon next met with the Arab delegation at 3:00 P.M, thirty minutes before the scheduled beginning of the Security Council meeting. He reassured them that their interpretation that the resolution called for Israel to withdraw from all of the occupied territories had not been prejudiced. Further, frantic negotiations ensued during the remaining minutes. Caradon compromised by agreeing not to write or state, as a response to what the Indian Ambassador might say, that "the Indian interpretation is not binding on the Council." In effect, Caradon's compromise was to neither accept, nor reject, the alternative Arab and Indian interpretation. Instead, each delegate was left to decide how the resolution should be interpreted. As it is has been left to the world ever since.

Based on Caradon's compromise, the Indian delegate agreed to vote in favor of the resolution and so informed the Soviet Union. At 4:00 P.M., thirty minutes later than scheduled, the delegates reconvened for the last time on the issue. No other nation formally placed another resolution before the Council. The vote was unanimous, fifteen to zero, in favor of passage. Resolution 242 was born.

The official languages of the Security Council were English and French. The Security Council used the English version of the resolution as the basis for the vote. Since it was the practice of the UN to make the draft which had been used as a basis for voting the official draft, the English version of Resolution 242 became the official, approved resolution. Subsequently, the English version was translated into French, Arabic, Chinese, Russian, and Spanish. All of those translations included, in their respective languages, the word "the" in front of "territories" despite the fact that much of the negotiations before the vote had focused on the absence of "the". To this day, those inaccurate translations have provided ammunition to some who debate the proper interpretation of Resolution 242. But there is no ambiguity as to which resolution was voted on and passed. It was the English version that did not contain "the" that passed with the full knowledge of the fifteen voting members who voted unanimously in favor that it.

Resolution 242 Aftermath

Resolution 242 was the parent of the concept "land for peace." However, the official version did not specify how much land nor how much peace. The resolution also contained a specific provision requesting the UN Secretary General to appoint a special representative to assist the parties. U Thant appointed Gunnar Jarring from Sweden. Jarring had worked with India and Pakistan to resolve their border in Kashmir. He also had many years of experience representing Sweden at the UN. But none of his experience prepared him for the powder keg of the Middle East. It was a difficult region, as Henry Kissinger noted when he said, "Most wars in history have been fought between countries that started out at peace; it was the special lunacy of the Middle East that its wars broke out between countries that were technically already at war."

The struggles over Resolution 242 and its passage did not bring peace or any meaningful negotiations to the Middle East. Hussein believed that the resolution meant that Israel had to withdraw completely. At least one West Bank leader who met with Hussein after the resolution passed was reported to say that Hussein told him he would not accept any deal that gave up any West Bank land or Jerusalem. If that was true, then there was no hope of resolving the dispute between Israel and Jordan in the aftermath of Resolution 242.

Nor did Resolution 242 have a calming effect on the virulence of Nasser's rhetoric, despite his acceptance of the UN resolution. It also did not change his directives to the Egyptian military. Nasser told his generals, "What has been taken by force can only be recovered by force." Clearly, he preferred war to recognition.

Neither did the resolution harm the future prospects of Fatah, Arafat's terrorist organization. Moderate Palestinians faced the brunt of its increasing power, as evidenced by the violence Fatah more and more directed their way. The home of one moderate leader was damaged by a bazooka shell fired by a Fatah member. Other moderate Palestinian leaders received death threats if they strayed too far from Fatah's party line. Fatah intimidation worked; diplomatic discourse diminished.

Nevertheless, Dayan tried to reduce friction with the Arab populace on the West Bank by granting them increased autonomy to run their own civilian affairs. Over the last several weeks of 1967 he removed most military staff officers assigned to civilian management of Arab affairs on the District level. The army remained on the West Bank for security purposes, but Dayan ordered the IDF to get out of governance. Still, violence increased. Between July 1 and the end of the year, Israel categorized forty-eight terrorist incidents as serious in addition to many more minor confrontations.

And, not only was Fatah gaining strength, it was beginning to make inroads on the hearts and minds of PLO adherents. In early December, the PLO executive Committee removed the incompetent and ineffective Shuqayri from office. At the same time, Fatah agreed to join the PLO as a member organization. In return, Fatah received 33 of the 57 governing seats allotted to guerilla groups in the PLO. That gave Fatah almost one third of the 105 total seats in the PLO's governing group.

But despite Fatah's growth in stature, Arafat's star had not yet risen to the top. He was not asked to be PLO's Chairman. And, in the middle of December, Arafat was almost captured by Israeli soldiers in Ramallah. Fortunately for him, he heard the voices of Israeli troops surrounding the building he was hiding in. When the soldiers burst into Arafat's hurriedly vacated apartment, all they found was a warm bed, sheets and a blanket strewn all over the floor, and tea in hot cups. Arafat was no longer there. He was hiding in a car on the street below after jumping from the second floor window. Shortly afterwards, he left the West Bank. Arafat did not return for nearly three decades.

At the end of 1967, Fatah stopped trying to run a home-based, Palestinian uprising from bases in the West Bank. Part of the credit belongs to the efficiency displayed by Israel's internal security agency, the Shin Bet. But Fatah also failed because of its own mistakes. Fatah organized its supporters into large groups that knew each other, rather than creating small compartmentalized units. Its members communicated in simple codes that were easy to break. Escape routes were not planned; safe houses were not so safe. And Fatah members were not trained to withhold information when interrogated. As a result, those caught by the Israelis revealed the identities of other Fatah members. Fatah's lack of professionalism was compounded by the willingness of many in the general populace, as a result of bribes or a different philosophy, to collaborate with the Israelis to identify terrorists in their midst.

Within Israel, there was the spark of political change. On December 15, 250 leading intellectuals placed a newspaper advertisement warning that the humane and democratic nature of Israel was endangered by the new settlements which had been established in the occupied territories. Nevertheless, the settlement movement continued to grow.

There also was change in the IDF. Yitzhak Rabin, the former leader of the Israeli armed forces in the Six-Day War, left the army near the end of 1967. Subsequently, Eshkol selected him to become Israel's next Ambassador to the United States. Rabin left an army that had absorbed more than eighty separate attacks listed as serious since the ceasefire. He had two main priorities as Ambassador. The **first** *was to ensure that Israel received the arms it needed from the United States along with the financial support required to purchase them. The* **second** *was to co-ordinate policies between the two countries, or, at worst, prevent them from diverging.*

Rabin's career as a soldier was over. His career as a politician was about to begin.

On the last day of the year, the Israeli cabinet met one more time. It was not for reminiscing over the cataclysmic events they had all gone through. In a few days, Eshkol was heading to the United States to spend time with President Johnson at his ranch in Texas. Much preparation was required. The cabinet tried to decide what Eshkol should tell Johnson of their plans for the territories. For the third time since the war ended, they could not reach a decision. Some historians, and others, maintain the reason was that Israel had nobody to speak to. Others have argued, in retrospect, that for the Arabs, Israel was not a willing partner. The truth is that there was no common ground between the two factions, and until the Arabs would be willing to speak **with** *Israel—* **not at it**—*there was little chance of finding any.*

CHAPTER TWENTY-FOUR
Phantoms

By early 1968, there seemed little likelihood that the confrontation between Israel and the Arabs would ease. The political process had frozen. Israel insisted on direct talks and a contractual peace agreement that assured her freedom of navigation in all international waterways. But Jordan and Egypt were not willing to go that far. Instead, they would only offer an agreement that would recognize Israel's right to exist, coupled with an ill-defined, pseudo peace cloaked in the ambiguous diplomatic term "non-belligerency." But they would not even offer that unless Israel first pulled back to the pre-war boundaries. And to make matters worse, Syria would not even offer the same, limited concessions Jordan and Egypt had grudgingly agreed to—not that the entrenched stance of the Syrians mattered. Those so-called concessions offered by Jordan and Egypt did not come close to enticing the Israelis. Until the Arabs would back up their words with deeds, Israel would insist on retaining the security buffer provided by the new territories. And exacerbating the divide, Arabs refused to be in the same room as Israelis—so complete was their disdain. The lone exception was King Hussein, and he would only do so secretly.

Hatred and desire filled the political void.

And the void left space for many Jews to succumb to the siren call of lands formerly denied to them—some for religious and cultural reasons, others for security and economic ones. Eshkol felt compelled to do something on their behalf. Before he departed for the United States to meet President Johnson, Eshkol approved two new settlements in the Jordan Valley on the eastern edge of the West Bank. He also pushed his cabinet to adopt policies promoting new construction of homes for Jews in both East Jerusalem and the former Jewish Quarter of the Old City (which the Jordanians had reduced to rubble after evicting all Jews in 1948). Eshkol also supported providing assistance to Arabs who wished to leave Gaza and settle in Jordan. Thousands took advantage of the opportunity. Israel paid for their transportation to the Jordan River. From there, Arab transport took many of them to a little-known refugee town on the West Bank that, several months later, became legendary for Palestinians—Karameh.

Meanwhile, as Eshkol maneuvered to strengthen Israel's permanent ties to the Old City, Moshe Dayan turned his thoughts to strategic issues. Dayan concluded that it was not necessary to hold on to all of the new territory to ensure Israel's security. He believed Israel should be willing to return the Golan to Syria, and most of the Sinai to Egypt, as part of a negotiated process. But he drew the line at Sharm el-Sheikh, from which Egypt had prevented shipping from using the Straits of Tiran to access Eilat's port. Dayan said, "If I had a choice between making proper peace that would require a withdrawal to the international border, or to reach an agreement accepted by both sides that would include freedom of navigations and half of Sinai—I would prefer this to a peace agreement." Dayan was similarly adamant about maintaining control of Gaza, Jerusalem, and parts of the West Bank necessary for Israel's security.

Of course, the political stagnation did not benefit Egypt. By January of 1968 her economic stability and political influence was on the decline. Closure of the Suez Canal, a significant decrease of tourism, and Egypt's desire to re-equip her military took a toll on the vitality of the country. More and more, Egypt became a supplicant, dependent on handouts from Arab oil-producing countries. When Syria and Saudi Arabia refused to attend an Arab summit scheduled for January 17, Nasser felt impelled to cancel the meeting. In contrast, however, as Egypt's strength diminished the power of Arafat's Fatah grew. Fatah's eviction from the West Bank by Israel's internal security department, the Shin Bet, was only one setback, more than balanced by the organization's many successes.

*Then, at the end of January, two events profoundly impacted the world and the Middle East. The **first** was that Arab oil-producing countries met and formed a new group known as OAPEC—the Organization of Arab Petroleum Exporting Countries. Their initial purpose was, of all things, to protect Western interests and to ensure an uninterrupted oil supply to the world. Members of OAPEC hoped the organization would provide a buffer that would insulate Saudi Arabia, Libya, and Iraq from pan-Arab problems that could jeopardize their stability. Things would soon change.*

*The **second** event happened far from the Middle East. North Vietnam launched the Tet offensive on January 30, 1968. For them, it was a military disaster, but that disaster was far outweighed by the political bonanza the communist regime secured. Even though the North Vietnamese were thoroughly defeated on the ground, many perceived them as victorious because they had not lost the means to continue to fight. The audacity of their attack psychologically devastated millions of Americans concerned by the number of her soldiers killed in a foreign land. As a result, that war occupied President Johnson's mind and soul, to the exclusion of most else. The Middle East became a sideshow he left alone to fester.*

But, before the Tet offensive started, Eshkol had a meeting scheduled with President Johnson for early January. Israel wanted to obtain fifty F-4 Phantoms, the extremely capable fighter jets America had first introduced into service in 1960. The Prime Minister was bound and determined to get them because the IAF needed new advanced aircraft. During the Six-Day War, the Arabs had shot down forty Israeli planes—twenty percent of Israel's air force. And, even though the Arabs lost hundreds of planes, Russia was in the process of restoring their losses. Throughout that war the IAF relied heavily on Mirage fighter jets purchased from France. In fact, before the war started, Israel had bought another fifty that the French had not yet delivered before the fighting started. But de Gaulle was no longer willing to do business with the Jewish State because, against his counsel, Israel launched her pre-emptive attack that started the Six-Day War. Therefore, he canceled the order. For the moment, the IAF still had air superiority because its pilots were much better than those the Arabs could muster. Eventually, however, they would be overwhelmed by the vast numbers of planes possessed by her enemies, unless Israel could procure more aircraft.

The answer to the IAF's dilemma was America's Phantom jet, the plane the IAF had coveted for many years because it was the world's best performing and most versatile warplane. In the hands of a proficient pilot it could vanquish any other plane. It could also fly long distances and carry a heavy payload of bombs and missiles to attack ground targets. Even though the United States had already agreed to sell Israel forty-eight Skyhawk jets of lesser quality, Israel needed the Phantoms.

Down on the Farm

On January 7, 1968, Eshkol met President Johnson at his ranch in Texas. An American government executive jet flew him there from New York. After the plane landed on a private airstrip, it taxied close to the front door of Johnson's ranch. Johnson was standing outside to greet Eshkol, while wearing a ten-gallon Stetson hat that made him seem even taller than his six-foot-four frame.

Johnson offered the prime minister a tour of the ranch. Eshkol accepted. What he didn't expect was that he would end up in the front passenger seat of a station wagon with the American president driving. In the back sat three of Eshkol's Israeli companions. Johnson took off at high speed without regard for the deep ruts in the dirt roads that bounced his passengers around. When one of the many cows along the way lingered, blocking their vehicle, Johnson honked his horn, nudged it aside with the car, and said with laughter, "That's Daisy, she's as pigheaded as a Texan senator with colic!"

Johnson had his own way of taking the measure of a man. He preferred one-on-one interaction in an informal atmosphere to fancy dinners in stuffy settings. Eshkol had a kindred spirit. He, like Johnson, felt at home on a farm. When Johnson proudly showed him his land, and the cattle grazing on it, Eshkol told Johnson the ranch reminded him of the Galilee. Since both areas were dry, Eshkol's comparison sparked a lively conversation about water and irrigation. Johnson spoke of the dams he constructed. Eshkol told Johnson about the national water carrier that stretched from the Sea of Galilee to the Negev which he had been instrumental in building. The two national leaders bonded. The press called it "barbecue diplomacy."

Their official meeting began in the living room of the president's ranch house. Eshkol sat on a sofa with plush cushions that settled low. Johnson parked himself in a rocking-chair that left him towering above the Israeli Prime Minister, forcing Eshkol to look up at him when they conversed. Eshkol told the President:

> "The heart of my mission is how to create peace in the Middle East at a time when the Syrian and Egyptian armies are being rebuilt at a menacing rate under Soviet guidance, so fast that the Arab leaders are contemplating renewed war."

He continued that the Arabs' air and tank forces were almost back to their pre-war levels and their navy was stronger than before. When Johnson asked about Russian personnel in Egypt, Eshkol responded there were 2,500.

Their conversation then turned to Israel's Air Force. Johnson asked what Israel had. Eshkol, his eyes locked into the President's, responded that Israel only possessed 150 planes, sixty-six of them almost obsolete. "In a word, Mr. President we presently do not have the minimum needs to defend ourselves."

Johnson then asked what Israel needed. Eshkol was clear and blunt, "Fifty *Phantoms* as rapidly as possible." Without them, he told Johnson, Israel would not have the minimum required for her security.

Eshkol also felt it important to emphasize his sincere desire for peace at the same time he was advocating for more weapons of war. Eshkol spoke of his relief when Israel had emerged victorious from the confrontation the previous June, and then said, "All my thoughts now are turned toward winning the peace—peace with honor between equals."

"It is important that you have your thoughts turned toward peace with honor," Johnson responded

Eshkol followed by expressing regret that he had to ask United States for help, but said there was nowhere else to turn. "Either the United States provides us with arms we need," he stated, "or you leave us to our fate. It's as simple as that."

Johnson listened and then candidly responded that he was bogged down with the Vietnam War, and America's resources were earmarked for that conflict. He suggested to Eshkol that he should look elsewhere as well. Eshkol smiled, "Please tell me where, Mr. President. I would be delighted to look elsewhere if you can give me an address."

Secretary of State, Dean Rusk, then chimed in. He expressed concern that, no matter how much the United States would provide Israel, the Arabs would then turn to the Russians and receive more. Referring to the newly occupied territories, he asked what kind of Israel the Arabs would have to deal with. Eshkol answered that Israel had not wanted a war with the Arabs. However, it was forced on them and only won at huge cost to the country. He continued:

> "It is inconceivable that we cannot win the peace. We want actual treaties of peace—After three wars—1948, 1956, 1967—Israel deserves peace. I will fight tooth and nail for peace. And in peace negotiations we will try to be as forthcoming as possible—but we must have the tools to deter another war."

After a break from their tense discussion, when the meeting resumed, Johnson suggested that, to avoid an arms race in the region, Israel's security might best be found by working with the Russians. Eshkol's answer did not directly address that advice. Instead, he said that he understood his country would never have a numerical arms advantage and that Israel could accept having only one-third of the planes the Arabs possessed. But, he warned, there was a limit to the extent good pilots could make up for numerical inferiority. Defense Secretary McNamara then picked up the thread of Johnson's remarks. He assured Eshkol that Israel would never be abandoned but prophesied that the more planes the Americans supplied the Israelis the more the Russians would send to the Arabs.

At that point, Mottie Hod, Israel's Air Force Commander, could not restrain himself. He told the Americans that the arms race had never been about the number of planes in Israel's inventory. Instead, it was about the Egyptian capacity to fly their planes. He plainly suggested that the Arabs had all of the planes they needed. The Russians did not need to give them more. The Egyptian problem was to increase the capability of their pilots flying them. Left unsaid, but understood by all present, was that there was nothing that would prevent the Arabs from improving the quality of their aviators in the future. And, if they did, that increased expertise, combined with a staggering numerical advantage, could spell disaster for the Jewish State.

Hod also had a response for McNamara's assurances that Israel would receive American help, if it ever was in need. "Might I suggest that the one way of guaranteeing ... and assuring that United States forces will never have to come to our rescue, is by keeping Israel's Air Force strong." Hod's comments seemed to have convinced the President. Johnson then suggested another break.

When they met a final time, Johnson told Eshkol that all of them should do what was needed to bring about a stable peace to the region. He also expressed his wish to prevent an arms race in the Middle East. But he then said the United States will ensure that the Israeli Air Force receives adequate equipment. While the President did not specifically mention the *Phantom* jets, Eshkol was satisfied.

Johnson suggested that part of the communique to the press at the end of the session should read:

> "The president agreed to keep Israel's defense capability under active and sympathetic review in light of all the relevant factors, including the shipment of military equipment by others into the area."

Eshkol understood what Johnson's comments meant even though it was not stated explicitly: America would supply the *Phantoms*. The Prime Minister responded, "Thank you, Mr. President. I thank you from the heart."

CHAPTER TWENTY-FIVE
Karameh

Israel's success in preventing Arafat and his Fedayeen group, Fatah, from gaining a foothold on the West Bank did not prevent terrorist attacks originating from bases in Jordan east of the Jordan River. An average of thirty terrorist bombs a month exploded in Israeli territory. Meanwhile, increasing numbers of West Bank Arabs accepted employment opportunities within Israel.

Hussein's goal was to stop Fedayeen from launching these attacks. He knew terrorism invited retribution. Politically, however, his situation was precarious. Many Palestinians believed that the terrorists were the only effective force fighting the Israelis. And, most worrisome to the king, many of Hussein's subjects and soldiers were Palestinian. Of those who were in the army, some turned a blind eye to terrorist activities, while others warned the Fedayeen of any Israeli troop movements that might harm them.

On February 8, a mine exploded south of the Sea of Galilee, killing three Israelis. Israel responded with airstrikes in Jordan that struck Palestinian targets. Because of that airstrike and others, some Palestinian refugees fled deeper into Jordan's heartland.

The town of Karameh was one of Fatah's main bases in Jordan. In February, Arafat sent Fedayeen stationed there into the West Bank to murder several Palestinian moderates. Those tasked with the mission suffered the same fate as many others; they were captured by Israeli forces. But some, on other missions got through to wreak mayhem. In response, the IDF planned for a much more forceful response than the sporadic airstrikes and artillery shelling it had previously employed to curtail terrorist attacks. Next time it would be different. The IDF hoped to disrupt the terrorists by sending ground troops into Karameh.

For months Israel had worked hard establishing countermeasures to prevent terrorists from crossing the Jordanian border into Israeli-held territory. The Israelis lined the Jordan River with military bases, barbed wire, and minefields. They also used sophisticated electronic surveillance to track terrorist attempting to cross. In addition, the Israelis bulldozed a dirt road adjacent to the border fence and kept it smooth and undisturbed so that infiltrators' tracks would be easily discovered. And, as another layer of protection, the IDF conducted nightly patrols to find Fedayeen who had slipped past the border defenses and searched caves and orchards to uncover terrorists and their weapons caches. Finally, to deter Arabs on the West Bank from helping terrorists, the IDF destroyed sympathizers' homes and undertook other reprisal measures. But terrorists still were getting through and were wreaking havoc. Something more needed to be done.

Israel began massing forces along the Jordan River on March 15, 1968. The Jordanians could plainly see that trouble might be coming their way. Their suspicions were reportedly confirmed by information received from the CIA. The Jordanian army alerted its troops in the area and deployed them to defend the Karameh region. The Jordanians also warned Arafat that Karameh was a potential target and suggested that he withdraw into the hills. Many in the Fatah leadership agreed, Arafat did not. He reportedly responded, "We want to convince the world that there are those in the Arab world who will not withdraw or flee."

On March 18, terrorists struck again. A bus carrying Israeli school children on a road in southern Israel close to the border with Jordan, hit a mine. Two adults on board were killed; twenty-eight children were injured. The deadly incident gave Eshkol the excuse he needed to launch a massive attack to punish Fatah, based in Karameh. Eshkol's Cabinet had rejected the same operation twelve days before, but the new attack on the bus made it clear that Hussein could not control the terrorists headquartered in his country. The cabinet was resolved—Israel would no longer limit her response to unrelenting terror to pinpricks. The cabinet approved the attack.

Karameh means either "honor" or "dignity" in Arabic. The town lies about four miles east of the Jordan River, opposite Jericho. Two bridges and several roads in the area afforded multiple routes for the IDF to reach the town. Further east, behind Karameh, rose steep mountains from which one could directly observe the Jordan River and the West Bank beyond. It was easy for Jordanians stationed on top of them to see the Israelis coming.

Since 1948, Karameh's population had swelled, primarily because thousands of Palestinian refugees from Israel's War of Independence took refuge there. The camp, built to provide temporary housing for them, took on a permanent look over time as a result of the mosques, schools, and a hospital built to accommodate the refugees. But proper investments were not made by the Arab world or the international community to relieve the squalid living conditions. The conduct of those Arab nations was quite a contrast to Israel, who during her first decade, had worked feverishly to ease the plight of hundreds of thousands of Jewish, refugee immigrants fleeing Arab lands. As a result, the inhabitants of the camps had a natural inclination to blame the Israelis for their plight and hate them for it. It was a growing hatred that served the purposes of Fatah and Arab leaders. Those feelings intensified when Israeli shells, fired in response to previous terrorist attacks, killed several girls leaving school. Meanwhile, even though Arafat had ordered the terror attack that invited the IDF's response, Karameh's inhabitants maintained their high regard for him. They did not feel the same way toward Hussein, however.

Many more hated the king than revered him. They blamed Hussein, not Arafat, for failing to protect them and for causing their problems.

King Hussein sensed that the ambush of the Jewish school bus might generate a significant Israeli response. The terrorists' use of a mine was an eerie reminder of the events leading up to Israel's reprisal raid on Samu in 1966. Hussein expressed his "shock and regret" for the most recent incident, but he did not condemn all terrorist attacks. For Israelis faced with unrelenting terror, his regrets were too little, too late. The terror needed to stop, not just be regretted.

King Hussein was not alone with his concerns. The United States also knew through intelligence sources that Israel was preparing for a large military response. It was not difficult to detect troop and tank movements in the barren valley between the mountains of the West Bank and the Jordan River. The Americans cautioned restraint. Under pressure, Eshkol waivered, but decided to move forward without the benefit of Moshe Dayan's counsel. The revered Defense Minister did not participate in the final discussions. Whether or not Dayan's absence motivated Eshkol to demonstrate he could act forcefully without leaning on his popular and dynamic Defense Minister is one of those "what ifs" which bedevils historians but which can never be answered with certainty.

Where was Dayan? On March 19, he was actively involved in planning the attack on Karameh. But on March 20, he was participating in one of his favorite hobbies—archeology. Or perhaps more appropriately said—digging for ancient artifacts that he had no right to keep, but because he was above the law at that point in his life, he kept anyway. That day, while deep in a pit with his shovel, the wall caved in burying him to his chin. He had trouble breathing and thought he would die. The more he tried to free himself, the more dirt filled in around him. Perhaps blissfully, he fell unconscious. But fortunately for him, two companions were nearby. They cleared dirt from his face, grabbed his arms, and pulled him out. Dayan had a weak pulse and was bleeding from the nose, but he was alive. Doctors at a hospital determined he had sustained two broken ribs, a damaged vertebra, and a paralyzed vocal cord. They placed him in a full body cast, and he was unable to return to work for three weeks. It was months before his symptoms stemming from the injuries dissipated. The Karameh operation went forward without him.

Early on March 21, 15,000 Israeli soldiers attacked. IDF soldiers crossed the Jordan River at multiple locations and came at Karameh from several directions. To complete its encirclement, helicopters landed paratroopers behind the town. The Israelis expected the Fedayeen to resist. What they did not expect was the Jordanian army to resist so ferociously.

The Fedayeen fought hard and often courageously. Some made suicide attacks on Israeli tanks. Seventeen guerillas dug entrenchments. They were killed while defending themselves with rocket-propelled grenades at close range against onrushing Israeli tanks. Several years later, Arafat named his security detail Force-17, in honor of their sacrifice. However, it is not certain that Arafat's bravery matched those of his Fedayeen soldiers. Some reports have Arafat staying and directing the fighting, although it is not clear to what degree. Another report has him fleeing on a bicycle. Nevertheless, nearly 100 of Arafat's followers died, and many more were injured. Despite being ill-equipped compared to the IDF, the Fedayeen managed to put up a strong fight.

While some of the battle went smoothly for the Israelis, some did not. The IDF took Karameh rather early in the day. Soldiers demolished most of the town other than the mosque and took care to avoid injuring the few civilians that did not flee before their arrival. As a result, Fatah's military base was destroyed, and many of its followers were killed or wounded in the fighting. Near 10:00 a.m., Eshkol even set foot on Jordanian territory for a short time.

The Jordanian army, however, posed a much greater problem than the IDF had anticipated. The Jordanians tenaciously defended the roads and hills. Without their help, most Fatah fighters would have been killed or captured. Hussein's soldiers sustained more than 200 casualties during the day and acquitted themselves as bravely as the Fedayeen. The fighting ended when the IDF withdrew in the late afternoon, though Arab soldiers harassed them with gunfire all the way back to Israel.

For the Israelis, the price of their victory was much higher than they anticipated. Twenty-eight IDF soldiers died in action, and the IDF abandoned two tanks and several trucks. Many other vehicles were beyond repair. One of the tanks left behind ended up on display in Jordan—complete with its dead Jewish driver still in the seat.

The Karameh battle was a "technical" victory for the Israelis, even though Fatah members swarmed back into the town the next day. Nevertheless, as a result of the attack, Arafat realized he should not base his forces so close to where Israeli troops were stationed. But, after moving his headquarters much farther away to a town named Salt, his Fedayeen had to traverse much more ground before reaching the border and crossing into Israel or the West Bank. That increased their exposure to interdiction by Jordanian units tasked to stop them. Therefore, Israel could argue her goals had been met.

However, despite Israel's "technical" win, the fighting that day was a major psychological boost for Fatah and Arafat. Arafat became a hero of the rank and file who believed his escape from death was a miracle. Public funerals for those killed kick-started public recognition for a new group of martyrs. Volunteers from the refugee camps, and from other Arab countries, flocked to join Fatah. Thousands came within days. Fatah's problem quickly became not one of manpower, but of training for its rapidly growing ranks.

The fight also restored hope among the Palestinian people. Some young Palestinian men said it:

- "Changed the Palestinian identity from refugee to revolutionary."
- "Gave me the answer to who I am."
- "Was the most important event not just in my life, but in all of our lives."

Many swore they had been in the thick of the fighting, even though they were nowhere near. Those statements embodied a respect for veracity not much different from bystanders who see a bus accident and claim to have been on board in order to press bogus injury claims. Nevertheless, after nine months of Arab shame stemming from their massive defeat in the Six-Day War, the "Arab street" brimmed with pride.

The sudden fervor induced by the battle among Palestinians created an environment that caused both concern and admiration in the Muslim world. Saudi Arabia agreed to impose a 7% tax on Palestinian nationals working in the country, which the Saudis would collect and remit to Fatah. Kuwait and the other Gulf States followed suit. Soon donations also arrived from wealthy Arab businessmen and countries as far away as Pakistan and Malaysia. Nasser saw opportunity, as well. He thought Arafat had the potential to open a second front against the Israelis that would help Egypt eventually recover the Sinai.

But King Hussein was worried, despite issuing a statement that said, "We have come to the point where we are all Fedayeen." He knew that his army was incensed because it was really the Jordanian armed forces that deserved most of the credit. But instead of seeing their efforts appreciated, the army faced increasing threats from within. Arafat's and Fatah's' popularity within Jordan had created an emerging, potentially potent, force to contend with.

That is not to say that Fatah was the only Palestinian movement thriving at that time. Even though the battle at Karameh quickly swept Fatah to the top ranks of recognized revolutionaries worldwide, there were other contenders. One was created by Syria, whose leaders were not so enamored with Arafat and Fatah. The Syrians wanted to control the movement, not be controlled by it. Therefore, they created an alternative Palestinian terrorist movement named al-Sa'iqa, which was based in Syria and entirely controlled by the Syrian leadership. Also, George Habash, a Palestinian doctor born in Haifa who fled to Lebanon with his family in 1948, continued to build his even more radical splinter group, the PFLP.

Israel faced censure in the UN as a result of her attack on Karameh. To some in the Security Council, the Israeli action appeared especially calculated because Jordan had predicted it before the terrorist mine blew up the Israeli school bus. However, the United States insisted that any resolution regarding Israel's attack into Jordan must also contain language that condemns the terrorist attacks that precipitated the Israeli response. The Arab and other Islamic nations countered that Israel acted like South Africa, and the attack on Jordan was no different than colonial aggression. The end result was stagnation. The only winner that emerged from the UN discussions was the Palestinian resistance movement. As a direct byproduct of their terrorism, the Palestinian cause had begun to seep deeply into the world's consciousness.

Israel won the military battle of Karameh; the Palestinians won their dignity and honor. Jordan won nothing and lost much. A new power was rising. Jordan would never be the same.

CHAPTER TWENTY-SIX
Dawn of the Settler Movement and the Rise of Fatah

A Hebron Home

Passover began at sundown on April 12, 1968. The eight-day holiday commemorates Jewish emancipation from slavery in Egypt thousands of years ago. For Moshe Levinger, the thirty-three year old Rabbi born in Jerusalem, Passover meant something else. It was an opportunity to reassert a Jewish presence in the ancient West Bank town of Hebron.

Hebron had once been part of the Kingdom of Israel before the Babylonians destroyed it. Much before that, Hebron's location was where Abraham lived after he purchased what is now called the *Cave of the Patriarchs* from the Hittites. After Abraham, Jews had lived in the area, almost without interruption, until 1929. In 1929, Hebron's Arab residents massacred more than sixty Jewish inhabitants living in the city and injured sixty more. Most of the several hundred surviving Jews fled. The British forcibly removed the remaining thirty in 1936. Hebron had been the city with the longest record of continuous Jewish habitation. The streak was at an end.

Levinger was determined to bring Jews back to Hebron. In late March, he toured the city along with companions that included an aging survivor of the Arab violence in 1929. The group pretended they were

Swiss sightseers who needed a place to stay. No apartments were available, but the Park Hotel was. The hotel was a square-shaped two-story stone building with small rooms. Levinger told the Arab owner that he wanted to rent the entire building for ten days with the option of staying much longer. The owner agreed.

On April 14, the eve of Passover, ten Israeli families registered at the hotel. Husbands and wives shared the cramped rooms with their children. Soon, more guests arrived. Before reaching Hebron all of them had obtained permission from General Narkiss, head of the IDF's Central Command, to stay overnight. They had to. At the time, Israelis were permitted to enter the West Bank during the day but needed approval to remain overnight. Narkiss thought they would leave the next day after the first Passover Seder.

Levinger, despite his determination to found Jewish settlements in the West Bank, did have some security concerns. He knew the small number of Jewish men, women, and children staying at the hotel could easily become victims at the hands of the large number of unfriendly Arabs living in Hebron. Therefore, before the holiday, he met with the Israeli military governor assigned to Hebron and asked him to provide security for the Seder. The Governor agreed and ordered some Druse border police in Israel's service to guard them. He also provided a few weapons to Levinger's group so they could better defend themselves.

The Seder proceeded without incident. Estimates of the number of participants range from forty to one-hundred. Simultaneously, on the Golan Heights, 117 Jews in a fledgling Jewish settlement also celebrated the Passover Seder. Meanwhile, along the border with Jordan, it was business as usual. The IDF foiled terrorists trying to sneak into Israel for a spectacular attack scheduled for the holiday.

The following day, Rabbi Levinger publicly announced that his group was re-establishing Jewish life in Hebron. Instead of leaving after a short visit, they intended to create a permanent settlement within the confines of the Arab town.

After declaring his intentions, Levinger was not one to refrain from publicly proclaiming his presence. He led the group at the hotel, singing and dancing, to Abraham's tomb. The tomb was also holy to adherents of Islam. On its grounds was the Ibrahimi Mosque. Previously, the mosque had been a church, built by the Byzantines and destroyed by Muslims after their conquest of the region—a fate Jewish religious sites experienced when they fell into Muslim hands in 1948. From the thirteenth century on, Muslims did not permit Jews to come closer to the tomb than the seventh step leading to its entrance. After the 1967 war, the Israelis vacated the rule prohibiting Jewish access. Levinger believed the image of joyous Jews at the holy site was the best way to promote his plans.

As the days wore on, some of Levinger's group left, but others joined him; and the Israeli government was not in a position to react quickly. The individual charged with responsibility for the territory was at home mourning his father's death, and Moshe Dayan was still in the hospital recovering from his injuries caused by the cave-in. In the absence of an official government response, public debate intensified.

Levinger sought to ensure that his group would not be evicted by telegraphing Labor Minister Allon and asking him for help. He told the minister that thirty families were planning to settle in Hebron. Allon was sympathetic. Previously he had pushed the cabinet to build a Jewish neighborhood near the city. Upon receipt of Levinger's telegram, Allon immediately traveled to meet with the would-be settlers. He told Levinger that, as Labor Minister, he would supply work permits for any members of the group who needed jobs. Allon then went to the Etzion Bloc where he told Hanan Porat, one of the people instrumental in re-establishing Kfar Etzion, to send guns to Levinger because they were in danger. Later, Menachem Begin visited Levinger too.

On April 20, the Labor Party held a meeting to discuss what had happened. Some complained about Allon acting on his own. Others expressed their opposition to permitting establishment of any settlement in Hebron. But the longer the Levinger group remained in the hotel, the more difficult it became, from a political perspective, to remove them. It also was clear that, if the government would not let them build a settlement, the authorities would have no choice but to remove them by force. Formed just before the 1967 war began, Israel's unity government contained both pro and anti-settlement forces that made coming to a consensus with regard to Levinger's gambit extraordinarily difficult. The problem was compounded because Jews had a historical claim to a presence in Hebron based on their more than two thousand year presence in the city, until evicted by Arab terror. Thus, it was an emotional issue that impacted many Jews, religious or not, who were determined to restore a Jewish presence there. However, the cabinet was also well aware that the Levinger group's presence risked inflaming the local Arab population to a degree that would create trouble. And the ministers knew they might also invite unwanted international scrutiny so soon after the fighting in Karameh had ended. In fact, that trouble had already begun. While the cabinet deliberated, conflicts between Levinger and Hebron's Arab Mayor increased.

Finally, on May 12, the cabinet sanctioned a negotiated compromise with Levinger. By then, one-hundred settlers were living in close quarters at the Park Hotel. Levinger agreed to move his group to an Israeli army base located where a former British fortress stood on the outskirts of town. But, the government cautioned, Levinger should not infer that the group was receiving permission to establish a town. After they moved, a recovering Moshe Dayan tried to induce them to leave quickly by making their living conditions uncomfortable. But Levinger's group persevered.

Eventually, the government gave up. The settlers received formal permission to build homes on the eastern side of Hebron, but not in the town itself. They named their settlement, Kiryat Arba. They were also told that they would not be permitted to establish business in Hebron so as to minimize contact with the Arabs. And, Dayan implored the settlers, "Don't raise your children to hate them."

A couple of months later on August 7, the Jews of Hebron celebrated the Katzovers' wedding. A thousand people attended, including most members of the cabinet. On the day of the wedding settlers set up tables outside of the Tomb of the Patriarchs, where the ceremony was held, to sell soft drinks. It was, however fleeting, the first Jewish business established in Hebron. The Israeli Military Governor ignored it. The next day the settlers set up tables again. This time the Governor ordered the drink-stand removed. A laughing group of Arab bystanders watched while Israeli soldiers shut it down after the settlers refused to do so voluntarily.

The next Jewish Holiday of consequence was Rosh Hashanah. Previously, Dayan had reached an agreement with the Muslims in charge of the mosque overlaying Abraham's Tomb that Jews could visit the areas sacred to them at any time except during Muslim prayers. The Hebron Jews wanted more. They asked the Military Governor for permission to pray all day at the tomb on Rosh Hashanah and Yom Kippur. Feeling emboldened when they did not receive a response, Jews stayed and prayed at the tomb the entire day on Rosh Hashanah, even during the Muslim prayers. Hebron's Mayor complained to Israeli authorities, to no avail. Afterwards, the Hebron Jews received permission from Israeli authorities to remain at the tomb all day on Yom Kippur.

Therefore, perhaps, it is no surprise that on October 9, during Sukkot, another Jewish holiday, a hand grenade was thrown into a largely Jewish crowd standing outside the Mosque waiting to enter and head for the tomb. Forty-seven were injured, mostly Jews.

The absence of a clear Israeli policy encouraged people like Levinger to push the limits of the law. Both in the West Bank and on the Golan "facts" were created on the ground, mostly by citizen action. During those heady days, one perspective is that Jews were returning to what had always been theirs prior to being evicted by Arabs and others over the past decades and millennium. Or alternatively, if your perspective is the opposite, Jews were confiscating Arab land, abusing Arab rights, and needlessly irritating the inhabitants. Both sides of the dispute had a point: The only sovereign nation ever to grace the West Bank was a Jewish one more than two thousand years before, but for hundreds of years Arabs had lived on the land in numbers that had significantly increased in the 1900's. Both sides had arguments; neither side had a solution that satisfied the other. And, in the absence of the conflict's resolution, the complexity of the problems Arabs and Jews would have to surmount in order to achieve peace increased with each passing month.

Arafat Goes Mainstream and the Fourth Palestinian National Assembly

By May, Fatah's influence within the Palestinian movement was on the rise; Arafat's popularity had surged despite the existence of other Palestinian groups and leaders. Although a Jordanian army unit fought with Fedayeen on May 28, the fighting did not stop Nasser from wooing the new star of the Arab world. Then, in early July, in light of America's imminent decision to send F-4 *Phantoms* to Israel, Nasser scheduled a trip to Moscow to obtain more arms deliveries. He asked Arafat to join him. Arafat could not turn down the offer, despite the proximity of the trip to the Fourth Palestinian National Assembly meeting scheduled to begin in Cairo on July 10. A meeting with the Russians would elevate his stature.

Nasser saw in Arafat the leader of a potential second front with Israel. Nasser's need to find a new ally had become increasingly apparent because of Syria's refusal to coordinate with him. Nasser told Arafat that Egypt had accepted Resolution 242, but that he doubted it was of any value in the ongoing conflict with Israel. And he emphasized to Arafat that 242 only involved the Arab nations and Israel—not the Palestinians. "You have every right not to accept it," he said. "There is no reason why you should publicly oppose the Resolution because it is not for you." Nasser also advised Arafat to remain independent of other Arab governments but to coordinate with them. He continued, "You must be our irresponsible arm. On this basis we will give you all the help we can." In a geopolitical sense he meant that Egypt would be the "good cop" and Fatah the "bad one".

Their plane left Egypt's airspace on July 3. It was a Russian plane because the Egyptians and Russians feared that Israel might shoot down an Egyptian aircraft flying over the Mediterranean. Arafat was disguised as a technician, and his passport contained a fictitious name, Musin Amin. During the entire time they were en route, Nasser was in great pain, which was nothing new. His health was another reason Nasser went to Moscow where he had scheduled a medical evaluation in a Soviet hospital.

Nasser met with the Russians on July 4. They mostly talked about money. Specifically, they discussed Egyptian payments for the additional arms requested and for the Russian advisors already in Egypt. The Soviet Union's willingness to help Egypt for geopolitical reasons did not come free; Russian communists knew how to be capitalists when it came to someone else's money. They required the impoverished Arab nations that received their help to pay the costs associated with their assistance.

Nasser introduced Arafat to the Russian leaders after lunch. Their meeting went well. The Russians agreed to assist Fatah. Two days later, after Russian doctors had examined the Egyptian President and diagnosed him with hardening of the arteries caused by his diabetes, Arafat and Nasser returned to Egypt. Arafat must have been buoyed by the support and recognition provided by the Russians but pre-occupied with his next challenge—the Palestinian Congress meeting scheduled to begin within a few days.

Fortunately for Arafat, despite his trip to the Soviet Union, he had sufficient time to promote his agenda when he returned to Cairo. The outcome of the meeting was a victory for both Arafat and Fatah. Fatah's seat total increased to thirty-eight in the PLO's governing body. Another ten seats went to Habash's PFLP, and other Palestinian Fedayeen movements received a total of twenty divided between them. The remaining thirty-two seats were awarded to members not necessarily affiliated with one of the Fedayeen liberation groups. With a total of sixty-eight out of one hundred seats, Palestinian guerilla control of the organization was assured and its focus remained liberation and self-determination. And among the Palestinian guerilla organizations, Fatah had gained, by far, the largest share of future influence.

The Palestinian Charter was also amended at the meeting. The most important amendments signifying the PLO's intent to end Israel's existence were:

- Article 6 - "The Jews who had normally resided in Palestine until the beginning of the Zionist invasion will be considered Palestinians."
- Article 9 – "Armed struggle is the only way to liberate Palestine…. They also assert their right to normal life in Palestine and to exercise their right to self-determination and sovereignty over it."
- Article 21 – "The Arab Palestinian people, expressing themselves by the armed Palestinian revolution, reject all solutions which are substitutes for the total liberation of Palestine."
- Article 28 – (This phrase was perhaps directed rather ominously towards Jordan) "The Palestinian Arab people assert the genuineness and independence of their national revolution and reject all forms of intervention, trusteeship and subordination."

Other provisions of the Charter that revealed the PLO's true colors remained intact. They included:

- Article 2, 3 and 20 which called for the end of the Jewish State and denied that the Jews had any rights of self-determination.
- Article 12 that warned other Arab nations not to absorb any Palestinian refugees into their own country (no wonder the Palestinians remained refugees—It was a cold calculation to use Palestinian suffering as a political weapon).
- Article 15 & 18 that called for all Arab nations to unite with the Palestinians in a war to liberate Palestine from the Israelis.

With its flanks protected, Fatah felt comfortable announcing that anyone attempting to set up a "counterfeit Palestinian entity" on the West Bank would be considered an enemy of the Palestinian people. King Hussein could not have been given a clearer warning. Any future attempt to return the West Bank to Jordanian control would be risky. It would meet resistance from Palestinian Fedayeen as well as Israel.

Shortly after the Palestinian meeting ended, Fedayeen stepped up the pressure. On July 23, the first and last successful hijacking of an El Al airplane occurred. El Al was Israel's national airline and a source of enormous pride for the Jewish State. Three members of the Popular Front for the Liberation of Palestine (PFLP) took over the plane shortly after it left Rome en route to Tel Aviv. One of them opened the unlocked cockpit door and struck the pilot with the butt of his pistol. The other two held the passengers at bay with guns and hand grenades. They ordered the pilot to fly to Algeria where the hijackers separated Israeli passengers from the others. The next day they gave the non-Israelis their freedom. Most of the Israelis were held for several weeks while the terrorists negotiated with Israel. They were only freed after Israel agreed to release twelve wounded Fedayeen from her jails.

Israel's government was adamant that the "Algeria affair" would be the first and last time Israel would agree to release detainees in the face of terrorist demands. To ensure that she would not have to face that choice in the future, counterterrorism quickly became Israel's top priority. Shin Bet, the Israeli organization responsible for internal security, sent operatives to Mossad stations around the world and set up shop independently in many countries. Most of their activity was in Europe where Israelis undercover agents played a deadly game of cat-and-mouse with Palestinian terrorists based there. Overnight, Israel built an organizational structure to protect her embassies, banks, airlines, and tourist offices. The security was multi-layered: Armed guards manned ticket counters and provided security at airports, and, on every El Al flight, armed sky marshals in plain clothes rode shotgun to ensure that no Israeli plane would ever be hijacked again.

Nineteen Israelis were killed and at least 180 others died as a result of terrorist attacks within Israel after the Palestinian Conference ended July 17. The worst event was the car bomb that went off in the crowded Mahane Yehuda market in Jerusalem that killed twelve and injured many more. Even though Israel had captured or killed 1,400 Fatah members since the beginning of the year, Palestinian terrorist activities were increasing, both domestically and internationally.

The rise of the PLO and its terrorist activities would have happened whether or not the incipient settler movement had achieved some success in 1968. During the year, the PLO became a recognized force on the world stage, while the desire of some Jews to build settlements in the occupied territories was merely a blip that had been bottled up, but then uncorked, by a reluctant government. Nor did those desires to create new Jewish homes in the newly won lands have a significant impact on West Bank residents at that time. In 1968, the settler movement did not create terrorists. Terrorist groups targeting Israel were already quite active and had been since Israel's founding in 1948. If anything, the terrorists created more settlers by adding substance to the argument of some that new settlements were needed to make Israel more secure. However, what was also becoming increasingly true was that the precarious political balance within Israel's unity government, formed by necessity before the Six-Day War, made it politically impossible to create a concrete policy for dealing with territorial demands of Jews who wanted to settle in the West Bank. Nor could the government agree on a negotiating policy for Arab nations that refused to negotiate directly with Israel. That political deadlock provided an opportunity for the nascent settler movement. Soon it would emerge as a potent political force.

CHAPTER TWENTY-SEVEN
The Canal Zone Heats Up in the Absence of Peace

During an interview with Look *magazine in March, Nasser retracted the false allegations he had made during the Six-Day War that American and British pilots had flown missions that, along with the IAF, destroyed Egypt's air force. He explained that his accusations were based on "suspicion and faulty information." But still, Nasser refused to meet with Israeli officials.*

Meanwhile, the Jarring mission had been sputtering along since the UN approved Resolution 242 in November, several months before. Jarring believed that Israel and the Arabs were not driven by logic but were prisoners of emotion and history. Nevertheless, in early March 1968, he thought he would be able to convince both sides to begin indirect negotiations on the island of Rhodes. Eshkol accepted the offer because he hoped it would lead to direct talks. But Egypt, in light of the three no's of Khartoum, and the prevailing view in the Arab world, did not want to risk sliding down a slippery slope that would end with direct meetings. Therefore, on March 7, Nasser rejected Jarring's proposal for peace negotiations. Instead, he turned up the heat. Egyptian commandos inflicted heavy casualties on the IDF when they attacked an Israeli tank unit along the canal. Israel retaliated with ten days of bombing and commando raids of her own. The Egyptians answered back by bombarding IDF positions with artillery shells. Russian advisors commanded the Egyptian artillery units.

On September 8, the fighting worsened. Egypt launched a massive artillery barrage on Israeli positions all along the Suez Canal. More than 10,000 shells landed over several hours, a pace in excess of twenty explosions every minute. IDF soldiers huddled in makeshift shelters; miraculously, only ten were killed and another eighteen wounded. The IDF responded swiftly and devastatingly. It shelled and demolished Egyptian oil refineries located in the canal cities of Ismalia and Suez. Israeli frogmen also swam into an Egyptian harbor where two Egyptian naval vessels were moored and destroyed them. The next day, several hundred Israelis landed in Egyptian territory on the western shore of the Gulf of Suez. To disguise themselves, they used Russian tanks and vehicles captured during the Six-Day War. For nine hours they marauded down the coastal road destroying missile sites, radar installations, and military vehicles along the way. Nasser was both embarrassed and furious.

Over the final months of 1968, the Egyptian army continued to fire on Israeli soldiers along the canal, and Israel continued to retaliate. Israel's goal was to deter the Egyptians by exposing their vulnerability to devastating air attacks. Egyptian fire eventually slackened but did not end. Nevertheless, Nasser's attempt to force Israel to retreat from the canal by bleeding her had failed. And it left Nasser's home front devastated. Subsequently, Egypt made no attempt to repair the refineries and the damage done to the cities along the eastern side of the canal. As a result of the destruction, 400,000 Egyptians fled the Canal Zone.

The IDF, however, recognized it needed to find a better strategy for defending the canal. The death of so many of their soldiers (only good fortune had prevented the loss of more) forced a search for a solution that would reduce the number of casualties if Egypt struck again. Internal discussions began within the IDF regarding two competing options: defend the canal with new fortifications built to withstand heavy artillery shelling, or pull the IDF eastward, out of range of artillery and rely instead on mobile patrols to secure the boundary along the canal.

Secret Meetings

In late January of 1968, King Hussein was frustrated because he saw no viable option for recovering his lost territory. Earlier that month, he had made a publicized offer. If Israel withdrew and permitted Jordanian civil servants to enter the West Bank, his army would stay put east of the Jordan River until a permanent settlement was concluded with Israel that resolved borders and refugees. Israel did not bite. The Israelis were very clear and consistent; there would be no withdrawal before direct negotiations and a binding peace treaty.

Hussein was also angry with the Americans, who refused to replenish the arsenal of weapons Jordan lost in the Six-Day War. Morale in his army, already impacted by the rise of Palestinian influence within Jordan, was dropping to levels that endangered his ability to retain his throne. The economic and political burden of the Palestinian refugees had overwhelmed Hussein's resources, and the increasing number of Fedayeen attacks had increased the likelihood of further conflict with Israel. Also, to the north, Syria was a constant threat; and the Iraqi troops still based within his country posed a danger to his rule, as well. Simply put, Hussein was threatened from all directions, including from within. If he could not strengthen his army, then, his chances of remaining in power were slim.

But Hussein had one trump card. He was a client of the western democracies and historically had close ties with England. And, fortunately for the king, his friend Jack O'Donnell, the CIA station chief in Amman, nurtured and protected Jordan's growing relationship with the United States. Still, Hussein was desperate for help. He decided to invite the Russians to send a high-level military delegation to meet with him. His plan to appeal for their help would have been music to Russian ears, if he would have followed through. It would have given the Russians an opportunity to wean away one of the few Arab countries left with close ties to the United States. However, O'Donnell and the American Ambassador managed to convince Hussein to hold off and pleaded with him to give America one more chance. The king agreed to refrain from contacting the Russians with one stipulation: If his delegation to

Washington, scheduled to get there in a few days, did not come back with all that he wanted, he personally would lead a Jordanian mission to Moscow.

On January 13, when Hussein traveled again to Cairo, Nasser greeted him warmly. Hussein told the Egyptian President that Jarring had tried to give him a letter sent directly by Eshkol but he had refused to take it. He also said that he told Jarring that passing such a message was outside the scope of the UN negotiator's mission. Hussein continued that he thought Jarring was trying to arrange a secret meeting between Israel and the Arabs. Even though Hussein sensed that he could only get his lands back if he agreed to direct talks with the Israelis, he knew he could not do that without Nasser's blessing. Perhaps Hussein advised Nasser of the Jarring note to probe whether Nasser would countenance him talking directly with the Israelis. But Nasser did not demonstrate any interest in the idea. Instead, the Egyptian leader reiterated that he did not support direct diplomatic contact with Israel.

However, even though he had no that hope Jarring would succeed, Nasser wanted to continue cooperating with him. His purpose was to convince the Soviets that diplomacy would not work and that only Soviet supplied arms would change facts on the ground. Nasser's long term strategy was to fight and win another war with Israel—a war he believed Egypt would not be ready to initiate for another three to five years.

The two leaders also discussed Hussein's need for new arms. Nasser advised the king that it was important for at least one Arab country to maintain her ties with the west and suggested that Hussein ask England for help if the United States continued to refuse him.

Nasser then brought up the subject of the Fedayeen. He asked Hussein to permit them to attack Israel from Jordanian soil. He pointed out that Jordan presented the only option for staging areas because the Syrians kept tight control on terrorists based in their territory, and Lebanon was too small and unstable to be a proper base for the

Palestinians. Hussein said no. He did not want to invite further Israeli retaliation raids on his soil, and he did not want to give the terrorists an effective vote on whether or not Jordan would accept a deal with Israel that restored his rule to the West Bank. As it was, it was bad enough having Iraqi troops on his soil. The Iraqis actively helped the Fedayeen by providing Iraqi uniforms for them to wear while infiltrating into Jordan. Then, when they entered one of the larger Jordanian cities, the Fedayeen took off their loaned uniforms and melted into the population.

Hussein's refusal of Nasser's request to permit PLO terrorists to operate freely on Jordanian soil proved prescient. Hussein's hold on his country was growing increasingly tenuous, especially after Fedayeen strength grew after the Karameh battle. The implicit threat to Hussein contained in Article 28 of the Palestinian Charter, approved four months after Karameh, left little doubt of Palestinian intent. Had Hussein cast his lot with the PLO, he would not have survived the massive growth of the Fatah movement that subsequently occurred within Jordan.

Thus, the king returned to Jordan without anything tangible to show for his efforts. Nasser had not given him clearance to talk openly with the Israelis. Nor did Hussein's plan for enticing Israel to withdraw spark any interest with the Egyptian President. The only good news Hussein received over the next several weeks was that the Americans offered Jordan enough military support to satisfy him. As a result, the risk that Jordan would fall under the sway of the Russian dissipated.

Meanwhile, Eshkol met with several Palestinian dignitaries in early February. The last meeting was with Anwar Nuseibeh, a powerful West Bank politician. Eshkol asked him to act as a conduit between him and Hussein. They spent an hour discussing various aspects of the Jerusalem issue and Eshkol's disappointment that Hussein, despite vowing not to, had decided to go to war with Israel in 1967. Nevertheless, Eshkol told Nuseibeh that he was prepared to offer Jordan sovereignty over the Islamic holy places in Jerusalem and to permit the Jordanian flag to fly above them. Nuseibeh responded that it was not enough. But, by the end of their conversation, Nuseibeh sensed that Eshkol might be willing to consider giving up much more land than he had yet offered; so much that he would insist on keeping very little other than Jerusalem.

Hussein asked Nuseibeh to meet with him on February 10. Violence almost intervened. When terrorist bombs went off in Israel killing four, Israel responded with artillery fire and airstrikes that precipitated a duel with Jordanian units. As a result, more Israeli soldiers died, and Arabs in a Palestinian refugee camp targeted by the IDF suffered many casualties. Even so, the king was still willing to meet with Nuseibeh.

Nuseibeh carried a note from Eshkol to Hussein suggesting that the Israeli and Jordanian military Chiefs of Staff meet secretly. The king responded favorably to the idea of bilateral meetings but suggested they be conducted at a lower level. Hussein nominated Colonel Daud as the Arab intermediary. Daud was well known to the Israelis: He had been Jordan's representative on the Mixed Armistice Commission which had worked to resolve disputes between Jordan and Israel before the outbreak of the 1967 war. Hussein thought that Daud would offer a measure of protection; if the talks were revealed he could explain they were just a continuation of Daud's pre-war role. Even though they considered the colonel a "very small and stale fish," the Israelis willingly accepted Hussein's alternative nominee.

The two governments scheduled the first meeting with Daud for two days later at the Allenby Bridge, which crossed the Jordan River and connects the West Bank to the East Bank. But Daud was in New York recovering from ear surgery and could not make the meeting. When Daud's deputy showed up late as a replacement, the Israelis were perturbed. They thought Daud's failure to appear indicated Hussein's lack of interest in Eshkol's initiative. They did not believe the Jordanian officer's excuses, and they decided that further discussions using that channel would be useless.

However, even though that meeting failed, Nuseibeh met again with Hussein on February 27. He conveyed Israel's minimum requirements for an agreement: peaceful borders, certain concessions, and direct negotiations. Hussein responded, as he had before, that he first needed to know the parameters of the deal that Israel would eventually agree to before committing. In effect, Hussein wanted to conclude the negotiations before they began. His was a request for Israel to reveal her bottom line while not revealing his own. It was a request Israel had consistently refused to honor before and would refuse once again.

Against the backdrop of escalating Fedayeen attacks and IDF responses, Israel's cabinet tried again to agree on a vision for the future of the West Bank. However, Allon and Dayan continued to clash over their competing plans. And Allon's plan had changed. His amendment called for twenty-five new settlements that would be built in the Jordan valley to increase protection of Israel's homeland from terrorist incursions. Eshkol favored Allon's proposal, but, once again, the cabinet was unable to reach a consensus. Thus the policy void remained; blood continued to flow, and the battle of Karameh, previously described, would soon follow.

Nevertheless, Hussein was still determined to try. He resolved to maintain a dual policy regarding future contacts with the Israelis; he would continue meeting secretly with high-level Israelis, while at the same time refuse to permit Jordan's Army Chief of Staff to meet with his Israeli counterpart. Hussein knew involving his army in high-level talks would not help his cause: The West Bank would not be recovered by winning a war. His task, he recognized, was to win the peace—a task that was his alone to accomplish.

On May 3, Hussein and his close friend and advisor, Zaid Rifa'I, met with Foreign Minister Eban and Herzog in England. Both sides wanted peace, but Israel wanted to hold onto Jerusalem and strategic portions of the West Bank. That did not sit well with Hussein who wanted every inch of his land back. The distance between their two positions was still too vast to overcome.

Eban told Hussein he had not come to make binding commitments. He only wanted the answer to two questions. **First**, would Jordan negotiate a peace agreement separate from, and not dependent on, her Arab neighbors? **Second**, what did the king intend to do to stop terrorists from launching attacks from Jordanian soil?

Hussein responded to the first question that it was possible; but, before he would commit to a peace process, he needed to know the specifics of the settlement Israel would offer. Eban answered evasively. He said there was no reason for his government to reach a decision on their final position before it knew that it had a serious partner. He told Hussein that, within the government, there were three schools of thought. The **first** was to keep all of the newly won territory. The **second** was to reach a settlement with the inhabitants of the West Bank. The **third** was to make peace with Jordan based on a new secure border that took into account history and Israel's security needs. The third group required, as a condition of reaching an agreement, that Jordan agree to demilitarized zones in the West Bank territories she would receive back and that Jerusalem would remain the united capital of the Jewish State.

In effect, Eban was telling Hussein that two factions of Israel's government did not want to negotiate with him at all, and the third was only willing to do so on terms that he would never accept. It should not have been a surprise that Hussein did not respond favorably. Hussein made no further attempt to find common ground. Instead, he suggested that the peace talks under the auspices of Jarring continue, and he told Eban that he would consult with Cairo before saying anything else. Hussein was not ending the discussions, but just buying time by and supporting Nasser's strategy to continue the hopeless, Jarring peace process.

Hussein, in light of the Khartoum "three no's," had no other choice. He needed Cairo's blessing before he could engage openly in talks with the Israelis. But on May 6, Rifa'I received an interesting message from Nasser for delivery to Hussein:

> Don't trust the Jews. First they will not carry out the Security Council Resolution. Second, they will not give up Jerusalem. Third, they will not give up Gaza. Fourth, they will not withdraw to the borders of 4 June 1967. This whole business is an illusion and a danger. But, if you insist, I, Nasser will order my permanent representative at the UN to meet with Jarring, not with the Israelis, and we'll see. I'll give you this chance.

Nasser's message obliquely suggested a two-step process. First, Jordan and Egypt would meet with Jarring in New York. Then Egypt would withdraw, and Jordan could continue with substantive talks. Nasser felt a moral debt to Hussein for dragging him into the war. He would do what he could, but no more, to give Hussein a faint opportunity to recover his lost lands.

While Jarring continued with his fruitless search for common ground, Hussein again met secretly with the Israelis in England. This time Allon joined the talks, and Eban, as happened in May, initiated the substantive discussions. He told Hussein they were there to discuss the possibility of finding a path to a permanent peace. But Eban warned, if rejected, Israel would seek an agreement with the West Bank's inhabitants without any consideration for Jordan's interests. Allon told Hussein that Israel required a contractual peace. A promise was not enough. He also asked the king if he could control Fatah and if he could sign an agreement without Nasser's consent.

Hussein responded that for peace to be genuine it had to be honorable. He warned that, although Israel was strong and might win many battles, if she lost one it would be catastrophic. It was a concern most Israelis were acutely aware of—but too many were overly-confident that if attacked they would win overwhelmingly.

Eban and Allon then outlined for Hussein six principles that guided their approach. Those principles were governed by Israel's need to implement significant boundary changes that would leave her with defensible borders for the future. And they made clear, without achieving their security needs there would be no concessions.

Hussein politely listened and then cautioned that security came from shared trust—not boundaries. Allon disagreed, and Eban reminded Hussein that Israel's principles were in line with UN Resolution 242. But, of course, that was his opinion, an opinion the United States also shared and which was based on the official text. But it was not the opinion of the Arabs and most other countries, who wrongly interpreted the resolution as requiring Israel to fully withdraw. However, the Jordanians remained calm even though the Israelis had not offered anything new.

Then Allon revealed a map that depicted his plan. Hussein gazed at the graphic depiction of Israel maintaining her occupation of the Jordan Valley, adjacent to the western bank of the Jordan River, and a slice of land that linked the valley to Jerusalem and bisected the West Bank. The map also showed other smaller areas that Allon wanted to continue to control. In all, Allon's plan reserved one-third of the West Bank for Israeli rule. It was too much for Hussein. Visualization of what he was being asked to accept hardened his resolve. He lost all interest in any further discussion.

The Israelis asked him to reconsider before giving a formal reply. Two days later Rifa'I responded in writing with a note: "The plan itself is wholly unacceptable since it infringes Jordanian sovereignty," he said. "The only way is to exchange territory on the basis of reciprocity."

Clearly, Allon's plan did not go over well with Hussein. The most the Jordanians had ever suggested they might concede was Israel's right to control Jewish holy sites. And the Jordanians had insisted that any border changes that gave Israel sovereignty over any West Bank land would have to be paid for by Israel's ceding to Jordan control of a reciprocal amount of Israeli territory. With both sides unwilling to compromise, the likelihood of Israel finding common ground with Hussein to sign a peace treaty was as far away as ever.

But Hussein's negative response did not end the contacts between him and high-level Israelis. On November 19, 1968, Hussein met again with Eban, Allon, and Herzog on board an Israeli ship in the Bay of Aqaba. By then the Fedayeen were a thorn deep in Hussein's side, but, due to their popularity within Jordan, he felt he had to negotiate a peace agreement with Israel before he could safely crack down on them. To improve his chances of doing so, Hussein planned to continue negotiating on two tracks, one with Jarring and the other, hopefully assisted by American pressure on Israel, with the Israelis privately.

Hussein kept a yacht moored at his villa close to Israel's border, near the port town of Eilat, which he used to cruise over to the Israeli boat where Herzog and the others waited. Once again, the Israelis had nothing new to offer. But Hussein did. He offered some territory on the West Bank in return for Jordanian sovereignty in Gaza, plus a land bridge on Israeli territory that linked Gaza to the West Bank. That would give Jordan direct access to the Mediterranean. Whether he would have been able to control Gaza, or even the West Bank, in the face of what might have been virulent Palestinian opposition is another story; but we will never know. The king's plan did not sit well with the Israelis. They were more interested in encouraging Gaza's residents to self-deport (a term used by Mitt Romney in the 2012 elections, but also descriptive of Israel's unrealistic policy at that time). In addition, Israel did not want to create a land-link that effectively would also link Jordan and Egypt via Gaza. The meeting concluded like all of the others in 1968. There were no substantive agreements, but their failure did not cause either side to lose respect for the other.

Despite the repeated failures to move forward on a contractual, peace deal, the Israelis saw value in talking to Hussein. While their conversations had little chance of yielding a peaceful resolution for the two countries—for Hussein required most, if not all, of his land returned—the talks were useful for pressuring Hussein to prevent the terrorists from attacking Israel. More than twenty-five years later, Hussein reflected back to those days and said:

> As far as I am concerned it was either every single inch that I was responsible for, or nothing.... [M]y grandfather eventually paid with his life for his attempts to make peace.... I could not compromise.

Assad

Syrian Defense Minister Hafez al-Assad was not happy. His relationship with Salah Jadid, the behind-the-scenes strongman leader of Syria, had worsened during the winter and early spring of 1968. Assad was obsessed with Syria's failure in the 1967 war and thirsted to recover the Golan Heights from Israel. Therefore, he believed it important to cultivate Syria's relationship with the Russians to assure the supply of weapons required to wrest back control of the Golan. However, he opposed Jadid's push to transform Syria into a socialist state. Also, Assad looked to partner with other Arab nations while Jadid favored a "peoples war" approach that led him to be more supportive than Assad of the various Palestinian terrorist organizations.

Quietly, Assad began to plot behind Jadid's back. He first moved to oust key Jadid supporters from their positions in the military and replace them with his own followers. His most important appointment was the new chief of staff, Mustafa Tlas. Since their days together at the military academy beginning in 1951, Tlas had been Assad's friend.

The fourth regional Congress of Syria's Ba'th party met in September. By then it was clear to many that Assad and Jadid were headed toward a clash. While Assad focused on recovering the Golan, Jadid was more concerned with transforming Syrian society. As a result they argued vociferously. Jadid only wanted adherents to the Ba'th party line to be eligible for membership in the party; Assad advocated embracing more people with differing views. Jadid denounced other Arab nations; Assad sought to enlist them in a common cause against Israel. Jadid's views prevailed. Even though Assad controlled the military, Jadid controlled the internal security and intelligence services. It was not yet Assad's time.

Rabin Comes to Washington

Rabin presented his ambassador credentials to President Johnson on March 6. Before then he had had no experience in the world of diplomacy and did not like what little he had already observed. Rabin had an impeccable reputation as a brilliant strategist and technician because he had been the man in charge of Israel's victorious armed forces in the Six-Day War. Dayan may have been lionized, but Rabin was revered by a grateful Israeli public, and he was well respected by the American military community. But still, his heavily-accented and not-so-fluent English caused some concern with regard to his diplomatic skills. His distaste for parties, reception lines, and formal wear magnified those fears.

Rabin bore his plainness proudly and encouraged others to think of him as only a temporary member of the diplomatic corps. But he had goals. They were to:

- Obtain economic and military assistance for Israel from the United States;
- Convince the United States to prevent Russian penetration of the Middle East; and
- Persuade the Americans that the countries in the Middle East should be allowed to resolve their disputes themselves rather than be dictated to by the superpowers.

Rabin came to enjoy his new responsibilities. His shyness did not impede him because he preferred slowly cultivating new relationships rather than embracing them without hesitation. Rabin also relished the freedom he felt in Washington, where he was not encumbered by an array of responsibilities as he was in Israel as IDF Chief of Staff.

Rabin got along well with Lucius Battle, the State Department official assigned to the Middle East. But when Battle resigned in October, his replacement, Parker Hart, was much less to his liking. Hart was an Arabist. Previously, he had been the ambassador to Turkey, and most of his international embassy postings had been in the Arab world. Rabin later said:

"I entered his office—and thought I must be having a heart attack.... On every wall, on every side, covering every centimeter, they were staring at me—Arab rulers, with and without Keffiahs, with and without moustaches, sheiks, princes, rulers, presidents. The only agreeable picture of the whole gallery was that of the Turkish President."

Terror

On December 26, two PFLP members threw hand grenades and opened fire on an El Al plane at the airport in Athens. Before Israeli security could stop the terrorists, one passenger was killed, and a flight attendant was badly injured. The terrorists had trained for their mission in Lebanon, and then flown from Beirut to Greece. Eshkol called a meeting with his military and intelligence chiefs to plan a response. "We can't just ignore this," he said. Enough was enough.

Just two days later, Israel responded. On December 28, Special Forces flew by helicopter to the tarmac of Beirut Airport. After a gun battle with Lebanese troops, they destroyed thirteen empty planes belonging to Arab airlines. No civilians were injured in the attack. World leaders and the international press condemned Israel for her actions. Israel responded that there was a vast difference between their reprisal and what the terrorists had done. The terrorists' plan was to murder innocent victims; the Israeli response was to destroy property of those who helped terrorism flourish. Israel could not be expected to remain on the defensive against terror attacks and stoically absorb the tragedies caused by those that got through. Only active cooperation from neighboring Arab nations could end the problem. By destroying the property of any Arab nation supporting terrorism, Israel reminded those countries that there was a price for their inaction. Hussein understood the message. Others did not, or refused to allow it to influence their behavior.

CHAPTER TWENTY-EIGHT
Phantoms and the Bomb

When France provided Israel with a nuclear reactor in the late 1950s (built in the Negev town of Dimona) Israel's dream of launching a nuclear weapons program became a reality. By 1968, the Central Intelligence Agency (CIA) felt fairly certain that Israel had produced at least one nuclear weapon. The CIA's suspicions were confirmed by Edward Teller, the father of America's H-Bomb, through his contacts with Israeli scientists. The State Department, however, told President Johnson that it did not agree with the CIA's assessment. But the State Department was missing one important piece of information; the CIA never divulged what Teller had told them.

Nevertheless, the State Department recognized it needed to know more about Israel's nuclear program. To do so, American diplomats used Israel's desire for American Phantom fighter aircraft as leverage to obtain more information about Israel's capacity to build nuclear weapons. When Johnson met with Eshkol on January 7, 1968, he raised concerns about Israel's nuclear program. The most the Israelis would say was that they would not be the first to "introduce nuclear weapons into the Middle East." What exactly did that mean? The Americans could not get clarification. But it is also conceivable that American officials did not want to know. They assumed that not introducing the weapons meant not testing them and not publicly revealing them. It is doubtful, however, that any American thought that, if they existed, they would not be used were Israel's existence in jeopardy.

As 1968 played out, the issue of the Phantoms loomed larger. President Johnson had intimated in January he would provide them, but then he surprisingly announced, at the end of a televised speech in late March, that he would not run for president in the fall. Instead, he explained, he would concentrate his efforts on bringing the Vietnam War to a conclusion. But what would Johnson's decision mean with regard to the Phantoms Israel coveted? In October, Dean Rusk met with Eban twice to discuss Israel's nuclear research. Rusk asked Israel to provide information concerning her nuclear program and to sign the international non-proliferation treaty. In return, Rusk suggested that the United States would sell Israel the Phantoms. Eban responded evasively. He would only provide the same old assurance that Israel would not be the first to introduce nuclear weapons to the Middle East.

Phantoms

By the beginning of November 1968, the Americans still had not given Israel a formal commitment to sell her the *Phantoms*. Yitzhak Rabin was charged with closing the deal. However, unbeknownst to Rabin, President Johnson had embarked on a secret gambit to avoid having to sell Israel the *Phantoms*—a gambit which had just failed. In October, Johnson sent a private note to Nasser suggesting he would withhold the modern jets from Israel if Egypt and Russia moderated their negotiating stance with regard to the Jewish State. But the note backfired. Instead of galvanizing Nasser into action, it incensed him. The Egyptian President was unwilling to offer more than what his interpretation of Resolution 242 called on him to do. Thus, he would accept nothing less than a full Israeli withdrawal accomplished without direct negotiations and without full recognition. When Johnson did not receive the response he had hoped for, the Americans turned their attention towards delineating the conditions they would require Israel to accept before selling them the *Phantoms*.

On November 4, the Israelis finally received word that the Americans were ready to commit to selling the planes. Responsibility had fallen to

Assistant Secretary for International Security, Paul Warnke, to lead the discussions with his Israeli counterparts concerning their nuclear weapons program and sale of the fighter jets. But when Rabin arrived at Warnke's office on November 5, prepared to sign an agreement, the document Warnke presented contained a catch in the third paragraph. In return for the *Phantoms*, Israel had to give the United States access to every location within the country connected to the development of nuclear weapons. Rabin recognized that, if he signed the document, the Americans would have unfettered access to Israel's airfields, ports, universities, corporate facilities, and the like. In addition, the United States would then be empowered to examine and monitor imports. And, even more, the document required that Israel sign the nuclear non-proliferation treaty and refrain from testing strategic missiles. It was a bridge too far for an Israel justifiably worried that she always was one step away from possible extinction. Rabin was furious. A few days later he told the Americans that his government would not sign the document.

But Rabin desperately wanted the *Phantoms*. And he was a military man. Rabin knew that frontal attacks frequently fail because that is where the enemy's defenses are strongest, but attacks from an unexpected direction often have a greater chance of success. He decided, after his meeting with Warnke, that he would have to influence the President indirectly in order to obtain the jets. Rabin asked friends—Abraham Feinberg, a wealthy, philanthropic supporter of Israel, and Arthur Goldberg, former Supreme Court Justice and U.S. ambassador to the UN—to urge the President to release the *Phantoms*.

After a week of maneuvering, Rabin met with Warnke on November 12. At that meeting Warnke tried to pin him down on the nuclear weapons issue. Warnke asked Rabin to clarify the meaning of two terms used in Israel's stock response that Israel would not be the first to "introduce nuclear weapons into the Middle East." Warnke wanted to know if Israel viewed a weapon held by a third country on Israel's behalf as an "introduction." He also inquired whether Israel considered an untested weapon to be a "nuclear weapon." Rabin, who was at the time pursuing his indirect strategy through Feinberg and Goldberg, responded ambiguously. Warnke, however, pressed further: "Then in your view, an unadvertised, untested nuclear weapon device is not a nuclear weapon. What about an advertised, but untested nuclear device or weapon, would that be introduction?" Rabin answered, "Yes," since the purpose of a nuclear weapon is to deter, and that requires public knowledge.

Israel's Nuclear Activity

While Rabin fended off American inquiries, other Israelis actively made arrangements for Israel to obtain the nuclear fuel required to make more nuclear weapons. France had supplied Israel with nuclear material when Israel's nuclear program began. After de Gaulle stopped shipments because Israel chose to fight rather than wait in 1967, the Israelis obtained twenty-one tons of heavy water from Norway. However, to speed production, Israel required uranium.

Zalman Shapiro had access to uranium.

Shapiro was an American Jew who grew up in Canton, Ohio. Many of his father's relatives had perished in the Holocaust. As a young man, he occasionally endured anti-Semitic insults that targeted him. In 1948, he obtained a Ph.D. in chemistry, and then Westinghouse Corporation hired him to help build the Nautilus, America's first nuclear submarine. In the mid-1950s, Zalman started his own company in Pennsylvania, the Nuclear Materials and Equipment Corporation (NUMEC); but the company had problems managing its nuclear materials. In 1962, regulators cited NUMEC for poor recordkeeping, and then in 1965, regulators discovered that 110 pounds of enriched uranium was missing. Enriched uranium is used to build nuclear weapons (in a later investigation, that took more than a decade to complete, the U.S. Atomic Energy Commission reported 587 pounds of uranium unaccounted for from NUMEC—enough to build up to eighteen atom bombs). Then, in 1968, four high level Israeli operatives paid a visit to NUMEC. It is no surprise that historians strongly suggest that Shapiro's NUMEC was a major supplier of other nuclear fuel for Israel's nuclear program.

But there were other sources, in addition to NUMEC, that likely fulfilled Israel's nuclear needs. Israeli officials purchased some uranium from South Africa, and Israel's nuclear scientists created nuclear material in the Dimona reactor from Israel's large phosphate reserves. And, in November of 1968, 200 tons of uranium oxide stored in 560 drums marked with the label PLUMBAT were purchased by a German corporation from a Belgium mining company. In Antwerp's harbor, dockworkers loaded the drums onto the deck of the *Scheersberg A*, a ship flying the Liberian flag. The *Scheersberg A* was supposed to go to Genoa. It never got there. Somewhere between Cyprus and Turkey it rendezvoused with an Israeli cargo ship. When the *Scheersberg A* eventually arrived in Turkey, the uranium oxide drums were no longer on board. Suspicions are strong, based on revelations from a part-time, Israeli, secret agent captured in Norway that the contents of the PLUMBAT drums made their way to Israel.

A Tumultuous Year Ends

1968 buffeted and distracted America. The year began with the North Vietnamese Tet offensive in late January. In April, a gunman killed Martin Luther King, setting off race riots in many American cities. Sirhan Sirhan, a Palestinian whose family left Jordan when he was twelve years old, assassinated Robert Kennedy on June 5. Many thought Kennedy was an inspirational leader, destined to win the presidency. The loss of both leaders left a pall over the country. Then in August, Russia invaded Czechoslovakia to put an end to the Czech democratic revolution. That Soviet aggressive act raised fears that America, overwhelmed by her internal divisions, would find her power and influence eclipsed in Europe.

And in Israel a new ruling political coalition emerged when three political parties consolidated to form the Labor party in January. Three months later, the new party wrestled to reconcile its members' conflicting views regarding what Israel's policy for the West Bank should be, but never reached an agreement. Without a meaningful Arab partner, and in the absence of any other external pressure, there was little to force a decision.

At least, however, the Israelis had the opportunity to become informed and entertained. On May 2, the Israeli Broadcasting Authority went live with Israel's first publicly available television channel.

On October 31, the cabinet met at Eshkol's home. Egypt's intransigence had altered the political climate. The ministers decided that Israel would no longer agree to pull back from the entire Sinai. Instead, peace with Egypt would require permanent changes to the international border: Gaza would have to remain controlled by Israel, and Israel would insist on retaining control of Sharm el-Sheikh, along with a territorial connection running from that crucial chokepoint to Israel, some 200 miles away. The implacable Arab stand that favored confrontation over compromise had had an impact—it whittled away the cabinet ministers' willingness less than seventeen months before, to withdraw entirely from the Sinai in return for peace.

However, even though his cabinet's views had hardened, Eshkol still held out hope for peace with Egypt. On November 9, he sent a private message to Nasser in which he wrote, "Mr. President, if you really want peace you will find us ready to agree to it with all our hearts and at any time." Nasser never replied.

Five days before that note, Richard Milhous Nixon was elected President of the United States. Nixon was a Republican with hardline credentials who had promised to change America's international policy from one of confrontation to negotiation. With regard to the Middle East, Nixon well knew that negotiation was necessary; the conflict in the Middle East contained the seeds for a superpower confrontation that he hoped to avoid.

Nixon's victory pleased Nasser. The Egyptian President remembered that President Eisenhower had forced Israel to withdraw from the Sinai in 1957. Nasser assumed that since Nixon had then been vice president he would be sympathetic to

Egypt's demand that Israel again withdraw from the Sinai. He also knew that a majority of American Jews did not vote for Nixon in the election. Therefore, he thought Nixon would not feel beholden to his Jewish constituents.

Rabin was also pleased that Nixon won. He had first met Nixon in 1962, while he was the IDF's Chief of Staff. After Nixon lost the 1960 presidential election to Kennedy, and also lost the California Gubernatorial election in 1962, the former vice president went on an international fact-finding trip with the hope of keeping his political future alive. One evening, Rabin found himself in the home of an American diplomat and seated at the dinner table with the former vice president. Nixon had just been in South East Asia. The only other dinner guest who had been there was Rabin. While neither Rabin nor Nixon engaged in small talk over dinner, they did begin conversing once the two discovered that they shared a common experience. During their conversation, Rabin offered Nixon a tour of Israel in a military helicopter. Nixon accepted the offer. Their flightpath included an aerial jaunt over the northern Galilee adjacent to the Golan Heights. Years later, when he returned to Israel shortly after the Six-Day War ended, but before he became president, Nixon said, "If I were an Israeli I would never give up the Golan Heights."

Rabin met Nixon again in August 1968, shortly before the Republican convention nominated him as their candidate for President. Rabin's first five months as ambassador had filled him with foreboding because he believed America was losing strength. Therefore, he was pleased when Nixon told him that one should not conduct negotiations unless from a position of strength. Nixon was referring to America; but, when Nixon was elected President, Rabin, remembering that conversation, believed that Nixon would understand and accept that the same policy was Israel's guiding light.

Then, on December 27, the same day three American astronauts orbited the moon for the first time, Eshkol finally heard the words he so desperately wanted to hear. President Johnson publicly announced, less than a month before the end of his term of office, that America would sell fifty Phantom jets to Israel for a little more than four million dollars apiece. Delivery was scheduled for late 1969 and 1970.

Thus, while 1968 ended with America committing to provide Israel with military hardware necessary for her survival, the year saw no progress toward achieving lasting peace in the region. Syria was still intransigent; and despite both Hussein's and Nasser's grudging private acceptance that Israel was there to stay, neither of them could summon the courage to publicly proclaim their acceptance of that inconvenient fact. Meanwhile, after Karameh, not only did the PLO gather strength and become increasingly popular, it also began to behave as a law unto itself within Jordan. The Jordanian army's hatred of Fedayeen conduct led to a confrontation on November 4 that left twenty-eight Palestinians dead before Hussein reined in his army. But because he restrained them, resentment towards the king grew within the military; and the Fedayeen, rather than cower, boasted they had fought the soldiers off. More fighting loomed on the horizon; it was just a question of when.

Also unfortunately, in 1968, local Arab leaders within the West Bank were too divided and too unrealistic to reach an agreement with Israel. For the second year in a row they had missed an opportunity by compromising too little and fearing Hussein and the PLO too much. The lack of movement toward resolution left too much space for some Israeli ministers to plot making Israel's presence in the West Bank more permanent and defensible. Those machinations gave rise to the government approving ten new Jewish settlements in the conquered territories within the first few days of the coming year. Eban subsequently said:

> *Many Israelis who had begun by regarding the occupied territories as cards to play at the peace table ended up by falling in love with the cards and embracing them so tenaciously as to eliminate their bargaining value.*

CHAPTER TWENTY-NINE
Nixon, Kissinger, and Rogers

In 1968, a peaceful resolution for the Middle East was not found. In 1969, the region paid a price for the failure.

Israel never wavered from her fundamental position that there must be direct negotiations between the Arabs and Israel that culminate in a binding, written agreement prior to any withdrawal. The Jewish State's caution was perfectly understandable when viewed through a historical prism composed of the animosity and mayhem which Arab nations had directed towards her. In 1957, under immense pressure from the United States, Israel reluctantly withdrew from the Sinai—and, in return, only received a promise of peace absent of concrete changes that would guarantee it. Then, instead of peace, Israel received more war—first in the form of terror and threats of destruction by Arab leaders that also egged-on the hatred their people had for Israel and Jews—then eviction of the international peacekeeping force in the Sinai, mobilization of the Egyptian army on the border, and an illegal embargo of the Jewish State's freedom to navigate in international waters.

Now, Egypt and Jordan demanded that Israel ignore that they had threatened Israel's existence in 1967. Without even an apology or a formal recantation of their policy to eviscerate the Jewish State, those nations insisted that Israel docilely return to the pre-1967 borders in return, once again, for a vacuous promise of peace far less worthy of trust than the international assurances Israel had received ten years before that had proved worthless. Not once did the Arabs recognize that it was their failure to honor their previous word that had generated much of Israel's reluctance to take risks. Not once did they address why their promises after the war they had instigated and lost should be believed this time, after they had broken their promises in the past. And in that poisoned environment, the refusal of Arab leaders to publicly negotiate a peace agreement with Israel fueled concerns among Israeli leaders. If the Arabs could not bring themselves to meet with Israelis, why should Israel believe their promises? How could future Arab leaders be trusted to keep promises of peace, if Arab leaders now did nothing to change the attitudes of their people? And what message is sent to the citizens of Arab nations when their leaders refuse to even speak with Israelis?

However, there was not an infinite amount of time available to overcome the basic differences dividing Israel and her Arab neighbors. Most of the leaders of nations in the region during 1968 changed in 1969. Those changes altered regional dynamics and impeded discerning, let alone following, a path to resolution.

But as she waited for the Arabs to talk peace, Israel suffered. From the end of the Six-Day War through December of 1968, 1288 documented incidents of Arab sabotage or terrorism killed nearly 300 Jews and injured more than 1,000. For comparison purposes, based on percentage of population, that was equivalent to more than 20,000 Americans killed and 100,000 injured. Given the American response to the horrific casualties of September 11, 2001, when nearly 3,000 died, it is no surprise that Israel refused to moderate her demands for withdrawal and responded to the violence aggressively. The cabinet believed that, even if a withdrawal would bring a short respite for an indeterminate period of time, loss of the land-buffer provided by the occupied territories would only make the terrorists' jobs easier and give rise to more Israeli deaths.

And Egypt's continued, vigorous artillery shelling of Israeli forces along the canal served to emphasize in Israeli minds that the Arabs could not be trusted. It also necessitated a costly change in defensive tactics. The lives of IDF soldiers forced to endure the shelling in their makeshift bases were at stake.

The question for Israel was what to do? Since the end of the War of Independence in 1949, IDF doctrine was to take the war to the enemy. There was no other choice, given the country's lack of strategic depth and long, indefensible borders. But the Sinai afforded both depth and a shortened, defensible border along the canal. General Bar-Lev, the Israeli Chief of Staff who succeeded Rabin after the Six-Day War, proposed a string of fortifications, each manned by fifteen soldiers, along the canal. The forts would be hardened to withstand Egyptian artillery. They would also provide an opportunity to observe military activity across the canal. Armored units, held further back, would patrol between the forts; artillery units, held even further back, would provide additional support to all. Then, in the event of an Egyptian attempt to cross the canal, troops in the forts would slow them and provide support for counterattacks.

General Sharon and others opposed building the forts. They argued that the fixed positions would give the Egyptians a target to focus their efforts on. Instead, they proposed constantly patrolling the water's edge of the canal with mobile units based beyond Egyptian artillery range.

Bar-Lev's views won the day because the cabinet felt it was important not to cede any territory to Egypt. Therefore, the ministers wanted to prevent the Egyptians from crossing the canal in small groups and then quickly pushing the U.N. to demand a ceasefire before Israel could respond. Construction of the fortifications began in late 1968 and was completed by the end of January 1969. Israeli engineers built thirty positions approximately three miles apart. They were placed on top of an artificial sand wall twenty-to-thirty feet high, facing the canal. Guns within the forts could effectively fire a half-mile in each direction. The sand wall that formed the forts' foundations sloped at a 45-degree angle to the canal. Such a slope would make it impossible for Egyptian vehicles crossing the waterway to climb up and over. The final plan also called for tanks to patrol between the forts and to reinforce the positions as needed. To the rear, two other defensive lines were built, as well as a new road network to shuttle reinforcements. Surprisingly, Egyptian forces did little to impede the construction.

Richard Nixon

Nixon's convoluted personality would eventually drive him both to success and to ultimate failure. But in January of 1969, he brought a new and unknown dynamic to the already complex, Middle East equation for peace. Although Nixon was known as a staunch anti-communist, he said in his inaugural address, "After a period of confrontation, we are entering an era of negotiation." More than academic studies, he often relied on instinct—formed in part by his impressions of the many world leaders he met before and after becoming president. He also had a reputation for toughness and decisiveness but believed foreign policy was best conducted in secret where he could be—and often was—more flexible.

Nixon proclaimed to some, as Nasser had suspected, that he was not beholden to Jewish interests because he had not received many Jewish votes in the election. That, however, did not prevent him from nominating Henry Kissinger, a forty-eight-year-old Jewish, Harvard professor of political science, to lead the National Security Council (NSC) and advise him on foreign policy matters. Kissinger was born in Germany. He immigrated as a child, along with his family, to the United States before World War II. Having informally advised Presidents Kennedy and Johnson, he was no stranger to presidential issues. Kissinger shared Nixon's abhorrence of nuclear war but had avidly studied nuclear policy. Both men believed that national strength and domestic support were necessary ingredients for diplomatic success.

Kissinger's nomination was important because Nixon planned to rely more on the NSC than the State Department for crafting and conducting major, foreign policy initiatives. Since the State Department bureaucracy traditionally was much more pro-Arab than Nixon, Kissinger's influence bode well for Israel's interests.

Both men's foreign policy strategy was driven by the concept of "linkage." Linkage meant that all issues between nations were related. Thus linkage meant that negotiation and resolution of one concern should not be done without reference to all other issues. By the same token, if America's adversaries resisted compromise in one area, America might use pressure on another matter to achieve a better result.

America's main adversary in the 1960's and 70's was the Soviet Union. And 1969 was an opportune time to pressure the Russians. The Soviets were greatly concerned by China's resurgence, with whom they had recently had frequent military clashes along their common border. Their weak economy was another problem for the Soviets. It required massive foreign investment to keep it going; but future, foreign investment was in jeopardy because Russia's international image had been tarnished by the Soviet invasion of Czechoslovakia which had ended the "Prague Spring" several months earlier. However, Russia was a nuclear power. Push too much, and the result could devastate the world. Therefore, since tendrils of the Russian-American confrontation stretched into the Middle East, one might think that resolving the Middle East dispute between Arabs and Jews before it caused a super-power confrontation would have been front and center on Nixon's agenda.

It was not.

Nixon's primary goal was to end the Vietnam War that had polarized America and cost her hundreds of soldier's lives each month. Therefore, he told Kissinger to focus on winding up that conflict. But Nixon did not lose sight of the risks the Middle East posed. He said it was "a powder keg—very explosive—it needs to be defused because the next explosion ... could involve a confrontation between the nuclear powers—which we want to avoid." Realizing Kissinger would be otherwise busy with his highest priority, Nixon tasked his Secretary of State, William Rogers, with the Middle East assignment. It was a poor choice, sort of like sending a pitcher just called up from the minor leagues to the mound with the bases loaded, none out in the ninth, and the World Series hanging in the balance.

Perhaps Nixon also chose Rogers because Kissinger was Jewish. Perhaps he selected Rogers because of their friendship that dated back many years. Or perhaps Nixon picked Rogers because he believed that the Israeli-Arab dispute was intractable, and he thought if Kissinger failed, it would taint his presidency. But Nixon's choice of Rogers may also have been due to the slight divergence between Kissinger's views and his own. Nixon understood that the more secure Israel felt the more likely she would be flexible in peace negotiations, but he also wanted to appear impartial as long as that stance would block Russian schemes to increase their influence in the region. Therefore, he may have felt that, since traditionally the State Department had advocated an evenhanded approach not too far afield from Nixon's view, that the secretary of state would be a better choice than Kissinger to lead the negotiations. "Even handed" meant two things. **First** that the U.S. should use as a "stick" the threat of stopping, or slowing, American arms deliveries to Israel to force her withdrawal from occupied territories. **Second** that the U.S. should not first supply to the Israelis a "carrot" of Arab commitments and recognition to the level that Israel demanded and needed. Of course, that was not evenhanded. What that really meant was that the Arabs should get what they want without Israel receiving much, if anything, of her core needs in return.

Kissinger, on the other hand, saw the Middle East as a key battleground for the rivalry between the Soviet Union and the United States. He believed it important that America never weaken her friends nor ever assist supporters of the Soviet Union. Therefore, he concluded that, until the Arabs distanced themselves from the Russians, the United States should not advocate on behalf of Arab interests. As such, he favored a much, more supportive policy towards Israel than Nixon was pre-disposed to embrace. Fortunately for Israel, he was well positioned to win the political tussle that would soon ensue. Even though Rogers had been charged by Nixon with finding a solution that would require Israel to disregard what her leaders regarded as vital interests, Kissinger, due to his daily access to the president, was in a position to undermine any of Rogers's initiatives that did not comport with his world view. Rogers's struggle and Kissinger's maneuvering soon began.

Meanwhile, Rogers's first task was to respond to a Russian initiative promulgated at the end of 1968. The Soviet proposal called for the United States and the Soviet Union to jointly work towards a peace agreement that included a complete Israeli withdrawal from all the newly won territories. Russia's strategy was to curry favor with her Arab patrons by imposing a superpower deal on the Israelis. What would Rogers do?

National Security Council, American Middle East Policy and Negotiations

Kissinger's NSC met on February 1 to formulate the framework for American policy in the Middle East, even though Nixon had selected Rogers to be in charge. The NSC's view was that the United States should take the lead in talks with the Russians. The Council agreed on the following principles to guide American participation:

- Even though conversations could begin between the superpowers, Israel must be involved and consent to any final deal.
- In exchange for an Israeli withdrawal, the Arabs could not just promise peace; they had to enter into some form of binding contractual commitment.
- Once an acceptable agreement was reached, Israel should withdraw from all of the Sinai, exclusive of Gaza where an "arrangement" should be made, and withdraw from the West Bank, except for minor territorial changes.
- Demilitarized zones should be created for critical areas.
- Jordan should have both a religious and civil role in Jerusalem.
- The refugee problem should be settled (the Council gave no guidance as to how).

The NSC envisioned that, once an agreement with the Russians was hammered out, it would be presented to Britain and France. The NSC did not want France or Britain involved at the beginning because it thought France pro-Arab and worried that, in concert with the Russians, the French would lean on the British. The last step of the NSC's plan was that once agreement was reached by the four powers, the final proposal would be given to Jarring to present to Israel, Egypt, and Jordan.

Over the next couple of months, American and Soviet negotiators met nine times regarding the Middle East. Conversations began on February 17, 1969, when Russian Ambassador Dobrynin brought a message to the White House that the Russians were willing to talk and would pressure their Arab allies towards making peace, in the right circumstances. Dobrynin received a curious response. Nixon told him that, even though Rogers was his close friend and foreign policy advisor from whom he would not hold back any secrets, he also wanted to institute an additional private channel between Dobrynin and Kissinger for sensitive issues. Dobrynin understood the significance of what Nixon was saying. Talks managed by the State Department would have less import than those through Kissinger; Rogers had been hamstrung without knowing it. For the next two months private, behind-the-scene negotiations paralleled Soviet discussions with the State Department.

The State Department's first formal meeting with the Soviets was on March 18 when Joseph Sisco, Undersecretary for Near Eastern and South Asian Affairs, met with Dobrynin. Dobrynin clung to the Russian position that the Arabs should not have to agree to anything until the Israelis withdrew. Sisco presented the American perspective:

- Final borders should be agreed on by the parties to the dispute with only minor adjustments.
- No settlement would be imposed.
- The final agreement must be reduced to a contract signed by all parties.
- Syria, Jordan, and Egypt must agree to peace prior to any Israeli withdrawal.

Sisco well knew that, only a few days previously, Eban had very clearly told Rogers that Israel opposed the superpowers' attempt to resolve the Middle East peace issues. Eban insisted that there could be no substitute for direct talks between Israel and the Arabs that would culminate in a contractual peace treaty. In addition, Eban conveyed his distaste for superpower guarantees in place of true, written peace agreements.

The Egyptians also had spoken privately with the Americans. Nasser's close advisor and former Foreign Minister, Mahmoud Fawzi, came to the United States to attend the funeral of former president, Dwight D. Eisenhower, after he died on March 28. Fawzi told Nixon that Syrian intransigence would not prevent Egypt from reaching a separate deal with Israel. But Fawzi also said that Egypt would not sign a jointly-written agreement with Israel, would not agree to begin diplomatic relations with Israel, and would not agree to a peacekeeping force in the region unless it could be removed with six months' notice.

Fawzi's statement was hardly a cause for optimism.

Over the next several weeks the Americans did not make any concrete proposals to the Russians, and the Russians continued to insist on specific Israeli actions unacceptable to the United States. Sisco could do no more without a specific plan rather than mere principles. The talks headed towards failure.

Kissinger, however, was not upset. He believed that to reach an agreement at present the United States would have to "deliver" Israel (force Israel to agree, against her will, to the Soviet's terms which reflected the desires of Russia's Arab patrons); and, if the U.S. did that, it would reward Arab nations that had broken relations with America. Since Kissinger thought Israel was not deliverable, and the Arabs not willing to commit to what was necessary for peace, he had believed all along that the talks were destined to blow up. His opinion was buttressed by Nasser's and Eshkol's public statements that included:

- **Nasser** proclaiming in an interview in February that total, Israeli withdrawal, pursuant to his interpretation of Resolution 242, was a pre-condition to fulfillment of the rest of 242; and
- **Eshkol** stating in an interview that, until Israel's requirements for peace were fulfilled there would be no withdrawal and that Israel would not return to the pre-war battle lines, would never give up the Old City of Jerusalem, the Golan Heights, or other areas needed to fulfill her security needs.

Kissinger also feared that the talks with the Russians carried the seeds of a potential disaster for American policy. If Israel were "delivered," then Arab radicals would see that as vindication for their intransigence, but might still block any proposed agreement. "Delivery" would also enhance Russian influence over her Arab client states. Additionally, if the talks failed, there was risk that the Americans would be blamed for the failure. Therefore, from Kissinger's perspective, since he was unable to stop the conversations from beginning; the faster they ended the better. He got what he wanted.

Against the backdrop of America's halting effort to jumpstart peace negotiations, Nixon established a cabinet-level taskforce to review the Eisenhower quota system for regulating imports of oil and to replace it with tariffs. His purpose was to protect domestic oil production. A report that America would need to import 27% of her oil consumption by 1980 drove the conversation. Perhaps Nixon's cabinet would have focused more on the problem, if the 27% forecast had been more accurate. America's ravenous need for oil would soon require vastly ramping up oil imports far more than that and at the same time the price for oil increased tenfold. But since there then appeared no need for urgency, cabinet discussions went nowhere, and the quota system remained. But, at least, the issue of oil imports was on Nixon's radar. In a few years, it would become a significant concern.

CHAPTER THIRTY
Eshkol Dies — Meir Emerges

Prime Minister Levi Eshkol was 73 when he died of a heart attack on February 26, 1969. Shortly before his death he asked some members of both the left and right wings of his cabinet whether Israel's actions were inflaming the sentiment of the Palestinian people toward the Jewish State. But he also unofficially adopted the Allon plan that called for settlement activity in the Jordan River valley to maintain control of the border. And he sent a note to President Nixon in which he suggested that the best way to prevent a new, Middle East war would be to keep Israel strong.

Eshkol's death put on hold the peace process promoted by Russia and reluctantly joined by the United States. It would have to wait until a new Israeli government could be formed. Then, while that political void existed, any fleeting thoughts the Nixon Administration had of Israel accepting an imposed solution in the wake of Eshkol's death were dispelled after Ambassador Rabin met with Kissinger, on March 4. Rabin told him that American discussions with the Russians undercut Israel's insistence that direct talks between the Arab nations and Israel was a precondition for a peace agreement. Rabin also emphasized that any guarantees dangled before Israel would not tempt her to soften her stance. Rabin later explained his reasoning, "We knew perfectly well that if an agreement was reached between the two powers, each would be obligated to induce its client to accept it." In reference to that conversation, and to many others with Rabin, Kissinger later wrote: "Yitzhak Rabin had many extraordinary qualities but the gift of human relations was not one of them"

On March 7, Golda Meir, almost seventy-one years of age, became Israel's new Prime Minister, and Israel's first, female head of state. Meir had resigned the year before from her political position as the Secretary General of the Mapai party because she suffered from a blood disease that required constant medical attention. When she received news of her appointment by Israel's Central Labor Committee, she sobbed uncontrollably in recognition of the awesome responsibility she was about to assume.

For Meir, "it" had always been about "security and survival." Born in 1898 in Kiev, a city in Ukraine that was part of what became the Soviet Union (and now no longer is), her family later moved to Pinsk. As a child, Meir witnessed local peasants launch anti-Semitic pogroms that targeted Jews living in the area—and saw the devastation, bloodshed, and constant fear that followed. She still had memories of hiding in an upstairs room while, below, violence raged, indiscriminately directed at Jews. When Meir was seven her family immigrated to America where she became active in the Zionist movement. When she was twenty-one, Meir moved to Israel and quickly rose to prominence. After Israel's independence, she became Israel's first ambassador to the Soviet Union. Thereafter, she held several ministerial and political positions.

Meir was tough and determined; and her view of the world was devoid of nuance. Because she possessed the capability to break down complex problems to simple choices, it enhanced her penchant to see things in black and white, rather than grey. Meir's reputation was that she was overbearing and intolerant when opposed. Perhaps that came from her dogged determination to prevail in arguments whereas Eshkol had tended towards compromise. Thus, when compared to Eshkol's apparent flexibility, she often appeared dogmatic and intransigent.

Meir's speech accepting her nomination did not mince words, "The government will regard … the settlement … of our sons on the soil of the homeland as of vital importance for the country's security and survival." Later, during a press briefing that same day, Meir said that to prevent the Arabs from obtaining a military advantage from any agreement, Israel must maintain control of the Golan and Sharm el-Sheikh. However, she also appeared open to doing whatever was possible to make it tolerable for Palestinians living on the West Bank to live under Israeli control. She even hinted that her government might be more forthcoming, if the Arabs chose to negotiate with Israel; but, until that time came, there was nothing to decide.

Meir's governing style relied on a "Kitchen Cabinet" composed of a select group of ministers and advisors. They met regularly at her home, usually on Saturday evening after Shabbat ended. The core group that regularly attended was sometimes augmented by select other individuals when the topic required their expertise. Its purpose was to develop a unified policy that would be presented to the entire cabinet the next day at its Sunday meetings. When the topics were political, Meir voiced strong opinions. But when the issue was a military one, she leaned heavily on the current IDF Chief of Staff.

The event that, perhaps, most shaped Meir's thinking was when both the United States and the Soviet Union forced Israel to withdraw from the Sinai in 1957, in return for guarantees that were not fulfilled when put to the test by Arab actions in 1967. Meir was determined not to countenance a similar withdrawal in 1969 unless Israel's Arab neighbors unambiguously acknowledged Israel's right to exist within secure and recognized borders. Meir understood and accepted that Resolution 242 called for substantial withdrawal, but she was adamantly against budging one bit until all the elements of a peace agreement, both those set to apply on signing and those that applied to future events, were clearly defined and made public.

For Meir, Israel's security was the central requirement around which all else revolved. This was a vital distinction, even if seemingly small, from Eshkol's focus on Israel's relationship with the Arab world. However, with regard to the West Bank, both perspectives merged. Neither Eshkol nor Meir wanted to annex the West Bank. They knew that would destroy the Jewish character of the nation. But Meir was adamant: without direct negotiations and a peace treaty, there would be no return to prewar borders. She said:

> The peace treaties must include agreements on final, secure and recognized boundaries. The peace treaties must annul claims of belligerency, blockades, boycotts, interference with free navigation, and the existence and activity of organizations and groups engaged in preparing or executing sabotage operations from bases and training camps on the territories of the states signatory to the peace treaties.

Over the next few years, Meir would not retreat from her fundamental principles, until the Yom Kippur war forced her to reexamine that policy. Subsequently she acknowledged her mindset when she said:

> And of course 'intransigent' was to become my middle name. But neither Eshkol or I, nor the overwhelming majority of other Israelis, could make a secret of the fact that we weren't at all interested in a fine, liberal, anti-militaristic, dead Jewish State or in a 'settlement' that would win us compliments about being reasonable and intelligent but that would endanger our lives … Israeli democracy is so lively that there were, and are, almost as many 'doves' as 'hawks,' but I have yet to come across any Israeli

who thinks that we should return ourselves permanently, into clay pigeons—not even for the sake of a better image.

Meir was able to form her policies at a time when the majority of Israelis had not reached a consensus as to what to do with the territories. But, on the political fringes, the Greater Israel Movement and the Peace Movement were polarizing forces with opposing views regarding Jewish settlement of the territories. Both at that time were mainly composed of intellectuals. Both drew members from all political parties. And both were ideological whereas Israel's leadership was still pragmatic. The center still ruled, but it would not be forever.

CHAPTER THIRTY-ONE
The Two-Power Talks Die

On April 25, 1969, Nixon gave Rogers permission to present a more comprehensive plan to the Soviets. Rogers's new plan used Resolution 242 as a baseline but then went further. He specified that there must be a formal state of peace that would include an end to Arab terrorist raids. His plan also envisioned that formal borders would be determined by negotiations between Egypt and Israel, but that Israel would maintain control of Sharm el-Sheikh. However, the devil was in the details.

Rogers Tries and Fails the First Time

At the behest of Rogers, Sisco met with Dobrynin during the first week of May to unveil details of his proposal to the Russians. When Sisco said Rogers's plan (hereinafter often described as "the *Rogers* plan") foresaw direct talks between the parties, Dobrynin downplayed their importance. More satisfying to the Russian was that, in response to his country's demands, the American proposal stated that a full Israeli withdrawal was "not necessarily excluded." However, Dobrynin opposed demilitarization of the Sinai as expressed in the *Rogers* plan, and, when asked to define what freedom of navigation meant to the Russians, the Russian Ambassador responded with calculated ambiguity.

Neither the Russians nor the Israelis liked the *Rogers* plan. The Russians wondered why the progress that they thought had been made during the previous, two months of negotiations with the United States had been ignored. They were also unhappy that the *Rogers* plan did not address Syrian and Jordanian issues. The Israelis were suspicious because the meaning of "peace" was not defined.

On June 17, the Russians made a counterproposal that disappointed the Americans. Four days before, Russian Foreign Minister Gromyko had ended his visit to Egypt with a jarring reference to what he thought must be done: "Liquidate the consequences of aggression." The new Russian plan spoke of a binding agreement and recognition of Israel; but it did not include direct negotiations, was not clear regarding what was meant by freedom of navigation, and did not include within its definition of peace any obligation for Arab nations to stop supporting terrorists, nor a requirement to prevent them from attacking Israel. The Russians also insisted that any agreement must include Syria and Jordan. Thus, for all intents and purposes, the new Russian proposal represented little more than a return to their December 1968 proposal.

Nevertheless, Rogers thought it was worthwhile to respond. He wanted to send Sisco to Moscow with what he thought would be a decisive American concession—Israel would fully withdraw in return for the Arabs agreeing to all other Israeli demands. But Kissinger opposed Rogers's strategy. He agreed that Sisco could go, but he did not want him to offer full withdrawal. Kissinger thought it premature, especially because the supposedly new Soviet reply/offer did not contain any real concessions. Nixon agreed with Kissinger. Dutifully, Sisco then went to Moscow but did not offer anything new with regard to final borders. Not surprisingly, the Russians remained wedded to their counterproposal. After Sisco briefed Nixon upon his return, the president responded, "Joe, the goddam Russians don't seem to want a settlement." They then agreed to do nothing more until September, when the Foreign Ministers would assemble at the UN for meetings.

Dobrynin followed Sisco's failed effort with an attempt, by contacting Kissinger, to resurrect the discussions through the backchannel Nixon had created. Dobrynin suggested to Kissinger that they either draft a joint statement for use as a guideline by the parties, or otherwise, assist the Jarring talks. Kissinger refused. Instead, he suggested that, until there was progress on resolving the Vietnam conflict, joint action to resolve other issues was unlikely. (It was linkage 101.) Dobrynin, however, was persistent. He again brought the subject up in a meeting with Nixon on October 14 when he read a statement from a prepared memo blaming the United States for the breakdown in the two-power talks. But Nixon, like Kissinger, was not buying it. The president told Dobrynin it was Egypt who lost the war, the Soviet Union that was inflexible, and that the Egyptians were in no position to be making demands.

However, Rogers would not accept that the Middle East crisis couldn't and shouldn't be resolved by working through the Russians. He did not see the Russian responses to his proposals as necessarily fatal to the process, and he did not recognize the increasing antipathy of Nixon, who more and more was falling under Kissinger's sway. Even though Rogers prevailed upon Nixon to permit him to try once more to work with the Russians, the President did so with little conviction. Later, Nixon told Jewish leaders that nothing would come of Rogers's latest plan.

On October 28, Sisco, per Rogers's instructions, presented a multi-point plan for a joint US-USSR working paper to Dobrynin. The important elements were:

- A full withdrawal of Israeli forces to the International Border.

- A binding, contractual agreement between the antagonists that would end the state of war and any subsequent conduct inconsistent with peaceful relations.
- A "fair settlement" of the Palestinian issues.
- A "Rhodes" type negotiation between Israel and Egypt (meaning an intermediary moving back and forth between their representatives until a final agreement was reached) to resolve issues involving Gaza and Sharm el-Sheikh, and a vague formulation for direct talks (which in practice meant that they would not happen).
- Freedom of navigation for Israel in the Straits of Tiran and the Suez Canal.
- Recognition of Israel's right to exist and live in peace.

Sisco told Dobrynin that all of the points in the new proposal were derivative of what had been discussed previously. Dobrynin disagreed. He said they might be derivative of the American position, but not the Soviet one.

The same day Sisco spoke to Dobrynin, Meir's Labor party won 56 out of 120 Knesset seats in Israel's national election. As a result, Meir had little trouble forming a majority, coalition government with other much smaller political parties. The cabinet she appointed included Dayan, Allon, and Eban. But something new was increasingly in the wind. Younger, non-establishment people from the National Religious Party, who embraced the "whole land" approach of keeping the occupied territories, began to flex their political muscles. They would only get stronger.

A little more than a week later, the Russians said to the Americans that the U.S. proposal was "unbalanced and unacceptable." They did not like that withdrawal from Gaza and Sharm el-Sheikh was left to the parties to work out, while Israeli withdrawal from other areas was tied to resolution of specific issues. The Russians knew that their position meant there was little prospect of reaching an agreement. Even so, they pushed Sisco to give more. He would not.

The two-power talks were dead.

Rogers Tries Again

The failure of the two-power talks did not end Rogers's involvement in Middle East issues. Sisco encouraged him to make a speech that outlined the steps the United States had taken to try to achieve peace. Otherwise, he said, the Russians would attempt to occupy the high ground in world opinion by blaming America for failure of the talks. Rogers felt the need to speak out too. He thought the United States had never announced support for a balanced position and believed it was time to do so. The plan he intended to make public was basically a rehash of what Sisco had presented to the Russians. Nixon agreed that he should. Kissinger did not.

Kissinger was not optimistic. "No scheme was conceivable that would bridge the gap between the two sides," he said. "It cannot produce a solution without massive pressure on Israel. It is more likely going to wind up antagonizing both sides. It may produce a war." Kissinger also thought it was a mistake to focus on Egypt first (in the years ahead he would change his views on that). He felt that Jordan's territorial issues should be given priority, and he believed that no deal could be made without Syria's involvement because the Syrians were largely at fault for starting the '67 war.

Egyptian Foreign Affairs Minister, Mahmoud Riad, voiced his opposition to the *Rogers* plan when Rogers briefed him. Riad argued that it left out Syria and Jordan, and it was incomplete because it left Gaza and Sharm el-Sheikh unresolved. Therefore, Egypt refused to respond until a more comprehensive proposal was put forward. Perhaps Egypt's actions spoke as loudly as her words. On November 16, Egyptian commandos sneaked into Eilat's harbor and sank three Israeli naval ships anchored in the sheltered waters.

Ambassador Rabin, not to be left out, also disliked the *Rogers* plan. By imposing solutions for most topics of contention, he thought it undermined any chance for negotiations between the Arabs and Israel. Rabin argued, as did Kissinger, why give the Soviets a concession by returning to the pre-Six-Day War borders when the Soviets had not offered any concessions that proved their clients' genuine desire for peace. In effect, the one concrete thing the plan required—Israel's full withdrawal—was balanced only by a number of negotiable principles laden with ambiguity. By requiring Israel's return to the June 4 borders, all that the Egyptians really wanted at that stage, the *Rogers* plan effectively eliminated Israel's leverage to obtain, through negotiations, concessions (not specified in the plan) that might have made a withdrawal worthwhile. Instead, Rogers would have had Israel give away up-front, without receiving anything of value in return, the principle of returning what Egypt craved and what Israel needed to protect her security. That would have left the difficult, more subjective, issues vital for Israel's future subject to tortured discussions with an Egypt that had already received what she wanted. That was a recipe for disaster for the Jewish State.

Nevertheless, despite negative reactions to his second plan from all quarters, including from within his own government, Rogers decided to press forward. He scheduled a speech at the Sheraton Park Hotel in Washington, D.C. for December 6. At that venue, he said that his plan was "balanced and fair" and that the Arabs must accept a "permanent peace." But, he also called on all parties to find a "just settlement" for Palestinian refugees without limiting that settlement to something that did not involve Israeli territory.

Then, also antithetical to Israel's interest, Rogers declared his support for what would be, in essence, a full Israeli withdrawal from occupied territories when he said:

> We believe that while recognized political boundaries must be established and agreed upon by the parties, any change in the pre-existing lines should not reflect the weight of conquest and should be confined to insubstantial alterations required for mutual security.... We do not support expansionism. We believe troops must be withdrawn.

Rogers tied Israel's withdrawal to acceptance by Israel's neighbors of her "territorial integrity." That was far short of Israel's requirement for a contractual peace. The Secretary of State also left out any details for resolving the dispute over control of Jerusalem, other than to say the Arabs should have partial control.

Rogers improvidently delivered his speech just as Meir's new government was being installed. Meir furiously lashed back despite Nixon's private assurances to her that he would not push the plan on Israel, and that Israel would not be sacrificed to major-power policy. Meir said the *Rogers* plan amounted to Arab appeasement. She told her cabinet, "If the [U.S.] proposal were implemented, it would be suicidal and would mean destruction of Israel. Any Israeli government which approved this proposal would be guilty of treason." Rabin piled on. He told Kissinger that Rogers's speech undercut Israel's ability to negotiate an acceptable agreement with the Arabs.

To Israel's relief, Egypt and Russia quickly rejected Rogers's publicized plan; ironically, both viewed it to be pro-Israeli and one-sided. Since it mainly addressed Egypt, Nasser read into the *Rogers* plan a call for direct negotiations at some point—a concession Nasser would not make. Therefore, he thought it a scheme to divide the Arabs and weaken them. Four days later, Egyptian emissaries met with their Soviet counterparts in Moscow. The Russians agreed to sell Egypt more arms.

On December 10, the NSC met to discuss Rogers's speech. Nixon expressed displeasure that, in the eleven months since he took office, the Soviet Union had become more dominant throughout the Middle East while American influence was diminishing in the moderate Arab states. He also was upset that the Russians had made no concessions in the two-power talks but were rewarded by Rogers's call on Israel to withdraw from all of the occupied territories. He said, "If the UAR [Egypt] comes out of the settlement whole and gives only vague obligations to peace in return, the Soviets come out looking good and the Israelis have little in return." Kissinger agreed, but then predicted that, the longer Israel remains where she is and does not withdraw, the less the Arabs will rely on the Soviet Union; for they will have been proved unable to deliver.

Rogers tried to defend himself. He argued that many believed the United States was not evenhanded with her support of Israel. He contended that was why America's position was worse than Russia's in the Arab world. But Nixon's response mirrored his worldview. For him it was not about resolving Middle East issues; it was the contest between America and Russia. Nixon said, "The Soviets should not come out ahead. The Arabs played a substantial part in bringing on the [Six-Day War], and the Soviets should pay some price for picking up the pieces."

But despite the criticism, Rogers plowed ahead. On December 18, he announced a parallel plan for Jordan and Syria. In it he called for only minor, territorial modifications for "administrative or economic convenience." The new plan called for a unified Jerusalem with Israel and Jordan sharing responsibility for its civic and economic administration. Rogers also suggested solving the refugee problem with annual quotas that would allow some to resettle within Israel, and compensation for those who did not return. Rogers's latest suggestions did little to relieve Meir's fury, but Hussein was pleased. And why not? If enacted, it would have amounted to a double, demographic win for Hussein: Israel would have to permit entry to thousands of people dedicated to her destruction, and Hussein would not have to worry about those same thousands, many of whom were also dedicated to his demise.

Afterwards, Meir was so incensed that, after calling Rabin to Israel for consultations, she sent him back to the United States to mount a public relations campaign against the *Rogers* plan. In a background press briefing on December 24, Rabin called the *Rogers* plan "an abrupt reversal of the principal that U.S. policy has hitherto proclaimed.... [It] undermines the principle of negotiation ... [and] comes close to the advocacy and development of an imposed settlement." Rabin coupled his public efforts with private comments to Kissinger:

> Let me tell you in complete frankness, you are making a bad mistake. In taking discussion of peace settlement out of the hands of the parties and transferring it to the powers, you are fostering an imposed solution that Israel will resist with all her might. I personally shall do everything within the bounds of American law to arouse public opinion against the administration's moves.

CHAPTER THIRTY-TWO
The War of Attrition

The Egyptians saw a juicy target coupled with an opportunity across the Suez Canal— Israeli soldiers huddled in the just-completed Bar-Lev forts. They were concentrated and stationary, not mobile nor in unpredictable locations. On March 8, 1969, the Egyptians struck. Their artillery rained high explosive shells on the Israeli forts. While the Soviet Union negotiated with the United States, the explosions heralded the opening of a new war between Arab and Jew, initiated by the Egyptians, just one day after Meir became Israel's Prime Minister.

Nasser announced that Egypt would engage in a sustained effort to inflict casualties on the Israelis. He called it "The War of Attrition," and contrasted the new effort from prior periods of conflict. He called the time just after the 1967 war to August of 1968, "The Period of Defiance," and then referred to the period between September 1968 and February 1969, "The Period of Active Defense." Beginning March 8, Egyptian artillery fired shells for eighty consecutive days.

The Egyptians had several goals. **First**, they hoped to destroy the just completed Bar-Lev line and prevent it from being rebuilt. **Second**, they wanted to make sure that the Bar-Lev line did not evolve into a de-facto border. **Third**, they were determined to make life miserable for Israeli soldiers guarding the canal. And **fourth**, they planned to use the fighting to set the stage for an offensive into the Sinai by inspiring the Egyptian military, and to use the confrontation to practice canal crossings with small-scale commando operations.

Nasser had decided that only a protracted military campaign could force Israel to withdraw. But he recognized that a lightning attack designed to retake territory lost to Israel would require Egyptian ground forces to have a two or three-to-one superiority of strength over the IDF, and that his air force would need to be able to launch an air strike that would destroy Israel's air force on the ground. However, Nasser knew Egypt's air force possessed neither the equipment nor the skill to succeed, and that his army was no match for the IDF. Nevertheless, Israel's sensitivity to casualties offered an opportunity. Rather than launch an offensive designed to take territory, Nasser decided to harass the Israelis with long-range artillery from fortified emplacements and augment those strikes with pinprick attacks with small ground forces that would wear the IDF and Israel's home front down. Victory would come not by defeating the Israelis, but by exhausting them.

On April 23, Nasser declared the 1967 ceasefire agreement that ended the Six-Day War null and void due to "Israel's refusal to implement the Security Council Resolution [242]." Dayan responded to the Egyptian attacks by asserting: "We must reply with a fighting refusal to any effort to push us off the cease-fire line." The IDF was his instrument. From the first day, it struck back at the Egyptians by firing artillery shells into Egypt, flying air strikes against the Egyptian military positioned along the canal, and sending commandos to wreak havoc behind Egyptian lines.

The fighting, however, did not end Meir's willingness to take a personal risk for peace. Before the 1948 War of Independence she sneaked into Jordan to meet with that nation's leader, King Abdullah, with the hopes of convincing him to stay out of any future Pan-Arab war against Israel. Once again, after the new shelling began, Meir demonstrated her willingness to take a personal risk for peace. She offered to travel to Cairo to seek a compromise. Nasser rejected her offer.

Fierce fighting continued into June and July. IAF pilots shot down nine Egyptian MiG 21s without suffering any losses of their own. On the ground, while Egyptian losses were even higher, IDF casualties were too significant for Israel to absorb indefinitely. Therefore, the IDF was determined to respond aggressively to force the Egyptians to stop. On July 20, Israeli airstrikes destroyed Egyptian SAM-2 (Surface to Air Missile) air defense system sites along the canal. That opened the door for deep penetration raids into Egypt's interior.

On September 9, the IDF launched one of its more audacious retaliatory raids. Naval assault vessels landed tanks on the Coast of the Gulf of Suez. They then traversed thirty miles into Egypt, destroying Egyptian military installations along their path. The raid lasted ten hours. A hundred Egyptians were killed and many more injured. The wreckage of Egyptian tanks and other vehicles left behind served as a monument to Egyptian ineptitude. Nasser was furious and fired his military Chief of Staff. And no wonder, the Israeli raid and ongoing retaliatory air strikes had produced an impact opposite to what Nasser had hoped for when he launched the war: Egyptian military morale, rather than Israeli morale, was crumbling.

September also saw the first F4 *Phantom* jet fighters coveted by the IAF arrive in Israel. The campaign Eshkol had begun in earnest when he met with President Johnson at his ranch in January of 1968 had, at last, borne fruit. But it was not enough for Golda Meir. She went to Washington seeking more.

Meir Visits Washington

Meir visited with Nixon on September 25. It was her first time in America as Prime Minister of Israel. Their meeting was cordial, and she acknowledged the American President as a friend to Jews. When the topic of Israel's nuclear weapons arose, the Americans tacitly accepted that Israel had them, agreed that Israel would not be forced to sign the nuclear non-proliferation treaty, and dropped their demands for Israel to permit U.S. experts to inspect the nuclear facility at Dimona. In return, Meir agreed that Israel would not publicize she had become a nuclear power, not test the weapons, and not provoke the Arabs by threatening use of them. The Israelis assured Nixon that the bombs would never come out of the closet unless there was a dire emergency. Nixon responded that as long as he was president he would ensure that Israel would never feel unable to defend herself with conventional weapons alone.

They also discussed the peace process. Meir argued that Nasser should not be permitted to duck responsibility for making peace by relying on others to negotiate the terms. Meir explained that the Russians needed to know that America would not permit Israel to be destroyed, and the Arabs needed to know that Israel was too strong to risk attacking. Nixon assured Meir it was his policy to keep Israel strong so that Americans would not have to fight. When Meir requested twenty-five more *Phantom*s and another 100 *Skyhawk* fighter-bombers, Nixon countered that he wanted "hardware for software." By saying that, he implied that the United States would supply military arms; in return, he expected Israel to exhibit flexibility with State Department proposals for peace. But Nixon watered down his admonition considerably when he added that even though Israeli representatives should continue meeting with Rogers, Ambassador Rabin was welcome to use Kissinger as a separate back channel into the White House.

Meir's meeting with Rogers at the State Department did not go as well as her meeting with Nixon. Rogers told Meir that, while he had some doubts whether Egypt and Russia desired peace in the region, a "Rhodes" style framework, in which a mediator shuttles between opposing sides at a negotiation, with neither party meeting directly, was possible to implement. Meir agreed to remain open to new ideas while the shuttle process was in the early stages, but insisted that, later in the process, Egypt and Israel must negotiate face-to-face. "Nasser has indoctrinated his people with the idea that Israel must be destroyed," she said. "He must now sit down with Israel to demonstrate that this is no longer the case." This concept that Arab leaders must publicly prepare their people for peace, not just pronounce their wish for it privately, is one strongly held to this day by Israel's present leaders regarding the Palestinians. Meir also told Rogers her test for Arab authenticity was whether they were willing to negotiate without preconditions. "Either they make war and pay the consequences or they face up to making peace."

By the time Meir returned home, the IAF thought it was well on the way to achieving its objective of punishing the Egyptians for starting the War of Attrition and deterring them from continuing. The Egyptian army near the Canal Zone had been mauled, and most of the SAM-2 sites near the canal had been destroyed. The cost in Israeli aircraft was steep—some fifteen planes lost by the end of the year—but acceptable. However, while Israel had achieved a tactical victory, she had not yet succeeded strategically. The Egyptian army continued to fire their artillery, and Israeli casualties on the ground mounted.

Nasser showed no hint of backing down. During his speech to the Egyptian National Assembly on November 6, he declared that he would reclaim the Sinai by "fire and blood." Nor was there any hint that he would consider ending the fighting soon when he said that he would not accept "half solutions," and would not consider concessions or negotiations with Israel for peace. And once again, Nasser could not resist blaming the United States: "The Americans are fighting behind the Israeli forces and supplying the planes which are being used against us." Thus, he saw no alternative other than "to open our own road to what we want, over a sea of blood and under a horizon of fire."

CHAPTER THIRTY-THREE
The West Bank, Jordan, and Settlements

Hussein did his best to look the other way when Israel struck PLO targets inside his country. On August 4, 1969, Israel launched a massive airstrike on the newly constituted PLO headquarters located within a city named Salt. Salt was located within Jordan, seventeen miles from the border with Israel. The attack killed civilians as well as members of Fatah, but did not succeed in catching Arafat, who had left only fifteen minutes before the bombs fell. However, the airstrike did reap international condemnation in the form of a UN Security Council resolution, which the United States had voted for. As a result, Hussein canceled another clandestine meeting with the Israelis, set for August 8, though he continued to communicate with them. Hussein had to posture displeasure, but by then his main concern was not Fedayeen casualties, but protecting his throne from a Fedayeen led revolt.

Throughout 1969, Hussein and the Israelis discussed matters of mutual concern in secret. But these conversations must be viewed against the backdrop of Arafat's increasing power, the emergence of Israel's settler movement, and the Israeli government's inability to agree on a coherent West Bank policy. That does not mean, however, that the government did not try to resolve settlement issues. Six months before the Salt airstrike, the Israeli cabinet met on January 26 to discuss proposals by Allon for more settlements in the Jordan valley, the Golan Heights, and in the Rafah area in northeast Sinai. The cabinet approved new settlements in all those areas, but the Rafah ones received the least priority. The cabinet did not discuss a framework for reaching a peace agreement with their Arab neighbors.

Two days later, on January 28, Hussein met with Herzog. Herzog told Hussein that, until the cabinet made a final decision regarding its position, he could not negotiate, but that Eshkol hoped their face-to-face discussions would continue. Herzog also expressed concern that Nasser had encouraged the terrorists with his inflammatory public speaking. Hussein responded, "Let us face facts. The man sometimes says crazy things and does crazy things."

The next month, Arafat was elected Chairman of the PLO. One of his first moves was to expand the presence of armed Fedayeen in Jordan—ostensibly to increase terrorist pressure on Israel. Hussein felt he had no choice but to agree. Arafat also recognized that he needed to shore up the PLO's finances. With Nasser's help, within weeks of becoming chairman, King Faisal of Saudi Arabia granted Arafat an audience. Faisal agreed to impose, collect, and remit to the PLO a five percent tax on the salaries of all Palestinians working in Saudi Arabia. He also agreed to give the PLO twelve million dollars (worth eighty million in 2016), weapons, and ammunition. The weapons, which passed through Jordan by truck, revitalized the PLO—as did the money. Soon, the PLO was firing Katyusha missiles from the West Bank that landed on Israeli targets. When Israel retaliated in response, Jordan became increasingly unstable.

When *Newsweek* magazine interviewed Prime Minister Eshkol on February 3, 1969, shortly before his sudden death, Eshkol said that Israel would never relinquish control of the Golan Heights, Sharm el-Sheikh, or Jerusalem. He also said, in de facto support of the Allon plan, that he wanted no part of the major Arab cities on the West Bank, but that Israel would need to maintain control of the Jordan Valley. An hour after that interview, Eshkol suffered a heart attack. While he convalesced in bed, his comments started a furor. Internationally he was perceived as intransigent. Domestically it was the opposite: Many Israelis were angered by his apparent intention to return much of the West Bank to Arab control.

On April 8, Hussein met with President Nixon. He told Nixon that he and Nasser were committed to accepting the dictates of Resolution 242. Hussein also said they would both sign documents with Israel, but not a peace treaty, and promoted what could be considered a land grab: If Israel would consign Gaza to Jordanian control he could agree to significant border changes on the West Bank. Furthermore, hoping to convince Nixon that the Arabs were reasonable, Hussein told the American president that, to resolve their differences with Israel, both he and Nasser were prepared to consider demilitarized zones, granting Israel freedom of navigation in the Straits of Tiran, and access to the Suez Canal. Hussein comments and demeanor made a positive impression on Nixon. But the king's comments were not matched by those of Fawzi, Nasser's close advisor, who had previously told Nixon that Egypt would not agree to establish diplomatic relations with Israel and would not sign any bilateral agreements as part of any deal.

Then, that May, seventy-three Nahal soldier-settlers established a new settlement eight miles from the old Sinai border in Rafah. The desolate, windswept settlement located amidst sand dunes was two miles from the Mediterranean. Months later, a local Israeli military commander issued decrees increasing its size and declared the area off-limits to civilians because it supposedly was a military area—a convenient cover used to deflect domestic and international criticism. Meanwhile, after being confined to a military base, the Levinger settlers in Hebron saw their conditions improve. The government granted them permission to move into prefabricated apartments. The settlement process, though still early and small, began growing roots.

Also in May, King Hussein flew his personal plane to Aqaba, adjacent to the Israeli city of Eilat. From there, he motored a twenty-eight foot boat out onto the bay at 8 p.m. in the direction of Coral Island, where he met with the Israelis. Hussein did not tell anyone on shore where he was heading—other than his friend Jack O'Connell, the American CIA agent assigned to Jordan. O'Connell remained behind on the beach with a walkie-talkie to summon help in the event Hussein did not return. Meir, the newly installed Israeli Prime Minister, was on the island along with Eban, Allon, and Herzog. Their talks accomplished nothing. But Hussein was not left unsated; Meir cooked him a huge dinner. Hussein returned to the Jordanian shore at 1:00 a.m., full but without anything new to resolve his deadlock with the Israelis.

During that time period Hussein was extremely sensitive to any Israeli actions that threatened the eventual return of the West Bank to Jordanian administration. To that end, on July 24, Amman radio issued a statement from the Jordanian government rejecting Israel's new plan creating a local Arab government authority to administer the West Bank. The Israeli government had called for the creation of three administrative districts governed by an individual—Governor, in Arabic, District Commissioner, in Hebrew—whose authority would be minimal, and who would be subject to the dictates of the Israeli military governor. Even though it was only a small step, the Israelis thought it would at least indicate some visible movement towards Arab autonomy. They also hoped that the threat of implementing the plan would pressure Hussein to be more forthcoming in future negotiations lest he risk diminishing his chances of once again controlling the West Bank. But Radio Amman's threat that the West Bank would never cooperate with the administrative plan was a not-so-subtle warning to West Bank inhabitants that worked. They feared retribution if Hussein ever regained control of the West Bank. Israel's plan collapsed.

However, while Hussein did not shy away from confronting Israel over his limited access to the West Bank inhabitants, he did have many cooperative discussions with the Israelis. Hussein was acutely concerned that Fedayeen elements plotted his demise and was worried that his Arab neighbors shared that same goal. He told the Israelis that he planned to deal with the PLO and asked for their help, if requested, to drive them into Syria. In addition, the IDF developed contingency military plans to respond in force if Syrian forces, or more Iraqi troops, moved into Jordan. The British, however, doubted that Hussein would keep his throne if there were a confrontation. That bothered them given their historical link to Jordan. Therefore, rather than developing plans to help the Jordanian army, the British government prepared to evacuate Hussein, his family, and his supporters should he be overthrown.

The PLO's threat to Jordan's ruling government was similar to the threat it posed to another nation in the region. Lebanon needed to find a better way to cope with the 300,000 Palestinian refugees living there. Their presence was upsetting the delicate political balance in that country to the extent that Nasser felt the need to intervene. Friction arose because of the Lebanese army's attempt to control the Palestinians "guests." In an attempt to resolve the dispute, on November 2, Arafat and the Lebanese Army finalized what was known as the "Cairo agreement." As a result, the PLO would take over responsibility for security of the Palestinians, and the PLO would have freedom to launch terrorist attacks into Israel. The agreement left the PLO in control of a "country" within a country. It was the same freedom that the Syrians refused to provide the PLO and that the Jordanians vigorously contested. It was also the beginning of the end for Lebanon's relatively peaceful existence.

Assad's Power Grows

The two most powerful men in Syria—Assad and Jadid— shared the same interim wish to confront Israel, although, they may have disagreed on future goals to some nuanced extent. Jadid firmly rejected both Israel's existence and the idea of a peaceful coexistence. Assad, on the other hand, was open to tactical compromises with the Jewish State, though only for a limited period and only so long as the temporary agreement fulfilled his sense of honor and was a step towards achieving his overall goals (recovery of the Golan and eventual Palestinian control of Israel as part of Greater Syria). They also disagreed on strategy. Jadid wanted to support and incorporate the various armed Palestinian groups in a clash with Israel. Assad believed unwavering support of the Fedayeen might draw Arab countries into a war with Israel they were still ill-prepared for. He preferred enlisting Jordan and Egypt in a joint effort to avoid Syria's being isolated and overwhelmed by Israel's superior military prowess.

On February 25, the day before Eshkol died, Syria's balance of political power shifted: Assad's brother received information suggesting that Jadid planned to kill Assad. The brothers reacted quickly to take power from Jadid. Jadid's power base was with Syria's internal security service. Many of them had a habit of filling up the gas tanks of their vehicles at the Defense Ministry—a facility controlled by Assad. On February 25, when they came one by one to get gas, rather than leaving with their tanks full of fuel, they were arrested. The chief of the Security Service, seeing the writing on the wall, committed suicide after learning his men had been detained. Meanwhile, troops supportive of Assad moved their tanks to key positions in Damascus. Very quickly, Assad assumed control of government buildings throughout the city and those loyal to Jadid who worked at newspapers and radios were ousted.

Then Assad paused. For the next eighteen months he did nothing to remove Jadid from his public leadership role. However, it was clear: the reins of power were firmly in Assad's grasp. Jadid had become nothing more than a figurehead. During his first few months at the helm, Assad toned down Syrian criticism of other Arab regimes and took baby steps towards cooperating with Iraq and Jordan to establish an eastern front against Israel. He also would only permit members of Palestinian groups he could control to enter Syria but refused them permission to carry arms in public or to assemble without his specific approval. Assad was determined to prevent the PLO-inspired anarchy in Jordan from spreading into Syria. He succeeded.

The Year Ends

Throughout 1969, terrorism directed at Israeli targets did not abate. On February 18, four PFLP Fedayeen gunmen attacked an El Al civilian passenger plane on the tarmac of Zurich's airport. They killed the pilot and wounded five passengers before an armed plainclothes El Al security guard killed one of the hijackers and stopped them. Though the security guard returned to Israel a hero, he could no longer function undercover, for his face had been pictured in the press. But he received an appropriate reward in the form of a highly sensitive new job—membership in Golda Meir's personal security detail. Incomprehensibly, the hijacker received a different type of reward, one that perhaps illustrates how little Jewish lives were actually valued by many: The Swiss authorities released him after he served just several months in prison.

On August 24, Arab hijackers struck again. Leila Khaled and other members of the PFLP hijacked a TWA jet traveling from Rome to Saigon. Khaled was born in Haifa in 1944. The young and beautiful Palestinian woman left Israel for Lebanon, where she became a member of the PFLP at the age of fifteen. The hijackers ordered the pilot to fly over Greece and then towards Israel, but were intercepted by Israeli fighter jets. The hijackers then ordered the pilot to change course towards Damascus, where they landed. The passengers and crew conducted an emergency evacuation, and the terrorists attempted to blow up the plane but only succeeded in destroying the cockpit. They then fired their guns at the fuselage in hope of igniting it. Within minutes Syrian security personnel arrived with busses that transported the passengers, crew, and terrorists to the terminal.

The Syrians released all of the hostages immediately—except for six Israelis. They had a plan for them. The Syrians demanded that their military pilots held by Israel after being shot down be freed in exchange for releasing the Israeli civilians. However, the issue of whether or not to release the Israelis got caught up in the power struggle between Assad and Jadid that began the day after the hijacking. Israel insisted that her citizens be released without any conditions. The United States, in support of Israel, threatened Syria with diplomatic isolation and blockage of its pending nomination to membership of the UN Security Council if the hostages were not freed. Syria backed down; the Israeli citizens were let go. But Khaled remained free to engage in new mischief—which she soon would.

As 1969 ended, the Egyptians continued to violate the June 1967 ceasefire by bombarding the IDF, which incurred significant casualties as a result. Diplomatically, Rogers's public speech had angered Meir and her ministers, but they remained comforted by the private assurances received from Kissinger and Nixon through the secret channel. And there were the gathering storm clouds on the horizon; the PLO was growing in strength, and more and more Israelis looked at the conquered lands—not as new territory to be incorporated or returned—but as old territory restored to its rightful owners.

Towards the end of the year the Israeli cabinet met and, at the urging of Rabin, decided to change its policies with regard to the War of Attrition. Rabin told the cabinet that Nixon would look favorably on Israel ramping up her air campaign, because it served America's strategic interests in the region to discredit the Soviet Union. One of the few who disagreed was Eban. He clairvoyantly foretold that the Russians would increase the quantity of arms made available to Egypt if the ferocity of Israel's retribution increased. A majority of the cabinet ministers, however, did not let Eban dissuade them. They ordered the IAF to conduct deep penetration raids into the interior of Egypt that targeted both military and economic sites. Their strategic aim was to make it so expensive for Egypt to continue the War of Attrition that Nasser would have to agree to a ceasefire. Then, they thought, Israel's future deterrent power would grow. In essence, they tasked the air force with breaking Egypt's morale. Should Nasser fall as a result—so much the better.

The raids were scheduled to begin in January.

Also, during those last weeks of 1969, the IDF conducted two operations that greatly increased its naval strength and the air force's ability to penetrate safely into Egyptian territory. The navy benefited from an audacious plot to take what Israel had purchased but had been denied. Before the 1967 war, Israel had contracted and paid for several French-built missile boats. After the war, de Gaulle refused to release them. A year-and-a-half later they remained anchored in Cherbourg Harbor on the French coast. On December 24, dozens of Israeli navy sailors sneaked into Cherbourg while wearing civilian clothing; their uniforms were tucked away in suitcases. They boarded the boats, took them to sea, and navigated them 3,000 miles to Israel. Other boats built by the French for the Israelis were purchased by a Scandinavian corporation that was a front for Israel. Those boats eventually arrived in Israel as well.

Then, on December 26, a commando operation landed IDF soldiers onto a seven-ton Egyptian radar station which had been sold to the Egyptians by the Soviet Union. After securing the site, the commandos used two helicopters to lift the entire installation—radar, rotating antennas, control panels, and all—into the sky and whisked it away to Israel. It was a treasure trove for Israeli and American technicians to study.

1969 was a climactic year for Israel. Her Prime Minister died and a new American president was elected. Then, shortly after Nixon was inaugurated, America embarked on a two-track political policy. One, led by Secretary of State Rogers, was more public and did not reflect Israel's needs or sensitivities. But the other, a back channel to the White House, led by Henry Kissinger, although still in its early stages, promised to be, at a minimum, a counterweight to what the Israelis perceived to be a heavy-handed approach by Rogers. But both paths led to President Nixon, whose central focus was the American-Soviet Union relationship. For him, Israel was a hammer, useful for achieving his ends that included détente with the Russians. And causing the diminutive chances for peace to diminish further, Nasser once again, like in 1967 before the Six-Day War, unilaterally declared the end to a ceasefire and initiated a bloody and destructive war. His refusal to back down coupled with the PLO's avid use of terrorism as a tool left little doubt that 1970 would be bloodier than 1969.

At least the Phantoms had begun to arrive.

CHAPTER THIRTY-FOUR
The War of Attrition Heats Up

New Year's Day 1970 did not herald a new beginning—only more of the same.

Nasser's war of attrition raged over the Suez Canal. Egypt was the gasping challenger punching wildly hoping to score points against Israel, the bloodied champion looking for a knockout blow to end her pain. Both sides were winning—and losing. Israel was scoring tactical victories that wreaked havoc on the Egyptian military, but Egypt's strategic goal to bleed the IDF in order to achieve political gains was progressing forward.

Meanwhile, America began to reexamine her policy of working with the Soviet Union to resolve the Middle East dilemma. The first week of January, Sisco wrote a memo to President Nixon in which he noted the Soviets had failed to deliver Egypt to the bargaining table. Therefore, he recommended the United States should move forward alone. Nixon replied, "Joe, I agree fully ... we're going to go at it alone in the peace process. The Soviets have had their opportunity."

And, for the time being, Kissinger still sat on the Middle East sidelines. Even so, in his capacity as National Security Advisor, he expressed doubt to Nixon that a settlement was then possible as long as Arab radicalism—spawned by Israel's existence, intensified by Israel's 1967 conquests, and made an attractive alternative by the social and economic hardships routinely experienced in the Arab world—remained a powerful force. Kissinger, however, did not identify the problem that forty-

five years later would supplant the Arab-Israeli conflict as the most combustible problem in the region—Islamic religious fundamentalism that rejects any government and anyone that does not comply with Sharia law. Kissinger then explained in his memo that radicalism doomed any agreement because it fomented opposition to anything involving the West and anything Arab moderates tried to achieve. Therefore, Kissinger, like Sisco, recommended cutting the Soviet Union out of any future peace process. And, in light of the other radical elements pervading the region, he added one other caveat: American policy should promote the concept that only Arab moderates held the key to resolving the region's problems, but it was a key that would only fit an American door.

Of course, both Kissinger and Nixon were still preoccupied with a problem much more important to them: The Vietnam War still raged, and the American incursion into Cambodia would soon begin. Perhaps because their attention was diverted they failed to recognize and react aggressively to what the oil companies knew; another crises loomed that had the potential to economically devastate the United States.

The first signs of a pending oil war appeared in late January when Libya demanded that the oil companies pay twenty percent more for the Libyan oil they pumped from the ground. In future months, the Libyans slashed their production to reduce global oil supplies and therefore create shortages which oil producers, including themselves, could take advantage of to charge even steeper prices. By September, the oil companies had knuckled under to Libyan pressure and agreed to pay more. That did not yet impact the United States because the new prices were still less than the cost of oil from wells in the United States. But the die was cast: domestic oil production in the U.S. was at its high point in 1970. As the power began to shift toward Arab oil producers, America was destined to become a nation that imported, rather than exported, one of the most valuable natural resources on earth. It was a destiny that only changed course with the advent of fracking in the twenty-first century.

But for the time being oil still flowed and the likelihood that the Arab producers could wield it as a weapon remained conjecture. Therefore, Nixon and Kissinger thought the Middle East was still a sideshow that did not require their full attention. They decided to wait for the Soviets or Egypt to make the next move. Meanwhile, the

United States would sit tight, and if there were any diplomatic discussions with the Arabs, they would be less public and less ambitious. Time, they thought, favored both American and Israeli interests; for the longer the Soviets failed to meet their patrons' goals, the more likely moderate Arabs would begin to turn to the United States. They may well have been right in that regard. But they also thought the complicated problems in the region would not become more entangled, more intractable. In that, they were wrong.

Things Get Ugly

Masses of Israeli planes raced over the Suez Canal into Egypt's heartland on January 7. Two days before, a nine-man Egyptian commando team had crossed the canal and attacked Israeli soldiers. The IAF planes bombed military bases and supply centers in Egypt's heartland. Their mission was a sharp break from Israel's prior practice that confined the IDF's military response to incessant Egyptian shelling and frequent commando raids to the Canal Zone. The purpose of Israel's expanded raids was to disrupt any Egyptian plans to attack across the canal in force, and to shock Nasser into ending the War of Attrition. Privately, the Israelis would not have minded if the concentrated attacks destabilized Nasser and led to his downfall.

The new attacks were a significant escalation—and were risky. The Israelis knew success might provoke an aggressive Soviet response. Also, Meir was still waiting for Nixon to respond to her request for twenty-five more *Phantom* F4s and 100 of the less-capable *Skyhawk*s. Nevertheless, when Rabin returned to Israel in late December to encourage the new policy, he heartily promoted the airstrikes.

Rabin forcefully argued to Meir's Cabinet that the risk was worth taking in order to end the War of Attrition on terms favorable to Israel. Rabin believed that the longer the war continued the more likely America would attempt to settle the Middle East crisis by striking an agreement with the Russians that his country would not be happy with. If, however,

Israel forced the Egyptians to honor the previous ceasefire they had since breached, it would reduce the likelihood that the two superpowers would impose a solution. Also, the private signals Rabin had received from the White House left him certain that President Nixon would welcome Nasser's downfall, as he would Russia losing its considerable grip on the Middle East.

A couple of months earlier Rabin had cabled Meir: "A man would have to be blind, deaf, and dumb not to sense how much the administration favors military operations;" and, some "sources have informed me that our military operations are the most encouraging breath of air the administration has enjoyed recently." Therefore, it is not surprising that, when discussing the Americans, Rabin predicted to the cabinet that "the[ir] willingness to supply us with additional arms depends more on stepping up the military activity against Egypt than reducing it."

Deputy Minister Yigal Allon, Rabin's former commander in the Palmach during the 1948 War for Independence, also argued in favor of escalating the attacks deep into Egypt. Allon observed that the Russians had never before sent their troops into a non-communist country; and because, if they did in the Middle East, it might result in a confrontation with the United States, they would refrain from doing so now. But Dayan and Eban felt otherwise. Eban, who was much less influential in Meir's Cabinet than when Eshkol was Prime Minister, said there was not enough evidence that the United States would favor the attacks. Dayan expressed concerns, despite what Allon and others believed, that the Russians would intervene.

After listening to the vigorous debate of her ministers, Meir said, "We shall not go into mourning if Nasser fails. I don't know if Nasser's successor would be any better than he is but I don't think he could be much worse." She then approved the air attacks that began on January 7. Those strikes did not end until more than 3,000 IAF sorties dropped

8,000 tons of explosives on targets scattered throughout the Nile Delta and the outskirts of Cairo.

The Russians are Coming

The intensified air strikes were devastating and achieved their short term goal. A panicked Nasser rushed to Moscow on January 22, only fifteen days after they began. Despite feeling the effects of his chronic illness, Nasser desperately requested the Russian leaders to begin discussions as soon as he arrived. He told them the fate of the Middle East depended on what happens within thirty kilometers of either side of the canal. He also warned that the Israeli aerial attacks were threatening his rule, and that he feared they would soon target the Aswan dam, whose destruction would devastate Egypt's economy. Nasser implored the Russians to provide Egypt the means to mount an effective response and rejected their assertions that the SAM-2s were sufficient. Instead, he insisted that Russia also provide SAM-3s, because the SAM-2s were only useful against planes flying at moderate or high altitudes; they were not effective against the low flying planes that the SAM-3s could interdict. Brezhnev, by then the predominant Russian leader, succumbed to Nasser's impassioned request and agreed to provide the SAM-3s. The two men then adjourned the meeting, leaving numbers and implementation issues for talks the next day.

When Nasser and Brezhnev met on the morning of January 23, Nasser shocked the Russian with a new request. He wanted Russian personnel to man the new missile sites for at least six months until Egyptians could be trained to take over. Brezhnev paused and then told Nasser that missiles alone would not be effective—planes would be required as well. "All right, send the planes too," Nasser responded.

But Brezhnev did not raise the issue of warplanes to complement the SAM-3s in order to expand the breadth of armaments Russia would supply Egypt. Instead, he expressed concern that sending Russian planes and pilots risked a serious confrontation with the United States. Perhaps he was seeking to find a way out of his commitment the day before to supply the missiles. But Nasser's next response tweaked his Russian benefactor: Nasser suggested that the Russians were scared.

Brezhnev responded forcefully, "We are not scared of anybody. We are the strongest power on earth." He then lectured Nasser that the issue was not fear, it was risk, and whether the risk was justified.

But Nasser was not intimidated. He answered, "Let me be quite frank with you. If we do not get what I am asking for everybody will assume that the only solution is in the hands of the Americans ... This means that there is only one course open to me. I shall go back to Egypt and I shall tell the people the truth. I shall tell them the time has come for me to step down and hand over to a pro-American president." Impacted by Nasser's emotional response, the Soviets asked for an extra day to consider his request; but Nasser would not agree to any further delay. Instead, the two leaders took a break during which the Russians discussed their response.

When the meeting resumed Brezhnev told Nasser the Russians would supply the missiles and planes, along with Soviet ground personnel and pilots to operate them. However, he made it clear to Nasser that Russian pilots operating from Egyptian bases would not attack Israeli ground targets or overfly Israeli airspace. They would restrict their operations to flying reconnaissance missions and intercepting Israeli attacks. But that was enough. As a result, Israel's gambit, so close to succeeding, failed. Egypt was not cowed into accepting a ceasefire; the Russians became more heavily involved in the Middle East, and Nasser remained in power.

Shortly after the Nasser-Brezhnev meeting, Israeli planes struck a training center close to Cairo filled with Russian advisors. Many Russians were killed or wounded. Within weeks the Soviets flooded Egypt with new SAM-3s and MiG-21 warplanes (not the more advanced MiG-23s that Nasser wanted) coupled with thousands of Russians to operate the equipment and pilot the planes. More arrived throughout the year as Israel and Russia crept closer to confrontation.

The Russians, however, remained concerned how Nixon would react to their provocative decision. On January 31, they used the back channel with Kissinger. Ambassador Dobrynin entered Kissinger's office carrying a note from Kosygin. By then the two men were accustomed to working with each other and they could speak directly without nuance. The note was aggressive and confrontational. It said in part:

> We would like to tell you in all frankness that if Israel continues its adventurism, to bomb the territory of [Egypt] and other Arab states, the Soviet Union will be forced to see to it that the Arab states have means at their disposal with the help of which due rebuff to the arrogant aggressor could be made.

The Russian note also accused Israel of deliberately targeting civilians, accused Nixon of conspiring with Israel, and demanded that the United States "compel" Israel to stop and speedily withdraw from all occupied lands.

The Soviet note created a storm of controversy at the highest levels in Washington. After being advised of its contents, Rogers told Nixon of the threatening note and said it meant that the Russians had already decided to supply more weapons to the Arabs. Kissinger also believed the note heralded more Russian arms for the Arabs. He told Nixon that it was the "first Soviet threat" during his administration and advised a reply should "come down very hard" on the Russians. But, he said, the U.S. should also ask the Russians to state what the Arabs would offer if the Israelis would agree to a ceasefire and withdraw from occupied territories.

Upon further reflection, Kissinger decided Russian policy might cause a no-win-situation for the Russians. If Israel reduced the level of her attacks, and Egypt still refused a ceasefire, then Russia would have no political maneuvering room to remain relevant. Israel would then not sacrifice another inch, and Russia's Arab patrons would recognize Moscow's inability to deliver an Israeli withdrawal. And further, the more equipment the Russians sent Egypt the less likely Israel would back off. Thus, an impasse would be created that the United States might exploit to marginalize the Soviet Union.

On February 4, Nixon responded to the Russian note. He said that Nasser was to blame for Israel's air strikes, and that the United States would provide weapons and other assistance to Israel, as needed, to maintain the military balance. He also lectured the Russians that the *Rogers* plan, which they had rejected, had met the legitimate needs of Russia's allies in the Arab world.

Subsequently, when the president presented to Congress his first annual report concerning foreign policy, it included the following statement: "The United States would view any effort by the Soviet Union to seek prominence in the Middle East as a matter of grave concern," along with a reminder that "any effort by an outside power to exploit local conflict for its own advantage or to seek a special position of its own would be contrary to that goal." His response could not have been clearer to the Soviets. The Americans would not back down.

Or would they?

Kissinger met with Dobrynin privately to discuss the Kosygin note and the American response. He assured the Russian Ambassador that Nixon would give "special attention" to Kosygin's message, but would not be pleased if Russian military personnel were sent to the Middle East. Kissinger also emphasized the special nature of the back channel, and that it should be used if talks with the State Department broke down. But Dobrynin did not take from their meeting the message Kissinger hoped to convey. Dobrynin believed the Kosygin note had succeeded in forcing Nixon to back Israel off. Therefore, rather than ratchet down their assistance, Dobrynin advised his government to act tougher and to send Russian pilots to Egypt.

The same day Nixon responded to Kosygin, the State Department summoned Rabin for a meeting. Rabin's comment that day to Rogers accurately reflected Israel's attitude. "To stop now would be a sign of weakness," he said, "particularly in light of [the] Kosygin approach." Rabin emphasized to the secretary of state the importance of teaching Nasser that continued fighting would be more costly to him than Israel. Rogers agreed that the United States should respond firmly to the Kosygin letter, but also hoped to pressure Israel to cease all deep bombing raids. He thought that Israel, which had spurned his proposals, was a large part of the problem. Nor did Rogers share Nixon's geopolitical view that placed Middle East issues within the context of the global struggle between America and Russia. Nixon's policy was to reduce Soviet influence in the region by weakening radicals and strengthening moderates, while ensuring that Israel would remain secure. Thus, predictably, their meeting consisted of no more than empty words meaninglessly intertwined in a desultory dance. Neither man was willing to listen to the other's arguments. But Rabin was unconcerned. While Rogers was important, and remained the public focal point for Middle East policy, Rabin knew communications received through the back channel reflected America's true policy.

Meanwhile, none of the diplomatic maneuvering made a difference on the ground. Russian pilots were on the way while Israel's attacks escalated further. Eight days after Nixon's response to Kosygin's note, IDF planes attacked deep within Egypt. The bombs dropped a mile short of hitting their stated military target—an Egyptian air force supply base—and instead struck a metallurgical plant just as a shift changed. Seventy Egyptian civilians were killed, and many others were injured. The Egyptians charged that the attack was designed to kill civilians, an accusation Israel denied. A few days later more bombs dropped from

IAF aircraft; clearly due to pilot error they struck a school almost seventy miles north of Cairo. Fifty children were killed or wounded.

As is so often Israel's cross to bear, by responding with military force to Arab attempts to kill Israeli soldiers and citizens, the international community labeled her callous, with no regard for the life of Arab citizens. Few nations were willing to recognize that, almost without exception, when Arab citizens were inadvertently killed by the IDF it was due to Israel's appropriately aggressive defensive response to Arab military operations and terrorist attacks. Instead, the international community held Israel to a standard that Arab nations, Palestinian terrorists, or even their own countries would never have matched, nor have matched since, with regard to their own conduct given the same provocations. For many Jews, those holding Israel to a higher standard than any other country was a strong indicator of anti-Semitic bias, bias that would appear unmasked a few years later in the halls of the UN General Assembly. The old refrain regarding disproportionate response is all well and good as long as it is not the families and property of the self-righteous accuser that is caught in the crosshairs of terror. Once again, as had been replayed through the course of history, how much did Jewish lives lost, or endangered, matter to the international community when it was the Arabs who initiated the killing and it was the Arabs who could have stopped the killing by directly negotiating with Israel in good faith?

Diplomacy

Despite Russia's stubborn insistence that Israel back down unilaterally, it appeared, by March 10, that Israel's deep penetration raids into Egypt had affected Russian policy. Dobrynin told Kissinger that if Israel stops her bombing campaign, Egypt would act with restraint. He also said that he was authorized to restart talks with Rogers based on two principles:

- A settlement that would not just end the war, but would establish the peace; and
- That Arab governments, as part of the agreement, would control the activities of terrorists on their territory.

Kissinger was elated, despite ironically noting that the Russian offer was the bare minimum required for any peace agreement between nations. He also shrewdly observed that Dobrynin had not promised to remove the Russian personnel stationed within Egypt.

Two days later, Kissinger met with Rabin and told him that Nixon, who acknowledged Israel's need to remain strong enough to take risks for peace, had agreed to replace the *Phantom*s and *Skyhawk*s Israel lost, and would provide more if Russia continued to send warplanes to the Arabs. It was not Rabin's nature to be loquacious in appreciation, nor was he. It was a trait Kissinger recognized in Rabin and noted in his memoirs:

> If [Rabin] had been handed the entire United States Strategic Air Command as a free gift he would have a) affected the attitude that at last Israel was getting its due, and b) found some technical shortcoming in the warplanes that made his accepting them a reluctant concession to us.

Kissinger also asked that Israel agree to stop the deep bombing raids and accept an undeclared ceasefire. Rabin responded by requesting that the Americans provide Israel with the additional armaments she had asked for. He told Kissinger that without further military assistance the Arabs would be encouraged to continue fighting, and the pressure on Israel to lash out to end the bloodletting would increase. Nevertheless, despite his misgivings that it might reward Nasser without Israel receiving anything in return, Rabin agreed to report Kissinger's request to Meir.

Five days later, Rabin returned to the United States after a quick trip to Israel. Surprisingly, he informed the Americans that Israel would accept an unofficial ceasefire. But their acceptance was short lived. American intelligence provided to the Israelis revealed a substantial new flow of Russian SAM-3s into Egypt. Accompanying them were 1,500 Russian experts tasked with operating the missiles. In addition, Russian pilots flooded the country. The pilots wore Egyptian uniforms and piloted planes marked with Egyptian insignia while flying aerial defense missions: And more were on the way. The Russians called their effort Operation *Kavkaz*.

The Russians coupled the arrival of Russia's military might in Egypt with a diplomatic offensive. Several days earlier they had released a plan at the UN for Israel and Jordan that, in many ways, mirrored the *Rogers* plan for Israel and Egypt. Excluding minor modifications to respective borders, it called for a full Israeli withdrawal.

Nixon and Kissinger were furious with the Soviet actions which they thought amounted to subterfuge. To discuss the matter, Nixon invited Rabin to meet with him. On March 18, he told the Ambassador, "I am aware of the Soviet SAM-3s and I hope you knock them out. You can't let them build up." Rabin responded, "Attack the Russians[?]" Nixon did not reply, leaving Israel free to formulate her own policy without any interference. Rabin left with assurances that America would both support Israel and desist from pressuring her to agree to a ceasefire.

On March 20, Kissinger tried pressuring the Russians. He told Dobrynin that Russian actions in Egypt were comparable to when the Soviet Union attempt to sneak nuclear armed missiles into Cuba touched off the Cuban missile crises. Therefore, even though the United States had looked favorably on a cessation of hostilities, the Soviet decision had caused the administration to change its mind—America would not push Israel to agree to a ceasefire. And Kissinger warned that Russia's aggressive acts might impact the prospects for détente, thus undermining the relationship both superpowers were striving for. Dobrynin responded that he was unaware of the SAM-3s, but that if the Russians did provide them, they were strictly for defensive purposes. Kissinger did not buy what Dobrynin was selling. He said that it appeared the only purpose of the ceasefire Russia sought was to improve Egypt's military position.

Nixon's fury with the Russians was not limited to directing Kissinger to speak harshly to Dobrynin. He told CIA Director Richard Helms to increase the level of covert operations against the Soviets. "Just go ahead," he said, "hit the Soviets and hit them hard." However, he did not want to get into a major confrontation with the Russians. Especially not with what was happening in Southeast Asia where, on March 21, Lon Nol overthrew Prince Sihanouk, the leader of Cambodia. Lon Nol did not want the North Vietnamese troops based in his country to remain. Therefore, as a result of Lon Nol's rise to power, a political opening was created for the United States to act aggressively. Nixon did not want to face a significant Soviet backlash if he did so. Less than two months later, American troops launched attacks from South Vietnam into Cambodia, directed against the North Vietnamese stationed there.

Then, on March 23, a policy decision promulgated deep in the bowels of the State Department, before the flagrant acts by the Russians that had provoked Kissinger and Nixon, manifested itself in a public display of the State Department's failure to coordinate policy with Nixon and Kissinger. Secretary of State Rogers announced that the United States would complete the promised shipments of *Phantom*s and *Skyhawk*s, but would not agree to fulfill Israel's requests for more.

In light of the back-channel conversations between Kissinger and Rabin, and between Kissinger and Dobrynin, there are three possible explanations for Rogers's announcement: Incompetence combined with Kissinger's lack of political strength or will to stop the process in its tracks; Rogers's moving forward purposively in ignorance because he had been kept out of the back-channel loop; or Rogers saw the growing crisis in Southeast Asia as an opportunity to reassert his primacy in Middle East policy while Nixon's and Kissinger's attention was elsewhere. Any one, two, or all three of these explain the inexplicable, a state department policy that was different from that of the White House.

Little more than a week later, in the beginning of April, there was another attempt to resolve the conflagration Egypt had instigated, and which had drained both Egypt and Israel. By then the Egyptians had suffered more than 10,000 dead or wounded as a result of the War of Attrition, and Israeli casualties numbered 2,000—almost as many as she suffered in the Six-Day War. In hopes of setting in motion a process for resolving the conflict, Dayan unilaterally announced that Israel would end deep penetration raids but would continue to attack and destroy targets near the Suez Canal, including any SAM sites built within thirty kilometers (about 18.6 miles) of the waterway. That last caveat was important because, if the Egyptians successfully placed SAM-2s and SAM-3s near the canal, their range would then extend into the Israeli-controlled Sinai. Israel needed to prevent establishment of a missile umbrella within that zone. Otherwise, Egyptian troops attacking across the Suez Canal would enjoy protection from IAF airstrikes. That would greatly enhance Egypt's chances of success.

The decision to halt the deep penetration raids was not a gratuitous one; Israel really had no choice. Russian SAMs were shooting down Israeli planes with regularity; Israeli pilots were increasingly exhausted by the round-the-clock operations, and Russian pilots flying defensive missions increased the likelihood of an Israeli-Russian confrontation. All of that made Rogers's announcement that no new arms requests would be honored even more concerning. On April 13, with the deep raids into Egypt terminated, Russia's intervention had succeeded.

The end of the bombing, however, did not bring an end to Israel's military problems. Arab artillery continued to strike Israeli targets.

Meanwhile, Soviet pilots were first identified flying over Egyptian airspace on April 18 when eight Russian-operated MiGs tried, without success, to shoot down two Israeli *Phantom*s returning to base from a mission. Rabin told Kissinger a week later: "Now there is a new element. Israel wants more planes."

Desperate for more warplanes, Rabin resorted to influencing American public opinion in order to loosen Nixon's grip on shipments of additional *Phantom*s and *Skyhawk*s. On April 29, Rabin publicly revealed how Russia had intervened over the skies of Egypt. The next day, Kissinger told Rabin to stop and said Nixon was sympathetic to Israel's needs, but would not welcome any pressure from Jewish constituents. It was an especially difficult day for the president. It was the same day American troops launched attacks into the "Parrots Beak" and other locations in Cambodia in order to stop North Vietnamese forces from using Cambodia as a sanctuary. Kissinger followed his admonition, however, with a much more favorable comment. He told Rabin that the United States would supply more planes despite the earlier announcement by Rogers, but it must not be publicized.

Nasser then tried to exert more pressure himself. During a public speech on May 1 he demanded that President Nixon order Israel to withdraw from "the" occupied territories (purposively ignoring that the official version of Resolution 242 had did not contain "the") and to suspend aid of any type if Israel refused. Otherwise, Nasser threatened, he would act under the assumption that American policy favored surrender of Arab land over Israel's continued occupation of the territories.

Israel reacted to Nasser's speech by asking the Rumanians to act as intermediaries to deliver a message to the Egyptian President. The Rumanian Foreign Minister told Nasser that Israel was willing to discuss all aspects of the problem with Egypt without any preconditions. The Israeli message also indicated that a new offer would be made once negotiations started, and conceded that the negotiations could be of a Rhodes model that would lead to direct discussions rather than start with them. The Rumanian Minister told Nasser:

> The problem is a matter of misunderstanding. The Arabs believe that Israel wants territorial expansion by using power. At the same time the Israelis believe that the Arabs want to destroy it as a state. That historic misunderstanding cannot be left as it is and should be put to a test, and tested by the parties themselves, who should not wait for a solution from outside. The United States and Soviet Union control the situation in the region, but we are the ones who are paying with our blood.

The Rumanian added that Israel would not agree to anything that would change the Jewish character of their nation and, therefore, would not annex the occupied Palestinian areas. He also said that Israel would offer solutions for all outstanding issues once negotiations began, but not before. In addition, the minister gave Nasser a personal note from his President indicating that he thought the Israelis were serious.

Unfortunately, Nasser refused to pursue the opportunity. He did not believe the Israelis were serious and thought that a majority of Israel's cabinet favored annexation. He also looked askance at any secret negotiations that, if revealed, would result in Egypt being ostracized by the Arab world and isolated. Nasser compared, with suspicion, Egypt's clear statement of goals to Israel's unwillingness to show her hand until negotiations commenced. But, of course, he did not care that Egypt's public position that Israel must withdraw from all occupied lands and solve the Palestinian refugee problem jeopardized the future existence of the Jewish State. Therefore, his was not a starting point for discussions because it was a veiled call for Israel's destruction. The Rumanian meeting ended with Nasser saying: "We want a peaceful solution, but I don't think it is obtainable now. And I don't think we are ready for negotiations with Israel, either open or secret."

Within the United States, Kissinger proposed a reevaluation of American policy in the Middle East. He told Nixon on May 12 that "[the U.S] had been wrong across the board." Kissinger said that it was a mistake to base policy on hopes that the Russians would pressure Nasser to reach an acceptable agreement, or to limit their involvement in Arab affairs. Nor, he said, would Israel accept any resolution imposed by the superpowers that was against her interests. He then suggested: "Perhaps it is time to shift our attention from the two-power and four-power exercises to direct action vis-à-vis the principal actors—Israel, the Palestinians, and [Egypt]."

Kissinger knew that the door for fruitful negotiations was closing. By the end of May, 150 Russian pilots patrolled the Egyptian skies, and the number of SAM-3 sites was growing. Meanwhile, IAF planes that penetrated beyond the Suez Canal risked encounters with the Russians; Egypt was no longer as concerned as she once had been, and Russian prestige was on the line. Furthermore, Kissinger knew Nixon was distracted. He later wrote, "The physical and mental toll of the Cambodia incursion was too great. Not until Watergate was Nixon so consumed and shaken; he was not prepared to add [the Middle East] to his problems."

But despite Nixon's preoccupation with Cambodia and Vietnam, he still found time to meet with Eban. Eban hoped to obtain reassurance that the planes and supplies would be delivered by the Americans, as promised. Nixon, perhaps sensitive to the ongoing agony of American troops fighting and dying in the jungles of Southeast Asia, along with the domestic unrest at home as a result of the incursion into Cambodia, asked Eban if it were still true that U.S. troops would never be required to fight for Israel. When Eban responded "yes" Nixon said, "Well, in that case, you will get the stuff so long as you don't insist too much publicly." In return, Nixon asked for Israel to publicly indicate her flexibility for negotiating a settlement with the Arabs. Within a few days Meir responded to Nixon's request with a public statement that Israel was still willing to settle all Middle East disputes based on Resolution 242, and that Israel would agree to something akin to a Rhodes formula for conducting talks. It was her first public acknowledgement that direct talks from the first moment would no longer be an Israeli precondition for negotiations. Within months the new *Phantom*s began to arrive.

Meanwhile, the War of Attrition raged on.

CHAPTER THIRTY-FIVE
Rogers's New Peace Plan

Secretary of State Rogers neither accepted nor realized that he would not play the leading role with regard to solving the Middle East crisis. On June 2, he called Ambassador Dobrynin without Kissinger's knowledge, and quite possibly without Nixon's. He told Dobrynin that the United States would not consider Russian forces in the Canal Zone defensive. His implicit message was that, elsewhere in Egypt, the Nixon administration would not object to a Russian presence. That thought was contrary to both Kissinger's and Nixon's stated views.

On June 25, after privately revealing his plan to Kissinger and the National Security Council, Rogers publicly suggested a ninety-day ceasefire, which could be renewed and would be coupled with a standstill for military forces. He suggested that the ceasefire should incorporate simultaneous indirect negotiations that would begin under the auspices of Gunnar Jarring after Egypt and Jordan publicly accepted Resolution 242 and its call for a "withdrawal from occupied territories." On Israel's behalf, he added that the United States would supply Israel three *Phantom*s in July as replacements for planes previously shot down, three more in August, and then four a month thereafter plus the requisite replacement number of replacement *Skyhawk*s. Future shipments, however, would be subject to review if negotiations successfully proceeded. That was diplomatic speak for saying that, if the negotiations failed, supply of the planes would continue. In essence, he called for a breathing space where the parties would "stop shooting and start talking."

Kissinger hated the idea. He felt that the United States should adopt a harder line, which included providing Israel with all the weapons she required. That would emphasize to Nasser that his path to recovering the Sinai was through the Americans—not the Russians. But, to Kissinger's surprise, Nixon supported Rogers's latest plan. Nixon was worried about a confrontation with the Soviet Union and was still smarting from repercussions emanating from the Cambodia incursion.

Meir instinctively opposed Rogers's new plan. She suspected it was a ploy that would morph into Rogers's 1969 plan, which sought to define permanent borders. Rabin met with Kissinger to explain Israel's objections. He emphasized that it left the Russians in place, abandoned any requirement for direct talks or implementation of the Rhodes formula, did not require the Arabs to agree to a formal contractual peace agreement; and, once again, limited shipment of the warplanes Israel required. The limitation of the planes was particularly galling to the Israelis because only weeks earlier Nixon had promised to sell the planes if Meir publicly proclaimed her flexibility with peace negotiations. If ever there was an armament yo-yo, the *Phantom*s were it. But Rabin did not submit a written objection to Rogers's new plan. He sensed then what he was later advised; it would not be in Israel's interest to be the first to reject it.

Kissinger agreed with Rabin, but refrained from telling him. He did tell Nixon that the Arabs would be foolish to refuse Rogers's ceasefire proposal because "we don't give the planes; Israel must accept the '67 border and all they [the Arabs] have to do is negotiate." Kissinger was especially critical of the part of Rogers's plan that suggested if the negotiations succeeded Israel would not get the warplanes. That was a disincentive for success when an incentive would be the better tactic. Nixon agreed. He told Kissinger to privately assure Rabin that the planes would be provided unless there was an extremely significant change that left Israel no longer needing them.

Fortunately for Israel, the Russians were outraged by the new Rogers initiative. They saw it as an attempt by the Americans to push forward a unilateral diplomatic initiative. On June 29, the Soviets received Nasser for an emergency discussion. Before leaving Egypt, Nasser told Vice President Anwar Sadat his thoughts regarding the likelihood of obtaining new armaments: "Anwar, the Soviet Union is a hopeless case." But Nasser was not just coming to Moscow to discuss the *Rogers* plan. He also badly needed quality medical treatment unavailable in Egypt. His high blood pressure and heart disease, exacerbated by incessant smoking and constant work, had worsened. He desperately needed an extended convalescence in a Soviet medical facility.

On the same day Nasser arrived in Russia, Meir delivered a speech to the Knesset. She called Rogers's proposed ceasefire "a trick" that would give Nasser an opportunity to prepare for war. She predicted that it would "facilitate the installation of Soviet missiles for the purpose of achieving an air umbrella … prevent our Air Force [from] silencing the Egyptian artillery aimed at our positions, and [enable] him to make an attempt to cross the Canal." She also charged that American policy mistakenly assumed that Nasser would miraculously change course and agree to negotiate with Israel. To buttress her argument, she quoted Nasser's speech in Libya a few days before in which he said, "[Egypt,] under no circumstances," would negotiate a withdrawal. Meir said that Nasser's policy was that Israel must withdraw from the Golan, Jerusalem, and the West Bank before there is talk of the Sinai. As a result Meir thundered, "Nasser is fanning the flames of hostility and taking pains to give the conflict a pan-Arab character."

That night, perhaps to emphasize Israel's refusal to back down, the IAF struck Egyptian SAM sites built within twenty miles of the canal. Eight missile sites were destroyed, but SAMs shot down five *Phantom*s. It was the biggest single loss of Israeli planes on any day since the Six-Day War. It was a loss rate she could not sustain. Israel's government and the IAF were stunned.

The next day, however, when Nasser met with Brezhnev before undergoing medical treatment in Russia, he shocked Brezhnev; Nasser told the Russian that he would accept Rogers's ceasefire proposal. Seventeen months of war had taken its toll on Egypt. Her oil refineries had been destroyed and the cities along the Suez Canal devastated. Civilians were paying a price, and, by then, military casualties neared 15,000. The country needed to heal. Brezhnev unhappily responded, "Are you going to accept a plan with the stars and stripes on it?" Nasser replied, "I am going to accept it precisely for that reason. A plan with an American flag on it is more likely to be binding on the Israelis."

While Nasser was still in the Soviet Union, Meir wrote a harsh letter to Nixon on July 2 that stated Israel would have to attack the SAM-2 and SAM-3 sites being installed near the canal without regard to the risk to Soviet personnel. The day before, Nixon had said, in response to an interview question about the Middle East that it "is like the Balkans before World War I, where the two superpowers, the United States and the Soviet Union, could be drawn into a confrontation that neither of them wants because of the differences there." Nevertheless, on July 10, Nixon ordered that delivery of the planes still due Israel, per the original agreement first approved by President Johnson in December 1968, be accelerated.

After having rested in a Russian hospital for nearly two weeks, Nasser met again with Brezhnev. He told Brezhnev that the Israeli raids were intended to disrupt Egyptian plans for an offensive into the Sinai, and he reiterated his decision to accept the ceasefire proposal. Nasser explained that the Americans would use an Arab rejection of the Rogers initiative as an excuse to provide Israel with more weapons. But, by accepting the ceasefire, the Egyptians and Russians could use it as an opportunity to improve their positions near the canal. Brezhnev was leery. "In other words," he said, "we exploit that period to reinforce our positions?" Then, despite his discomfort with agreeing to an American led initiative, Brezhnev gave reluctant blessing to Nasser to accept the ceasefire.

On July 23, Nasser publicly announced acceptance of Rogers's ceasefire proposal. He told students at Cairo University that it was Israel's "last chance," and "while we inform the United States that we have accepted its proposals, we also tell them that our real belief is that whatever is taken by force cannot be returned except by force." Palestinians, however, angrily expressed their opposition to his decision. Nasser responded by refusing to see Arafat when he came to Cairo a few days later. Nor did Nasser leave it at that. After Arafat left Cairo, Nasser gave Hussein a tacit green light to deal forcefully with his Fedayeen problem.

By then the IAF had lost three more planes to Russian SAM missiles. Upon hearing of Egypt's acceptance, Nixon sent Meir a message acknowledging that she opposed the *Rogers* plan. Nevertheless, Nixon indicated he expected a "prompt affirmative reply" from her and expressed hope that it would lead to productive negotiations under Jarring.

But Nixon understood that pressure alone would not obtain Israel's grudging acceptance; a sweetener was needed as well. So, in addition, he told Meir, "Our position on withdrawal is that the final borders must be agreed between the parties by means of negotiations under the aegis of Jarring." In addition, Nixon informed Meir that he would not push any resolution of the Palestinian refugee issue that would "fundamentally alter the Jewish character of the State of Israel or jeopardize Israel's security." Finally, Nixon assured Meir that he would not insist on any

Israeli withdrawal "until a binding contractual peace agreement satisfactory to you has been achieved."

Though Nasser had agreed to the *Rogers* plan, Kissinger was still unhappy. He saw that it left the Russians in place without restrictions. Kissinger believed that the lesson to be learned from past Russian behavior was that the Russians would take small steps followed by larger ones if they did not meet resistance (a fitting description of Putin's behavior during the twenty-first century). Therefore, he believed it would only be in America's interest to pressure the Israelis to agree to the plan if the Russians also agreed to remove their combat personnel from Egypt. Kissinger's thought was to eventually secure Israeli agreement to withdraw in the Sinai in return for providing her a massive quantity of American arms and securing Egypt's agreement to enter into a contractual peace agreement. But Kissinger had no room left to maneuver. The Egyptians had foreclosed that option by accepting the *Rogers* plan.

The Ceasefire

Meir was instinctively suspicious of any peace plan with Rogers's name on it. While she considered her options, and Nixon's message, the threat of confrontation with the Russians increased. On July 30, two Soviet-piloted MiG-21s unsuccessfully attacked two Israeli *Skyhawks* near the Suez Canal. Four days later all hell broke loose. Sixteen warplanes—eight Russian and eight Israeli—engaged in a short, but dramatic, air battle over the canal. The Israelis had laid an ambush for the Russians. While four IAF planes attacked ground targets, four other Israeli planes waited high above in the skies. The IAF placed their best pilots in the planes at high altitude designated as the ambushers. When the Russians went after the quartet at low altitude, the Israelis, lying in wait up high, pounced. Within minutes they shot down four Russian planes.

Their success boosted Israeli confidence, but brought danger as well. Russia was not likely to back down. In the face of frequent Egyptian attempts to establish missile sites near the canal, and determined Israeli airstrikes to block them, more confrontations between Israel and Russia were bound to happen. At some point a confrontation would ensue. It would be a fight that, without America's support, Israel could not win.

Feeling the pressure, Meir announced the next day that she would accept the ceasefire. Unfortunately, things did not go smoothly from there. Egyptian acceptance was tied to a document written by Jarring for UN Secretary General U Thant. Meir's acceptance had been based on a letter Rabin had given Rogers on August 4 that included specified reservations to specific words in the Jarring document that Israel disapproved of. Given the contrived controversy over many nations' attempts to add the word "the" to Resolution 242 before "occupied territories", Meir's concerns had merit. Sisco, however, worried that, before the formalities of the ceasefire would be completed, some violent act would occur that would re-ignite the fighting. Therefore, he thought time was of the essence and discounted the importance of the wording differences between the Jarring document and the Israeli letter to Rogers. Thus, in the interest of finalizing the agreement without any further delay he instructed the American mission to the UN to tell U Thant that both parties consented to the Jarring document. Sisco didn't realize the importance Meir attached to her reservations because Meir's American contact, through which she accepted the ceasefire, had not been him—it was the American Ambassador to Israel.

Meir reacted furiously when she learned what had happened. She instructed Rabin to convey the following to Sisco: "The Prime Minister has told me to tell you that the conduct of the U.S. government is an insult to Israel, its government, and its people. You have taken upon yourselves to place words in the mouth of the government of Israel which we have never agreed to say." But Meir would not leave it at that.

She called Sisco and got into a shouting match with him. Neither would listen to the other, nor could they understand each other's positions. Sisco argued that if Meir tried to accept something different than what Nasser had already accepted it would open the whole process up again. But Meir refused to allow herself to be consoled because the language she had agreed to had been ignored.

Rabin met with Kissinger later that night to explain the Prime Minister's fury. But Kissinger was not buying what Rabin told him. Instead, he lost his composure because he could not understand the difference between the Israeli letter and the Jarring document. Rabin responded with an example—the words "just and lasting peace" were in the Jarring document, but not defined. However, Rabin refused to put Israel's complaints in writing, justly fearing that by highlighting the differences and the ambiguities it might bind Israel to an unfavorable interpretation of a document she had not consented to but was stuck with.

The circle of anger grew when Rogers learned that Kissinger had met with Rabin. Rogers was not angry with the Israelis, but with Kissinger. Rogers well knew that the more Kissinger was involved the more his own political power diminished. He argued that the Israelis needed to learn that they could not go to two different places to sound their grievances, unless the president specifically authorized the second channel. Of course, despite probably sensing it, Rogers did not know that Nixon had specifically already done that.

The next day, Meir backed down. She really had no choice. The IAF had been straining to maintain its pace of operations, casualties were increasing; and a confrontation with the Soviets was just around the corner. Her cabinet voted to accept the ceasefire even though Minister Begin argued vociferously against doing so because he thought it would lead to returning "not all of the territories, but undoubtedly most of them" on the West Bank. When his arguments did not prevail he and five other ministers resigned in protest. That ended Israel's unity government, in existence since the dark days shortly before the 1967 war.

Egypt and Russia Cheat

The ceasefire took effect the next day on August 7. The agreement specified that it would expire after three months and included a standstill of military forces for approximately thirty miles (50 kilometers) on each side of the Suez Canal. Rogers announced that neither party could "introduce or construct any new military installations within these zones" and could only engage in activities involving maintenance or resupply of existing locations. Each side was permitted to use aircraft to verify compliance as long as they did not fly closer than 6.2 miles (10 kilometers) from the front lines. But Meir's government thought the term "standstill" seemed too vague to restrain a party that was determined to cheat. Therefore, Israel clarified with the United States that "standstill" included no movement of anti-aircraft missiles closer to the canal. By the time that clarification was communicated to the Egyptians, it was thirty-six hours after the ceasefire had taken effect. By then, with Russian assistance, Egypt had massively cheated.

Egypt's actions appeared premeditated—just as Meir had feared and predicted, and just as Brezhnev and Nasser had schemed previously. Immediately after the ceasefire took effect, Russian and Egyptian convoys began moving towards the canal. Within hours new missile batteries were installed in the "standstill" zone. Israeli intelligence and American satellites detected the violations immediately. Shortly thereafter, Rabin told Kissinger "an entirely new defense configuration has developed." The fourteen new Egyptian SAM sites discovered were a clear violation of both the spirit and the intent of the ceasefire. Despite Israel's request for the clarification, there was no ambiguity in the term "standstill" that Egypt could legitimately claim.

Due to the violations, the United States convinced the British to permit American U2 high-altitude reconnaissance planes to take off from their bases in the Mediterranean and overfly the Canal Zone. The American operation "*Even Steven*" found that the Egyptian violations were worse than previously thought. The operation confirmed that twenty-three SAM-2 sites and five SAM-3 sites, finished by August 10, had not been operational when the ceasefire took effect on August 7. They either had been built or completed subsequent to the ceasefire date. Photographs taken later in the month found even more.

The Israelis were furious and did not spare Kissinger their anger. Rabin told Kissinger on August 15 that "Israel is now under the direct threat of a Soviet pistol, not merely an Egyptian military threat, but a Soviet threat—a threat which is designed to bring Israel to its knees." Rabin further complained that America's failure to respond publicly in the strongest of terms proved that the U.S. did not understand the severity of the violations nor their implications. Three years later, when the Yom Kippur War broke out, Rabin's prognostication proved all too true.

For the most part, Kissinger agreed with the Israelis. He told Nixon: "This has serious consequences for our current initiative in the Middle East, for the longer term prospects for the area generally, and for US-Soviet relations." But Rogers felt differently. Although he acknowledged that the Egyptians and Russians had clearly violated the ceasefire agreement, he felt the violations did not substantially change the military balance. Instead of complaining about past transgressions, Rogers preferred to push forward towards finding a path to peace. He was so narrow-minded concerning his goal that he failed to properly weigh Israel's existential concerns for her survival in a neighborhood devoted to her destruction. It is a failing that many continue to display to this day.

Nevertheless, despite Egypt's having flagrantly broken an agreement within hours of its onset, Israel respected the ceasefire and made no attempts to destroy the new missile sites. However, Israel's decision not to reflexively respond with force to Arab provocations, as she had in the past, was probably not because of a new passivity. Instead, it more likely was necessitated by the exhaustion of the IAF, coupled with the lack of any new additional American promises for arms to placate the Israelis after Egypt had violated the ceasefire. As a result, Israel eventually received the latest American weapons systems, and the friendship between the two countries, both furious with Egypt and Russia, grew closer.

Of course, the Egyptians denied violating the agreement. Nor did they stop construction of more illegal missile sites. Instead, they tried to mask their perfidy with specious arguments that all they were doing was rotating men and equipment in and out of the Canal Zone while maintaining or repairing existing sites. And rather than admit guilt, the Egyptians engaged in a verbal offensive. They lashed out that the new arms the Americans agreed to provide the Israelis violated assurances given Egypt by Rogers in order to obtain Nasser's agreement to the ceasefire. The Russian response to American complaints was technical and underwhelming—they pointed out that they were not signatories to the agreement.

Within two months of the ceasefire, the Egyptians, with Russian assistance, established ninety new missile sites in the Canal Zone that incorporated hundreds of missile launchers. Many of the new sites were so close to the canal that their range extended an additional twelve miles into Israeli air space. As a result, Israel lost unrestricted control of the skies over her soldiers manning the Bar-Lev forts strung out along the canal and miles back. Meanwhile, more Russians continued to pour into Egypt.

On September 6, Israel announced that because of the Egyptian violations she would not participate in talks with Jarring until Egypt stopped adding more military installations in the Canal Zone and dismantled those that had been built after the ceasefire. Meir pointed out that, "If they did not [dismantle the illegal missile sites and stop building new ones in the Canal Zone], what would be the point of any agreements they would ever sign?"

CHAPTER THIRTY-SIX
Hussein Takes Matters into His Own Hands

Dawson's Field

The same day Israel announced her official refusal to participate in the Jarring talks until Egypt complied with the terms of the ceasefire, a new crisis unfolded. On September 6, gunmen from the PFLP hijacked two American civilian airliners and one Swiss plane. The PFLP was the second largest terrorist group under the PLO umbrella; only Fatah, led by Arafat, was bigger. Two other PFLP hijackers had tried to take control of an El Al plane as well, but the pilot thwarted them when he put the aircraft into a steep nosedive. The precipitous descent distracted one gunman's attention. That provided an opportunity for a brave passenger to hit the hijacker with a bottle of whiskey, after which the plane's crew shot and killed him and wounded the other. The wounded hijacker was none other than Leila Khaled, who had helped hijack an airliner the year before.

Meanwhile, the hijackers in one of the commandeered American planes, a Pan Am jumbo jet, took it to Cairo, where, after permitting all 170 on board to evacuate, they blew it up. That may have been done to convey the PFLP's disdain for Nasser's decision to enter into a ceasefire with Israel. The hijackers in the other two planes had a different agenda.

They directed them to Dawson's Field (renamed by the hijackers "Revolutionary Airport"), a small airstrip in a remote desolate area of Jordan. It was only five days after assassins had almost taken Hussein's life.

Before the hijackers would release the passengers, they insisted that several demands had to be honored, including:

- Release of Leila Khaled, held in a British jail after her failed hijack attempt;
- Release of three terrorists held in Germany and three others imprisoned in Switzerland; and
- Release of an undefined number of terrorists in Israeli jails in return for release of the American and Israeli passengers.

If not, they threatened to blow up the planes and passengers early on the morning of September 10. But Habash's PFLP, was also motivated by something other than release of terrorists in various jails. By being more militant than the other Palestinian groups, the PFLP hoped to trigger a confrontation with King Hussein that, with the help of Syria and Iraq, would remove him from his throne.

Subsequent negotiations led to the terrorists moving 127 non-Jewish women and children passengers to a hotel in Amman on September 7. Six men—including three Americans, two rabbis, and another Jewish man—were taken to a separate location as insurance against a surprise attack. The rest of the men and the Jewish women and children remained on the planes.

In the United States, Kissinger, Rogers, Richard Helms (Director of the CIA), and Melvin Laird (Secretary of Defense) met on September 8 in Rogers's office. The discussions were only noteworthy for some of the wild ideas thrown about, including use of nerve gas to paralyze the hijackers. But in the end, and again after a meeting with Nixon in the afternoon, they accepted that they were largely powerless to change the course of events.

Use of military force was not an option. Most American soldiers and Special Forces were already committed to the Vietnam conflict or required for other roles. Unfortunately, in 1970, the United States did not have highly specialized soldiers ready to act at a moment's notice to free passengers from hijackers. The only available forces were four brigades that constituted the entire American strategic reserve. Of them, those soldiers based in Germany would take forty-eight hours to reach Jordan; those in the United States would take seventy-two hours to get there. Then, once in Jordan, they would face the challenge of maneuvering, surviving, and receiving supplies in potentially hostile territory. They also might have faced opposition from the 17,000 strong Iraqi military force still stationed in the country. Therefore, the Americans could do little more than posture by sending an aircraft carrier from the Sixth Fleet closer to the Lebanese Coast and pressure the Europeans to not make separate deals with the hijackers. Military force would only be considered if it appeared King Hussein was about to fall from power.

Then, on September 9, terrorists hijacked another plane. It too was taken to Dawson's Field where the 115 passengers and crew on board joined the 177 people still held hostage there. Shortly afterwards, the terrorists agreed to extend their deadline to September 13. But tension continued to mount at Dawson's Field and also in Amman where the king's army strained at the bit to put down the increasingly audacious Fedayeen, who, from its perspective, were infesting the city.

The sight at the isolated airstrip was something to behold. Fedayeen patrolled the airfield where they held over 300 passengers captive on the three planes for days in deteriorating condition. The passenger jets were jarringly out of place and forlornly parked in the barren desert location. Jordanian troops surrounded them, but refrained from firing out of fear of harming the hostages. While the standoff continued, Hussein fumed and denounced the terrorists, calling them the "shame of the Arabs."

The PFLP reacted to international pressure by releasing all of the Jewish women and children on September 12 along with many of the men. But they continued to hold fifty-six males (Jews and crew members) that had American, British, and Israeli passports. They also destroyed the three planes. Eventually, most male passengers and crew were released, except for sixteen not freed until September 25. Six days later England released Leila Khaled without comment; British silence did little to hide what was obvious—a deal had been made.

The Dawson's Field hijackings spurred increased fighting between Fedayeen and the Jordanian army. The specter of a de-facto Palestinian army holding hundreds of innocent passengers on Jordanian soil had highlighted Hussein's apparent impotence. His initial response did little to dissipate that impression. Hussein was furious, but soberly understood that if he took action hundreds, if not thousands, of civilians would be killed or wounded. Thus, when the king received information that a Jordanian army column was heading towards Amman to fight the Fedayeen, he rushed to stop them after they had ignored his brother's orders to turn back. When Hussein reached the column, he noticed a radio antenna with a women's bra flapping in the breeze and asked why it was there. His soldiers responded it was because their king was a woman, afraid to fight Jordan's enemies. After three hours of argument, Hussein convinced them to turn back. But the writing was on the wall. The army's faith in their king was rapidly diminishing.

Finally, recognizing the danger of further restraint, Hussein agreed the Fedayeen had to be stopped—no matter the cost—and gave the army a green light. The generals planned to attack the PLO on September 16, but postponed it one day. Why? Because Hussein's sister, who lived in England at the time, met with a fortune teller who told her the sixteenth would be a bad day for the king, but the next day had prospects for good fortune. Hussein, not wanting to tempt fate, decided to wait one more day.

On the fifteenth, Hussein announced the formation of a military government and told his people: "We find it our duty to take a series of measures to restore law and order to preserve the life of every citizen, his means of living and his property."

On September 17 the army began its effort to restore Jordanian control to Palestinian areas. Its commanders forecast it would take two-to-three days to drive the 52,000 Fedayeen, of which 12,000 were believed to be full-time soldiers, out of the city. But, as military operations often are, it was more difficult than anticipated. Hussein's admonition to minimize civilian casualties coupled with the stone homes, deep ravines, and narrow streets of the refugee camps within and around Amman, made progress difficult. The army also needed to deal with Fedayeen located in other towns and cities. And Jordanian military planners were concerned about what the Iraqi troops stationed on Jordanian soil would do; how Syria would react, and that Israel might see the fighting as an opportunity to push into Jordan to take strategic areas near the northern part of their common border. In addition, to make matters even more worrisome, Hussein could not be certain of the loyalty of all of his soldiers since many were Palestinian (amid the fighting, 5,000 had switched to the Palestinian side or stayed home).

America's ambassador to Jordan tried to reassure the king in his time of need. He told Hussein the United States would assist his efforts with material support, if requested. By then the fighting had spread to other cities, including Irbid in the north. To underscore the ambassador's point, the Americans sent two more aircraft carriers towards the Lebanese coast along with other naval support ships and a marine contingent. Although the U.S. did not make the naval movements public, the Russians were surely aware. Nixon also spoke off the record, but for publication, that, if Iraq or Syria turned against the Jordanians, the Americans or the Israelis might intervene.

Syria Attacks

By September 18, the Jordanian army was making slow progress, and the PLO was running out of ammunition. However, there were ominous signs. Syrian tanks were massing in increasing numbers along her shared border with Jordan, and Hussein had received reports of Iraqi troop movements. And because most international news reporters covering the story were based in a hotel within PLO controlled area, their reporting tended to be one-sided and reflective of the dire situation the PLO found itself in (an eerie forerunner to correspondents based in designated locations in Gaza reporting on Israeli strikes against Hamas decades later). As a result, leaders of other Arab nations felt pressured by their populace and their own convictions to intervene before the Palestinians were slaughtered.

The Syrians were determined to prevent the Jordanians from dismantling the PLO. As a first step, Syrian Defense Minister Assad had already facilitated movement of military equipment from Syria's inventory to the Fedayeen. Assad also had implored Iraq's defense minister to use his troops stationed in Jordan to help the PLO, but the Iraqis would not commit. However, as the PLO weakened in the face of the Jordanian army's ferocious onslaught, the Syrians recognized that only if they intervened with their army could they reverse the course of events.

Fortuitously, when the conflagration erupted in Jordan, Golda Meir was in Washington to meet with Nixon and Rogers. But Jordan was not the topic; Egypt was. Meir had brought with her maps that showed Egyptian missile sites moving closer to the Suez Canal, thereby violating the ceasefire.

"What disturbs us immensely is the preparation for future shooting," she told Nixon. "When this starts, it may be much more serious than before."

Nixon assured her that, because of the violations, Israel's requests for aid would receive his "sympathetic attention." Neither of them knew that three years later Meir's prediction would come to pass, and Nixon's promise would be tested.

While Meir and Nixon spoke, the Syrians completed final preparations to move their forces into Jordan. In the early hours of September 19, Palestinian Liberation Army troops supported by Syria, crossed into Jordan from Syrian territory. The next day, Syrian troops and tanks also crossed the border and headed towards Amman. Iraqi troops stationed within Jordan did not participate in the fighting, but yielded to permit Syrian troops space to maneuver. With most of the Jordanian army concentrated close to Amman and the other Fedayeen concentrations throughout the country, little was left to block the initial Syrian thrust. One Jordanian tank commander said, "I didn't give much for our chances." By nightfall, despite their superior military training, the exhausted Jordanian troops in the area were barely able to contain the Syrian advances. Arafat declared northern Jordan liberated.

Hussein was desperate. He asked the American Ambassador to tell President Nixon that conditions were deteriorating, and only an intervention on the ground and in the air would stem the tide. He told the British the same. Pointedly, Hussein did not dismiss the idea of Israel saving him.

Nixon felt the need to react to the invasion of Jordan. He saw Syria's incursion as a Russian-inspired attempt to unseat a pro-Western government. Years later he wrote in his memoirs: "We could not allow Hussein to be overthrown by a Soviet-inspired insurrection. If it succeeded, the entire Middle East might erupt in war ... it was like a ghastly game of dominoes, with a nuclear war waiting at the end." The Americans responded by openly raising the alert level of one of their airborne divisions and moving the Sixth Fleet towards the region. They also quietly warned the Soviets to restrain the Syrian regime and then reached out confidentially to Israel for assistance. Nixon and Kissinger agreed that Israel had the means to apply military pressure on the Syrians that would keep the Jordanian crisis from exploding. But would Israel come to the aid of an Arab country that had attacked her three years earlier?

As luck would have it, it was an opportune moment for quickly coordinating with the Israelis. Meir, after meeting Nixon on the eighteenth, was accompanied two days later by Rabin in New York to a dinner sponsored by the United Jewish Agency. Kissinger called Rabin at 10:00 p.m. and said he needed to see him urgently in Washington. After a series of discussions concerning whether the Americans would support Israel if she agreed to launch airstrikes against the Syrian army in Jordan, Rabin went to the airport and boarded a plane supplied by the White House.

When Rabin arrived in D.C., Kissinger informed him that only the Israelis could stop the Syrians from advancing on Amman. Rabin responded that Israel would need the Sixth Fleet to help protect her from a Russian response. Kissinger agreed to Rabin's request. He also assured the Israeli Ambassador that the United States would restore any material losses Israel sustained while fighting the Syrians. Later that night, Rabin told Kissinger that Meir had agreed to fly air reconnaissance at first light. She would then decide on a course of action after the IDF analyzed its findings.

Israeli air reconnaissance on the twenty-first confirmed that up to 300 Syrian tanks were operating within Jordan and suggested the possibility that the Iraqis were also involved. When the Israeli cabinet met without Meir, who was in the U.S., they were divided. Some, including Allon and Eban (as well as Meir and Rabin in absence), wanted to help Hussein. Others, including Dayan, Peres, and Sharon, saw the turn of events as an opportunity to end Israel's West Bank problems by staying on the sidelines and thus giving the Palestinians an opportunity to create a new state on the ruins of Jordan. However, all of the participants agreed that, if they decided to intervene, air strikes alone would not be enough to stop the Syrians. Before making a final decision, they decided to ask the Americans several questions and to inform them that Israeli ground troops would be required to stop the Syrians. Their questions boiled down to:

- Would King Hussein ask for Israel's help so Israeli intervention would not be seen as an invasion?
- How would the United States stop the Soviets from intervening?
- Would the United States veto any Security Council resolution condemning Israel or demanding her to withdraw?
- Would Israel be held responsible for the fate of the remaining unreleased Dawson's Field hostages if she intervened?

Nixon responded that the Israelis should not use ground troops in Jordan unless it was a last resort. He added that, although air strikes within Syria to support operations would be acceptable, use of ground troops within Syria, as opposed to Jordan, would not. Kissinger felt impelled to tell Rabin not to extract too many conditions before moving. "Conditions don't mean much anymore," he said. "If you lick the Syrians that will count."

Although the Israelis were not totally satisfied with America's responses, they mobilized troops along the Syrian and Jordanian border. From the outset, the Israelis planned to use both air and ground forces to stop the Syrians. But they also made contingency plans to permanently take strategic portions in Jordan should the Jordanians fall apart in the face of the Syrian onslaught and the internal civil war. During the evening, Allon contacted Hussein to reassure him that Israel would help and would not take advantage of his weakened state. Hussein responded within the hour that he appreciated Israel's willingness to assist him but, although the situation was precarious, there was a chance he would be able to contain the Syrians on his own.

Shortly after dawn, Jordan's air force, coupled with Jordanian tanks and artillery, took a huge toll on the Syrian expeditionary force. Perhaps emboldened by the prospect of Israeli help, the Jordanian army stopped the Syrians from advancing further. The Syrians may also have been demoralized after being pounded by sonic booms from a squadron of Israeli planes that flew low over them and then disappeared over the horizon. By the end of the day, the Syrian forces began a hasty withdrawal.

Also, the Jordanians were more effective than had been expected due to the conspicuous absence of the Syrian Air Force. Assad later said, "It was a difficult predicament. I was distressed to be fighting the Jordanians whom we did not think of as an enemy. I didn't bring up our own stronger air force because I wanted to prevent escalation." He explained that the reason Syrian troops moved into Jordan was not to overthrow Hussein, but to protect Palestinians from being massacred by creating a safe haven in the north from which they could negotiate a resolution to the confrontation. Others have suggested that Assad purposively withheld the air force to weaken Jadid, his chief rival, or because he feared that employing Syria's air force would have drawn America or Israel into the battle. Another explanation, argued by some, is that the Syrian air force's failure to appear over the battlefield might have been due to Russian pressure induced by American threats. However, whatever the reason, without having to fear air strikes, and assisted by their own air force, the beleaguered Jordanians repelled the invaders.

Iraqi neutrality was also crucial to Jordan's success. Iraq's 17,000 troops and 200 tanks based inside Jordan could have tipped the balance, but the Syrian and Iraqi regimes hated each other. Each suspected the other of plots to take over Jordan. Therefore, despite Iraq's support for the PLO and opposition to Hussein, the Iraqi leadership's dislike of the Syrian leaders won out. Other than tacit assistance to the Syrians, Iraqi troops stayed out of the fray.

By late in the day on September 23, 1970, all remaining Syrian forces were back behind the Syrian border. Later, in a magnanimous gesture,

Hussein permitted the Syrians to recover their burned-out and damaged tanks from Jordanian territory. Hussein then turned his full attention back to the Palestinian uprising.

The crisis changed regional dynamics. Arafat discovered he could not count on the Syrians to come to his aid, and Assad received confirmation for his concern that an unrestrained PLO could pull Syria into conflicts she was not prepared for. As a result, Arafat and Assad's relationship deteriorated. And American ties with Israel deepened. Also, the Americans and Israelis found they could work together in pursuit of common strategic interests. Kissinger called Rabin with a message for Meir: "The President will never forget Israel's role in preventing the deterioration in Jordan and in blocking the attempt to overturn the regime there ... These events will be taken into account in all future developments."

Hussein to Cairo

With the Syrians out of the picture, the PLO could not stand up to a determined and vengeful Jordanian army. However, a savior appeared in the form of the Sudanese president who tried to broker a ceasefire on September 24 that required:
- The Fedayeen to leave the cities;
- The Jordanian army leaving the cities after the Fedayeen did;
- Jordan recognizing that the PLO was the sole legitimate representative of the Palestinians; and
- The PLO's agreement to abide by Jordan's laws.

When Arafat first heard the terms he rejected them, but then changed his mind the next day when he realized the PLO would otherwise be destroyed. (Subsequently, the PLO disingenuously said that the Jordanians refused the ceasefire at first, not them.) After agreeing to the Sudanese proposal on September 25, Arafat went to Cairo where Nasser treated him as if he were a head of state. Nasser had no love for Arafat but felt he had no choice but to support him. Otherwise, he feared, the PLO's defeat might cause Arafat to lose control of the organization. Then, he would be replaced by somebody much more hardline such as George Habash, leader of the PFLP.

But Nasser had his work cut out with Hussein. The king was not in a conciliatory mood having barely survived a PLO inspired civil war and having emerged with the upper hand. Nasser had previously praised Hussein for his patience with the Fedayeen. But now he worried that, if the Jordanians killed many more Palestinians, Egypt would be forced to intervene. And if Egypt did, Nasser knew that might cause the Israelis to respond, pushing him into a full-scale war he was not yet ready for. Therefore, Nasser gambled. He threatened Hussein with intervention if the king did not stop fighting the PLO, but he invited Hussein to Cairo for an Arab Head of State meeting the next day. Hussein agreed despite opposition voiced by many of his advisors.

On September 27, Hussein personally piloted his plane to Cairo. By the time he arrived, Arafat had already had two days alone with the other Arab leaders to convince them that the Jordanian regime was brutal. Nasser's demeanor suggested he believed Arafat. Although he went to the airport to meet Hussein, he was cool and distant to the Jordanian king.

The conference convened at the Cairo Hilton. Each Arab leader had the use of an entire floor for his entourage that included guards and advisors. The meetings started at 1:30 p.m. in one of the hotel's conference rooms. Both Hussein and Arafat wore guns. The leaders of Saudi Arabia, Kuwait, Libya, Yemen, and Lebanon, along with Nasser, joined them. The table where they sat was horseshoe shaped with Nasser in the center. Hussein and Arafat were at each end.

The talks lasted six hours. Nasser looked exhausted, but assumed the role of peacemaker. He castigated Hussein for the brutality his soldiers had shown towards the civilian population, but he expressed sympathy for the humiliation the hijackings had caused Hussein. Others accused Hussein of attempting to exterminate the Palestinians. The king responded bitterly, mentioning "Syrian butchers" and accusing them of naked aggression. The angry rhetoric continued, but the participants did not formally censure Hussein. Nor did they offer to help him financially or offer material assistance to care for the hundreds of thousands of Palestinian refugees within his country.

Finally, the attendees reached an agreement even less favorable to Jordan than the terms of the ceasefire proposed by the Sudanese president a few days before. It placed restrictions on both Fedayeen and Jordanian army movement. The agreement also required that the new ceasefire begin immediately and that prisoners of war were to be released by both sides. Then, to ensure that the agreement would last, it included establishment of an Arab commission charged with supervising the peace. No requirement was placed on the Fedayeen to respect Jordanian authority, and no recompense provided for the burden Jordan sustained as a result of trying to minister to the needs of Palestinian refugees. Nor was there any admonition against the PLO continuing to mount its terrorist attacks into Israel from Jordanian territory, even though everyone knew that would invite an Israeli response detrimental to Jordan. The agreement concluded: "Full support of the Palestinian revolution is ensured to enable it to carry out its sacred duty, the liberation of the land." Then the Arab leaders convinced Hussein and Arafat to reluctantly shake hands (It was an eerie precursor to a day fifteen years later, on the White House lawn, when Rabin reluctantly shook Arafat's hand at the urging of President Clinton).

Arafat had won the political battle. His allegations of Jordanian army impropriety were exaggerated. Hussein was sensitive to minimizing the suffering of his people and had issued orders to prevent wanton destruction and mayhem. But, as Hamas and Hezbollah would do decades later, the PLO chose to establish its bases within populated areas.

Therefore, civilian casualties were impossible to avoid. Arafat had put the two days he had in Cairo before Hussein's arrival to good use. Also, as would be repeated in ensuing decades to Israel's detriment, the PLO had taken great advantage of the proximity of the international press corps to tell its side of the story, unfettered by other perspectives that would have revealed a different reality. The king was made to appear the villain when he was really the victim. It was vilification built on a reversal of truths similar to what Israel has endured to this day. Only in this early case, it was an Arab leader who bore the brunt of that cynical and fraudulent strategy.

In the aftermath of his titanic struggle with the Palestinians, Hussein renewed dialogue with the Israelis. On October 3, he met with Allon and Herzog in an air-conditioned car parked in the desert north of Eilat, in southern Israel, where they spoke for ninety minutes. Hussein thanked them for their willingness to come to his aid. He said that his actions had preempted a Palestinian plan to instigate a general revolt against his rule. He also divulged that his army had discovered weapons in more than 300 secret caves along with documents that would be helpful for tracking down many remaining insurgents. And he told the Israelis that he was determined to rebuild Jordanian society and rid the country of the Palestinian terrorists. The king called Arafat a liar who bore the main responsibility for the confrontation and insisted that he must be dealt with. He also assured the Israelis that he would work hard to expel the Iraqi military contingent from his country.

Hussein addressed the peace process too. He said he wanted to resume the peace talks through Jarring but could not until Egypt did as well. However, given the political upheaval in Egypt (see the next chapter), that did not seem likely soon. Then, Allon presented his new Palestinian West Bank autonomy plan that might eventually link West Bank residents to Palestinians in Jordan. Hussein refused to divulge whether he thought it a good idea, but he agreed to consider it after hearing more details. However, because Israel's cabinet had no interest, Allon's thoughts comprised only a vague skeleton of an idea that he never had the political backing to flesh out.

Less than two weeks after meeting with the Israelis, Hussein signed another agreement with Arafat. The document called for the Fedayeen to respect Jordan's laws and codified that the Fedayeen could not wear uniforms or bear arms in public. But, in return, Hussein gave Arafat what he most wanted: Jordan would recognize the PLO as the sole representative of the Palestinian people. Since more than half of Jordan's resident population was Palestinian, at the very least the document made Arafat a de-facto co-leader of Jordan's populace.

As a result, any hope of Hussein resolving the Palestinian crisis unilaterally with the Israelis independent of the PLO, was extinguished.

CHAPTER THIRTY-SEVEN
The New Arab Leaders

Sadat Becomes President

Despite his obvious mounting fatigue, Nasser saw each Arab leader off, individually, the day after the Arab Summit conference concluded. On his final trip to the airport, he accompanied the Kuwaiti Emir to his plane. The last few days had exhausted the Egyptian president. Nasser uttered, "What I need is a long deep sleep." His legs were aching so much that he could no longer stand and could only get into his car with difficulty. Finally, near 3:30 p.m., Nasser made it home. He was so tired that he refused any food.

Within a half hour of reaching his residence, Nasser suffered a massive heart attack. He died less than an hour later. That night, elite members of the Egyptian government gathered around his bedside. Vice President Sadat kissed his face and his hand. He then pulled the blanket over his president's dead body. The Nasser era had come to an end; Sadat's was about to begin.

For many, Sadat's accession to leadership was a temporary measure that would only last until a real leader was chosen. Sadat was born in 1918. He lived in poverty within the Nile Delta, with twelve brothers and sisters, for the first seven years of his life. Sadat's parents then moved the family to Cairo, where he developed a hatred for the British who occupied Egypt at the time. When Sadat was eighteen, he enrolled in the Royal Military Academy where he studied history and concluded that the British would never leave Egypt unless forced out by violent means. After graduating from the Academy, he became a second lieutenant and was posted to the Sudan. While there, Sadat met Nasser and joined with him to form the secret, anti-British, free officers' movement.

During World War II, Sadat collaborated with the Nazis rather unsuccessfully and eventually was arrested by the British on charges of treason. After the war ended, Sadat plotted with Nasser to overthrow Egypt's King Farouk. When their plans came to fruition in 1952, Sadat announced the successful coup to the masses on Cairo radio. In 1964, Nasser appointed Sadat as his vice president and reappointed him five year later. Sadat's position, however, was largely for show; he was powerless, and it was never clear whether Nasser considered him his heir apparent since Sadat had little or no involvement with developing or executing Egyptian policy. As a result, most Egyptians and foreigners, including those in the Arab world, knew little about him. After Nasser died, most viewed Sadat as a transitional figure, at best, who would not last more than a few months.

The Russians were especially concerned by Sadat's rise to power. They knew he did not hold them in high regard. In fact, during Nasser's funeral, Sadat took the American representative at the proceedings, Elliot Richardson, aside and expressed his desire for closer relations with the United States. The Russians preferred Ali Sabry to Sadat. Sabry, who also held the title of vice president and was Chairman of the Arab Socialist Union, promoted pro-Soviet policies in Egypt.

Sadat pledged in his first few speeches as president not to depart from Nasser's primary mission—liberation of all Arab land occupied by Israel in 1967. However, he astutely realized even then that, although the Russians might be more willing to provide the military equipment required for the Israelis to take him seriously, only the Americans could deliver the political pressure needed to influence Israel to withdraw.

But, to Sadat's dismay, America's policy was unaffected by recent developments. The ceasefire along the Suez Canal, resolution of the crisis in Jordan, his conversation with Richardson, and even the death of Nasser; none brought change in American policy. In fact, many American policymakers believed the Middle East to be less volatile as a result of the turn of events. Therefore, rather than focusing on Arab-Israeli relations, they turned their attention to resolving the Vietnam War, opening diplomatic connections with the Chinese, pursuing détente, and scheduling a Summit Conference with the Russians. As for the Middle East, Nixon planned to remain close with the Israelis, push for a resumption of the Jarring talks, and convince Sadat that the Russians could never provide him with the means to achieve his goals. None of those policy objectives dovetailed with what Sadat wanted. And complicating matters for him, the Americans were still angry with the Egyptians and Russians for sneaking the SAMs closer to the Suez Canal immediately after the ceasefire came into effect. Therefore, the United States agreed within weeks of Nasser's death to provide Israel more *Phantom*s, 200 tanks, and a combination of loans and foreign aid to pay for them. Rabin's argument that a stronger Israel was more likely to take risks for peace had borne fruit in the form of weapons needed for war. Time would tell whether they would promote peace.

Sadat had two issues to deal with immediately after assuming power. The **first** was whether or not to extend the ninety-day ceasefire along the canal that would end in November. Israel reached out to him through a Rumanian diplomatic representative at Nasser's funeral in hopes of getting off on the right foot with Sadat. The Rumanian took the new Egyptian president aside and said the Israelis had asked him to convey to him the following message:

We understand your feelings at this moment and the sorrow that the loss of President Nasser has brought. The Israeli government sends you assurances that it will not exploit any resulting confusion. We look eagerly to better times when we can establish contacts for dealing with our joint causes.

Perhaps due to the message, or perhaps due to his need to focus first on internal politics, Sadat proclaimed in early November that he would renew the ceasefire, due to expire November 6, for another ninety days. He also suggested that the Jarring talks should resume during those three months. Meanwhile, through low-level diplomatic contacts, Sadat privately told the Americans that he would favorably consider any idea that included an Israeli interim withdrawal to the mountain passes as the first stage of a full withdrawal to the border that predated the Six-Day War. And later in 1970, Sadat sent a letter to Nixon which emphasized that Egypt was outside the Soviet's sphere of influence, and that if Nixon wished to talk with Egypt, he should do so through Cairo—not Moscow. "Our own decisions [are made] freely and independently," Sadat reiterated, "so that if you prove friendly to us, we shall be ten times as friendly."

Sadat also had a **second** problem, more pressing than extending the ceasefire decision. How would he hold on to his position and power? To forestall his opposition, Sadat strove to reach agreements with his political rivals. All agreed that they would abide by the Egyptian Constitution, which required sixty-days to pass after the vice president assumed control of the government on a temporary basis before a permanent president could be selected. When, at the end of those two months, nobody came forward to contend for the presidency, Sadat's position as the head of state was affirmed. Still, many believed that his reign would be short-lived, and that he could easily be manipulated.

They soon found their assessment wrong.

Assad Takes Over

On November 13, fifteen days after Nasser's death, Assad made his move to take complete control of Syria. For twelve days the Syrian Ba'ath party Congress had met during which Jadid and Assad had clashed continuously over Syrian policy. Jadid, aware of his opponent's growing power within the military, had attempted to limit Assad's influence by prohibiting officers from transferring between posts. But Assad, realizing that the moment for decisive action had arrived, turned the tables on his opponent. Pro-Assad forces arrested Jadid and placed him in jail where he languished for the next twenty-three years until his death. No blood flowed, but Syria had a new leader.

After Assad had Jadid arrested, Libyan leader Muammar Gaddafi flew into Damascus airport on a previously planned visit to Syria. Assad forces had completed the final stages of the coup only a few hours earlier, and the Syrian leadership change had not yet been publicized. Nevertheless, Assad went to the airport to greet him. After informing Gaddafi that he had taken power, Assad quipped, "It's a good thing you didn't arrive half an hour earlier."

Assad was only forty years old. He had five children, four of whom were sons. And he was not one to permit any challenge to his rule. However, rather than just using brute force, he also sought popular support for his rule. In that regard, he enacted some reforms and relaxed the Syrian police state, because despite his disdain for democracy, he hoped to rule by general acclaim. Perhaps his desire to please the Syrian rank and file was due to his minority religious background. Assad, like Jadid, was an Alawite—a religious sect much more akin to the Shiite branch of Islam rather than to Syria's Sunni majority. But unlike Jadid, he did not employ a powerless Sunni front man to deflect religious-based opposition to his rule. Therefore, Assad not only wanted support from all Syrians, in order to rule effectively he needed it.

Assad, despite his less openly virulent nature than Jadid, had no real interest in signing a peace treaty with Israel. His first priority was to recover the Golan because it was Syrian land. It was a goal he fully expected to have to achieve through force. Equally important to Assad, was to eliminate the lingering sting of dishonor that Israel's overwhelming victory over Syria had caused. Therefore, as opposed to Hussein and Sadat, Assad did not want to sign an agreement with Israel before winning a military confrontation with the Jewish State. Nor did he have an interest in permanent peaceful co-existence with Israel. That is why he reaffirmed Syria's rejection of Resolution 242. (I am mindful of the failed negotiations between Israel and Syria that subsequently occurred in the 1990's, but whether the talks signaled a change in Assad's thinking rather than a tactic to recover lost lands we will never know for sure—but it appears doubtful given his life's record.) However, it was not hatred for Jews in general that motivated Assad (as opposed to Jadid who believed that Jews wanted to control the world). Instead, Assad's hatred was for the Jewish Zionists who created Israel. The existence of Israel drove his strategic perspective and planning.

In late November, Assad flew to Egypt to make common cause with Sadat. He knew that Syria had no hope of successfully confronting Israel alone. Therefore, coordinating with Egypt was a strategic necessity, especially given Syria's failed attempt to support the PLO at Hussein's expense a few months before. Since both leaders were new to their roles, an early meeting was crucial for developing a mutually beneficial relationship. And Assad knew Syria needed to maintain a strategic relationship with the Soviets. He had no love for Marxist ideology unlike his predecessor, but he needed Russian weapons. While in Egypt, Assad told Sadat that Syria would join a proposed Federation of Egypt, Libya, and the Sudan. He also signed a military agreement with Sadat. The crescent of hatred bordering Israel was re-forming and re-energizing.

End Year Review

From Israel's perspective, the first overtly ominous signs that the UN was tilting further towards an anti-Semitic abyss appeared in 1970. The General Assembly passed a resolution expressing concern for people struggling to attain self-determination and specifically referenced and castigated the governments of South Africa and Israel for denying those rights. With regard to Israel, the General Assembly called for her to immediately take steps to implement the "return of the displaced persons." The resolution had little legal impact, but served to highlight the plight of Palestinians. By doing so, the UN implicitly labeled Israel, a constituent member of the organization, the sole stumbling block even though Arafat had shown no interest in easing Palestinian suffering in any manner that did not include ending the existence of the Jewish state. Thus, a process that had begun with Israel's strike on Karameh in 1968, which had raised Arafat's profile, up through 1970, when Hussein's confrontation with the PLO raised the Palestinian cause to the top of the international agenda, the future of the PLO—despite numerous challenges on the horizon—grew brighter than ever.

On December 28, Meir succumbed to American pressure. She announced her willingness to return to the Jarring talks. Her decision was predicated on America's commitment to maintain the balance of power in the Middle East and to permit Israel to negotiate freely on borders and refugees. She also affirmed that America had committed to support Israel's base requirement—until there was a contractual written agreement between Israel and the Arab countries, not one Israeli soldier would withdraw.

Throughout the year, Egypt was a mess, its economy in ruins. Egypt continued to lose revenue for numerous reasons including: shut-down of the Suez Canal, inability to access oil in the Sinai, and the loss of tourism because Egypt had become a war zone. Those factors and others created an economic tsunami that rolled relentlessly over the country, affecting both its infrastructure and the culture at large. As a result, inflation raged; and Egypt's lack of exports created a huge balance-of-payments gap. Any resources left were drained by the military. Only ten percent of the 50,000 young men and women that graduated from Egyptian universities every year could find jobs commensurate with their education. Rather than achieving independence, those newly-educated youths had to live at home with their parents where they shared the common plight of most—filthy conditions, scarce housing, and no money to marry. Simmering rage that could threaten the government and social stability threatened to boil over. One way to contain it was state-sponsored hatred. The remaining 3,000 Jews in Egypt bore the brunt of that. But even so, some Egyptians began to question whether it was worthwhile to continue support for the Palestinians. They recognized that the PLO was free to instigate trouble, but it was Egypt that paid the price.

Militarily, the end of the year found the Russians tightly entwined deep within Egypt's armed forces. Anonymously, 200 Russian pilots flew Egyptian airplanes, bought and paid for, from the Soviet Union. In addition, thousands of Russian instructors taught the Egyptian army while thousands more manned the SAM sites. The Russians were attached to every sinew of the Egyptian military but were not always welcome. And they treated their Egyptian counterparts with disdain.

Meanwhile, the political sphere had not yet solidified. By the end of the year, Sadat was still an unknown quantity. His continued rule was by no means certain, his people were increasingly restless, he faced an increasingly confident Israel, and a Russian cancer threatened to usurp Egypt's independence.

Something needed to change.

CHAPTER THIRTY-EIGHT
1971 — Trying for Peace

Overview

Hussein's accord with Arafat in late September of 1970 did little to settle their dispute. The Fedayeen continued to demonstrate disrespect for the Jordanian government; as a result, Hussein felt compelled to drive the PLO from Jordan. In October 1970, he appointed Wasfi al-Tal Prime Minister. Tal was a strong believer in law and order. Beginning in November of 1970, and increasingly during the first months of 1971, Hussein and Tal drove the PLO out of the major cities in Jordan. And despite calls for his overthrow from other Arab leaders, Hussein persevered. Unfortunately, even though an end to the PLO's stranglehold on Jordan was in sight, Hussein's success transferred the problem to another Arab nation in the region. Palestinians, driven from their homes and refugee camps in Jordan, and denied entry by Syria, found a new land to establish refugee camps and create havoc—Lebanon.

Before large numbers of Palestinians arrived, Lebanon was an Arab nation, already teetering on a narrow political precipice created by a political compromise between its Christian and Muslim inhabitants. That agreement had barely averted the nation tumbling into the abyss of sectarian warfare. Although the massive influx of Palestinians into Lebanon included many desperate for a respite from the fighting in Jordan, it also included others determined to use Lebanon as a primary post from which they could attack Israel. Unfortunately, Lebanon had neither the strength nor the unity to control her new residents, and Israel would not passively accept being targeted by them. As a result, in less than a decade the Palestinian migration unhinged Lebanon's political balance, causing the small nation to spiral into dissolution and despair.

Assad was active as well. He used the first few weeks of 1971 to shore up his relations with the Soviet Union; his visit to Moscow yielded a new arms deal. Assad needed Russian arms to build a credible threat to Israel, but he also knew the Russians sought a stable base in the heart of the Arab-Israeli dispute to offset American influence and to insert themselves into the peace process. Therefore, in return for the arms he permitted Russian military advisors to enter Syria and endured their patronizing attitude towards the Syrian army. But Assad would only go so far. He refused a Soviet request for him to sign a Treaty of Friendship and Cooperation because he did not want to give Moscow an opportunity to interfere in Syria's internal affairs.

Meanwhile, Sadat solidified his control of Egypt. And he experimented during his first few months in power, like Assad, with reducing the government's stranglehold on dissent. Sadat's loosening of strings included releasing hundreds of members of the Muslim Brotherhood from jail and permitting them to move about. The Brotherhood was an ultra-conservative religious movement that pushed for integration of Egypt's legal framework with Islamic law. Nasser's secular government had suppressed it. Sadat's strategy was to relieve some restrictions on the Brotherhood while removing from government many old-school members of Nasser's Nationalist party. He hoped that by weakening the old order's stranglehold on organizations while simultaneously supporting religious students within the country, he would avoid a confrontation and achieve a balance that would blunt the forces opposing him. Sadat might also have concluded, despite having a more secular than religious philosophy, that he would never garner support from Nasser's adherents, and that his rule would be strengthened by currying favor with the Brotherhood. While that strategy worked for Sadat in the short run, just over a decade later it cost him his life. It also opened the door to promulgation of increasingly radical forms of Islam that would bedevil the world in the twenty-first century.

Sadat was also aware of the deepening relationship between Israel and America, where domestic politics strongly favored the Jewish State. If there was any doubt whether the American administration was angry with Egypt for violating the ceasefire along the canal, the volume of modern weapons the United States was shipping to Israel provided a clue. Although Sadat knew that only the Soviet Union would make available to his country the means to fight, he also knew that the path to Egypt's recovery of the Sinai led through Washington, not Moscow. Ironically, just as Sadat had advised the Americans that if they wanted to talk to him they should do so directly—not through Moscow—if Sadat wanted to recover the Sinai, he would have to deal directly with the Americans if he wanted them to apply enough pressure on Israel to force her to withdraw. Therefore, Sadat decided he needed to create, with Russia's help, a credible military threat that would impel Israel to negotiate, but do so while simultaneously enlisting the Americans to lean hard on the Israelis. It was a dangerous game that risked angering one or both superpowers, since he planned to convince both countries individually that they were Egypt's friend, much to the detriment of the other. But he had no choice. For his plan to succeed he needed both the United States and the Soviet Union to act independently in Egypt's interest.

Also, in early 1971, the Western world increasingly realized that oil resources in the Arab states would soon be needed to power their economies. That created a strategic dilemma for the United States since the Arab nations with oil had virulent anti-Israel policies. Even so, Vice President Agnew and Secretary of State Rogers visited King Faisal of Saudi Arabia to deepen America's relationship with the Saudi nation and to discuss how the United States could ensure Saudi security. They went despite Faisal's public statement that labeled Israel "a cancer in the body of the Arab states," and even though Faisal encouraged all Saudi government officials to contribute one percent of their monthly salaries to Palestinian charities while knowing full well that those charities were fronts for the Fedayeen. However, the United States simply could not ignore that Saudi Arabia possessed at least one-third of the proven oil reserves in the world. Years later, Kissinger told Saudi officials, "Most countries have the problem of finding resources to meet your ambitions; you have the problem of finding ambitions to meet your resources." Kissinger was partly wrong, or else duplicitously diplomatic.

One of Saudi Arabia's greatest ambitions was restoration of control of Jerusalem to the Arab world and the creation of a Palestinian State on the ruins of the Israeli one. However, the other part of his comment was correct; the Saudis possessed a burgeoning fortune to spend towards achieving their goals.

The New Year also brought another round of diplomacy. The most recent extension of the ceasefire along the Suez Canal was due to expire February 6, 1971. During the first month of January there was much international speculation as to whether Sadat would renew it. On January 4, U Thant issued a report on the Jarring mission that warned, "[Egypt] and Jordan for their part insisted that there could be no question of discussion between the parties until the Israeli forces had been withdrawn to the position occupied by them prior to June 5, 1967." But a few days later an interview aired that Sadat gave to Walter Cronkite, the respected journalist from CBS News, in which he claimed to be "totally in favor of a peaceful settlement." And to encourage the United States, he emphasized his independence from the Soviet Union when he said "our policies are made in Cairo, made by us, and never made by other countries." But he did not clarify what a peace settlement meant to him. Would it mean a contractual agreement, direct negotiations, or just an Israeli withdrawal with no concrete assurances for the future?

Israel, rather than stating her goals publicly, gave Jarring a written document that outlined Israel's view of what was essential for peace. It contained nothing new or surprising. Essentially, it called for what amounted to establishment of normal relations between Israel and the Arab nations, no different than that between most other countries. Specifics included:

- An end to belligerency.
- An end to terrorism, economic blockades, and boycotts.
- Establishment of good relations and cooperation.
- Secure and recognized borders that were agreed to and that were accompanied by suitable security provisions (from Israel's perspective that meant continued control of some Egyptian territory).

Similar to Israel, the Egyptian official position did not change either. Egypt continued to insist that Israel unilaterally withdraw to the pre-Six-Day War *boundaries and repudiate any desire for territorial expansion. Perhaps Egypt's inflexibility was motivated in part by an unauthorized comment Rogers made to the Egyptian Foreign Minister in January. Rogers told him that the Americans would make an all-out effort in 1971 to achieve a negotiated settlement on the basis of his previously stated proposals. But there really was little chance of that. The Nixon administration, strongly influenced by Henry Kissinger, would not push Israel hard as long as Egypt remained a de facto military base for the Russians. Kissinger was content with a stalemate in the region until the Russians offered a compromise. Or better yet, until moderate Arabs decided their best path was through the United States, rather than the Soviet Union.*

Thus, as a result of the positions taken by all sides, the first round of Jarring discussions deadlocked.

Sadat Renews the Ceasefire Agreement

Late in 1970, Moshe Dayan floated a suggestion that Israel withdraw several miles from the Suez Canal in return for the Egyptians making a similar military concession on their side. Doing so would permit Egypt to reopen the canal, which would generate sorely needed income from the transit fees ships paid to pass through its waters. Dayan thought that if the canal were to reopen and Israeli troops withdrew to the mountain passes, Sadat could be nudged into grudgingly accepting Israeli's long-term presence in the Sinai. He argued that once the Egyptians reaped the monetary benefits stemming from putting the Suez Canal back in business, Egyptian leaders would not risk losing them again to another war. Neither Israel's cabinet nor most Egyptian government officials were interested in Dayan's plan, but Sadat was. He never wavered from his goal of removing Israel's presence from the Sinai but saw merit in initiating movement short of that. That is what impelled him to publicly state in late 1970 that he would react favorably if Israel, as a first stage of an eventual total withdrawal, withdrew to the passes.

But Sadat's pressing decision did not require finalizing his long-term strategy; he first needed to decide whether to renew the ceasefire once more. Much like the American government shutdown talks during the Obama administration that came to a head in 2013 after previous short-term fixes, each time the ceasefire provision had previously been renewed for a stated period it relieved pressure for the short-term, but served in the long run to just kick the can down the road. That caused renewed tension and anticipation as each new deadline approached. By early 1971, nothing had changed from three months before when the same issue was before Sadat.

On February 4, 1971, hours before the ceasefire was scheduled to end, Sadat told the Egyptian National Assembly, and by extension the world, that he would extend it another thirty days. He also said that if Israel withdrew he would reopen the Suez Canal. However, Sadat insisted that the IDF must withdraw all the way to El Arish—much further than the passes. He coupled his initiative by indicating his acceptance of Resolution 242. But of course he failed to acknowledge, or accept, Israel's and America's interpretation, based on the official text, that the resolution did not call for a withdrawal from all territories. Also missing from Sadat's offer was willingness to begin direct negotiations that would not be saddled with another deadline for renewing the ceasefire. Instead, he only proposed restarting the Jarring talks. Thus, Sadat's offer meant little. His proposal amounted to a demand for a significant Israeli pullback to positions difficult to defend because they would lack any natural defensive barriers. In return he would only promise to negotiate while holding a gun to Israel's head and in a forum that had only seen failure. Israel was not enticed.

However, Sadat's offer may have been a veiled attempt to push Israel's cabinet to approve Dayan's suggestions. It also may have been meant to signal the United States that he was prepared to formulate his own policy independent of the Soviet Union or other Arab nations. But, whatever his intent, Sadat's offer did represent a clear change from Nasser's policy since initiating the War of Attrition. Previously, Egypt's position had been that she would only reopen the canal after Israel withdrew completely from the Sinai to the pre-Six-Day War borders. That reflected Nasser's strategic plan to foment international pressure on Israel by imposing an economic burden on the world community whose shipping was forced to take a much more circuitous, and therefore more expensive route around the horn of Africa than the shortcut the canal provided. But in truth that strategy cost Egypt far more in lost income than political support gained. That deepened Egypt's poverty to a far greater degree than the burden placed on any one individual nation by the increased cost for shipping.

And also fundamentally important, by accepting Resolution 242 as a basis for future negotiations, Sadat implicitly accepted an end to the state of belligerency and Israel's "right to live within secure and recognized boundaries." That was a distinct change of policy for Egypt. It was one that Sadat hoped would lead to a new relationship with the Americans. He also made sure to let the United States know that if his proposal was accepted and led to an Israeli withdrawal, he would resume diplomatic relations with the United States. But Sadat was one to cagily cover all of his bases during his dangerous dance with the superpowers. The same day he introduced the new plan and extended the ceasefire, he also reached out to the Soviets. Sadat told them that Egypt and the Soviet Union needed to continue to stand together against America and Israelis in the face of the "treacherous alliance of the enemies of peace, freedom and progress."

Israel responded to the Sadat initiative with tentative, tongue-in-cheek encouragement. The Israelis did not comment on Sadat's demand for withdrawal but hinted that a permanent resolution might include a complete withdrawal from the Sinai, except for Sharm el-Sheikh. Issues involving Gaza and the West Bank, the Israelis suggested, should be left for subsequent negotiations.

Unfortunately, Jarring then opened his mouth and dashed any chance for Israel and Egypt to explore the possibilities presented by their competing proposals. On February 8, he publicly proclaimed his solution for the Middle East conundrum. He suggested that:
1. Egypt give Israel assurances of peace, recognition, and an end of the war between them;
2. Israel tell Egypt it would withdraw behind the pre-1967 war lines; and
3. Israel permit Gaza to return to Arab rule.

Jarring's solution undercut the official interpretation of Resolution 242. In effect, he endorsed a full return of Arab territory without direct negotiations and without requiring a contractual written peace agreement.

Sadat was displeased with Jarring's suggestion, as were the Israelis. Speaking to his National Assembly on February 14, he said, "We shall not be the generation that gave up on the Palestinian's peoples' rights." To this he added a demand that Israel resolve the Palestinian refugee problem in accordance with UN resolutions. But he also said, "Egypt will be ready to enter into a peace agreement with Israel containing all the aforementioned obligations provided for in Security Council Resolution 242."

Sadat's response left much to be desired from Israel's perspective because of his focus on Palestinian issues. But it did appear that he might be amenable to a contractual agreement because of his reference to Resolution 242. As such, in some small part, it represented a step forward.

Israel swiftly rejected the basic premise of the Jarring proposal because it ignored her core requirements. In response to Jarring's initiative, Israel announced she would withdraw to borders she considered secure and that were recognized, but "will not withdraw to the June 4, 1967 lines." In addition, Meir made clear that Israel would not withdraw at all until Israel and Egypt settled on the contours of a final agreement. However, in a slight softening of her previous public position, Meir stated that once an agreement was reached she would consent to an initial partial pullback in order to reopen the Suez Canal.

Both Jarring and Sadat considered Israel's response a rejection of their individual proposals. Many believe Sadat focused on Israel's insistence that she would not return to the pre-war borders. But, if Sadat was then truly prepared to negotiate, the opening was there. Israel clearly had indicated a desire to negotiate. The problem was that Jarring's plan was tougher on Israel than Sadat's. Jarring did not insist on a contractual agreement; Sadat had hinted that he might agree to that condition. Jarring insisted that Israel withdraw fully; Sadat's initial offer was much fuzzier on that issue. Sadat's suggestions contained an interim measure designed to build confidence—acceptance of 242 as a basis for negotiation—from which further negotiations would ensue. By contrast, Jarring's proposal required Israel to move, in one step, well beyond her declared bottom line.

The byproduct of Jarring's intervention was that both Sadat and Meir hardened their public attitudes, positions from which they both would find it difficult to unwind. The impact was little different than decades later when President Obama delivered a speech in Cairo that included a demand for Israel to stop settlement activity in the West Bank. That was a demand that the Palestinians had not previously made a pre-condition for negotiations, but they had no choice but to adopt it after an American president had indicated his support for it.

Jarring never understood that he had become an impediment rather than a cohesive force. He viewed the Egyptian response in a positive light because he believed Sadat had committed to make peace. From his perspective, the Israelis were the problem because they would not commit to full withdrawal. Israel's twenty-three-year experience of being on the precipice of destruction at the hands of neighbors filled with implacable hatred for the Jewish State was lost on him. Because of his failure to fully understand the real and emotional needs of both parties, Jarring's failed initiative widened rather than narrowed the impasse.

Secretary Rogers, having seen the Jarring discussions unravel, refused to give up. After learning that Israel rejected Jarring's plan, he spoke with Ambassador Rabin on February 24. Rogers accused Israel of being evasive. Rabin responded that the Israeli response was no different than her prior publicly announced positions. Soon, their conversation degenerated. "It is just an evasion," Rogers yelled at Rabin. "It is only a matter of time before your hand will be disclosed. Sooner or later you will have to face up to it." He also threatened Israel, telling Rabin that if his country remained inflexible the military arms the administration had promised to deliver might not arrive on time. Rabin was in a quandary. Although he knew there were two avenues of communication to Nixon in Washington, one through Rogers and the other through Kissinger, he had no idea whether Rogers's message was an expression of American policy or one man's frustration with his diminishing influence. Nevertheless, Rabin responded vigorously. He told Sisco, Rogers's assistant, that cutting off supplies would be seen as abandonment of an ally and diminish Israel's ability to cope with the massive numbers of Russian arms and pilots flooding the region.

After his conversation with Rabin, Rogers tried to convince Nixon to stop arms shipments to Israel. But Nixon, even though he shared some of Rogers's frustration, understood why Israel was so adamant. On the heels of Egyptian perfidy after the ceasefire that ended the War of Attrition, he found it easy to appreciate why the Israelis did not trust the Egyptians. In addition, he knew Egypt's breach of the agreement that produced an Israeli pullback after the 1956 war, an agreement brokered while he was vice president, had led directly to the Six-Day War. Therefore, there was no reason to be confident that Egypt would not break future agreements—if not by Sadat, then by a future Egyptian leader. And with the Russians still heavily involved, Nixon was not about to leave Israel dangling. For the time being, Nixon would continue to honor the American commitment to supply arms to Israel despite Rogers's protestations.

Sadat to Moscow

On March 1, Sadat visited Russia. He hoped to adopt a joint military and political strategy with the Russians. He also wanted to obtain from them weapons in greater quantity and quality that would permit Egypt's military to successfully confront Israel's formidable forces. But when Sadat arrived in Moscow, things got off to a bad start. Brezhnev berated the Egyptian president because he had not yet announced that he would again renew the ceasefire, due to expire on March 7.

Sadat ignored the frosty greeting and bore straight ahead with his request for modern offensive arms. One of Sadat's highest priorities was for bombers capable of reaching and devastating targets in Israel to the same degree that the Israelis had achieved when the IAF attacked Egyptian targets deep within Egypt's interior. The Russians thought that supplying the bombers would be provocative and dangerous. They insisted that they would only supply them with significant strings attached, strings which would prevent the Egyptians from using them to attack Israel without Russian permission. Those restrictions would include requiring that the planes remain under Soviet control to ensure they could only be used by the Egyptians with Soviet approval. Sadat thought that the Russian proposal would reduce him to a puppet on a string. He responded that given their position he might consider switching his allegiance to the Americans. He also said, "You are destroying yourselves by keeping me two steps behind Israel. America is doing everything for Israel. And you are going to be the losers." Sadat continued that the presence of larger numbers of Soviets within Egypt would be counterproductive for it would reduce any American inclination to pressure Israel to withdraw. Then Sadat declared, "I am the head of an independent country, and I can't surrender any part of my independence of action."

Brezhnev could see the conversation was leading towards weakening rather than strengthening the ties that bound Egypt to Russia, so he did what he could to mollify the Egyptian leader. For the most part the Russians reluctantly complied with Sadat's requests for more and better armaments. But they refused to supply the advanced bombers requested. Even though Sadat went home seemingly placated, he was not. The encounter accelerated his mounting concern over the previous few months that he had been relying on the wrong superpower. After returning to Egypt, Sadat drafted a letter to Nixon asking that America support his February 4 initiative.

Upon receipt of Sadat's request, the Americans reached out to the Israelis. Realizing that Israel had only responded to Jarring's proposal and Egypt's response to Jarring's proposal, the Nixon administration asked Israel to issue an official response to Sadat's February 4 speech. That was the speech that proposed a deep Israeli withdrawal in the Sinai in exchange for reopening the Suez Canal. Coming so soon after the clash between Rogers and Rabin, it was not a time that the Israelis felt particularly trusting of the American administration. Israel's answer reflected that harsh fact. Meir insisted that, in return for an unspecified limited withdrawal, Israeli troops must be permitted to remain in the Bar-Lev fortifications along the canal, Egyptian troops must withdraw from the Canal Zone, and Israel must receive assurances that Israeli shipping would be permitted through the canal when it opened. The Americans did not deliver Israel's answer to Sadat because they knew it would needlessly inflame tensions before he announced whether he would renew the ceasefire scheduled to lapse in early March.

On March 7, the ceasefire agreement lapsed, but fighting did not resume.

On March 13, Meir responded publicly to an inquiry as to what her peace map would look like. Meir said that Israel must retain Sharm el-Sheikh and control an access road that stretched from the city to Israel's border. She added that the Sinai must be demilitarized; and, to protect Eilat, Israel's border nearby with the Sinai had to be changed. Meir also declared that for security reasons Israel must retain control of the Golan and Gaza, and that a final agreement would have to incorporate border changes on the West Bank. Hers was a maximal demand, no different and no more helpful than Sadat's minimalist offer. Unless Sadat stated with clarity an acceptable vision of what the permanent relationship between Israel and Egypt would become, few Israelis would give serious consideration to a withdrawal that would give up the security provided by crucial defensive positions in the Sinai. Meir's and Sadat's public statements were both examples of attempting to appear reasonable without revealing bottom lines. But there was one salient difference between the two plans that scuttled any real hope for resolving their differences. Israel insisted on eventually, as part of the process, having direct talks. Egypt still refused. Sadat wanted Meir to trust him but was unwilling to look her in the eye. It was a hurdle that made the gap too large to jump. One day Sadat would change his mind with regard to that crucial step, but that would be years in the future and after much blood from Israel's and Egypt's young men drained onto the desert sands.

Sadat, recognizing the impasse, declared 1971 the year of decision, but did little to back up his implied threat of war. The Israelis, however, knew the clock was ticking. Even though they felt safe and secure behind defensible borders, many Israeli leaders understood that the vast numbers of Palestinians comprised a demographic time bomb. (In recent years there has arisen some legitimate debate as to whether that demographic time bomb will create the level of disparity first thought.)

In addition, an American political vise began to squeeze them. Rogers, despite his weakened position of influence, pressured for a more forthcoming response to Sadat's February 4 offer. On March 22, the Israeli cabinet met to discuss the matter. However, Meir refused to consider any withdrawal prior to a peace treaty. Nor would she consider anything the Arabs might say, if linked blithely to Resolution 242, a concession. That was because the Arabs interpreted the resolution to require Israel's complete withdrawal. In addition, she adamantly opposed any agreement that permitted Egyptian troops to cross the canal and operate on the West Bank.

Dayan pushed back against Meir. He advocated a limited withdrawal in return for something less than peace. He again suggested that the IDF withdraw just under nineteen miles (thirty kilometers) to the eastern edge of the mountain passes that faced the canal. In that way Egypt could open the canal and renew normal civilian life alongside it. Dayan conditioned his proposed on obtaining a guarantee from the United States that the Americans would provide Israel long-term military assistance.

After much discussion, Meir's cabinet caved. It accepted the concept of a limited withdrawal within the context of a limited agreement. No longer would a contractual peace treaty be a pre-condition. It was a huge concession with tremendous implications: Israel would not demand at the outset that its Arab interlocutors guarantee they comply with whatever was agreed in a binding manner. But there was still much dispute as to the depth of the withdrawal. Many were not willing to pull back as far as Dayan recommended.

It took another month, until April 19, for Israel to deliver her formal response to Washington. The Israelis indicated they would be willing to consider a very limited withdrawal and re-opening of the Suez Canal if the Egyptians agreed to:

- Make a public commitment to end the state of belligerency between their two countries.
- A ceasefire of unlimited duration.
- No Egyptian military forces on the East Bank (Israel's side of the Suez Canal).
- Thin out Egyptian forces based close to the canal's west bank.
- Release Israeli prisoners of war still held by Egypt.

In addition, the Israelis asked the Americans to reaffirm all assurances the United States had previously provided concerning arms and future negotiations.

Sadat responded a few days after the Americans transmitted Israel's proposal to him. He stated that Egyptian forces must be permitted to cross the canal and control the Mitla and Giddi passes, but that demilitarized zones could be established. He did agree that Israel could continue to control Sharm el-Sheikh during the first stage of implementation, but that within six months a final settlement had to be reached that would include a full Israeli withdrawal. Sadat's response proved that he had not changed his tune and that for him the Israeli offer was a nonstarter. Nor did it provide a basis for further discussion. Rather than offer Israel any lasting reassurance, Sadat continued to insist on getting everything he wanted—his land back—without meeting Israel's basic needs. Kissinger knew that it meant there was no chance for a solution at that time. But Nixon did not prevent Rogers from trying again to find one.

CHAPTER THIRTY-NINE
Another Failed Try for Peace

Secretary of State Rogers arrived in Cairo on the afternoon of May 5, 1971. It was the first time that an American secretary of state had met with the leader of a country with which the United States did not have diplomatic relations. Rogers had secured Nixon's permission for him to go in April. The secretary of state hoped to reignite the process for reaching an agreement between Egypt and Israel. It was a precipitous moment. Two days earlier Sadat had removed from government office his rival, the pro-Russian minister, Ali Sabry. Sadat may have fired Sabry for self-preservation; he may have meant it as a signal to the Americans that he was prepared to speak seriously with them, or Sabry's dismissal may also have been a message to the Soviets that they should only communicate with Sadat, not with their sympathizers. In any event, Sabry was gone and so was Russia's highest ranking protégé in the Egyptian government.

When Rogers met with Sadat on May 6, Sadat told him, "I know what's uppermost in your mind and I want to talk about it at once … and that's the Soviet Union." Sadat then explained, "I don't like the fact that we have to depend on the Soviet Union as much as we do … I don't want to have to depend on anyone else. The only reason I have is because we were humiliated and I had no place to turn."

Sadat complained that the Russians had deepened his economic problems. Not only was Egypt paying for the military hardware Russia supplied, she also was reimbursing the Russians for the cost of providing advisors to the army. Sadat told Rogers he knew that the Soviet Union's main goal was to increase Russian presence in the region. Recovery of lost Arab lands was not the Politburo's primary objective; it was merely a pretext to achieve Russian goals. The Egyptian leader concluded his comments by requesting that America be evenhanded while navigating between Arab and Israeli interests. And he assured Rogers, if an interim settlement were achieved, he would evict all Soviet personnel—excluding their pilots—from Egypt within six months.

Rogers responded that the main stumbling block was the presence of the Soviets in Egypt. He admitted his own frustration with Israel, but said the Israelis would be supported politically and militarily as long as the Russians were in Egypt. However, "once they've left, or most of them, it's a different ballgame." Sadat responded, "I don't want to bother Israel … I'll sign an agreement … I just want my land back." As the meeting was ending Sadat told Rogers that, if an interim agreement could be achieved, he thought both Egypt and other Arab nations would agree to resume diplomatic relations with the United States.

Rogers left Cairo for Israel. He told Meir that Sadat was willing to be the first Arab leader to make peace with the Jewish State and would force the Russians to leave his country if Israel and Egypt concluded an agreement. He also advised Meir that he believed Sadat would probably remain in power for a long time.

But Meir was not convinced. She told Rogers that Sadat was only interested in land, not peace. Meir's memory was long and her diplomatic experience extensive. She had been integrally involved in both the 1949 Armistice agreements and the 1957 concessions Israel made in return for promises that proved empty in 1967. She told the American secretary of state, "I can only say this. We have to learn from our experiences." She also reminded Rogers of Sadat's public statements that Israel "will not escape punishment, no matter how long it takes," and of Sadat's references to total war that would ravage every Jewish town. She summarized her concerns with a short statement that said much: "Which Sadat are we to believe?" Their meeting ended with Meir's refusal to negotiate partial agreements for which she would have to pay for with partial withdrawals. Israel wanted to end the fighting forever, not wait from increasingly-weaker defensive positions with bated breath for the outcome of each new stage of negotiation. For Meir it was an issue of existential survival, not an exercise in confidence-building measures whose efficacy she had reason to doubt.

Rogers was dejected as he left the building. He failed to understand that Sadat's position, not Israel's, made achieving an agreement impossible because he was too focused on the present; and he did not understand, or else discounted, the searing impact previous Arab perfidy had wrought on the Israeli psyche. Of course, Meir could have knuckled under to Sadat's demands, but that would have meant taking a chance on Israel's continued existence. A risk that would not be reciprocally shared by Sadat since Egypt's future survival was not in doubt.

The next day, Rogers was scheduled to meet with Meir again. Just before the meeting, his assistant, Sisco, met with Dayan. Dayan was much more willing to compromise than Meir and, consistent with his past views, was willing to consider an interim Suez agreement coupled with demilitarization zones.

In fact, Dayan had two ideas in mind. The **first** could be implemented if Egypt was only willing to agree to an extension of the ceasefire for a limited period. In that event, Dayan suggested that Israel could safely withdraw a distance short enough that the IDF could shoot its way back to the canal waterline if Sadat renewed hostilities. However, diverging from his previous suggestions, Dayan told Sisco that Israeli troops must also remain in the Bar-Lev forts to keep the canal under constant direct observation. The **second** idea, Dayan stated, could be executed if Egypt agreed to an unlimited ceasefire extension and would be based on the IDF never returning to the canal. He said he would support withdrawing the IDF more than six miles—as long as Egyptian civilians were the only ones permitted to cross the canal; i.e. both Soviet and Egyptian military forces would be barred from crossing its waters. Instead of an Egyptian or Soviet military presence to safeguard the area, Dayan envisioned creation of a UN peacekeeping force that would stand between IDF forces that had pulled back and a thinned out Egyptian force on the west bank of the canal. However, Dayan was adamant on one thing: the first step had to be Egypt's agreement to a permanent ceasefire. In the absence of a final contractual peace treaty, his second option required a permanent ceasefire that ended hostilities once and for all.

Few in the cabinet were as flexible as Dayan. And when Meir continued to oppose his plan, Dayan did not ask the cabinet to vote on it. However, Dayan's perspective did subtly change Meir's views. When she met with Rogers on May 7, she told him she had reconsidered. Israel would reluctantly withdraw from the Suez Canal in return for an interim agreement. But, she insisted, the Egyptians must first agree to an indefinite extension of the ceasefire, reopening the canal to Israeli as well as other international shipping, and no troops on the canal's eastern bank in the areas from which Israel would withdraw. Meir was still concerned that after Israel would withdraw, Sadat, or some other future Egyptian leader, might have a change of heart that would lead to war. But she said, "We are prepared to move from the [c]anal. We do not want any more shooting," and then clarified that because she did not trust the Egyptians, "we do not want military personnel to cross the [c]anal. If we have to face the Egyptian army we would rather face them across the [c]anal."

Rogers was euphoric over Meir's sudden turnabout. He sent Nixon a message, "We hit pay dirt," and reported that there was "helpful Israeli flexibility." Rogers, feeling the joy of a long distance runner seeing the finish line, sent Sisco back to Cairo to see if he could bridge the differences between Egypt's and Israel's positions. Unfortunately, Sisco suggested a bridge too far. He told Sadat that Israel might be willing to withdraw east of the mountain passes. It was a suggestion no Israeli had given voice too, and it fell far beyond what the Americans could ever hope to convince the Israelis to do as a first step. When word leaked of Sisco's erroneous formulation to the Israelis, they reacted furiously and never trusted Rogers again. Sadat felt let down as well. He also learned from the experience that he could not rely on what Rogers conveyed, even though he continued to maintain faith in Nixon. Nevertheless, a frustrated Sadat abandoned the Rogers initiative.

Rogers's failure in May marked the beginning of the end for his role in Middle East diplomacy. Kissinger assumed responsibility but reasoned the time was not yet ripe for success. He understood that as long as Israel perceived she was too weak to take risks and the Russians were inside Egypt, there was little chance that Israel would make concessions that magnified the threat of their annihilation. Kissinger's antidote was to supply sufficient arms to keep Israel strong while patiently waiting for an Egyptian leader who, before negotiating, would expel the Russians from his country. Until then, he thought a meaningful deal impossible to attain.

Kissinger was also very critical of how Rogers had conducted his diplomacy. He thought Rogers became too involved in the substance of negotiations at too early a stage. Kissinger doctrine was that only when parties near agreement should America come forward with substantive recommendations. Otherwise, America's ability to gain the trust of both sides would be imperiled. Kissinger also criticized the public style of diplomacy Rogers practiced. Kissinger much preferred private discussions leading to public concessions. For the past three years, in his opinion, public negotiations had invariably failed since negotiating parties, due to their domestic politics, could only express extreme positions that disregarded the sensitivities of the other side.

But Nixon, reflecting his secretive manner, was not yet totally willing to cut Rogers out of the loop. He sent Rogers an "eyes only" memo that opened a window into his thinking and encouraged Rogers, despite his failure. In it he said, "Under these circumstances it is essential that no more aid programs for Israel be approved until they agree to some kind of interim action on the Suez or some other issue. In the month of June or July [the Israelis] must bite the bullet as to whether they want more U.S. aid at the price of being reasonable on an interim agreement or whether they want to go at it alone." But he also advised, "Where the Soviet Union is obviously siding with Israel's neighbors it serves our interests to see that Israel is able to not only defend itself but to deter further Soviet encroachments in the area."

Nixon's worldview prioritized maintaining peaceful relations with the Soviets while besting them strategically. Those priorities dictated his short-term policy of siding with the Israelis. However, when he said, "the interests of the United States will be served ... by tilting the policy ... on the side of 100 million Arabs rather than on the side of two million Israelis..." that evinced his willingness to change his policies toward Israel if he thought it would not jeopardize his other goals.

Nixon also felt the pressure of his looming 1972 re-election campaign. Therefore, if he could not achieve a deal in 1971, he knew he would be constrained politically in 1972 from applying the pressure on Israel necessary to coerce Meir to accept an agreement she did not feel was in Israel's interest. But more delay increased the risk of Russia becoming further entrenched in the region. Therefore, contrary to Kissinger's opinion, Nixon thought time was not on America's side.

The last part of May brought exactly what Nixon feared. The Russians engaged in frantic diplomatic activity designed to shore up

Egyptian support in the face of Rogers's visit earlier in the month to Egypt. Russian President Podgorny traveled to Egypt on May 25, hoping to smooth over the rift between their two countries which had developed earlier that year in the aftermath of Sadat's meetings with Brezhnev. To achieve his goal, Podgorny arrived bearing gifts. Moscow agreed to immediately deliver modern MiG-23 fighter jets to Egypt. In addition, he offered Sadat a fifteen-year Treaty of Friendship and Cooperation. The treaty offer implicitly sent Sadat the message that his dismissal of Sabry at the beginning of the month would not negatively impact relations between the two nations. It also provided for Soviet economic assistance, military aid, and training that would strengthen the Egyptian army. In return, Sadat's signature would commit Egypt to pursue socialist policies no matter who was in power. Sadat did not take time to deliberate. He signed the treaty on May 27. The Russians were elated. They believed they had shored up a wavering ally. Sadat, on the other hand, viewed things differently. He had pragmatically done what he had to do to dance with two suitors diametrically opposed to each other. That is why within days of signing, he told the Americans he was still interested in an interim agreement.

Then, perhaps emboldened by Nixon's memo and aware of Sadat's most recent overture, Rogers once again attempted to shape Israel's behavior by using arms shipments as leverage. He warned the Israelis that *Phantom* F-4 shipments could be suspended if they did not agree to make further concessions to Egypt as part of a peace process. Having tried in 1970 to push for a reduction of arms shipments once there was peace, this time Rogers took the opposite tack. He told the Israelis that, until there was peace, they would not receive any more arms. That strategy failed for the same reason his last attempt to manipulate the Israelis with arms supplies failed: Both strategies highlighted the uncertain world Israel had to navigate just when she needed the opposite, a heightened level of confidence that the nation would always possess the overwhelming strength necessary to embark on a risky future course.

But Rogers no longer had a relatively free hand. Kissinger got wind of the secretary of state's attempts to coerce the Israelis. Emboldened by Nixon's increasing reliance on his advice, Kissinger sought the president out to again emphasize the need to keep Israel strong. It was so important and of such immediate concern to him that he conveyed his views to Nixon on the morning of June 12—the day Nixon's daughter, Tricia, was married in the Rose Garden.

Kissinger's attempt to minimize Rogers's influence on the Middle East peace process was not entirely successful. Sisco went to Israel once again at Nixon's request. Nixon's instructions were to push Meir hard for more flexibility but not cause a blowup. He wanted to avoid overshadowing the recent public disclosure of his breakthrough upcoming trip to China in early 1972. But Meir proved a hard sell. She would not let sweeteners soften her requirements for an interim agreement. She also argued that any interruption of American arms shipments to Israel exacerbated tension and risked war. Meir told Sisco, "If I were Sadat I would say to myself, I am now in a position where Israel is not getting any planes. What am I waiting for? Until the U.S. will begin to deliver planes? This is the time." She also said that in light of Sadat signing the Treaty of Friendship with the Russians, Egypt would not cut ties with the Soviets. Therefore, without believable assurances of more arms, Israel would not budge.

Sisco came home empty-handed.

CHAPTER FORTY
Hussein and the PLO

Hussein's campaign to expel the Fedayeen from Jordan gained steam in 1971. On March 8, an embattled Arafat visited Sadat. Sadat advised him to avoid indicating approval of any Jordanian agreement with Israel even though it was possible that Hussein, as the sovereign ruler of Jordan, might sign one. The Egyptian leader made clear it was up to Arafat to ensure that the Palestinian cause did not die. But when one of the Palestinians in Arafat's entourage pushed Sadat to convince Hussein to end his campaign against the Fedayeen, he refused, despite having no love for Hussein.

Sadat's issues with the Jordanian king were in part caused by Hussein's designs on Gaza, territory that Sadat considered Egypt's. Sadat also did not want to give Hussein a political opportunity to raise Kuwait's refusal to pay the subsidies promised to Jordan as part of the 1967 Khartoum agreement made famous by the "three nos." But Sadat's main reason to hold Hussein at arm's length was that he did not want to get entangled with anything that would impede recovering the Sinai. Sadat knew there was no path to a peaceful resolution of the Palestinian-Jordanian drama other than a joint confrontation with Israel. If he became embroiled in that dispute he knew it would end his hope to recover the Sinai soon.

On April 6, Hussein increased pressure on the Fedayeen by ordering them out of Amman. Hussein said, "The land where the weapons should be wielded and resistance should be planted is the Occupied Territories so that every citizen here may live in peace and security." The Fedayeen, by that time weakened by a determined and united Jordanian army, meekly let the Jordanians herd them onto busses and transport them to outlying areas in rough and remote terrain. Within days the 5,000 Fedayeen in Amman were gone.

But the Fedayeen could not overcome their nature. On June 1, they killed a Jordanian farmer. That murderous act gave Hussein the impetus he needed to clear the nation of what he viewed as a cancer. The Jordanian army pushed the Fedayeen into an indefensible triangular area. Besides issuing vociferous calls to overthrow Hussein, no Arab country lifted a finger to help the embattled Palestinians. Meanwhile, Fedayeen stocks of ammunition dwindled while shipments from the United States augmented Jordan's armaments. The savagery with which the Jordanian army dealt with the irregulars caused a few to seek asylum with their hated enemy, Israel; they feared their fellow Arabs more. In the end 3,000 Palestinians died in the last few weeks of fighting, and another 2,000 escaped to Lebanon by way of Syria.

By July 18, all organized Palestinian Fedayeen in Jordan were gone. Years later, in retrospect, one PLO leader said:

> We dug our own graves in Jordan. We were welcomed as heroes after Karameh and then driven out like thieves in the night three years later.... Some of them [Jordanians] had been living in Jordan for centuries and resented our appropriation of the country.... The same thing was to happen in Lebanon.

Since Assad refused the Fedayeen permanent resettlement in Syria because of their resistance to control by their host country, the Fedayeen had no choice but to move to Lebanon where refugee camps had already filled with their brethren. Over the next several years the Palestinians destabilized their new host nation, provoked Israel into staging multiple reprisal raids and invasions, and created conditions that gave rise to increased Syrian influence, weakening of the Christian Phalange, and the emergence of Hezbollah. That, however, is another story, in a time not the subject of this book.

The fighting took a toll on Hussein's ability to dominate affairs on the West Bank. More than one out of five families in the occupied territories had relatives directly impacted by the violence in Jordan. Their sympathies lay with the Fedayeen, and despite Arafat's defeat they viewed Hussein as the enemy and Arafat as a savior. The king had depended on the allegiance of local leaders to maintain his influence on the West Bank, but the local population's hostility towards him weakened those leaders' resolve to spout Hussein's virtues. In addition, Arafat threats directed at those that adopted policies contrary to the PLO's had cowed them. Previously, Nasser had been a powerful check on PLO influence. When he died there was no other force left capable of capturing Palestinian allegiance; thus Arafat's grip on the West Bank's leadership tightened.

But Arafat had difficulties too. After losing his base of operations, he would have to play his dwindling cards deftly if he wanted to remain relevant on the international stage. Arafat knew that to be successful he would need to embrace diplomacy on the ground while covertly employing terrorism to maintain the momentum and vibrancy of the Palestinian movement before the world. And he knew he could not count on his Arab brethren. There had been little Arab response to the most recent round of fighting that ended the PLO's presence in Jordan even though Syria had closed her borders with Jordan, broken diplomatic relations with Hussein, and perfunctorily fired some artillery shells at a few Jordanian towns; and Iraq had withdrawn her remaining expeditionary force present in Jordan since 1967 and closed her border with Jordan. For Hussein, the Iraqi withdrawal was a positive development he had sought for years. Thus, Jordan felt little pain and the PLO derived little benefit from Syria and Iraq's response.

However, even though Sadat did not offer the PLO any help during its final struggles in Jordan, he did show his disdain for Hussein. On November 28, Jordanian Prime Minister Tal was in Cairo. It was Tal who bore much of the responsibility and reaped much of the credit for the Jordanian army's success fighting the PLO. But, while walking through the Sheraton hotel where he was attending the Arab League Summit, four assassins from a newly-formed terrorist group called Black September shot him dead. Tal's last words were reported to be, "They've killed me. Murderers, they believe only in fire and destruction."

Black September was nominally created:
- To avenge the death of a Palestinian leader in Jordan.
- As a response to Hussein's imposition of martial law in September 1970.
- In reaction to the eviction of the PLO from Jordan.

As such, it was a militant offshoot of the PLO that moderate PLO members either tolerated or encouraged and was supported with intelligence and financing from Arafat's Fatah contingent.

One of the assassins, not content with just killing Tal, knelt and "lapped with his tongue the blood flowing across the marble floor." Egyptian police arrested the murderers. Egyptian authorities then released the killers four months later after they posted the minimal bail ordered by the court. They then fled the country and disappeared into the mists of history.

Egypt's refusal to keep custody of the four who slaughtered the Jordanian Prime Minister was a vivid example of how low Hussein's favor had fallen since Nasser appreciatively supported him shortly after the 1967 war. The other Arab nations didn't care that Jordan had paid a price for supporting the Palestinian cause—a cause they were all too happy to promote with their money and rhetoric as long as it was Jordan's sovereignty at risk and not their own.

CHAPTER FORTY-ONE
The US and USSR Dance

Gromyko, the Russian Foreign Minister, arrived in Washington in late September. Soon the superpowers would announce their agreement to hold a summit meeting. On September 29, Gromyko went to the White House to discuss outstanding issues. After assuring Nixon that the Russians wanted to reach agreement on arms reduction, reduce tensions between east and west, and end the Pakistan-India crisis, he dramatically asked to speak to Nixon alone. Alone meant no note takers, no Rogers, no Kissinger, and no Dobrynin.

Once the room cleared, Gromyko presented Nixon with Russia's new secret plan for peace in the Middle East. The Russians had sensed their relationship with Sadat was different than what they had had with Nasser. And worse, they could feel Sadat pulling further away. Therefore, they were eager to deal themselves back into the diplomatic process so that Sadat would view them as a necessary party. In an attempt to do so, Gromyko told Nixon that Brezhnev wanted to complete a peace deal in the Middle East before their Summit meeting. He then revealed the new Soviet plan, which included:

- Israeli agreement to a total withdrawal from all of the occupied territories.

- Withdrawal of all organized Russian military units from Egypt and Syria except for some advisors.
- An end to Russian supply of military arms to the region once the conflict is resolved.
- A security guarantee for Israel and the Arabs that Russia would be part of.
- Agreement that all of Russia's proposals could be incorporated into an interim accord if that agreement contained instructions for reaching a final settlement.

Gromyko also requested that future discussions with regard to implementing the Russian plan only be held in the back-channel between Kissinger and Dobrynin, thus effectively cutting Rogers and the State Department out.

Nixon thought the offer an excellent starting point. Kissinger, when he learned of it, saw positive new elements in it too because it included that the Russians would remove their military forces. The next day Kissinger met with Gromyko to confirm details and suggested that Egypt should permit Israeli ships to traverse the Suez Canal as soon as an interim agreement was implemented. But, he told Gromyko, a comprehensive deal would have to wait until 1973 because of Nixon's upcoming trip to China in February 1972, and the presidential elections in November 1972. Gromyko was not optimistic that he could sell Israeli access to the canal to his Arab allies but left believing the Americans viewed his proposal in a positive light. Thus, Gromyko felt encouraged that the Russian plan might win the day. And, from Kissinger's perspective, there was one other positive element tied to the plan. He would be more firmly in control of U.S. Middle East policy than ever before.

Two weeks later, Nixon announced he had accepted the Russian invitation to visit the Soviet Union in May of 1972. Although the impending summit was viewed favorably by most of the world, Sadat was devastated. He feared that if an agreement with Israel was not reached before the superpower meeting, the Americans and Russians would put Egypt's issues on a back burner while they focused on items that more directly impacted them. That would leave Israel in control of Egyptian territory for at least another year.

The Russians had their own worries related to further delay. They feared that if Israel and Egypt did not reach an agreement before the summit it would impel Sadat to launch an attack on Israel that would end in defeat. And, because an Arab attack on Israel risked causing a confrontation between Russia and the United States, there was a chance that Nixon might, as a result, cancel the summit meeting that the Russians desperately wanted. It was partly for fear that if they supplied the weapons Sadat continued to demand that he might use them, and because that might cause the summit to be canceled, that the Russians continued to resist Sadat's requests for more offensive weapons.

In October and November of 1971 various individuals trod three different paths in hopes of resolving the woes of the Middle East. **One**, once again, was Rogers. In early October, unaware of the secret offer Gromyko had made on behalf of Russia, Rogers delivered a speech to the UN calling for Israeli troops to pull back from the canal and for Egypt to then reopen access to the waterway. He argued that would lead to implementation of Resolution 242 if talks between Israel and Egypt subsequently began in New York. Conspicuous by their absence were details regarding whether Egyptian troops would be permitted to cross the canal and occupy any territory from which Israel pulled back. Meir responded two days later that Rogers's speech encouraged Egyptian intransigence, and she reiterated that Israel would not pull back under any circumstances if Egyptian troops could cross the canal as a result. She further informed the Americans privately that Israel would not consider any withdrawal unless the United States resumed shipment of the F-4 *Phantom*s.

The **second** track involved four African leaders sent by the Organization of African States on an independent peace mission. They visited Israel in hope of ending the stalemate. They proposed that Israel and her neighboring Arab nations agree to speak to each other directly under UN auspices. Unfortunately, from the Arab perspective, that was a nonstarter.

The only track that really mattered, however, was the **third**, which was Kissinger's. On November 5, he met with Rabin to communicate the new Soviet plan to the Israelis. Kissinger told Rabin that it boiled down to concluding an interim agreement immediately and a final agreement that would result in Israeli withdrawal after the American election of November 1972. By saying the withdrawal would be roughly to the pre-war lines of June 4, Kissinger soft-pedaled the extent of the eventual withdrawal. He tried to convince Rabin of the plan's merit by emphasizing its main virtue: the Russians would significantly decrease their presence in the region. But Rabin immediately sensed the risk the deal would impose on Israel. He also did not trust Brezhnev, despite Kissinger's assurances that he would not negotiate with Russia without Israel's full involvement. And the mere mention of returning to pre-war borders left Rabin with a stern expression of disinterest on his face. Kissinger, seeing Rabin's discomfort, told him, "I understand your difficulties, and if Israel replied to the Soviet proposal in the negative, I wouldn't blame her. I would seek ways of preventing American-Soviet negotiations on Brezhnev's proposal."

Despite his misgivings, Rabin went back to Israel to discuss the Russian plan. It was a terrible deal from Israel's perspective, notwithstanding Nixon's enthusiasm, because it required Israel's full withdrawal without a peace agreement. Furthermore, to rub salt in their wound, Israeli intelligence received word that two weeks earlier the Russians had agreed to a new arms deal with the Egyptians. When Rabin returned to the United States he knew that Israel would reject the Russian offer. But it was not for him to convey the news. Meir insisted that she wanted to communicate her rejection directly to Nixon during her scheduled visit to Washington in early December.

Meir and Nixon

On December 2, Meir met with Nixon at the White House. Her goal was to ensure that American delivery of critical arms would resume, and she hoped to convince the president to abandon both the *Rogers* plan and the Russian proposal. Prior to meeting with Nixon, she complained to Rogers that the flow of Russian arms was continuing and that Sadat had reportedly told his army in a speech, "We will meet the Israelis in the Sinai." She told Rogers, "We don't believe that he thinks he can win, but we must be prepared because he can start at any time."

Nixon asked Meir to be flexible. He told her that if a deal was not implemented then it was sure to be a topic at the summit. But Meir made clear, "There will be no American-Soviet deal contrary to Israel's wishes." Her response persuaded Nixon not to pursue the Russian plan. Instead, he decided to limit his efforts to achieving an interim solution.

Nixon also told Meir that, from then on, main responsibility for the Middle East would shift from Rogers to Kissinger. He said Kissinger would communicate with both Rabin and Dobrynin and then, only if there was a breakthrough would there be further talks between the United States and Egypt in which Rogers's assistant, Sisco, might play a role. In addition, he conveyed to Meir the news she desperately wanted to hear. The United States would send the IAF forty more *Phantom*s and seventy additional *Skyhawk*s.

A few days after seeing the president, Meir met with Kissinger. By then, as a result of her successful meeting in the White House, she was willing to be more flexible. She told Kissinger that Israel would agree to an interim withdrawal short of the mountain passes in the Sinai and to a ceasefire of 18-24 months duration. In addition, she said she might consider accepting a few Egyptian soldiers on the Israeli side of the canal as part of an interim deal. She also indicated it would be acceptable to link an interim deal to a final agreement provided the *Rogers* plan was dead. But, Meir made it very clear, there could neither be an implied nor an explicit link between the interim deal and a withdrawal to the pre-war borders. And she was insistent; the final borders must be determined in a direct negotiation between Israel and Egypt.

Meir also expressed skepticism that there was no difference in risk associated with an IDF withdrawal of a few miles versus a withdrawal all the way to the passes. Nevertheless, she signaled her willingness to listen and moderate Israel's position. It was a significant concession by a Prime Minister suspicious of the motives of anyone outside of Israel. It only happened because of Nixon's agreement to supply additional war planes, to back away from the Russian plan, and to not jam the *Rogers* plan that required complete withdrawal of Israeli forces from the Sinai down Israel's throat.

Kissinger chose to pocket Meir's willingness to offer the Egyptians more and never communicated it to Cairo. Perhaps it was because Sadat's views had hardened by then. Perhaps it was because Kissinger favored immediate direct talks. But most likely it was because Kissinger continued to believe the longer the delay the more Egypt would feel the need to drop the Russians and depend solely on the United States. It was a "Game of Kings" and Kissinger was determined to use Israeli occupation as a lever to push Russia out of the Middle East.

1971 Year End

The year ended without progress between Israel and the Arab world. Sadat's promise that 1971 would be the "Year of Decision" turned into the year of indecision. Cairo's citizens mocked him for extending the year of decision by presidential decree. Of the Arab nations, only Jordan had solidified her position in 1971: The PLO was finally out of the country, albeit at the cost of Hussein having lost influence on the West Bank and becoming estranged once again from the Arab world. Throughout 1971, Hussein had focused his efforts on survival and consolidation. He succeeded, but the price paid was the West Bank. He would never return to power there.

Meanwhile, the struggle between the Soviet Union and the United States on the world stage manifested itself in the sands of the Sinai where the superpowers wrestled for position. Too many agendas intermingled in a kaleidoscope of intrigue that resulted in stalemate. Israel was still in control of the east bank of the Suez Canal; the Egyptian economy was reeling, and the parties were no closer to achieving resolution of the conflict. Israel's fundamental issue was trust; Sadat's and Assad's issue was honor. The superpowers were unable, or unwilling, to effect change.

One positive development, however, was Kissinger's assuming control of the Middle East account. The Israelis did not trust Rogers's motives, and Sadat did not trust his veracity. Kissinger, by contrast, had the ear of President Nixon and the respect of Meir and Rabin. But it was still too early for him to have an impact, especially since he viewed all issues first through the prism of American interests and only then took into account Israeli concerns.

However, a new problem had also emerged due to Jordan's victory—the PLO's transition to Lebanon. Although it was much more difficult for the Fedayeen to mount attacks into Israel from their new home, the PLO eventually destabilized Lebanon instead. By wielding its Black September terrorist unit, the PLO also found a way to make sure the world would not forget Palestinian concerns. Forty-five years later, Lebanese and the world still pay the price of Lebanon's unraveling. In only nine months, Israeli Olympic athletes would pay the price for the emergence of Black September.

Also, the Arabs began learning how to wield a new weapon that was destined to disrupt the world's economy within two years. Early in 1971, Arab countries started to reap greater economic benefits from the oil pumped from their lands. First individually, and then as a cohesive group through OPEC (the Organization of the Petroleum Exporting Countries), Arab countries negotiated price increases and equity ownership of their oil production facilities. Soon oil would become a devastating political weapon linked to the Arab-Israeli crisis.

CHAPTER FORTY-TWO
Stalemate — 1972

On January 1, forty-six-year-old David Elazar became Israel's ninth chief of staff. Elazar, known affectionately by his friends and admirers as "Dado," was born in Sarajevo. When a new government came into power on the eve of World War II in Yugoslavia in 1939, all but a small percentage of the Jewish students were expelled from Yugoslavia's secondary schools. Dado, along with several others, left the country in 1940 bound for Palestine. He wrote to his father who had been called up in the reserves, "There's nothing left for me in a country where you are good enough to serve in the army, but I am not good enough to be accepted in a high school."

At the age of twenty-one, Dado joined the Palmach, the elite strike force of the underground organization Hagana, which was the precursor to the IDF. There, he began his military career. His first notable moments as a commander came while leading small units during the struggle for Jerusalem in 1948 and 1949. When Israel's War for Independence ended, twenty-three-year-old Dado Elazar found himself serving as an officer in a brigade commanded by twenty-six-year-old Yitzhak Rabin.

The official ceremony to commemorate Elazar's appointment as the chief of staff of the IDF began in Meir's office. Present were the cabinet ministers and the other officers on the General Staff. Also present was Chaim Bar-Lev, the retiring chief of staff whom Elazar was replacing. It was a special moment for both men. Bar-Lev had been Elazar's childhood friend in Sarajevo. He had immigrated to Palestine a few years before Elazar's arrival in Israel. During the 1940s they renewed their friendship. It was a close relationship that continued throughout their careers. Less than two years later, Elazar would rely heavily on Bar-Lev when Israel's survival was at stake.

One of the cabinet members at the ceremony was Defense Minister Dayan. By then Dayan had been in his position for more than four years and still was the dominant military personage in the government. As defense minister, all new appointments to the General Staff had to be approved by him. As a result, by 1972, Dayan had largely shaped the entire staff. Elazar, who became a member of the General Staff in 1961, was the only remaining member that had not gone through Dayan's gauntlet. That created a tricky playing field for Elazar to navigate; to have his views heard he had to maneuver through the cabinet and other members of the General Staff, many of whom were under Dayan's political influence. Fortunately, he had direct access to the highest-ranking politicians because of a tradition started by Prime Minister Eshkol that the chief of staff would be invited to attend most cabinet meetings.

At Dado's first meeting with his General Staff he told them, "We are definitely entering a period when the possibility of war is very likely. In the immediate future we must say to ourselves that 'There may be a war'…" Dado believed it likely that the Egyptians would conduct deep raids in combination with low-level harassment designed to cause Israeli casualties. He also was concerned that the Egyptians might try to take control of a narrow strip of land on the Israeli side of the Suez Canal. Therefore, he wanted to deter them by ensuring that the IDF maintained its offensive capability to conduct raids into Egypt's interior and wreak havoc on Egypt's cities near the canal.

Dado concerned himself with defensive measures too. He was a proponent of Bar-Lev's controversial line of fortresses along the canal, even though Ariel Sharon, the Sinai-front commander in the south, as well as others, had opposed the fortress plan. Instead, they had favored a mobile defense that would not provide stationary targets for the Egyptians to attack. But Elazar did not have to deal with the question of whether or not to build the strongholds; Bar-lev had already taken care of that. He *just had to decide whether to keep using them. From Elazar's perspective, the fortresses had worked the prior year. And, even though the IDF had incurred casualties, Egypt's frequent raids had not taken any ground. Also, there was no certainty that a strictly mobile defense of roving tanks would perform better, and with fewer casualties, than the fortresses had. Elazar viewed the strongholds as a fixed component of a mobile defense that would be augmented by tanks and the IAF as conditions required. And in the event of an imminent, full-fledged war, he thought the Bar-Lev line could always be evacuated. While Elazar was right about many things, he would soon find that he was wrong about that.*

Another thorn Elazar had to deal with was Israel's border with Lebanon. Assad wanted Syria to have a special, dominant relationship with Lebanon. One day he hoped to place Syrian troops in Fatahland, in southern Lebanon, near Israel's border. He also provided material support to the PLO, newly-located in Lebanon after Hussein had evicted them from Jordan. As a result of Assad's help and the PLO's industriousness, during the first two months of 1972, the number of raids by Fedayeen terrorists into Israel from Lebanon increased. In retribution and defense, Israel launched a punitive attack into Lebanon designed to destroy PLO bases near the border. History was repeating itself, little different from events in past years along Israel's and Jordan's border.

Overall, however, Israel felt little pressure to break the stalemate with her Arab neighbors. Nor did Meir feel the nation's existence was threatened in early 1972. But, within Israel, domestic forces that favored settling the occupied territories became more powerful, and political pressure from within the government to create new Jewish settlements in the Sinai grew. On January 14, bulldozers and troops removed thousands of Bedouin from their homes by force in an eighteen-mile section of the Rafah plain that extended west from the Gaza strip. Since many of those Bedouin were employed as cheap labor by Israeli settlements in the Negev, the government's actions angered many of the Kibbutzim in the area who had depended on them. General Sharon's excuse for clearing the land and fencing it off was that it was required to prevent terror attacks and smuggling into Gaza. The reality was that the unpublicized eviction of the Bedouin was the first step towards Dayan's dream to create a permanent presence in occupied Sinai.

Several months later, nine Bedouin sheiks petitioned Israel's Supreme Court to stop the expulsions. They took advantage of a provision of Israeli law that permits any person to petition the court directly if they are victims of a perceived injustice by the executive branch of government. The sheiks argued that their expulsion violated Geneva Convention agreements regarding transfers of populations in occupied territories. The IDF responded with its "security" explanation. Before final arguments were presented to the court, the lawyer representing the sheiks died of a heart attack. A year later the Supreme Court ruled against the petition: The Bedouin could not return. But the side effect of the litigation was that it helped tip off the media to Dayan's master plan to create a seaport in the area called Yamit. The public opposed the idea immediately; under significant pressure the cabinet shelved those plans, but not forever.

Nor did the New Year bring increased urgency from the United States to prod nations in the region towards a peace agreement. The State Department, true to form, did continue to push the proposition that only by withholding arms would Israel become more diplomatically flexible. But the newly-ascendant Kissinger resisted. He continued to maintain that the only way to influence Israel was to keep her feeling strong and instinctively felt a weakened Israel would be less willing to take a chance for peace that risked her destruction. Kissinger also maintained his belief that the longer the stalemate endured the more likely the Arabs would realize that the Russians could not deliver what they wanted—the return of their lands. Then, in frustration if not friendship, Kissinger thought they would turn to the United States.

Meanwhile, the Russians tried to impress on the Americans the need for haste to find a Middle East solution. Brezhnev wrote to Nixon expressing concern that he had not received a response from Gromyko's proposal a couple of months earlier. He told Nixon, "It is important to act without delay." But Nixon had other things on his mind. On January 25, he announced that Kissinger had been holding secret talks with North Vietnam since June of 1971. Finding an honorable way out of the Vietnam morass was at the top of Nixon's agenda. Finding a path to a diplomatic relationship with China was very important to him, too. Finding a solution to the Middle East was much further down Nixon's list of priorities—especially since it was an election year. Nixon was not willing to risk angering significant portions of the electorate to pursue an uncertain outcome. That could wait until 1973.

January and February

Sadat did not have the luxury of waiting for the superpowers to deal their Middle East cards. Previously, he had declared 1971 the year of decision. Instead, it had been the year of indecision. Protests by 6,000 college students at Cairo University demonstrating against the "no war, no peace" status quo reminded him of his failure. They wanted action. So did Sadat.

In February, Sadat returned to Moscow where he again demanded aircraft capable of bombing targets within Israel's heartland, which would then give the Egyptian military a strategic offensive option. He also requested pontoon bridges so that the army could attack across the Suez Canal. But Brezhnev did not want to do anything that might give the Americans a reason to cancel his historic summit with Nixon scheduled for May. Achieving and deepening détente between Russia and the United States was Brezhnev's priority. And it had to be. The cost of the nuclear arms race was further damaging the Soviet Union's already-faltering economy; survival of the communist system was at stake. Brezhnev believed that détente would be a tool for fixing his economic problems because it would bring better trade relations with the West that would help revitalize his moribund economy.

Brezhnev tried to mollify Sadat. He told Sadat that he would exert pressure on the Americans at the summit to work towards an agreement that would return the occupied Arab lands. He also tried to appease the Egyptian leader by agreeing to send more tanks, some old technology MiG-21 fighters, and a few of the bombers the Egyptians coveted. But Sadat, who wanted parity with the Israelis, was not satisfied. He felt treated like a child told to be a proverbial good boy until after the summit. It was a measure of disrespect that would backfire for the Russians.

Israel did not remain dormant while Sadat maneuvered and fumed. The IDF conducted an intricate war game in February called "*Oz*" which meant courage. The IDF trained to launch an offensive across the Suez Canal in response to an Egyptian attack. To prepare for the exercise, the army dug a huge ditch at great expense in the middle of the desert that the IDF used to simulate a crossing of the canal. Meir and Dayan watched the exercises. The vast movement of arms and men remained vivid in Dayan's mind. A year later he cockily said that if the Egyptians began a war, "I don't rule out planning to reach the Nile."

The IDF did not just conduct the *Oz* exercise. They concocted "*Iron Ram*" and other simulated events as well. The premise of *Iron Ram* was that Israel would uncover an Egyptian plan to attack twenty-four hours before it was scheduled to start. Because of the surprise, IDF reserves would not reach the canal front until two days after the Egyptians attacked. The exercise assumed that the Egyptians would gain control of the Bar-Lev strongholds. Nevertheless, *Iron Ram* purportedly proved that the IDF could and would counterattack and begin crossing the canal on the third and fourth days of war. It would not be too long before those conclusions would be tested.

However, Sharon, still commander of the Southern Front, did not content himself with just planning how to defeat the Egyptians. He had a vast number of Palestinians in Gaza to worry about too. Shortly after the *Oz* exercise ended, he established a new Nahal outpost within Gaza. It had fifteen tents, a perimeter fence, and was deliberately placed in close proximity to the Arab population to prevent Gaza City from spreading south. The courageous members of the new settlement were part of Sharon's "fingers" strategy designed to break up the Gaza strip into separate areas that would restrict travel and be more easily controlled.

That same February, Kissinger was busy on things other than Israel and the Arabs. During the first twenty days he was preoccupied with Nixon's upcoming trip to China on February 21. The opening of a dialogue with China was a stunning political achievement that demonstrated Kissinger's and Nixon's mastery of diplomatic skills. Coming months before the first summit meeting with the Russians, it was a clear signal to the Soviets that not all of America's marbles were in the Russian basket.

Nevertheless, Kissinger found time to muse over what steps to take in the future to resolve the Middle East conundrum, which he knew might flare up again at some point. He proposed to Israel that she agree to separate the concept of sovereignty from that of security. Simply put, sovereignty meant ownership. Along those lines, he suggested that Israel permit Egypt to regain sovereignty over the Sinai in return for the IDF retaining some strategic security positions. In Kissinger's view, his idea would facilitate an Israeli withdrawal to the west edge of the mountain passes (Suez Canal side) in return for a ceasefire that extended to at least early 1974. Egypt would then be permitted to move police, but no military forces, into the Sinai, and could reopen the canal. All the while, explicit linkage to a final settlement could be left vague. Ambassador Rabin and Moshe Dayan were interested in exploring Kissinger's concept.

But while Egypt, Israel, America and Russia pondered the future, a growing darkness ominously swept outwards from Lebanon. Black September began terrorist activity in Germany. Bombs exploded outside of factories in Cologne, and, on February 22, Black September members hijacked a Lufthansa Boeing 747. The passengers were eventually released, but not before a German government official delivered a five million dollar ransom to a man in a black coat sitting in a car outside of Beirut airport. By doing so, Germany established the precedent that the country would yield to terror. It was a precedent that would soon come back to haunt the Germans.

Hussein Has a New Plan

King Hussein began 1972 as confident as ever. His battles with the PLO were behind him; he had ripped the PLO from Jordanian soil. Therefore, he felt able to turn his focus to recovering his lost territories on the West Bank.

In March, Hussein unveiled a new plan that would create a United Arab Kingdom under his leadership. He proposed to join the occupied West Bank with the rest of Jordan east of the Jordan River in a federalist structure in which each region would have its own governor, courts, parliament, and right to manage local issues. Hussein, along with a National Parliament, would remain responsible for economic issues, defense, and foreign policy. Under the king's formulation, Amman would be the capital of all of Jordan, and East Jerusalem would be the capital of the Palestinian region. The army would be composed of citizens from the entire newly-united Jordanian nation. Hussein also suggested that the Gaza strip could be included along with the West Bank.

The Arab world did not like Hussein's plan. Most Arabs were inclined to support the PLO over Hussein, either out of conviction or out of concern for their personal survival if they did not. Arab leaders condemned Hussein for trying to steal land (the West Bank) that did not belong to him. Many believed the king's plan was part of a plot concocted by him, the United States, and Israel. Syria, Algeria, Iraq, and Egypt responded by severing diplomatic relations with Jordan, although Syria and Egypt threw him a spurious lifeline. They informed Hussein that they would resume relations with him if he allowed the Fedayeen to return to Jordan—something that Hussein, after having fought to evict them, would never agree to voluntarily. For Hussein, that was not just a matter of conviction. A return of the PLO would have meant the end of his rule and probably the end of his life.

Sadat, burned by the PLO's fiery objections to his agreement to extend the ceasefire in February 1971, was only too happy to side with the PLO to turn their wrath from him to Hussein. In addition, Sadat was angry with Hussein's transparent attempt to negotiate his own separate deal with the Israelis. Similarly, the king had valid concerns that Sadat was pursuing a separate deal with Israel which, if concluded, would lessen Jordan's chances of recovering the West Bank. Israel, of course, had no difficulty dealing separately with the two nations. But in the absence of a true peace overture ending in a contractual peace, neither Egypt nor Jordan had any chance of convincing Meir to withdraw the IDF.

The PLO joined the strident anti-Hussein chorus by declaring that only the Palestinian people had the right to decide their future. Rather than seeing Hussein's idea as a way to free Palestinians from Israeli rule, they denounced Jordan and charged she was "offering [her]self as an accomplice to the Zionist entity." The PLO also called for the forceful overthrow of King Hussein. Nor did Palestinian residents on the West Bank support Hussein's proposal. The mayor of Hebron used an old Arab saying to register his disapproval. He said Hussein's idea was like "selling fish to the sea."

In a speech to the Knesset on March 16, Meir rejected Hussein's proposal as well. Meir had always been against a separate Palestinian option and had previously said,

> It is not as though there was a Palestinian people in Palestine considering itself as a Palestinian people and we came and threw them out and took their country away from them. They did not exist.

And she was convinced that a separate state would never succeed for both demographic and geographic reasons. Meir was, however, willing to accept some form of Jordanian jurisdiction over the West Bank as part of an overall agreement because, in her mind, she thought it the only viable solution to a nearly intractable problem. Thus, Meir rejected Hussein's plan because it violated a core principle of hers; she would not agree to transfer any land before first reaching an agreement with the king that would lead to a peace treaty between Israel and Jordan.

Arafat, for his part, was relieved that Meir had rejected the plan. He believed that, if Israel had accepted Hussein's idea, it would have been the end of the PLO. He later stated, "Sometimes I think we are lucky to have the Israelis as our enemies."

On March 21, Hussein and Meir again met secretly at a location south of the Dead Sea. Meir believed the intermittent secret direct conversations with Hussein, though not always fruitful, worthwhile. That was also her opinion in 1947 when she sneaked into Jordan to meet with Hussein's grandfather. She knew it was unlikely that the meetings with Hussein would solve the main issues that divided them, but they did serve to resolve smaller issues ranging from fighting terrorists to mosquito control. Since the 1967 war, bridges over the Jordan River had been opened, and unofficial trade between Jordan and the West Bank had proven fruitful. In essence, the two countries exhibited many traits of a peaceful relationship, even though Jordan would not publicly recognize the Jewish nation. Thus their private discussions were a vital mode of mutually beneficial communication.

When they met in March, Meir complained that Hussein had not given her advance notice of his Federation plan. Hussein apologized and then clarified he intended for it to be implemented after a peace agreement with Israel. Meir responded by highlighting a speech Hussein had given where he referred to liberating all of the occupied territories. She then inquired, "Maybe you meant Tel Aviv as well?"

Hussein answered indirectly. He asked if she would give him access to the people on the West Bank in order to build support for his plan.

Meir neither agreed nor disagreed. Instead she fended him off by saying it was a complex issue. Israel's leader then asked the king if he would sign a separate peace treaty with Israel. Hussein said yes, but only within a proper framework.

Meir pushed further. Could a peace treaty include significant border changes?

Hussein responded in the negative. But to ease Israel's security concerns he agreed that both the West Bank and Gaza could be demilitarized and that Jerusalem could serve as an undivided capital of both Israel and the Palestinian region.

Meir made no promises in response to the king's answers but agreed to think about his proposals. However, by refusing to consider Israel's territorial needs, and by requiring that Muslims control both the Muslim and Christian quarters of Jerusalem, King Hussein doomed any chance of getting the Israelis on board.

Meir and Hussein met again in late June. At that meeting she urged Hussein to make a deal with Israel but insisted that it would require significant border changes. Hussein would not agree. But, when asked by Dayan whether Jordan would join in the fight if Egypt and Israel ever went to war again, Hussein said he would not. A peace agreement was not achieved, but their relationship reduced the prospect that Israel and Jordan would ever again fight a war against each other.

Kissinger and Sadat Go to Russia

In advance of the upcoming summit, Kissinger secretly arrived in Moscow on April 22 to find solutions for issues dividing Russia and the United States. Prior to Kissinger's arrival, Sadat sent Brezhnev a note that, among other things, declared: "Any new American policy will certainly be against our interests." Sadat then accused the Soviets of not supporting him to the same extent that the Americans supported Israel's interests. He further warned about Jewish immigrants leaving Russia for

Israel: "Some of them are young men, intellectuals and scientists, who are going to be of great material assistance to Israel." The issue of Jewish emigration from the Soviet Union would soon come to haunt U.S.-U.S.S.R. relations.

Brezhnev gave Kissinger a paper upon his arrival that outlined Russia's position on resolving the Israeli-Arab dispute. As usual, it called for Israel to withdraw completely from the occupied territories. It also included a suggestion to establish a demilitarized zone on both sides of the shared borders, possibly patrolled by UN troops. Even though the text did not incorporate Gromyko's previous offer that Russia would withdraw from Egypt in the wake of a peace agreement, Gromyko assured Kissinger it was still part of the deal the Russians were proposing.

Kissinger read the document but was determined to put off any serious discussions until late fall after the U.S. elections. He also knew the Israelis would not agree to pull back to the pre-1967 war borders, and that Israel would almost certainly not accept any proposal that would extend a demilitarized zone into her much smaller land mass (compared to Egypt's). And, after having gone to war in part over Egypt's closure of the Straits of Tiran, he knew that the Israelis would not accept losing control of Sharm el-Sheikh. Thus, Gromyko's missive was a non-starter.

Kissinger responded to the note the next day. He hoped to signal that Brezhnev should not hold out much hope that their discussions on April 24 would significantly advance resolution of problems in the Middle East. He said, "We cannot ... go to war with Israel in an attempt to reach a settlement," and further warned, "It may turn out to be an insoluble problem. Within that framework, we are prepared to have discussions."

But Brezhnev was not deterred by Kissinger's remarks to Gromyko. When he met with Kissinger the next day, Brezhnev said,

> As we understand it the agreement reached between the president and Gromyko in Washington last fall remains fully

valid, and now the question is how to formalize that understanding without making public the main substance.

Kissinger responded that Brezhnev had the wrong impression of the outcome of those talks. He said Nixon did not agree to Gromyko's proposal—only that he would consider it. Kissinger also clarified the timing of any serious peace negotiations,

> As an objective reality, it will be impossible to complete any agreement before mid-1973. We cannot do it before the elections, and cannot do it immediately after the elections. November and December will be taken up constituting a new government. And the agreement can be done only by a new government.

Kissinger then added, with reference to the upcoming summit, that Nixon must be able to return to the United States and honestly say there had been no "secret agreements" with regard to Israel and the Arab nations. The only way to ensure that, he said, was to keep any discussions within the preliminary realm. "Then, when I come back in September, we can talk about completing an agreement. We will keep our word."

Brezhnev unambiguously displayed his frustration with Kissinger's response before the translation was completed. Once the translator finished he responded, "I'll tell you honestly; I certainly cannot say that satisfies me." He then criticized the United States for not pressuring Israel and for being unwilling to agree to a framework for an agreement in advance of the summit. Brezhnev warned that only a summit agreement would restrain the Arabs from launching a war. "As things stand now, I do not know how to talk to Sadat, in particular. If I'm deprived of this weapon, that is the agreement with you, I don't know how we can approach the Arab leaders without causing an explosion." And he added, "An army as big as that cannot stay tranquil all the time, especially in these conditions."

Kissinger remained unfazed. He knew the Israelis would not agree to most of the proposed Russian framework, nor did he blame them. Therefore, instead of counter-productively working on an agreement that would not only cause a political uproar but had no chance of being successfully implemented, he played for time. Besides, Kissinger still believed that the longer progress was delayed, the more likely the Egyptians would move closer to the Americans' orbit.

After Kissinger left the Soviet Union, Sadat arrived. None of the Russian leaders were on hand at the airport to greet him. That must have increased his apprehension regarding how reliable the Soviet Union was as an ally. Sadat suspected that the Russians were more concerned with implementing détente than resolving his territorial problems. Alternatively, he feared—as did the Israelis for similar reasons—that the Americans and Soviets would reach an agreement that he did not approve of—and at his expense.

While Sadat was in Russia, a high-level Egyptian general communicated to the United States that his president wanted to establish contact on a presidential level with the United States. The general indicated that Sadat had an interest in a secret meeting, but not until after the US-USSR summit coming up in Moscow in May. Until then, Sadat had been having difficulty divining America's true intent. The information he received concerning America's intentions had come from the State Department, secret channels, and filtered intelligence through Soviet sources. Since he was worried that the Soviets might agree to maintain the "no peace, no war" status quo, despite Brezhnev's willingness to supply some of the arms he had requested, Sadat decided to take steps towards developing a new option: A dialogue with the Americans.

After meeting with the Soviets, Sadat visited Rumanian President Nicolas Ceausescu. Since Rumania still had diplomatic relations with Israel, Sadat used Ceausescu as a conduit to deliver a message to Meir that conveyed his willingness to be the first Arab leader to recognize Israel and its borders. "But," he warned, "I do not want to end up as King Hussein, completely cut off from the Arab world." A week later the Rumanian leader delivered the message to Meir. She later wrote, "After so many years it really looked as though the ice were about to break." Ceausescu told Meir that Sadat would be willing to permit international troops based in the Sinai to supervise an agreement. Meir responded that Ceausescu could tell Sadat that she would meet with him whenever and wherever he chose. Sadat never responded. Perhaps the personal risk of meeting the head of an Israeli government while Israeli troops still occupied the Sinai was too much for him to risk.

On May 8, four members of Black September hijacked a Sabena airline plane heading from Brussels to Tel Aviv. Eighty-six other passengers were on board. The Black September leader was experienced; he had participated in the hijacking of the El Al plane in 1968. The Sabena plane landed at Lod (now Ben Gurion) Airport, and the terrorists threatened to kill the passengers unless 317 terrorists held in Israeli jails were freed. Many of the imprisoned terrorists had Jewish blood on their hands.

That same day, while the hostage crisis brewed, President Nixon went on American TV to announce that the American military would mine North Vietnam's ports in an attempt to prevent supplies from arriving. Since most of those military supplies were transported to North Vietnam by Russian ships, the threat of a superpower confrontation was in the air. In addition, Nixon announced that he would commence bombing of the rail network inside North Vietnam.

In May of 1972, Israel's policy was clear; Israel would not negotiate with terrorists. An elite Israeli team that included two future Israeli prime ministers, Ehud Barak and Bibi Netanyahu, gathered at the airport. The next day the specially-trained Israeli unit dressed in white overalls to masquerade as airport maintenance personal. In the late afternoon they stormed the plane and killed two of the terrorists and wounded two others. Only one of the innocent hostages died during the rescue. Afterwards, several countries decided they needed to create similar elite groups trained to respond to terrorist acts; West Germany and England sent designated Special Forces to Israel to learn how to storm a hijacked airplane without killing hostages.

Unfortunately, Israel's rousing success did not translate into even one more peaceful month at Lod Airport. On May 30, three Japanese members of the terrorist Red Army group carried weapons hidden in baggage they brought with them onto a plane that landed there. The Red Army had allied itself with George Habash's PFLP. When they reached the terminal, mayhem ensued. Twenty-seven passengers died from bullets spit from the terrorists' guns; most were Christian pilgrims from Puerto Rico. The one surviving terrorist confessed that the operation was revenge for Israel's success in freeing the passengers on the Sabena plane three weeks before.

CHAPTER FORTY-THREE
Egypt Takes a Bold Step

The Summit Meeting in Russia

The summit meeting between Nixon and the Soviet Union's leadership began in Moscow on May 22. Brezhnev, who by then controlled the Politburo, took the lead for the Russians on military and political issues; Kosygin was relegated to economic concerns.

Nixon and Brezhnev spoke about the Middle East only one time, on May 26. The next day, they were scheduled to sign the Strategic Arms Limitation Treaty. With regard to the Middle East, Nixon told Brezhnev, "Putting it cold turkey, we can't settle before the election, but after that we can make progress, in a fair way," and then, "We are not in a position to settle it today because frankly we're not in a position to deliver the Israelis on anything so far proposed." But Nixon did not dismiss Brezhnev's concerns. He recognized that the longer the problem lingered, the more likely it would incite a conflagration.

Nixon's deferral frustrated Brezhnev, as had Kissinger's the month before. But Brezhnev's highest priority was reaching an agreement on a treaty for nuclear arms. Therefore, since he had little interest in causing a confrontation that would jeopardize his primary goals of signing the treaty and hosting a successful summit, Brezhnev did not push Arab issues. Upon the summit's conclusion, the Americans and Soviets issued a joint, rather-bland statement that reaffirmed their mutual support for Resolution 242 and the Jarring mission. Afterwards, a pleased Soviet Politburo, more concerned with Russia's relationship with the United States than assisting their Arab clients, concluded, "You can do business with Nixon."

Sadat, however, had no interest in superpower relations. He wanted his land back—all of it. The absence of anything in the joint superpower communiqué that signaled movement regarding his fundamental issue left Sadat embittered and disillusioned. He called it a "violent shock." His 1971 "Year of Decision" was rapidly morphing into a subsequent year of indecision. However, none of the obvious paths for him to tread were promising. **One** choice would have been to do nothing and instead place his faith in the superpowers eventually focusing on Egypt's needs. But that would have risked his overthrow by an increasingly angry and frustrated populace. **Alternatively**, he could have made what he knew was a bad and dishonorable deal with Israel. But, if he had done that, he would have been viciously attacked politically by other Arab nations for achieving so little while acting alone. And, as with inaction, he probably still would have been overthrown. **Or**, he could have chosen to immediately go to war with Israel. But he knew that Egypt was too weak to win and that his army would probably have been destroyed as a result.

So Sadat thought out-of-the-box. Knowing he needed to do something imaginative to change the dynamic, he decided to break with the Soviets. Sadat knew it would weaken Egypt militarily in the short run, but he thought it would demonstrate his resolve to the Russians and teach them that ignoring Egypt's needs on the altar of détente comes with a price. It also would send a message to the Americans that Egypt was not inalterably tied to the Russians. Sadat knew that, as long as the Soviets had military bases and considerable influence within his country, America would not consider helping him at Israel's expense. By throwing them out he thought it would teach Russia the peril of ignoring his requests and would potentially sow the seeds for a new relationship with an even more powerful friend, a friend that just might deliver what he needed—Israel's withdrawal from the Sinai.

Sadat Kicks Them Out

One week after the summit, Sadat sent his emissary to Moscow with two simple requests and a threat. The **first** request was for the Russians to honor their arms supply commitments in their entirety and to supply Egypt with the offensive weapons he needed to take Israel on. The Egyptian army had advised Sadat that over the past three years their military capabilities had not drawn closer to Israel's. That was not acceptable. Sadat needed to have a war option in order to pressure Israel to make concessions.

The **second** request was for Russia to reschedule loan repayments for money Egypt had borrowed from the Soviet Union to purchase armaments delivered by the Russians. Egypt borrowed the money because Russia had insisted on being paid in full for the weapons supplied and for the cost of housing Russian "advisors" in Egypt. The Egyptian economy was being crushed by the burden of making these payments.

Sadat's threat was blunt. His representative told the Russians that if they failed to comply with the Egyptian demands, Sadat would kick them out of Egypt. But the Soviets were not intimidated. They were convinced that Sadat lacked the political strength and fortitude to execute such a power play, even though his survival in office for two years after Nasser's death suggested otherwise. Moscow's opinion of Sadat was not unique. Few believed him a strong leader. Therefore, Brezhnev would not buckle in the face of Sadat's threats. He refused both requests.

Brezhnev's refusal was not entirely because of his desire to maintain good relations with the United States. It also reflected a Russian reality: her inability to fulfill the armament needs of all of her allies in addition to those of the Russian military. It must have been frustrating to the Politburo since much Soviet foreign policy depended on supplying weapons. But foreign demands were a huge drain on Russian industrial output for several reasons. **First**, the Vietnam War still raged leaving North Vietnam in great need. **Second**, given Russia's hope to build a relationship with India, weapons were required to grease those wheels after India had just finished fighting a war with Pakistan in late 1971. **Third**, the Warsaw Pact nations' needs were a constant drain. Therefore, even if Brezhnev had enthusiastically supported supplying advanced weapons to Egypt, there is significant question whether Russian factories would have been able to build them while still satisfying the other demands being placed on them.

But Moscow's problems meant little to Sadat. He despaired over his failure to obtain more arms and became increasingly resolute that he had to break with his communist benefactor because of her refusal to provide the support he demanded.

Also, the manner in which the Russian advisors treated the Egyptians made evicting them all the sweeter. Problems between Egyptian and Russian military personnel began in the 1950s, before the 1956 war, when many high level Egyptian officers received training in Russian military academies. The translators provided by the academies were not very capable. That caused the Egyptian officers to seem less knowledgeable and more hesitant. In part, as a result, younger Russian officers treated them contemptuously. Also, the language barrier prevented the Egyptians from receiving their instructions in classrooms alongside other Russian officers. Therefore, the Egyptians were frequently taught in substandard classrooms. Matters were made even worse by the poor living conditions the Egyptians were forced to endure by their hosts.

After the Six-Day War, problems between the Egyptian military and the Russians intensified. Egyptian officers charged that inferior Russian equipment was part of the reason for the 1967 debacle. They contended that some of the tanks the Soviet Union provided were more suited for arctic conditions than the desert, especially those that lacked proper ventilation. In addition, Egyptian soldiers that had experienced the tumult of war began to resent their Soviet advisors who pompously instructed them even though they themselves had never been in combat

Russian arrogance was also a significant issue. Soviet military bases on Egyptian soil were off-limits to the Egyptian military. Egyptian civilians and military personnel were even sometimes blocked from using Egyptian highways when convoys of Russian personnel moved on them. There were also allegations that Russian soldiers smuggled Egyptian gold out of the country when they went home.

But before making a final decision with regard to the Russians, Sadat met with his Armed Forces Council on July 6 to take stock of the capabilities of Egypt's armed forces. The head of Egyptian military intelligence told him that, mostly due to Israel's air superiority, they could not attack and win. After listening to his generals Sadat said:

> We must distinguish between politicians and soldiers. You soldiers must concentrate your efforts on preparing the troops for the coming battle. I realize, and General Sadiq agrees with me, that we must not go into battle unless we have the capacity to deter Israel from attacking our interior. The problem which confronts us is what to do if we are obliged, politically, to go to war before we have that deterrent?

Meanwhile, Sadat maneuvered in hopes of avoiding having to break with Moscow. He sent the Soviets two letters asking for their views on the outcome of the summit and how agreements reached there would impact the Middle East. Moscow's replies were evasive; they just promised Russia's good will.

The Russian responses angered Sadat so much that he overcame any remaining inhibitions. Sadat summoned Soviet Ambassador, Vladimir

Vinogradov, to a meeting at the Presidential Palace on July 8. There, Sadat told Vinogradov that all Soviet experts must leave the country in a week and that Russian equipment could either be sold to Egypt or removed. When Vinogradov tried to change Sadat's mind without success, Sadat told him, "After studying the situation in all its aspects and in full appreciation of the tremendous aid the Soviet Union has extended to us, and while fully anxious for the friendship of the Soviet Union, the time had come for objective pause in that friendship."

Coincidently, Syrian President Assad, embroiled in his own confrontation with the Soviets, was in Moscow the same day Sadat summoned Vinogradov. Assad wanted arms; in return the Soviets were pressuring him to sign a Treaty of Friendship like Sadat had done the year before. But Assad's response was, "Friendship needs no treaty." Their discussions became increasingly confrontational, to the point that Assad prepared to leave. But after news of Sadat's decision reached Moscow, Brezhnev intervened; the pressure to sign the treaty dissipated. Instead, Brezhnev asked the Syrian leader to fly to Cairo and try to help the Soviet Union get back in Sadat's good graces. Assad agreed.

Sadat publicly announced his expulsion of the Russians on July 18. By then more than 10,000 Russians had already left or were in the process of leaving. Sadat would only permit a few Soviet troops in supporting roles to stay. He did, however, permit the Russian navy to continue to use Port Said. The Egyptian president told the Central Committee of the Arab Socialist Union (Egypt's only recognized political party at that time) that he was kicking the Russians out because of Russian refusal to supply modern offensive arms. But in a speech on July 24, Sadat further intimated that his decision was really a byproduct of the détente between the Soviets and the Americans:

> "Perhaps to [the Russians] the Middle East problem is not the number one problem—but to me, the problem of the occupation of the land and the Middle East problem is not only the number

> one problem but is sleep, life, food, waking hours, and water. It is my problem. It is the problem of my occupied land."

Sadat added in another speech that he could not accept continuation of "no war, no peace" and charged that Russia's support for Egypt fell far short of American support for Israel.

Sadat's speeches explained why he evicted the Russians. They also contained a hint that if the Russians supplied more military arms he might reverse his decision. Meanwhile, by kicking the Russians out Sadat was able to deflect pressure to immediately start a war that he would lose but still preserve his option to do so later if the Russians changed their policies and Egypt's military strength increased as a result. But until then, he would be free to explore an alternative way forward with an American administration happy to see the Russians lose influence.

The announcement electrified the Egyptian population, and editorials effusively praised their president. The Arab street had no love for the Russians because they had treated the Egyptians condescendingly. Therefore, they applauded Sadat's courageous move in response to Russia's refusal to help the Egyptian people. Sadat's popularity soared; no longer would he be viewed as a weak-kneed president with a tenuous hold on power.

Nixon, fearing accusations of collusion, quickly assured the Soviet Union that he had nothing to do with Sadat's decision. Brezhnev tried to mask the Russian failure. He wrote in a message to Nixon that it was a "unilateral move" by the Russians in fulfillment of Gromyko's suggestion that the Soviet Union would leave Egypt as part of a Middle East settlement. Nobody believed him.

In Israel, most saw only one thing: the Russian menace had been removed from their borders. Whatever the future might bring, it appeared that it would include an Egypt whose military had been significantly weakened. But Israel's analysis was too shallow as Sadat explained in his memoir:

The Soviet Union, the West, and Israel misinterpreted my decision to expel the military experts and reached an erroneous conclusion which in fact served my strategy, as I had expected—that it was an indication that I had finally decided not to fight my own battle. That interpretation made me happy. It was precisely what I wanted them to think.

Meir did hope, however, that Sadat's eviction of the Soviets would present an opportunity for peace. She held out the barest of olive branches to test the waters. In a speech to the Knesset on July 26, she said, "It would seem that this hour in the history of Egypt can, nay, should be the appropriate hour for change, and if it truly is the hour for change, let it not be missed."

But Sadat was not inclined to contact the Israelis after throwing the Russians out. Instead he focused his efforts on the United States. On July 19, he sent a message to the Americans. Kissinger responded that he was willing to engage in confidential talks with the Egyptians, but he would not have any new proposals until he could determine if there were areas where the Egyptians and Israelis could reach an agreement. Kissinger was reluctant to engage with the Egyptians because he was not prepared at that point to offer any new ideas. Six weeks went by without Sadat's answer.

Israel's Knesset acted in the absence of any public peace overtures from Egypt, Syria, and Jordan. Led by the Labor Party ministers that controlled the chamber, it directed substantial sums towards developing the newly-conquered territories. The Knesset planned for dozens of settlements, an industrial center on the Golan, and commercial and industrial sectors in the Jordan Valley and East Jerusalem. The legislators also targeted the Sinai for substantial development. Time was not standing still—Jews began moving into the occupied territories in great numbers.

Meanwhile, a political storm brewed in the shadow of the wildly successful, superpower summit and the calamitous departure of Soviet forces from Egypt. On June 17, five men broke into the Watergate offices of the Democratic National Party headquarters. Their bumbling attempt to photograph documents and install listening devices on telephones was compromised by an alert security guard. The guard called the police, and the men were arrested. The men were acting on behalf of the Committee for Re-Election of the President.

CHAPTER FORTY-FOUR
Munich

Just after 4:00 a.m. on September 5, eight men dressed in tracksuits resembling those worn by returning athletes strode to the base of a six-foot high chain link fence surrounding the Olympic Village in Munich. The fence was supposed to protect the thousands of athletes sleeping within the compound. The men carried large sport bags within which they hid guns and grenades underneath other clothing. The eight men were members of Black September.

Black September, along with other small, organized groups of Palestinian Fedayeen, comprised Arafat's secretive terrorist arm. Abu Daoud, the Commander of Fatah forces in Jordan before Hussein had evicted them, said about the group's history: "There was a need to find a meaningful way of pursuing the struggle." So, Daoud and others

> decided to form a group with no link to Fatah. The group would take a role in drawing attention to the significance of the struggle and then return to the mother organization, Fatah. So we set up an organization called Black September. It was separate from Fatah so that Fatah and the PLO would not have to carry opprobrium for our operations. The group as individuals and as a leadership was responsible for its own successes and failures

without compromising the legitimate leadership of the Palestinian people.... There is no such thing as Black September. Fatah announces its operations under this name so that Fatah will not appear as the direct executor of the operations.

By 1972, Arafat agreed with Daoud that, for the sake of its international standing, the PLO should no longer be tied to terrorism. But he firmly believed in the value of politically motivated violence. Therefore, Arafat never raised a hand to stop terrorist elements in the PLO, certainly knew who was involved, benefitted from their successes that raised awareness of the Palestinian cause, and did not overly concern himself with their failures because those failure had a by-product of weakening opposition to him within the PLO. It was a cagey calculation by a master politician little concerned for the lives of those that opposed him.

Black September's target for terrorism during those early morning hours was 31 Connolly Street, the apartment block assigned to the Israeli delegation. But first, the men assigned to the mission had to negotiate the fence surrounding the residential area and the deserted streets beyond. While climbing the barrier, they helped several drunk American athletes returning from a night of merriment cross over. The inebriated Americans were useful, if unexpected, cover. Several German officials saw the two groups going over the fence rather than returning through a designated gate but thought nothing of it. After all, the officials thought, if German security had so little concern that those charged with guarding the compound carried walkie-talkies rather than guns, why should they be apprehensive? After entering the compound, the Americans walked with the Palestinians for a short while, and then went their separate way—the Americans to their beds, the Palestinians to their mission.

A few minutes later, the terrorists entered the central foyer of their target through an unlocked door. They then headed towards Apartment #1. Inside seven Israeli athletes were sleeping, but Yossef Gutfreund, his curiosity sparked, wandered into the communal lounge after being awakened by the sounds of people entering the building. Through sleep-laden eyes he saw the door to the apartment opening, and beyond, men with assault rifles. His stupor dissipated in a heartbeat. He instantly recognized them for what they were—terrorists. "Take cover boys," he shouted while simultaneously trying to slam the door shut with his body. Gutfreund, six-foot-three and 290 pounds, was a wrestling referee. His considerable frame and determination presented a formidable obstacle to the oncoming Palestinians. Gutfreund's desperate warning saved his roommate who woke up, saw what was happening, screamed to the others, and then dove out the window to freedom. But there was no time for organized resistance to form. The terrorists used the barrels of their rifles to wedge the door open. Within ten seconds, rifles blazing, they pushed their way into the room.

Immediately, the eight Palestinians fanned out and went from room to room to round up the remaining Israelis. Most stayed submissive while traveling their unwelcome cognitive journey from dreamland to harsh reality, but Moshe Weinberg fought back. Grabbing a knife, he slashed at the first terrorist that burst into his room but was shot by another. The bullet tore through his mouth and exited his skull.

The terrorists tied up the captured Israelis with pre-cut lengths of rope. Then, several of the Black September operatives went to Apartment #3 where they captured six more Israelis and forced them to join the others in Apartment #1. For some reason, they made no attempt to enter Apartment #2, where five other Israeli athletes slept, including the fencer, Dan Alon.

In 2012, forty years after witnessing the terrorist invasion, Alon spoke in Jackson Hole, Wyoming about the events of that day. His memories were clearly etched on his facial expressions while he spoke slowly and movingly from the Wort Hotel podium. His horror was Israel's horror, shared by all Israelis, Jews, and many others who heard the news when they woke up on the morning of September 5, 1972; memories of Nazi concentration camps closed fewer than three decades before were still profound. The sight of Jews once again singled out on German soil horrified them. Its impact on Israelis was no less than the impact the assassination of John F. Kennedy had on Americans that fateful day in November 1963.

Not all of the Israelis who were bound remained docile. American-born David Berger whispered, "Let's pounce on them! We have nothing to lose!" But his captors heard him and redoubled their guard. Another, the five-foot-four-inch wrestler, Gad Tsabari, broke for freedom. He shoved one of the terrorists aside as they led him down the steps from Apartment #3 and ran into the parking lot underneath the building. Another fired his rifle at Tsabari while giving chase. But the concrete support pillars rising from floor to ceiling that broke up his route to freedom offered protection too. Whether it was Tsabari's zigzag race for life or the obstacles that absorbed many of the bullets, it was not Tsabari's day to die. He escaped outside.

Then, once more, another Israeli captive fought back. Again it was Moshe Weinberg, who only a few moments earlier had been holding a scarf against his head to control the bleeding from the gunshot wound he had just sustained. Weinberg launched himself at another terrorist, tackling and then punching him. Weinberg's fists broke his target's jaw, sending his teeth flying. But his satisfaction was fleeting. Bullets from the other terrorists' guns tore into his body. He crashed to the floor, reduced to a bloody pulp of flesh, bereft of life.

The Black September operatives gathered the remaining Israelis together in an upstairs room. There, one more doomed, courageous Israeli tried to fight back. Yosef Romano lunged for one of the rifles. He successfully grasped one of the guns with his hands, but before he could make use of it more bullets flew, and his dead body slid to the floor.

Once things settled down within the apartment the terrorists turned to the next part of their mission. A little after 5:10 a.m. a German police officer approached the building with his hands raised. A two-page ultimatum fluttered down from a window above. A few minutes later a much more macabre sight greeted a second policeman that arrived on the scene; the Palestinians dumped Moshe Weinberg's naked bloody corpse at the feet of the Germans below.

The ultimatum contained a demand to release 234 terrorists held in Israeli jails and two in German prisons. One was Kozo Okamata, a Japanese Red Army member that participated in the massacre in May at Lod Airport near Tel Aviv. The two imprisoned in Germany were members of the Baader-Meinhof Gang that focused on domestic terror operations within Germany. The deadline was nine a.m. Their threat clear: "Free all those prisoners or all the hostages will die."

The Germans successfully played for time as morning droned on. Repeatedly, but with mounting suspicion, the terrorists agreed to extend their deadline while the German government searched desperately for a solution. Complying with the ultimatum was not an option. Israel's government had declared it would not release the terrorists in their jails to satisfy Black September's demands. Prime Minister Meir said, "If we should give in, then no Israeli anywhere in the world can feel his life is safe." The Germans rejected storming the building after the police studied the approaches to the apartment and determined they could not mount a successful assault.

Outside, people gathered and voyeuristically looked on from balconies, streets, and open grassy areas. Their deportment was more akin to viewers of a sporting event than an unfolding horror. Children roamed the village eating candy, couples hugged and caressed each other, and athletes took the opportunity to sunbathe.

Within the apartment complex at 31 Connolly Street, nine Israeli athletes remained alive. They were bound, frightened, menaced by guns pointed in their direction—and had bloody reminders of their friends' deaths in full view. It is inconceivable to think what must have been going through their minds, helplessly facing their likely demise while the innocent sounds of human beings at play filtered through the walls.

A stone's throw away from the hostages, the Olympic Games continued. Prime Minister Meir, burning with rage that the suffering of her athletes could be so trivialized, thundered, "It is inconceivable that Olympic competitions should continue while Israeli sportsmen are threatened with murder." Finally, and with great reluctance, Olympic Director Avery Brundage succumbed to mounting political pressure and moral indignation. That afternoon, he temporarily suspended the games.

German officials approached the terrorists once again at 11:45 a.m. They asked for another extension, this time falsely blaming Israel for needing time to gather cabinet ministers so that the government could obtain authority for release of its prisoners. The subterfuge gained another hour, but this time the terrorist leader warned that if there was no progress, two hostages would be executed. To emphasize the point he held up two fingers. Those watching thought he was displaying a "V" sign for victory—not realizing it was the meant to show the number of hostages marked for imminent death.

By having successfully strung the terrorists along, the Germans grew increasingly hopeful that they could resolve the crisis without further loss of life. But Meir was not so optimistic. She ordered an Israeli elite commando unit, the *Sayeret Matkal*, to prepare to fly to Germany. The unit specialized in rescuing hostages and counted among its leaders future Israeli Prime Minister, Ehud Barak. The Israelis pleaded with German Chancellor Willie Brandt to permit the unit to enter Germany and participate in the rescue of their countrymen. But the Germans, who had no police or military unit trained for, or with experience for, such a mission, refused to allow *Sayeret Matkal* into the country. It was not only a matter of German pride; it was a constitutional problem. The German

Constitution did not permit involvement of the Federal Government in what they deemed local problems. The German authorities told the Israelis, "[Our] security forces [will] handle the problem." The *Sayaret Matkal* remained grounded in Israel.

After several more hours filled with extensions and negotiations, the terrorists grew increasingly suspicious that Israel would never agree to their demands. Each excuse the Germans provided for Israel's delay served to heighten the captors' desperation. The terrorist leader stabbed his finger at one of the Germans at 4:35 p.m. when they met and shouted, "You're not going to trick us. You're trying to play around with us!" When the Germans began to respond to the accusation, the terrorist leader drew a cigarette, took a long pull, and then went back into the apartment building. Minutes later he returned with a new proposal. He demanded an airplane to fly his men and the hostages to Cairo, where, he threatened, if Israel did not release her prisoners as demanded, Black September would kill all of the hostages.

The German officials conferred privately for a few minutes and then returned. They told the terrorists they would only agree to the plan if they could see the Israeli captives first. The Palestinians responded by pushing one Israeli, Andre Spitzer, to a window and permitted him to speak with the Germans. The Germans asked him if everyone was okay. Spitzer tried to answer, his face drawn with tension. But when he began, "Everybody is okay except for one," he suddenly stopped after being struck in the back with the butt of a rifle by one of the hostage takers. After some audible mumbling in the background he began again, "All the hostages who survived the dawn attack are alive and in fair condition." Then the Palestinians pushed him away from the window and drew the curtain closed. Spitzer's wife, Ankie, watched the conversation from the television she was glued to in Holland. It was the last time she would see his face.

The stilted conversation did not satisfy the Germans. They demanded to see all of the hostages. The terrorist leader acquiesced, realizing that it was part of the puzzle he needed to piece together to accomplish his goals. He allowed two German representatives to enter the apartment where the Israeli athletes were held. Romano's body was lying on the floor with a gaping hole in his groin from gunshots. Bullet holes raked the walls, and blood stained the floor. The stench overwhelmed them. All nine living Israelis were bound. One German later said, "This picture of the room ... will stay with me as long as I live. I will never forget those faces, full of fear, and yet full of hope." After a short conversation, the terrorists hustled the Germans from the room.

Police commanders immediately debriefed the two upon their return to the crisis center. Because the German government had decided it would not permit Arab terrorists to leave Germany with Jewish hostages, their only alternative left was to plan a rescue. For those charged with executing the mission, it was crucial to determine the number of terrorists present; the two officials reported seeing four or five.

While planning continued, Chancellor Brandt hoped to play another card that might defuse the crisis. He tried to contact President Sadat in Egypt for help. But Sadat would not take his call. Instead, Brandt spoke with a lower-level Egyptian Minister who showed little interest in helping. Brandt later said, "I was flatly informed that Cairo wanted nothing to do with those people."

Eventually, the terrorists and the Germans agreed on a plan to transport the hostages and their captors to an airport by helicopter. The Germans hoped to ambush them somewhere along the nearly 200-yard walk from the apartment to where the helicopters would wait. Five sharpshooters positioned themselves along the way. But at the last minute the terrorists changed their minds. They insisted that, rather than walk, a bus must transport them to the helicopters. The sudden switch required a change in plans. The bus would shield the terrorists from attack. The sharpshooters quickly moved to the airport where they knew the terrorists would have to walk onto the tarmac to enter the airplane designated to take them to safety. Meanwhile, the Germans delayed the bus from reaching the apartment complex until the sharpshooters had an opportunity to reach their new positions within range of the runway.

Just after 10:00 p.m. the bus arrived in front of 31 Connolly Street. The Palestinians pushed the Israelis three at a time, blindfolded and bound, into the bus. After the vehicle completed its short journey, the terrorists shoved the Israelis into the waiting helicopters in front of thousands of bystanders thronging behind police barricades. The charged atmosphere more resembled a circus spectacle than a somber moment of madness. The terrorists cavorted as if they were heroes. Flashbulbs spewed light that captured images of shackled Jews trundling into the waiting helicopters as if they were animals being taken to slaughter. Zvi Zamir, head of Mossad, Israel's intelligence Service, said, "After the Holocaust … Jews once again walking tied on German land. It was something I'll never forget…"

But the Germans in charge of the rescue operation were not distracted by the revelry when the terrorists exited the bus. They were alarmed. They counted eight terrorists, not five. That was a problem because only five sharpshooters were present at the airport to take them down. But no time remained to develop a new plan and to position more sharpshooters. Moments later the helicopters took off. They hovered over a road that led towards the airport and then moved forward following its path. After a short time the road branched. The branch they followed led to the airport, the other to Dachau (a town near which the Nazis built Dachau concentration camp to imprison and exterminate Jews when Hitler ruled Germany).

The German plan to free the hostages at the airfield had two components. Both depended upon one or two of the terrorists exiting the helicopters and personally checking the Boeing 727 provided for their flight from Germany. Police waiting in ambush on the plane would capture or kill any terrorists inspecting the inside of the plane. The five sharpshooters then intended to shoot and kill the remaining three terrorists who would be visible to them through the helicopter windows. But the scheme did not account for the fact that there were three more terrorists than expected.

And then their plan quickly unraveled.

When the helicopters arrived at the airport, the tarmac was completely dark rather than flooded with light from spotlights as it should have been. In addition, the helicopters did not land where the sharpshooters had anticipated. As a result the pilots and one of the sharpshooters were in the line of fire of some of the others tasked with gunning down the terrorists. And to complicate things further, despite the terrorists' promises to the contrary, the four helicopter pilots were not permitted to immediately walk away. Suddenly, there were thirteen hostages instead of nine.

But far worse, the German plan had begun to crumble even before the helicopters arrived. The police had refused to set a trap in the jet airliner. They had pointed to the difficulty of hiding on the plane and the likelihood the terrorists would use their guns and grenades to defend themselves. The police then argued that, even if their officers were not shot in the anticipated melee, the thousands of gallons of fuel in the aircraft's tanks presented too great a risk of explosion. Therefore, they refused to fulfill their role in the plan.

Thus, when the two helicopters landed and one terrorist headed towards the waiting plane, less than half of the needed firepower was in place. Nor were any police hiding on the plane waiting to grab some of the hostage-takers while they were divided. The plan to free the Israelis had unraveled before it could be set in motion.

For some reason the terrorist leader sensed a trap while he was on the aircraft checking it out for flight. Perhaps his fears began when the helicopter flight took much longer than he had anticipated. Whatever the reason, he came running back to the others. His running, like the flight of a prey animal from a carnivore, set events in motion. The German Commander, believing he had no choice at that point, ordered his men to fire. But the shooting was not coordinated. Inexplicably, none of them had radios for communication. Therefore, only those within earshot started firing. And their firing was not accurate, perhaps because their rifles were not compatible with long-distance marksmanship. And to make matters worse, despite the darkened environs, none of them had infrared gun sights.

The fighting raged for more than an hour, during which the Germans never attempted a direct assault. Even so, the Israeli captives remained alive during that time. A bit later, a little after midnight, German armored cars arrived and began maneuvering towards the terrorists who were still fighting back. Only then did the terrorists appear to recognize that their struggle was coming to an end. One left his sheltered position and entered one of the helicopters. He fired his machine gun, killing three bound Israeli captives and wounding the other. He then threw a grenade into the cabin and leapt to the tarmac below moments before a massive explosion followed by flames enveloped the helicopter. Later, when the Germans searched the scene for the bodies of the hostages, only burned remains could be found. Another terrorist, perhaps inspired by his comrade, burst into the other helicopter. He sprayed bullets from his machine gun throughout. From their hiding places the Germans could hear the bound captives' screams.

At 12:30 a.m., almost two hours after the first shots broke out, quiet reigned over the field. The Germans took three terrorists prisoner. None of the Israelis had survived. The German police chief said that the spectacle caused him "a deep depression, which stays with you for the rest of your life … the rest of your life."

Perversely, an hour before the battle ended, at 11:30 p.m., false reports issued by some news media proclaimed that the hostages had been rescued and were fine. Rejoicing broke out in Israel. Relatives of the hostages, along with Israel's citizens and the Israeli government—including Gold Meir—felt a generous measure of relief.

But no hostages emerged from the shadows. It soon became apparent something was wrong. At 3:00 a.m. Meir received a call from Zamir in Germany. He informed her tersely that all the hostages were dead and that he had witnessed it himself. At 3:17 a.m. news media began issuing reports reversing the 11:30 pronouncement. Jim McCay, the American spokesmen for ABC television said in a downtrodden tone, "When I was a kid my father used to say our greatest hopes and our worst fears are seldom realized. Our worst fears have been realized tonight ... They're all gone."

The Aftermath

The next day, the Olympic Committee held a memorial service. Eleven seats were left empty to commemorate the dead Israeli athletes. But Olympic Chairman Brundage callously proved his lack of concern for the dead and their loved ones. Instead of focusing on the tragedy alone, he downplayed the horrific acts witnessed by the world. Insensitively he declared at the service that the Games had been held victim from two savage attacks, one by the terrorists, the other a political attempt to bar Rhodesia from the Games. He then stated, "The Games must go on ... We declare today a day of mourning and will continue all events one day later than originally scheduled."

Brundage's decision to continue the Olympics in the face of such barbaric acts was controversial for many, but defensible in the minds of some. It is for each person to determine in his own heart whether the moment required a public demonstration of disgust and vilification of terrorism, emphasized by canceling the games; and whether that need outweighed arguments that terrorism should not be permitted to overwhelm the dreams of so many who had sacrificed so much to prepare for the competitions. But indefensible was Brundage's linkage of the loss of eleven Jewish lives on German soil, singled out for their national origin, to a political protest by African nations. Millions were upset by the comparison, but not the Arab delegations, most of who had boycotted the memorial service. Perhaps the Saudi delegation's response to whether they intended to attend the memorial service expressed their beliefs best, "What service? What shootings?"

Within Israel, grief and anger were widespread. One editorial of a major Israeli newspaper said, "The time has come for a major stocktaking, settling the one and only account we have with the guerillas and the dispatchers." Meir "took it personally" and reacted swiftly. She established a new position entitled the "Prime Minister's Advisor on Counterterrorism." In addition, she charged a group of operatives with creating Committee X. Their task? Track down and kill any Black September operative directly or indirectly involved in the massacre. They made no plans for capture—only revenge.

On September 16, the IDF launched attacks into Lebanon that lasted more than twenty-four hours to root out Palestinian terrorists. That operation followed IAF strikes on September 8 against Palestinian terrorist targets in both Lebanon and Syria. When the UN Security Council discussed the ongoing violence, its debate was only about Israel's response to terrorism—not the tragedy Israel had just lived through and the need to prevent it from happening again. Thirteen nations supported a vote to condemn Israel's retaliatory attacks, but it did not pass because the United States vetoed the resolution.

Israeli preparations for revenge did not immediately prevent new terrorist plots from reaching fruition. On September 19, a terrorist letter bomb killed an Israeli diplomat in London. Within months terrorists sent more than fifty other letter bombs to Jewish targets in Europe. Soon, a covert war between terrorists and Israeli intelligence operatives flared throughout Europe.

Little more than a month later, two Palestinian terrorists hijacked a Lufthansa Boeing 727 jet. They demanded release of the three surviving Black September members from the Munich massacre. The Germans quickly agreed to their terms. Many Israelis and members of the German government believed the hijacking was an arranged sham. Black September had threatened Germany with a terrorist bombing campaign. It was all too convenient that within hours of the hijacking the terrorists that left such a supposed black mark on German honor were freed. Meir later admitted she "was literally physically sickened by their release." Any reluctance she might have harbored to track and kill those involved with the attack was now gone. She called her intelligence team into her office, looked them in the eye, sighed, and then uttered with complete conviction, "Send forth the boys."

Because of the location, public stage, and pure audacity of the attack, along with Germany's failure to both protect the athletes and respond to the terrorists competently, the Munich tragedy seared Gold Meir's consciousness forever. For Israelis and Jews everywhere it was a sharp reminder of their isolation: when it came to ensuring their safety; they could count on no one other than themselves. But, in truth, the lives of the eleven Israeli athletes had no more meaning than the lives of the thousands that fell victim to terrorism before them and the thousands that have fallen since. The athletes' suffering was no less poignant and no more worthy of remembrance than that of all other Jews who have fallen to Arab terrorism. Their story, however, is presented in detail because it must be remembered that shocks such as the Olympic massacre change minds, change perceptions, and could not help but change the calculus of Israel's leadership when their nation was faced with challenges from the Arab nations and pressure from the superpowers.

Within months, Meir faced new choices whether or not to bend to external pressures that risked Israel's existence. If there were times Israel may have seemed intransigent, much of the reason is rooted in Jewish blood having been wantonly shed by her enemies in Munich, shed in Hebron in 1929, shed by Nazis during World War II, shed in the convoys of 1948, and shed throughout the land from Israel's inception to the present. There is no escaping it. Israel's policies were, and always will continue to be, based on preserving her ability to ensure her survival—and to depend on no other.

CHAPTER FORTY-FIVE
Egypt Prepares for War

On September 6, 1972, Sadat sent Henry Kissinger a message. The Egyptian president was hoping that Kissinger would meet with his foreign minister, Ismail, and explained that he had expelled the Russians for Egyptian national purposes—not to please or displease anyone, but to pursue his own policy independent of the wishes of any other nation. He also hoped it would signal his desire to engage in discussions with the United States while simultaneously emphasizing his commitment to furthering Egypt's core interests. But Kissinger was not interested in immediate talks; his priority was the Vietnam War. He did not want to become embroiled in Middle East issues until after the American presidential election in November. In his vague response to Sadat's overture, Kissinger neither foreclosed the possibility of eventually meeting nor indicated any desire to meet immediately.

On September 8, just before Rosh Hashanah (a holiday that marks the beginning of a new year in the Jewish religion) began, Meir disclosed her view of the future in an interview. Still smarting from the Munich tragedy three days before, she declared that Israel required three things for her security: retention of the Golan, West Bank borders "with as few Arabs as possible" in accordance with the Allon plan or some other, and control of Sharm el-Sheikh along with a land connection to it stretching from Israel. She then said with regard to Egypt:

If I were an American, I would say: let Sadat stew in his own juice. Let him sit and reflect and take stock of himself and his world. And then, when he's finished contemplating and decides that he really wants to have done with war, then he has to sit down at the negotiating table.

Evolution of Israel's Policy in the Occupied Territories

The Labor party was still the dominant political party in Israel. But five years after the end of the 1967 War it had yet to agree on definitive guidelines for Israel's policy in the occupied territories. President Lyndon Johnson's question several years before, "What kind of Israel do you want?" remained unanswered.

In September 1972, 170 members of the Labor party, including Prime Minister Meir, gathered with the hope of answering how Jews and Arabs in the occupied territories should live together prior to a peace agreement. Conditions for a future peace treaty and establishment of definable borders were not part of the discussion. The Secretary General of the Labor party informed them that 160,000 Arabs were available for labor, of whom 50,000 or more were already working within Israel. The Minister of Finance, Pinchas Sapir, then warned that Arab labor was mostly confined to dirty work, and that a social, political, and moral danger was being created as a result, with the "dirty" work being relegated to the Arabs and the "clean" work to the Jews. Therefore, he cautioned, nobody should expect a surge of work opportunities for the Arabs to create an improved standard of Palestinian living which might rid the populace of nationalist aspirations. He ended his remarks with an admonition that Palestinians, if the occupied territories were included, would comprise almost 50% of the population of Israel by 1998 at current rates of birth, death, and immigration. Thus he warned, Israel faced the existential question whether to deny the Palestinians equal rights and make Israel no different than "countries whose names I don't even want to say in the same breath," or risk that Jews might become a minority in the Jewish homeland.

Shimon Peres, who at that time was politically allied with Dayan and had much less liberal views then than he would come to hold much later, accused Sapir of weakness. Peres predicted that Jews would come in large numbers from the Soviet Union, Europe, and the United States. As a result, Arabs could live in the Jewish State as a minority with equal rights in an expanded Israel. Peres then referred approvingly to the peaceful borders with Jordan across which "terror has almost stopped…. And all this is when Jerusalem is united, a Jewish neighborhood has been established in Hebron, and settlements have been established…" despite the lack of a peace treaty.

Unfortunately, but not surprisingly, the group could not agree on a future course that provided a solution to the growing problem. Instead, Israel's settlement and occupation policy would continue to be buffeted and twisted by events, politics, short-term needs, and messianic dreams.

Egypt Begins Preparations

Despite Sadat's protestations for achieving his goals peacefully, he prepared for war. He had no choice: 1971 had passed without action, 1972 was almost over, Israel seemed unlikely to bend to his will, and the expectations of the Egyptian people would not permit him to remain complacent much longer. And rubbing salt into growing Egyptian perception of his impotence, his people were enduring economic hardships that had no end in sight. Much of that suffering was due to the Suez Canal being closed and the cost of advanced weaponry purchased from the Russians. Sadat was simply running out of time.

On October 24, Sadat met with Egypt's highest ranking military officers at his home in Giza. A week earlier he had sent his Prime Minister to Russia to see if the Soviet Union would loosen its hold on offensive weapons. But the Russians again refused, even though they did agree to supply spare parts, tanks, and SAM-6 mobile batteries. The ice was beginning to thaw between Russia and Egypt, but much frost still divided them.

Sadat called for a limited war at the Giza meeting. He told the generals, "The 1967 defeat has made enemy and friend doubt that we would ever fight again.... I will not sit at a table with Israel while I am in such a humiliating position because that means surrender." Sadat was determined to liberate at least a smidgen of land on the east bank of the canal in hope of strengthening his hand in the negotiations that would follow. He said it was his goal to upset the balance that existed in the region in order to initiate a process that would lead to Israel's leaving the Sinai. But, to achieve that, he believed that it would require convincing Israel that the cost to her in men and material for staying put would be more than she was willing to bear. Therefore, Sadat argued, a limited attack was the necessary first step toward liberating the entire Sinai.

Many of the generals objected to Sadat's plan. They feared Israel's airpower would inflict devastating losses on the Egyptian army. Sadat responded, "We are confronted with a challenge. 'To be or not to be'. A partial solution has been presented to me [by the Americans].... But, I am not going to accept it. We will simply have to use our talents and our planning to compensate for our lack of equipment."

Egyptian Defense Minister and Commander of the armed forces, General Sadek, was not convinced. He vociferously argued that Egypt did not have the strength to hold Israel's response within limits that the Egyptian nation could absorb. He feared that Israel would resume the deep bombing raids that had devastated Egypt during the war of attrition. Sadat angrily responded to his skepticism and that of many of other generals, "You don't have to tell me what to do and what not to do.... Keep to your limits. You are a soldier, not a politician." Sadek apologized, but two days later Sadat forced him to resign and replaced him with a new chief of staff, General Saad el-Shazly.

Shazly had distinguished himself in the 1967 War in which he commanded the only Egyptian unit that crossed into Israeli territory. When Shazly received the general order to pull back, he successfully withdrew his unit and kept it intact throughout its retreat across the Sinai and over the Suez Canal despite attacks from Israeli planes. After the war, he carried out his duties with distinction and was recognized in the Egyptian army as a rising star. Shazly's only problem with being appointed chief of staff was that Sadat appointed General Ahmad Ismail to fulfill Sadek's second role as minister of war. Ismail and Shazli were much more enemies than friends. Both of them had to put aside their differences due to their shared responsibility for planning a dangerous military operation that matched Sadat's needs for a limited, but successful, war.

The name of the new attack plan they worked on was "*High Turrets.*" Its goal was to recover an approximately five-mile-wide band of land stretching east along the entire length of the canal. By holding the Egyptian army back from moving further inland, the land forces would stay under the protective range of Egyptian SAM emplacements and artillery located along the west bank of the canal. In essence, their plan called for the Egyptians to cross the canal en masse, inflict as many Israeli casualties as possible without unduly risking their forces, and then dig in under a missile shield that would deflect any attempts by Israeli planes to destroy them. The Egyptians considered Israel's hope of avoiding heavy casualties her greatest weakness. They thought that if the Egyptian army could establish a continuous line of dug-in infantry, with prodigious numbers of artillery tubes and anti-tank weaponry to support them, it would force an exhausted Israel, bled white from futilely trying to retake the lost ground, to agree to a ceasefire. Beginning in November, the Egyptians increased the pace of their maneuvers to train for their future attack. They preferred maneuvering openly so that the Israelis could observe them and become used to what they were doing. That way, when it became time for the attack, the Israelis would complacently think the mobilized Egyptian troops were just engaging in another military exercise.

The *High Turrets* plan replaced the old *Granite-2* plan. *Granite-2* incorporated a lunge for the mountain passes after crossing the canal. For the Egyptian army to penetrate into the heart of the Sinai and towards Israel's border, holding the passes was a pre-requisite. However, the passes ranged from nearly thirty to as many as sixty miles away from the canal. If Egyptian tanks and troops successfully penetrated that far, they would be exposed to aerial strikes from IAF warplanes, to which they had no answer. In addition, they would face the superior maneuverability of Israel's armored and infantry forces. The *High Turrets* plan played to Egypt's strength of numbers, especially in the opening days of the war when Israel might not have yet mobilized all of her reserves and missile defense. The *Granite-2* plan exposed Egypt's weaknesses. It risked a replay of the devastating Six-Day War outcome.

Sadat's political problem was Syria. He very much wanted, and needed, Syrian participation to succeed in a war with Israel. Sadat knew that a Syrian offensive along the Golan, an area much closer to Israel's populated heartland, would prevent the IDF from concentrating most of its strength against the Egyptian army. He also knew that Syria was rapidly re-arming with Russian help and that Russia had increased the number of her advisors in Syria. Furthermore, Sadat was aware that after Israel raided targets in Syria in retaliation for Munich, the Russians had increased both the quantity and the pace of SAM shipments to the Syrians. Therefore, he knew the Syrians were well on their way to be ready for war.

But Sadat had a problem. Assad would only participate if he believed the Egyptians were "all in." Otherwise, his smaller army, which shared the same weaknesses as the Egyptians', would risk destruction in the face of a focused IDF response. If the Syrians knew that the Egyptian plan only contemplated a short advance, and then to hold fast, they would never go to war. That was because an Egyptian halt would make it too easy for the Israelis to leave minimal forces in the south facing Egypt while using the majority of the IDF's power to destroy the Syrians. Sadat's answer to this dilemma was to lie. Syria would be told that *Granite-2* was the plan, but the Egyptian army would plan for *High Turrets*. If conditions later became favorable for *Granite-2*, plans could always be changed.

Ashraf Marwan, the presumed super spy for Israel, told the Israelis about Sadat's October 24 meeting with his generals in Giza. He also warned them that Egypt might attack in December and later disclosed Egypt's and Syria's plan to jointly launch an offensive. Previously he had leaked details of the *Granite-2* plan to the Israelis. But, out of either ignorance or intent, Marwan did not disclose the new *High Turrets* plan.

1972 Draws to an End

The year wound to a close with more diplomatic maneuvering that amounted to nothing.

On November 19, King Hussein and Prime Minister Meir met again. The king continued to push his plan for incorporating the Gaza Strip into "Greater Jordan." This time he requested that Meir consider permitting creation of a land corridor between Gaza and the West Bank for the Palestinians to use. Meir demurred. She suggested leaving that option for later stages of negotiations. Instead, she pressed Hussein to commit that the Jordanian army would never cross the Jordan River in the event that Israel went to war with Egypt or Syria. She also proposed a peace plan between Israel and Jordan in which, in addition to already-established settlements, only the unpopulated areas on the West Bank would remain in Jewish hands. Her proposal did not mention Jerusalem. That thorny issue remained to be dealt with. And the plan she proposed did not have the backing of her government. But she lost any motivation to seek authority from the ministers to formally propose her new idea when Hussein rejected her suggestion out of hand—even though it was better for Jordan than Allon's plan. Hussein had made clear during their meeting that he could never agree to significant border changes and expect support from the Arab world.

Meanwhile, over the last two months of the year numerous "battle days" between Syrian and Israeli forces along the Golan kept tension running high between the two countries. Syria invariably initiated the fighting—always in specific areas along the border between the Golan Plateau held by Israel and the Damascus Plain below. And always, the Syrians would incur significant losses. On November 21, during one such fight, the IAF shot down six Syrian MiG-21s, and the IDF destroyed numerous Syrian tanks and artillery emplacements. The attacks were dangerously annoying for the Israeli troops that thinly manned the border. But they bred confidence too; the few Israelis present with their limited equipment had no trouble throwing the Syrians back.

By December, Sadat realized that he had to do something to increase the quantity and quality of arms flowing from the Russians. He reached out to Moscow with an offer to extend the agreement which was coming to an end that gave the Soviets the right to use Egyptian naval bases for five years. His gesture bore fruit. Arms flow from the Soviet Union picked up, and in early 1973 increased numbers of defensive SAMs and offensive FROG ground-to-ground missiles, useful for striking deep into Israel's industrial heartland if Israel were to launch attacks against Egypt's infrastructure, began to arrive. Finally, Egypt was on the road to receiving the defensive missiles she needed and the offensive deterrent Sadat desired.

And, on December 18, the UN General Assembly passed Resolution 3034. The member nations had debated it for several months. The resolution expressed the need for international cooperation to bring international terrorism under control. But the third and fourth clauses gave Israel cause for great concern. The **third** *clause referred in part to "the inalienable right to self-determination and independence of all peoples under colonial and racist regimes and other forms of alien domination" and upheld those peoples' rights to struggle for liberation. The* **fourth** *clause denounced "the continuation of repressive and terrorist acts by colonial, racist, and alien regimes in denying peoples their legitimate right to self-determination and independence and other human rights and fundamental freedoms."*

Seventy-six nations supported the resolution; thirty-five voted against it and seventeen abstained. Many nations, including France, believed that the PLO's support of terrorism could not be separated from the cause and therefore voted in favor of it along with all Arab and most African nations. Others, including the United States, Israel, and many western and Latin nations voted against it. They objected because the tone of the resolution's denouncement of terrorism was too watered down by its emphasis on liberation and, by doing so, the resolution had morphed into a thinly veiled attempt to excuse Palestinian terror.

The truth was that Palestinians engaged in terror operations against Jews long before Israel was a state, and that they continued doing so for the nineteen years from Israel's independence until the 1967 war. That terror was directed at destroying a member state of the United Nations. Long suppressed by Jordan, Palestinian "liberation" idealists had rejected a state of their own in 1948 because that mean accepting Israel's existence. The Palestinians then lost another opportunity for self-government that they might have attained on the West Bank shortly after the 1967 war ended had they chosen to negotiate and explore possibilities instead of choosing violence to chase an impossible dream. Resolution 3034, which the U.N. passed while Jews were still living well within the emotional and political shadow of the Munich nightmare less than four months before, sent a strong reminder to Israelis of what they already well knew—they could only count on themselves.

CHAPTER FORTY-SIX
Preliminaries — 1973

The Year Begins

On the first day of the New Year, Henry Kissinger could look back on his major accomplishment of the previous year with pride—he had successfully orchestrated détente between Russia and the United States. The agreements America and Russia had forged were in large measure due to his prodigious effort to convince the leaders of both sides that they benefited more from cooperation than confrontation.

For the last two years the Russians had worried about their economy and about the Chinese. Détente provided a path for alleviating both concerns. The arms-reduction treaties that followed gave the Soviets an opportunity to reduce their spiraling defense costs. Détente also provided a foundation from which the Russians hoped that the Americans would grant the Soviet Union "Most Favored Nation" status which would facilitate trade between the two countries and bolster Russia's economy. And because China had been increasing her contacts with America, the Kremlin also recognized that improved relationships with the West would help the Soviet Union to focus her effort against the Chinese, especially should differences with their fellow communist behemoth explode into a full-fledged war.

Détente also alleviated concerns held by the United States. The fighting in Vietnam, Laos, and Cambodia, along with an unrestrained arms race, were open sores that not only sapped America's strength, but threatened mankind in general.

Also, European security, due to Europe's proximity to Russia's massive military, presented a problem that had no clear solution short of threatening use of nuclear weapons in difficult times. Therefore, since that would risk a devastating, nuclear war spanning the globe, America as well as Russia had much interest in perpetuating and strengthening détente.

But the Middle East stalemate still continued. More than four years after the 1967 War, the Arabs still refused to recognize the legitimacy of the Jewish State; and Israel still occupied Sinai, Gaza, the West Bank, and the Golan. Kissinger, however, still was in no rush. He continued to think that further delay played into the hands of both Israel and the United States. Further stalemate, he assumed, would drive Egypt towards America and, therefore, away from Russia, because only America could solve Sadat's problems with Israel. Kissinger also thought that the same dynamic would cause Arab intransigence to transition towards moderation. Thus, he thought, Israel would be able to negotiate a better deal if she waited for the political atmosphere to change. His strategy was bold and far-sighted, but contained much risk. What if Sadat no longer wanted to wait patiently for America's help? What if Sadat's domestic situation was such that time was running out?

Thus, nothing had changed between the Arabs and Israel. Egypt, Jordan, and Syria desperately wanted to recover their lost lands, but none of their leaders were then willing to do the one thing that would have created movement toward achieving their goals—publicly recognize Israel's right to exist without pre-condition; and without knowing with certainty before entering into negotiations what that would get them. In effect, Resolution 242, which had been approved in November 1967, had become a hindrance rather than a road map. Israel insisted on recognition as a pre-condition, the Arabs insisted on return of their lands as a pre-condition. The only crack in the Arab façade was Egypt's and Jordan's private suggestions that they might recognize Israel, in some form, and end their belligerency, but only if their lands were returned. But even then, the Egyptians and Jordanians were only willing to consider signing a full contractual peace once the Palestinian problem was resolved, and that did not seem likely.

Egypt faced the most internal pressure. Her economy was a wreck. The army had been mobilized since 1967, and some soldiers, including many university graduates, had been conscripted for several years with no hope of their servitude ending in sight. Partly as a result, the vast majority of her people lived in poverty with little hope for change. And meanwhile, as a constant reminder of the futility of their sacrifices, Israel still sat in the Sinai, an ongoing, humiliating reminder of their loss. Sadat sensed the unrest of his people.

Sadat hoped his eviction of the Soviets in 1972 would induce the America to get involved in 1973, even though she had not during the latter part of 1972. The rest of the Arab world would only accept an Egyptian agreement with Israel if it included complete return of the Sinai to Egyptian control. To achieve that, Sadat knew that he needed America to pressure Israel to acquiesce to his aims. However, he was disappointed and concerned with the lack of political movement over the last few months of 1972. Sadat feared that the price Egypt might pay for détente was an imposed superpower resolution not to his liking, or no superpower involvement at all because the United States and the Soviet Union did not want to jeopardize their improved relationship. And he could not remain in a state of "no war and no peace" forever without risking being deposed. Therefore, the Egyptian leader resolved he would not permit 1973 to pass without achieving tangible progress. He would actively plan a military solution but would simultaneously pursue a peace process. And there would be no more delay. The army would strike as soon as it was ready. He would only hold it back if a peaceful solution that met his needs was found first.

Both Israel's political and military leadership recognized there was a significant chance that Egypt and/or Syria would start a war with Israel to recover their lost lands, and possibly more. The question was when. Every six months Israeli military intelligence prepared an assessment of the likelihood that Egypt would renew hostilities in order to take back the Sinai. The estimate, approved by Eli Zeira in January 1973, stated the chance of war was farther away than ever before. The report's conclusion was heavily impacted by the "concept."

Dayan had appointed Eli Zeira as Director of Military Intelligence in October of 1972. Zeira was the leading proponent of the "concept." The "concept" was based on the fact that Egypt had no defense to Israeli air attacks against its rear-area infrastructure. Although Egypt had a sufficient number of SAMs to protect forces arrayed along the Suez Canal from air attacks, she did not have enough to prevent bombing raids on important economic and military targets deep within the country. Israeli planes had devastated those targets during the War of Attrition, and Zeira believed that Egypt would not risk them being struck again. The "concept" that resulted from that analysis contained three assumptions:

- Egypt would not start a war with Israel until her military had the ability to strike Israeli economic and military targets within the pre-1967 border in order to deter Israel from doing the same to Egypt.
- Egypt had no chance of achieving the ability to attack deep within Israel until 1975 at the earliest, and, even then, only if Russians supplied Egypt with appropriate equipment (advanced warplanes and/or sufficient numbers of capable ground-ground missiles).
- Syria was willing to fight Israel, but would not do so unless in concert with Egypt.

Much of the basis for the "concept" came from information provided by Dr. Ashraf Marwan. This supposed Israeli spy was a roving ambassador-trouble shooter for Nasser and then Sadat. He had provided many written Egyptian reports and summaries of communications between Egyptian and Russian leaders to Israeli intelligence. The documents painted a stark picture; Egypt wanted to go to war to recover her lost land but held back because of Israel's superior air force. However, Marwan never told the Israelis about the meeting Sadat held with his Generals on October 24, 1972. Thus, while the "concept" that pervaded Zeira's thinking may have accurately portrayed the thoughts of Egyptian military leaders at one point, it did not reflect Anwar Sadat's current thinking.

Israel's civilian leadership also did not think the chances of war were high and, therefore, were not prepared to water down their requirements for withdrawing from any territory. Meir said in her autobiography:

> Intransigent was to become my middle name. But neither Eshkol nor I, nor the overwhelming majority of Israelis, could make a secret of the fact that we

weren't at all interested in a 'settlement' that would win us compliments about being reasonable and intelligent but that would endanger our lives.

Dayan later described Meir as "a courageous, stubborn, determined women blessed by the Lord with the capacity to see the world in bold black and stark white, free from the range of twilight shades." Thus, since there was no political or military imperative that would motivate Israel to make significant withdrawals, consideration for that would wait until the Arabs were willing to publicly recognize Israel and agree to a contractual peace.

Israel's concern over the aggressive intentions of Egypt and Syria did not extend to Jordan. Secret contacts with Hussein had not generated a peace agreement, but they did foster a relationship with the king that made war between the two nations unlikely. In addition, Hussein was deeply appreciative of Israel's willingness to come to his aid in 1970. The threat the IDF had posed to the Syrian expeditionary force had bolstered both the king and his small army. Nothing that had happened since made it likely that Hussein would risk his soldiers and kingdom again as he had in 1967.

Amidst the backdrop of an uneasy "no war no peace" with Egypt, intermittent battle days with Syria along the Golan, and private accommodation with Jordan—the shadow war between Israel and the Palestinians continued into 1973. On January 9, a bomb exploded at the Jewish Agency in Paris; and, ten days later, terrorists attempted to sabotage Schonau castle in Austria. Schonau was a key transit point for Jews fleeing the Soviet Union, of which many ended up immigrating to Israel. Other terrorist attacks were foiled as well, including one in New York and several that employed letter bombs sent to targets throughout Europe. But tragically, others succeeded.

However, even if inertia on the diplomatic front did not impact Israel's security, it did impact Israeli domestic politics. 1973 would be the last year that settlements in the occupied territories were only a minor issue, instead of a barrier, for achieving peace. At the beginning of the year only 7,000 Israelis lived in the West Bank and Gaza. Therefore, an opportunity still existed for bordering Arab nations to recover most of their lost lands without Israel's having to face a significant domestic backlash caused by forcibly removing Jewish settlers. The Arab nations would only have had to ignore *their extremists and make an offer Israeli moderates could support. But Arab political courage and/or desire was lacking. Meanwhile, the number of Israelis that supported the siren call for settlements in the occupied territories continued to grow. Every day's delay made the next day more difficult to achieve peace than the last.*

On January 12, Dayan made an appearance on Israel's lone television station. "At the moment," he said, "there is no Arab State ready for peace with significant border changes. Thus, we must plan our lives in accord with the existing situation for a long period." Proposals for vacation resorts at Sharm el-Sheikh and for more settlements in the Sinai became commonplace. Slowly, but surely, barren parts of the conquered territories began to fill with Israelis who had religious fervor, a pioneering and patriotic spirit, or a strong emotional link to ancient lands that once again were under Jewish rule. It would not be long before those same forces set their sights on areas populated by Palestinians—areas with both recent and ancient links to the Jewish people.

Maneuvering and Remaining in Place

Kissinger was happy, or at least may have rationalized he was happy, that until late 1972, Nixon had given Rogers the lead for implementing American foreign policy in the Middle East. Since he did not believe negotiations should be rushed, Kissinger had accepted Rogers's primacy, safe in the knowledge that the secretary of state's efforts would probably go nowhere. But in 1973, Rogers was no longer the prime contact, and all of the interested parties knew it. That is why, on January 27, Sadat rejected another attempt by the State Department to restart talks leading towards an interim agreement. Sadat wanted to see what he could accomplish with Kissinger rather than Rogers.

For Kissinger, January 23 marked the day for what he viewed as one of his many triumphs. It was the date the ceasefire agreement was signed by the United States and North Vietnam. But that was not all that happened then. On that same day Kissinger initiated contact with Sadat's National Security Advisor Hafez Ismail. Kissinger felt Sadat had displayed patience, realizing that the U.S. would not make any definitive moves in his direction until Nixon had been reelected and the Vietnam negotiations were concluded. But Kissinger also knew Sadat's patience would quickly wear thin now that both reasons for delay had disappeared. Therefore, he agreed to meet Ismail secretly in the United States on February 25 and 26. Kissinger did not conceal his knowledge of the secret meeting from the Israelis, but neither he nor Nixon informed Secretary of State Rogers.

The day after Kissinger spoke to Ismail, he met with Israeli Ambassador Rabin in the map room of the White House. The two discussed strategy for the upcoming Kissinger-Ismail meeting and the approaching visit of Prime Minister Meir with President Nixon. The following day, Rabin met with Nixon. He told the president it was most important that Egypt realize she does not have a military option. He emphasized that only then would Egypt agree to a partial pullback in the Sinai that could lead to re-opening the Suez Canal. Later, Rabin cabled back to Meir, "[Nixon] will understand even if the Prime Minister is not able to bring anything new."

But, despite Kissinger's having agreed to meet with Ismail, as Sadat had previously decided, Egypt prepared for war. To further his plans, ministers from various Arab states met in Cairo. They appointed Egypt's War Minister Ismail Ali (a different man from Hafez Ismail) commander in chief of the Syrian, Jordanian, and Egyptian fronts. That announcement was mere window dressing. It mattered little because Syria fiercely maintained her independence, and Hussein would never again permit an Arab general from another country to command his troops. Nor would he permit the Fedayeen to be reintroduced into his country.

After his appointment, Ismail Ali traveled to Syria to discuss a joint war effort. He arrived shortly after publication of a new constitution had threatened Assad's rule. The unrest began because the new constitution did not require that the president of Syria be a Muslim, as all prior versions had. Assad was an Alawite, a sect that had similar but different religious beliefs from those of Sunni Muslims who comprised the majority of Syrians. As they did regarding Shiites Muslims, Sunni Muslims looked down on Alawites due to their religious differences. The problem was solved when a Shiite cleric issued a Fatwa that declared Alawites were Muslims.

Assad happily agreed with Ali to join with the Egyptians to wage war against Israel and hoped to recover the Golan in one quick lunge. But Assad bluntly told Egypt's war minister that Syria could not be ready by May, Sadat's targeted time period. Later, Sadat agreed to wait until October for war.

On February 6, King Hussein came to the United States and expressed concern that Egypt and Syria would soon launch a joint military action against Israel. Hussein predicted that the Russians would supply more arms to Egypt and Syria in order to maintain their relationship with the two countries. He did, however, make clear that he would not participate and stated that he hoped to ensure that diplomatic efforts would prevent any future war from breaking out.

Hussein also conveyed his frustration. He spoke of his desire to make peace with the Jewish State, and acknowledged that, while he wanted to recover lost lands, his army was too weak to fight Israel. Nor, he said, could he make the type of far-reaching concessions the Israelis demanded without endangering his throne. However, it was also clear that Israel could not afford, while still having to worry about Egypt and Syria, to make the deep concessions with Jordan that Hussein required. It would be too risky for the Jewish State to retreat to a long difficult-to-defend border facing Jordan while still having powerful enemies on its flanks. Kissinger suggested to Hussein that he should devise a new plan. But Hussein knew that his only alternative would be to collaborate with Sadat, and Sadat did not like him or want to be tied to him. Sadat's reason may have been personal, but he also had pragmatic ones. The Egyptian president knew that Hussein would never permit the PLO to gain power again inside Jordan, and Sadat needed the PLO's support for his own purposes. The irony is startling—in a sea of radical Arab monarchs, presidents, and sheikhs, the two most moderate leaders, leaders with the most to gain by finding peace with Israel, were not on speaking terms.

Two days after Hussein came to the United States, Hafez Ismail arrived in Moscow to meet with Brezhnev. They agreed that a partial Israeli pullback was unacceptable. And so the frosty relations between Russia and Egypt continued to thaw; Soviet armaments began to flow into Egypt in robust quantities.

Meanwhile, many Israelis in government still felt the status quo favored them. They believed the Arab world knew they could not resolve their problem with Israel by using force. Rabin expressed his view that détente between the superpowers was a good thing for Israel because neither party would want to get deeply involved in the Middle East dispute. He stated, "Small nations that are determined and able to fight for their positions will have more freedom of action." Another luminary, Zvi Zur, the assistant defense minister said, "It may take another five or six years before we arrive at some magic formula for an agreement with the Arabs, but in the meantime things aren't so bad in Israel from any point of view."

Dayan echoed the views of Rabin, Zur, and others. He stated, "With the borders we occupy today, in the short run there is no military threat—meaning that if they attack us, they will be defeated," and continued that, if Israel withdrew, peace might be achieved at first, but it would not last long. Dayan added:

> I think it is necessary to draw a new map of the State of Israel.... [I]f we really want to honor all the sovereign rights of the past and all the desires of every Arab in each period and every place, we won't be able to have a Jewish State here."

And further, Dayan said on February 2, "Pressures or no pressures, we're ensconced in Sinai, and that's that! If Egypt wants to talk to us, by all means let her do so...."

But while Israel was confident that the IDF would defeat anything the Arabs might try, the IDF knew it was crucial that it receive warning of an impending attack early enough to mobilize the reserves. That would give the civilian government the opportunity to head off a war with last minute diplomacy and to save the lives of many soldiers if diplomacy failed. The IDF, however, did not worry. It was confident it would receive sufficient warning.

Dayan's suggestion to draw a new map was certainly acceptable to some Israelis. On February 2, fifteen young couples gathered with other youthful singles in an apartment in Kiryat Arba. Their goal was to duplicate in Nablus, a populous Arab city on the West Bank, the fledgling Jewish settlement of Kiryat Arba, adjacent to Hebron, a city that also had a large Arab population. Nablus was located where the biblical city of Shechem once stood and where Jewish tradition holds that God promised Abraham that his descendants would settle the land. Israeli government policy had been to prevent settlement in the northern West Bank. Allon supported that policy, but Dayan and Shimon Peres were open to the idea. Slowly, the cracks in the wall preventing significant Jewish settlement in the West Bank multiplied and deepened. Soon, the wall would crumble.

CHAPTER FORTY-SEVEN
Two Israeli Successes and One Large Failure

During the early morning hours of February 17, four IDF helicopters loaded with specially trained personnel crossed the Gulf of Suez west of Suez City. They were on a highly secret mission critical to Israel's security. After landing, they labored the rest of the night to attach special listening devices to communication cables connected to the Egyptian army's ranking headquarters. The mission went forward without a hitch. By morning, Israeli intelligence had the technical means to listen to the Egyptian military's highest-level communications. To conserve the limited power available to run the equipment and limit the chance of being detected, the devices would only be activated in the event of an emergency. But they were there, ready to be used, as a precaution against any surprise attack. Or so the Israelis thought.

A few days later the IDF conducted a major raid against terrorist bases located in and around Tripoli, Lebanon. Simultaneously, soldiers attacked seven different targets successfully. The operation again proved that no terrorist base was safe from Israel's long arm. But the next day, Chief of Staff Elazar's euphoria over successful completion of the two operations in Egypt and Lebanon came to a crashing halt.

A Libyan civilian jet liner took off from Benghazi on its way to Cairo. The plane registered on Israeli radar when it crossed the ceasefire line and then flew deep into the Sinai. Since the Six-Day War, no other civilian plane had flown over the Sinai into what was known internationally as a closed military space. The Libyan plane was far to the east of its intended course. Rather than descending towards Cairo, it headed towards Dimona, Israel's secret nuclear site in the Negev.

The IAF send two *Phantom* fighter jets to intercept the aircraft and force it to land at an Israeli military airfield. Israeli intelligence had previously obtained information that warned of terrorist plots to blow up an airplane over Tel Aviv or crash one into a target in Israel (an eerie foretelling of the events on September 11, 2001). The IDF worried that the Libyan plane was part of that plot.

When the *Phantom*s rendezvoused with the civilian airliner they reported that the curtains were drawn on all the windows and no passengers could be seen. That increased Israeli concerns. The *Phantom* pilots then flew within yards of the plane's cockpit and signaled to the Libyan pilots to land. At first they seemed to comply; the plane began to descend and its landing gear dropped. Then it turned west at high speed and appeared to be trying to escape. Elazar's suspicions were heightened by the fact that Egypt's military had not re-acted earlier when the plane had crossed over its closed military space. Therefore, he was determined not to let it get away and ordered it shot down.

Elazar's decision had grievous results; 113 civilians were on board. Only five, including the co-pilot, survived the crash. The plane had lost its way due to a sandstorm that required the pilots to rely on instrumentation. The co-pilot later stated that he and the pilot were aware that the Israelis were signaling them to land, but because of the state of relations between Israel and Libya, they thought it better to flee.

Once again, the world condemned Israel for its actions. Henry Kissinger told Ambassador Rabin, "I am glad to hear that your military are just as stupid as ours." Rabin responded that Israel had made a serious error.

However, if viewed through the context of September 11, 2001, perhaps Israel's actions were not so plainly wrong. After two jets plowed into the World Trade Center and another into the Pentagon, Vice President Cheney issued orders to shoot down any other civilian jets acting suspiciously. If the passengers of US Air 91 had not taken matters into their own hands causing it to crash, it may well have been shot down by American fighter jets. If the American military could shoot down its own civilian aircraft to ward off potential terrorist acts that would cost more lives, should Israel be criticized for its resolve to do the same to a foreign aircraft from a nation with a virulent anti-Israeli leadership? Did the fact that the plane had turned away make a difference?

Elazar felt badly but didn't second guess his decision. Meir told him several days later, "I don't just appreciate you. I admire you. And I don't just believe in you. I have full confidence in you."

CHAPTER FORTY-EIGHT
Hafez Ismail Comes to Washington

In the early days of 1973, Sadat was still angry that the United States and Secretary of State Rogers had not "deliver[ed]" Israel the previous year. But his two-pronged strategy required giving America another chance while also preparing for war.

*Three things are now clear in retrospect but were largely unknown in 1973. **First**, Sadat would not allow the year to pass without making significant progress towards recovering all of the Sinai. **Second**, if diplomacy did not yield recovery of the Sinai, Sadat's alternative plan for war was to launch a surprise attack on Israel to achieve his goal. His innovation was to limit his aim to retaking a small sliver of territory and use that success as a wedge to force open the diplomatic process. **Third**, he was willing to cancel the attack if, and only if, diplomacy delivered significant progress towards recovering the Sinai before his army was ready to strike. After his war minister consulted the Syrians and he received input from the Egyptian military, Sadat set the deadline for attacking to September or early October. Thus, two "concepts" hurtled towards a climactic clash: Israel's concept that the Egyptians would not start a war without the means to deter Israel from responding with strategic strikes, and Sadat's concept to use a war with limited goals as a tool for his diplomacy.*

Ismail Meets with Nixon

Foreign Minister Ismail led Sadat's last-ditch effort to use diplomacy to recover the Sinai. Egypt and the United States agreed that Ismail would meet with Nixon and Rogers on February 23, and then, two days later, secretly with Kissinger.

Nixon was predisposed to pushing Israel hard to reach an agreement. He had told Kissinger shortly after his re-election in November 1972:

> Henry, the time has now come that we've got to squeeze the old woman [Meir]. I am determined to bite this bullet and do it now because we can't let the thing ride and have a hundred million Arabs hating us and providing a fishing ground not only for radicals but, of course, for the Soviets.

However, Kissinger continued to resist his boss. He calculated it would be better to delay negotiations until after Israel's elections, in October 1973, when he believed the Israelis would be more flexible and the Egyptians more desperate. To further his plans he would rely on his mastery of oratorical obfuscation.

When Kissinger met with Rabin to discuss Ismail's upcoming visit, he asked the Israeli Ambassador, "Is it worth my while to become a central figure in dealing with the Middle East?" Rabin answered, "[You] must not undertake the responsibility for achieving a political solution. Nonetheless, it would be more than essential, perhaps fateful for Israel."

Rabin continued that Kissinger must take the lead in American policy because Kissinger understood that Sadat would be deterred from starting a war by an Israel kept strong with American arms. Kissinger responded reassuringly, saying he would tell Ismail that, having just returned from the Far East, he was not yet sufficiently familiar with Middle East issues. Therefore, he would use their talks to listen and learn. If Ismail put forward new ideas, Kissinger said that, rather than respond directly to them, he would tell Ismail that he would need time to study them. Further, he said he would warn Ismail that the situation would not change overnight. Vietnam had taken four years, and he would not succumb to any pressure to act before he was ready. However, neither Kissinger nor Rabin had any inkling that Sadat's clock was ticking.

Ismail arrived at the White House during the late morning of February 23. His meeting with Nixon lasted for an hour. Ismail told Nixon that he did not understand why the United States permitted Israel to continue to hold Egyptian land and implored the president to adopt a more evenhanded policy. Then, in hope of signaling reasonableness, he told Nixon that, if Israel withdrew from the Sinai, Cairo would discuss both security guarantees and an agreement to end the state of belligerency between Israel and Egypt. However, he still clung to Egypt's stance that the Palestinian problem was a core issue. Therefore, Egypt would not enter into a formal peace treaty with Israel unless the Palestinians resolved their issues with Israel. That, in effect, meant that a formal peace treaty would be captive to Palestinian approval—an impossible condition for Israel to accept. Ironically, despite Assad's willingness to join Sadat in attacking the Jewish State, Ismail did not make Assad's major goal—the return of the Golan Heights—an issue.

Nixon dominated the conversation with Ismail as their meeting came to a close. He did not promise a speedy resolution but indicated he hoped that serious discussions would ensue. Nixon then outlined the framework for those future discussions. He told Ismail that there would be two tracks—a public one with the State Department and a private one with Kissinger. He also encouraged Ismail to speak frankly with Kissinger during their upcoming, two-day, secret meeting and to agree on long-term goals that would entice Israel into a phased settlement. "Let us see," Nixon said, "whether in that format whether we can find some way to help. I don't want to indicate that I have a solution … but the only way to find out is to have a frank discussion." Nixon concluded with a warning to Ismail that, despite Egypt's fear that an interim solution might become a final one—one that did not return all of the Sinai—little else seemed possible at the time. "We must do some walking," he said, "before we run."

After his discussions with Nixon, Ismail headed to the State Department for a two hour meeting with Rogers. Ismail knew their talks would be meaningless but were necessary for public consumption. Rogers did not. The secretary of state had no knowledge of Ismail's forthcoming two-day meeting with Kissinger, nor did Ismail inform him.

While Ismail was with Rogers, Nixon and Kissinger spoke about the upcoming secret meeting. Nixon's attitude, despite his neutral tone with Ismail, had not changed since having previously told Kissinger, "We've got to take a very strong line with the Israelis ... we cannot let Mrs. Meir come here and take the same hard-nose line about the election. That's all done now. Right now, this is going to be settled," and also:

> The time has come to quit pandering to Israel's intransigent position. Our actions over the past have led [Israel] to think we will stand with them regardless of how unreasonable they are.... You know my position of standing firmly with Israel has been based on broader issues than just Israel's survival. Those issues now strongly argue for movement toward a settlement, this is the time to get moving.

One of the "issues" Nixon alluded to was oil. Saudi Arabia's King Faisal had begun to speak publicly about using oil as leverage to force Israel to withdraw. Domestic production of American oil had lessened, and global demand, including that of the United States, for Arab oil was increasing. Oil prices were going up, and oil companies were becoming concerned about the stability of the Middle East. The possibility of the Arab-Israeli confrontation inspiring an oil crisis loomed on the horizon.

Ismail Meets with Kissinger

The Central Intelligence Agency (CIA) handled the details of the Kissinger-Ismail meeting. The agency chose to hold the conference at the stately home of Donald Kendall, the CEO of Pepsi. Kendall supported Nixon in the 1972 elections and was a strong advocate of improving U.S.-Egyptian relations. Woods surrounded Kendall's home in the town of Armonk, a suburb of New York City. It was the perfect location for a clandestine meeting in comfortable surroundings.

On February 25, the participants arrived in two groups. First came Kissinger, along with his secretary and two aides from his National Security staff. Next, Ismail's group of five entered the grounds. Ismail was tall, thin, and had a full head of greying hair. He had risen to his position as a principal advisor to Sadat more due to his education, reputation for honesty, and long service to the government than on a quick and flexible intelligence. Ismail was noticeably courteous, more comfortable with explaining a prepared position than engaging in back and forth repartee.

Kissinger and Ismail spent the first few minutes sitting by a fireplace in the living room while getting to know each other. They then moved to the dining room for more formal talks. During their opening discussions, Kissinger emphasized that the secret channel with him would parallel the more public talks with the State Department but might contain different content. He also told Ismail that the process could not move quickly because he had not had an opportunity to sufficiently prepare any new ideas, and that he was only there to listen. Kissinger then referenced his busy schedule but emphasized he had found time to start the discussions, rather than delay them, because of the importance he attributed to them. Of course, that was a diplomatic white lie; Kissinger was very prepared but was enacting his strategy of delay.

Kissinger then tried to reassure Ismail that their meeting had much value by suggesting that, at subsequent meetings, they could further discuss the ideas discussed during their two days together. He also suggested that their next secret meeting could be held in Europe when other matters provided cover for his being there. Kissinger then delivered a bombshell. He expressed concern that it would be difficult to achieve anything with Israel until after the Israeli elections in October. Finally, Kissinger delivered one of his trademark lines that he used in negotiations. He stated that he would only get further involved in resolving the dispute if he thought there was a real opportunity to reach a solution, and he would not promise anything that he could not deliver. "Otherwise," Kissinger said:

> we will just be buying ourselves three months of good will, and great distrust afterwards. You must have a sense that when you deal with the White House our word counts. I would rather tell you honestly that we can't do something than to tell you something we can do and later we would not deliver.

Since he did not know at this point the limits to which Israel would go, Kissinger told Ismail there was no value at present to refer to maps. Instead, they should speak in general principles. Kissinger concluded his opening remarks by offering Ismail coffee. The foreign minister of Egypt preferred tea.

Ismail responded to Kissinger's oration by presenting what amounted to a five-point proposal and indicated where Egypt might have some flexibility.

First, Ismail told Kissinger that Sadat knew the issues between Israel and Egypt must be dealt with separately from the issues between Israel and the rest of the Arab world. He said Sadat would try to maintain his standing with the other Arab nations by presenting his agreement with Israel as a model for others. Therefore, Sadat did not intend to raise Syria's issues with the Golan Heights or Palestinian and Jordanian issues concerning the West Bank. Ismail also made an effort to assure Kissinger that those matters would not interfere with resolving Egypt's issues with Israel and recognition of the Jewish State. However, he was not reassuring about East Jerusalem. Ismail demanded that it be returned to Arab control.

Second, Ismail indicated that Sadat understood Israel's security concerns. He assured Kissinger that Egypt would demonstrate flexibility regarding instituting demilitarized zones, provided they were on both sides of the border. He also said that Egypt would consent to a continued Israeli presence at Sharm el-Sheikh and some other key points in the Sinai during stages of a complete withdrawal—but would not agree to an interim agreement that was not part of an overall deal (Kissinger well knew that demilitarized zones extending into Israel were a non-starter. Since 1956, Israel had categorically refused any such zones in Israel because the danger emanated from Egypt, not them. However, he remained silent as Ismail continued).

Third, Ismail assured Kissinger that an agreement would include recognition of Israel. Ismail defined recognition to include freedom of navigation of the Suez Canal and the Straits of Tiran. He declared that, after an agreement, Egypt would not partake in anymore negative propaganda and boycotts, would make a concerted effort to stop terrorist activity emanating from Egypt, would not claim Gaza, and would accept increased contacts between the two nations. But, Ismail also emphasized, recognition did not include full normalization of relations and an exchange of ambassadors. That would only come once Israel made similar agreements with her other Arab neighbors—thus, the Egyptian offer fell short of Israel's minimum demand. It was an offer to move towards regular relations, but that goal would remain hostage to Israel satisfying her other Arab neighbors. Nevertheless, Kissinger saw opportunity where he knew Israel would see a closed door. Kissinger believed the absence of normal relations in Egypt's offer gave Israel an opening to insist on maintaining much more of a physical presence in the Sinai than Egypt might otherwise be willing to permit.

Ismail's **fourth** requirement was that talks should continue exclusively between the United States and Egypt until an agreement of principles had been reached. Only then should the Israelis be brought into the discussions. In essence, the Egyptians wanted to foreclose Israeli involvement and avoid direct discussions until it was too late for Jerusalem to change America's position. By doing so, the Egyptians would neatly sidestep Israel's fundamental demand—that if Arab nations wanted peace and return of their lands, then they would have to speak directly with Israel.

Ismail's **fifth** point was perhaps the most crucial and most subtle. Ismail emphasized three times that progress could not wait for Israel's elections in October. He said, "We think before the first of September we should have the preliminary phase agreed." Ismail then doubled down on the target date when he stated:

> The principles of the agreement could be formulated until the end of May. The details for a comprehensive settlement could be discussed until September, 1973, and Israel had to make its partial withdrawal from the Suez Canal by then.

Of course, Ismail did not say why September was so important, or what would happen if that date passed without substantial progress.

Besides Egypt's willingness to enter into a separate final deal with Israel, Kissinger heard little that was new in Ismail's presentation. And he recognized the central problem: When, if ever, would the relationship between Israel and Egypt be no different than the normal diplomatic relationship between nations? Ismail admitted, "It will be sometime before Madame Meir can come to Egypt to shop." Kissinger, seeking an answer to the dilemma he saw, pressed Ismail to explain what Egypt had really meant by saying it was willing to recognize Israel if they reached an agreement. Ismail responded that Egypt's agreement to Resolution 242 implicitly recognized Israel. Kissinger answered, "But you are not recognizing Israel as a state." He then continued, "If we are candid with each other—the genius and the disaster of [the] Resolution is its vagueness."

Kissinger and Ismail continued to debate until an exasperated Kissinger exclaimed that Egypt was the defeated side and ought not to "make demands acceptable only from victors." But Kissinger's remarks did not make any impression on Ismail. Instead of bowing to pressure to soften Egypt's demands, Ismail responded that Kissinger needed to personally push the Israelis to make more concessions.

The two men met for a total of twelve hours over the two days. Kissinger knew that there would only be rapid progress if Egypt offered full recognition in return for full withdrawal. Anything short of that would require slow torturous negotiation and concessions from both sides that could never be finished, and probably not even begun, before the Israeli elections in October. The deal Egypt offered contained too many qualifications to be acceptable to the Israelis. In essence, Kissinger said later, "Ismail had come less to discuss mediation—and therefore compromise—than to put forward a polite ultimatum for terms beyond our capacity to fill." Therefore, Kissinger devoted most of the second day to further deflating Ismail's hopes that progress would be quick.

Nevertheless, despite their failure to reach an agreement, the two men did not part on unfriendly terms. They agreed to meet again April 10, to exchange correspondence before the next meeting, and to keep their talks secret. Ismail also agreed Egypt would not provide much detail of the discussions to the Russians, and Kissinger agreed not to update Israel on the contents of the talks. Both broke their promises. Kissinger promptly divulged to the Israelis everything said in Armonk, and Sadat broke Ismail's pledge to keep the talks secret when he granted *Newsweek* an interview and said that the Americans refused to push the Israelis to make concessions.

Still, Kissinger was happy with the results of their meeting. He thought he had succeeded in holding the Egyptians off and was pleased the Egyptians had indicated willingness to reach an individual agreement with Israel separate from any other Arab nation. Kissinger also believed he had identified an opportunity that might form the basis for future negotiations, and was confident, given time, that he could move Egypt closer to satisfying Israel's basic requirements. He was confident because he had divined that Egypt's bottom line was sovereignty over all of the Sinai; Israel's was security. That opened the door to satisfying the needs of both countries. What if Egypt received sovereignty relatively early in the process, but Israel maintained security control of selected areas for an extended transitional period? Ismail had shown some interest in the idea, but had made no commitment.

Sadat, however, did not share Kissinger's happiness regarding the meeting results. In fact, he was bitterly unhappy. Sadat had expected a new offer from Kissinger that reflected knowledge gained from the last five years of failed peacemaking. He had hoped the offer would be one he could sell to his government and people. Instead, all he received was a pronouncement of further delay.

On February 27, Sadat held a three-hour meeting of more than one hundred Egyptian media personalities and other individuals who shaped public opinion. He told them Egypt's choice was capitulation or war in 1973. He then said, "I am not the right man for capitulation. The decision therefore has been made and it is something unavoidable … we will defeat the Zionists in a third war." But Sadat clarified that he regarded war as only one of the tools in his tool belt. He assured them he would prepare for both the "unavoidable battle" and the diplomacy that would be required, "before, during, and after the battle."

At 8:30 p.m. on February 26, Kissinger returned to the White House to brief Nixon regarding his meeting with Ismail. Kissinger recommended that Nixon empower the State Department to pursue an interim agreement under his (Kissinger's) direction while he labored in the secret channel to achieve a full agreement. Kissinger also attempted to pull Nixon away from his predisposition to pressure the Israelis. He told the president, "To threaten to cut off aid to Israel is—we could do it, but such action would lead to an uproar." But Nixon was clearly impatient. He told Kissinger, that if the Israelis agreed to anything, then "we've got to tell 'em we're not squeezing them, and then squeeze 'em."

CHAPTER FORTY-NINE
Meetings with Hussein and Meir

King Hussein

On February 27, just one day after saying goodbye to Ismail, Kissinger met with King Hussein. Hussein objected to Sadat unilaterally entering into a peace agreement deal with Israel. He knew that, if Israel had a deal in place with Egypt, it would become much more difficult for him to achieve a satisfactory outcome for his negotiations with Israel. Their conversation then moved to Hussein's issues, at which point Kissinger asked the king if he had any new ideas.

Hussein responded by indicating willingness to negotiate directly with Israel. He advised that he would permit Israel to keep troops, and even settlements, in enclaves along the Jordan River as part of any peace plan. Hussein also agreed to permit settlements already in existence to remain intact and that Jews with residences in Hebron, Nablus, and the Old City of Jerusalem could keep them. But he insisted that all of that territory, including where the settlements and residences were, must come under Jordanian sovereignty and control.

In addition, Hussein said he would be amenable to making border changes on the West Bank that favored Israel, but only if he obtained sovereignty over Gaza. With America's help, Hussein said he would also build an overpass road that would cross Israeli land to connect Gaza and the West Bank. The king emphasized, however, that his ideas could succeed only if they were portrayed as an American plan rather than a Jordanian one. And he warned, if there was no diplomatic movement he believed there would be an explosion within two-to-three years. Kissinger responded that he thought Hussein's ideas were fair. Kissinger did not say that everything would have to wait until after Israel's elections in October. And he never pursued Hussein's proposal.

After meeting with Hussein, Kissinger met with Rabin. To some extent they rehashed the conversation they had had by phone after Kissinger's briefing of Nixon the night before. And they arranged a follow-up meeting to coordinate the upcoming meeting of Meir and Nixon. But, before Rabin and Kissinger would meet again, an important decision needed to be made in Israel. To help her, Meir discussed the matter with Zvi Zamir. The issue was whether or not to provide the Americans with intelligence received from their secret agent, the Egyptian, Ashraf Marwan. Zamir had been the head of Mossad, Israel's secret intelligence service, since 1968. He was born in Poland, joined the Palmach in 1946, and commanded a brigade responsible for supplying and defending the Etzion Bloc before it fell in 1948. Later he headed Israel's Southern Command and held diplomatic positions at various posts, including one in England. Zamir was against sharing the intelligence with Americans; he feared doing so risked exposing Marwan.

Meir overruled Zamir. She thought Marwan's information proved that the Egyptians were using the Americans to shield them while preparing for war. One of the documents that Marwan had provided and that Meir ordered turned over to the Americans, was a report from Ismail to Sadat summarizing his meetings in Moscow. Another document she gave the Americans was a letter from Brezhnev with several interesting revelations. **One** committed Russia to supplying advanced MiG-23 fighter jets and SCUD missiles to Egypt. The advanced MiGs would give

Egypt a better chance of achieving air superiority, and the SCUDs could be used to attack Israel's heartland. Both were Egyptian prerequisites, according to Israel's "concept," that needed to be fulfilled before Egypt would consider attacking Israel. The Russian letter also contained **two other items**: a warning to Sadat that Egypt should not start a war without first coordinating it with the Soviet Union, and a discussion concerning the feasibility of limiting Arab oil exports as an economic weapon for furthering Arab political purposes. **Finally**, it also contained a statement that the Soviet Union did not oppose the supposedly secret talks between Ismail and Kissinger. That detail suggested Ismail had ignored his promise to not give the Russians full details of their meeting

The letter did not surprise Kissinger. Two days before his meeting with Rabin, the Soviets had informed him that Egypt was preparing for war, as an alternative, if talks did not work. The truth was that the Russians did not want the Arabs to attack Israel. They feared a confrontation that would risk détente and feared Russia would again be humiliated if, and when, Western weapons trumped their own.

Kissinger responded to the letter Rabin handed over by teasing him that Egypt was now America's friend. But behind the teasing, Rabin saw danger. Rabin thought the Egyptians were merely currying America's favor as a prelude to war, but he also recognized the telltale signs that the United States was developing a new relationship with the Egyptians.

And Rabin did not accept Kissinger's assertions that Ismail had offered something new, despite Kissinger's attempt to cast a promising light on his meeting with the Egyptian envoy. Rabin first received a written summary of the Kissinger-Ismail meeting two hours before he met with Kissinger. After reviewing it, he told Kissinger when they spoke, "There is nothing new here." To which Kissinger responded, "For me there is something new." Kissinger explained that the distinction Egypt made between a state of peace and the normalization of relations presented an opportunity. Because Sadat would not agree to normalize relations until some indeterminate time in the future, he argued the door was left open for Israel to demand that the IDF maintain a long term presence in the Sinai at sensitive positions crucial to Israel's security, positions especially critical if normalization broke down and war threatened. But Rabin recognized that to walk through the door Sadat held open, the Israelis would have to relinquish the entire Sinai. That was something Israel was not willing to do.

The discussion between the two men then turned to the posture Meir should take when she met Nixon. Kissinger advised that she should convey willingness to agree to a partial settlement in order to buy Israel time. By doing so, the secret channel could continue, and the Soviets would be kept out of the negotiations.

However, for no apparent reason, throughout his face-to-face discussions with Rabin, and in their telephone conversation the day before, Kissinger artfully left out one detail. He never mentioned that King Hussein had come to Washington, D.C. for an update on the Ismail meetings. In diplomacy there is never complete transparency.

Meir

The next day, Rabin hosted a meeting at his home. Meir and Kissinger were present, along with Simcha Dinitz, whom Meir had appointed to soon replace Rabin as the new Israeli Ambassador to the United States. Kissinger well knew Meir's goals: maintain the flow of economic and military aid and continue the status quo, at least until the elections. "We never had it so good," Meir believed at the moment.

Kissinger recognized that discussions with Meir would be difficult. For a pioneer such as she, returning territory would be painful, especially because the increasingly long period that Israel had controlled the occupied territories had made it more difficult politically and emotionally for her to conceive giving them up (and would even more so for Israel in the future as the occupation continued). Kissinger also knew Meir would skillfully express herself and would push hard for direct negotiations with the Arabs and ironclad guarantees of security in return for any pullback. Meir ridiculed those who were more moderate than she and who advocated a withdrawal without direct negotiations. She felt strongly that if she reluctantly agreed to Arab demands without obtaining full normalization of relations and unqualified recognition for her country it would risk Israel's eventual destruction. For her, there was no middle ground when the Jewish State's existence was in question.

After the meeting started, Rabin sensed that America's resolve to delay the peace process was softening, even though Kissinger had again committed before his talks with Ismail to not actively seek a solution before Israel's elections. It was an important commitment, because Meir would not be able to face, or appease, domestic critics of a peace deal without roiling the political process during the run-up to elections. Therefore, Rabin asked Kissinger why he would consider changing their 1971 agreement to delay negotiations. Meir made a demand linked to Rabin's question. She insisted that the Americans keep their promise not to pressure Israel to withdraw from the Sinai until after the October elections. Kissinger responded, "In the talks with Ismail, I can apply my regular delaying tactics." But he recommended not doing so. Kissinger told them what he had already told Rabin privately: Sadat had left an opportune opening between normalization and a state of peace. Kissinger continued that Ismail had requested a paper specifically outlining Israel's security needs and then said, "It is possible to get changes in the Egyptian position, but again, I would only try if you and I agree."

Meir wasted no time in rejecting Kissinger's notion. Where Kissinger saw an opportunity, Meir saw subterfuge. For her it was a repeat of 1957 when the IDF, due to pressure from President Eisenhower, withdrew from the Sinai in return for an agreement with the Egyptians that brought peace but not normalization. Ten years later there was another war as a result. "The trouble with Egypt," she began, "is they want to end before they begin." Meir continued, "It is simply incredible, the Egyptians behave as if they had won the war and as if their troops were staying in Petah Tikvah for the last six years. There is no realism. Do we really have to take all this?"

When Kissinger responded that he believed the Egyptians would demonstrate more flexibility, Meir answered, "I can see no flexibility whatsoever." She saw Sadat's offer as a disingenuous ploy to recover what Egypt had lost.

Kissinger then tried a different tactic. He confided to Meir that they were likely to get more by dealing with the Egyptians through his secret channel than if he failed and they had to deal with the Russians in a different forum. Kissinger's argument was a calculated plea in keeping with his strategic plan to stop Russian involvement and keep him as the lead interlocutor between the parties. His strategy served American interests because it reduced the risk of a major confrontation with the Soviets.

But again, Meir was not convinced. She responded, "I ask you: Should Israel voluntarily put itself in a more difficult, or even fatal, position?"

Kissinger then realized he could not change Meir's mind. Therefore, he warned her that Nixon would not accept the status quo without a plan; the president required a vision for resolving the debacle. Kissinger said she needed to be prepared to respond to questions about future strategy and asked which of the following choices she preferred:

- A complete standstill that would be unacceptable to Nixon;
- Discussions with the Egyptians; or
- Discussions with the Russians.

"The trouble is that they do not want us there," Meir responded. "Whatever they will sign, tomorrow they will go on trying to get us out." Nevertheless, she indicated that she understood the predicament and was willing to begin discussions of an interim agreement as long as it would not lead to a peace agreement that failed to include full Arab recognition of Israel.

Later that day, Meir met with other branches of the American government, including the State Department. What she heard in those meetings reinforced her fear that Israel faced a risk that the United States would become less sympathetic to Israel's plight and increasingly hostile to Israel's negotiating position. She was correct. Unbeknownst to her, Nixon had suggested to Kissinger that same day that they should consider increasing the pressure on Meir by again halting the orderly flow of warplanes he had previously agreed to supply. Once again Kissinger objected to that tactic, saying if Israel felt weaker she would be less flexible, not more. Nixon responded that supplying warplanes had not worked so far, implicitly suggesting that it might be time to move in a different direction.

Rabin and Kissinger met again at 7:30 p.m., but, before that, a despairing Meir had expressed her frustration and fears generated by her meetings with the State Department. "I am ready to pack my things and go home," she said, "even before the meeting with the president tomorrow morning—if the meeting with him is anything like what I had today from the members of the administration." Meir's comment may not have completely revealed the depth of the depression she had sunk into. Another event earlier in the day must have contributed to her emotional outburst. An American government representative announced that the United States would support a UN Resolution that condemned Israel for shooting down the Libyan plane over the Sinai and that demanded an investigation. Was that a signal of what was coming?

Rabin knew he was walking a tightrope between Nixon's need for something positive and Meir's legitimate reluctance to give away something for nothing. He told Kissinger that, if Nixon asked, he had formulated a response for Meir that Israel would not oppose the United

States' and the Soviet Union's continuing discussions based on the December 1971 understandings. In other words, Israel would not oppose those discussions as long as an agreement wouldn't be shoved down her throat and as long as Israel continued to receive warplanes from the United States. Nor would Israel oppose further conversations between Kissinger and Ismail. However, Rabin emphasized, Meir would insist that the United States not adopt a position that would impact Israel without first obtaining Israel's agreement. In addition, Rabin told Kissinger that Meir would brief Nixon on the substance of Israel's secret conversations with Hussein. Kissinger responded that Rabin's formulation would not interrupt the flow of armaments. It would also permit the secret channel to continue, and as a result, they could delay the process to fulfill Israel's need to wait until after the elections.

Kissinger knew that further delay increased the chance for war. He did not forget Ismail's insistence that there must be significant progress by September, two months short of what Israel's domestic political situation required. But Meir's focus was not just on remaining in power. Her need to wait before making concessions reflected a keen appraisal of what she could politically accomplish at that time. Israelis were rightly suspicious of any concessions made to the Arabs. They had lived in fear and had been victimized by terrorist attacks for far too long to be charitable to Arab sensibilities. To interject the uncertainties and revelations of an ongoing negotiation to an election campaign was a bridge too far. It was one Nixon had not wanted to cross in 1972; it is not surprising that Meir did not want to cross it in 1973.

Meir's meeting with Nixon began on March 1 at 11:00 a.m. Kissinger called Rabin beforehand to tell him that Nixon approved the formulation he had presented the night before. To achieve Nixon's agreement, Kissinger had told him that Meir intended to run for office again and that it would be politically impossible to move precipitously in the shadow of pending elections. That was politics Nixon well understood. Kissinger also reiterated his plan that had the State Department working somewhat publicly towards an interim solution while he would keep momentum moving forward privately for the real deal in the secret channel. Then, when the moment was ripe, the two tracks could merge. Nixon agreed despite two comments he scribbled in the margins of Kissinger's position paper: "The time had come to quit pandering to Israel's intransigent position," and a prophetic note, "This thing is getting ready to blow."

When they met, Meir and Nixon first exchanged pleasantries. Nixon reassured her with regard to the Libyan plane, "Things like that happen.... I have no doubt that you didn't do it intentionally." Meir then flattered Nixon and Kissinger by congratulating them on having successfully negotiated with North Vietnam. Nixon followed by offering Meir a carrot: He said he would continue providing Israel with economic and military armament assistance, and he reaffirmed the importance of Israel remaining strong enough to defend herself. When Nixon told Meir that it was in Israel's interest to move towards a solution, he opened the door for her to state her position on peace talks. "I will not squeeze you," Nixon said, "but you must conduct diplomatic activity even if it is only so that you will be seen doing it."

Meir answered that Israel was willing to engage in negotiations at any time.

Nixon then outlined the two tracks for negotiations Kissinger championed—one public and one private. And he confirmed that Kissinger, not the State Department, would control the process and that Israel needed to be prepared to move forward after her elections. He then said, "Henry is a master of fuzzy language ... and [is] the only man who can talk for one and a half hours without saying anything."

Meir responded that she would not oppose the Kissinger-Ismail talks as long as they remained general and Israel was timely informed of what had been said. But Meir's basic position never wavered; resolving the dispute once and for all required direct negotiations between Israel and Egypt.

The neglected backdrop to their meeting was how Israel would respond if attacked by Egypt. In 1971, Rabin had told Kissinger, "There is no doubt that we will hit them hard if attacked. We won't let Egypt choose the rules of the way and the manner it is fought." In response, Kissinger said that if would be helpful if Israel waited "more than two hours" before launching a retaliatory response. Kissinger's "two hour" request was an implied quid pro quo for the United States providing military assistance to Israel and refraining from exerting unwelcome political pressure on the Jewish State. It was a request that Meir never forgot. And it was a request that would have a profound impact on a decision Meir would have to make on October 6, 1973.

Near the end of their meeting, Meir suggested publicizing Israel's willingness to partially withdraw in the Sinai and permit some Egyptian police—but not the Egyptian army—to cross to the east bank and, therefore, create conditions necessary for the Egyptians to open the Suez Canal. But, she added, she would not agree to what the final borders would be before beginning direct negotiations with Sadat. From her perspective, the "trouble with Egypt is that they want the end before they begin."

Her offer, though important, was an empty one. She knew Sadat would never make concessions in return for a partial withdrawal unless she guaranteed that Israel would eventually fully withdraw. The meeting ended with Nixon assuring Meir, once again, that America would continue to provide assistance to Israel.

After the Israelis had left, Kissinger and Nixon spoke. Kissinger said that Israel would not agree to anything that permitted Egyptian soldiers to cross the canal, but that the more difficult issue was making a connection between an interim and final agreement. He explained that the Egyptians would refuse an arrangement that was not linked to a final agreement that returned all of the Sinai. He followed by explaining his strategy which was to get Egypt to agree to something that contained vague references to a comprehensive final deal and then go to the Israelis. If he then could get their agreement, the stage would be set to move forward.

Nixon responded once again with one of his favorite lines: "We've got to tell 'em [the Israelis] we're not squeezing them and then squeeze them."

Meir left Washington happy with the outcome of her meeting with Nixon. And why wouldn't she be? She had been assured that she would not have to face any American diplomatic pressure for most of 1973, and that economic and military assistance would continue to flow. But Meir failed to recognize the seriousness of Ismail's insistence that there must be progress by no later than September. Since the Ismail meeting had been secret, and perhaps because Meir saw no significance to his demand, the Egyptian foreign minister's insistence on the need for political movement by September was never conveyed by her, or any of her advisors aware of Ismail's declaration, to Israel's military intelligence services. Nor was it conveyed to Elazar, the IDF's highest ranking officer. Therefore, neither Elazar nor military intelligence had reason to question the "concept" that shaped their analysis as to whether Egypt would go to war. It was a tragic mistake.

Shortly after Kissinger left the White House, he learned of some terrible news. An eight-man Black September squad had shot its way into a farewell party for an American diplomat held in the Saudi embassy in the Sudan. Five hours after Kissinger informed Nixon, the terrorists killed the American Ambassador to the Sudan, his *Charge' du Affairs*, and the Belgium ambassador.

Sadat was extremely unhappy with the outcome of the Ismail talks and Nixon's meeting with Meir because Kissinger had not exhibited any urgency to move forward. In addition, as was the case every time the Americans agreed to supply more military jets to Israel, the news that America would send more planes to Israel burned Sadat like a blowtorch. He said, "Every door I have opened has been slammed in my face." As a result, he was more certain than ever that his only option for achieving something in 1973 required military force. When Arnaud de Borchgrave interviewed him for Newsweek magazine, Sadat said, "Everything is now being mobilized in earnest for the resumption of the battle—which is now inevitable." And, "Everybody has fallen asleep over the Middle East crises, but they will soon wake up. The time has come for a shock."

Kissinger's determination to delay the process did not impede his planning. He beguilingly wrote to Ismail that he was in the process of determining what Israel's position was and building the principles of an agreement based on their discussions in Armonk. Of course, he did not tell Ismail of the three-stage approach he envisioned. **First***, he and Ismail would meet secretly in April, and he would promise Ismail that the United States would work towards achieving sovereignty for Egypt over the entire Sinai, but not Gaza.* **Next***, at the end of the upcoming superpower summit between the U.S. and the Soviet Union, the powers would officially endorse the sovereignty concept.* **Third***, in November after Israel's elections, Egypt and Israel would begin negotiations towards a comprehensive peace that contained provisions for Israel's security in the Sinai and that included a long-term presence of Israeli military forces in areas under Egypt's sovereignty. In essence, Kissinger envisioned three zones in the Sinai:*

1. *A narrow area that Israel controls but under Egyptian sovereignty;*
2. *A large demilitarized area, comprising most of the Sinai, under Egyptian control; and*
3. *A third area under Egypt's unrestricted control.*

Kissinger also envisioned the possibility of some very minor border adjustments and a long period during which Israel and Egypt would move towards normalizing relations.

On March 9, Rabin met with Kissinger the day before his ambassadorship ended. Rabin told Kissinger, "To come out publicly with principles, say July or August, will be very unpleasant to the Prime Minister. That is two or three months before our election." At the end of their meeting, Kissinger asked if Israel would be willing to give up her demand for significant border changes in the Sinai. Rabin had no answer.

Afterwards, Rabin discussed Kissinger's ideas and questions with Meir in a long telephone conversation. Her answer was a definite no. Meir's position was clear; she would not agree to anything approaching full return of the Sinai to Egypt prior to negotiating.

In Rabin's last act as Israel's ambassador to the United States, he told Kissinger that Meir would require significant border changes in the Sinai as part of any deal. Kissinger responded by reiterating the threat that always implicitly existed. He warned that a failure to move forward could bring the State Department back into a lead role and convince Nixon to slow or stop the shipment of arms until Israel demonstrated more flexibility. Kissinger concluded their conversation with news that he would meet with Ismail again in April and that Israel would then have another opportunity to change her position. Afterwards, Rabin left for Israel. Kissinger would have to work with a new Israeli Ambassador, Simcha Dinitz.

Kissinger knew he did not have 'buy in" from the Israelis. He also understood that he needed to delay the Arabs until the time came that Meir could be more flexible. It is a sometimes difficult truth in a democracy that controversial decisions often require majority support. Also, change does not come if the leader that pushes a new agenda fails to remain in power. That required winning elections. And, fortunately for the prospects of negotiating an agreement with Sadat, some powerful domestic Israeli political forces did want to move quickly to find peace. They included Yigal Allon who worried that the longer it took to reach an agreement on the Sinai where there were fewer security concerns than on the West Bank and the Golan, the more likely that Israelis would come to regard the Sinai as holy land that they could never part with.

But Meir faced many domestic forces that opposed reaching any agreement with Egypt that would give up the Sinai. Moshe Dayan, who still enjoyed tremendous public support and was an important part of Meir's coalition government, had said previously, "I prefer the existing situation over a complete or almost complete withdrawal to the previous lines." Therefore, Kissinger knew that Meir's refusal to consider a significant withdrawal in the Sinai was not only based on a visceral lack of *trust of Sadat, but also based on cold, hard, political reality. She had to find a way to credibly avert, for a while, making concessions as a result of pressure emanating from Egypt and Russia. Then, after the elections were over, when she would also be subjected to intense American pressure, she could be more flexible. Therefore, at the last minute, Kissinger postponed his April meeting with Ismail. In addition, he decided to deflect Russian attempts to push hard for an agreement before the summit. Since there was another superpower summit already scheduled for the summer of 1973, there would not be any serious political engagement concerning Middle East issues until November. Israel's request for a delay would be honored.*

CHAPTER FIFTY
Most Favored Nation

Russia was in trouble. Her economy was struggling due to poor productivity and the increasingly expensive arms race that would contribute to her downfall two decades later. That was a main reason why détente was a priority for Brezhnev, as were the accompanying Strategic Arms Limitation Talks. But also high on his list was convincing Congress not to enact legislation preventing Nixon from designating the Soviet Union eligible for Most Favored Nation Status. If Russia attained that status, it would end American trade restrictions which impeded the Soviet Union's ability to import grains to feed its people.

The issue of Jewish emigration from Russia stood squarely in the way of Russia's receiving *Most Favored Nation (MFN)* Status. Since the days of Stalin, those who wished to leave Russia were considered "traitor[s] to the motherland." Rather than receiving permission to leave they were sent to jail or exile for merely making the request. After Stalin died, some were permitted to exit the country, but it remained difficult. Soviet Ambassador to the United States, Anatoly Dobrynin, later wrote that it was "not much easier to emigrate than to qualify for cosmonaut training."

By 1973, Russian attitudes towards preventing Jewish emigration had not diminished. Anyone who expressed the desire to leave was still considered a traitor. Some governmental officials were apprehensive that

Jews who had worked on government science or military projects would expose state secrets. Other worried that émigrés would join anti-Soviet campaigns abroad. Also, the Russians were concerned that it would anger Arab countries if Russia relaxed her barriers to emigration. The Arabs feared that many would move to Israel, thereby strengthening their enemy. But, perhaps most of all, the Russians worried that the Jews would be the tip of the iceberg. Their departure might spark others to leave who also felt deprived. If that happened, it would create a demographic death spiral that the Soviet Union would not survive.

Nixon promised Brezhnev at their June 1972 Summit that he would not make Jewish emigration an issue. And by the beginning of 1973, after Soviet authorities had lessened their intimidation, the flow of Jews leaving Russia had quietly increased from 400 to 35,000 a year. However, even though the Soviets loosened some restrictions, they had also created a new impediment. On August 3, 1972, the Soviet Presidium imposed a tax on those wishing to emigrate that required them to reimburse the government the value of the free education they had received. That financial burden prevented many from leaving. It also lit a fire in the United States.

On March 15, 1973, Senator Scoop Jackson and seventy-three other senators introduced the Jackson-Vanik amendment. The amendment prohibited the president from granting the Soviet Union *MFN* Status until Russia eliminated her barriers to emigration. That concerned the Russian Politburo. The Politburo worried that the amendment would impair their ability, by reaching economic agreements with Nixon at the upcoming summit in the summer, to achieve economic progress and raise the standard of living for their people.

In an effort to find an answer to the growing clamor in the U.S. Senate, the Soviet Union, at the end of March, informed the Nixon administration that between 1971 and then, 60,000 Jews had emigrated. The Russians also committed to repealing the education tax. But when the Nixon administration told Senator Jackson of the Russian disclosure, Jackson was not persuaded. He did not believe that the Soviet Union had changed her emigration policy because the Russians had not publicly committed to permitting emigration of a large, stated number of Jews.

While the proposed Jackson-Vanik amendment fanned the flames of anti-Soviet sentiment, Ismail quietly responded to Kissinger's message of March 9 that informed the Egyptians that he would explore Israel's position regarding negotiations. Ismail's response warned that America's decision to supply more warplanes to Israel would imperil the secret channel. But Ismail's answer did not motivate Kissinger to move faster. Instead, Kissinger told Dinitz, Israel's new ambassador to the United States, "We are pushing nothing, we are wasting time. I will take no initiatives. I will react in a slow moving way to their proposals. If it moves slowly and drags through the summit, that is their problem. I am not aiming at a Nobel Prize on the Middle East."

CHAPTER FIFTY-ONE
War Approaches

On April 8, 1973, England's *Sunday Times* published an article declaring that Sadat intended to launch a limited attack to break the deadlock, but that he did not aspire to destroy Israel. On April 9, *Newsweek* published an interview with Sadat under the headline, "The Battle is Now Inevitable." The following day, Libya sent sixteen *Mirage* fighter planes previously purchased from France to Egypt. The planes were of the same type that France had refused to ship to Israel after the Six-Day War.

Sadat matched his public rhetoric with private preparations. On April 5, he received his cabinet's approval to go to war. He also redoubled his effort to coordinate with the Syrians. Sadat had several reasons, however, for not trying to enlist King Hussein. First and foremost, they did not personally get along. He also disapproved of Hussein's handling of the PLO issue. And Sadat believed Hussein was willing to cut a separate deal with Israel to recover the West Bank. The irony of that is overwhelming. Sadat had already tried to negotiate a separate deal to recover the Sinai that gave lip service to Jordanian and Syrian concerns. Of course, practicalities made it easy for Sadat to be holier than thou. He knew that the Jordanian army was not prepared for war with Israel and that, even if asked, Hussein would refuse to join with Egypt in an attack.

During that spring Israel received warnings that Egypt was preparing for war, and would attack in mid-May, most likely on May 19. The information came from Marwan. Since he was the reason Israel possessed a copy of Egypt's *Granite-2* plan, the IDF thought it knew how the attack would unfold. After having consulted with the Egyptians, so did the Syrians. The plan in Israel's possession included precise details concerning the number of divisions and tanks that would be employed as well as specifics concerning planned commando raids deep into the Sinai. It also outlined the Egyptian strategic goal which was to take the territory between the canal and the Mitla and Giddi passes some forty miles beyond. Other information in Israeli hands included details concerning Syria's plans to take back the Golan Heights.

At first, Israel essentially ignored Marwan's warnings. The IDF even closed some of the Bar-Lev forts per its decision made earlier in the year. In addition, the IDF did not reverse its choice, made several months before and scheduled to begin soon, to shorten compulsory service for draftees by three months. Marwan's warnings also had little impact on Zeira, who said during a meeting with Meir, Dayan, and Elazar in the middle of April, "I am sure that if Egypt intended to launch a massive crossing of the Suez Canal we would know about it in advance, and we would be able to give a warning, not only a tactical one but also an operational one, i.e. a number of days in advance."

Zeira also expressed doubt that the Egyptians would foolishly start a war they knew they would lose. He added, in light of the upcoming Kissinger-Ismail meeting in May (re-scheduled from April) and the next U.S.-Soviet summit in June, that an imminent war was unlikely. He also warned that if Israel voiced concern it might motivate the Americans to seek significant concessions from Israel to head off a war that would not happen. Dayan agreed with Zeira's analysis. Elazar was not so sure but decided there was no need to make additional preparations; if Zeira was wrong, he thought, they still would have sufficient warning to respond to any surprise attacks launched by the Arabs.

In fact, rather than focusing on the drumbeat for war emanating from Egypt, Israel's cabinet addressed property issues on the West Bank. Moshe Dayan had proposed permitting Israeli businesses and individuals to buy land from Arabs living there. Hussein panicked when he heard of the proposal. He feared poorer Arabs would sell out of concern that their land would be confiscated otherwise. Then, Hussein postulated, once they sold their land those former Arab owners would constitute another wave of refugees that would descend on Jordan. Meanwhile, Jewish settlers would move in, making it even more difficult to pry Israel out of the West Bank.

Many Israelis shared Hussein's views with regard to land purchases on the West Bank. They thought it would create a new class of Israelis opposed to withdrawal for personal financial concerns derived from their land ownership rather than their ideology or thoughts of national security. Also, land ownership was contrary to traditional Labor Party policy that stood for land being owned by the State on behalf of all Jewish people rather than by private individuals.

The United States also opposed the land purchase plan. But Dayan contended that the most important reason that the Arabs had not started another major war was the land-buffer Israel held. He argued that finding a peaceful resolution of the Arab-Israeli dilemma might take a generation or more and that by settling the land Israel would have a greater claim. As for losses suffered by Arab residents of the West Bank, Dayan thought they would be compensated more than fairly by the improved economic conditions that development would bring.

Meir concluded that there was no need to make such decisions at present. She sensed that it was a dangerous time during which Israel needed more unity and less division. And she knew that if her government made a decision, Israel's internal domestic political conflicts would increase to the detriment of Israel's security. Of course, a decision would also have had an unpredictable impact on her re-election prospects. The prime minister's arguments prevailed. The cabinet took no position on Dayan's proposal which, in effect, was a vote against it.

Against the backdrop of Sadat's preparation for war and Israel's failure to recognize its coming danger, Ismail sent a reply on April 7 to Kissinger's message in March. In his response Ismail did not agree to the time framework that Kissinger suggested. Instead, he asked Kissinger to pick a date that they could meet that month. He also wrote that he assumed Kissinger's letter was predicated on a decision that the United States would become involved, and that Israel had provided Kissinger with sufficient assurances to make it worthwhile to do so. Ismail knew that for their talks to be successful from Egypt's perspective, it would require major concessions from the Israelis. Therefore, he tried to obtain a negotiating advantage by carefully crafting his response to the Kissinger letter. In it, Ismail outlined his expectations for their future talks. If then Kissinger had confirmed those expectations, Ismail would have been able to pocket them as concessions without having given anything in return.

Kissinger answered Ismail's response promptly, saying that May 9 (rather than a date in April) would be a good date for them to meet. He also chose to not respond to Ismail's assumptions concerning Israeli assurances, thus deftly avoiding Ismail's subtle diplomatic tactic. Kissinger did, however, address one issue head on when he expressed displeasure that the Egyptians had disclosed the existence of the secret channel to Saudi Arabia. Kissinger had learned of the leak when the Saudis warned the Americans to push for an agreement or risk the outbreak of war.

On April 10, Israel launched another commando raid, titled "*Spring of Youth*," against targets in Beirut. Israeli commandos attacked multiple points with the express intent of killing PLO terrorist leaders involved with planning the Munich massacre. Future prime minister Ehud Barak led the operation. Part of the plan required him and two others to dress as women. Three PLO leaders were killed along with many PLO soldiers. The operation also unearthed documents that led to the arrest of many terrorists living in areas under Israel's control. The successful mission was part of what motivated Dayan to say in a subsequent speech on Masada (where 1,000 Jewish zealots committed suicide two thousand years before rather than permit the ancient Romans to capture them after a three-year siege), "We will establish a new Israel, with wide borders, not like in 1948." Meanwhile a storm brewed in Cairo and Damascus that would endanger Dayan's homeland despite the wide borders he trumpeted.

May Warnings and Information Withheld

Kissinger could read what was happening. He knew, despite having reluctantly agreed with Israel to hold off the Egyptians, that the political standstill was increasing the risk of war. Since he had agreed to a meeting with Ismail the following month, he thought it time to see if the Israelis would be more forthcoming. On April 11, he and Ambassador Dinitz held their second working meeting since Dinitz took over for Rabin. Kissinger warned that he had held the Russians off for a year-and-a-half and the Egyptians for almost a year, but was concerned that if he continued to do so "the Egyptians would open fire, even though it was clear to them that they could not achieve any advantage by doing it, and at the same time, they would focus on pressure using the oil issue." Kissinger then asked how Israel thought the peace process should begin and proceed. He also solicited suggestions for an interim agreement that might break the impasse.

Kissinger's meetings did not go unnoticed. When Secretary of State Rogers learned of his secret channel from the CIA, he immediately went to Nixon to complain and receive clarification. Rogers knew the secret channel undercut him and thereby threatened his power and influence.

Nixon explained that the secret channel was part of a "double game" to publicly maintain the appearance of activity that would cover a private attempt to build momentum towards a solution. In essence, the public path was to demonstrate that each side was trying but would not require disclosing any controversial solutions that could be derailed by hardliners from all sides. The private path was for finding the answer before those same hardliners could interfere. Nixon's explanation mollified the secretary of state, but Rogers extracted a commitment that he would be kept informed of any private-channel activity. That compromise did not make Kissinger happy. He believed secrecy was crucial to success and did not trust the State Department's ability to keep confidential information passed to them. Kissinger thought it best if his actions were kept secret from everyone other than Nixon. And Rogers was not the only statesman concerned about the information flow coming through Kissinger. Meir's antenna was up too. She was increasingly concerned that Kissinger did not convey to Israel every detail of his communications with Ismail.

Meir, Elazar, Dayan, and others met informally in Meir's home on April 18 to discuss the questions Kissinger posed to Dinitz regarding the peace process and an interim agreement. The "Kitchen Cabinet" was in session. Meir made clear from her tone and comments that she did not want war. Zeira, in what was becoming a routine for him, reassuringly expressed certainty that neither Egypt nor Syria would go to war. He also added that the Soviets did not want a war either. Zeira's conclusions were predicated on Egypt's not yet possessing the pre-requisites for war as required in the "concept" and Syrian's weaknesses that left her needing to act in concert with Egypt to have any hope of recovering the Golan. Elazar agreed with Zeira but spoke of his increasing belief that, given the past few years without war, the warnings received from Marwan should be taken seriously. Dayan chimed in, "If I'm asked whether they go now for war or not—I believe they go for a war."

The conversation then turned to a specific response to Kissinger's questions. The "Kitchen Cabinet" concluded that war with Egypt was preferable to an American-mediated withdrawal from the Sinai to the international border, even if Israel remained in control of some strategic positions in the Sinai as part of the negotiated agreement. Elazar understood that their decision meant that the risk of a conflagration would increase. Therefore, he began to prepare for a conflict. Meanwhile, the "Kitchen Cabinet" members kept their discussions private; they did not share their conclusions with the rest of the cabinet.

However, the warnings from Marwan and the decision not to change their position on withdrawal was not all that was withheld. Only Meir and Dayan knew that Israel had committed to Kissinger that, even if an Egyptian attack was imminent or launched, Israel would absorb the strike for two hours before hitting back. Most importantly, the reader should remember, Elazar did not know that. The two-hour commitment was the price for America's agreeing not to force Israel into an unwanted settlement with Egypt, and to continue delivering warplanes. It was a price that only the top layers of Israel's government knew of. Because Elazar, the man in charge of commanding the IDF, was unaware of the commitment, he based his plans on a preemptive strike strategy that would never be permitted. Therefore, unlike 1967, political considerations meant that a new war would be fought first on Israeli-held territory rather than on the Arab side of the border. Meir's and Dayan's failure to inform Elazar would have deadly repercussions. Elazar would not have a chance to prepare for a war as it would have to be conducted.

And to make matters worse, only Meir, Dayan, and Rabin knew about Sadat's September deadline that Ismail had communicated to Kissinger in February. Zamir, the head of Mossad, had no knowledge of that, nor did Zeira or Elazar. As a result, Sadat could attack at a time and place of his own choosing, but those charged with evaluating the likelihood of an attack and how to respond did not have vital information required to make the sound judgments the IDF depended on.

The secret two-hour commitment was held so close that Dayan even permitted the IAF to rely, in the case of war, on intricate plans it had developed that were based on false assumptions. The reason for the IAF's meticulous planning was the SAMs Egypt and Syria possessed. To provide aerial support for the army, the SAMs needed to be overcome. Israel had constructed jamming devices for the SAM-3 missiles that shot down so many Israeli planes during the War of Attrition. But no electronic jamming answer had been found for the newer SAM-6 missiles that Russia began supplying to Egypt and Syria in 1972. Traditional bombing methods, the IAF had concluded, would result in the loss of one plane per missile site. Since Egypt and Syria possessed at least 87 forward SAM batteries and another 95 batteries behind the lines, one plane shot down per site would be too high a cost for destroying the SAMs in the traditional manner. Another answer was required. Otherwise, Israeli soldiers outnumbered on the frontlines would not receive air support and might be overrun as a result.

The IAF's solution was a complex plan that required hundreds of planes flying in a coordinated manner over several hours. The plan for the Egyptian front was called *Tagar*, and the Syrian front plan was called *Dougman*. Both efforts required good weather, sun in the defender's eyes, and preparation. Many thought the plans, which demanded precision flying techniques, were too complex; but they were the only solutions to the vexing SAM problem the IAF had found. Peled, the IAF Commander, knew how precarious they were. On the first day Peled took command, he told Dayan, "You should know that these plans aren't worth the paper they're written on unless we get permission to strike first," and:

> Sir, you must understand that this whole opera will be conducted according to plans only if we are the initiators. There's a helluva

difference between us initiating and choosing the day and the hour, the weather, the position of the sun, the right intelligence, the visibility. If we don't have that choice the system will not work and you will have a hell of a time and we shall have to take not one day, it will take three or four days to clear things.

Dayan responded with a dangerous lie: "Benny, my dear friend, do you really think that if we believe that the Arabs are planning to attack us, the air force won't get approval to attack? Don't be a fool." A mollified Peled said, "From your mouth to God's ears. So be it."

After the "Kitchen Cabinet" meeting, the instructions Meir sent to Dinitz were: "The prime minister has determined that, although we are sure of victory, it is our greatest interest to prevent a war, as far as it is in our power." She then emphasized that "a) we estimate that there is a low probability of renewal of fighting by Sadat; b) we are completely certain of our strength."

Meir's instructions downplaying the chance of war were designed to avoid any pressure from America to moderate her positions during negotiations—pressure that she thought would increase if Israel indicated the likelihood of war were high. Meir had mainly relied on Zeira's analysis which was based on incomplete information since Sadat's September deadline had been kept from him. It was a tragic way to formulate policy.

However, despite Zeira's reassuring tones, Elazar decided after the meeting, in an abundance of caution, to prepare for the worst—an all-out war in May on both the Sinai and the Golan—by reinforcing the IDF on both fronts. And, when speaking to news correspondents, he said: "We are taking his speeches seriously, and we are maintaining an alert. The IDF will be prepared. We never disregarded Sadat's threats in the past and we aren't now either."

But Elazar refrained from mobilizing the reserves. He thought there would be enough time for that after May 1.

Assad and Sadat Plan a War

Assad secretly flew to Egypt on April 23. Egyptian Air Force commander and future president, Hosni Mubarek, escorted him to Sadat's residence west of Alexandria. A political dispute divided the two leaders because of positions their predecessors had taken. Nasser had accepted Resolution 242 in 1967, Syria had not. The supposed implication of Egypt's agreement was that the Egyptians would no longer attempt to destroy Israel. Syrian leaders, however, still dreamed of Israel's demise. But Syria's dreams were mitigated by her weakness. Assad knew that he could not retake the Golan unless Egypt attacked at the same time, which would defuse the IDF's strength.

Sadat said to Assad, "Hafez, I am going to war this year. What do you think?" Without hesitation Assad replied, "I am with you."

However, they still needed to agree on goals. Otherwise the joint project would fall apart. With effort, Sadat convinced Assad to confine his war plan to recovering Syria's lost land on the Golan—at least at the beginning of the war they were planning.

Sadat told Assad that he planned to strike for the Mitla and Giddi passes during the first stage of his attack, tens of miles from the Suez Canal, and then advance towards Israel during the second stage of fighting. What Sadat described was Egypt's discarded *Granite-2* plan. Sadat knew Assad would only agree to fight if Egypt's plans were ambitious because Assad would not be willing to confront Israel alone in later stages of the war. To do so would be suicide. If Assad would have known that Egypt intended to only carve away from the Israelis a narrow strip of land across the canal and then to stop carrying the fight to their enemy, he would then have realized Syria would be left fighting alone within a couple days of the war's outbreak. That scenario would not have tempted him to join with Sadat.

So Sadat lied. He convinced Assad that the war would be one of liberation. Sadat left out of their conversation that the fighting was really only meant to jump-start negotiations. Of course, the Egyptian army did consider *Granite-2* a contingency plan if all went well after the initial crossings. But as Egyptian Chief of Staff General Shazly said, "The truth was that neither I nor any of my subordinates dreamed the second phase would be carried out."

Assad did harbor concerns that neither Egypt nor Syria would be ready to attack in May. Therefore, he questioned the Egyptian Minister of War closely, not realizing that Egyptian preparations were geared towards a much more limited operation than the one Sadat had led Assad to believe. And, as their discussions continued, it became clear to both leaders that neither country was ready for war yet. The two presidents agreed to delay their joint attack until the fall so that more equipment could be acquired, primarily from the Soviets. Both men would use the next few months to coordinate their efforts and hone their plans.

Assad wasted little time. Shortly after the meetings ended he went to Russia to obtain more arms. By the end of May he received the armaments he needed. All that remained was to train the troops to use them.

Therefore, after the two-day Arab secret summit ended on April 24, there was no chance that the Arabs would start a war in May. But Egypt's and Syria's preparations were becoming increasingly visible. Also, Israeli intelligence received additional information about Syria's war plan that was coupled with evidence that the Syrians were ready to attack at any time. As a result, unaware of the Arab decision to defer their offensive, the Israelis became further alarmed. On May 3, they gave Kissinger detailed information that suggested Egypt planned to start a war in May. Eventually, however, Marwan reported the war date had been postponed: first to late May, then early June, and then for some time in the future.

But before it became clear that there would not be an Arab attack, despite Zeira's objections, Elazar continued to prepare for a possible battle in May. The army resolved that, within 72 hours of being notified that war was imminent, elite standing units would replace reserve forces in the strongholds. In preparation, IDF Southern Command moved its tanks forward. In addition, the general staff drew up plans that would permit armored forces to intervene within minutes of a breakthrough, and in concentrated armored fists within a few hours.

Meanwhile, the same day Assad arrived in Egypt, Sadat attempted to push forward his parallel political track. Ismail sent Kissinger a letter confirming their May meeting. Kissinger, however, was still playing for time. He postponed the meeting to May 18 and then May 20. His excuse was that he needed to go to Russia on May 9 and 10 to prepare for the upcoming, second summit between Nixon and Brezhnev (He went to Moscow on May 4—whether or not he was intentionally disingenuous about the date with Ismail is not clear.).

Nixon's involvement in Middle East issues diminished during this period, quite probably because he was distracted; Watergate was heating up. On April 30, Nixon accepted the resignation of his two closest domestic advisors, H.R. Haldeman and John Erlichman. Meanwhile, White House counsel John Dean, who told Nixon on March 21 that there was a "cancer [growing on the presidency]," was singing to the FBI in exchange for his freedom. That night, Nixon went on television for his first address to the American people concerning the scandal. He said that the resignations were not an admission of guilt by his assistants and:

> I will do everything in my power to ensure that the guilty are brought to justice and that such abuses are purged from our political processes in the years to come, long after I have left this office.

Nixon added that he intended to return to his responsibilities as a president. Unfortunately, for him and the country, the unfolding crisis increasingly made that impossible, sapped his energy, and diverted his focus.

Israel Still Believes War is Imminent

On May 9, Meir visited the "Pit," Israel's war room buried deep under Tel Aviv, where Zeir briefed her on the current military situation.

* Egypt had 2,100 tanks and 1,000 artillery pieces in the canal zone, plus another 700 tanks and 300 artillery pieces near Cairo, about 100 miles from the front lines;
* Syrian forces arrayed near the Golan included 700 tanks and 600 artillery pieces. Farther back, but still close-by, the Syrians had another 400 tanks and 300 artillery pieces in Damascus. The Syrians also possessed several hundred more tanks based elsewhere.
* Confronting the Egyptians were 300 Israeli regular army tanks in the Sinai that were outnumbered seven-to-one; far fewer faced the Syrians on the Golan where they were outnumbered more than ten-to-one. And of concern, Israeli reinforcements would take some time to reach the critical zones after they were mobilized.

Nevertheless, Zeira still spoke strongly against the likelihood of war. Elazar, however, interjected that, if war did break out, it would do so on both fronts simultaneously. He knew that if the reserves did not mobilize early, only massive assistance from the air force would enable the IDF to stop such a large Arab force.

The IDF called Israel's basic defensive plan "*Rock*." Planning for it had begun in 1968. The *Rock* plan took into account the fact that most of Israel's combat power was in the reserves, which would be mobilized in the event of war, and that the IDF believed it would need five days to fully complete their mobilization. However, the IDF thought that significant forces could reach the Golan within thirty-six hours and the Suez region within forty-eight hours. *Rock* planners envisioned that the standing army, with the assistance of airpower, would stop the Egyptians at the canal's edge and at the crest of the Golan facing Syria. The reserves, after they reached the fronts, would then go over to the offensive together with the standing army. IDF planners assumed that Israel would receive at least forty-eight hours warning before an Arab attack, and that Israel would not call up reserves earlier or initiate a ground attack before receiving warning. They did not prepare plans for a war that would begin without any warning. Elazar called that scenario a "catastrophe" that would require the air force to hold the line and require a mad rush for the fronts by the reserves. Even worse, the planners did not know that Meir had promised Kissinger that Israel would stay on the defensive for two hours. Therefore, the IDF's plans, so heavily dependent on an IAF first strike to take control of the skies, were fundamentally flawed.

Throughout May, secret Israeli intelligence sources (including Marwan) continued to report a high likelihood that the Arabs would attack but kept moving the date later in the month and then into June. The evil tidings concerned King Hussein. He even traveled secretly to Tel Aviv to warn Meir and Dayan of Egyptian and Syrian preparations for war. Shortly afterwards Hussein provided the Americans with a detailed report along the same lines. He also added that he would not participate in the coming war nor would he place his military under an Arab joint command. In short, the king would not repeat his mistake of 1967. Hussein made it very clear that he would not fight unless Israel threatened to advance into Jordan.

As evidence of Arab readiness grew, Israel intensified her preparations. Unaware that Assad and Sadat had put off the attack Sadat had hoped to launch in May, Elazar secured permission to mobilize some of the reserves. And the IDF enhanced its ability to cross the Suez Canal by finishing construction of a huge roller bridge earlier than planned and by training armored units to move it. Military equipment dumps for reserve units were also moved closer to the fronts to shorten the mobilization time required for reinforcements to reach the front lines. In addition, the army created new units and strengthened existing ones. It all cost money—lots of it.

But, when May passed, the urgency lessened. On June 8, the IDF released some of the soldiers it had mobilized. By August 12, the IDF reverted to its pre-alert readiness. The crisis was over—or so Elazar believed. Many criticized the money wasted by the alert. And, as a result, Zeira's hand was strengthened. He had proved to be right, and others, including Elazar, wrong. Having cried wolf once, would Elazar and others do it again in the face of opposition from Zeira and without clearer indications than those that existed in May? But at least the alert provided one benefit, even though nobody knew it at the time. The dry run was a stripped-down rehearsal of what would be required for the trials the IDF would face very soon.

In 1973, Arafat's power to influence the region had waned, evidenced by Sadat and Assad excluding him from their war plans. Plus, Sadat had little interest in helping Arafat's cause or tying his mission to recover the Sinai to Palestinian causes. And Assad, instead of incorporating PLO forces into his army, evicted remaining PLO members from Syria in May. From Syria, most found their way to Lebanon where they did receive Syrian arms. Assad was all-too-happy to have them in place as a thorn in Israel's side that protected his right flank, but he did not want to let them into Syria where they might foment unrest as they had in Jordan.

But the influx of Palestinians into Lebanon destabilized that country. Initially, it was because PLO terror raids generated Israeli reprisals. The destruction those reprisals caused motivated the Christian Lebanese to push their government to stop the PLO from mounting raids on Israel. Things would spiral downhill from there as the demographic balance between Muslims and Christians unraveled, partly because of the influx of Palestinians.

Meanwhile, on the West Bank, some residents challenged the PLO's desire to be the sole representative of the Palestinian people, and the Mayor of Bethlehem called for negotiations before Israel took all of the land. In addition, some members of the PLO considered challenging Arafat's rule. Arafat's rejection of any attempt to negotiate the Palestinian issue that did not involve him faced some danger of being challenged from within.

CHAPTER FIFTY-TWO
Final Negotiations Before the Deluge

Kissinger Goes to Russia

Kissinger went to Moscow in early May to ensure that the summit meeting scheduled for June would run smoothly. America's main focus was to end the war in Vietnam, but the United States also shared Russia's desire to conclude the trade agreement granting *MFN* status to the Soviet Union. Both Kissinger and Nixon believed the agreement to be crucial for furthering détente and making progress in other areas, including Vietnam. However, several U.S. senators still stood in the way because Russia would not publicly commit to unfettered Jewish emigration. Kissinger's solution was to enlist Israel to lobby the senators. In return, he promised the Israeli government he would continue to freeze diplomatic activity in the Middle East.

The Russians, however, still hoped they could quickly resolve the issues of their Arab allies in a manner they favored and reap the credit for doing so. To prepare for the summit, on May 4 Gromyko gave Kissinger, before he left for Moscow, a proposal that contained nine principles for settlement of the Israel-Arab dispute. New was a call for Israel to withdraw, without exception anywhere, to the June 4, 1967 lines that predated the Six-Day War. The document also made reference to "legitimate rights of the Palestinians." And it declared that if one side did not comply with the requirements they agreed to, then the other side would no longer be bound by their commitments. That would make it too easy for the Arab countries to void any promises they made whenever it suited them.

When Kissinger arrived in Moscow, Brezhnev took him to his hunting lodge at Zavidovo, a location akin to Camp David, for their meetings. After discussing various world issues, Brezhnev focused on the Middle East. The KGB had told Brezhnev that Egypt and Syria were preparing for war and that Egypt had a detailed plan to cross the Suez Canal. Therefore, Brezhnev pushed Kissinger to be more flexible regarding American willingness to pressure Israel. And he told Kissinger that Russia would continue to try to restrain the Arabs from initiating military action but that it was becoming increasingly difficult to do. Brezhnev then suggested that they both push the Arabs and Israelis to reach an agreement based on a set of principles agreed to by the United States and the Soviet Union.

Kissinger did not express any interest in Brezhnev's requests. Instead, he told the Russian leader, "It is hard to convince Israel why they should give up territory in exchange for something they have [a ceasefire], in order to avoid a war they can win only to negotiate with the most intransigent element of the Arabs [the PLO]." Kissinger continued that American intelligence had deduced that Egypt and Syria would not win a war and were unlikely to start one before the summit. But Kissinger did dangle one enticing detail. He said that after Israel's elections he planned to push them hard to make necessary concessions but did not hint what those concessions would be.

The two continued dancing the same dance they had repeated many times. Brezhnev was no stranger to Kissinger's delaying tactics, including Kissinger's argument that he could not influence Israel, at least before their elections. On the other hand, Kissinger was accustomed to hearing

Russians remonstrate that war was imminent and that they had difficulty controlling the Arabs or changing their views. And so, the band played on repeating the same tired songs.

After returning to the United States, Kissinger met with Dinitz. During their conversation, Kissinger asked whether Israel had anything to offer in response to his request for something new to bring to his next meeting with Ismail. Interestingly, Kissinger did not contact Israeli Foreign Minister Eban because Dinitz had previously asked him not to tell Eban about the Ismail meetings. Meir had her own back-channel that left Eban out in the cold as the public figurehead while the real diplomatic effort was done behind the scenes through Dinitz. One would guess that Eban and Rogers would have had much to commiserate about over dinner and drinks should they have been of a mind to do so.

Meir had told Dinitz not to voluntarily offer anything new when he met with Kissinger. If pushed, she instructed him to respond that Israel might agree to a partial settlement along the lines of what was discussed in 1971 but would not agree to one that led to a comprehensive deal that did not fulfill Israel's needs. Meir also told Dinitz to emphasize that Israel did not subscribe to Kissinger's strategy of "sovereignty in return for security." When Dinitz conveyed what he had been instructed, Kissinger responded with frustration, "I don't share Israeli optimism about the low probability of the war being renewed and I don't believe that you can continue to stay calm and comfortable without moving." Kissinger reminded him, "Thanks to me there has been a standstill for twenty months and that is above and beyond what can be imagined.... Now it is going to end." Kissinger also warned that further delay may not work in Israel's favor. He counseled Dinitz that the Watergate scandal posed a threat to Nixon's presidency, and, if there was a change, a new president may not be as favorable to Israel.

Kissinger met afterwards with the staff of his Washington Special Actions Group (the *WSAG* was a National Security Council subcommittee tasked with contingency planning and crisis management). They discussed the risks of war after taking into account Sadat's public statements, Hussein's warnings, Russian fears, the exchanges with Ismail, and the input of American intelligence agencies along with other indicators. They concluded that war would not break out in the near future. There was still time—or so they thought.

On May 14, just a few days after Kissinger successfully parried Brezhnev's thrusts, Moshe Dayan stirred the pot during an interview on the BBC. Despite his overwhelming popularity, Dayan seemed satisfied to remain defense minister in Meir's government rather than try to replace her as prime minister. Perhaps that is why he felt comfortable to espouse controversial views in the hope of influencing government policy. He told the BBC that the West Bank "is our homeland." However, Dayan also expressed hope during the interview that Israel could reach an agreement with Jordan that would permit Israel to keep her Jewish character, to settle Jews in the West Bank, and that would allow the Arab inhabitants to retain their Jordanian citizenship instead of becoming citizens of Israel. Of course, he could not state how that would be accomplished in the face of Hussein's convictions and Palestinian desires.

Dayan also moved towards fulfilling his dream of settling the Rafah approaches, just south of the Gaza strip. Meir's finance minister opposed him but failed to block disbursement of the funds needed to build Dayan's dream town of Yamit along with an accompanying seaport. Nor did Israel's Supreme Court interfere with Dayan's plan when it had an opportunity. A case came before the Court that involved a military order that expelled Bedouin living in the area planned for the new city. The Supreme Court reaffirmed it had the power to review and overrule decisions by the IDF, but it did not find sufficient basis to reverse the IDF's decision. The Bedouin could not go home, and Jewish settlement in the Sinai became a reality.

Kissinger Meets with Ismail

On May 16, Ismail arrived in Paris under the guise of meeting with the president of France. His real purpose was to meet with Kissinger. On May 19, Kissinger first saw Le Duc Tho, North Vietnam's representative, to engage in more discussions regarding ending the Vietnam War. Their meeting was public knowledge. Kissinger's meeting with Ismail, scheduled for the next day, was not.

The Kissinger-Ismail meeting took place at an ancient home south of Paris. They spent five hours together. First they ate lunch and then they walked to an outdoor garden to engage in private talks under the warmth of a bright sun. Ismail seemed less interested in substance and more in the role America would play in future negotiations. He expressed doubt that America would push Israel and also said that Egypt would make a final peace agreement contingent on resolution of the Palestinian issue. Kissinger responded that the United States had no interest in Israel's maintaining a presence in the Sinai but that progress must be made "step by step" and would take longer than Egypt wanted. Kissinger clarified this meant that an interim agreement could not be reached until 1974, after Israel's elections; and a comprehensive one would take another year.

Kissinger, aware that direct negotiations were important to Israel, asked Ismail if Egypt wanted the United States to act as an intermediary. Ismail responded, "You have expressed your desire so many times to be go-betweens." To which Kissinger said, "Nonsense. You don't need us to convey messages to Israel. I am not a postman. You want us to convince Israel of your point of view. We are ready to back a solution, but a solution discussed by the parties."

A dismayed Ismail warned once again that there would be war if there were no solution. And again, Kissinger was unimpressed. He later said of that time, "We all thought he [Sadat] was a fool, a clown, a buffoon who goes on every stage every other day to declare war."

Kissinger then tried a different tactic. He suggested that the United States and Egypt try to agree on a general set of principles for a peace agreement that the United States could announce, but Ismail saw through that delay tactic. Kissinger also pressed his step-by-step concept for resolution of the crisis and inquired whether Egypt might permit Israel to retain defensive positions in the Sinai under the umbrella of Egyptian sovereignty. Ismail responded that he would speak to Sadat. Sadat's response a few days later lacked any hint of enthusiasm for Kissinger's ideas.

The only thing Ismail said that Kissinger found productive was that Egypt would not take any military action before the June summit between the superpowers.

After Kissinger left, Ismail remained in the garden alone—his hands supporting his drooping head. American intelligence agents later indicated that Ismail's face was etched in despair. In retrospect it is clear; Ismail knew his diplomatic mission had failed, and the United States would not honor Sadat's deadline. War would ensue.

With seeming clairvoyance, Dayan met with Israel's military General Staff on May 21. On that day, his public confidence did not match the depth of his private concern. Rather than addressing the ongoing alert, Dayan predicted a dim future:

> You have to take into consideration a renewal of the war in the second half of this summer. We the government tell you, the General Staff: Gentleman, please prepare for war in which those who threaten to start a war are Egypt and Syria.

Dayan added that he did not think Jordan would participate in the attack. It was the closest he would come to telling the IDF of the September deadline delivered by Ismail to Kissinger in February.

Dayan ordered the generals to prepare an overwhelming response that would crush their attackers and that would include crossing the borders into Arab territory. He predicted that a future war would be short and would be stopped by a ceasefire pushed by the United States and the Soviet Union. He further warned that the oil-producing Arab nations would probably use their oil reserves as a political weapon. Therefore, he stated that Israel needed to become less dependent on Iranian oil by increasing oil production from sources in the Sinai (even though Iran was not an Arab nation, Dayan recognized that oil imports from there might easily be impacted by an Arab oil embargo).

But Dayan's private conversations with American officials did not always mirror his tough approach with the generals or his demeanor in public. Nor did they deflect his determination to set up settlements and a port in the Sinai. Dayan told some American diplomats that he would consider permitting Egyptian sovereignty over land devoid of an Egyptian military presence. He also said if Israel maintained control of key positions, and if settlements in the Sinai remained under Israeli civil administration, he could agree to Egyptian sovereignty over much of the Sinai if it included demilitarized zones. Dayan also accepted that some land transfers of Israeli soil might be required to compensate Egypt for the few settlements in occupied territories that would remain under Israel's control.

If you, the reader, are confused you have a right to be. It was as if Dayan had two opposing agendas and wanted credit for both. Whether Kissinger ever knew of all of Dayan's ideas is not clear, nor is it clear that it would have made any difference.

War Preparations Continue

Sadat did not publicly back down after receiving the bad news from Ismail. Towards the end of May he told a German journalist, "Egypt wants through action—regardless of what it will cost—to show the world that it has a problem…" He then warned ominously, "Israel thwarted all our efforts to make peace based on justice in the area."

During the late spring and throughout the summer, the Egyptian army accelerated its preparations for the oncoming conflict. The Egyptian approach was methodical, detailed, and focused on achieving its primary task—to cross the Suez Canal en masse and in a manner that the IDF could not dislodge them. To do so, the Egyptian army trained each soldier thoroughly for his specific job rather than attempt to enhance his ability to perform multiple missions. Drills duplicated what was demanded of each soldier during the first phase of the war. They had to learn how to cross the canal safely, break through Israel's defenses, and then tear gaps in the massive sand ramparts that ran parallel to the canal. Once the soldiers breached those sand walls, engineers would construct bridges that led to the openings, after which tanks and other motorized vehicles would cross.

But crossing the canal presented much difficulty. The tides caused canal water to rise and fall precipitously every six hours, up to six feet in some places, only a few inches in others. And the speed of currents in the canal varied based on proximity to the lakes within the canal system. The currents also changed direction with the tides. As a result, it was not easy to row a straight course or build a bridge quickly, especially because conditions changed so drastically based on time and location. The Egyptians planned to assemble 2,500 small craft for their initial wave. Practice for the operation was exhaustively repetitive; some practiced more than 300 times crossing the canal in a location that mimicked conditions they would face.

The first impediment the Egyptians would encounter were sand ramparts, by then at least sixty feet high, built by the Israelis along the shoreline of the canal. The edge of the ramparts facing the water contained mines, other booby traps, and barbed wire. It also sloped at a forty-five degree angle, enough to prevent any vehicles from climbing up it to the top. Israeli soldiers manned the Bar-Lev fortifications which were built into the ramparts every few miles. Behind the main sand wall, the IDF built a second sand barrier about 300-to-500 yards back from the canal. It was not as massive as the ramparts, but along its length were 240 ramps from which tanks could engage oncoming troops from protected positions. Behind that the IDF constructed a third set of sand walls that protected the roads leading out of the canal area into the interior of the Sinai.

For training purposes, the Egyptians built replicas of the Israeli defensive zone along tributaries of the Nile River. The men in the first wave had to hone skills needed to execute a plan that demanded that they row across the canal in rafts. Then, with sixty pounds of equipment and supplies on their backs, they would have to hurriedly climb the sand barrier in front of them using ladders built of bamboo and rope. It is no wonder that the Egyptians felt the need to drill their men over and over again.

The IDF thought that it would take Egyptian bulldozers at least twelve hours to tear through the sand walls to such an extent that motorized vehicles crossing on hastily constructed bridges could get through. But the Egyptians had found a better way. They had learned while building the Aswan dam that water pumped through high pressure hoses would effectively move large concentrations of sand. Through experimentation, they discovered that by using the same technique on Israel's sand barrier along the canal they could cut the time it would take to punch through from half a day to three or four hours. The discovery made mincemeat of IDF planning that assumed it would have at least twelve hours after hostilities began to get its tanks into position on the ramps along the second line of defense. As a result, when the IDF's proposition was tested by war, armored units stationed far back in the Sinai found that they did not have enough time to beat the Egyptians to their pre-planned defensive sites from which they could have mounted an effective response.

The Egyptians, however, did see some value in the sand ramparts, so they constructed their own. Once completed, those ramparts interfered with IDF soldiers' ability to directly observe Egyptian movements; they also protected Egyptian troops from Israeli fire and secured favorable positions for their artillery and tanks to fire down at Israeli soldiers on the other side of the canal.

Kissinger was unaware of Egypt's meticulous preparations to attack the Israelis. He still believed that time remained for diplomatic maneuvers. On June 2, he met with Dinitz to discuss his conversation with Ismail the previous month. Kissinger said he would ward off any Russian pressure at the upcoming summit by saying he was waiting to hear how Egypt would respond to Israel's need for an agreement that incorporated defensive arrangements in the Sinai. However, the same day Kissinger met with Dinitz, a message arrived from Ismail. In it the Egyptian made clear that his president needed action, not words. Sadat wanted to reach an agreement with the United States on principles for resolution of the impasse with Israel rather than some form of non-binding American declaration that would guide future discussions. Ismail also advised that Sadat had asked the Russians for assistance and for them to bring up Egypt's issues at the upcoming summit. Separately, Ismail told a State Department officer in Cairo that Egypt preferred war to the present state of "no peace and no war." The State Department never reported that conversation to Kissinger.

On June 5, Sadat gave his army final orders to prepare for war. It was plain to Israeli observers that something was afoot. And if any doubt still remained, Marwan provided another warning that should have raised concerns. When he met with his Israeli handlers on June 14, he declared that Sadat and Assad had decided to launch an attack in late September or early October. But, instead of redoubling their vigilance, Israel's army stood down from their May alert.

The June Summit

Three days before the summit meeting was scheduled to begin, Kissinger spoke with Dinitz to coordinate strategy. They discussed whether Kissinger should attempt to reach an agreement with Gromyko on a set of principles to guide resolution of Middle East issues or to gamble and leave it to Nixon and Brezhnev to work that out without knowing what, if anything, they would agree to.

The next day, Kissinger met with Dinitz for the purpose of further clarifying Israel's needs. By then, Meir had formally responded she did not agree to the proposal made by Gromyko in 1972 and that she preferred that a jointly-produced document not be drafted at the summit. Subsequently, Meir clarified that, if something needed to be agreed upon for show, it should be limited to a reference to Resolution 242. And while preparing for the summit, Kissinger received another message from Ismail. That communication relayed Sadat's suspicions that America lacked sincerity with regard to pushing Israel to reach an agreement with Egypt.

Brezhnev arrived in Washington, D.C on June 17. For a president beginning to feel under siege, Brezhnev's visit came at a good time because the pomp and ceremony that heralded the summit hid the disarray poisoning Nixon's administration. Three days before, Jeb Magruder, a former White House aide and deputy director of Nixon's reelection campaign, had testified before the select Senate Committee investigating Watergate. He asserted that Attorney General John Mitchell and White House Counsel John Dean knew the break-in to the Democratic headquarters had been conducted by the Nixon reelection campaign and that they had participated knowingly in its cover-up. The committee scheduled Dean to testify on June 25, at the end of Brezhnev's visit. As a result, the Watergate scandal was blowing up and impacting Nixon's concentration. Kissinger later wrote that Nixon was "troubled and distracted." Fortunately, however, even though the Russians were aware of the scandal, they did not understand its impact. Nor did they recognize that they had an opportunity to achieve much if they focused on deftly playing Nixon's emotions and political needs for their own benefit.

Brezhnev's arrival in the Unites States did not stop Meir from taking an important political step. She announced that she wished to continue as prime minister after the elections in October. She did not disclose, however, that she suffered from an inoperable cancer for which she made regular visits to Hadassah hospital for treatment. Instead, each time she went to the hospital she said she was visiting a sick friend. Meir declared privately, "It's very exhausting, sometimes to death," but, "I will get over it."

The summit schedule called for eight days of meetings—first at the White House, then Camp David in Maryland, and finally ending at Nixon's home in San Clemente, California. During their days together the two leaders signed nine agreements which included principles for limiting nuclear weapons, an agreement to prevent nuclear war, and an agreement to conduct scientific and cultural exchanges. In the midst of that process, on June 22, the summit delegations flew to San Clemente. The next morning, Gromyko broached the topic of the Middle East for the first time, but he and Kissinger did not reach an agreement. Their discussion centered on what an end-of-summit statement should say about the Middle East. Gromyko did not want it to contain any reference to Resolution 242. Kissinger, however, insisted it should because an Arab commitment to Israeli sovereignty behind secure and recognized borders was the cornerstone to any agreement. Realizing they could not agree, the two of them deferred their discussions to later in the day.

That afternoon, all of the summit participants attended a poolside cocktail party loaded with elite Hollywood personalities, and then joined together for a private dinner. The next day, Brezhnev planned to return to Washington for a day of relaxation before flying to Europe. Therefore, he asked that dinner be held early so he could get sufficient rest for the next two days of travel. After the meal, Brezhnev gave Nixon's wife a gift, hugged the president, and went to bed. It was 7:15 p.m. Kissinger thought he had dodged any conflict over Middle East issues.

Just after 10:00 p.m., something unusual happened. Kissinger received word from the Secret Service that Brezhnev had awakened and demanded to meet with Nixon, who by then had fallen asleep. Kissinger later said, "It was a gross breach of protocol. For a foreign guest late at night to ask for an unscheduled meeting with the president on an unspecified subject on the last evening of a state visit was then, as it has remained, unparalleled."

Kissinger had no choice but to awaken the president. Nixon sat up in his pajamas and asked, "What are they up to?" to which Kissinger responded, "Who knows, but I fear we are not going to get through the summit without a dacha session." Kissinger's comments referred to the last summit in Moscow when Brezhnev emotionally and bitterly confronted Nixon about Vietnam.

Nixon and Brezhnev met in Nixon's private study. But for the darkness, they would have seen the Pacific Ocean from the window. Present, in addition to the two leaders were Kissinger, Gromyko, and Dobrynin. Nixon's valet started a fire, fixed a round of drinks, and left the room.

Brezhnev began, "I would be glad to hear your views on the Middle East problem." Kissinger sat in fury, not showing his anger. To him the Russian leader's strategy was plain. He hoped to catch Nixon off guard, unprepared, and not at his best after drinking in the afternoon and early evening, and then hopefully not alert after falling asleep. But Nixon was ready for Brezhnev. He responded in part:

> The main problem in our view is to get the task started. Once we get them started, we would use our influence with the Israelis and you with the Arabs. But if we just talk about principles we'll never

get [there] …. We can do nothing about it in the abstract, we need a concrete negotiation.

Brezhnev was not mollified. He wanted a rock-solid agreement with Nixon that the two of them could impose. He argued that the Arabs could not enter into peace negotiations without knowing the principles that would guide the talks. Therefore, Brezhnev wanted Israel's agreement to a full withdrawal. In return the Soviet Union and the Arabs would give Israel security guarantees and free shipping through the Straits of Tiran and the Suez Canal. He added that a full, contractual peace would depend on negotiations with the Palestinians. Brezhnev beguilingly suggested that their deal could be kept secret and need not be reduced to writing. A gentleman's agreement would suffice. Then it could be implemented by Kissinger and Dobrynin after Israel and the Arabs had a chance to study the details of its implementation.

Clearly, Brezhnev did not want to go home empty-handed.

But Nixon resisted the Russian. He refused to be pinned to a policy that he had not prepared for and would not support. Nixon knew the Israelis would resist initiating negotiations before their election and that he had little domestic strength, due to Watergate, to force Meir to begin them earlier. Therefore, he responded, "On a subject as difficult as this, we cannot say anything definitive." However, he assured Brezhnev that he would study the proposal and that he was not just putting him off.

Brezhnev was not placated. Emotionally, he warned that the Americans did not appreciate the position the Arabs felt they were in and predicted the result would be war if the superpowers did not resolve the dispute.

Their impromptu meeting lasted three-and-a-half-hours, until two a.m. During the discussions, Dobrynin acted as translator and frequently edited some of Brezhnev's more emotional remarks, fearing that Nixon would be insulted. Their informal talk ended when Nixon declared, "We can't settle this tonight," and further, "We don't owe anything to the

Israelis. That means I am interested in a settlement ... That will be our project this year. The Middle East is the most urgent place." The Russians, however, (despite Nixon's assurances that he would seriously consider their comments, suggestions, and concerns) did not believe him.

Kissinger viewed the Russian gambit harshly. He believed it a thinly-veiled attempt to reassert their influence with the Arabs by forcibly inserting themselves into the process to obtain what they wanted. Kissinger later said, "Twenty-four hours after renouncing the threat of force in the agreement on the prevention of war, Brezhnev was in effect menacing us with a Middle East war unless we accepted his terms."

When the summit ended the two superpowers issued a 3,000-word communiqué summarizing its successes and the agreements reached. Only eighty-nine words were devoted to the Middle East. None of them were meaningful. There would not be any more diplomatic efforts to resolve Middle East issues before another war broke out.

Post Summit Maneuverings

On July 3, Dinitz flew to the West Coast to meet with Kissinger for a post-summit review. Meanwhile, Nixon, exhausted by his meetings with Brezhnev and the stress of Watergate, developed pneumonia and had to rest. Kissinger told Dinitz that he had successfully resisted Russian attempts to use their 1972 proposal as a basis for a new agreement. He also said that Rogers had tried, without success, to convince Nixon to force Israel and Egypt to begin negotiations immediately. Rogers had wanted those talks based loosely on Resolution 242, but without the United States taking a position on whether the resolution required Israel to return all of the occupied territory.

Dinitz responded, "A version like this one will not be agreed to. I will not ... accept a document which says that the 1967 lines are not rejected."

In Israel, the cabinet was relieved that the summit had ended without threat of new diplomatic pressure. Their joy led them, without basis, to minimize fears that the Arabs would soon start another war. Perhaps it was because negotiations with an unacceptable starting point had not been forced down Israel's throat. Perhaps it was just due to the constant tension that created the perception of a new norm. Or, perhaps, it was just wishful thinking that failed to take into account the determination of their adversaries.

Several weeks before, Dayan had warned IDF Generals to prepare for a war with Egypt and Syria that might break out later in the summer. But his remark to Elazar while discussing the planned reduction of compulsory military service terms due to take effect in 1974 exemplified the new prevailing mood, "A preplanned total war with all of the Arab states on all of the fronts—this does not seem to be on the horizon in the near future." Dayan also predicted to *TIME* magazine that there would not be a major war in the region for the next ten years and that boundaries would remain frozen during that time.

Rabin, back in Israel, was optimistic too. In an article written for *Ma'ariv*, an Israeli newspaper, he chimed in confidently:

> Our present defense lines give us a decisive advantage in the Arab-Israel balance of strength. There is no need to mobilize our forces whenever we hear Arab threats, or when the enemy concentrates his forces along the ceasefire lines. Before the Six-Day War, any movement of Egyptian forces into Sinai would compel Israel to mobilize reserves on a large scale. Today, there is no need for such mobilization so long as Israel's defense line extends along the Suez Canal.
>
> We are still living within a widening gap of military power in Israel's favor.

The Arabs have little capacity for coordinating their military and political action. To this day they have not been able to make oil an effective political factor in their struggle against Israel.
Renewal of hostilities is always a possibility, but Israel's military strength is sufficient to prevent the other side from gaining any military objective.

However, despite Israeli complacence, when the June summit ended the last realistic chance to channel Sadat away from war also ended. Sadat stopped talking war. There no longer was any purpose in threatening violent actions; it then became more important for him to mask his intent. Instead, Sadat declared his renewed friendship with the Soviet Union. The Syrians, however, were not so circumspect. Their bellicose statements increased, and Syrian soldiers and military equipment moved to positions near the Israeli-held Golan. In addition, a second contingent of Moroccan troops arrived in Syria. Anyone with a set of store-bought binoculars could plainly see from IDF strongpoints that Syria was preparing for war.

On July 13, Ismail arrived in Moscow to meet with Brezhnev. When he left, their talks were described as "frank and friendly" rather than "warm and friendly." Probably, Ismail told the Russians that Egypt would soon start a war, and the Russians were not pleased. But despite his displeasure when he heard what Ismail had to say, Brezhnev had no leverage that he was willing to wield to dissuade the Egyptians. Brezhnev wanted to support Russia's Arab friends, and he did not want to risk another rupture of relations with Egypt. On the other hand, he did not want a confrontation with the United States that would risk détente as a result of a war he thought the Arabs were destined to lose. Stuck between two competing interests, Brezhnev sent a futile note to Kissinger and Nixon after Ismail left that said, "The situation in the Middle East is very complicated and fraught with danger of serious explosion."

The Israeli government's confidence was mirrored by the IDF's. Since its awareness of Arab military preparations was not matched with understanding Arab political intent, the IDF saw no reason to delay or alter a planned change of command. Ariel Sharon, Commander of the Southern Front facing Egypt, was perhaps the most experienced and capable war fighter in Israel. In 1973, he resigned when he learned he would never be appointed chief of staff. Rather than remain in the regular army (Sharon remained a reserve commander of an armored division), he stepped down to reshape his nation's political landscape. Sharon hoped to unite the conservative political parties into a coalition that could challenge the Labor party in the upcoming elections. His creation was called the Likud Party.

Shmuel Gonen became the new Commander of the Southern Front on July 15. In 1967, Gonen was the first brigade commander to break through Egyptian lines and reach the Suez Canal. At the end of that war, Gonen said, "We looked death in the eye and it averted its gaze." Gonen was brave, but he also had a prickly, demanding aspect to his personality that subordinates found difficult to deal with and approached abusiveness. General Adan, Commander of the Armored Corps, affronted by evidence that Gonen's soldiers feared telling him news he did not want to hear, told Elazar, "Gorodish [Gonen] has no place in the IDF."

When Sharon learned of Gonen's appointment he warned Dayan that Gonen was not ready to handle the job. Sharon said, "I believe you are making a grave mistake. If we have a war here, and we might have one, Gonen does not have the experience to handle it." Dayan responded, "Arik, we aren't going to have any war this year. Maybe Gonen is not too experienced. But he'll have plenty of time to learn." Thus, within two months of telling his general staff to expect war, Dayan backtracked and then weakened Israel's ability to defend herself by permitting appointment of a potentially unfit commander to a critical front.

Dayan's newfound confidence that there would not be a war may have stemmed from his belief that Sadat would eventually recover, through diplomatic means, most of the Sinai. Until then, the United States had proven her friendship and willingness to abide by the agreement with Israel to put off negotiations with Egypt until after Israel's election in the fall of 1973. When Sadat called Israel "world's biggest bully" and pushed the United Nations to debate Israeli policy, America's special relationship with Israel became evident. That debate led to a Security Council resolution on July 26 condemning Israel for continued occupation of the territories. Even though the United States vetoed the resolution, Dayan knew that, after Israel's election in late 1973, Nixon would probably put tremendous pressure on Israel to be more forthcoming. Therefore, why would Sadat fight a war now for what he could soon obtain peacefully without risk?

Dayan's confidence in the status quo extended to the West Bank. In late July he declared that he was not sure whether he would run on the Labor ticket because "the territories are not a deposit to be held temporarily." Instead, Dayan advocated that Israel build cities beyond the 1967 lines, permit private purchases of land from Arab owners, and speed the construction of Yamit and a seaport in the Sinai. In a conversation with a *TIME* Magazine correspondent he said, "There is no more Palestine. Finished." His statements echoed comments he made months before to the *BBC*, "Israel should remain for eternity and until the end of time in the West Bank."

Not surprisingly, Arafat was unsatisfied with the status quo. Pressured by the lack of movement for Palestinian causes, he decided to test a diplomatic option. America's ambassador in Iran, Richard Helms, reported to his superiors that an Arafat confidant had approached one of his aides at the end of July. Helms said the PLO appeared to be asking for a dialogue with the United States based on two principles: Israel would continue to exist, and Jordan should be the permanent home for Palestinians. In addition, the PLO wanted clarification of what was meant in the post-summit joint superpower communiqué by "Palestinian interests?" The message's implication was that Arafat thought Jordan could become a home for Palestinians after deposing Hussein. The PLO passed a similar message to the United States through Morocco in August. America's policy, however, was to refuse to talk with the PLO as long as it publicly disavowed Israel's right to exist and was a terrorist organization. Nevertheless, Kissinger instructed Helms to respond that the American goal was peaceful coexistence for Israel and the Palestinians and that he would be interested how the PLO thought that could be achieved. Kissinger would not talk, but he was willing to listen.

On August 10, Dayan told Israel's military staff college, "The balance of forces is so much in our favor that it neutralizes the Arab considerations and motives for immediate renewal of hostilities." But Dayan did not know that Sadat had met with King Faisal of Saudi Arabia and said to him that war was coming soon. Faisal told Sadat that he approved of his decision and recommended that the war should last long enough for Arabs to build a united front. Nor was Dayan aware that when Syria moved her army into position near the Golan late in the summer, as had been done every year for training since 1968; this time it was for something much more.

Dayan was part of one of the three groups in Israel responsible for obtaining and analyzing intelligence. The **first** was the Mossad, run by Zvi Zamir, who enjoyed Meir's trust. He ran Israel's most important intelligence source, Ashraf Marwan. The **second** branch was military intelligence headed by Eli Zeira. That branch collected information from multiple sources, but was so wedded to Zeira's allegiance to the "concept" that it operated with blinders. The **third** group was the political sphere. Its most important evaluators were Meir and Dayan who also were the decision makers. And they were the only ones who received all of the information uncovered by all three groups, including Ambassador Dinitz's reports.

Unfortunately for both Zamir and Zeira, they never received the political information to which Meir and Dayan were privy. They never knew that Ismail had told Kissinger that Sadat's deadline for an initial agreement, and at least a partial withdrawal from the Sinai, was September. Meir and Dayan chose to sit on that information rather than share it. Perhaps, for political reasons, they wanted to keep their sources and conversations confidential. However, whatever their reasoning, the impact was devastating—the professional intelligence-gatherers and evaluators were left ignorant of the key they needed to match capability with intent.

On August 10, Israeli military intelligence received reports from a source within the PLO that George Habash, the leader of the PFLP branch of the PLO, was on an Iraqi civilian plane headed from Beirut to Tehran. Zeira informed Elazar who immediately decided, "We will intercept him" and force the plane to land. Both Meir and Dayan approved.

However, there was a mechanical problem with the plane while it was still in Lebanon. The resulting delay caused airline officials to replace the Iraqi plane with a Lebanese one. After it departed, IAF jets intercepted the civilian airliner and forced it to land at an Israeli military airbase. Commandos burst into the plane, but Habash was not onboard. He had canceled his ticket when the flight was delayed.

Once again the UN Security Council debated (whether nations debate or pontificate at the UN when it comes to Israel is open to question) a resolution condemning Israel for forcing down a civilian plane from another country. This time the United States did not veto the forthcoming resolution condemning Israel. But privately Nixon was not upset by Israel's attempt. Twelve years later President Ronald Reagan would do the same when he ordered U.S. warplanes to intercept an Egyptian airliner carrying four Palestinian terrorists that had murdered an elderly American tourist, Leon Klinghoffer, after hijacking a cruise ship, the Achille Lauro. That plane was forced down on Italian soil. No UN censure against the United States was ever sought.

CHAPTER FIFTY-THREE
Final Preparations

Egyptian and Syrian Generals Meet

On August 21, six of Syria's highest ranking military officers boarded a Soviet passenger ship at the Syrian port of Latakia. Although they wore civilian clothes, the men were decidedly on a military mission. After the boat docked at Alexandria in Egypt, with little fanfare, they headed separately to a hotel often used by Russian officers and advisors. The next day they met with eight of their counterparts in the Egyptian military. They were in Egypt to finalize plans for their joint attack on Israel.

The Egyptians worked hard to keep everything secret: They only permitted one person to take notes during the meetings, banned all electronic devices from the conference site, and several times each day technicians swept the meeting room for electronic bugs. Nor did those security concerns end at the door; once they left the room, none of the participants were permitted to contact each other in any manner when they went back to their quarters to rest.

In addition to completing their battle and deception plans, the participants had to decide what day and time they would attack. After analyzing tide charts and the phases of the moon, war planners had identified two appropriate time periods from which to choose: September 7-11 or October 5-10. But further complicating the problem, the assembled generals thought that they needed at least twenty days' prior notice of the designated date (later reduced to fifteen) to fully deploy Syria's army because it had not yet fully massed close to the Golan Heights. Egypt did not share the same time constraints because Sadat's forces were already arrayed along the Suez Canal. Still, the requirement of a twenty day notice ruled out the September dates. That left October 5-10 for consideration.

But the Syrians were not satisfied with just knowing the approximate date. They demanded to be told the actual date at least five days before their joint offensive would start—that would give them enough time to drain all the oil from their refinery at Homs. The Syrians feared that if the oil was not removed Israeli bombing raids, as part of a campaign to damage Syria's infrastructure, would cause massive damage to the refinery. The Egyptians voiced no objection to their request.

Finding agreement for the time of the attack proved more vexing. The Egyptians wanted to attack in the late afternoon so that they would have a couple hours before dark to establish positions on the east bank of the canal and then six hours of moonlight to construct bridges and move men and tanks across the waterway with minimal interference. Syria wanted to attack at dawn because the direction of their attack was from east to west. A dawn attack would put the rising sun behind them and in the eyes of the Israelis. Compromises floated at the meeting included having the Syrians attack at sunrise and the Egyptians much later in the day. But the Syrian officers worried that if the two countries did not start fighting at the same time, Israel would focus on them. The Egyptians then suggested that they start in the late afternoon and the Syrians attack the next day at dawn. The Syrians did not like that suggestion either, because the delayed attack would eliminate their advantage of surprise. When the generals realized they had reached an impasse, they agreed to kick the problem upstairs; resolution of both the date and time would be left to Assad and Sadat.

After the meeting ended, General Tlas, Commander of the Syrian army, flew back to Syria. Sadat was already there. He had first attended meetings in Saudi Arabia and Qatar to mask the reason for his last stop in Syria. Soon after his arrival, Tlas met with Sadat and Assad to relay the outstanding issues they needed to resolve. The two presidents agreed the attack would begin between October 5 and 10. They did not resolve what time or the exact date the offensive would start. However, their inability to agree would later prove auspicious after the fighting began.

While the Arab generals met an important change happened in the United States—Nixon announced that Kissinger would replace Rogers as secretary of state and would retain his position as head of the National Security Council. Kissinger finally had what he wanted—full control of American foreign policy, including policy in the Middle East.

Settlements

Even though his philosophy had transformed over the years, Dayan's threat to leave the Labor Party and the cabinet in August unsettled Meir. During the first days of the Six-Day War, Dayan had been reluctant to take any territory other than the Sinai. But by 1973, he had become focused more on creating facts on the ground in the occupied territories than finding permanent solutions. That was much different than dovish members of Meir's cabinet. Those ministers, such as Eban, believed the territories a burden and therefore advocated for less rather than more presence on the West Bank, in the Sinai, and the Golan. In furtherance of their beliefs, the doves resisted integrating the newly-won lands with Israel's economy. But the liberal element had a problem: there were no partners for peace. No Arab leader had come forward and offered a palatable deal that included recognizing Israel as a permanent member of the Middle East. As a result the elements of Israeli government and society that advocated annexation, settlements, and/or more economic links with the territories were becoming increasingly difficult for the doves to resist or placate. Therefore, Meir asked Minister Yisrael Galili to draft a document to bridge the gap.

Galili finished his work on August 23. He opined that the government should permit the number of settlements in the occupied territories to increase dramatically from forty-six to seventy-six. He also supported developing Yamit in the Sinai with sufficient housing for 3,000 residents but suggested waiting three years before building a port there. And he declared that all approved settlements, including Yamit, should remain part of Israel after any agreement with the Arabs. However, Galili was less supportive of Jews purchasing Arab land, calling for strict controls to prevent speculation.

For the most part, Galili's attempt to find a compromise between hawks and doves supported Dayan's position. Liberal political elements opposed his proposals vigorously. So did the Arabs, who viewed it written proof that Israel did not want to negotiate a peace agreement. Israeli newspaper editorials fanned the flames, chiming in that Yamit would house the first of a quarter million Jews in the Sinai.

Although a cursory analysis might leave a different impression, the Labor Party did not provide significant support to Galili's report. When the party adopted his document, it had 161 members in its governing body. The vote on September 4 in favor of incorporating Galili's views into the Labor Party platform was seventy-eight to zero. But that left eighty-three party members that chose to abstain rather than risk a political backlash from voting against it. Meanwhile, Ariel Sharon kept busy. Labor's weakness provided the right-wing an opportunity. Sharon worked tirelessly to unite the opposition right-wing parties into one new movement named Likud, the Hebrew word for consolidation.

By September, Dayan had transitioned from being concerned about the military intentions of Egypt and Syria, to being overconfident that the status quo would continue until after the elections were completed. Dayan knew Kissinger planned to revitalize talks with Egypt after the elections and would push Israel hard to make dramatic concessions. And he assumed the Egyptians knew that too. Therefore, Dayan saw no reason for Sadat to instigate a war to recover the Sinai—a war he could not win—when he could wait a few months for a negotiation in which he very well could get his way. But Dayan did not know that his plans for Yamit and a seaport had emphasized for Sadat that there was nothing to be gained by deferring his decision for war. Sadat saw it as a signal that Israel would never withdraw from the Sinai. At least not without first being administered a shock.

Although Dayan's plans had hardened Sadat's views, Dayan's optimism helped Labor's political position. One lesson of 1967 was that war drums created pressure to unify the government. When Egypt moved into the Sinai in May 1967, Eshkol responded by bringing the conservative right-winger, Menachem Begin, into a coalition government to unify the country in the face of Arab threats. Another war scare would create pressure to create another coalition government. That pressure would inevitably weaken the party's still overwhelming hold, a hold that already had begun to show signs of slippage. Therefore, the political prospects of both Meir and Dayan were aided by the illusion of peace. That is why, even as late as September 20, one of Labor's political ads read, "On the Banks of the Suez all is quiet." An image of an Israeli soldier relaxing on a wicker chair overlooking the canal with an Uzi submachine gun between his legs accompanied the text. It may also be why Meir and Dayan kept private Ismail's warning that peace would be the casualty of a September that passed without significant movement towards Israel's withdrawing in the Sinai.

Sadat and Assad Meet Once More about War

On September 10, Assad traveled to Cairo to discuss war plans with Sadat. By then, Sadat's determination to go to war coursed through him. He knew his supportive relationships with other Arab countries would never be better, his military had the equipment and training needed to succeed, and Egypt's relationship with Russia had returned to satisfactory levels. And, with his domestic constituency, he had run out of time. Unless Israel changed her political stance in a manner that left no doubt she would return the Sinai to Egypt, Sadat would not be swayed from his path.

Sadat and Assad invited King Hussein to meet with them in Cairo, but they did not include him in their war planning sessions. Nor did they tell him that they planned to attack Israel. Instead, their overt purpose for inviting him was to welcome the king back into their good graces. Their actual reason, however, was to shore up Syria's southern flank. For that they didn't need Hussein to attack; they only wanted to ensure that he would not permit Israeli forces to outflank the attacking Syrians by moving through Jordan.

Hussein welcomed the invitation. It had been three long years since he last was in Cairo. After he had evicted the PLO in 1971, his four years of relatively good relations with Egypt following the 1967 war had reverted to the cold peace he had endured before the war. Hussein thought the September meeting a success; both Egypt and Syria agreed to resume normal diplomatic relations with Jordan after he committed to release hundreds of Black September operatives that had languished in Jordanian jails for years.

But Hussein also heard tidings that unsettled him. He deduced that Egypt and Syria were actively considering an offensive against Israel, and he wanted no part of it. Therefore, even though neither Assad nor Sadat had told him they were planning for war, Hussein declared that he would not participate in any attack on the Jewish State. The king had learned the lesson of 1967 when his cooperation with Egypt had cost him Jerusalem and the West Bank. He had also appreciated the support Israel and the United States gave him in 1970. In addition, Hussein knew that if he joined with Syria and Egypt he would also have to permit PLO fighters to operate from Jordanian soil. That was a risk he would never take. However, he did say what the other two Arab leaders hoped to hear; Jordan's army would block any Israeli attempt to attack Syria by way of Jordanian soil.

Sadat and Assad were pleased with the direction their talks with Hussein took. But Hussein was not the main item on their agenda. They needed to agree on the day and time to start the war. They had that discussion outside of Hussein's presence.

Assad's motivation for going to war was simple. He wanted the Golan back and perhaps more. He knew that he would never achieve his aims by negotiation, nor was he disposed to try. For him, war was the only path. In contrast, Sadat's views were radically different. His reason for war was to revitalize negotiations already started with the United States. Therefore, he did not need a huge victory, only a small success that bloodied the Israelis, restored Egyptian pride, and sent the Israelis a message that the status quo could not continue without significant cost.

Since Sadat knew they measured success differently, he again lied to Assad about the goal of his offensive. Assad later said:

> The goal was the retrieval of territory which Israel occupied in 1967. Each country was free to plan its offensive on its own front, but it was agreed that Syria's aim was the recovery of the

> Golan while the Egyptian objective was to reach the Sinai passes in the first stage before regrouping for the re-conquest of the whole peninsula. This was what Sadat and I decided and it was on this principle we went to war.

Sadat, on the other hand, knew he did not have the strength to reach the passes, much less reconquer the entire Sinai. Thus, during those days in September in Cairo, Assad and Sadat hid their plans from Hussein, and Sadat hid his plans from Assad.

And Sadat's subterfuge was not just directed towards the Syrians. He also fooled the Russians. Sadat needed massive quantities of Russian arms to ensure success. He didn't tell the Russians that he would attack in the near future but did disclose to them Egypt's *Granite-2* war plan that entailed reaching the Sinai passes. What he didn't say was that the plan that he would put into effect was much more limited. However, because *Granite-2* required a tremendous amount of military equipment, it provided a reasonable basis for Sadat's demand to Brezhnev for more arms. That demand would have been less well received if he had disclosed that his real plan was only to take a small slice of land across, and immediately adjacent to, the canal. In essence, Sadat asked for more knowing he would receive less. Thus, even though Russia invariably would never provide all that he had asked for, Egypt's needs for the less ambitious *High Minarets* plan would be satisfied.

On the last day of their meetings, Assad and Sadat decided they would launch their attack against Israel on October 6. That date had two auspicious attributes, neither of which was why they selected it, but both laced with meaning. For the Arabs, the significance of October 6 was that it was the tenth day of Ramadan and the anniversary of the Battle of Badr, won by the prophet Muhammad in A.D. 626. For the Israelis, it was Yom Kippur, also known as the Day of Atonement—the most solemn religious day of the year for Jews.

However, the two leaders failed to decide what time of day the hostilities would begin. Their continued indecision turned out to be a blessing that greatly contributed to their initial success.

Tension Mounts

Egypt's plans for deception long included mobilizing her forces every year for normal autumn maneuvers per the code name *Liberation 23*. Israel knew of the planned exercises and had become used to them. In 1973, the Egyptians used those training activities as a launching pad to position their army for war. But the Egyptians did not anticipate their cause would be aided by a series of events that would give Syria and Egypt an excuse to move their troops to forward positions. Nor did they anticipate that those events, as was subsequently alleged, would enhance the credibility of Marwan, Israel's supposed superspy.

On September 5, five Arab terrorists hoped to use ground-to-air, handheld, missile launchers to shoot down an Israeli El AL passenger jet taking off from Rome. Thanks to information provided by Marwan, they were arrested before they could fire the rockets. That was not the first time information from Marwan had prevented a terrorist attack. In April, possibly at Sadat's request, Marwan passed Israel information that thwarted a Syrian-supported terrorist attack on the cruise ship *Queen Elizabeth*.

Then, on September 13, the day after Assad and Sadat agreed on the date to initiate hostilities, a climactic event occurred over the skies of Syria. It began when two Israeli *Mirage* fighter jets carrying photographic gear flew into Syrian airspace on a reconnaissance mission. After crossing the Syrian coastline, they circled left. At the same time four IAF *Phantom* fighter jets flew low over the ocean, crossed into Lebanon before entering Syria, and then increased their altitude to 40,000 feet to join with the two *Mirage*s. Together, they raced across Syria towards Turkey before turning back to Israel. Eight more Israeli jets were aloft, flying some distance away, but close enough to provide quick support should the Syrians cause trouble.

The Syrians decided to fight. Sixteen Syrian MiGs took off. Once airborne, they dropped their extra fuel tanks and energized their onboard electronic tracking systems. Soon, sixteen Arab planes and twelve Israeli jets tangled in an aerial ballet that lasted several minutes. Nine Syrian planes went down in flames. One Israeli plane joined them.

The Syrians knew the Israeli pilot of the IAF's one crashed plane was floating in the ocean waiting to be rescued. They were determined to capture the pilot to wrest some honor from the dismal day. The Syrians sent a helicopter to find him, along with four MiGs to provide cover. The Syrians could not find the pilot floating in the fog offshore. But four Israeli *Phantom*s found the Syrians. Soon, four more Syrian planes were downed.

An IDF helicopter returning to base low on fuel reversed course to rescue the IAF pilot. Floating a few hundred yards away was a downed Syrian pilot. The helicopter picked up both. Israeli television and radio publicized the successful encounter—thirteen Syrian jets downed against one Israeli—and the Israeli pilot of the downed plane saved.

The dogfight increased Israel's confidence, but it also provided cover for Syria's pre-planned massive movement of her army towards the Golan. Was Syria just planning a demonstration of her strength, a limited battle day much like the ones she had initiated previously, or a full-fledged war? Israel's intelligence had the task of discerning Syrian intent. Capability was less of an issue. The growing threat was plain to see.

Time Runs Out

Kissinger met with Dinitz on September 10. He emphasized to the Israeli Ambassador how important it was for Meir to provide guidance how she would protect her core needs when America pressured her to exhibit flexibility after the Israeli elections. Subsequent to their meeting, Dinitz said to news reporters, "It is clear that Professor Kissinger intends to initiate a new diplomatic offensive in the Middle East after the Israeli election." Two days later Kissinger said in Senate confirmation hearings for his appointment as secretary of state, "Israel and the Arabs must be ready to carry out difficult decisions resulting from the agreement," and Dinitz told the cabinet ministers during a trip back to Israel, "The Americans are talking a lot about the need for progress in political initiatives, and they expect Israel to be the one to make this progress."

Dayan knew Israel would have to respond in a manner that the United States would perceive positively. He leaned towards embracing Kissinger's idea of trading sovereignty over the land in return for satisfying Israeli security issues that included IDF control of strategic points for an extended period. What that would have meant for Dayan's pet project, Yamit, is not clear. But, since the proposed location of Yamit was a strategic location just south of Gaza, Dayan probably planned to keep it under Israel's control.

Nevertheless, despite clear public pronouncements that America would soon make a vigorous attempt to solve Egypt's problems with diplomacy, Sadat was no longer willing to wait. And he felt justified. For three years he had announced it was the "Year of Decision." For three years he had deferred. No more. In the middle of September Sadat had everything in place that was required to maximize prospects for his plan's success. Russia had provided most of what his army required, the morale and training level of his army was high, and, most importantly, Syria was eager to fight. Any further delay risked dissipation of the optimum conditions that then existed. And Sadat knew those conditions might never appear so well aligned again, especially if Assad were to learn that his goals were much different from what he had told the Syrian leader.

Sadat also planned an Arab diplomatic campaign designed to make Israel appear the intransigent party in order to provide political cover for the offensive he would soon launch. To further that political aim, Sadat focused some of his attention on the UN General Assembly during those final weeks before war. In addition, he hoped to mobilize Arab oil producers to embargo their oil in order to create economic pain for the West at the same time as he bloodied Israel. That combination, he thought, would push the West to pressure Israel to make concessions while the flow of Jewish blood greased the way.

Kissinger, pre-occupied with his confirmation, did not anticipate what was about to happen. In August, in furtherance of his plans for later in the year, Kissinger asked the Iranian ambassador in Washington to inquire whether Sadat was willing to agree to a step-by-step approach to resolve Egypt's dispute with Israel. The Ambassador reported back on September 15 that Egypt was open to such an approach but would not wait on sovereignty. He told Kissinger, "Egypt wants all of the salami on the table and to slice it. The Egyptians are not ready for the salami to be kept outside the room with an additional slice brought to them each time."

Dinitz's next meeting with Kissinger was scheduled for September 30. Kissinger could not meet before because he was busy taking the reins of his new position as secretary of state. Unfortunately, we will never know if a meeting on that day would have changed the course of history because it never happened. Dinitz's father died causing Dinitz to head home to Israel for the funeral. He did not return to the United States until after war broke out.

However, as September droned on, Dayan's confidence that Egypt would not attack before the elections weakened. On September 17, Dayan again met with Zeira concerning the advanced stage of Arab deployments. But once more Zeira's philosophical "concept" held the day over a common-sense analysis based on what was known about the preparations of Syria's and Egypt's military. Then, on September 20, Israeli intelligence analysts began poring over aerial photographs of Syria's build-up. They saw that it had reached alarming proportions. For the first time three full Syrian divisions were arrayed close to the thin IDF line; a storm was brewing on the Damascus plain before a scant thin line of Jewish tanks and soldiers—a line far too weak to stop Syria from advancing deep into the Golan. Still, Israel's military and political leadership remained complacent.

King Hussein, however, knew that evil tidings were in the air; a Jordanian intelligence officer had received information from a Syrian military commander that Syria was preparing to invade Israel in conjunction with Egypt.

A storm was coming.

Kissinger achieved high office on September 22. Before hundreds of guests, the first person of the Jewish faith was sworn in as an American secretary of state. The same day, Egyptian generals received their attack orders for October 6.

CHAPTER FIFTY-FOUR
War Approaches

Israel's Worries Increase

On September 24, the IDF General Staff met for a second time concerning Egypt's and Syria's unprecedented marshaling of forces on Israel's borders. It was two days before Rosh Hashanah, the Jewish New Year. The buildup worried General Hofi, the IDF's Northern Commander, who said, "To my mind the Syrians are more dangerous to Israel than the Egyptians." He knew that the Egyptian army needed to penetrate 150 miles to reach Israel. The Syrians only needed to advance fewer than twenty.

Hofi ticked off a frightening list of developments to support his thesis that soon the Syrians might launch a limited attack on IDF positions in the Golan:

- The Syrians had moved artillery to forward positions that normally were stationed further back.
- Syrian SAM-6s, based in the valley close to Israel's positions on the Golan since August, could reach the air space over the entire Golan Heights. Therefore, any IAF planes that would attempt to provide air support risked being shot down.

- More Syrian troops and tanks were positioned adjacent to the ceasefire lines than ever before.

However, General Elazar and most of the General Staff were not concerned. They knew the IDF had recently built roads on the Golan, had improved bridges spanning the Jordan River from northern Israel to the Golan so that military vehicles could cross at a faster rate, and had moved reserve depots closer to the front lines. All of that would enable the IDF to deploy reinforcements, when needed, faster than ever. In addition, adjacent to the Syrian border, IDF engineers had recently completed a series of tank ramparts overlooking the Syrian plain below, increased the density of the minefields, and finished the anti-tank ditch. As a result, they felt confident that the standing army could contain any attack until reservists arrived and the air force could assist.

Elazar tried to soothe Hofi by telling him that intelligence sources would provide advance notice of an attack. Then, Elazar thought, once it was clear the Arabs were about to strike, the civilian leadership would give the IDF the greenlight to react preemptively with devastating air strikes, which would eliminate Syrian SAM defenses. Therefore, he assured Hofi, the air force would be available to destroy onrushing Syrian forces well before the end of the first day of fighting.

Hofi's concerns, however, did not fall on deaf ears. They impacted Dayan, who told Elazar:

> If I were in your place I would follow this scenario. I wouldn't take a Rosh Hashanah vacation—not even a break. Either you or the general staff prove that Hofi's and my evaluation is mistaken, or find a practical solution to the possibility that the Syrians might actually do that.

Elazar responded, "If the question is one of war, in my opinion, this deployment does not change the air force's ability to finish Syria off in a day and a half."

Most of those present viewed their discussions as theoretical. Very few thought war was imminent.

Hussein Comes to Israel

King Hussein had no wish to again face the difficult choices that a conflict between neighboring Arab countries and Israel would present; and, to make matters worse, he was not on good terms with the Arab countries involved. Earlier that month, in Egypt, he had met with Assad and Sadat—an encounter that, coupled with information provided by Jordanian intelligence, served to intensify his concern. On September 23 he reacted. Hussein contacted the Israelis and requested an emergency meeting with Prime Minister Meir.

Two days later, an IDF helicopter landed near the Dead Sea. Waiting, was another helicopter piloted by King Hussein that had left from a helipad near his home and penetrated Israeli air space. Hussein, along with his prime minister and chief of intelligence, entered the cabin of the Israeli craft. The helicopter then took off; its destination was Tel Aviv. From there, Israeli security whisked the Jordanians to Herzliya to meet with Meir.

Hussein appeared anxious and nervous. Some Israelis present felt the same. Intelligence sources had revealed that Egyptian troops were deploying in forward positions. Hussein's concerns, however, were not based on Egypt's activity. The impetus for his request for an emergency meeting was information he had received about Syria. The source was a major general in the Syrian army the Jordanians had recruited two years before. The general was related to a woman married to a Jordanian intelligence officer. From him, the Jordanians received the newly-drafted Syrian war plan which had been created after the meeting between Syrian and Egyptian generals in August.

Hussein sat down with Meir and Israel's Director-General Gazit. The Jordanians did not know the Israelis filmed and recorded the meeting but probably suspected it. A closed-circuit TV connection transmitted the proceedings to eager observers in another room.

In great detail, Hussein described his meetings with Assad and Sadat in Cairo two weeks before. The king told Meir that the Egyptian and Syrian leaders were not willing to accept much longer the no peace–no war state of affairs that had existed since the conclusion of the Six Day War. Nor, he said, could he blame them. However, he assured Meir that when Assad and Sadat asked him if he would open an eastern front along the Jordan River if war were to break out, his response was "leave me alone." Hussein made clear to Meir that he "had already paid a high price for such partnership in 1967." He would not do it again.

Hussein said that information from a "very sensitive source in Syria" gave him concern that Syria might use its present military exercises as a cover to conceal Assad's intent to launch a surprise attack with troops already in position. "Does this have any significance or not? No one knows," said Hussein. "But I have my doubts. In any case no one can know for sure. We can only relate to facts."

Meir responded with a question: "Is it conceivable that the Syrians would start something without the full cooperation of the Egyptians?"

"I don't think so," Hussein replied. "I think they are cooperating."

Hussein did not reveal when an attack would occur, nor did he intimate that an Arab strike was imminent. But he did suggest that Egypt and Syria were cooperating. That information alone should have shaken adherents to the "concept" that held as one of its basic tenets that Syria would not fight without Egypt.

While the Meir/Hussein meetings were underway, Zamir, the director of Mossad, met separately with his Jordanian counterpart. Zamir focused their conversations on Palestinian terrorist groups rather than the likelihood of war. As a result, an independent opportunity for assessing the risk of war was lost.

Later that evening, near midnight, Meir called Dayan to provide him with details of the meeting. Neither viewed Hussein's comments as a warning of imminent war; others, who had overhead the conversation, agreed. In fact they did not regard Hussein's information as anything new. But what must be remembered is the urgency that Hafez Ismail attached to the message he had conveyed in February to Kissinger that there was a September deadline. Only Meir and Dayan knew that. The others listening and analyzing the conversation with Hussein did not.

Hussein's revelation was a crucial clue that should have unlocked the meaning behind the September time limit Ismail had hinted at (and was conveyed by Kissinger to the Israelis). The essence of the king's message was that Syria and Egypt were cooperating. Israel already knew Syria's troops were in positions from which they could attack. Egyptian forces were also known to be moving forward. The dots were not difficult to connect through the proper lens. But Israel's military commanders, including Elazar and Northern Commander Hofi, were not given the key that would have made it easier to divine the coming deluge. Along with all of Israel's intelligence analysts and leaders, they were never told of Ismail's literal drop-dead date—a crucial fact which, in conjunction with all other information gathered, might have revealed what would soon befall them.

The next day, Syria and Egypt issued press releases announcing military maneuvers. Both Israel and the United States knew that Egypt had been conducting maneuvers periodically for the last few months. Thus, the announcements alone meant little. But Israel and the United States were not aware that at the end of each exercise some Egyptian troops would return to their bases, but not all. Insidiously, Egyptian troop presence along the Suez Canal surreptitiously grew.

However, Dayan and Elazar did not totally ignore the growing Arab concentrations along Israel's southern and northern borders. In response to the increasing possibility of a surprise attack signaled by the placement of Arab forces, they ordered a partial alert of the regular army, but refrained from mobilizing any reserve forces because they did not believe the Arabs intended to attack. Their response was little more than flexing their muscles in the face of a horde that would soon engulf them.

Dayan and Elazar also visited the north, where they toured the Golan frontline and met with Hofi. From the Golan, they saw the massive Syrian military force only a few miles away. Again, Hofi expressed his apprehension. At that moment all he could muster to defend the forty-mile front with Syria was an infantry brigade and an understrength, armored brigade, which had at the moment only 75 working tanks at its disposal. Those few tanks could not hope to provide significant support to the infantry, mostly spread-out in small fortified strongholds along the front. Arrayed against them were 1,500 Syrian tanks, 800 of which were in forward positions, and tens of thousands of infantry.

Their discussion convinced Elazar to send reinforcements. To do so, he ordered mobilization of reserve elements of the Barak Brigade manning the Heights. In addition, Elazar sent to the Golan a battalion of the elite Seventh Armored Brigade, stationed in the Sinai, along with a small number of artillery units. Elazar said, "We will have one hundred tanks against eight hundred Syrians. That's enough."

For his part, Dayan thought that if he sent the right indirect message it would deter the Syrians and might back them off. Therefore, he met with Israeli residents of the Golan at Kibbutz Ein Zivan and invited news media, including an American television crew, to cover the event. Dayan's comments publicized Israel's awareness of the massive Syrian forces close-by and the IDF's ability to respond forcefully. The message was meant to convey that we know what you are thinking of doing and we are ready. But did Israel really knowing what the Syrians were doing? And was the IDF really ready?

On September 28, while tensions rose in the Middle East, Russian Foreign Minister Gromyko visited Nixon at the White House. He warned the president, who was in the midst of battling the Watergate scandal, they might wake up to a war between Arabs and Jews. Nixon promised to push forward resolution of the Arab-Israeli issues. To further that prospect, he agreed to schedule preliminary talks with Moscow in November, and then more in January when Kissinger was scheduled to visit the Soviet Union. Neither knew that the next day Sadat would tell Russian Ambassador to Egypt, Vladimir Vinogradov, that Egypt would soon break the ceasefire. But even though Sadat tipped off the Russians, he did not do the same for his own foreign minister who was in New York and scheduled to meet Kissinger on October 5. Sadat did not want to burden his representative with having to keep that secret.

CHAPTER FIFTY-FIVE
The Austrian Divergence

On the same day that Gromyko had visited Nixon, two Palestinian terrorists hijacked a train in Austria loaded with thirty-nine Jews escaping Russia. They selected seven of them for hostages, including an old man, a sick woman, and a three-year-old child. The Palestinians demanded that the Austrians shut down a transit camp at Schoenau Castle near Vienna. The castle housed and processed Jews who had left Russia until their transport to Israel could be arranged. The terrorists believed that every Jew that immigrated to Israel strengthened the Jewish State and weakened the Palestinian cause. Therefore, they threatened to kill their hostages and launch a wave of terrorist attacks on Austria if their demand was not met.

Chancellor Bruno Kreisky led the Austrian government. After meeting with his cabinet, he announced that the Austrians would yield to the terrorists' demands. The next day the Austrians announced they would close Schoenau Castle and then provide the terrorists safe passage to Libya. The Arab world erupted in ecstasy. Golda Meir was enraged.

Meir responded by first flying to Strasburg to address the Council of Europe. She then planned to go directly to Austria to meet with Kreisky.

Meir's speech on October 1 to the Council broke with tradition. Rather than read from a prepared statement, she spoke from her heart: "Since the Arab terrorists have failed in their ghastly efforts to wreak havoc in Israel, they have of late taken their atrocities against Israeli and Jewish targets into Europe, aided and abetted by Arab governments."

She then recounted the Munich outrage in 1972 and Germany's release of the surviving terrorists in response to the Lufthansa hijacking. She also empathized with the attendees. Meir told them she understood their desire to be spared from involvement with the conflict between Arabs and Jews. But, in a mocking tone, she explained that to do so they had to make a moral decision that would declare their countries off-limits to Jews, or perhaps at least Israeli ones. Meir concluded with a thundering warning:

> European governments have no alternative but to decide what they are going to do. To each one that upholds the rule of law I suggest there is but only one answer—no deals with terrorists; no truck with terrorism. Any government which strikes a deal with these killers does so at its own peril. What happened in Vienna is that a democratic government came to an agreement with terrorists. In so doing it has brought shame upon itself. In so doing it has breached a basic principle of the rule of law, the basic principle of the freedom of the movement of peoples—or should I say the basic freedom of Jews fleeing Russia? Oh, what a victory for terrorism this is!

Meir left to applause. Her next stop was Austria and Kreisky.

Chancellor Kreisky was Jewish by birth but not practice; he had turned agnostic in 1936. Shortly after the Germans incorporated Austria into the Third Reich, he escaped to Sweden where he spent the war years. Kreisky returned to Austria in 1946, after which, he rose to power. The Chancellor opposed Zionism but, curiously, not the existence of the State of Israel. And, some believed, he was too accommodating to former Nazi Party members who lived in Austria.

Meir extended her hand to Kreisky when she entered his office on October 2. The well-dressed but overweight man in his mid-sixties rose to shake her hand with a slight bow, but never emerged from behind his desk.

After some pleasantries that included reference to Kreisky's Jewish roots and lack of interest in Israel, Meir said, "We are grateful to your government for all that it has done to enable thousands of Jews to transit through Austria from the Soviet Union to Israel."

Kreisky's response showed no appreciation for Meir's gratitude: "But the Schoenau transit camp has been a problem to us for some time."

"What sort of problem?" Meir asked.

"For a start it has always been an obvious terrorist target …"

An upset Meir cut him off "Herr Kreisky, if you [close] down Schoenau it will never end. Wherever Jews gather in Europe for transit to Israel they will be held ransom by the terrorists."

Kreisky responded that Austria should not have to bear the burden. He suggested that Jews be flown directly from Russia to Holland.

But Meir admonished him that the Soviet Union would not permit Jews to leave by plane, only by train—a train running to Austria. Otherwise "we would fly them directly to Israel."

Kreisky said, "So let them be picked up by your own people immediately upon arrival in Vienna and flown straight to Israel."

"That's not practicable," Meir responded. And then:

> You know and I know that it takes guts for a Jew to even apply for an exit permit to leave Russia to come to us. They lose their jobs, they lose their citizenship, and they are kept waiting for years. And once a permit is granted most are given hardly more than a week's notice to pack up, say their goodbyes, and leave. They come out to freedom in dribs and drabs, and we never

know how many there are on any given train arriving in Vienna. So we need a collecting point, a transit camp. We need Schoenau.

Kreisky remained unmoved. He accepted his country's duty to provide humanitarian aid to refugees, but not when it put Austria at risk.

"And is it also not a humanitarian duty not to succumb to terrorist blackmail, Herr Chancellor?" Meir asked.

The formal meeting was growing increasingly nasty with each exchange.

"Austria is a small country," Kreisky answered angrily, "and unlike major powers, small countries have few options in dealing with the blackmail of terrorists."

Meir vehemently disagreed. "There can be no deals with terrorism whatever the circumstances. What you have done is certain to encourage more hostage-taking. You have betrayed the Jewish émigrés."

Kreisky shot back, "I cannot accept such language, Mrs. Meir. I cannot...."

Again Meir sharply interrupted him. "You have brought renewed shame on Austria," she said. "I've just come from the Council of Europe. They condemn your act almost to a man. Only the Arab world proclaims you their hero."

The Austrian responded without emotion. "Well, there is nothing I can do about that." He then shrugged and said, "You and I belong to two different worlds."

"Indeed we do, Herr Kreisky," an exasperated and drained Meir responded. "You and I belong to two very, very different worlds."

Meir then grabbed her handbag and rose to leave. As she did so an aide to the chancellor entered the room. He told the two leaders that media had gathered for a joint press conference. Meir saw no point in a charade that would only enhance Kreisky's image in the Arab world. She turned to her aide and whispered in Hebrew, "I have no intention of sharing a platform with that man. He can tell them what he wants. I'm going to the airport." To Kreisky she said, with contempt, "I shall forego the pleasure of a press conference. I have nothing to say to them. I'm going home." Meir left by a back stairway.

Five hours later Meir arrived at Ben-Gurion airport. She told the waiting Israeli press, "I think the best way of summing up the nature of my meeting with Chancellor Kreisky is to say this: he didn't even offer me a glass of water."

Meir's caustic confrontation with Kreisky and her speech to the European Council did have a salutary effect. It aroused protests around the world against Austrian plans to summarily close the transit camp. As a result, Kreisky felt compelled to offer an alternative arrangement to Jews hastily leaving the Soviet Union. Many weeks later the Austrians found a less prominent location that permitted discretion. But meanwhile, something much more dire had intervened to divert Meir's attention.

Pressure Builds

The IDF did not remain idle while Meir was in Europe. During the evening of September 30, its top generals met again. By then the tank reinforcements Elazar ordered had arrived on the Golan, but their crews were permitted to return to their base in Beersheba more than a hundred miles away. His minimal response was influenced by the attitude of Zeira, the IDF's intelligence chief who remained unfazed by the Arab military buildup. Zeira continued to insist that Syria would not attack alone and that, per the "concept," Egypt would not attack because she did not possess the weapons needed to strike Israeli air bases and economic targets.

However, perhaps sensing Hofi's continued unease despite Ziera's assurances, IAF Commander Peled boldly declared that, if the Syrians attacked in the morning, he would only need four to six hours to destroy their anti-air missile batteries, and no more than two hours if they struck at night. Either way, he was confident the IAF would be able to support the ground troops on the Golan once the missiles were disposed of. But, until then, any troops stationed on the Golan would have to fend for themselves. And, if Peled's assumptions were wrong, it would be for much longer.

Unbowed, Hofi's chief intelligence officer refused to remain silent in the face of what he could see with his own eyes and feel in his heart. Zeira's confident assertions did not translate into a proper analysis of the facts clearly evident on the ground. Hofi's subordinate said, "I don't need any more warning signs. All of the attack elements that they need, they already have. For me, the signs are all there."

When the generals' discussion turned to whether the standing army could block a Syrian advance while it waited for the air force and mobilized reserves to provide support, Elazar reluctantly decided that more strength was needed on the Golan. He ordered a reserve tank battalion, already in training, to remain in place on the Golan, and then added additional artillery units. The extra forces would provide a thicker crust, slightly harder to penetrate, but still lacking in depth and resilience. It would be sufficient for the best-case scenario, in which the IAF controlled the skies and unloaded its firepower upon onrushing Syrian tanks and infantry. But what if events did not meet those expectations?

Dayan was not present at the meeting, but he most certainly was informed of the generals' conclusions. With Meir out of the country, Yigal Allon served as acting prime minister in her place. He, like everyone in the military, did not know about Ismail's September deadline. During Meir's absence, only Dayan was aware of both Ismail's statement and all of the current military developments. That information he kept to himself.

In Washington, D.C., Kissinger intuitively felt uneasy on September 30. The Syrian build-up on the Golan concerned him. His alarm prompted him to ask for an interagency assessment. The response generated by his inquiry was that there was no reason to believe war would breakout imminently. Ambassador Dinitz, with whom Kissinger had met the same day, echoed those assurances.

Meanwhile, some lower-level elements of Israel's intelligence apparatus felt the need to sound an alarm. They knew that on October 1 the Egyptian army would begin its already-announced large-scale military exercises. They also were aware that many of their brethren attributed the Syrian military alert to the devastating losses Syria had incurred during the air battle on September 13 in which the IAF shot down thirteen Syrian warplanes. Still, sensing something was not quite right, they tried to warn their superiors but were thwarted at every turn. The "concept" was too powerful for them to overcome. Even news that arrived at 2:00 A.M. on October 1, from a well-regarded Mossad agent, did not shake the "concept" most subscribed to. That startling information revealed that the Egyptian military exercises along the Suez Canal would not end on October 7, as previously thought, but instead would be the launching pad for an attack with the objective of taking control of the mountain passes in the Sinai. That sounded a lot like Egypt's *Granite-2* plan, of which Israel was already aware.

All of the warnings and premonitions induced the IDF to increase preparations, but did not change its beliefs. Those at the highest levels of Israel's intelligence arm still thought that no definitive evidence existed that Egypt and Syria intended to act together. Likewise, they felt certain that Egypt did not possess the means to protect her infrastructure in a conflict with Israel. Therefore, Zeira still felt on the morning of October 1 that the likelihood war would break out in the near future remained small. Dayan, Elazar, and Allon allowed themselves to be assuaged by his assurances. None of them knew that the Egyptians thought that the small number of Mirage attack planes received from Libya (the same type of planes that De Gaulle had withheld from Israel in 1967) coupled with a brigade of ground-to-ground Kelt missiles delivered by the Soviets, gave them the ability to strike deep into Israel if provoked. Nor did the Israelis recognize that possession of those arms made the Egyptians confident that they could deter the Israelis from striking Egypt's core. Those Egyptian beliefs, whether accurate or not, meant that the conditions preventing an Egyptian attack, as stated in the "concept," had been met.

What Egypt did not know was whether Assad would follow through with his commitment to go to war. In 1967, the Syrians left Egypt in the lurch. Even though Syria had played a major role in instigating the 1967 crisis, Syrian forces had, for the most part, remained comfortable in their fortified holes while Israel pummeled Egypt and Jordan. Egypt's military wanted to make sure history did not repeat itself. To that end, the army summoned the Egyptian military attaché in Syria to Cairo for a debriefing.

During the evening of October 2, Dayan and Elazar met again. Meir, due to return from Austria, had not yet arrived. Earlier in the day, Sadat had secretly advised his War Council that the countdown to war had begun. Then human error intervened. The Middle East News Agency issued a news bulletin that the Egyptian 2nd and 3rd armies had been placed on alert. The bulletin was only supposed to go to a specified few. Instead, it was issued to all subscribers to the news agency. It was an important public clue that something was up. Still, Dayan and Elazar remained complacent. Elazar saw no evidence that Egypt would start a war and, due to the "concept," that Syria wouldn't without Egypt.

Dayan was not overly concerned either. "At the moment, I don't propose anything else," he said. He was satisfied with plans to strengthen the anti-tank ditch, pave an access road, and add more mines. Those new, relatively inconsequential measures would take several more days to finish.

During the time Meir had spoken to Kreisky, and while she was in the air returning home to Israel, lower-level intelligence officers received more information that supported their belief that Egypt's actions were not just exercises but instead presaged an imminent attack. They learned that Egyptian soldiers had broken down sandbag walls leading to the canal at forty different locations. In addition, massive quantities of ammunition on overloaded trucks flooded through Egyptian checkpoints that had received no advance warning of their arrival. Meanwhile, in Syria, troops moved to positions indicated as jumping-off points on Syrian attack plans (of which Israel had possession). Suspiciously, Syrian wireless radio traffic also decreased. That led some to speculate that the Syrians were trying to mask what they were doing. Still, those intelligence officers who sensed the coming storm failed to convince their superiors that something was awry.

When her plane landed in Israel following her exhausting trek, and she stepped onto Jewish soil, Meir was unaware of the danger her country was in. To this day, hard evidence has not surfaced to support well-reasoned suspicions that the Syrians ordered the terrorist attack in Austria to provide a distraction that would divert attention from the last part of their mobilization. Circumstantial evidence, however, is in no short supply.

The terrorists that took the hostages were members of Al-Sa'iqa, a Palestinian terrorist group established by Syria, supported by Syria, and based in Syria. It is inconceivable, especially given Israel's proclivity to retaliation against their host country, that Sa'iqa's leaders would undertake a high profile mission without the approval of their Syrian masters. It is quite conceivable, however, that the Syrians ordered a terrorist incident that would give them an excuse to bring their army to its highest state of alert and to mass along the Golan border. Since Israel often retaliated for terrorist attacks, what better cover for Syria's surprise attack than a manufactured need to defend herself?

Whether a planned diversion or a fortuitous event, the hijacking of the train had another consequence. At a critical stage Meir's attention was diverted by events, travel, speeches, and high profile meetings. At a time when Arab armies were massing, King Hussein was taking extraordinary steps to relay his concerns; lower-level Israeli intelligence evaluators were struck by the mounting danger; and Israel's northern commander was doing everything he could to push for help—Israel's prime minister was focused on the plight of Russian refugees and European terrorism. Would Meir have otherwise sniffed the danger in time to react? We will never know. But she was one of only a few who sat at the apex of Israel's intelligence machine. With her energy and emotions out of the loop for a few crucial days, one more opportunity to right the ship was lost.

CHAPTER FIFTY-SIX
Last Days

Three Meetings

On October 3, after returning from Austria, Meir met with several advisors at her home to discuss developments on the front facing Syria and, to a lesser extent, Egypt. In attendance were Dayan, Galili, Allon, Elazar, Peled, and Arye Shalev. Shalev stood in for Zeira, who was ill. Shalev reviewed recent events that led up to Arab forces massing along the ceasefire lines with Syria and Egypt, but only Allon appeared to be listening intently. Shalev concluded by saying it was feasible for the Syrians and the Egyptians to start a war from their present deployments, but not likely. Instead, he advised, the Egyptian deployment was a military exercise, not a run-up to war; and the Syrian deployment, was a response to the air battle in September.

Elazar then indicated that despite the information pouring in he was not convinced that the Arabs intended to start a war. Elazar noted that Marwan, Israel's trusted super-spy, had not given any warnings whereas, previously, Marwan had provided warnings for specific dates. Therefore, he concluded, there was not enough evidence to suggest war was imminent, or that Syria and Egypt were colluding; and he was confident that Israel would detect an attack. "We have good ... information. And, when you operate a big machine, it is likely that you'll have leakage."

Nevertheless, Elazar admitted that if the Syrian army did attack, it could force its way across the ceasefire lines. But even if that happened, he was convinced the IDF would expel the Syrians after deploying additional regular armored and artillery forces. It was a bold statement that suggested nothing else needed to be done.

Though Dayan agreed with Elazar's assessment, he disagreed with Elazar's reasoning. Dayan thought that Sadat would not attack because it didn't make sense politically; he thought that, even though he was acutely aware of Sadat's implicit threat to use force stemming from Ismail's revelation of the September deadline. But Dayan deluded himself into thinking that by procuring America's promise to help influence Israel, Sadat had already achieved a modicum of success. He also knew that the United States would pressure Israel to moderate her position following the Israeli elections. It made little sense to Dayan to think Sadat would not remain patient for another month. In fact, Dayan may have secretly hoped that Egypt would attack. Later he said:

> If the Egyptians cross the Suez tomorrow ... and [reach] up to the Mitla pass ... they will find themselves in a very uncomfortable position after that first step. There are many traveling expenses in crossing the canal, and afterwards, working in an area that has no end and we are coming at them from all sides ... a situation in which the Egyptians ... are not solving anything [not receiving any political benefit or retrieving the Sinai] and they are in a much more difficult situation than they are now, when the Suez Canal is protecting them. If they cross the Suez ... they are exposing themselves, so that there are quite a few people who are not stupid saying: 'Let them come, because if they cross—all of the tanks will advance on them,' etc.

However, Dayan was not so sanguine towards Syria:

> The Syrians are facing a situation in which everything that it lost in the Six-Day War it can theoretically capture in one step, protected by a missile deployment and the artillery it presently has, and after that, it has a relatively good defensive line, a natural obstacle—the Jordan—and it has solved its national problem in freeing the Golan Heights from our control.

But Dayan did not question Elazar. He thought Elazar's plans sufficient to hold the Golan.

Dayan's and Elazar's views won the day. Nobody suggested mobilizing the reserves, and Meir said:

> I accept the 'conception' of the difference between Egypt and Syria one hundred percent. I think that no argument can be made against it. To cross the canal, the Egyptians can and will be farther from their base and what will it give them in the end? On the other hand, the situation is completely different from the Syrians. Even if they wish to take all of the Golan, if they succeed in holding on to a few settlements, for each step over the line, if they can succeed in holding on to it—it exists in their hands.

In essence, Meir rationalized that the Egyptians had an opportunity to recover their lost lands diplomatically; Syria had none. Therefore it made no sense that the Egyptians would risk suffering devastating losses, even though the Syrians might be willing to do so.

Meir did, however, accept Allon's recommendation to schedule a cabinet meeting for Sunday, October 7 to discuss the situation. But, as she left the room, Meir turned to Shalev with appreciation and shook his hand. "Thank you," she said, "you calmed me down."

That same day, Egyptian Defense Minister Ahmad Ismail Ali flew to Damascus. He told the Syrians that Egypt planned to start the war on October 6. Not happy since it would take five days to remove all the oil from the tanks in the Homs refinery, the Syrians requested a two day delay. The Syrians feared that if Israeli planes were to attack before the combustible fluid was drained they would destroy not only the refinery but also the surrounding areas. Yet the Egyptians didn't care—any further delay was a risk they weren't willing to take.

However, not all of the news Ismail brought to Damascus was bad. The Egyptians had insisted the war begin at 6:00 p.m. and vigorously opposed Syria's request that it begin at dawn. One reason the Egyptians dismissed Syria's request was because, at sunrise, Israeli airbases would be shrouded in fog, which would prevent Syrian planes from accurately bombing the IAF's bases. Ismail suggested a compromise: both nations would attack at 2:00 p.m. even though then Israeli defenders would not face the glare of a setting sun during the critical first hours of the attack while the Egyptian army crossed the canal (which would have been the case were the Egyptians to attack nearer to 6 p.m.). Assad accepted the compromise. He had already decided that he would not permit last minute obstacles to derail their joint attack.

The Syrians and Egyptians also discussed strategic bombing of Israeli cities. The Syrians suggested they refrain from doing so initially in the hopes that the Israelis would refrain as well. Ismail agreed.

On October 3, Sadat held his own short, but important, meeting in which he told the Russian Ambassador that he had decided to go to war, and then asked, "What will the Soviet attitude be?" Sadat did not reveal when they planned to attack; that honor would go to Assad who was scheduled to meet with the Russian Ambassador to Syria the next day. Given Syria's superior relations with Moscow, both men felt that was the correct approach.

October 4 - The Russians Leave

On October 4, Assad told Russia's Syrian Ambassador that war would break out in a few days and that he envisioned it lasting no more than two days. The Syrian leader further advised that his primary goals were to recover the Golan and protect Palestinian rights. He then asked that the Soviet Union request a ceasefire from the Security Council once his army recovered the Golan. That would prevent an Israeli counterattack.

Assad never communicated his ceasefire plan to Sadat. He wanted the Egyptians to keep advancing, which would draw the Israelis to the Sinai and limit the amount of firepower directed at his own army. The request for a ceasefire was Assad's insurance plan if things did not go as well as he hoped. Of course, Assad was unaware that Sadat was also not telling him everything. He did not know that Sadat intended to move only a few miles from the Suez Canal, after which Syria would be on her own.

In Egypt, the Russian chief leading the Soviet military mission called on Egypt's minister of defense. He asked for permission to evacuate Russian families of servicemen working in Egypt. Ismail granted the request. Later that night planes loaded with Russian women and children began to leave Egypt and Syria.

On October 4, Brezhnev's response to Sadat's question about the Soviet Union's attitude arrived. He wrote that it was up to Egypt to decide how to resolve her own "vital issue." The decision to fight was Egypt's to make, and the Soviet Union would support Egypt as a friend. But Brezhnev advised that political means were preferable to war—especially if Egypt suffered a setback in the fighting. In that case, Egypt's opportunity to recover her territories would be lost.

Despite détente, Brezhnev did not feel any obligation to alert the Americans, which is not surprising, unless, of course, his decision to permit the evacuation of Soviet citizens was driven by more than his concern for their welfare. One would think no brighter signal could be sent of the risk of war than the sudden emergency evacuation of all noncombatant Russian personnel. Sadat and Assad could not have been pleased with how the Russians responded after being trusted with a heads-up about their surprise attack. They knew that both the Americans and the Israelis would detect the hasty departure of Russian non-combatants. Sadat's chief of staff later said, "So far, to our amazement, the enemy had not guessed the truth. If anything could now persuade him, this panicky action would." Since the Russian military advisors stayed behind at their posts, one could argue that the Russians thought that their actions would be interpreted only one way—a war was about to begin. That would have been a crafty, subtle way to signal the United States that something significant was about to happen.

Dayan met with Elazar, Hofi, and others during the morning of October 4. "My trauma is not about the Heights but about the settlements there whether they break through or not," Dayan told them. They must devise a solution, he added, one that would ensure the Syrians could not seize the settlements before Israel's reserves had the chance to mobilize and arrive. But nobody offered a suggestion. Nor did they feel any sense of urgency. Instead, their conversation consisted more of a theoretical discussion about the future than an exchange of ideas for how to respond to the present emergency.

However, as the day wore on, the information arriving was more ominous. Aerial reconnaissance missions finally succeeded in taking pictures of Egyptian deployments near the canal. An attempt to do so on October 1 had been thwarted by cloud cover; another try on October 3 had failed due to a faulty camera. But they were successful on the third attempt. As soon as the plane landed, the air intelligence unit began developing the pictures. Late in the evening, they were first disseminated to military intelligence and then to higher-level headquarters. The pictures revealed Egyptian crossing equipment staging closer to the water and Egyptian troops and equipment in battle positions. Still, some analysts credited their presence to a training exercise—which Egypt had announced would soon conclude with the troops returning to their bases.

Almost at the same time as the reconnaissance photos were being interpreted, Israeli intelligence learned of the Soviet evacuation. First, news arrived that the Soviets were leaving Syria. Then, by 10:00 p.m., Israeli military intelligence discovered that the same was happening in Egypt. The Israelis identified five Russian planes tasked for the mission in Syria and perhaps seven in Egypt. The question was: who was leaving and why? If the experts and advisors were on the planes along with their families then that might signify another upheaval in Syrian-Soviet relations. Since Israeli intelligence thought that the transport planes arrived later in Egypt than in Syria, might that then indicate Egyptian support for Syria's decision? On the other hand, if just families were leaving, some analysts thought that would mean Russia was aware fighting might soon break out between Israel, Syria, and possibly Egypt.

General Mendler commanded the armored division of Israel's regular army based in the Sinai. It was his task to hold off an attacking Egyptian army long enough for reserves to mobilize and arrive. On October 4, a farewell party was held for Mendler, whose reassignment to other duties was scheduled to begin four days later. During the party, he told his subordinate officers that he did not think he would be leaving so soon because the Egyptians, he felt, would attack before his departure.

Earlier in the day, Mendler had tried to convince Shmuel "Gorodish" Gonen that war was imminent. Gonen, who commanded the Southern Front, which included all Israeli forces in the Sinai, was not convinced. But inexplicably, he had only visited the Suez front once during that trying week. As a result, his views were shaped by Zeira's "concept" rather than his personal observations. Gonen rejected Mendler's request to move his division's two reserve brigades further forward into the Sinai so they could react faster to an Egyptian attack. Neither did he permit Mendler's warnings, or the increasing volume of troubling information that was pouring into the intelligence branches, to trouble him. Nor did he spend the night at his headquarters. Instead, Gonen visited friends in Haifa, even further from the canal.

As night turned into early morning, lower-level analysts sounded increasingly-loud alarms. And their superiors were no longer so confident that a war wasn't impending. Still the "concept" held—shaken but still preserved.

Just after midnight, a troubling warning reached a different branch of Israeli intelligence when Marwan relayed to his Mossad handlers that the Arabs were accelerating their preparations for war. He did not use the designated code word for signaling an imminent attack. Nor did he provide the date when war would break out. But he did ask to meet with Zamir, the head of Mossad, the next day in London—the evening of the fifth. By then, in Israel, night would already have fallen.

CHAPTER FIFTY-SEVEN
The Day Before

The Early Hours

On October 5, at 1:00 a.m., Eli Zeira telephoned Zamir. It was the first time Zeira had felt compelled to interrupt the sleep of his counterpart in the Mossad, but he was shaken by the news of the Soviet evacuation. He still was not ready to change his mind about the likelihood of war, but knew the development merited further discussion. An hour earlier, Zeira had ordered activation of the special listening devices affixed by Israeli Special Forces to the telephone lines running to the Egyptian military's main headquarters. Zeira's decision to activate them betrayed his heightened concern because the batteries that powered the devices would last for less than a day, and, once activated, they could be detected. As such, they were a onetime insurance policy reserved for true emergencies. By 1:45 a.m. they were operational.

Zamir listened to Zeira, but did not divulge the startling development that Marwan had contacted Mossad last night with an urgent request to meet. Why didn't Zamir tell Zeira? Most likely because Marwan had not used the designated code words indicating that an Egyptian attack was imminent. Previously, Marwan had been more specific when he had requested a meeting. Thus, Zamir may not have wanted to fuel speculation before he had hard information. Alternatively, Mossad and military intelligence were, in some ways, competing intelligence services. Zamir might well have wanted an opportunity, after learning what Marwan had to say, to form his opinion, and advocate for it, before Zeira had an opportunity to weigh in.

Two hours later Zamir's attitude changed. He received a call from a respected high-level analyst within Mossad who indicated that Marwan's meeting request probably meant the Arabs would attack soon. Zamir immediately called Zeira back, told him that he would be leaving for London in the afternoon to meet with Marwan, and then said to Zeira, "This means war; we don't have a date because a hint is not a date."

Meanwhile, new disturbing information continued to pour into Israel's military intelligence group. Between just before midnight and 3:30 a.m., five Russian planes landed at Damascus airport to receive passengers. An hour later, the last aircraft landed at Cairo airport to transport Russian family members out of Egypt. Seven Soviet ships prepared to leave the Egyptian port of Alexandria in the morning. Then, at 5:45 a.m., military intelligence distributed a report detailing its review of reconnaissance photographs taken over the Suez Canal. It said, in part: "The Egyptian army on the Canal front is in emergency formation, the magnitude of which has never been seen before."

Morning Meetings

General Elazar met with Zeira and Air Force Commander Peled at 8:25 a.m. He found Zeira still clinging to his "concept." Before the meeting, Zeira discussed the implications of the Soviet evacuation with analysts at military intelligence. He did not tell them that Marwan had asked for a meeting. Nothing the analysts said swayed him. Of course, the analysts did not have the full picture.

Zeira was not worried about the huge numbers of Egyptians staged so close to the canal. But Elazar was no longer willing to silently accept Zeira's analysis. Elazar said: "I don't have enough evidence that all these signs do not signal an intention to attack." His attitude had plainly changed.

Elazar decided to take some protective measures. He ordered the IAF to go on full alert. The alert effectively canceled the vacations of all members of the air force—even though Yom Kippur, the most important holiday of the Jewish people, would begin less than twelve hours later at sundown. Elazar also ordered the personnel of the entire Seventh Brigade to fly to the Golan, initiated planning for another armored brigade to move to the Sinai, and declared a "C" alert for the first time since the Six-Day War. A "C" alert required that those people necessary to coordinate a full mobilization of all reserve units be called into active service. Leave for IDF forces already stationed on the Golan and in the Sinai was also canceled. Elazar's office informed Meir's military assistant what he had done.

Little more than thirty minutes later, Elazar and Zeira met with Dayan. Elazar opened the meeting by focusing on the Russians' hasty departure. He told Dayan it could mean an Arab attack was forthcoming, or it could be a symptom of a diplomatic rift between the Arabs and the Soviet Union. But, he pointed out, there was no evidence of a diplomatic problem. Elazar then added: "Another sign tells me that this is not a political rift, because it is with the Syrians and the Egyptians at the same time."

"A diplomatic rift is not with women and children," Dayan responded, "it is with men. This could be a result of their fear that we will attack."

Elazar then told Dayan the measures he had ordered, saying, "[I am] choosing the stricter way." Dayan listened, then looked at intelligence reports describing developments on the Syrian and Egyptian fronts and said, "Just looking at the numbers could bring on a stroke."

Zeira, stubborn to the end, emphasized that there still was no positive proof that the Arabs would attack; but he no longer sounded so certain. Dayan responded by asking if anything had been heard. He was alluding to the "special source" listening devices. "Complete quiet," Zeira answered.

Missing from both conferences was any discussion of Marwan's request for the urgent meeting, which Mossad had interpreted as a warning of war. There was no discussion because incomprehensibly, Zeira did not inform the military chief of staff or the defense minister. That startling news might well have been sufficient for them to connect dots that would have led to an accurate and more sinister interpretation of what Egypt and Syria had planned. The only sensible explanation for Zeira's omission is that he felt too much ownership of the "concept" to allow others to form an independent opinion based on their analysis of all of the evidence. As long as he controlled the information flow, he controlled the conclusions.

Dayan told Elazar he supported the orders the general had issued. However, if Zeira had mentioned Marwan's communication, then Elazar, and perhaps Dayan, would have pushed for a more robust mobilization at an earlier date. Absent that information, Dayan may have remained reluctant because of his memory of "Duck" night in April 1959, when the military had ordered a general mobilization exercise without approval from Prime Minister Ben-Gurion. The citizen soldiers, suddenly racing to their military bases without prior notice, alarmed Israeli citizens and caused great tension with neighboring Arab countries. Dayan was also acutely aware of the disruption a sudden mobilization would cause just as Yom Kippur prayers were to begin, and things were already tense with the Arabs. A mistake could cause another "Duck" night, but this time on steroids. With Israel's elections scheduled for the end of the month, the risk of that particularly troubled Dayan. What impact would a needless mobilization have on voters? Would it harm Labor's chances to win?

The next meeting began at 9:45 a.m. This time Elazar, Zeira, and Dayan met with Meir. Zeira repeated his view that "our feeling is that they are not going to attack." He continued, "Perhaps the Russians think that they are indeed going to attack because they do not know the Arabs very well." And then, for the first time that morning, Zeira made an oblique reference to Marwan. He said that Zamir would be meeting with an important source who had reported, "Something is going to happen."

Elazar followed Zeira's comments by explaining the difference between having proof that the Arabs wouldn't attack and having to deal with their ability to attack. That was why he had placed the standing armed forces on high alert—because the Arabs could potentially attack. Dayan indicated he agreed with Elazar's decision and then added his explanation why, despite the high alert, reserves should not be mobilized: "We are not worried at the Egyptian front, and in the Golan Heights, we are worried all year around."

Dayan then suggested a political effort be made to forestall an Egyptian attack—if one was imminent. He recommended they ask the Americans to work with Russia to inform Egypt that Israel had no plans to attack, but also to warn them that, if attacked, the response would be devastating. The unsaid subtext of Dayan's proposal was that Kissinger should contact the Egyptians directly through his secret channel to Ismail. Dayan could not mention it explicitly, though, for the only other person in the room aware of the arrangement was Meir. But Dayan had a problem to surmount before his suggestion could be implemented. Who would carry the message to Kissinger? Very few people were cleared to know about it. Dinitz was in Israel rather than the United States because of his father's death. Foreign Minister Eban was in New York, but Eban had no knowledge of the secret channel. Dayan and Meir eventually decided to employ Dinitz's assistant. But, by the time that could be arranged, it would prove too late. The meeting concluded with Meir accepting Dayan's proposal to hold an immediate emergency cabinet session.

At 11:30 a.m., the six cabinet ministers who had planned to spend Yom Kippur eve in Tel Aviv gathered in Meir's office. The other cabinet ministers had already scattered throughout Israel to observe the holiday.

The six ministers met with Meir, Elazar, Zeira, and other IDF generals. During the meeting they learned of the increased tensions along Israel's borders and of the Soviet evacuation. Zeira then gave them his more upbeat assessment of the situation, and Elazar spoke again about the difference between capability and intent. He told the gathering that the Syrians and Egyptians both followed Soviet military doctrine, which expressly provided for moving rapidly from defensive positions to the offensive. However, unless he received more troubling information, he also said he would not recommend mobilization beyond what was called for in a "C" alert.

The group then discussed who had the authority to order a general mobilization, should it be required, especially on Yom Kippur. They agreed Meir could do so without obtaining any additional authorization from other cabinet ministers. Meir told them she hoped to refrain from ordering a general mobilization unless absolutely necessary. She then reminded them of the three weeks in May 1967 that preceded the Six-Day War:

> There is something, there are points that repeat themselves from the 5th of June, 1967. There were, here and there, messages that the IDF was reinforcing the Golan. Now we have a piece in the Egyptian press that says that the IDF is deployed on the Golan and that Israel has concentrated more forces along the lines, under a constant air umbrella ... it reminds me so much of what we had at ... the beginning of mid-May until June 5, that this should tell us something.

The necessary general mobilization in 1967 had caused hysteria across the nation, devastated the economy, roiled the political process, and, in the end, left Israel facing an existential threat that gave her no choice but to attack. Meir was determined to do all she could to make sure that the Arabs were aware that Israel had no intent to launch an offensive. She also wanted to avoid a general mobilization that, if it lasted too long because of how the Arabs reacted, might leave the IDF having no choice but to go to war.

Kissinger Becomes Concerned

At 11:40 a.m., Meir sent a cable to Mordechai Shalev, who was in charge of the Israeli embassy during Dinitz's absence, ordering him to arrange an urgent personal meeting with Kissinger. She further instructed him that a second cable would soon arrive with the reason and information required for the meeting. Since both Kissinger and Eban were in New York for the UN annual General Assembly meeting, Meir told Shalev to meet with both of them together if Kissinger did not return to Washington, D.C. beforehand.

The second cable did not leave Israel until 6:10 p.m. (12:10 in the afternoon in D.C.). It was delayed because it was rerouted, without Meir's knowledge, through Israel's military intelligence (AMAN) for comments. As a result it arrived in two parts. The **first** contained Meir's personal statement concerning the Arab deployment, assurances that Israel had no thought of attacking, a request that Kissinger ask the Russians to tell the Arabs that Israel would not attack; and an admonition that, if attacked, Israel would respond, "strongly and vehemently." However, the **second** part written by AMAN, significantly watered down Meir's concerns. It included AMAN's estimate that the Egyptian mobilization was due to a military exercise and fears that Israel would attack. It further included AMAN's speculation that the Russian departure might be due to a political crisis between the Soviets and the Arabs. Therefore,

AMAN's addition, an addition neither Meir nor Dayan was aware of nor would have approved, significantly undercut the message's purpose by minimizing the apparent need for Kissinger to promptly respond.

By the time Eban received the cable from Shalev, it was too late to reach Kissinger. Kissinger's assistant told Eban that he was unavailable and that the message could be given to his aide, Brent Scowcroft, instead. It appears Scowcroft received the message around 8:00 p.m. on October 5 in New York (2:00 a.m. on October 6 in Israel). Kissinger did not see it until after the war began.

However, earlier that day, Kissinger did learn of the Russians evacuating their families. Concerned, he asked the CIA for an assessment as to whether that meant war. The CIA responded, "It appears that both sides are becoming increasingly concerned about the activities of the other.... The military preparations that have occurred do not indicate that any party intends to initiate hostilities." The cable that Kissinger's assistant had read that night, which, Meir hoped, would inspire an urgent reaction but which was softened by AMAN, seemingly supported the CIA's analysis. Much later, despite not having seen the cable in a timely fashion, Kissinger reflected on October 5 and criticized himself for not anticipating what was about to occur.

Israeli Preparations

After Elazar had ordered the "C" alert, and the Seventh Brigade and other units began to move; the IDF increased its number of tanks on the Golan from 100 to 180 within hours. The next day, the full complement of 300 regular army tanks in the Sinai would be in place. It would prove enough to shield the country from certain calamity, like the end of Israel, by the narrowest of margins. But not enough to deflect a disaster of monumental proportions.

The Seventh Brigade was able to move into position so rapidly because IAF transports moved the men in the unit from the Sinai; their tanks and vehicles stayed behind. Then, rather than use their own equipment, they drew on pre-positioned stocks near the front earmarked for reserve units. As a result the Seventh Brigade was fully in place within twenty-four hours of Elazar's orders.

Late in the day, General Eitan, IDF Commander of the Golan region, received permission from Hofi to concentrate the entire Seventh Brigade near Nafekh, the central crossroads where Eitan's headquarters on the Golan Heights was located. When war broke out the next day, events would prove that Hofi guessed wrongly where the main axis of the Syrian attack would be. He would have to scramble because no second line of defense existed. However, the few forces available on the north were well-prepared for war and positioned close enough to the front to make a difference. They saved the nation.

The same cannot be said for the IDF defenders in the Sinai.

Strung out along the canal, the Bar-Lev line was in a state of neglect. In the event of war, the fortifications were supposed to be occupied by a regular army infantry unit, at full strength, and at the height of its training. On October 5 and 6, they were not. Instead, 450 members of a reserve unit from Jerusalem manned the Bar-Lev line, and many of the fortifications were closed. Those men who garrisoned the open forts were in their 30s and no longer in the best of fighting trim. And some of the fighting positions were in disrepair: the trenches had collapsed, and many positions lacked sufficient sandbags to provide protection. The forts also did not have enough ammunition, and the men did not have enough recent training to use the little weaponry they did have as effectively as a younger, regular army unit would have been able to.

The troops occupying the Bar-Lev forts had the misfortune to be there because it was their turn, based on a peacetime rotation plan. Their mindset was focused on how to occupy their time, not on how to prevent themselves from being overrun by the enemy. They had brought books and fishing rods. Aggressive instincts some might have possessed when first drafted many years before had naturally dissipated with age and a soft civilian life. Shockingly, they were the only soldiers Israel had on the frontline to oppose 100,000 men, more than 1,300 hundred tanks, and massive amounts of Egyptian artillery. A superior, who previously served reserve duty along the Jordan River where fighting could be expected, told the unit's most senior company commander before he and his men were stationed along the canal: "This time, I'm sending you to the canal and you can rest."

Elazar fretted from morning to afternoon. At 12:30 p.m., when he met with his General Staff, he told them he did not think war would break out within twenty-four hours. He also expressed hope that, if war were imminent, he would receive more than one day's warning. However, he was not satisfied that he had done enough. To ensure that the air force would be at full strength if fighting started, Elazar ordered mobilization of the several thousand additional reserve personnel required to bring the IAF to maximum readiness. He did so even though he did not have the authority to do it without the political leaders signing off.

The Marwan Meeting

By 5:00 p.m. in Israel, the stream of incoming intelligence had turned even grimmer. A report had arrived from an Arab source that the reason the Russians were evacuating was because Syria and Egypt intended to attack Israel. Bureaucratic impediments prevented the message from being transmitted and interpreted promptly, and analysts did not deliver the message to Zeira until 11:00 p.m. As a result, Zeira had already heard rumors of the war warning from another source before officially receiving it. Even so, Zeira decided not to tell Elazar, Dayan, Meir, or anybody else in leadership positions until he heard from Zamir following his meeting with Marwan.

Zeira later said that he did not contact Elazar because the chief of staff had already taken the necessary steps to protect the nation. In addition, he did not believe that the source was reliable enough that the information added anything to what was already known. Thus, Zeira ignored what he had heard Elazar say he needed: more verification of Arab intent. Later, after the war ended, Elazar testified that, if he had known of the warning Zeira received that night, he would have ordered the army to mobilize its reserves. Elazar's opinion was that, even at that late date, full mobilization would have prevented catastrophe on the Golan and in the Sinai. As Elazar put it, the Egyptians would not have broken through the Bar-Lev line "as if they were on parade." But because of Zeira's stubborn adherence to his crumbling "concept," Elazar never received the information he needed to objectively confirm what his intuition already told him—war was on the horizon.

Zamir arrived in London at noon. His meeting with Marwan was scheduled for 10:00 p.m. (11:00 p.m. in Israel).

Marwan was born in 1944 to an Egyptian family of moderate means. He studied chemistry and served in the Egyptian army. His rise to fortune did not commence as a result of his intellect or military service. Instead, he married well. His wife was President Nasser's third daughter. Two years after they married, Marwan began working at the Presidential Information Bureau. His job was to gather intelligence. The bureau's function was to brief the Egyptian president on all the information it collected and analyzed. Within a year, Marwan moved to London where he combined studying for a Master's degree with undertaking diplomatic missions for his father-in-law, President Nasser. But soon Marwan had a third purpose. Twice he contacted the Israeli Embassy with hopes of speaking to the Israeli intelligence representative in order to offer his services as a spy. The third time he succeeded.

Generally, walk-in spies are greeted with suspicion. If it seems too good to be true, there likely is something wrong. That is especially true in the intelligence world. Past history guides that walk-ins volunteering their services as spies frequently are double agents, pretending to work for their new masters while still in the employ of their own country. Once a double agent gains the trust of an intelligence service, that person can inflict great damage by spreading disinformation to mask what is real. Of course Mossad was wary, but Marwan's connection to Nasser's family overcame their initial reluctance to trust him.

But before they would rely on Marwan, Mossad—the Israeli intelligence service that along with AMAN (the military intelligence service) and the Shin Bet (responsible for internal security) comprised Israel's intelligence umbrella—had to evaluate the risk that he was a double agent. To do that, they needed to obtain satisfactory answers to three questions.

Mossad analysts **first** asked themselves: what was Marwan's motive for betraying his country and his father-in-law? It appeared the answer was money.

The analysts' **second** question was whether the Egyptian intelligence services were sophisticated enough to mount a high-level espionage operation for an extended period of time, with Marwan as the spearhead? Their answer, which mirrored the disdain that most Israeli branches of government felt about their Egyptian counterparts, was a resounding no. And even more, they doubted whether the Egyptians would be willing to risk the safety of a person so closely connected to their leadership.

Their *third* question was whether the information Marwan provided was important and accurate. The answer to that question was a resounding yes. Marwan brought access to valuable material and insights from the beginning. Mossad's analysts deemed the information too vital to Egyptian interests to be used as cover to convince them of the bona fides of a double agent. In support of their conclusion, whenever alternate sources brought information on the same topic as that received from Marwan, what Marwan provided always was consistent with what was provided from those other sources. And, when his handlers asked him to obtain specific information, Marwan did. Very quickly he gained Mossad's trust.

Mossad used the code name "Angel" when referring to Marwan. The name was a takeoff of the Roger Moore character, Simon Templar, in the popular James Bond copycat television show of the time, "The Saint." To motivate Marwan by impressing him with his importance, Zamir would often take the unusual step of meeting with the spy himself rather than assigning the task to a lower-level agent. Zamir also had another motive. He needed the constant contact to assuage his nagging concern that Marwan was a double agent.

After Nasser died, Sadat promoted Marwan to run the Egyptian Information Bureau. The new position gave Marwan ever better access to Egypt's secrets. In August 1971, he handed over to Mossad Egypt's war plan to regain control of the Sinai. The contents of that plan helped birth the "concept;" Egypt would not attack until it had offensive weapons that could deter the Israelis. If the "concept" was correct, then, in theory, all Israel needed to do to obtain advance warning of an attack was to monitor Egyptian airfields and ports for the arrival of planes and scud missiles capable of bombing Israel's cities.

Marwan's new position inspired confidence within Israel's intelligence community that he would provide warning of any planned Egyptian attack. In fact, Marwan warned in November 1972, that the Egyptians would soon begin a war with the Israelis, and then again in April and May 1973, as well as on other occasions. One time, he warned of a specific date for an attack, May 19, 1973. Each time, Israel responded with some form of heightened alert or mobilization that turned out to have been needless but cost a significant sum.

On October 4, Marwan had contacted his Mossad case officer in Paris. He did not mention anything about the joint Syrian and Egyptian meetings in Alexandria in August, or about Sadat's meeting with Saudi

King Faisal in late August where he was present and war was discussed. But Marwan did say he wanted to meet and talk about "lots of chemicals," the code word for a war warning. And he said that he wanted Zamir at the meeting. However, he did not use the code words that Mossad had provided for an imminent, emergency war warning.

Their late night meeting did not begin with a discussion of a possible war. Instead they spoke of the rocket attack Palestinians had attempted in Rome, which had been foiled thanks to information Marwan provided, and whether it would somehow cause suspicion to fall on him. Then Marwan turned to the real reason he had requested an urgent meeting. He told Zamir that Egypt and Syria would attack Israel the next day. He said the attack would unfold pursuant to plans Egypt had previously developed. He advised Zamir that he was uncertain whether Egypt would stop her advance a few miles from the canal, or if the Egyptian army would try to reach the mountain passes. He followed his pronouncement with a proviso:

> I must tell you that if political or military conditions were different, if there was a decisive and important change in the military or political conditions, Sadat would stop everything.

Marwan also indicated that the Egyptian leadership was surprised that, given the concentration of their forces along the canal, Israel had not changed her military deployments. During the meeting the spy handed over an update of the Egyptian war plan. Nothing in it was markedly different from the one already known to the Israelis.

After the meeting ended, Zamir pondered their conversation for a few moments before writing a report for delivery to Israel. Zamir's contemplation centered on his concern over whether Marwan had "cry wolf syndrome." Marwan had delivered erroneous war warnings many times in the past. Therefore, Zamir could not help but speculate about the accuracy of Marwan's information. But this time was a particularly dire moment, Zamir knew, because of the other indicators, that once Israel's leadership received Marwan's warning, Israel would initiate a full-scale mobilization. Such a sudden mobilization could cause the war Israel hoped to avoid.

Quickly, however, Zamir overcame his doubts and decided that he should not discount Marwan's warnings. He then called his bureau chief to pass on a preliminary report that Israeli decision makers could use as a basis to act expeditiously while waiting for his more detailed, written report. Zamir placed the call on an international line. However, the switchboard operator, rather than immediately completing the connection, tried to convince Zamir that nobody would answer. After all, it was Yom Kippur and a Jew was not likely to pick up the telephone. But Zamir was insistent. The call had to go through. The Mossad bureau chief was expecting to hear from Zamir. He picked up the phone. It was 2:30 a.m. in Israel. Zamir told him with 99.5 percent certainty that the Egyptians, in accordance with the Granite-2 war plan, would begin the attack that evening.

Almost thirty-five years later, a body hurtled toward the street from a fifth floor apartment balcony in London. It hit the ground with a thud. The body was that of Ashraf Marwan. The day before, Marwan had had a lengthy phone conversation with Ahron Bregman, an Israeli historian based in London. Previously, Bregman had written a book revealing Marwan's name as an Egyptian double agent spy (working for Egypt while pretending to spy for Israel) who had tipped off Israel that Egypt would attack. They discussed the memoir Marwan was working on, which detailed his life as a double agent. It was provisionally titled "What Happened in October 1973." The two men had agreed to meet, but Marwan never showed up at the appointed time and place. London police investigating Marwan's death did not find his manuscript nor did they determine what caused Marwan to fall.

Was Marwan a double agent after all? The debate still rages. Zamir later said about their meeting in October: "I did not ask him how long he had known, both because it would not have made any difference and also because I did not see any point in initiating a discussion that would create tension between us." Marwan did not divulge the exact time of the attack, but did say it would be at sunset. Sunset on October 6 was at 5:20 p.m., and last light was at 5:44 p.m. The Granite-2 plan specified a sunset attack. Somehow, Zamir reached the conclusion that the Egyptians would attack at 6:00 p.m. He was wrong, and Marwan's suggestion that the attack would begin at sunset was either a mistake based on old information or a lie. One thing, however, is certain. The timing error was fatal for many soldiers, and almost fatal for Israel. Zamir had passed on an erroneous estimate based on a false premise in a manner that suggested certainty.

If Marwan was a double agent what advantage could Egypt have hoped to gain by divulging a portion of their war plans, and that they were planning to attack the next day? **One** *answer is that perhaps, even at the last moment, Sadat hoped for a diplomatic resolution. Marwan signaled those hopes with his suggestion that, even though time was swiftly running out, war could be averted with the right diplomatic moves. Perhaps the Egyptians had discounted the harm that disclosing the information would cause because they may have believed that, by then, Israel would already have detected and determined the true reason for their mobilization. That is especially true because, even now, with the benefit of hindsight, it is virtually impossible to understand why the urgent Russian evacuation on October 4 did not tip off the Americans or the Israelis to Egypt's and Syria's nefarious intent. Sadat may also have hoped to obscure his ultimate goals by hinting at Granite-2 while withholding the High Minarets plan, which the Egyptian army had developed to seize only a sliver of land. And* **second***, by not revealing the time of the attack at the same time the attack was revealed, Egypt gained the tactical advantage of surprise: the Egyptians could attack earlier than Israel had expected them to, based on the plans Marwan had provided. It was an advantage that, in the first few hours of war, did much to help ensure their success.*

On the other hand, the reason the double agent theory makes no sense is that the Egyptians would have known that the information Marwan revealed would trigger an accelerated IDF mobilization that might thwart Sadat's plans. In addition, over the years, Marwan had provided Israel with information that proved crucial to her security.

Would Egypt have risked giving up so much in order to gain, what the Egyptians must have realized, might be so little?

The argument continues to this day. After the war, Zeira, the vilified main proponent of the "concept" and also the first to reveal the existence of the high-level Arab spy, clung to his theory that Marwan was a double agent. Part of the evidence he marshaled was that Marwan, on two occasions, failed to reveal crucial information that he definitely knew: **first***, the meeting of the generals in Alexandria, on August 23, 1973, when they planned the war;* **second***, Sadat's meeting on August 28 with King Faisal that included Marwan and during which Sadat revealed his plan to go to war "soon, very soon." However, it's not surprising that Zamir, who relied on Marwan and also maintained extensive personal contacts with him, has continued to maintain that he was not a double agent. Zamir's perspective was strongly supported by a book published in 2016 entitled "The Angel" written by Uri Bar-Joseph. The truth may well have been that Marwan was both a spy and a double agent, depending on what suited him at the moment. He lived for years after his identity was revealed. Yet, did the Egyptians permit him to live because killing him would only corroborate the truth that he was a spy? Or did the Egyptians kill him because they did not want him to reveal that he was a double spy?*

The day after Marwan's funeral, Hosni Mubarak, who at the time was the president of Egypt, said: "Marwan carried out patriotic acts which it is not yet time to reveal." The controversy continues.

CHAPTER FIFTY-EIGHT
The Wrong Countdown Begins

October 6, 1973 was a Saturday. It also was Yom Kippur, the most solemn holiday in the Jewish religion. Another name for it is the Day of Atonement, a day of contemplation and repentance. Traditional observance requires fasting for twenty-four hours and prayers. Even most secular, non-religious Jews observe the holiday. In Israel, during the early morning hours of Yom Kippur in 1973, the roads were empty, and most were sleeping. Their last meal had been before the sun went down the night before. For many, their last thoughts before the sun's rays slipped below the horizon were whether to take a last bite or a last sip. They went to bed contemplating the long day at the synagogue ahead and the pangs of hunger they would face while waiting for the day to end so they could eat and drink again. None of them expected the sunset that day would be different from all others. Rather than feeling the refreshing satisfaction of that first sip of water or coffee and the invigorating wave of energy from their first morsel of food in twenty-four hours, instead they would face their nation's mortality and endure a desperate fight for survival.

In this chapter I will depart from the style of this book to this point. Instead we shall move, moment by moment, from Israel's first recognition of the tsunami barreling towards her until the first shells were fired as the Arab wave of lead, steel, and determined soldiers rose and crashed over the Jewish State's borders. The story unfolds both in Israel and on the east coast of the United States where the clock was six hours behind Israel's.

Countdown

Israel, shortly after 2:30 a.m.—The Mossad bureau chief, soon after speaking to Zamir, quickly disseminated the startling news to Israel's military and political leaders that Egypt and Syria would launch a surprise attack at 6:00 p.m. No time was wasted waiting for Zamir's notes to arrive so that intelligence analysts could pick over, cross-check, and interpret the meaning of Marwan's revelations before news of the imminent attack was revealed to those who needed to know. Zamir opposed that sort of pre-processing because he thought that, if raw details were left unvarnished by military intelligence, it would help Meir, Dayan, and other members of the leadership team to sense Sadat's mood and the political environment in Egypt. But it also meant relying on two things: Marwan's ability to accurately express sensitive and colorful information and Zamir's ability to convey it; and dispensing with a third thing: having the information evaluated by dispassionate analysts trained to uncover inconsistencies that might question Marwan's veracity and reveal inaccuracies.

Israel, 4:00 a.m.—Aides awakened Meir, Dayan, Elazar, and Zeira to inform them, based on the intelligence provided by Marwan and reported by Zamir, that Syria and Egypt would launch an attack on Israel at 6:00 p.m.

"Yisrael, what do we do now?" Meir blurted to her military secretary. Zeira's immediate reaction was to call Elazar. Elazar sprang out of bed to summon his staff for a meeting.

Israel, 5:00 a.m.—Elazar told Peled to prepare to attack Syrian missile sites. Peled responded that the IAF would be ready by 11:00 a.m.

Israel, 5:50 a.m.—Elazar met with Dayan in the Defense Minister's office. Elazar wanted to mobilize 200,000 men that would comprise four divisions plus supporting forces. He also pushed for permission to launch a preemptive air strike on Arab SAMs and airfields. Elazar had not forgotten that he had previously promised Peled the IAF would have the opportunity to destroy Egypt's and Syria's SAMs before having to provide air support to the ground troops.

Elazar's promise had been a response to Peled's warning that, if he did not strike preemptively, he would be unable to provide the troops with air-to-ground support for several days. Therefore, since Israel's defense plan was predicated on achieving air superiority, a decision not to preempt by launching air attacks before the Arabs struck could cost the lives of hundreds, if not thousands, of IDF soldiers, and potentially risk the nation's existence. Moreover, the need to preemptively attack was even greater than had been anticipated because the Israelis had taken far too long to properly interpret signs of the surprise attack. This failure would result in there not being enough troops on the front lines to blunt or deflect the Arab attacks that would soon come. Elazar knew that, without the IAF's help, the few soldiers in place might be no better than a speed bump that would scarcely impede the Arab assault. However, until the SAMs were destroyed, the ground forces would not get the support they needed. That is why Elazar so badly wanted to unleash Peled immediately.

But nobody had told Elazar about the promise Kissinger had extracted from Meir at the end of 1971—Israel would not preempt and, if attacked, would not respond for two hours. If Elazar had known, he certainly would have pushed much earlier for at least a partial mobilization.

Dayan, who knew that Israel's hands were tied by Meir's promise, did not reveal the secret understanding in those early morning hours. But he was adamant that he would not countenance any form of preemptive strike. When Elazar pushed hard to change his mind, Dayan responded: "[O]ur political situation does not enable us to do what we did in 1967." And then Dayan came close to revealing the secret that he had held close for far too long: "Even if the Americans are 100 percent sure [that Syria and Egypt will attack that day] they will not let us attack first."

Dayan was equally resistant to full mobilization. He told Elazar that "the entire IDF should not be mobilized for Zamir's stories." Dayan was alluding to Marwan's warnings months before which had not proved true, and to Marwan's suggestion that Sadat could still change his mind, if the political situation warranted it. And since Dayan knew that Kissinger had a secret channel to the Egyptians, he may also have believed that, even if the warnings were accurate, the Americans, acting on Meir's request from the day before, would forestall the Egyptians. He did not know that Meir's request, watered down by AMAN, had not yet been delivered to Kissinger.

Therefore, at first, Dayan would only give Elazar permission to mobilize 30,000 reserves. After more discussion he agreed to 60,000. That would be enough for two divisions, one to reinforce each of the two fronts.

However, Elazar persisted. He wanted more. It would take two days for eighty percent of the army to reach the frontlines if full mobilization began immediately. Elazar told Dayan that, while an extra division on each front would have been enough with a proper warning, it was not under the present circumstances. Because the reinforcements would not arrive for another twenty-four hours, they had to expect that the Arabs would occupy some territory. Therefore, the IDF would have to counterattack. More men would be required for those attacks to succeed.

Dayan derisively responded, "The Chief of Staff wants to mobilize forces for a counterattack in a war that did not start?"

In the end, all Dayan and Elazar could do was agree to disagree, leaving the decision regarding mobilization to Prime Minister Meir. Tragically, nobody sent call-up notices after the meeting for the men needed to man the two divisions to which Dayan had consented. Thus, the IDF did not mobilize anybody until after Dayan and Elazar met with

Meir. Crucial time was lost that would cost lives, territory, and post-war political advantage.

Israel, 6:45 a.m.—Fog and bad weather covered the Syrian missile sites. Elazar approved Peled's request, if sanctioned by the cabinet, to change the initial target of the IAF's preemptive attack to Syria's airfields. The new plan required reconfiguring the armament load for each plane, altering the sequence of attack, and changing the composition of formations that would comprise the strike. Peled advised Elazar that he would not be ready to launch until noon.

Israel, 8:05 a.m.—Meir arrived at her office and immediately met with Dayan, Bar-Lev, Elazar, and Zeira. Soon after, Galili and Allon joined them. It was the first time Meir had seen Dayan since she had learned of Marwan's warning. She had asked Dayan to meet with her earlier but he had turned her down, citing other commitments.

Dayan spoke first. Surprisingly, he ignored the armies about to invade and instead focused on the children living in settlements on the Golan Heights, settlements which, he feared, the Syrian tanks would overrun. Dayan wanted to ensure that the children would be removed from danger by bringing them to Israel's interior. Next, he briefly spoke about coordinating intelligence with the United States and Jordan. Then he objected to the IAF launching a preemptive attack. He also argued against a general mobilization, which he felt would wrongly signal that Israel wanted to go to war—something he still hoped to avoid. Recognizing the unease his restrained approach might cause the Prime Minister, Dayan reassured Meir that, if war broke out, they could easily switch to a general mobilization. He concluded saying, "It is almost a tradition in the IDF for the military chiefs to urge more activity: I speak as a former chief of staff. It is for the political authority to impose limitations when necessary."

Elazar shot back:

> The reserves we do not call up now will not be able to take part in the war by tomorrow.... I favor a call-up of 200,000 soldiers ... if we don't have a large call up, then I don't see less than 70-80,000. From the standpoint of international impact, it doesn't matter if we call up seventy thousand or two hundred thousand.... It's better if they say that we started it and then we win. That is what they will in any case.

Elazar continued, "With regard to a preventive strike ... that would save many lives.... We don't have to decide that now. We have four hours to consult with the Americans."

Meir repeatedly asked Elazar if holding back from attacking would jeopardize Israel's survival; Elazar responded each time that it would not. When Elazar was asked how much advance time the IAF would require, he answered that Peled would be ready by noon and then optimistically predicted that the IAF would require three hours to destroy airfields and missile sites. But, he warned, if the political leadership waited until 1:00 p.m. to give permission to preempt, it would be too late to destroy the SAM air defense systems on either front before the Arab attack would begin.

Meir then asked Zeira to state his views. Zeira responded cautiously that the Arabs had everything in position to launch an attack but "[Sadat] has not given the order to proceed. Perhaps at the last moment he will draw back. We may be able to influence what he does or decides." Zeira then suggested they call up the reserves, which would deter an attack, while also asking the Americans to use diplomacy to prevent one.

The discussion left Meir with three competing perspectives. Elazar thought in terms of capabilities. He insisted that Israel be prepared to respond to what the Arabs could do—which is why he wanted to both mobilize and preempt. Zeira had shifted from denying the likelihood of war to recognizing the need to deter the Arabs from starting one. Therefore, he supported mobilization but still retained hope of using diplomacy to avoid war. Dayan was focused on a political solution. He feared a significant mobilization would cause the war they hoped to avoid. He was more willing to gamble that the Arabs would give in to pressure from the superpowers not to attack, so long as Israel refrained from provoking them in the meantime. And, if he was wrong, Dayan believed that the standing IDF forces could hold off the Arab onslaught until reserves had the chance to mobilize and reach the frontlines. In essence, he was willing to gamble Israel's security on the Americans being able to forestall the Egyptians, while knowing full well that, if his roll of the diplomatic dice failed, the lives of thousands of IDF soldiers would be at risk.

Not totally satisfied with the options before her, Meir proposed another idea. She suggested leaking information to the press to let the Arabs know Israel was prepared and ready. She asked, "Inasmuch as this doesn't harm us, if they know that we know, does that make things difficult for us or not?" It is not clear whether her question, similar to one posed by Minister Galili, ever received any consideration or response.

Dayan then sensed that Meir was close to making a decision. So he told her, "If you approve a large call-up, I will not resign." He did not know that Elazar, who had become more and more nervous that nothing had been done for the last few hours, had already covertly ordered the mobilization of 70,000 men.

Meir finally made her decision near 9:00 a.m. Because of her promise to the Americans, she knew she could not preempt. It is the burden of leaders to compare the short-term costs of their decisions with the long-term goals of their country, and to determine how many lives can be put at risk, if any, to preserve the future of their people. If Israel preempted, and the war went long or not well, Meir feared that an angry President Nixon would not provide sorely-needed military supplies coupled with the diplomatic support Israel might need to prevail. Therefore, she felt she had no choice but to refuse to preempt. But she endeavored to soften the blow to Elazar, whose military planning and decision-making till then had been predicated on using the IAF to preempt. It was a plan that Dayan had disingenuously acknowledged his support of to Peled months before. Meir told Elazar, for whom she had a soft place in her heart,

> Dado [Elazar], I know all the arguments in favor of a preemptive strike, but I am against it. We don't know now, any of us, what the future will hold, but there is always the possibility we will need help, and if we strike first, we will get nothing from anyone ... with a heavy heart I am going to say no.

But Meir also told Elazar regarding preemptively striking, "My heart is drawn to it; we'll see." Meir held Elazar in such high esteem that it troubled her to disappoint him. However, her rejection had also contained a hint that she might change her mind. That hint contributed to the IAF's confusion in the early hours of the coming war.

Meir did respond more sympathetically to Elazar's request for mobilization. She thought, during those difficult moments when she had to choose between two respected military experts with vastly more experience than her, "My God. I have to decide which of them is right." Therefore, Meir compromised. Despite her concern about the economic impact of a large mobilization, she approved an immediate call-up of 100,000 -120,000 reservists. The meeting broke up with a self-serving statement by Dayan to Elazar designed to deflect any potential future criticism for mobilizing too many or too little, "The Chief of Staff will mobilize the entire number as proposed by the Chief of Staff." He said that, knowing that the compromise number was only half that Elazar originally requested.

Israel, 10:15 a.m.: U.S., 4:15 a.m.—Kenneth Keating, the American Ambassador to Israel, arrived at Meir's offices at her urgent invitation. "We may be in trouble," she said. Meir told Keating about Egypt's and

Syria's deployments, about Israel's belief she was about to be attacked, and that Israel had decided to partially mobilize in response. She asked Keating to make sure that the United States would tell Russia and Egypt that Israel is only mobilizing to defend herself and would not attack. Meir warned, however, that, if attacked, the result for Egypt and Syria would be devastating.

Meir certainly hoped that diplomatic channels would prevent war. But she also was unwilling to change Israel's policies to anything near what Sadat would require to call-off Egypt's attack.

Israel, 11:00 a.m.: Elazar met with his generals and Dayan in the command headquarters known as the "Pit." Orders for the partial mobilization had already gone out. Because of the holiday, it was easier to locate those that needed to be contacted in synagogues than it otherwise would have been on a regular day. The clear roads eased movement of military vehicles and mobilized personnel. But radio and TV broadcasts were not functioning normally. Nor were many people listening to them. They were in synagogue instead. That hindered the smooth operation of the portions of the mobilization plan that depended on coded words broadcast over the airwaves.

Elazar told the assembled officers about the Marwan warnings and the 6:00 p.m. attack time. However, when he said that he wanted to send fighter planes into the air to patrol Israel's skies, Dayan responded that he should do so, if they were needed, but they were not required to deter the Arabs. Dayan then told the officers that the Americans had been informed about the developments and were in the process of telling the Egyptians and Syrians that Israel was aware of their plans and was ready.

Surprisingly, Dayan asked when the reserves would arrive at the Sinai front. As defense minister, and having been the main proponent of limiting Israel's mobilization, his inquiry was as disturbing as it was surprising. Without knowledge of how long it would take for mobilized forces to reach the fronts, how could he have advocated against mobilizing more when he did not know the implications of his recommendation? Elazar responded that 300 tanks would arrive at the front within twenty-four hours and 300 more within forty-eight hours.

Dayan then asked Elazar, "What happens if, on the night following Yom Kippur, at midnight, it becomes clear there is no war?"

Elazar answered, "The release of the reserve soldiers will [the translator's interpretation was 'will not' rather than 'will' but that probably was an erroneous translation or a typographical error] take place less than forty-eight hours later."

Dayan retorted, "A hundred thousand men will wander around for a full day before being sent home?"

An annoyed Elazar shot back, "They won't just wander around: They will also be sent to the front. If it becomes clear that there is no war, we will release them within forty-eight hours."

Months later Elazar described those hours. He said the atmosphere was electric: "Everyone is running and we carry out many activities in parallel." In short, it was a madhouse.

Egypt, 11:30 a.m.: Sadat spoke to the Soviet Ambassador. He told him, "You have been very quick about your civilians but not so quick about the stuff I asked for." With war about to break out Sadat was in no mood for further delays of Soviet shipments of arms and ammunition.

Israel, 12:00 p.m.: U.S., 6:00 a.m.—Keating's telegram to the State Department, containing a summary of his conversation with Meir, arrived in the United States. Kissinger's assistant, Joseph Sisco, formerly undersecretary of state for Rogers, but now working for Kissinger, received the telegram first. Within fifteen minutes, he was banging on the door of Kissinger's suite at the Waldorf Astoria in New York. The night before Kissinger had spent a peaceful night by himself. It was his first night since being appointed secretary of state that he had relaxed, eating dinner alone and not taking any work with him into the suite. The urgent noise emanating from Sisco's hands beating on the door woke him from a sound sleep. It was probably the last sound sleep he would have for a long time. Nevertheless, the next several months would see Kissinger at his finest, displaying a whirlwind brand of diplomacy that he drew from his vast reservoirs of intellect and energy.

Israel, 12:30 p.m.: U.S., 6:30 a.m.—Gonen, the IDF Southern Front Commander, decided not to permit General Mendler to move his tanks into position until 5:00 p.m. Gonen also failed to reinforce the 450 men of the second-rate reserve, Jerusalem Brigade, which was manning the Bar-lev line. Instead, he ordered those men to continue their regular routines until 4:00 p.m. and to wait until 5:00 p.m. to begin preparing for an artillery bombardment. At 10:00 a.m., General Mendler had received his first warning that fighting would break out at 6:00 p.m. The frontline commanders did not receive their warning until noon. Even then, there was no further information about what to expect: an artillery barrage, a battle day, or a full-fledged war.

Throughout the days leading up to October 6, Gonen never requested reinforcements. With the crisis at hand, he contented himself with making last minute decisions, all of which heavily relied on the accuracy of the intelligence being provided to him. Because of his failure to command effectively, and presciently, hundreds, if not thousands, of soldiers would be killed, wounded, or captured.

Gonen's failures were in direct contrast to Northern Command, where General Hofi reinforced the outposts on the Golan. In preparation for the coming attack, Hofi ordered the Seventh Armored Brigade to remain in reserve in the center and the Barak Brigade to split its battalions and deploy: tasking one battalion to cover the border in the northern half of the Golan and the other to protect the southern half of the border.

Local commanders on the Golan took the alert seriously. "All right, let's get down to business," said Colonel Avigdor Ben-Gal at a 10:00 a.m. meeting with officers under his command (Ben-Gal was commander of the crack Seventh Brigade recently transferred to the Golan from

Southern Command). And, "Gentleman, war will break out today." Ben-Gal ordered them to go back to their units, prepare, and reconvene with him at 2:00 p.m. Still, many IDF soldiers in the north did not prepare themselves mentally for an all-out war. They were anticipating one of the intermittent battle days that the Syrians had instigated from time to time over the past couple of years.

Israel, 12:40 p.m.: U.S., 6:40 a.m.—Kissinger called Dobrynin. Just like Kissinger, the Russian Ambassador had been sleeping. He was groggy and had trouble understanding Kissinger and the information he was trying to convey. Finally, an exasperated Kissinger said, "If this keeps up … there is going to be a war before you understand the message."

Kissinger attempted to impress on Dobrynin the importance he attached to Russia helping to stop the outbreak of war. Kissinger said, "I would like to tell you as you no doubt know—that this is very important for our relationship, that we do not have an explosion in the Middle East right now."

Dobrynin fought for time to stall the charged-up Kissinger, telling him that communications were slow. But Kissinger would not fall for that ploy. He countered that Dobrynin was welcome to use the White House switchboard if he wanted to.

Israel, 12:55 p.m.: U.S., 6:55 a.m.—Kissinger told Shalev, Ambassador Dinitz's stand-in, that he had been in touch with the Russians and the Egyptians. Kissinger said that the Soviet Union would cooperate to prevent the outbreak of hostilities. He also emphasized Israel must not to take any preemptive action.

Israel, 1:00 p.m.: U.S., 7:00 a.m.—Peled finally learned that Elazar would not give him permission to preempt. Therefore, his planes, laden with munitions for bombing airfields, had to change quickly to interceptor configurations. For some, it was the third configuration change of the day. To do so, airbase commanders had to call back jets that were lined up or taxiing on runways. The control towers had no choice but to break radio silence to order the pilots to bring their planes back to the underground bunkers to refit with different weapons. One author described the confusion, "The air force command had never been shaken to this extent. Never had it had to struggle for balance as it did on that fateful day."

Imagine the chaos that must have ensued. Think of a commercial airport with lines of civilian airliners taxiing out to their runways and waiting on line for takeoff. Imagine further that each plane has explosive devices strapped to its wings, and that there are twenty or thirty planes. Then, think what would happen if every one of them had to reverse course and return to their hangar. Would they use the runway, a narrow taxiway, or both? Would it be orderly or mass chaos? And realize that all of that movement had to happen quickly to minimize the time they were exposed to possible enemy air attacks raining destruction from the skies above. It was a miracle there were no reported mishaps during the turn-around. But it was no surprise that much of Israel's air strength would not be available for more than an hour.

Thirty-one years before, in 1942, the Japanese navy lost four aircraft carriers at the Battle of Midway. Their airplanes were caught on deck by the fortuitously timed arrival of American attack planes just as the Japanese were in the midst of multiple weapons configuration changes of their airplanes required by rapidly changing orders. The confusion and haste caused by urgently and abruptly changing their missions left bombs and torpedoes scattered all over the flight decks and the hangars below. When American bombs fell amongst them, the combustible items left exposed outside the storage bays multiplied the damage wrought by America's explosives. It did not take long for the Japanese aircraft carriers to sink. The IAF was indeed fortunate that no Arab warplanes appeared over its airfields during those harrowing minutes when Israel's Air Force was similarly exposed.

Israel, 1:00 p.m.: U.S., 7:00 a.m.—Kissinger called Egyptian Minister of Foreign Affairs, Mohammed El-Zayyat, who also was in New York to attend the General Assembly meeting. Kissinger didn't have anybody specific to call within the Syrian delegation. When his staff tried to make contact with them nobody answered the phone. For that he would have to depend on the Russians. Zayyat sounded surprised and indicated the same when Kissinger told him Egypt was planning to attack Israel. Zayyat's astonishment was real. Sadat had informed his government of the date of the attack after Zayyat left for New York. Sadat intentionally did not tell Zayyat so that he would not be burdened with keeping it secret while pursuing his normal diplomatic activities. Kissinger reiterated the message he had received from the Israelis and asked that the minister pass their message to Sadat. Zayyat tried to contact Sadat within a half hour of speaking to Kissinger, but he was unavailable. Sadat had already left for his war headquarters. Hafez Ismail received the message in Sadat's place.

Egypt, 1:30 p.m.—The Egyptians issued a press statement falsely accusing the Israelis of attacking them. Meanwhile, Egyptian soldiers strolled along the canal without weapons or helmets. It was the last Egyptian deception and one of the final moments of peace.

Egypt, 1:35 p.m.—The Soviet Ambassador called the Egyptians and asked to see Sadat, but Ismail said that he was unavailable. The Russian Ambassador told Ismail that the Israelis had warned that the Egyptians were about to attack them. Ismail responded that it was the Israelis who were attacking.

Israel, 1:45 p.m.—Israeli intelligence analysts finished their written analysis of the notes received from Zamir that described the meeting with Marwan. Their conclusion was that Sadat would limit his aims to grabbing a small sliver of territory six miles deep across the canal. The analysts predicted that the Egyptians would not head for the mountain passes during the first stages of the war. They were correct, but it was too late.

Israel, 1:47 p.m.: U.S., 7:47 a.m.—Kissinger spoke again to Dobrynin, who was much more alert now. They assured each other that the appropriate messages to head off the Arabs had been sent. Kissinger added that he had spoken to Zayyat. "You spoke with him on the telephone?" Dobrynin asked with astonishment. The surprised Dobrynin was not aware that Kissinger had a relationship with the Egyptian. Kissinger knew he was taking a calculated risk revealing information that could tip-off his secret channel with the Egyptians, but the urgency of the moment outweighed the risk.

Golan and Sinai, 1:55 p.m.—Planes took off from airfields in Syria and Egypt, and the first shells burst from Arab guns on their way to carpeting IDF military positions on and near the border with explosives.

Israel, 2:00 p.m.: U.S., 10:00 a.m.—Meir convened a meeting of the cabinet ministers in Tel Aviv. Their discussion focused on topics such as: should Israel attack Syria if only Egypt attacks? They also considered whether Meir had the right to unilaterally decide whom to attack and when.

Suddenly, sirens wailed. It was a clear sign that the war had started. Meir's military secretary reported that Syrian planes were taking off from their bases, and that the Arabs had started shooting. One participant remembered that Meir murmured, in Yiddish, "That's all I needed."

She then added, in English, "They'll be sorry for this."

Israel, 2:35 p.m.: U.S., 8:35 a.m.—Kissinger contacted Alexander Haig, President Nixon's Chief of Staff. He told Haig they might have a Middle East war on their hands.

Final Thoughts

The first seven years of Israel's pivotal years saw her rise from a budding powerhouse, uncertain of her strength, to a confident nation deeply desiring peace with her neighbors. But justifiably, after the Six-Day War, Israel was unwilling to return to little more than a truce, which would leave implacable neighbors, hungering to destroy the Jewish State, virtually a stone's throw away from vital Israeli population centers. Nevertheless, under the right conditions, although Jerusalem would never be returned to Arab rule, Israel was willing to part with most, if not all, of the Sinai and the Golan, as well as vast tracts of the West Bank. As such, Israel pursued a policy of willingness to take risks for peace, but only for a real peace accompanied by all the trappings of peaceful co-existence between nations: including face-to-face negotiations, exchange of ambassadors, trade relations, peace treaties, and other written documents and exchanges that would codify permanent, peaceful intent and that are standard fare in the international community.

Unfortunately, there were no takers.

Syria and Egypt remained focused on recovering every inch of their lost territory but were unwilling to enter into the relationship with Israel that would enable them to do so. Meanwhile, King Hussein tried to straddle five worlds: that of Egypt and Syria, his domestic populace, the outside Arab world, Israel, and the Palestinians in the West Bank. He successfully managed to survive those competing forces, but only by not overcommitting towards any until the Palestinians in his own country forced his hand.

As a result of the stalemate, Israel's improved geographical position masked the increasing risks she faced. More and more, Israel became increasingly dependent on the United States for military arms and political support while simultaneously becoming less able to recognize the danger she was in. The IDF's relatively easy victory in the Six-Day War, coupled with the buffer provided by the occupied territories, created the conditions from which sprung the political/military leadership's over-reliance on the intelligence services being able to separate Arab intent from Arab capability. This led to a profoundly, devastating war which is covered in the first half of Volume Two of *The Pivotal Years*. But that war did lead to an Arab leader becoming willing to do what was necessary to find peace with the Jewish State. It also led to the rise of the PLO and a fundamental change in Israeli politics that opened the door for the Settler movement. And, unfortunately, it also was a period in which Israel's standing in the world plummeted even further.

However, through it all, Israel's principles never changed. Israel coveted peace, but would not comprise her security for the sake of a temporary respite. No matter how strong the outside political pressure, no matter how strident the enemies she faced, Israel would never, and will never, take the route of Czechoslovakia before World War Two. That was the correct policy and the only sensible policy. But it was sorely tested as is revealed in Volume Two of *The Pivotal Years*. I hope you will read Volume Two because knowing what happened and why between 1973 and 1977 is necessary for fully understanding the importance of the pivotal years and their impact on what is happening now.

Glossary of People, Places, Things and Entities

Glossary — People of Influence or Interest

Note on spellings - Accurate spelling for those individuals with Arabic names presents a challenge when one wishes to convert them to English in a manner that is easy to read and remember. Authors have taken several approaches to the problem, ranging from popular forms to literal ones. During my research for this book it was not uncommon to find the same person's name spelled multiple ways. Accordingly, with apologies to the individuals named and their loved ones, I have chosen to use a more readable and easy to remember format. Usually, that includes eliminating portions of their name such as "al-" or "el-".

Adan, Avraham (Bren) – In 1973, the IDF armored corps commander and commander of a reserve armored division in the Sinai.

Allon, Yigal – Became Commander in Chief of the Palmach, an elite irregular fighting force of the Israeli underground before Israel's establishment of a regular army, in 1945. Subsequently, between 1966 and 1977, he served in multiple positions; including: labor minister, deputy prime minister, and foreign affairs minister. He also was the author of the Allon plan that called for Israel to pull back from portions of the West Bank but not the rest.

Amer, General Abdel Hakim – Commanded the Egyptian army during the Six-Day War. Before that he played a leading role in the 1952 coup that brought Nasser to power and became a powerful political force within Egypt. He was arrested in August of 1967 for allegedly planning with others to overthrow Nasser.

Amit, Meir – Director of Mossad from 1963 to 1968.

Arafat, Yasser – Leader of Fatah and then elected Chairman of the Palestinian Liberation Organization (PLO) in February 1969.

Assad, Hafez – Defense minister of Syria in 1966 and then took power

in 1970 before assuming the title of president in 1971.
Bar-Lev, Haim – From 1968 to 1971 he was Chief of Staff of the IDF and championed what became known as the Bar-Lev line along the Suez Canal. During the 1973 war, Elazar appointed him de-facto commander of Israeli forces in the Sinai.
Begin, Menachem – Leader of the Irgun during the period leading up to Israel's victory in the 1948 War for Independence. Subsequently, he became a minister in the Knesset where he led the Herut political party. Just before the 1967 war, Eshkol asked him to become a cabinet member as part of a coalition government. Subsequently, he led the Likud party that formed after the Yom Kippur War and became Prime Minister in 1977.
Ben-Gurion, David – Israel's revered first Prime Minister.
Brezhnev, Leonid – He became General Secretary of the Central Committee of the Communist Party of the Soviet Union. By the early 1970's he was the undisputed leader of the Communist party.
Brundage, Avery – Elected president of the International Olympic Committee in 1952. His statements in the face of terrorism during the 1972 Munich Olympics created much controversy. He retired shortly thereafter.
Caradon, Lord – British Ambassador to the United Nations from 1964 to 1970.
Dayan, Moshe – Appointed defense minister just before the Six-Day War and continued in that role until 1974. In 1977 he became Foreign Affairs minister under Prime Minister Begin.
De Gaulle, Charles – President of France between 1958 and 1969.
Dinitz, Simcha – Named as Israel's Ambassador to the United States in 1973.
Dobrynin, Anatoli – Soviet Union's Ambassador to the United States.
Eban, Abba – Foreign minister of Israel from 1966 to 1974.

Eitan, General Rafael – IDF division commander on the Golan in 1973.

Elazar, David (Dado) – Northern Commander of the IDF in 1966 and 1967. He was appointed IDF Chief of Staff in 1972 and resigned under pressure in 1974.

Eshkol, Levi – Prime Minister of Israel from 1963 until his death in 1969.

Faisal, King of Saudi Arabia – He was the king of Saudi Arabia from 1964 to 1975. His full name was Faisal bin-Abdulaziz al-Saud.

Fawzi, Mahmoud – Appointed Prime Minister of Egypt by Sadat in 1972 and subsequently held the position of Vice President until 1974.

Fedorenko, Nikolai – Soviet Union Ambassador to the United Nations 1963-1968.

Galili, Yisrael – Minister without portfolio in Meir's government and a trusted member of her "Kitchen Cabinet."

Gamasy, Mohamed – Held a leadership role in the Egyptian military during the 1973 Yom Kippur War and was appointed Chief of Staff of the Egyptian armed forces after the war ended.

Goldberg, Arthur – Resigned from the Supreme Court to become the United States Ambassador to the United Nations 1965-1968.

Gonen, Shmuel – A celebrated brigade commander during the 1967 Six-Day War, he was appointed Southern Commander for the IDF in July, 1973. He bore the brunt of much criticism for his conduct during the Yom Kippur War. After the war, he lost his positon and left Israel, never to return.

Gromyko, Andrei – Soviet Union's foreign minister, 1957-1985.

Gur, Mordechai – During the Six-Day War he commanded the brigade that took back the Old City of Jerusalem. Later he was IDF Chief of Staff in 1976 when the IDF rescued hostages in Entebbe, Uganda.

Habash, George – A Christian Palestinian politician who founded the terrorist Popular Front for the Liberation of Palestine (PFLP).

Herzog, Chaim – IDF general who became a radio military commentator during the Six-Day War and afterwards was appointed Military Governor for the West Bank. In 1975 he served as Israel's Ambassador to the United Nations.

Herzog, Yaakov – Served in several senior roles in Israel's government. On behalf of the government he met secretly with King Hussein on multiple occasions.

Hod, Mordechai – Became commander of the IAF from 1966 to April 1973. During the Yom Kippur War, he was recalled to assist the IDF's Northern Command with air operations.

Hofi, Yitzhak – Head of the IDF's Northern Command during the Yom Kippur War.

Hussein, King – King of Jordan. His full name was Hussein bin Talal.

Ismail, Hafez – Sadat's national security advisor.

Ismail, Ahmad – The Egyptian defense minister during the Yom Kippur War.

Jadid, Salah – Strongman who led Syria from 1966 until he was overthrown by Assad in 1970.

Jarring, Gunnar – Appointed by the UN to facilitate negotiations between Israel and the Arabs.

Johnson, Lyndon – President of the United States from 1963 until January 1969.

Khaled, Leila – PFLP terrorist who twice hijacked an airplane.

Kissinger, Henry – President Nixon appointed him national security advisor in 1969. He continued in that role until Nixon appointed him secretary of state in 1973. Kissinger remained secretary of state during President Ford's term of office that ended January, 1977.

Kollek, Teddy – Mayor of Jerusalem.

Kosygin, Alexsei – Held the post of Premier in the Soviet Union. By the early 1970's, his power was eclipsed by Brezhnev.

Laner, General Dan – IDF division Commander on the Golan during the Yom Kippur War.

Levinger, Moshe – Zionist and orthodox Rabbi who became a leader in the settler movement after the 1967 war.

Marwan, Ashraf – A spy. It remains an open question whether he worked for Israel or Egypt.

McNamara, Robert – Served as secretary of defense under Presidents Johnson and Kennedy.

Meir, Golda – Prime Minister of Israel from 1969 until she resigned in 1974.

Mendler, Avraham – IDF commander of an armored division in the Sinai during the Yom Kippur War.

Mubarak, Hosni – Commander of Egypt's Air Force from 1972 to 1975 and then Vice President of Egypt from 1975 to 1981. In 1981 he became President of Egypt after Sadat was assassinated.

Narkiss, Uzi – Central Front Commander during the Six-Day War.

Nasser, Gamal Abdel –The charismatic President of Egypt from 1956 until his death in 1970. Most believed that for much of that time he was strongest leader of the Arab world.

Nixon, Richard – President of the United States from January 1969 until he resigned in 1974 in order to avoid impeachment as a result of Watergate.

Nuseibeh, Anwar – A leading Palestinian moderate who had contacts with Israel and King Hussein after the 1967 war.

O'Donnell, Jack – An employee of the CIA who served in Jordan from 1963 to 1971. He became very friendly with King Hussein.

Peled, Benny – Commander of Israel's Air Force (IAF) during the Yom Kippur War.

Peled, Moussa – IDF commander of an armored division initially stationed along the Jordanian border in 1973.

Peres, Shimon – A minister in the Knesset. Over the years, he served in many positions, including that of Prime Minister of Israel from 1990 to 1992. During Rabin's first term as Prime Minister from 1974 to 1977, Rabin appointed Peres as defense minister.

Podgorny, Nikolai – Chairman of the Presidium of the Supreme Soviet, but lost power to Brezhnev in the early 1970's.

Porat, Hanan – A leading figure in the settler movement and a founder of the *Gush Emunim* (the bloc of the faithful) movement that aggressively pushed for settlement of territory captured in the 1967 war. As part of his activities he worked with others to establish *Kfar Etzion*, the first settlement on the West Bank. It arose on the foundations of a Jewish settlement destroyed by Arabs in 1948.

Rabin, Yitzhak – Chief of staff of the IDF from 1964 to 1969, Israel's Ambassador to the United States from 1968 to 1973, and Prime Minister from 1974 to 1977 (He served again as Prime Minister from 1992 until he was assassinated in 1995).

Riad, General – Just before the Six-Day War, Nasser sent General Riad to Jordan to command the Jordanian armed forces.

Riad, Mahmoud – Egyptian minister of foreign affairs from 1964 to 1972.

Rifa'I, Zaid – Close confidant of King Hussein and at times the Jordanian Prime Minister.

Rogers, William – Appointed secretary of state by President Nixon, he held that position from 1969 to 1973. He authored the controversial Rogers plan.

Rusk, Dean – Secretary of state from 1961 through 1968.

Sabry, Ali – Head of Nasser's Socialist Union and a strong advocate of the Soviet Union.

Sadat, Anwar – Vice President of Egypt while Nasser lived, and then became President of Egypt in 1970.

Shapiro, Zalmon – Founded the Nuclear Materials and Equipment Corp. (NUMEC).

Sharon, Ariel – IDF commander of a division in the Sinai in 1967, Southern Front Commander from 1969 to the summer of 1973, and then commander of a reserve division in the Sinai during the Yom Kippur War. Also, in the latter part of 1973, he was a prime organizer for the Likud party. Subsequently, he became the minister of agriculture under Menachem Begin and was a prime supporter of the settler movement. In 2001 he became Prime Minister of Israel, a position he held until suffering a massive stroke in 2006.

Shazly, Saad – An Egyptian field commander during the Six-Day War, he rose to chief of staff of the Egyptian army in 1971 until he lost power during the latter stages of the Yom Kippur War as a result of a dispute with Sadat.

Shuqayri, Ahmad – In 1964 he became the first leader of the PLO.

Sisco, Joseph – Held various titles as a high-level employee of the State Department. Under both secretary of state Rogers and Kissinger he served as a point man for many Middle East issues.

Tal, Yisrael – IDF division commander in the Sinai during the Six-Day War, he had crucial influence on the development of Israel's armored corps and served as deputy chief of staff during the Yom Kippur War.

Tal, Wasfi – Served at the pleasure of King Hussein as Prime Minister and defense minister of Jordan from 1970 to 1971 until he was assassinated by Black September murderers.

Tlas, Mustafa – Syria's defense minister from 1972 to 2004.

U Thant – Secretary-General of the United Nations 1961 to 1971.

Vinogradov, Vladimir – Russian Ambassador to Egypt 1970 to 1974.

Waldheim, Kurt – Secretary-General of the United Nations 1972-1981.

Zamir, Zvi – Mossad (Israel's intelligence agency) director from 1968 to 1974.

Zayyat, Mohammed – Egyptian minister of foreign affairs from 1972 until shortly after the Yom Kippur War.

Zeira, Eli – Director of military intelligence (AMAN) from 1972 to 1973 and prime supporter of the "concept."

PLACES

Abraham's Tomb (Tomb of the Patriarchs) – Located in the heart of Hebron and beneath a mosque. Among many Jews, it is believed that Abraham, Sarah, Isaac, Rebecca, Jacob, and Leah are buried there.

Abu Ageila – Road junction in the Sinai.

Allenby Bridge – Bridge that crosses the Jordan River from the West Bank to Jordan.

Amman – Capital of Jordan.

Artillery Road – A road in the Sinai running six to seven miles from the Suez Canal.

Bar-Lev Line – A sand wall with interspersed fortifications that the IDF built along the length of the Suez Canal.

Cairo – Capital of Egypt.

Damascus – Capital of Syria.

Dawson's Field – A remote desert airfield in Jordan.

Dimona – Site of Israel's nuclear reactor and nuclear weapon program in the Negev.

Eilat – Israeli port located at the northern tip of the Red Sea on the Gulf of Aqaba.

El Arish – Located in the Sinai along the Mediterranean Coast, about thirty-one miles from Gaza.

Etzion Bloc – Four Jewish settlements in the Judean Mountains that were overrun by Jordan's Arab legion in 1948 and then rebuilt by Jews after the Six-Day War.

Galilee – An area comprising much of northern Israel.

Gaza – Small thirty-two mile by seven mile strip of land along the Mediterranean that is northeast of the Sinai and that juts into Israel.

Giddi Pass – A mountain pass in the Sinai.

Golan Heights – This elevated plateau was part of Syria and bordered Israel, Lebanon, and Jordan. It was captured by Israel during the Six-Day War.

Gulf of Aqaba – Sea leading to Eilat. It is bordered by Egypt, Jordan, Saudi Arabia, and Israel. It is also known as the Gulf of Eilat.

Hebron – A large Palestinian city located in the southern portion of the West Bank.

Ismailia – A city in northeast Egypt located along the western bank of the Suez Canal roughly half way between its northern and southern terminuses.

Jerusalem (New City and Old City) – It is the Capital of Israel. Before the Six-Day War the Old City (including the Jewish Quarter within) was controlled by the Jordanians. After the Six-Day War the Old City came under Israeli control.

Jordan River – A 156 mile long river that divides Jordan from the West Bank and flows into the Sea of Galilee and then below to the Dead Sea.

Karameh – A Jordanian town located near the Jordan River and the Allenby Bridge.

Kiryat Arba – Israeli settlement located in the West Bank in close proximity to Hebron.

Kuneitra – The Syrian Capital of the Golan until the IDF took the city during the Six-Day War. Israel returned it to Syria as part of the disengagement agreement with Syria after the Yom Kippur War in 1973.

Lateral Road – A road in the Sinai that runs parallel to and approximately twenty miles from the Suez Canal.

Latrun – A strategic point overlooking the road running from Tel Aviv to Jerusalem.

Lexicon Road – Road running north and south, approximately six-tenths of a mile from the Suez Canal.

Lod Airport – Israel's main airport, now known as Ben Gurion Airport.

Missouri – An Egyptian military position in the Sinai that threatened Israel's crossing site over the Suez Canal during the Yom Kippur War.

Mitla Pass – A mountain pass in the Sinai.

Mount Hermon – The highest mountain in the region (composed of three summits), it borders Syria and Lebanon. After the Six-Day War Israel controlled its southern slopes.

Nablus – A populous Palestinian city in the northern part of the West Bank.

Naffakh – Located at a central point in the Golan Heights, it was where the IDF's command structure for defense of the Golan was located during the Yom Kippur War.

Negev – Desert region located in southern Israel.

Northern Galilee – Located in northern Israel.

Pit – The underground bunker, located in Tel Aviv, used by the IDF as a headquarters when at war.

Purple Line – Ceasefire line between Israel and Syria after the Six-Day War.

Samu – A village in the West Bank less than five miles from Israel's border and almost fifteen miles south of Hebron.

Sea of Galilee – Israel's largest freshwater lake. It is located in northeast Israel and is also called Lake Kinneret.

Sharm el-Sheikh – A city located at the southern tip of the Sinai that overlooks the Straits of Tiran.

Soviet Union – During 1966 to 1977 it was the most powerful communist nation in the world, one of two superpowers, and was composed of multiple republics. For the purposes of this book the terms Soviet Union and Russia mean the same nation.

Straits of Tiran – The narrow sea passage situated between the Sinai and the Arabian Peninsula. It must be navigated to reach Eilat.

Suez City – A seaport in northeastern Egypt located on the northern coast of the Gulf of Suez near where the Southern portion of the Suez Canal lets out into the sea.

Tel Aviv – Along with Jerusalem and Haifa, one of Israel's three largest cities. It is located along the shores of the Mediterranean and a short distance from the West Bank.

Yamit – An Israeli settlement in the northern portion of the Sinai Peninsula established after the Six-Day War ended. It was bulldozed by the Israelis prior to returning the land to the Egyptians in 1982.

Yemen – An Arab country in the southern portion of the Arabian Peninsula.

Things and Entities

Al-Sa'iqa – A Syrian sponsored Palestinian terrorist group.

Arab Street – As described by Thomas Friedman, it is a descriptive term for Arab public opinion as opposed to the Government's.

Ba'th party – An Arab political party founded in Syria that mixed nationalistic, pan-Arab, socialist, and anti-imperial ideals. Another branch of the party took root in Iraq but did not see eye to eye with the Syrian Ba'ath party.

Brigade – A large military unit, usually consisting of a few thousand soldiers that is part of a division.

Division – A large military unit usually consisting of multiple brigades or regiments and comprising 10,000 to 20,000 military soldiers.

Druse – A religious group that split from Shiite Islam a thousand years ago and has its own independent religious beliefs. Druse communities exist in Syria, Lebanon, Israel, and Jordan.

El Al – Israel's national civilian airline.

Fedayeen – Palestinians that participated in violent operations–generally against Israeli military and civilian targets.

Haganah – A Jewish defense force that operated before Israel's Independence and that formed the core of the IDF when Israel proclaimed its independence.

Holocaust – The descriptive term for the systematic murder of six million Jews (as well as many others) during World War Two by the Germans and those that assisted them.

IAF – Acronym for Israel's Air Force.

IDF – Acronym for Israel's Defense Forces.

Knesset – Israel's legislature.

Likud – An Israeli right-wing party founded in 1973.

Mirage – French fighter jet sold to Israel.

MiG 21 – Russian fighter jet that first appeared in 1955.

MiG 23 – Russian fighter jet first produced in 1970.

Mossad – Israel's national intelligence agency responsible for intelligence collection, covert action, countering terrorism, protecting Jews in other countries, and bringing Jews to Israel from countries that refuse to permit Aliyah agencies on their lands.

Most Favored Nation Status (*MFN*) – A country that receives *MFN* status is guaranteed trade terms as advantageous as any other country given *MFN* status.

Nahal – Acronym for Fighting Pioneer Youth, an IDF paramilitary force that combines military service with the establishment of settlements.

NSC – Acronym for the National Security Council (an entity devoted to considering foreign policy and national security issues for the President of the United States).

OAPEC – Acronym for the Organization of Arab Petroleum Exporting Countries. This entity was originally conceived to ensure that an oil embargo would not be used frivolously for political purposes. It subsequently became the political vehicle for implementing the oil embargo imposed by Arab oil producers during the Yom Kippur War.

October War – See Yom Kippur War.

OPEC – Acronym for the Organization of Petroleum Exporting Countries.

Passover Seder – The feast that marks the beginning of Passover. Its ritual includes retelling the story of Jews liberated from slavery in Egypt.

PFLP – Acronym for the Popular Front for the Liberation of Palestine.

Phantom F4 – A two-seat aircraft fighter bomber developed by the United States. It was the most capable warplane in America's inventory in the 1960s and early 1970s.

PLO – Acronym for the Palestinian Liberation Organization.

Rhodes Formulation – In order to overcome Arab refusal to meet directly with Israel, this diplomatic construct incorporated an intermediary moving back and forth between the parties until a final agreement is reached. It avoided direct negotiations.

Rosh Hashanah – Jewish New Year and the beginning of the High Holidays.

Sagger missiles – Soviet produced, wire-guided, antitank missiles.

SAM-2 – Russian surface-to-air missile primarily designed to shoot down attacking aircraft at medium to high altitudes.

SAM-3 – Russian surface-to-air missile primarily designed to shoot down attacking aircraft at low to medium altitudes.

SAM-6 – Mobile Russian surface-to-air missile designed to shoot down attacking aircraft from low to high altitudes and at ranges of up to fifteen miles.

SAM-7 Strella – Russian surface-to-air handheld missile (also referred to as SA-7 Strella).

Shabbat – The weekly day of rest for Jews. It extends from Friday sundown to Saturday sundown.

Shin Bet – Israel's internal security service.

Six-Day War – The war between Israel and many Arab nations that began on June 5, 1967.

Sixth Fleet – Headquartered in Italy, it is the name the U.S. navy gives to a group of American naval ships primarily responsible for protecting American interests in the Mediterranean.

Skyhawk – A versatile attack aircraft developed in the United States.

Sukkot – A joyous Jewish holiday that commemorates the forty years Jews wandered in the desert and lived in temporary shelters.

Three no's – It is the term used to refer to the part of the Khartoum Resolution issued September 1, 1967 after the 1967 Arab League Summit ended that stated Arab policy to be "no peace with Israel, no recognition of Israel, no negotiations with it."

UN – Acronym for the United Nations.

UNEF – Acronym for the United Nations Emergency Force established to help maintain peace between Egypt and Israel in 1956 until evicted by

Nasser in 1967. A second force was created after the Yom Kippur war to supervise the ceasefire between Egypt and Israel.

U.S.S. Liberty – An American intelligence gathering ship that operated off the coast of the Sinai in 1967.

Yom Kippur – Holiest day of the year for Jews. It is a day of fasting and prayer that completes the High Holy Days, which begin with Rosh Hashanah when God inscribes each person's fate. On Yom Kippur the verdict is sealed.

Yom Kippur War – The war that began with a surprise attack on Israel by Egypt and Syria. It is also called the October War.

A Note about Footnotes

You might have noticed an absence of footnotes in this book. It is certainly fair to ask why?

When I first embarked on this writing odyssey I thought much about whether to include footnotes. By the time my research ended, I had made 3,648 entries, ranging from a few words to pages of text, into a specially designed database. Each entry was coded as to time period, source, page number, etc. In addition, I have maps, website references, and the like.

As an avid reader of history books I must admit that I often flick to the back of a book when there is a footnote that interests me or a passage I question. However, I must also admit that I am rarely satisfied by what I find. Usually it is a bland reference to page(s) in a book, a document, or an interview. Sometimes it is an interesting, more detailed explanation, but even that often leaves something lacking. But rarely is the footnoted reference one that would be easy to locate for the average reader. And even if it is, how many feel the need to do so? How many willingly break their concentration on what they are reading to check the source? I think very few. So why include them?

For the historian doing research the answer is easy, without footnotes the author's assertions and conclusions cannot be verified. But for most readers will they bother to do so? Is that a sufficient reason to omit them? Footnotes add credibility. They make a book appear scholarly. Perhaps they demonstrate the seriousness of the author. But is the state of mind they create a sufficient reason to add them? And is that state of mind a false comfort? How is the reader to know unless she takes the time to check them, consider whether they accurately portray the intent of the source, and decide whether the sources used present only one side of the argument? But even if the reader does that (which I strongly doubt will be the case for most) she will likely lose the flow of the story.

Therefore, I decided to opt in favor of readability. Frankly, my goal was to present a very complex topic in detail, but in a fair and digestible manner. It was not to write a boring historical tome for researchers. That is not to say that I don't feel footnotes are important. They certainly are. And that is why after the Kindle version is finished, and before the print version of this book is released, footnotes for all quotes and some selected passages will be my website, **www.CliffordSobin.com**. I will also place on the website a bibliography sorted by chapter and topic so that if readers want to explore certain issues in more detail, your ability to do so will be facilitated. However, in the interest of providing additional sources from which the reader can gain a more comprehensive picture of The Pivotal Years, at the end of this book I included a selected bibliography of the most important sources for this work.

Bibliography Most Relied On

Aburish, Said K. *Arafat From Defender to Dictator*. Great Britain: Bloomsbury Publishing, 1998

Aronson, Shlomo. *Conflict & Bargaining in the Middle East - An Israeli Perspective*. Baltimore: The Johns Hopkins University Press, 1978

Ashton, Nigel. *King Hussein of Jordan A Political Life*. New Haven: Yale University Press, 2008

Avner, Yehuda. *The Prime Ministers*. Jerusalem: The Toby Press LLC, 2010

Bar-Zohar, Michael. *Yaacov Herzog*. London: Halban Publishers Ltd, 2005

Bartov, Hanoch. *Dado: 48 Years and 20 Days*. Israel: Ma'ariv Book Guild, 1981

Ben-Ami, Shlomo. *Scars of War, Wounds of Peace – The Israeli-Arab Tragedy*. Oxford: Oxford University Press, Inc., 2006

Bowen, Jeremy. *Six Days How the 1967 War Shaped the Middle East*. New York: St. Martin's press, 2003

Brecher, Michael. *Decisions in Crisis – Israel, 1967 and 1973*. Berkley: University of California Press, 1980

Chamberlain, Paul Thomas. *The Global Offensive: The United States, the Palestine Liberation Organization, and the Making of the Post-Cold War Order*. New York: Oxford University Press, 2012

Cobban, Helen. *The Palestinian Liberation Organization*. Cambridge: Cambridge University Press, 1984

Cohen, Eliezer. *Israel's Best Defense*. New York: Crown Publishers, Inc., 1993

Daigle, Craig. *The Limits of Detente: The United States, the Soviet Union, and the Arab-Israeli Conflict, 1969-1973*. New Haven: Yale University Press, 2013

Dunstan, Simon. *The Six-Day War 1967: Jordan and Syria.* Long Island City: Osprey Publishing Ltd., 2009

Dupuy, Trevor. *Elusive Victory: The Arab-Israeli Wars, 1947-1974.* New York: Harpers & Row, 1978

Eban, Abba. *Personal Witness, Israel Through My Eyes.* New York: G. P. Putnam's Sons, 1992

Gilbert, Martin. *Israel a History.* New York :William Morrows and Company, Inc., 1998

Gorenberg, Gershon. *The Accidental Empire.* New York: Henry Holt and Company, 2006

Gorenberg, Gershon. *The Unmaking of Israel.* New York: HarperCollins, 2011

Ginor, Isabella and Remez, Gideon. *Foxbats over Dimona.* New Haven: Yale University Press, 2007

Gold, Dore. *Tower of Babble How The United Nations Has Fueled Chaos.* New York: Crown Forum, 2004

Halabi, Rafik. *The West Bank Story.* Orlando: Harcourt Brace Jovanovich, Inc., 1981 (paperback)

Hammel, Eric. *Six Days in June - How Israel Won the 1967 Arab-Israeli war.* New York: Charles Scribner's Sons, 1992

Heikal, Mohamed. The Road to Ramadan. London:Times Newspapers, Ltd., 1975

Glassman, Jon. *Arms for the Arabs – The Soviet Union and War in the Middle East.* Baltimore: The Johns Hopkins University Press, 1975

Karpin, Michael. *The Bomb in the Basement.* New York: Simon & Schuster, Inc., 2006

Kipnis, Yigal. *1973 The Road to War.* Charlottesville: Just World Publishing, LLC, 2013

Kissinger, Henry. *White House Years.* Boston: Little, Brown & Company, 1979

Kollek, Teddy. *For Jerusalem, A Life. Tel Aviv.* Tel Aviv: Steimatsky's Agency Ltd., 1978

Lall, Arthur. *The UN and the Middle East Crisis, 1967.* New York: Columbia University Press, 1968

Laquer, Walter. *The Road to Jerusalem.* New York: The Macmillan Company, 1968

Laqueur, Walter and Rubin, Barry Editors. *The Israel-Arab Reader – A Documentary History of the Middle East Conflict.* New York: Penguin Group, 2008

Louis, Wm. Roger and Shlaim, Avi, Editors. *The 1967 Arab-Israeli War Origins and Consequences.* Cambridge: Cambridge University Press, 2012

Ma'oz, Moshe. *Syria and Israel.* New York: Clarendon Press, 1993

Meisler, Stanley. *United Nations – The First Fifty Years.* New York: The Atlantic Monthly Press, 1995

Morris, Benny. *1948 The First Arab-Israeli War.* New Haven: Yale University Press, 2008

Mutawi, Samir A. *Jordan in the 1967 War.* Cambridge: Cambridge University Press, 1987

Neff, Donald. *Warriors for Jerusalem.* New York: Simon & Schuster, 1984

Nutting, Anthony. *Nasser.* New York: E.F. Dutton & Co., Inc., 1972

O'Connell, Jack. *King's Counsel.* New York: W.W. Norton & Company, 2011

On Line Prime Minister's Office

Oren, Michael. *Six Days of War June 1967 and the Making of the Modern Middle East.* New York: Oxford University press, Inc., 2002

Oren, Michael. *Power, Faith and Fantasy - America in the Middle East 1776 to the Present.* New York: W.W. Norton & Co.,

Pollack, Kenneth. *Arabs at War.* Lincoln: University of Nebraska Press, 2002

Primakov, Yevgeny. *Russia and the Arabs.* New York: Basic Books, 2009

Prittie, Terence. *Eshkol: The Man and the Nation.* New York: Pittman Publishing Corporation, 1969

Quandt, William B. *Peace Process: American Diplomacy and the Arab-Israeli Conflict Since 1967.* Washington, D.C.: Brookings Institution Press (Paperback), 2001

Quandt, William, Jabber, Fuad, Lech, Ann Mosely. *The Politics of Palestinian Nationalism.* Berkeley: University of California Press, 1973

Rabinovich, Itamar and Shaked, Haim. *From June to October, The Middle East between 1967 and 1973.* New Brunswick: Transaction Books, 1978

Edited by Rabinovich, Itamar and Reinharz, Jehuda, Editors. *Israel in the Middle East Second Edition.* Waltham: Brandeis University Press, 2008

Raviv, Dan and Melman, Yossi. *Every Spy a Prince.* Boston: Houghton Mifflin Company, 1989

Raz, Avi. *The Bride and the Dowry – Israel, Jordan, and the Palestinians in the Aftermath of the June 1967 War.* New Haven: Yale University Press, 2012

Ro'I, Yaacov and Morozov, Boris, Editors. *The Soviet Union and the June 1967 Six-Day War.* Washington, DC: Woodrow Wilson *Center Press,* 2008

Sachar, Howard. *Egypt & Israel.* New York: Richard Marek Publishers, 1981

Sakal, Major General Emanuel. *Soldier in the Sinai.* University Press of Kentucky, 2014 (Offers a much more negative view of General Elazar than mine)

Schiff, Zeev and Rothstein, Raphael. *Fedayeen – Guerillas against Israel.* New York: David McKay Company, Inc., 1972

Seale, Patrick. *Asad, The Struggle for the Middle East.* Los Angeles, Berkley: First University of California Press Edition, 1990 (paperback)

Segev, Tom. *1967 - Israel, the War, and the Year that Transformed the Middle East.* New York: Henry Holt and Company, LLC, 2007

Sharon, Ariel with David Chanoff. *Warrior.* New York: Simon and Schuster, 1989

Sharon, Gilad. *Sharon - The Life of a Leader*. New York: HarperCollins, 2011

Shlaim, Avi. *The Iron Wall, Israel and the Arab World*. New York: W.W. Norton & Company, Inc., 2001

Shlaim, Avi. *Lion of Jordan: The Life of King Hussein in War and Peace*. New York: Penguin Group, 2007

Slater, Robert. *Rabin of Israel*. New York: St. Martin's Press, 1993

Slater, Robert. *Warrior Statesman, The life of Moshe Dayan*. New York: St. Martin's Press, 1991

Stein, Kenneth. *Heroic Diplomacy - Sadat, Kissinger, Carter, Begin and the Quest for Arab-Israeli peace*. New York, NY: Routledge, 1999

Stein, Leslie. *The Making of Modern Israel 1948 – 1967*. Cambridge, UK: Polity Press, 2009

Time Magazine September 1 and November 25, 1966 editions

Tyler, Patrick. *A World of Trouble The White House and the Middle East – From the Cold War to the War on Terror*. New York: Farrar, Straus and Giroux, 2009

Viorst, Milton. *Sands of Sorrow – Israel's Journey From Independence*. New York, New York: Harper & Row, 1987

Yonay, Ehud. *No Margin for Error*. New York: Random House, Inc., 1993

Wasserstein, Bernard. *Divided Jerusalem, The Struggle for the Holy City*. New Haven, Conn.: Yale University Press), 2001 (paperback)

Wawro, Geoffrey. *Quicksand America's Pursuit of Power in the Middle East*. New York: Penguin Press, 2010

A Final Word and Request

If you enjoyed this book I hope you will be kind enough to write a review on Amazon. And, if you would like to email me questions or suggestions, sign up for my newsletter which I will begin issuing monthly in 2017, or just check me out you can head over to **www.cliffordsobin.com** or my Amazon Authors website at **Amazon/CliffordSobin**.

Thank you again for reading this book, I am not the one who first said "knowledge is power," but I deeply believe it.